VISUAL QUICKPRO GUIDE

MACROMEDIA FLASH MX 2004 ADVANCED

FOR WINDOWS AND MACINTOSH

Russell Chun
with Joe Garraffo

 Peachpit Press

Visual QuickPro Guide
Macromedia Flash MX 2004 Advanced for Windows and Macintosh
Russell Chun with Joe Garraffo

Peachpit Press
1249 Eighth Street
Berkeley, CA 94710
510/524-2178
510/524-2221 (fax)

Find us on the World Wide Web at www.peachpit.com.
To report errors, please send a note to errata@peachpit.com.
Peachpit Press is a division of Pearson Education.

Published in association with Macromedia Press.
Copyright © 2004 by Russell Chun

Editor: Rebecca Gulick
Production Editor: Lisa Brazieal
Contributing Writer: Joe Garraffo
Copy Editor: Judy Flynn
Technical Reviewers: Sharon Selden and Hiroko Takada of Macromedia, Inc.
Compositor: Owen Wolfson
Indexer: Rebecca Plunkett
Cover Design: The Visual Group
Cover Production: Nathalie Valette
CD-ROM Mastering: Jay Payne

ISBN 0-321-21341-6

9 8 7 6 5 4 3 2

Printed and bound in the United States of America

Thank you

Many thanks to everyone at Peachpit Press, especially my dedicated and long-time editor, Rebecca Gulick. Thanks also to Judy Flynn for putting the polish on my words and to Lisa Brazieal and Owen Wolfson for piecing this beautiful book together. And thanks to Marjorie Baer, Nancy Davis, Nancy Ruenzel, Rebecca Ross, Gary-Paul Prince, and Kim Lombardi for their tremendous support.

Special thanks to Joe Garraffo for his enthusiasm and tireless, late-night efforts. His contributions made the formidable task of bringing in new content possible.

For keeping an eye on accuracy and best practices, thanks to the technical reviewers at Macromedia: Sharon Selden and Hiroko Takada, whose attention and suggestions were invaluable.

I'm grateful to the numerous people and friends who lent their time and talents to text, video, sound, photos, and illustrations: Steve Vargas, Eric Stickney, Josh Frost, Ross "Hogg" Viator, Khin Mai Aung, David Harrington, SadSadFun, Derek Jimenez, and Tim Cramer. Additional images and sound provided courtesy of Benjamin Cummings, Corel Photo, Gary Fisher bikes, Music4Flash.com, RocketClips.com, and Kim Steinhaug and SubReal from Flashkit.com. I would also like to especially thank my parents, Dolores and David, for all they have given me.

And to the Flash community (that includes readers like you!), thank you for the time, creativity, and energy that you've poured into your movies, sharing with the world the amazing things Flash can do. I hope this book inspires even more to do the same.

–Russell Chun

Thank you

To my soul mate, my best friend, my wife, Nicole, thank you for your constant support, love, friendship, and really just for being you! To my daughter (the star of a few pictures), Madison Rae, thank you for your smiles, laughter, and hugs. You truly are the most incredible thing that has ever happened to me.

To my parents, Jim and Marie, the two most amazing people on the face of the earth. If it weren't for your belief in me this would never have happened. Thank you for always standing by my side. To Steven, Stacy, Gary, and Carol, thank you for being the best family that anyone could ask for. To my nieces and nephews, Danielle, Bryan, Sarah, Timmy, Arianna, and Taylor, you guys rock! To my in-laws, Sal and Gail Ciaravino, thank you for your help with the baby, the dinners, and the constant encouraging words.

A very special thank you to all the people who have made the Long Island Flash User's Group a reality. It is because of LIFUG that I have had the privilege of working with Susan Nixon, Ed Sullivan, and Amy Brooks. I'll never forget the constant support from my friends, David Cappelli and Bruce MacArthur.

Thank you to Jason McGuigan and John Herringer for your help with the video footage; to Anthony Petosa and Stephen Rosenberg for your assistance; to my friend and mentor, Rob Reinhardt, you have been a huge part of my learning over the years.

And finally, heartfelt thanks to Russell Chun for allowing me to work with you on this project. It has been an honor to work with someone as knowledgeable as you. To Rebecca Gulick, for always being there to answer my questions and guide me in the right direction. Thanks for your patience, tips, and support for those late-night questions or Sunday evening questions.

–Joe Garraffo

TABLE OF CONTENTS

INTRODUCTION

Macromedia Flash MX 2004 is one of the hottest technologies on the Web today. Leading corporate Web sites use its streamlined graphics to communicate their brands; major motion picture studios promote theatrical releases with Flash movies; and online gaming and educational sites provide rich user experiences with Flash interactivity.

As a vector-based animation and authoring application, Flash is ideal for creating high-impact, low-bandwidth Web sites incorporating animation, text, video, sound, and database integration. With robust support for complex interactivity and server-side communication, Flash is increasingly the solution for developing Internet applications as well. From designer to programmer, Flash has become the tool of choice for delivering dynamic content across various browsers and platforms.

As the popularity of Flash increases, so does the demand for animators and developers who know how to tap its power. This book is designed to help you meet that challenge. Learn how to build complex animations, integrate sophisticated interfaces and navigation schemes, and dynamically control graphics, video, sound, and text. Experiment with the techniques discussed in this book to create the compelling media that Flash makes possible. It's not an exaggeration to say that Flash is revolutionizing the Web. This book will help you be a part of that revolution. So boot up your computer and get started.

Who Should Use This Book

This book is for the designers, animators, and developers who want to take their Flash skills to the next level. You've mastered the basics of tweening and are ready to move on to more complex tasks such as importing video, masking, controlling dynamic sound, or detecting movie-clip collisions. You may not be a hard-core programmer, but you're ready to learn how ActionScript can control graphics, sounds, and text. You're ready to integrate interactivity with your animations to create arcade-style games, to create complex user-interface elements like pull-down menus, and to learn how Flash communicates with outside applications such as Web browsers. If this description fits you, then this book is right for you.

This book explores the advanced features of Flash MX 2004, so you should already be comfortable with the basic tools and commands for creating simple Flash movies. You should know how to create and modify shapes and text with the drawing tools and be able to create symbols. You should also know how to apply motion and shape tweens, and how to work with frame-by-frame animation. You should know your way around the Flash interface: how to move from the Stage to symbol-editing mode to the Timeline, and how to manipulate layers and frames. You should also be familiar with importing and using bitmaps and sounds, and assigning basic actions to frames and buttons for navigation. Review the tutorials that come with the software, or pick up a copy of *Macromedia Flash MX 2004: Visual QuickStart Guide* by Katherine Ulrich.

Goals of This Book

The aim of this book is to demonstrate the advanced features of Flash MX 2004 through a logical approach, emphasizing how techniques are applied. You will learn how techniques build on each other, and how groups of techniques can be combined to solve a particular problem. Each example you work through puts another skill under your belt, so by the end of this book you'll be able to create sophisticated interactive Flash projects.

For example, creating a pull-down menu illustrates how simple elements—invisible buttons, event handlers, button-tracking options, and movie clips—come together to make more complex behaviors. Examples illustrate the practical application of techniques, and additional tips explain how to apply these techniques in other contexts.

How to use this book

The concepts in this book build on each other, so the material at the end is more complex than that at the beginning. If you're familiar with some of the material, you can skip around to the subjects that interest you, but you'll find it most useful to learn the techniques in the order in which they appear.

As with other books in the Visual QuickPro Guide series, tasks are presented for you to do as you read about them, so that you can see how a technique is applied. Follow the step-by-step instructions, look at the figures, and try them on your computer. You'll learn more by doing and by taking an active role in experimenting with these exercises. Many of the completed tasks are provided as FLA and SWF files on the included CD-ROM; those tasks that have accompanying files are identified with this icon. ⊚

Tips follow the specific tasks to give you hints on how to use a shortcut, warnings on common mistakes, and suggestions on how the technique can be extended.

Occasionally, you'll see sidebars in gray boxes. Sidebars discuss related matters that are not directly task-oriented. You'll find interesting and useful concepts that can help you better understand how Flash works.

What's in this book

This book is organized into five parts:

- **Part I: Approaching Advanced Animation**

  This part covers advanced techniques for graphics and animation, including strategies for motion tweening, shape tweening, masking, and using digital video.

- **Part II: Understanding ActionScript**

  This part introduces ActionScript, the scripting language Flash uses to add interactivity to a movie. You'll learn the basic components of the language and how to use the Actions panel to construct meaningful code.

- **Part III: Navigating Timelines and Communicating**

  This part teaches you the ways in which Flash can respond to input from the viewer and how complex navigation schemes can be created with multiple Timelines. You'll also see how Flash communicates with external files and applications such as Web browsers.

- **Part IV: Transforming Graphics and Sound**

  This part demonstrates how to dynamically control the basic elements of any Flash movie—its graphics and sound—through ActionScript.

- **Part V: Working with Information**

  The last part focuses on how to retrieve, store, modify, and test information to create complex Flash environments that can respond to changing conditions.

- **Appendixes**

  Two appendixes give you quick access to the standard object name extensions and key code values.

What's on the CD

Accompanying this book is a CD-ROM that contains nearly all the Flash source files for the tasks. You can see how each task was created, study the ActionScript, or use the ActionScript to do further experimentation. You'll also find trial version of Flash MX 2004 as well as a list of Web links to sites devoted to Flash and showcasing the latest Flash examples, with tutorials, articles, and advice.

Additional resources

Use the Web to your advantage. There is a thriving international community of Flash developers; within it you can share your frustrations, seek help, and show off your latest Flash masterpiece. There are free bulletin boards and mailing lists for all levels of Flash users. Begin your search for Flash resources with the list of Web sites on the accompanying CD and with the Help panel in the Flash application, which provides a searchable ActionScript dictionary and Flash manual.

GOALS OF THIS BOOK

Flash MX 2004 and Flash MX 2004 Professional

What's the difference between Flash MX 2004 and Flash MX 2004 Professional? And which version is right for you? First of all, both versions are new upgrades from Flash MX. Flash MX 2004 contains many new features, such as the Behaviors panel and the Video Import Wizard, and new ActionScript elements that expand Flash interactivity. Flash MX 2004 Professional has all of these same new features, plus additional tools that will primarily interest advanced developers of Internet applications and professional video. Among the additional tools that Flash MX 2004 Professional provides are a forms-based environment to create applications, a slide-based environment to create presentations, additional components for database integration, and a video encoder to export FLV files from professional video editors.

If your main interest is in manipulating graphics, animations, sound, text, and video, and integrating them with ActionScript, then Flash MX 2004 is for you. If, instead, your main interest is in developing applications such as Internet chat rooms or e-commerce sites where connectivity to databases is essential, then Flash MX 2004 Professional is for you. This book covers the features common to both versions.

Keep in mind that, while the name of the authoring application is Flash MX 2004 or Flash MX 2004 Professional, the Web browser plug-in that plays media authored in either version is called the Flash Player 7.

What's New in Flash MX 2004

Whether you're a beginner or an advanced user, or a designer or a programmer, a number of new features in Flash MX 2004 will appeal to you. The following are just a few that make Flash MX 2004 even more powerful, flexible, and easy to use.

New productivity tools

New features such as Behaviors, Timeline effects, and the History panel can make your life as a Flash animator and developer much less tedious. Behaviors can automatically assign basic interactivity to keyframes, buttons, and movie clips, while Timeline effects can automate common animation effects such as transitions or special effects such as blurs and explosions. The History panel keeps track of every move you make in Flash, making your Undo commands more precise and letting you create custom commands for repetitious work.

Improved media support

You can now import Adobe PDF and Adobe Illustrator 10 files, making workflow across applications much easier and simpler. You also have many more options for importing digital video with the new Video Import Wizard. The Video Import Wizard walks you through the video import process, allowing you to edit, change dimensions, crop, do color correction, or customize compression settings, with full support for QuickTime, MPEG, AVI, and DV formats.

Expanded interactivity

There are even more ActionScript classes, properties, methods, and events to bring your Flash project to life. For example, detecting the mouse wheel, customizing the contextual menu, and controlling movie clip depth levels are but a few of the many capabilities new to ActionScript. Also new are language elements that make possible strict data typing and a more robust way of creating custom classes; a change in the language dramatic enough to warrant identifying it as a new version of ActionScript, called ActionScript 2.0. In addition, a new Actions panel provides a more streamlined way to script. Enter code directly into the Script pane without relying on the field-driven interface of Normal mode from the previous versions.

Part I: Approaching Advanced Animation

BUILDING COMPLEXITY

1

The key to creating complex animations in Flash is building them from simpler parts. You should think of your Flash project as being a collection of simpler motions, just as the movement of a runner is essentially a collection of rotating limbs. Isolating individual components of a much larger, complicated motion allows you to treat each component with the most appropriate technique, simplifies the tweening, and gives you better control with more-refined results.

To animate a head that's turning quickly to face the camera, for example, you would first consider how to simplify the animation into separate motions. Animating the entire sequence at the same time would be difficult, if not impossible, because the many elements making up the head change in different ways as they move. The outline of the head could be a frame-by-frame animation to show the transformation from a profile to a frontal pose. Some of the features of the face could be symbol instances that you squash and stretch in a motion tween to match the turn of the head. And the hair could be a shape tween that lets you show its flow, swing, and slight bounce-back effect when the head stops.

Learning to combine different techniques and break animation into simpler parts not only solves difficult animation problems, it also forces you to use multiple layers and establish symbols of the component parts. By doing so, you set up the animation so that it is easy to manage now and revise later.

This chapter describes approaches to building complex animations through layering, combining, and extending basic Flash capabilities.

Motion-Tweening Strategies

Motion tweening lets you interpolate any of the instance properties of a symbol, such as its location, size, rotation, color, and transparency. Because of its versatility, motion tweening can be applied to a variety of animation problems, making it the foundation of most Flash projects. Because motion tweening deals with instance properties, it's a good idea to think of the technique in terms of instance tweening. Whether or not actual motion across the Stage is involved, changing instances between keyframes requires motion tweening. Thinking of it as instance tweening will help you distinguish when and where to use motion tweening as opposed to shape tweening or frame-by-frame animation.

Creating seamless animated loops

Animated loops are important because they provide a way to continue motion by defining only a few keyframes. You see animated loops in interface elements such as rotating buttons and scrolling menus, as well as in cyclical motions such as a person walking, a butterfly's wings flapping, or a planet revolving. The important point in making seamless loops is making sure that the last and first keyframes are identical (or nearly identical) so that the motion is continuous.

This section shows you how to make two of the most common types of animated loops: scrolling graphics and graphics on closed motion paths. Scrolling graphics are familiar effects in interface elements such as menu options that cycle across the screen. You can also use this technique to create background animations that loop endlessly, such as a field of stars behind a spaceship or scenery passing by a car window.

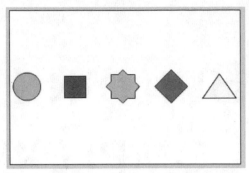

Figure 1.1 Five objects placed across the Stage as they would appear when they begin scrolling across from right to left. The objects could be buttons or simple graphics.

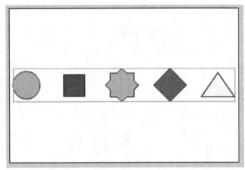

Figure 1.2 Group the objects by choosing Modify > Group.

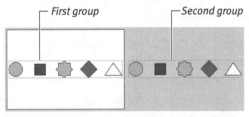

Figure 1.3 Create a pattern by copying and pasting the group.

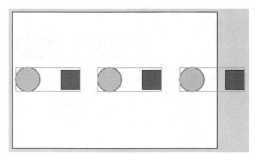

Figure 1.4 This group has only two objects. Place copies of it to extend well past the Stage.

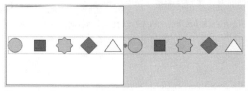

Figure 1.5 Create a graphic symbol of the entire pattern.

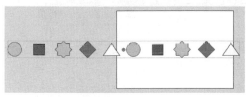

Figure 1.6 The second repeated group is moved where the first group was originally.

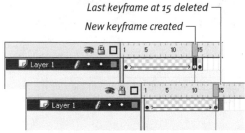

Last keyframe at 15 deleted

New keyframe created

Figure 1.7 Create a new keyframe (top), and delete the last keyframe (bottom).

To create a continuous scrolling graphic:

1. Create the elements that will scroll across the Stage, and place them as they would appear at any given moment (**Figure 1.1**).

2. Select all the elements, and choose Modify > Group (**Figure 1.2**).

3. Copy the group, and paste the copy next to the original group to create a long band of repeating elements.

   If your elements scroll from right to left, for example, place the second group to the right of the first group (**Figure 1.3**).

   Your scrolling elements usually will be larger than the Stage, but if your first group is smaller, you'll need to duplicate it more than once to create a repeating pattern that extends beyond the Stage (**Figure 1.4**).

4. Select all your groups, and convert your selection to a graphic symbol (**Figure 1.5**).

   An instance of the symbol remains on the Stage, allowing you to apply a motion tween.

5. Create a keyframe at a later point in the Timeline.

6. Select the instance in the last keyframe, and move it so that the second repeated group of elements aligns with the first.

   When you move your instance, use its outlines to match its previous position (**Figure 1.6**).

7. Apply a motion tween between the keyframes.

8. Insert a new keyframe just before the last keyframe, and remove the last frame (**Figure 1.7**).

   When you use this technique, the animation won't have to play two identical frames (the first and the last) and a smooth loop is created.

MOTION-TWEENING STRATEGIES

A motion path in a guide layer provides a way to create smooth movement along a path from the beginning point to the end point. If you make the end point of the path match the beginning point, you can create a seamless loop and effectively close the motion path.

To make a closed motion path:

1. Create a graphic symbol, and place an instance of it on the Stage (**Figure 1.8**).

2. Create a guide layer by clicking the Add Motion Guide icon below your layers.

   A new guide layer appears above the first, and your first layer becomes a guided layer (**Figure 1.9**).

3. Draw an empty ellipse in the guide (top) layer.

4. With the Snap to Objects modifier for the Arrow tool turned on, grab your instance by its registration point and place it on the path of the ellipse (**Figure 1.10**).

5. Add frames to both layers, and create a new keyframe in the last frame of the guided (bottom) layer.

   The first and last keyframes remain the same to create the animated loop (**Figure 1.11**).

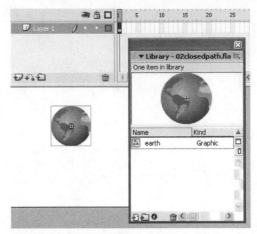

Figure 1.8 An instance of a graphic symbol is placed on the Stage for motion tweening along a path.

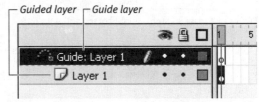

Figure 1.9 The guide layer above Layer 1 will contain the motion path.

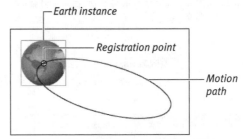

Figure 1.10 The registration point of the earth instance snaps to the motion path.

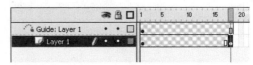

Figure 1.11 The position of the earth at keyframe 1 and at keyframe 18 in Layer 1 are the same.

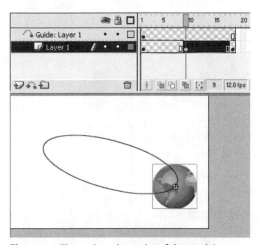

Figure 1.12 The registration point of the earth in the middle keyframe is positioned at the far side of the ellipse.

6. Select the middle frame of the guided (bottom) layer, and insert a new keyframe, moving your instance in this intermediate keyframe to the opposite side of the ellipse (**Figure 1.12**).

7. Select all the frames between the three keyframes, and in the Property Inspector, choose Motion Tween.

Your instance now travels along the path of the ellipse, but it returns on the same segment of the ellipse rather than making a complete circuit (**Figure 1.13**).

8. Grab the instance in the last keyframe of the guided (bottom) layer, and move it slightly closer to the instance in the middle keyframe while maintaining its registration point on the path (**Figure 1.14**).

continues on next page

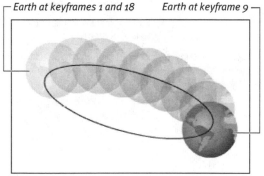

Figure 1.13 The earth bounces back and forth on the same segment of the ellipse.

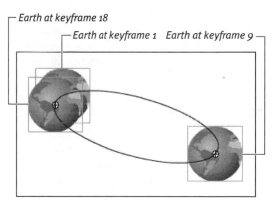

Figure 1.14 The three keyframes of the earth. The first instance is closer to the middle instance on the top path of the ellipse, and the last instance is closer to the middle instance on the bottom path of the ellipse.

MOTION-TWEENING STRATEGIES

Flash tweens two instances by taking the most direct path, so by shortening the distance between the last two keyframes on the bottom segment of the ellipse, you force Flash to use that segment of the ellipse.

Your instance now travels along both sides of the ellipse (**Figure 1.15**).

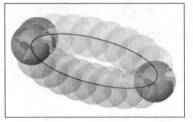

Figure 1.15 The earth moves around the closed path.

✔ Tip

■ You can accomplish the same kind of looping effect by deleting a small segment of your path. When you create a gap, you essentially make an open path with beginning and end points for your instance to follow (**Figure 1.16**).

Using multiple guided layers

A single guide layer can affect more than one guided layer, letting multiple motion tweens follow the same path. This approach is good for creating complex animations that require many objects traveling in the same direction, such as soldiers marching through a field, blood cells coursing through an artery, bullets flying through the air, or cattle stampeding in a herd. Although the individual instances may vary, you maintain control of their general direction with a single guide layer.

Several leaves blowing across the Stage could be animated to follow one guide layer, for example. The guide layer establishes the wind's general direction; the leaves could have slight individual variations by being offset in separate guided layers. Just by changing the path in the guide layer, you make all the leaves change accordingly. Using a single path to guide multiple layers this way is an example of how you build complex animations (in this case, swirling leaves) from very simple parts (one guide layer and one leaf symbol).

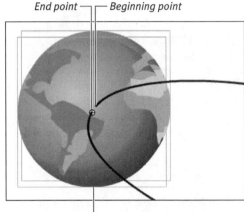

End point ─── ┌─ Beginning point

─── Earth at last keyframe attached to end point of path

Figure 1.16 A tiny gap provides beginning and end points for your motion path.

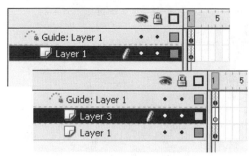

Figure 1.17 Selecting the guided layer (Layer 1 above) and inserting a new layer automatically modifies the new layer as a guided layer (Layer 3).

Drag Layer 3 under the guide layer

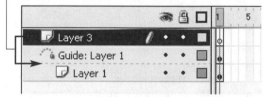

Figure 1.18 A normal layer (Layer 3) can be dragged below the guide layer to become a guided layer.

Instance in leaf 2 layer
Instance in leaf 1 layer   Motion path

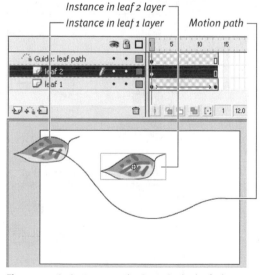

Figure 1.19 An instance on the Stage in the leaf 2 layer.

To assign a second guided layer to a guide layer:

◆ Select the first guided layer, and click the Insert Layer icon.

A second guided layer appears above the first (**Figure 1.17**).

or

◆ Drag an existing normal layer below the guide layer.

The normal layer becomes a guided layer (**Figure 1.18**).

To offset a second guided layer:

1. Create the second guided layer as described earlier in this section, and drag in an instance that you want to tween (**Figure 1.19**).

2. Select the instance in the second guided layer, and choose the Free Transform tool in the Toolbox.

Control handles appear around your instance, along with a white circle in the center marking the current registration point (**Figure 1.20**).

continues on next page

Free Transform tool

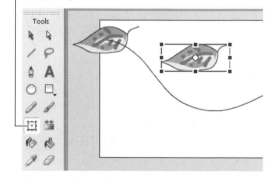

Figure 1.20 Select the instance in the second guided layer, and select the Free Transform tool in the Toolbox.

MOTION-TWEENING STRATEGIES

3. Drag the registration point to a new position.

An instance's registration point can lie anywhere, even outside the boundaries of the Free Transform tool's control handles.

The new registration point will be set where you just placed it (**Figure 1.21**).

4. Now select the Arrow tool to exit the Free Transform tool, and make sure that the Snap to Objects modifier is turned on.

5. Grab the instance by its new registration point, and attach it to the beginning of the guide-layer's path (**Figure 1.22**).

6. Insert a new keyframe into the last frame.

The newly created instance in the last keyframe will have the same registration point as the edited instance.

7. Now attach the instance in the last keyframe to the end of the guide-layer's path, and apply a motion tween between the two keyframes.

The motion tween in the second guided layer follows the same path as the first guided layer. The new registration point of the instance in the second guided layer, however, offsets the motion (**Figure 1.23**). 🎧

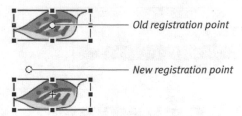

Old registration point

New registration point

Figure 1.21 Change the registration point of your instance by moving the white circle.

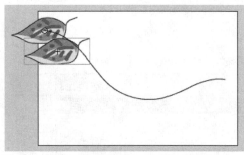

Figure 1.22 The registration point of the leaf, shown selected here, is attached to the path.

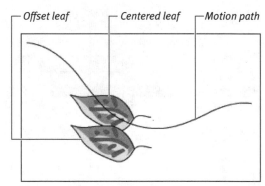

⌐*Offset leaf*   ⌐*Centered leaf*   ⌐*Motion path*

Figure 1.23 The two tweens follow the same motion path. The second leaf is offset because of its moved registration point.

Instance in leaf 2 layer ⎯ *Instance in leaf 1 layer*

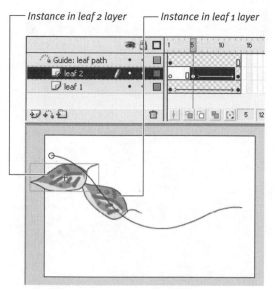

Figure 1.24 The leaf in the leaf 2 layer follows the motion path only after the one in the leaf 1 layer has already started.

Last keyframe moved from frame 13 to frame 10 ⎯

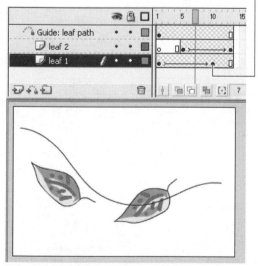

Figure 1.25 Move the last keyframe in the leaf 1 layer closer to the first keyframe.

To vary the timing of a second guided layer:

1. Continuing with the preceding example, drag the first keyframe of the second guided layer to a later point in time.

The motion tween for that guided layer will begin after the first one starts, but both of the animations will end at the same time (**Figure 1.24**).

2. Drag the last keyframe of the first guided layer to an earlier point in time.

The motion tweens following the path in the guide layer are staggered relative to each other (**Figure 1.25**).

3. Refine the timing of the motion tweens by moving the first and last keyframes in both guided layers.

✔ Tip

■ Create variations in the second guided layer by placing the instances on any point along the path in the guide layer. The instances do not have to lie at the very beginning or end of the path for the motion tween to work.

You can increase complexity by using animated graphic symbol instances along the guide layer's motion path. Animated loops within graphic symbols provide localized motion that still follows the guide layer in the main Timeline.

To add local variations to multiple guided layers:

1. Enter symbol-editing mode for the graphic symbol you use on the motion path.

2. Select the contents of this symbol, and convert it to a graphic symbol.

   You create a graphic symbol within another graphic symbol, which allows you to create a motion tween within your first graphic symbol.

3. Create a looping motion tween (**Figure 1.26**).

   This type of animation ends where it begins.

4. Exit symbol-editing mode, and play the movie to see how the motion tween of the graphic symbol gets incorporated into the motion tween on the main Stage (**Figure 1.27**).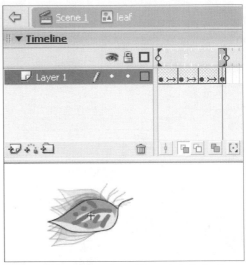

✔ Tips

■ In the Property Inspector, adjust the play-mode option and First parameter to vary how the animated graphic instances play (**Figure 1.28**). By having your loops begin with different frames, you prevent them from being synchronized with one another (**Figure 1.29**).

■ Rotating your instances at this point can produce even more complex, interesting, and seemingly random movements. Experiment with rotating your instances as they travel along the motion path.

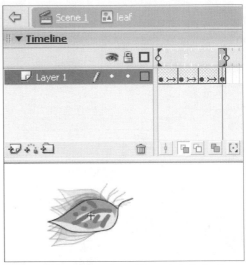

Figure 1.26 An animated graphic symbol of a leaf moving up and down.

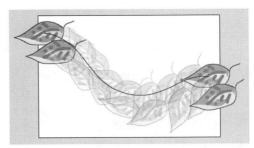

Figure 1.27 Play the movie to see how the leaves follow the motion path while going through their own animation.

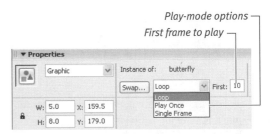

Figure 1.28 The First parameter is set to 10 so that the leaf graphic will loop beginning with Frame 10. The other play mode options in the pull-down menu include Play Once and Single Frame.

MOTION-TWEENING STRATEGIES

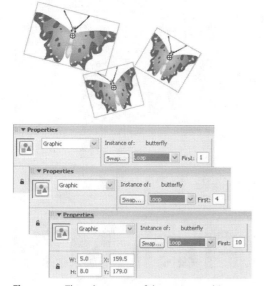

Figure 1.29 Three instances of the same graphic symbol with different first-frame play options. The left butterfly loops beginning with Frame 1; its wings will start to close. The middle butterfly loops beginning with Frame 4; its wings are already closed and will start to open. The right butterfly loops beginning with Frame 10; its wings are opening.

Figure 1.30 Breaking apart a block of static text (top) results in static text of the individual letters (bottom).

Animating titles

Frequently, splash screens on Flash Web sites feature animated titles and other text-related materials that twirl, tumble, and spin until they all come into place as a complete design. Several techniques can help you accomplish these kinds of effects quickly and easily. The Break Apart command, when applied to a block of static text, breaks the text into its component characters while keeping them as live, editable text. This command lets you painlessly create separate text fields for the letters that make up a word or title. You can then use the Distribute to Layers command to isolate each of those characters on its own layer, ready for motion tweening.

When you do start applying motion tweens to your individual letters or words, it's very useful to think and work backward from the final design. Create an end keyframe containing the final positions of all your characters, for example. Then, in the first keyframes, you can change their positions and apply as many transformations as you like, knowing that the final resting spots are secured.

To animate the letters of a title:

1. Select the Text tool, and make sure that Static Text is selected in the Property Inspector.

2. On the Stage, type a title you want to animate.

3. Choose Modify > Break Apart (Cmd-B for Mac, Ctrl-B for Windows).

   Flash replaces the static-text title with individual static-text letters (**Figure 1.30**).

continues on next page

MOTION-TWEENING STRATEGIES

4. Choose Modify > Timeline > Distribute to Layers (Cmd-Shift-D for Mac, Ctrl-Shift-D for Windows).

Each selected item on the Stage is placed in its own layer below the existing one. In this case, the newly created layers are named with the individual letters automatically (**Figure 1.31**).

5. Create keyframes at a later point in the Timeline for each layer.

6. In the first keyframe of each layer, rearrange and transform the letters according to your creative urges.

7. Select all the frames in the Timeline, and apply a motion tween.

Flash automatically converts the static text elements to graphic symbols and stores them in the Library. Your movie animates all these text elements coming together as a complete title (**Figure 1.32**).

✔ Tip

■ Make sure that you select all the frames in step 7. If you don't include the last keyframe, Flash will leave those text elements as static text while converting the elements in the first keyframe to graphic symbols. In that case, you'll end up with motion tweens with different elements in the first and last keyframes, which could foul up future tweening in those layers.

Figure 1.31 Distribute to Layers separates the selected items in their own layers.

Figure 1.32 These letters tumble and fall into place at the last keyframe.

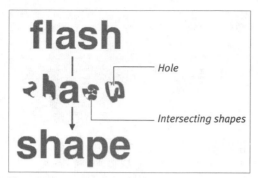

Figure 1.33 An attempt to shape-tween *flash* to *shape* all at once in a single layer. Notice the breakups between the *s* and the *p* and the hole that appears between the *h* and the *e*.

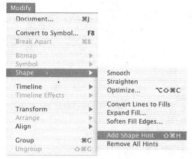

Figure 1.34 Select the first keyframe of the shape tween, and choose Modify > Shape > Add Shape Hint.

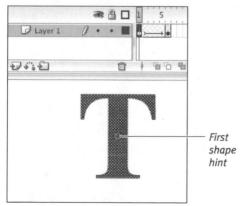

Figure 1.35 The first shape hint appears in the center of the Stage in the first keyframe.

Shape-Tweening Strategies

Shape tweening is a technique for interpolating amorphous changes that can't be accomplished with instance transformations such as rotation, scale, and skew. Fill, outline, gradient, and alpha are all shape attributes that can be shape-tweened.

Flash applies a shape tween by using what it considers to be the most efficient, direct route. This method sometimes has unpredictable results, creating overlapping shapes or seemingly random holes that appear and merge (**Figure 1.33**). These undesirable effects usually are the result of keyframes containing shapes that are too complex to tween at the same time.

As is the case with motion tweening, simplifying a complicated shape tween into more basic parts and separating those parts in layers results in a more successful interpolation. Shape hints give you a way to tell Flash what point on the first shape corresponds to what point on the second shape. Sometimes, adding intermediate keyframes will help a complicated tween by providing a transition state and making the tween go through many more-manageable stages.

Using shape hints

Shape hints force Flash to map particular points on the first shape to corresponding points on the second shape. By placing multiple shape hints, you can control more precisely the way your shapes will tween.

To add a shape hint:

1. Select the first keyframe of the shape tween, and choose Modify > Shape > Add Shape Hint (Cmd-Shift-H for Mac, Ctrl-Shift-H for Windows) (**Figure 1.34**). A letter in a red circle appears in the middle of your shape (**Figure 1.35**).

continues on next page

2. Move the first shape hint to a point on your shape.

Make sure that the Snap to Objects modifier for the Arrow tool is turned on to snap your selections to vertices and edges.

3. Select the last keyframe of the shape tween, and move the matching circled letter to a corresponding point on the end shape.

This shape hint turns green, and the first shape hint turns yellow, signifying that both have been moved into place correctly (**Figure 1.36**).

4. Continue adding shape hints, up to a maximum of 26, to refine the shape tween (**Figure 1.37**). 🖱️

✔ Tips

- Place shape hints in order either clockwise or counterclockwise. Flash will more easily understand a sequential placement than one that jumps around.

- Shape hints need to be placed on an edge or a corner of the shape. If you place a shape hint in the fill or outside the shape, the original and corresponding shape hints will remain red, and Flash will ignore them.

- To view your animation without the shape hints, choose View > Show Shape Hints (Cmd-Option-H for Mac, Ctrl-Alt-H for Windows). Flash deselects the Show Shape Hints option, and the shape hints are hidden.

- If you move your entire shape tween by using Edit Multiple Frames, you will have to reposition all your shape hints. Unfortunately, you cannot move all the shape hints at the same time.

Figure 1.36 The first shape hint in the first keyframe (left) and its matching pair in the last keyframe (right).

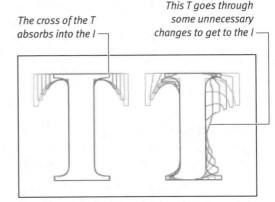

The cross of the T absorbs into the I

This T goes through some unnecessary changes to get to the I

Figure 1.37 Changing from a *T* to an *I* with shape hints (left) and without shape hints (right).

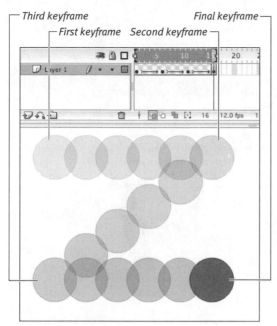

First keyframe   Second keyframe
Third keyframe   Final keyframe

Figure 1.38 A complicated motion tween requires several intermediate keyframes.

Intersecting shapes

Figure 1.39 Changing a *Z* to an *S* all at once causes the shape to flip and cross over itself.

Figure 1.40 An intermediate shape.

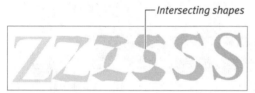

Figure 1.41 The *Z* makes an easy transition to the intermediate shape (middle), from which the *S* can tween smoothly.

To delete a shape hint:

◆ Drag the shape hint off the Stage.

The matching shape hint in the other keyframe will be deleted automatically.

To remove all shape hints:

◆ Choose Modify > Shape > Remove All Hints.

Using intermediate keyframes

Adding intermediate keyframes can help a complicated tween by providing a transition state that creates smaller, more-manageable changes. Think about this process in terms of motion tweening. Imagine that you want to create the motion of a ball starting from the top left of the Stage, moving to the top right, then to the bottom left, and finally to the bottom right (**Figure 1.38**). You wouldn't create just two keyframes—one with the ball at the top-left corner of the Stage and one with the ball in the bottom-right corner—and expect Flash to tween the zigzag motion. You would need to establish the intermediate keyframes so that Flash could create the motion in stages. The same is true of shape tweening. You can better handle one dramatic change between two shapes by using simpler, intermediate keyframes.

To create an intermediate keyframe:

1. Study how an existing shape tween fails to produce satisfactory results when tweening the letter *Z* to the letter *S* (**Figure 1.39**).

2. Insert a keyframe at an intermediate point within the tween.

3. In the newly created keyframe, edit the shape to provide a kind of stepping stone for the final shape (**Figure 1.40**).

The shape tween has smaller changes to go through, with smoother results (**Figure 1.41**).

Sometimes, providing an intermediate keyframe isn't enough, and you need shape hints to refine the tween even more. Here are three ways you can add shape hints to a shape tween that uses an intermediate keyframe.

To use shape hints across multiple keyframes:

◆ Select the intermediate keyframe, and add shape hints as though it were the first keyframe.

Keep track of which shape hint belongs to which tween by noting their respective colors. Yellow is the shape hint for the beginning keyframe, and green is the shape hint for the ending keyframe (**Figure 1.42**).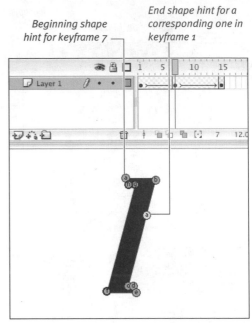

or

◆ Insert a new keyframe adjacent to the second keyframe, and begin adding shape hints.

A new keyframe allows you to add shape hints without the confusion that overlapping shape hints from the preceding tween may cause (**Figure 1.43**).

or

◆ Create a new layer that duplicates the intermediate and last keyframes of the shape tween, and begin adding shape tweens on this new layer.

By duplicating the intermediate keyframe, you keep shape hints on separate layers, which also prevents the shape hints from overlapping (**Figure 1.44**).

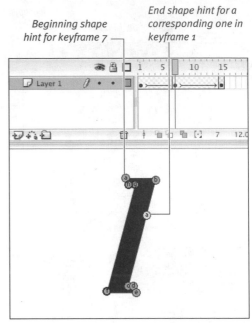

Beginning shape hint for keyframe 7

End shape hint for a corresponding one in keyframe 1

Figure 1.42 This intermediate keyframe contains two sets of shape hints. Some are the ending shape hints for the first tween; others are the beginning shape hints for the second tween.

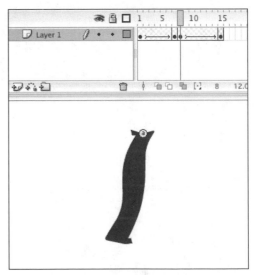

Figure 1.43 A shape hint in a new keyframe.

Shape hints in Layer 2

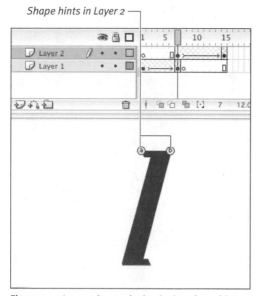

Figure 1.44 Layer 2 keeps the beginning shape hints for the tween from Frames 7 to 15 separate from the end shape hints for the tween from Frames 1 to 7.

Using layers to simplify shape changes

Shape tweening lets you create very complex shape tweens on a single layer, but doing so can produce unpredictable results. Use layers to separate complex shapes and create multiple but simpler shape tweens.

When a shape tween is applied to change the letter *F* to the letter *D,* for example, the hole in the last shape appears at the edges of the first shape (**Figure 1.45**). Separating the hole in the *D* and treating it as a white shape allows you to control when and how it will appear. Insert a new layer, and create a second tween for the hole. The compound tween gives you better, more-refined results (**Figure 1.46**). 🔊

Figure 1.45 A hole appears at the outline of the first shape when a shape tween is applied to change an *F* to a *D*.

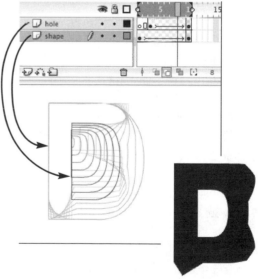

Figure 1.46 The hole and the solid shapes are separated on two layers.

Using shape tweens for gradient transitions

It helps to think about shape tweening as a technique that does more than just "morphing," or interpolating one amorphous contour to another. After all, shape tweening can be used on any of the attributes of a shape, such as line weight and line color (but not line style) and the fill color, including its alpha or gradient. In fact, you can create interesting effects just by shape-tweening color gradients. For example, changing the way a gradient is applied to a particular fill using the Fill Transform tool can be an easy way to move a gradient across the Stage; combined with changing contours, it can be a way to produce atmospheric animations like clouds or puffs of smoke.

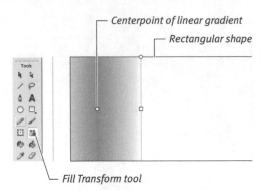

Centerpoint of linear gradient

Rectangular shape

Fill Transform tool

Figure 1.47 Use the Fill Transform tool from the Toolbox to move the gradient fill of the rectangle to the far left side.

To create a gradient transition with shape tweening:

1. Select the Rectangle tool, and draw a large rectangle on the Stage.

2. Fill the shape with a radial or linear gradient.

3. Select the Fill Transform tool, and click the rectangle on the Stage.

   The control handles for the Fill Transform tool appear for the gradient.

4. For this example, move the center of the gradient to the far left side of your rectangle (**Figure 1.47**).

5. Create a new keyframe later on the Timeline.

6. Select the last keyframe, and click on the rectangle with the Fill Transform tool.

   The control handles for the Fill Transform tool appear for the gradient in the last keyframe.

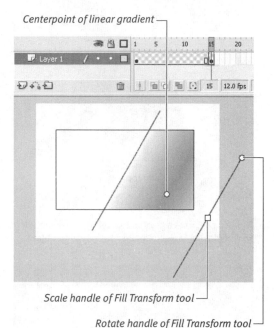

Centerpoint of linear gradient ⎯

Scale handle of Fill Transform tool ⎯

Rotate handle of Fill Transform tool ⎯

Figure 1.48 In the last keyframe, use the Fill Transform tool to change the way the linear gradient fills the rectangle. Here, the linear gradient is moved to the far right side, tilted, and made wider.

7. Move the center of the gradient to the far right side of your rectangle and change the rotation, scale, or angle of the gradient as you desire.

Your two keyframes contain the same rectangular shape, but its gradient fills are applied differently (**Figure 1.48**).

8. Select the first keyframe, and in the Property Inspector, choose Shape Tween.

Flash tweens the transformation of the gradient fills from the first keyframe to the last keyframe. The actual contour of the rectangle remains constant.

9. Delete the outlines of the rectangle.

The gradient moves from left to right (**Figure 1.49**).

✔ Tip

- You cannot shape-tween between different kinds of gradients; that is, you cannot shape-tween from a radial gradient to a linear gradient or vice versa.

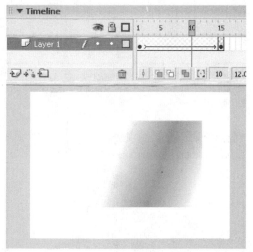

Figure 1.49 The final shape tween makes the gradient twist, widen, and move across the rectangle.

SHAPE-TWEENING STRATEGIES

Creating Special Effects

Because Flash's drawing tools are vector based, you normally wouldn't think of incorporating a special effect, such as a motion blur, which is associated with bitmap applications such as Adobe Photoshop or Macromedia Fireworks. But integrating special effects is possible simply by importing a bitmap that has been altered by a special-effect filter. This technique can give your Flash movie more depth and richness by going beyond the simple flat shapes and gradients of vector drawings.

The following examples demonstrate a motion blur and a blur-to-focus effect. A *motion blur* is a camera artifact produced when something moves too fast for the film to capture; you see a blurry image of where the moving object used to be. Often, these images overlap, creating a streak that trails the fast-moving object. Cameras do create motion blurs automatically and unintentionally, but in Flash, you must put them in yourself.

A *blur* is an effect that occurs when the camera is out of focus. Blurs are particularly effective for transitions; you can animate a blurry image coming into sharp focus.

To create a motion blur:

1. Create the image to which you want to apply a motion blur, and convert it to a graphic symbol (**Figure 1.50**).

2. Copy the graphic, and paste it into a new document in Photoshop.

    The new Photoshop document should be in RGB, the resolution should be 72 dots per inch (dpi), and the size should be the same as your copied Flash graphic.

    The Flash graphic appears in the Photoshop document.

3. Choose Image > Canvas Size.

    The Canvas Size dialog box appears.

Figure 1.50 Create a graphic symbol. This snowboarder will be moving fast enough to cause a motion blur.

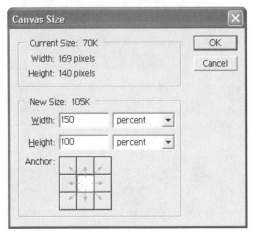

Figure 1.51 In Photoshop, change the canvas size in the direction of the blur. This canvas will get wider on either side by 150%.

Figure 1.52 The image in Photoshop needs room on either side to make room for a horizontal blur.

Preview window

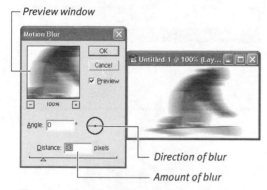

Direction of blur

Amount of blur

Figure 1.53 The Motion Blur filter in Photoshop provides options for the direction and amount of blur, as well as a preview window of the effect.

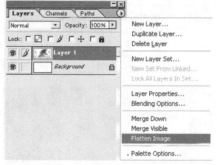

Figure 1.54 In the Layers palette of Photoshop, flatten your image to a single layer.

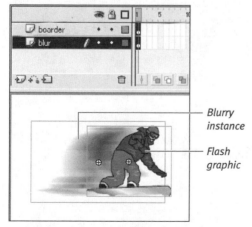

Blurry instance

Flash graphic

Figure 1.55 The motion blur is positioned behind the image of the snowboarder. Both instances are on separate layers, in preparation for motion tweening.

4. Increase the canvas by about 150 percent in the direction in which you will be applying your motion blur (**Figure 1.51**); then click OK.

The background of your graphic increases so that you have room for your motion blur (**Figure 1.52**).

5. Choose Filter > Blur > Motion Blur.

The Motion Blur dialog box appears.

6. Change the angle of the blur to match the direction in which your image will be moving, and set the amount of blur to about one-fifth the overall size of your image (**Figure 1.53**); then click OK.

The image becomes blurry in one direction only, simulating the speed streaks from a camera.

7. Choose Layer > Flatten Image (**Figure 1.54**).

8. Choose Select > All (Cmd-A for Mac, Ctrl-A for Windows), copy the image, and then paste it back into your Flash file in an empty layer.

The motion-blurred bitmap image appears on the Stage and in your Library.

9. Convert the blurry bitmap image to a graphic symbol.

10. Move the blurry instance below the original Flash graphic so that the streaks extend in the direction opposite from which the graphic will move (**Figure 1.55**).

11. Create keyframes for both layers later in the Timeline, move both instances across the Stage, and apply a motion tween to both layers.

The original image and the blurred image move together, but the combined effect isn't quite convincing yet.

continues on next page

12. Adjust the timing of the keyframes so that the blurred image starts a few frames later and the original image finishes a few frames earlier, and add an empty keyframe in the last frame for the blurred image (**Figure 1.56**).

Having the blurred image lag behind the original graphic makes the streak more of an afterimage and completes the special effect.

✔ Tip

■ This technique works only if your Stage is a solid color because the Photoshop filter produces a bitmap that blurs the image to the background.

To create a blur-to-focus effect:

1. As in the preceding example, copy and paste an image from Flash into Photoshop.

2. Adjust the canvas in both width and height to make room for the blur effect.

   For an image that bleeds on all four sides like the example shown here, however, increasing the canvas size isn't necessary.

3. In Photoshop, choose Filter > Blur > Gaussian Blur.

   The Gaussian Blur dialog box appears.

4. Enter a pixel amount that determines the amount of blurring you desire (**Figure 1.57**); then click OK.

   The image blurs.

5. Make sure to flatten the image by choosing Layer > Flatten Image.

6. Select the entire image; then copy and paste it back into Flash in an empty layer.

   This Flash file contains your original, focused image.

7. Convert the blurry imported bitmap to a graphic symbol.

Figure 1.56 Play with the timing of the motion tween of the blur so that it appears when the snowboarder is in motion but disappears when he stops.

Figure 1.57 The Gaussian Blur filter in Photoshop makes the entire image unfocused.

CREATING SPECIAL EFFECTS

Figure 1.58 Place the blurry instance over the original image. In this figure, the two images are not yet aligned, so you can see their overlapping positions.

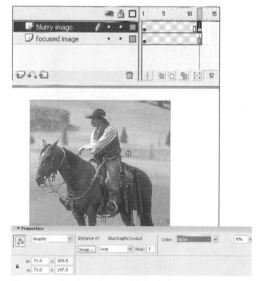

Figure 1.59 In the Property Inspector, the alpha value of the top, blurry image is set to 0%, exposing the original, focused image in the bottom layer.

8. Align the original, focused image and the blurry image, with the blurry image in the topmost layer (**Figure 1.58**).

9. Later in the Timeline, insert a keyframe into the layer that contains the blurry image and add a matching number of frames in the layer that contains the focused image.

10. In the last keyframe of the blurry image, change the image's alpha value to 0% (**Figure 1.59**).

    The blurry image in the last keyframe becomes transparent, exposing the focused image in the layer below.

11. Apply a motion tween to the layer that contains the blurry image.

    As the blurry image slowly disappears, it shows the unaltered image, making it seem as though you have one image with a change in focus (**Figure 1.60**).

✔ Tips

- Try increasing the initial size of the blurry image slightly to add a subtle zooming-in effect, which enhances the blur-to-focus transition.

- You can use any Photoshop filter in this manner to create a transition. Experiment with the numerous available filters to suit your movie.

Figure 1.60 The result makes an effective transition.

CREATING SPECIAL EFFECTS

Animated and Complex Masks

Masking is a simple way to reveal portions of a layer or the layers below it. This technique requires making one layer a mask layer and the layers below it the mask*ed* layers.

By adding tweening to either or both the mask layer and the masked layers, you can go beyond simple, static peepholes and create masks that move, change shape, and reveal moving images. Use animated masks to achieve such complex effects as moving spotlights, magnifying lenses that enlarge underlying pictures, or "x-ray" types of interactions that show more detail within the mask area. Animated masks are also useful for creating cinematic transitions such as wipes, in which the first scene is covered as a second scene is revealed, and iris effects, in which the first scene collapses in a shrinking circle, leaving a second scene on the screen.

You can add even more complexity to animated masks by inserting layers above and below them. A shape filled with an alpha gradient, for example, can make the hard edges of a mask fade out slowly for a subtle spotlight.

Using movie clips in mask layers opens even more possibilities: multiple masks, masks that move on a motion guide, and even dynamically generated masks that respond to the user. Because dynamic masks rely on ActionScript, however, they'll be covered in detail later (in Chapter 7) after you've learned more about Flash's scripting language.

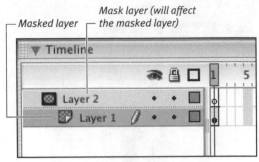

Figure 1.61 Layer 2 is the mask layer, and Layer 1 is the masked layer.

Diver in Layer 1 — Shape tween in Layer 2

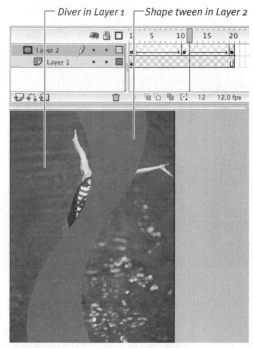

Figure 1.62 A shape tween of a moving vertical swirl is on the mask layer. The diver image is on the masked layer.

Figure 1.63 The shape tween uncovers the image of the diver. The portion of the mask that does not reveal the photo is the color of the Stage.

To tween the mask layer:

1. In Layer 1, create a background image or import a bitmap.

2. Insert a new layer above the first layer.

3. Select the top layer, and choose Modify > Timeline > Layer Properties.
   or
   Double-click the layer icon in the top layer.
   The Layer Properties dialog box appears.

4. Select Mask Type.

5. Select the bottom layer, and choose Modify > Timeline > Layer Properties.

6. Select Masked Type.
   The top layer becomes the mask layer, and the bottom layer becomes the masked layer (the layer that is affected by the mask) (**Figure 1.61**).

7. Create a shape tween or a motion tween in the mask layer (the top layer) (**Figure 1.62**).

8. Insert sufficient frames into your masked layer (the bottom layer) to match the number of frames in the mask-layer tween.

9. Lock both layers to see the effects of your animated mask on the image in the masked layer (**Figure 1.63**).

continues on next page

ANIMATED AND COMPLEX MASKS

✔ Tips

■ Place duplicate images that vary slightly in a normal layer under both the mask and masked layers. This technique makes the animated mask act as a kind of filter that exposes the underlying image. Add a bright image in the masked layer and a dark version of the same image in a normal layer under the masked layer, for example. The mask becomes a spotlight on the image (**Figure 1.64**).

Explore other duplicate-image combinations, such as a sharp and a blurry image, a grayscale and a color image, or an offset image (**Figure 1.65**).

■ Place a tween of an expanding box in the mask layer that covers the Stage to simulate cinematic wipes between images (**Figure 1.66**).

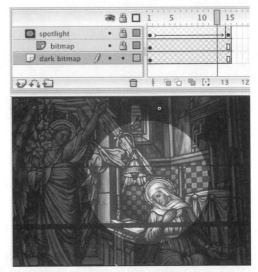

Figure 1.64 The moving spotlight in the mask layer (spotlight) uncovers the stained-glass image in the masked layer (bitmap). A duplicate darker image resides in the bottom, normal layer (dark bitmap).

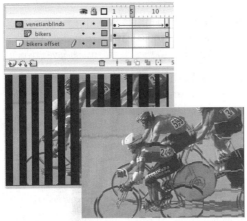

Figure 1.65 The moving vertical shapes in the mask layer (venetianblinds) uncover the image of bicyclists in the masked layer (bikers). A duplicate image in the bottom normal layer (bikers offset) is shifted slightly to create the rippling effect.

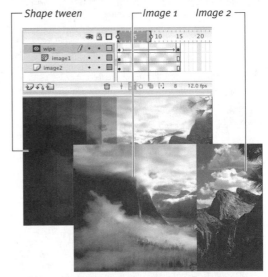

Figure 1.66 The mask layer contains a large shape tween that covers the entire Stage. This technique creates a cinematic wipe between an image in the masked layer (image 1) and an image in the bottom, normal layer (image 2).

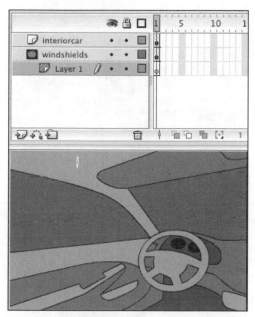

Figure 1.67 The windshield shapes are in the mask layer called windshields. The drawing of the car interior is in a normal layer above the windshields layer.

To tween the masked layer:

1. Beginning with two layers, modify the top to be the mask layer and the bottom to be the masked layer.

2. Draw a filled shape or shapes in the mask layer (the top layer) (**Figure 1.67**). This area becomes the area through which you see your animation on the masked layer.

3. Create a shape tween or a motion tween in masked layers (the bottom layers) that pass under the shapes in the mask layer. You can have as many masked layers as you want under a single mask layer (**Figure 1.68**).

4. Lock both layers to see the effects of your animated masked layers as they show up behind your mask layer (**Figure 1.69**).

continues on next page

Figure 1.68 Several motion tweens in masked layers (tree, cow, ground, and sky) move under the windshield shapes in the mask layer.

Figure 1.69 The images of the tree, cow, ground, and sky move under the mask, creating the illusion of the car's forward motion.

ANIMATED AND COMPLEX MASKS

✔ Tip

- This approach is a useful alternative to using shape tweens to animate borders or similar types of objects that grow, shrink, or fill in. Imagine animating a fuse that shortens to reach a bomb (**Figure 1.70**). Create a mask of the fuse, and animate the masked layer to become smaller slowly, making it look like just the fuse is shortening (**Figure 1.71**). Other examples that could benefit from this technique include trees growing, pipes or blood vessels flowing with liquid, and text that appears by filling in with color. Just remember that Flash doesn't recognize strokes in the mask layer, so if you want to create thin lines in the mask layer, use fills only.

Figure 1.70 The fuse of a bomb shortens.

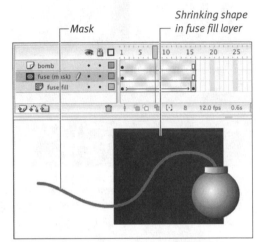

Figure 1.71 The bomb's fuse is a thin shape in the mask layer. The rectangular tween in the masked layer shrinks, making it appear as though the fuse is shortening.

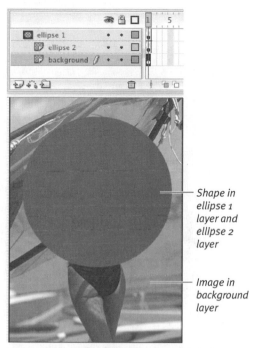

Shape in ellipse 1 layer and ellipse 2 layer

Image in background layer

Figure 1.72 The same ellipse appears in both the mask layer (ellipse 1) and the top masked layer (ellipse 2). The image of the windsurfer is in the bottom masked layer (background).

100% alpha

0% alpha

Figure 1.73 A radial gradient with a transparent center in the top masked layer.

In the mask layer, Flash sees all fills as opaque shapes, even if you use a transparent solid or gradient. As a result, all masks have hard edges. To create a softer edge, place a gradient with a transparent center either under or over the mask to hide the edges.

To create a soft-edged mask:

1. Create a mask layer and a masked layer.

2. Place or draw a background image in the masked layer (the bottom layer).

3. Draw an ellipse in the mask layer (the top layer).

4. Copy the ellipse.

5. Insert a new layer between the mask layer and the masked layer.

   Your new layer will become a masked layer.

6. Choose Edit > Paste in Place (Cmd-Shift-V for Mac, Ctrl-Shift-V for Windows).

   A new ellipse appears in the new masked layer, right under the ellipse in the top mask layer (**Figure 1.72**).

7. Fill the pasted ellipse with a radial gradient, defined with a transparent center to an opaque perimeter, in the same color as the Stage (**Figure 1.73**).

continues on next page

8. Lock all three layers to see the effects of the mask (**Figure 1.74**).

The mask layer lets you see through an elliptical area. The top masked layer hides the edges of the ellipse by creating a gradual fade toward the center. The bottom masked layer holds the contents of your background image (**Figure 1.75**).

Figure 1.74 The resulting soft-edged mask.

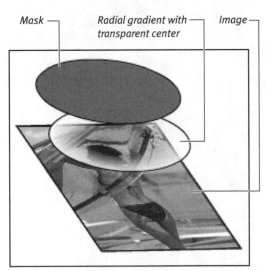

Mask — Radial gradient with transparent center — Image

Figure 1.75 The soft-edged mask is the combination of the mask in the top layer (mask layer), a radial gradient in the middle layer (top masked layer), and the background image in the bottom layer (bottom masked layer).

Figure 1.76 An irregular shape in the top masked layer above an image in the bottom masked layer.

Empty rectangle ──┐　　┌── Irregular shape

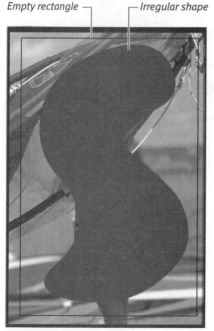

Figure 1.77 An empty rectangle drawn around the irregular shape.

Creating soft edges with radial transparent gradients works well with circular masks, but if the shapes of your masks are more complicated, you'll need to resort to customizing the fades of your edges.

To create a soft-edged mask with an irregular shape:

1. Create a mask layer and a masked layer.

2. Place or draw an image in the masked layer (the bottom layer).

3. Draw an irregular shape in the mask layer (the top layer).

4. Copy the shape.

5. Insert a new masked layer between the mask layer and the first masked layer.

6. Choose Edit > Paste in Place.

   Your irregular shape appears in the new masked layer right under the original shape in the top mask layer (**Figure 1.76**).

7. With the Oval or Rectangle tool, draw an outline around your shape (**Figure 1.77**).

continues on next page

8. Fill the area between your shape and the outline with the background color, and delete the fill in the original shape.

Your irregular shape is now the "hole" of a larger shape (**Figure 1.78**).

9. Select the entire shape, and choose Modify > Shape > Soften Fill Edges (**Figure 1.79**).

The Soften Fill Edges dialog box appears (**Figure 1.80**). The Distance option determines the thickness of the soft edge. The Number of steps option determines how gradual the transition from opaque to transparent will be. The Direction option determines which way the edge softening will take place.

Figure 1.78 By filling the area between the shape and the rectangle and then deleting the shape, you create a hole.

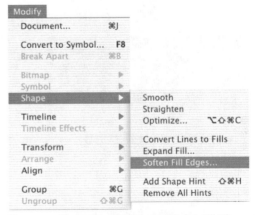

Figure 1.79 Choose Modify > Shape > Soften Fill Edges.

Figure 1.80 The Soften Fill Edges dialog box.

Figure 1.81 The softened edges expand into the "hole," where it is visible through the mask in the top mask layer.

Figure 1.82 The soft edges of an irregular mask created with Modify > Shape > Soften Fill Edges.

10. Enter the distance (in pixels) and the number of steps, and choose Expand for the direction.

All the edges around your shape soften. Because the entire shape expands, the actual hole shrinks (**Figure 1.81**).

11. Lock all three layers to see the effects of the mask (**Figure 1.82**).

Although Flash allows multiple masked layers under a single mask layer, you cannot have more than one mask layer affecting any number of masked layers (**Figure 1.83**). To create more than one mask, you must use movie clips. Why would you need to have multiple masks? Imagine creating an animation that has two spotlights moving independently on top of an image (**Figure 1.84**). Because the two moving spotlights are tweened, they have to be on separate layers. The solution is to incorporate the two moving spotlights into a movie clip and place the movie clip on the mask layer.

You will learn much more about the movie clip in Chapters 4 and 7. If you'd like, skip ahead to read about movie clips and return when you feel comfortable.

To create multiple masks:

1. Create a mask layer and a masked layer.

2. Place your image on the masked layer (the bottom layer).

3. Choose Insert > New Symbol (Cmd-F8 for Mac, Ctrl-F8 for Windows).
   The Create New Symbol dialog box appears.

4. Enter a descriptive name and choose Movie Clip (**Figure 1.85**); then click OK.
   Flash creates a movie-clip symbol, and you enter symbol-editing mode for that symbol.

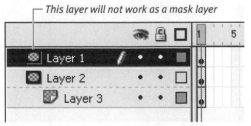

This layer will not work as a mask layer

Figure 1.83 Layer 1 and Layer 2 are both defined as mask layers, but only Layer 2 affects Layer 3—the masked layer.

Figure 1.84 Two independent spotlights moving, each uncovering portions of the image.

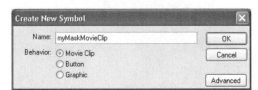

Figure 1.85 Choose Movie Clip to create a new movie-clip symbol.

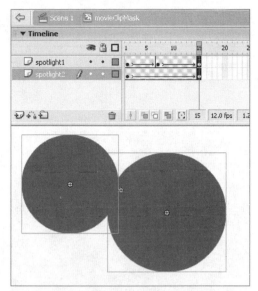

Figure 1.86 The two moving spotlights are motion tweens inside a movie clip.

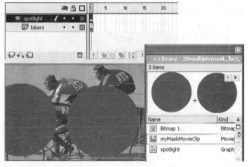

Figure 1.87 An instance of the movie clip is in the top (mask) layer, and the image of the bikers is in the bottom (masked) layer.

5. Create two motion tweens of spotlights moving in different directions on the Timeline of your movie-clip symbol (**Figure 1.86**).

6. Return to the main Stage, and drag an instance of your movie-clip symbol into the mask layer (the top layer) (**Figure 1.87**).

7. Choose Control > Test Movie to see the effects of the movie-clip mask.

  · The two motion tweens inside the movie clip both mask the image on the masked layer.

continues on next page

✔ Tips

- To see what your masks are uncovering, use a transparent fill or choose the Outlines option in your Layers Properties dialog box (**Figure 1.88**).

- To prevent the animation inside the movie clip from looping constantly, add a keyframe to its last frame and add a `stop` action.

Outline of spotlight 2 layer in a movie clip
Outline of spotlight 1 layer in a movie clip

Figure 1.88 Viewing your masks as outlines lets you see the image underneath; choose the Outlines option in the Layers Properties dialog box, or click the Show as Outlines icon in your layer.

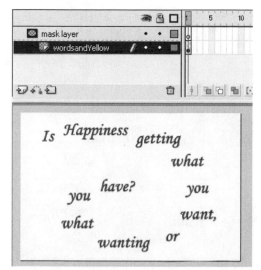

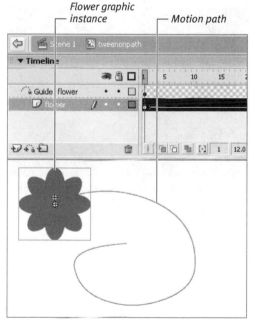

Figure 1.89 The words of this interesting question and a background fill are put on the bottom (masked) layer.

Flower graphic instance — Motion path

Figure 1.90 Inside a movie clip, the flower graphic instance follows a motion path.

Putting a movie-clip instance inside the mask layer not only makes multiple masks possible, it also provides a way to have a mask follow a motion guide. Build your tween that follows a motion guide inside a movie clip. Place that movie clip in a mask layer on the main Stage, and voilà—you have a mask that follows a path.

To guide a mask on a path:

1. Create a mask layer and a masked layer.

2. Place your image on the masked layer (the bottom layer) (**Figure 1.89**).

3. Create a new movie-clip symbol.

4. Inside your movie-clip symbol, create a motion tween that follows a motion guide (**Figure 1.90**).

continues on next page

5. Return to the main Stage, and drag an instance of your movie clip into the mask layer (the top layer) (**Figure 1.91**).

6. Edit the motion path to get it exactly the way you want, relative to the other graphics on the Stage, by choosing Edit > Edit in Place or by double-clicking the instance (**Figure 1.92**).

Flash dims all graphics except for the instance you are editing.

7. Choose Control > Test Movie to see the effect of your movie clip on the mask layer.

The animation follows its path in the motion guide, and at the same time, it masks the image in the masked layer on the main Stage (**Figure 1.93**).

Figure 1.91 The movie clip containing the moving flower is in the mask layer and positioned over the words.

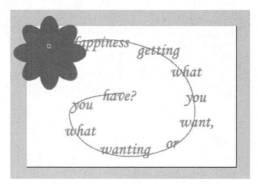

Figure 1.92 Edit in Place allows you to make changes in your movie-clip symbol and see the graphics on the main Stage at the same time.

Figure 1.93 The moving flower exposes the question as it moves along its motion path.

WORKING WITH VIDEO

2

This chapter explores the exciting possibilities of integrating video in your Flash project. Flash makes importing video easy with the Video Import Wizard, which takes you step by step through the process and gives you options for editing, cropping, changing color balances, and setting levels of compression. When you combine digital video with Flash, you can develop imagery with all the interactivity of Flash ActionScript but without the limitations of the Flash drawing or animation tools. You can create truly interactive movies, for example, by importing your videos into Flash and then adding buttons and hotspots, sounds, and vector graphics. You can export this combination of video and Flash as either a Flash movie or a QuickTime file. More possibilities of integrating an imported video include using it as a guide for your Flash animation or transforming the video completely by applying Flash's editing tools to turn it into vector drawings. Use this effect to give short animated sequences a live-motion feel while maintaining manageable file sizes.

Importing Video into Flash

Everybody loves movies. So when you can add video to your Flash Web site, you'll likely create a richer and more compelling experience for your viewers. Several popular formats for digital video are QuickTime, MPEG, AVI, and DV. Fortunately, Flash supports all of them. Flash also supports its own video format, the Flash Video (FLV) format, which we'll discuss in Chapter 6. You can import any of these digital video formats into Flash; you can add Flash graphics, animation, and interactivity; and in certain cases, you can even apply motion tweens to your imported video. You can import video into Flash by embedding it or, if you are using the QuickTime format, linking to the video.

Embedding puts the video file inside your Flash project, increasing its file size just as importing a bitmap does. Linking, on the other hand, maintains your video as a separate file outside Flash. Flash keeps track of the video with a path to the filename. If you link a video, however, several restrictions exist. You cannot apply motion tweens to a linked video, and you *must* export your Flash project as QuickTime. (Linked videos will not work in SWF format.) Moreover, the QuickTime format doesn't support the full functionality of Flash ActionScript (see the sidebar "Not All Flash Features Work in QuickTime" later in the chapter). It's safe to say that if you want to create fully functional SWF movies, always embed your videos rather than link them.

You have several ways to acquire digital video. You can shoot your own footage using a digital video camera, or you can shoot with an analog video camera and convert the video using a digitizing board that you install in your computer. Alternatively, you can use copyright-free video clips that have already been digitized and are available on CD-ROM from commercial image stock houses. Any way you go, adding digital video is an exciting way to enrich a Flash Web site.

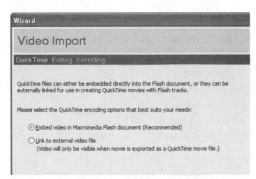

Figure 2.1 For video in the QuickTime format (.mov), the Video Import Wizard lets you choose to embed the video or link to it.

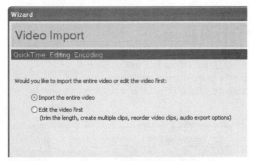

Figure 2.2 You can choose to either import the video "as is" or edit the video first, before importing.

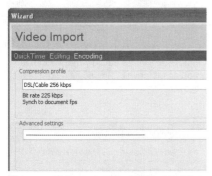

Figure 2.3 The compression setting is set for a DSL or cable download speed (top drop-down list). No Advanced setting profile is selected (bottom drop-down list).

To embed a digitized video in Flash:

1. From the File menu, choose Import > Import to Stage (Command-R for Mac, Ctrl-R for Windows).

   The Import dialog box appears.

2. Select the file you want to import, and click Import (Mac) or Open (Windows).

   The Video Import Wizard appears. If your video file is in QuickTime (MOV) format, you are asked whether you want to embed the video or link to it (**Figure 2.1**).

3. Choose Embed video in Macromedia Flash document, and click Next.

   The Video Import Wizard proceeds to the Editing options (**Figure 2.2**), asking whether or not you want to import the entire video or edit the video first.

4. Choose Import the entire video, and click Next.

   The Video Import Wizard proceeds to the Encoding options (**Figure 2.3**), giving you the option to set the compression profile, where you set the trade-offs between image quality and file size. You can also set the advanced settings, where you can crop your video or edit its color.

   continues on next page

5. Choose a Compression profile setting to best match your file needs (**Figure 2.4**). **Table 2.1** lists all of the Compression profile settings.

Flash uses the Sorenson Spark codec (*compression-deco*mpression scheme) to import and display video. This codec is lossy, meaning some of the less important or less visible data are discarded in order to make the file smaller. The rebuilt movie appears similar to the original, but not exactly the same. The compression profiles are based on bandwidth, in kilobits per second, which is a measure of how much data can download per second. Flash may alter the quality of individual frames in order to keep the download at a consistent speed. Remember, the higher the kbps preset setting, the larger your file size and the higher quality your video will be.

6. Click Finish.

Flash embeds the video in your document, putting a video symbol in your Library and an instance of the video on the Stage in the active layer (**Figure 2.5**). If you do not have enough empty frames to accommodate the entire length of your video, a dialog box appears (**Figure 2.6**). If this happens, click Yes.

Table 2.1

Default Compression Profile Settings	
LABEL NAME	BIT RATE
56 kbps modem	34 kbps
Corporate LAN 150 kbps	150 kbps
DSL/Cable 256 kbps	225 kbps
DSL/Cable 512 kbps	450 kbps
DSL/Cable 786 kbps	700 kbps

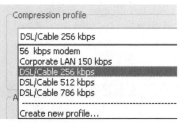

Figure 2.4 The default compression profiles that ship with Flash mimic the most common download speeds. The preset profile is DSL/Cable 256 kbps.

Figure 2.5 Importing a video puts a video symbol in the Library and an instance of the movie on the Stage in the active layer.

Figure 2.6 Flash will ask you whether it can add enough blank frames to the Timeline to accommodate the video.

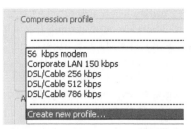

Figure 2.7 Select Create new profile from the Compression profile drop-down list to customize your own compression settings.

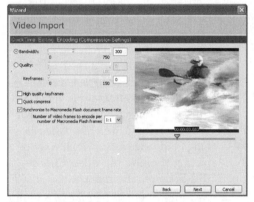

Figure 2.8 With the compression settings, you can decide to have the quality of your video be determined by bandwidth (maintaining a consistent download speed) or by quality (the integrity of the video image). You can also choose different frame encoding options.

✔ Tips

■ Macintosh users can import a file quickly by simply dragging the video file from the Desktop to the Stage.

■ Flash can't display the soundtrack of imported videos, so if your original video file has sound, you won't hear it within the authoring environment of Flash. When you publish your Flash movie or test it by choosing Control > Test Movie, the sound will be audible again.

■ If you have more frames than are needed in a layer containing an embedded video, Flash will display the last frame of the video until the end of the Timeline. To end the Timeline exactly where the video ends, select the excess frames and choose Edit > Timeline > Remove Frames.

To select your own compression settings:

1. From the Encoding options of the Video Import Wizard, choose Create new profile from the Compression profile drop-down list (**Figure 2.7**).

    The compression settings for your new profile appear (**Figure 2.8**).

    continues on next page

2. Choose between Bandwidth or Quality. Bandwidth compresses your video to maintain a consistent download speed while Quality compresses your video based on image quality. Choose from these settings to affect the quality, length, and file size of your imported video.

▲ **Bandwidth.** Determines the quality of video based on download speeds measured in kilobits per second (kbps). The larger the kbps, the higher the image quality and larger the file size.

▲ **Quality.** Controls the amount of compression that is applied to your video and, hence, the quality of the image. A value of 100 is the best quality but results in a large file; a value of 0 is the worst quality but produces a small file.

▲ **Keyframes.** Determines the keyframe interval, or how frequently complete frames of your video are stored. The frames between keyframes store only the data that changes from the preceding frame. A keyframe interval of 24, for example, stores information on the complete frame every 24 frames of your video. If your video contains the action of someone raising his hand between Frames 17 and 18, only that portion of the image where his hand is being raised is stored in memory until Frame 24, when the full frame is stored. The lower you set the keyframe interval, the more keyframes are stored and the larger the file will be. A keyframe setting of 0, however, will store no keyframes and will result in the smallest file.

▲ **High quality keyframes.** Select this option if you are compressing the video using a Bandwidth value to ensure consistent image quality in keyframes. Using a Bandwidth value can degrade keyframe quality if you do not select this option.

▲ **Quick compress.** Choose this option to speed up the compression time. Quality, however, may suffer.

▲ **Synchronize to Macromedia Flash document frame rate.** Choosing this option matches the frame rate of your video to the frame rate of your Flash movie. This option ensures that a video plays at its intended speed even if the frame rates between it and Flash differ. A video shot at 30 frames per second (fps) and brought into a Flash movie running at 15 fps will play twice as long (and twice as slowly) if you do not synchronize the video. Choose this option for normal use.

▲ **Number of video frames to encode per number of Macromedia Flash frames.** Controls the mapping of frames between the video Timeline and the Flash Timeline. Choosing a ratio in which the first number is smaller than the second number makes the video display fewer of its frames than Flash. The ratio 1:2 for example, results in one frame of your video playing for every two frames on your Flash Timeline. This setting results in a smaller file (because there are fewer video frames to encode) but a choppier playback. It does *not* affect the duration of your video. Choose 1:1 for normal use.

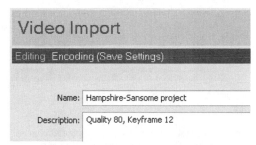

Figure 2.9 Enter a name and description of your custom compression settings. This can be useful if you need to import many video files for a single project that must maintain a uniform level of quality.

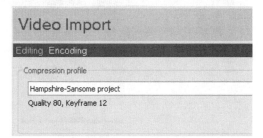

Figure 2.10 Your custom compression profile appears as a choice in the drop-down list.

3. Click Next.

The Video Import Wizard proceeds to the Save Settings options.

4. Enter a descriptive name for your custom compression profile in the Name field and any comments in the Description field (**Figure 2.9**).

5. Click Next to save your custom compression profile for use in future video imports needing the same treatment (**Figure 2.10**).

What Makes a Good Video?

We all know a good video when we see one. But how do you create and prepare digitized videos so they play well and look good within Flash? Knowing a little about the Sorenson Spark compression that is built into Flash will help.

Sorenson compresses video both spatially and temporally. Spatial compression happens within a single frame, much like JPEG compression on an image. Temporal compression happens between frames, so the only information that is stored is the differences between two frames. Therefore, videos that compress really well are ones that contain localized motion or very little motion (such as a talking head) because the differences between frames are minimal. (In a talking-head video, only the mouth is moving.) For the same reasons, transitions, zooms, and fades do not compress or display well, so stick with quick cuts if possible.

Here are a few other tips, not related to compression, for making a good video:

◆ Keep the size small (320 by 240 maximum) and the length of the video short. Often, just a few well-placed moments of video is enough to heighten the drama of your Flash movie.

◆ Maintain reasonable frame rates. Although video may run at about 30 fps, use 12 to 15 fps.

◆ Shoot in digital. You'll get a cleaner image by using a digital source rather than filming in analog and then converting to digital.

Advanced color, size, cropping, and tracking options

In many situations, you may need only a cropped portion of a video, or the video at a smaller size, or you may want to apply some color corrections to it. Using the Video Import Wizard, you can make the necessary adjustments to color balance, brightness and contrast, scale, and cropping; you can even choose to import the video to different Timelines inside your Flash movie. All of these options are available from the Advanced Settings Encoding stage of the video import process. You can create and save new Advanced settings profiles to apply to multiple video imports.

To change color balance, dimensions, or tracking:

1. From the Encoding options of the Video Import Wizard, choose Create new profile from the Advanced settings drop-down list (**Figure 2.11**).

   The Advanced settings for your new profile appear (**Figure 2.12**).

2. Adjust the Color, Dimensions, and Track options settings. Each adjustment can be viewed in the preview window.

   ▲ **Hue.** Determines the color shift of your video, and it is measured from -180 degrees to 180 degrees.

   ▲ **Saturation.** Determines the purity of color, and it is measured from -100 to +100. Choose -100 to strip all color and create a black-and-white video.

   ▲ **Gamma.** Determines the relative proportion of light and dark in your video, and it is measured from 0.1 to 1.8.

   ▲ **Brightness.** Determines the amount of light and dark in your video, and it is measured from -100 (completely black) to +100 (completely white).

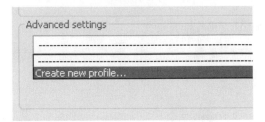

Figure 2.11 Select Create new profile in the Advanced settings drop-down list to make changes to color, dimensions, or tracking options.

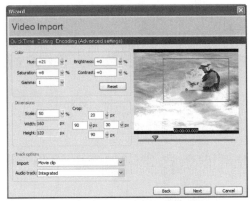

Figure 2.12 The Advanced settings options let you tweak color shifts and proportions of light and dark (top of window), set scale and cropping options (middle of window), and control how the video and audio will be imported into the Flash Timeline (bottom of window). The preview window to the right shows the effects of any cropping or color changes.

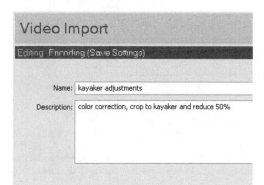

Figure 2.13 Enter a name and description to identify your Advanced settings customizations.

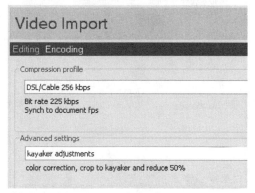

Figure 2.14 Your custom Advanced settings profile appears as a choice in the drop-down list.

▲ **Contrast.** Determines the contrast between light and dark in your video, and it is measured from -100 (no contrast) to +100 (high contrast).

▲ **Scale.** Sets the size of your video from 1% to 100% of the original size. The Width and Height fields display the pixel dimensions of the new video size.

▲ **Crop.** Sets the top, bottom, left, and right pixel dimensions of the amount of video information to crop. Guidelines in the preview window show the cropped image area.

▲ **Import.** Determines where the imported video will appear. In the Import drop-down list, you can choose the current Timeline, the Timeline of a new movie-clip symbol, or the Timeline of a new graphic symbol. When importing video into either a movie clip or a graphic symbol, Flash sets the registration to the upper-left corner for that symbol.

▲ **Audio track.** Determines where the sound from your video will appear. You can choose to keep the sound integrated with the video, strip your video of sound and create a separate sound symbol, or strip your video of sound entirely and make it silent.

3. Click Next.

The Video Import Wizard proceeds to the Save Settings options.

4. Enter a name and description for your newly created profile (**Figure 2.13**).

5. Click Next to save your Advanced settings profile and continue importing your video into your Flash movie.

The profile that you just created is now available for use in future projects (**Figure 2.14**). 🕸

To link a QuickTime video in Flash:

1. Choose File > Import > Import to Stage to open the Import dialog box.

2. Select the video file you want to link in Flash.

   The Video Import Wizard dialog box appears.

3. Choose Link to external video file (**Figure 2.15**), and click OK.

   Flash imports a link to the video into your document, putting a video link symbol in your Library and an instance of the video on the Stage in the active layer (**Figure 2.16**).

   If you do not have enough empty frames to accommodate the entire length of your video, a dialog box appears, asking to insert frames for the video automatically. If this happens, click Yes.

   Linked videos are visible only when your Flash project is exported as QuickTime (see how to do this later in this section). Be sure to set your publish settings (File > Publish Settings) to Flash Player 5 or earlier before exporting a linked video to QuickTime. QuickTime 6 only supports Macromedia Flash 5 functionality.

✔ Tip

- Unlike with embedded videos, if you have more frames than are needed in a layer containing a linked video, Flash displays an empty placeholder that looks like a rectangle with an *X* through it (**Figure 2.17**). To end the Timeline exactly where the video ends, select and delete the excess frames.

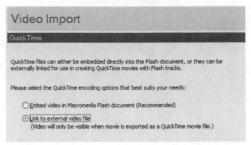

Figure 2.15 Select Link to external video file to link the external QuickTime movie to your Flash document.

Figure 2.16 The Library shows the linked video.

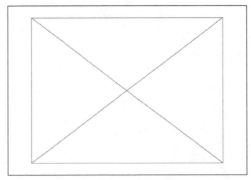

Figure 2.17 The placeholder on the Stage means you're past the end of the linked movie and there are no more frames available to display.

Editing Video

If you want to edit your video before importing it into your Flash project, you can do so with the Video Import Wizard. Create smaller clips of your video, delete selected portions, or rearrange video sequences in order to import just the video you need, the way you want it. The Editing (Customize) options of the Video Import Wizard provides all the tools you need to edit your imported video (**Figure 2.18**). Establishing the video's In and Out points is the first step in doing any video edits. The In and Out points identify the beginning and the end of a video segment you wish to save in the Video Clip window. You can import your video clip into Flash, or once you have several video clips in the Video Clip window, you can import them as separate videos or rearrange them and combine them into one single video to import.

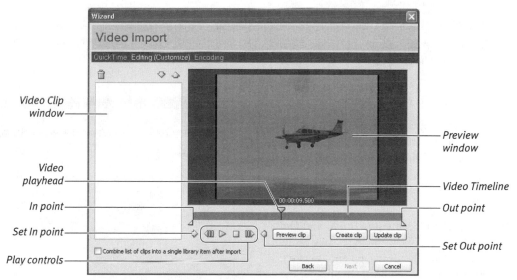

Figure 2.18 The Editing (Customize) options of the Video Import Wizard. Here you can select shorter sequences of your video to import or rearrange them as needed.

To create a video clip:

1. From the Editing options of the Video Import Wizard, choose Edit the video first, and click Next (**Figure 2.19**).

    The Editing (Customize) options appear, with the video selected for import displayed in the preview window. The In point is located to the far left of the video's Timeline, and the Out point is located to the far right. This shows that the entire video is currently selected to be imported.

2. Drag the In and Out points where you want your movie to start and finish.

    or

    Move the video playhead and click the Set In Point button (the right-pointing arrow) and the Set Out Point button (the left-pointing arrow) to establish the In and Out points (**Figure 2.20**).

    You can preview your selected video clip by clicking the Preview clip button under the video Timeline.

3. Click Create Clip.

    The new clip appears in the Video Clip window, to the left of the preview window (**Figure 2.21**).

4. Click the Next button.

5. Make any adjustments you want to make to the compression profile or Advanced settings, and click Finish.

    Your video clip is imported into Flash.

✔ Tip

- For precise placement of the In and Out points, select one of them so they remain highlighted. Then, click on the Advance One Frame or Step Back One Frame button to step through your video and move the In and Out points frame by frame.

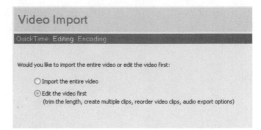

Figure 2.19 Choose the Edit the video first option.

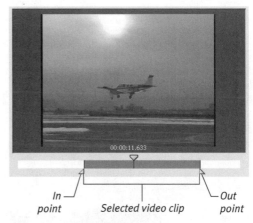

Figure 2.20 The highlighted portion of the Timeline, bounded by the In point on the left and the Out point on the right, shows the selected video clip.

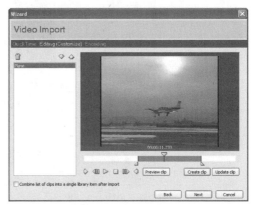

Figure 2.21 New video clips are placed in the Video Clip window.

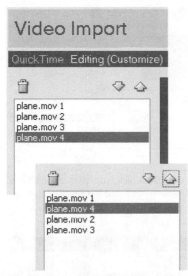

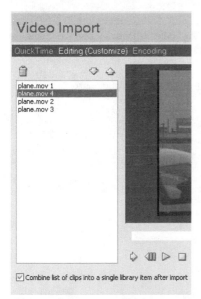

Figure 2.22 A selected video clip (top) can be moved to a different position (bottom) using the Up or Down arrow.

Figure 2.23 If the check box below the Video Clip window is checked as it is here, Flash will combine the separate clips in the order that they appear in the list and import a single video. If the check box remains unchecked, the four video clips will be imported as separate video symbols in the Library item and only the first clip will be placed on the Stage.

To change the In and Out points of a video clip:

1. Select the video clip in the Video Clip window.

2. Set the In and Out points to new positions.

3. Click the Update clip button.

   The video clip is updated to reflect the new In and Out points.

To rearrange video clips:

◆ Select a video clip in the Video Clip window and click the Up arrow.

   The selected video clip moves ahead one position (**Figure 2.22**).

◆ Select a video clip in the Video Clip window and click the Down arrow.

   The selected video clip moves behind one position.

To delete a video clip:

◆ Select a video clip in the Video Clip window and click the trash can button.

   The selected video clip is deleted from the Video Clip window.

To combine several video clips into one video:

◆ Click the check box under the Video Clip window (**Figure 2.23**).

   Flash will combine all the video clips in the Video Clip Library in the order that they appear into a single video. If this option is not checked, Flash will export the video clips as separate Library symbols.

EDITING VIDEO

Updating and replacing imported videos

When you make changes in your original video file, you'll want those changes to be reflected in your Flash movie as well. Luckily, Flash makes updating your imported videos easy, whether the videos are embedded or linked in Flash. For an embedded video, you can update it or reimport it to modify the compression settings. For a linked video, you can update the path to the file if it's been moved or renamed.

If you've linked your video, you can also edit your original video with either QuickTime Player or another external digital video editor. When you do, Flash updates your video symbol in the Library automatically. Note that if you use QuickTime Player, you will need QuickTime Pro (the upgrade you buy from Apple) to do any copying, pasting, or resaving of files.

To update an embedded video:

1. Double-click the video icon or the preview window in your Library.

    or

    Select the video symbol in the Library; then, from the Library window's Options menu, choose Properties (**Figure 2.24**).

    The Embedded Video Properties dialog box appears, showing the symbol name and the original video file's location (**Figure 2.25**).

2. Click Update.

    Flash finds the video file and reimports it, using the original compression settings. Any changes you have made in the video are updated in Flash. The video must be in the same file path as the original video you imported. If not, you cannot use the Update button to update the video.

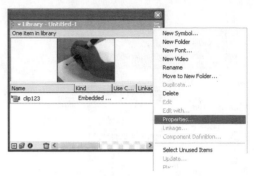

Figure 2.24 Choose Options > Properties in the Library window to get information about the selected symbol.

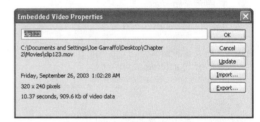

Figure 2.25 The Embedded Video Properties dialog box shows the name of the symbol and the location of the original video file, as well as the properties of the compressed video (dimensions, time, and size).

54

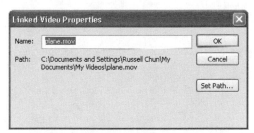

Figure 2.26 The Linked Video Properties dialog box shows the name of the linked file and the path to it. Click the Set Path button to change the path if the file has been moved.

Figure 2.27 In the Library window, choose Options > Edit with QuickTime Player or Edit with to use another application to make changes in your linked video file.

To set a new path for your linked video:

1. Double-click the video icon or the preview window in your Library.

   or

   Select the video symbol in the Library; then, from the Library window's Options menu, choose Properties.

   The Linked Video Properties dialog box appears, showing the symbol name and the original video file's location (**Figure 2.26**).

2. Click the Set Path button.

3. Navigate to the new location or renamed video file, select it, and click Open.

   The new path and filename appear in the Linked Video Properties dialog box next to Path.

4. Click OK.

   Flash will now be able to locate the video.

✔ Tip

■ The name in the Name field in the Linked Video Properties dialog box is not the name of your original video file; it's the name of your symbol in the Library. These two names can be different as long as the path to the video file is correct.

To edit a linked video:

1. In the Library, select the linked video symbol you want to edit.

2. From the Library window's Options menu, choose Edit with QuickTime Player or Edit with (**Figure 2.27**).

   The external application launches and opens your video file.

3. Edit the video file, and save it.

4. Return to Flash, delete the current instance of the video on the Stage, and drag a new instance from the Library to see the changes in your video.

   Flash will use the new video file that you just edited and saved.

EDITING VIDEO

Adding Flash Elements to Your Video

After you have imported your video into Flash, you can add Flash elements such as titles, labels, and animated special effects over the movie. Add graphics next to a talking-head video to mimic a newscast, for example, or use labels to point out important features as they appear in an instructional video on fixing a bicycle.

Put your embedded video inside a graphic symbol, and you can also apply motion tweens to create transitions with the alpha or color effect or create funky rotations, skewing, scaling, and even horizontal or vertical flips.

Add interactivity by integrating buttons or frame actions that control the playback of the video content. Create your own Pause, Stop, Play, Fast Forward, and Rewind buttons to customize the video-playback interface. You can even convert your video to a movie-clip symbol and have at your disposal the methods, properties, and events of the Movie Clip class. Create drag-and-drop video puzzle pieces as a twist on standard puzzles, for example. You will learn much more about the Movie Clip class in later chapters, so be sure to return here after reading about it to see how you can incorporate it into imported videos.

Titles and border added on top of video

San Francisco

Skateboarding

Smoke added on top of video — Imported video in the bottom layer

Figure 2.28 Add Flash graphics and animation over your imported video. This example shows two animated titles, a mask that uncovers a border, and the special effect of the shape-tweened smoke behind the skateboarder's foot.

Convert to Symbol

Name: inLineSkaterVideo

Behavior: ○ Movie clip   Registration: ▢
         ○ Button
         ● Graphic

OK
Cancel
Advanced

Figure 2.29 Convert your embedded video to a graphic symbol so you can apply motions tweens.

To overlay Flash elements on a video:

1. For this example, set the Stage to the same size as the imported video file (320 by 240 pixels), and position an imported movie to cover the Stage exactly.

2. Lock the layer that contains the video to prevent it from being moved accidentally.

3. Add separate layers over the video layer to create animated titles, graphics, or special effects.

   Figure 2.28 shows a few animated elements superimposed on the imported video file. Check out the Flash and video files provided on the CD.

To apply a motion tween to an embedded video:

1. Select the video instance on the Stage.

2. Choose Modify > Convert to Symbol (F8). The Convert to Symbol dialog box appears.

3. Enter a descriptive name, choose the Graphic option in the Behavior section, and click OK (**Figure 2.29**).

   A warning dialog box appears, asking whether you want to insert enough frames into the new graphic symbol to accommodate the length of your video.

4. Click Yes.

   The video on the Stage is now an instance of a graphic symbol to which you can apply motion tweens.

continues on next page

ADDING FLASH ELEMENTS TO YOUR VIDEO

5. Create new keyframes along the Timeline, and modify the instance by changing its color effect, position, scale, rotation, or skew.

6. Apply motion tweens between the keyframes (**Figure 2.30**).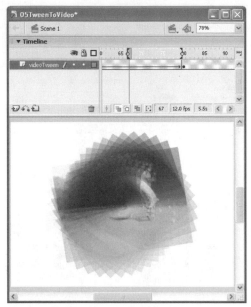

✔ Tips

■ You cannot apply tweens to a linked video clip; they will not show up in the final exported QuickTime file.

■ You can always add layers and drag out more instances of the graphic symbol containing your video and your video will play in all the instances. Be aware, however, that new keyframes of the same instance will make your file larger.

■ The First parameter in the Property Inspector, which normally establishes which frame of a graphic instance will begin playing, will not affect the playback of the video.

To create interactive controls for a video:

1. Create four buttons: a Play button, a Pause button, a Skip to End button, and a Skip to Beginning button.

2. Place your four button instances in a new layer above the layer containing an imported video file (**Figure 2.31**).

3. Add a third layer, and insert a keyframe at the last frame of the Timeline.

Figure 2.30 This video of an inline skater coming toward the viewer is given a motion tween that rotates and enlarges it, enhancing the excitement.

Four button instances placed on a layer above the video ⌐

Figure 2.31 Add button instances to let your users navigate the video. These buttons are placed on a separate layer.

Figure 2.32 In another layer, label the start of the Timeline start (top) and the end of the Timeline end (bottom). This method will make assigning frame destinations for your buttons easier.

Figure 2.33 The exported SWF file plays your video while buttons and actions you've customized control its playback.

4. Label the first keyframe start, and label the last keyframe end (**Figure 2.32**).

5. Assign actions to all four button instances by selecting them individually and then opening the Actions panel.

▲ Give the Play button these actions:
`on (release) { play(); }`

▲ Give the Pause button these actions:
`on (release){ stop(); }`

▲ Give the Skip to End button these actions:
`on (release) { gotoAndStop("end"); }`

▲ Give the Skip to Beginning button these actions:
`on (release) { gotoAndStop("start"); }`

For more information on the Actions panel, see Chapter 3.

6. Test your movie to see how your custom Flash buttons let you navigate to different spots on the Timeline and control the playback of the video (**Figure 2.33**).

Exporting to QuickTime, QuickTime video, and AVI

Most of the time, you will publish your Flash movie as a SWF file to play with Flash Player in a browser. On some occasions, however, you will need or want to export your Flash movie in alternative formats. The three video formats available for export are QuickTime, QuickTime Video (Mac only), and AVI (Windows only). What are the differences among these file formats, and how do they differ from SWF? To help sort out the confusion, see the sidebar "QuickTime, QuickTime Video, and AVI" in this section.

If you linked a video in Flash, you must export your Flash project as one of these three movie formats for the linked video to display.

If you want to rasterize all your Flash content so that earlier versions of QuickTime Player can display your movie, you will want to export a QuickTime video or an AVI.

To export your Flash movie as a QuickTime video or AVI:

1. Choose File > Export > Export Movie (Ctrl-Alt-Shift-S for Windows, Command-Opt-Shift-S for Mac).
   The Export Movie dialog box appears.

2. Choose a destination folder and name, and choose QuickTime Video from the Format drop-down menu (Mac) (**Figure 2.34**) or choose Windows AVI from the Save As Type drop-down menu (Windows).
   The Export dialog box appears (**Figure 2.35**).

3. Select your export settings, and click OK.
   Flash exports your Flash movie as a QuickTime video or AVI.

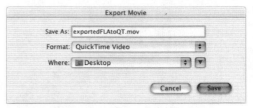

Figure 2.34 The Export Movie dialog box.

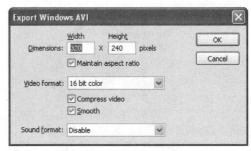

Figure 2.35 The Export Windows AVI dialog box.

✔ Tip

■ If you have animations inside movie clips, only their first frames will display in a QuickTime video or AVI. In the Property Inspector, set their behavior to graphic symbols to play as Loop and they will play when you export to a QuickTime video or AVI.

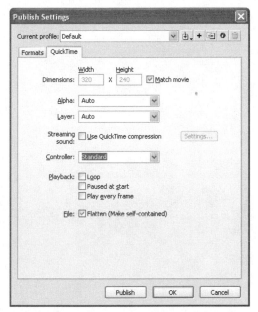

Figure 2.36 The QuickTime tab of the Publish Settings dialog box.

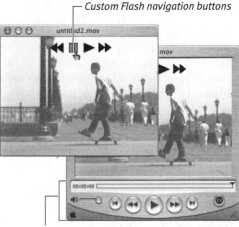

Custom Flash navigation buttons

Standard and QuickTime playback controls

Figure 2.37 Two QuickTime movies, with (bottom) and without (top) the standard playback controls.

To export your Flash movie as a QuickTime file:

1. Choose File > Publish Settings.
   The Publish Settings dialog box appears.

2. Select the Flash tab, and change the Version option to Flash Player 5 or earlier.
   Currently, QuickTime 6 supports only Flash 5 functionality.

3. Select the Formats tab, check the box next to QuickTime, and uncheck the others.

4. Select the QuickTime tab, and set the following parameters for QuickTime (**Figure 2.36**):

   ▲ **Dimensions.** Allows you to set alternative height and width in pixels.

   ▲ **Alpha.** Controls how the Flash elements are displayed with the QuickTime movie. Choose Copy to make the Flash Stage opaque. Choose Alpha-Transparent to make the Flash Stage transparent. Choose Auto to make the Flash Stage transparent or opaque, depending on the stacking order of Flash graphics and the QuickTime file.

   ▲ **Layer.** Controls where you want the Flash track to lie in the exported QuickTime file. Choose Auto for the layering to follow your Flash layers.

   ▲ **Streaming sound.** Lets any sounds in Flash be converted to a QuickTime sound track using QuickTime compression settings.

   ▲ **Controller.** By choosing None, you can create a QuickTime file that doesn't contain the standard QuickTime playback controls. Use this option if you've created custom navigation buttons with Flash (**Figure 2.37**).

continues on next page

ADDING FLASH ELEMENTS TO YOUR VIDEO

▲ **Playback.** Choose these options to control how the movie will play. Avoid checking the Play every frame check box because it will disable any audio in the QuickTime sound track.

▲ **File.** The Flatten (Make self-contained) check box creates a single file incorporating all externally referenced media, eliminating the need to keep the original imported QuickTime file together with the final exported QuickTime file. The Flatten option also makes the file compatible for both Mac OS and Windows.

5. Click OK or Publish.

    or

    As an alternative to steps 3 through 5, choose Export Movie from the File menu. In the Export Movie dialog box that appears, choose the destination folder, name the destination file, and choose QuickTime from the pull-down menu. The Export QuickTime dialog box appears to let you set the same QuickTime parameters that appear in the Publish Settings dialog box.

Not All Flash Features Work in QuickTime

It's very important to understand that QuickTime 6 supports only a subset of current Flash features. The latest QuickTime Player is usually a version or two behind the Flash Player, so QuickTime 6 supports some Flash 5 features. As a result, many of the more complicated interactive functions and new features in Flash MX 2004 movies won't work properly or at all when exported as QuickTime files. Embedded videos, for example, are not supported by QuickTime 6.

You should design your Flash files with these limitations in mind if your intended destination is QuickTime Player. Test early and often, check with Apple for QuickTime updates, and try to stick with basic ActionScripting that controls the playhead of the main Timeline.

QuickTime, QuickTime Video, and AVI

The Export Movie and Publish options give you the choice of QuickTime and either QuickTime Video or AVI, depending on whether you're using a Mac or a Windows computer. These options produce very different formats even though they are all "movie" files.

The QuickTime option allows you to put your Flash content in a separate track of a QuickTime file. The Flash content maintains its functionality and its vector information, so the Flash graphics are still resolution independent. At the same time, a separate video track plays the bitmap information.

On the Mac, the QuickTime Video option rasterizes your Flash content and puts it on the video track along with the imported QuickTime movie. All interactivity is lost, and buttons become simple graphics that are locked in at a set resolution (**Figure 2.38**). Choose this option if you want to create simple, linear movie files from Flash that don't require the latest version of QuickTime Player.

Figure 2.38 QuickTime (top) separates Flash content on a different track, maintaining Flash's vector information. QuickTime Video and AVI (bottom) combine Flash graphics with the video so that vector information is lost. Recompression of the original imported video file also results in degraded picture quality.

On a Windows computer, you have the option of exporting a movie in AVI format. This format also rasterizes Flash content into a linear movie and disables all interactivity (refer to Figure 2.38).

Tables 2.2 and **2.3** will help you decide what kind of export format you need.

Table 2.2

Export Movie Options for Windows

IMPORTED VIDEO	EXPORT FORMAT	COMMENTS
Embedded	SWF	Flash 6 Player required
	AVI	No interactivity
Linked	QuickTime	Limited interactivity
	AVI	No interactivity

Table 2.3

Export Movie Options for Mac

IMPORTED VIDEO	EXPORT FORMAT	COMMENTS
Embedded	SWF	Flash 6 Player required
	QuickTime Video	No interactivity
Linked	QuickTime	Limited interactivity
	QuickTime Video	No interactivity

Rotoscoping

Rotoscoping is a traditional animator's technique that involves tracing live-motion film to create animation. This process is named after an actual machine, the Rotoscope, which projected live-action film onto an animation board. There, an animator could easily trace the outline of an actor frame by frame to get natural motion that would be too difficult to animate by hand. The old Disney animators often used rotoscoping to do studies, and feature movies and commercials rely on rotoscoping even today.

You can use Flash to import and display digitized videos of actors or moving objects and then do the rotoscoping yourself.

To copy the motion in an imported video:

1. Import a video as described earlier in this chapter (**Figure 2.39**).

2. Lock the layer that contains the video.

3. Add a new layer above the layer that contains your video.

4. Begin tracing the actors or the action in the new layer in keyframe 1 with any of the drawing tools (**Figure 2.40**).

Figure 2.39 A video that is good for rotoscoping contains dramatic or interesting motion with a clear distinction between background and foreground.

Lock the layer containing the video to prevent you from moving it accidentally

A simple tracing of this gorilla was made with the Pencil tool set on the Smooth modifier

Figure 2.40 Zoom in to the area you want to trace, and use the imported video file as your guide.

Figure 2.41 Rotoscoping this gorilla results in a layer of keyframes with drawings that follow its gait.

Figure 2.42 When you play the finished rotoscoped animation, see how natural the animation appears even if the tracings are very simple.

5. Add a blank keyframe by choosing Insert > Timeline > Blank Keyframe.

   An empty keyframe appears in Frame 2.

6. Trace the actors or action in the empty keyframe you just created.

7. Continue the process of adding blank keyframes and tracing until your sequence is complete (**Figure 2.41**).

8. Delete the layer that contains the imported video to see the final rotoscoped animation (**Figure 2.42**).

   In this example, rotoscoping produces a very simple outline of the action, but you can trace any level of detail depending on the desired effect.

✔ Tips

- To make it easier to see the video below your tracings, you can use the Show Layers As Outlines option in your active layer, or you can use a semitransparent color until you finish the entire sequence.

- Use the Onion Skin buttons (**Figure 2.43**) to help you see your drawings in the previous keyframes.

- Use the comma (,) and period (.) keys to move back or forward on the Timeline in one-frame increments. This technique will help you go back and forth between two frames rapidly to test the differences between your drawings, much like a traditional animator flips between two tracings.

Sometimes, the video you are trying to rotoscope has too many frames, making the motion unnecessarily smooth and the tracing too tedious. You can reduce the number of frames that the video occupies in the Flash Timeline by reimporting your video and changing the video-frames-to-Flash-frames ratio in the Video Import Wizard dialog box.

To reduce the number of available frames to trace:

- ◆ Re-import your video into Flash. In the Compression settings options in the Video Import Wizard, choose a lower ratio in the Number of video frames to encode per number of Macromedia Flash frames pull-down menu.

  Choosing 1:2, for example, will play one video frame for every two Flash frames, effectively halving the number of tracings. The total length of the video remains the same.

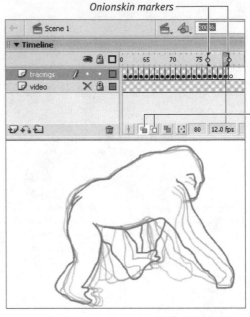

Onionskin markers

Onion Skin buttons

Figure 2.43 Use the Onion Skin buttons below the Timeline to show multiple frames in front of or behind the current frame. Move the onionskin markers to show less or more frames. This onionskin shows three frames behind the current frame 80.

ROTOSCOPING

Simulating Video

Although Flash can display video directly within Flash Player, there are times when you'll be looking for a more artistic effect than straight video can provide. Converting video to a sequence of bitmap images to create a short frame-by-frame animation is a very effective technique to simulate video and gives you some flexibility to modify the imagery. Although this process can be laborious and relatively low tech, the rewards are enormous. When you work with bitmap sequences, you can use the Trace Bitmap command to convert them to vector shapes. In the process, you can reduce the number of colors and shapes to create stylized images with posterized effects or delete background shapes to isolate dramatic silhouettes. You can better integrate these short sequences into your Flash movie without being limited by the rectangular boundaries of a direct video. It is also a way to simulate video if you are creating content for Flash Player 5 or earlier.

To create sequential bitmaps from a video:

1. Import a video file, and embed it in your Flash movie.

   You eventually will be importing the same number of bitmap images as you have frames of video, so take care not to import too long a video segment. If possible, reduce the frame rate of your video by using a video-editing application such as Adobe Premiere or Apple's QuickTime Pro.

   continues on next page

2. Change the dimensions of the Stage to fit the dimensions of your imported video.

3. Choose File > Export > Export Movie.

The Export Movie dialog box appears. This dialog box lets you choose a file format and destination folder.

4. Click New Folder to create a new destination folder.

5. Enter a name for your exported image files.

6. From the Format or Save as Type pull-down menu, choose PICT Sequence (Mac) or Bitmap Sequence (Windows) (**Figure 2.44**).

7. Click Save.

The Export PICT (Mac) or Export Bitmap (Windows) dialog box appears.

8. Click the Match Screen button to make sure the width, height, and resolution numbers match your Stage at screen resolution (72 dpi).

9. From the Color Depth pull-down menu, choose the appropriate bitmap level.

24 bits is the color depth for millions of colors.

10. In the Options section, check the Smooth (Windows) or Smooth bitmap (Mac) check box (**Figure 2.45**).

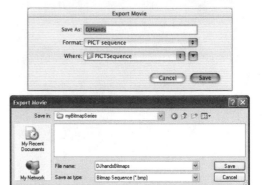

Figure 2.44 The Export Movie dialog box for the Mac (top) and Windows (bottom). The Format and Save as type pull-down menus give you the choice of export file types. Choose PICT sequence for the Mac or Bitmap Sequence for Windows.

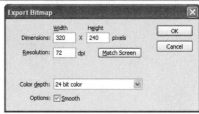

Figure 2.45 The Export PICT dialog box for the Mac (top) and the Export Bitmap dialog box for Windows (bottom).

SIMULATING VIDEO

Figure 2.46 The warning dialog box. Click Yes to import the entire sequence.

Each keyframe contains one bitmap

14 individual bitmaps are saved in the library

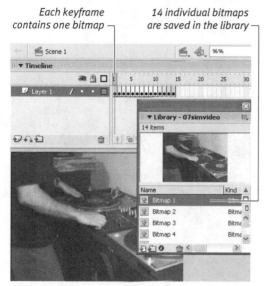

Figure 2.47 After you import a bitmap series, each image is placed in a separate keyframe and also is saved in the Library.

11. Click OK.

Flash exports a series of bitmap images and appends a numerical extension to the filenames to keep them in a series.

12. Open a new Flash file, and import the first of the images you just created.

Flash recognizes that this first image is part of a sequence (**Figure 2.46**) and asks you whether you want to import the entire sequence.

13. Click Yes.

Flash places each bitmap in a new keyframe and aligns them all in the active layer (**Figure 2.47**).

To convert the bitmaps to simplified vectors:

1. Select the first keyframe or bitmap on the Stage.

2. Choose Modify > Bitmap > Trace Bitmap. The Trace Bitmap dialog box appears (**Figure 2.48**). The parameters in the dialog box determine how accurate the tracing will be to the bitmapped image.

3. Set the following options:

   ▲ **Color threshold** (a number between 1 and 200). Controls the tolerance level when Flash is deciding whether neighboring pixels should be considered to be one color or two colors. Flash compares the RGB values of two neighboring regions, and if their difference is less than the color threshold, the color is considered to be the same. The lower the color threshold, the more colors Flash will see and reproduce.

   ▲ **Minimum area** (a number between 1 and 1000). Controls how large an area Flash will consider when making the color calculations.

   ▲ **Curve fit.** Controls the smoothness of the contours around shapes.

   ▲ **Corner Threshold.** Determines whether Flash will create sharp or smooth corners.

4. After making the first tracing, select the bitmap in the next keyframe and apply Trace Bitmap.

   Continue this process until all the bitmaps in the sequence have been traced (**Figure 2.49**).

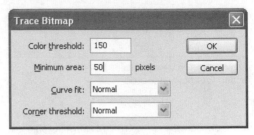

Figure 2.48 The Trace Bitmap dialog box.

Figure 2.49 This image is the result of a color threshold of 150 and a minimum area of 50.

The background in the traced bitmaps is deleted ⌐

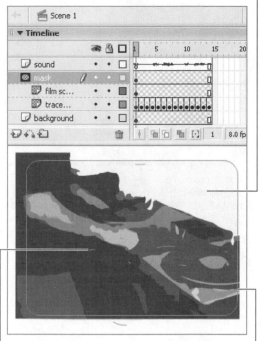

⌐ *Animated random lines give the effect of film scratches*

A rectangle with rounded corners will mask the traced bitmaps ⌐

Figure 2.50 Deleting the background in every traced bitmap of the sequence lets you experiment with a more dynamic, animated backdrop. This example masks the traced series and adds sound and other animated elements.

5. Add, delete, or change shapes and colors as needed in each keyframe by using the drawing and selection tools in the Toolbar (**Figure 2.50**).

Look at the finished Flash file on the CD that accompanies this book to see how this short traced video has been modified. ⌑

✔ Tips

■ The Trace Bitmap menu command doesn't have a default keyboard shortcut, but you can create one yourself by choosing Edit > Keyboard Shortcuts (Windows) or Flash > Keyboard Shortcuts (Mac). When you create a keyboard shortcut for Trace Bitmap, the process of converting a long sequence of bitmaps becomes much easier.

■ To save time performing repetitive tasks like tracing bitmaps, you can save the Trace Bitmap step from the History panel as a command and then replay it. This eliminates the need to go through the Trace Bitmap dialog box for each step. Alternatively, you can click the Replay button in the History panel for the Trace Bitmap step.

■ You should be careful not to select too low a color-threshold value. A traced bitmap that has too many shapes will be a huge drain on performance and often makes the Flash file larger than if you used the bitmap itself.

Although they are vector shapes, sequences of traced bitmaps still can take up a fair amount of space, so it's important to consider ways to maximize their use and get the most bang for your buck.

Copy your keyframes containing the traced animation, and paste them into a graphic symbol or a movie-clip symbol. This technique allows you to treat the keyframes as a single instance, which makes them easier to manipulate.

Following are a few simple strategies you can use to make your one traced animation symbol seem like many different clips (**Figure 2.51**). 🎧

To use the traced animation:

◆ Try to keep your simulated video sequences short and small. Most times, you only need a few frames (fewer than 10) to suggest a particular motion if you focus on the most dramatic action of a central character.

◆ Modify the instances by changing the brightness, tint, or alpha effect. Repetition of graphics with color variations can create interesting designs and maintain really small Flash files.

◆ Transform the instances by flipping them horizontally or vertically or by changing rotation or scale. An enlarged mirror-image animation can provide a dramatically different backdrop.

◆ Apply motion tweens to the instances. Create more variety by moving something that's already moving. Tweening instances of an Olympic-diver sequence, for example, can result in many dive varieties.

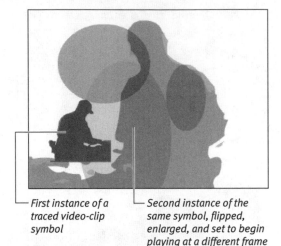

First instance of a traced video-clip symbol

Second instance of the same symbol, flipped, enlarged, and set to begin playing at a different frame

Figure 2.51 A single traced video clip of a DJ spinning some records gets reproduced twice on the Stage. The background instance has been flipped horizontally, enlarged, and made transparent. The foreground instance moves across the Stage and begins looping at a different frame. The circles are extra animated elements.

◆ Keep some of the instances static in different frames while looping others with different starting frames. In the Property Inspector, choose among three play options (Loop, Play Once, and Single Frame), and designate the First frame to play. Setting these play-mode options will prevent multiple instances on the Stage from being synchronized.

Part II: Understanding ActionScript

GETTING A HANDLE ON ACTIONSCRIPT

3

ActionScript is Flash's scripting language for adding interactivity to your graphics and movies. You can use ActionScript to create anything from simple navigation within your Flash movie to complex interfaces that react to the location of the viewer's pointer, arcade-style games, and even full-blown e-commerce sites with dynamically updating data. In this chapter, you'll learn how to construct ActionScript to create effective Flash interaction. Think of the process as learning the grammar of a foreign language: First, you must learn how to put nouns and verbs together and integrate adjectives and prepositions; then you can expand your communication skills and have meaningful conversations by building your vocabulary. This chapter will give you a sound ActionScripting foundation upon which you can build your Flash literacy.

If you are familiar with JavaScript, you'll notice some similarities between it and ActionScript. In fact, ActionScript is based on JavaScript, which is a popular object-oriented programming language for adding interactivity to a Web page. Whereas JavaScript is intended to control the Web browser, ActionScript controls the interactivity within Flash content, so the two scripting languages have slight differences. But the basic syntax of scripts and the handling of objects—reusable pieces of code—remain the same.

Even if you've never used JavaScript, you'll see in this chapter that Flash makes basic scripting easy. You'll learn about the logic of objects and how the Actions panel can automate much of the scripting process while giving you the flexibility to build more sophisticated interaction as your skills improve.

About Objects and Classes

At the heart of ActionScript are objects and classes. *Objects* are data types—such as sound, graphics, text, and numeric values—that you create in Flash and use to control the movie. A date object, for example, retrieves information about the time and the date, and an array object manipulates data stored in a particular order.

All the objects you use and create belong to a larger collective group known as a *class*. Flash provides certain classes for you to use in your movie. These built-in classes handle a wide range of Flash elements such as data (Array class, Math class) and sound and video (Sound class and Video class).

Learning to code in ActionScript centers on understanding the capabilities of objects and their classes and using them to interact with one another and with the viewer.

In the real world, we are familiar with objects such as a cow, a tree, and a person (**Figure 3.1**). Flash objects range from visible things, such as a movie clip of a spinning ball, to more abstract concepts, such as the date, pieces of data, or the handling of keyboard inputs. Whether concrete or abstract, however, Flash objects are versatile because after you create them, you can reuse them in different contexts.

Before you can use objects, you need to be able to identify them, and you do so by name just as we do in the real world. Say you have three people in front of you: Adam, Betty, and Zeke. All three are objects that can be distinguished by name. All three belong to the collective group known as humans. You could also say that Adam, Betty, and Zeke are all *instances* of the Human class (**Figure 3.2**). In ActionScript, instances and objects are synonymous, and the terms are used interchangeably in this book.

Figure 3.1 Objects in the real world include things like a cow, a tree, and a person.

Figure 3.2 Adam, Betty, and Zeke are three objects of the human class. Flash doesn't have such a class, but this analogy is useful for understanding objects.

Human class

Properties — Height
Weight
Sex
Hair color

Adam	Betty	Zeke
Height: 69	Height: 68	Height: 66
Weight: 140	Weight: 135	Weight: 188
Sex: M	Sex: F	Sex: M
Hair color: black	Hair color: black	Hair color: brown

Figure 3.3 Adam, Betty, and Zeke are human objects with different properties. Properties differentiate objects of the same class.

✔ **Tip**

■ It helps to think of objects as nouns, properties as adjectives, and methods as verbs. Properties describe their objects, whereas methods are the actions that the objects perform.

About Methods and Properties

Each object of a class (Zeke of the humans, for example) differs from the others in its class by more than just its name. Each person is different because of several defining characteristics, such as height, weight, gender, and hair color. In object-oriented scripting, we say that objects and classes have properties. Height, weight, sex, and hair color are all properties of the human class (**Figure 3.3**).

In Flash, each class has a predefined set of properties that let you establish the uniqueness of the object. The Sound class has just two properties: duration, which measures the length of a sound, and position, which measures the time the sound has been playing. The MovieClip class, on the other hand, has many properties, such as _height, _width, and _rotation, which are measures of the dimensions and orientation of a particular movie-clip object. By defining and changing the properties of objects, you control what each object is like and how each object appears, sounds, and behaves.

Objects also do things. Zeke can run, sleep, and talk. The things that objects can do are known as *methods*. Each class has its own set of methods. The Sound class, for example, has a setVolume method that will play its sound louder or softer, and the Date class has a getDay method that retrieves the day of the week. When an object does something by using a method, we say that the method is called or that the object calls the method.

Understanding the relationships between objects, classes, properties, and methods is important. Putting objects together so that the methods and properties of one influence the methods and properties of another is what drives Flash interactivity. The key to building your ActionScript vocabulary is learning the properties and methods of different classes.

Writing with Dot Syntax

As with other foreign languages, you must learn the rules of grammar to put words together. *Dot syntax* is the convention that ActionScript uses to put objects, properties, and methods together into statements. You connect objects, properties, and methods with dots (periods) to describe a particular object or process.

```
Zeke.weight = 188
Betty.weight = 135
```

The first statement assigns the value **188** to the weight of Zeke. The second statement assigns the value **135** to the weight of Betty. The dot separates the object name (Zeke, Betty) from the property (`weight`) (**Figure 3.4**).

```
Betty.shirt.color = "gray"
```

In this statement the object Betty is linked to the object shirt. The object shirt, in turn, has the property `color`, which is assigned the value `"gray"`. Notice that with dot syntax, you use multiple dots to maintain object hierarchy. When you have multiple objects linked in this fashion, it's often easier to read the statement backward. So you could read it as "Gray is the color of the shirt of Betty."

Betty.weight = 135   Zeke.weight = 188

Figure 3.4 The hypothetical `weight` property describes Betty and Zeke. In Flash, many properties of objects can be both read and modified with ActionScript.

Mouse.hide ( )

Adam.run ( )

Figure 3.5 Dot syntax lets you make objects call methods. Just as the hypothetical method run() could make the Adam object begin to jog, the real Flash method hide(), when applied to the Mouse object, makes the pointer disappear.

Symbols and Classes

Symbols are not classes. Symbols are not even objects. It's true that movie clips and buttons are both symbols and objects, but these elements are exceptions—and perhaps the source of some confusion. Graphics, sounds, bitmaps, and imported video clips are all symbols that appear in the Library, but they are not objects or classes because they do not have methods and properties that you can control with ActionScript.

Some parallels exist between classes and symbols. Symbols are reusable assets created in or imported to the Library. You create instances, or copies, of the symbols to use in your movie. As you have seen, you can also create instances of classes to use in your movie.

Now consider the following statement:

`Zeke.run ()`

This statement causes the object Zeke to call the method `run ()`. The parentheses after `run` signify that `run` is a method and not a property. You can think of this construction as noun–dot–verb (**Figure 3.5**). Methods often have *parameters*, or arguments, within the parentheses. These parameters affect how the method is executed.

`Zeke.run (fast)`

`Adam.run (slow)`

Both of these statements will make the Zeke and Adam objects call the `run ()` method, but because each method contains a different parameter, the way the run is performed is different: Zeke runs fast, and Adam runs slowly.

Each method has its own set of parameters that you must learn. Consider the basic Flash action `gotoAndPlay("Scene 1",20)`. `gotoAndPlay` is a method of the MovieClip class. The parenthetical parameters, `("Scene1", 20)`, refer to the scene and the frame number, so the playhead of the object will jump to Scene 1, Frame 20, and begin playing.

✔ Tip

■ The dot syntax replaces the slash syntax used in previous versions of Flash. Although you can still use the slash syntax, the dot syntax is recommended because it's more compatible with all the new actions. Use slash syntax only if you are authoring for the Flash 4 Player or earlier.

More on Punctuation

Dot syntax allows you to construct meaningful processes and assignments with objects, properties, and methods. Additional punctuation symbols let you do more with these single statements.

The semicolon

To terminate individual ActionScript statements and start new ones, you use the semicolon. The semicolon functions as a period does in a sentence: It concludes one idea and lets another one begin.

```
stopAllSounds ();
play ();
```

The semicolons separate the statements so that all the sounds stop first and then the movie begins to play. Each statement is executed in order from the top down, as with a set of instructions or a cookbook recipe.

✔ Tip

■ Flash will still understand ActionScript statements even if you don't use the semicolons to terminate each one. It is good practice, however, to include them in your scripts.

Curly braces

Curly braces are another kind of punctuation that ActionScript uses frequently. Curly braces group related blocks of ActionScript statements. When you assign actions to a button, for example, those actions appear within curly braces in the on (release) statement.

```
on (release) {
    stopAllSounds ();
    play ();
}
```

In this case, both the stopAllSounds action and the play action are executed when the mouse button is released. Notice how the curly braces are separated on different lines to make the related ActionScript statements easier to read.

Commas

Commas separate the parameters of a method. A method can take many parameters. The gotoAndPlay () method, for example, can take two: a scene name and the frame number. With commas separating the parameters, the ActionScript code looks like this:

```
gotoAndPlay ("Scene 1", 20);
```

Some methods may have three, four, or perhaps even 10 parameters, but as long as you separate the parameters with commas, Flash knows how to handle the code.

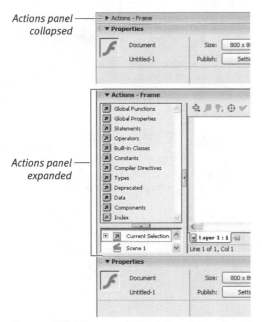

Actions panel collapsed

Actions panel expanded

Figure 3.6 Click the arrow in the Actions bar to expand or collapse the Actions panel.

The Actions Panel

The Actions panel is the Flash dialog box that lets you access all the actions that will control your Flash movie. Depending on your level of expertise, you can choose ActionScript commands from a hierarchical list or you can simply write ActionScript code directly. If you're uncomfortable with the ActionScript rules of grammar, the Actions panel can provide hints as you enter code and also automate some of the formatting. The ActionScript panel can also give you anytime access to the ActionScript Reference Guide.

In Flash, the name of the Actions panel appears as either Actions-Frame, Actions-Button, or Actions-Movie Clip, depending on which element you have selected. In any case, the contents of the panel remain the same, so in this book it is always referred to as the Actions panel.

To open the Actions panel:

◆ From the Windows menu, choose Actions (F9).

or

Click the right-facing triangle in the Actions bar.

The Actions panel expands, and the triangle points downward (**Figure 3.6**).

or

Alt-double-click (Win) or Option-double-click (Mac) an instance on the Stage or a keyframe in the Timeline.

The Actions panel appears so that you can attach actions to either the keyframe or the instance.

To undock the Actions panel:

◆ Drag the Actions panel by the bumpy area in the top-left corner.

Your pointer will change (hand for Mac, arrow for Windows), indicating that you can undock the Actions panel (**Figure 3.7**).

To redock the Actions panel:

1. Grab the Actions panel by the bumpy area in the top-left corner, and drag it over the different panels on your desktop.

Those areas highlight with a bold outline.

2. Drop the Actions panel.

The Actions panel docks with the high-lighted panels. In Mac OS X, the Actions panel cannot dock with the Property Inspector or the Timeline.

✔ Tip

■ You can disable docking of all your panels by choosing Edit > Preferences and choosing Disable Panel Docking in the General tab of the Preferences dialog box. (This option is available only on Windows.)

Area to grab to dock or redock Actions panel

Figure 3.7 The Actions panel can be undocked from the Property Inspector (Windows only).

Actions panel layout

The Actions panel features several sections and multiple ways to enter ActionScript statements (**Figure 3.8**). The Actions toolbox on the left side displays all the available commands, organized in logical categories. At the bottom of the categories, an index lists all the ActionScript commands in alphabetical order. You can choose actions from this categorized list. In the right section, your completed script appears in the Script pane. You can use the Script navigator in the lower-left portion of the Actions panel to navigate to different scripts within your Flash movie.

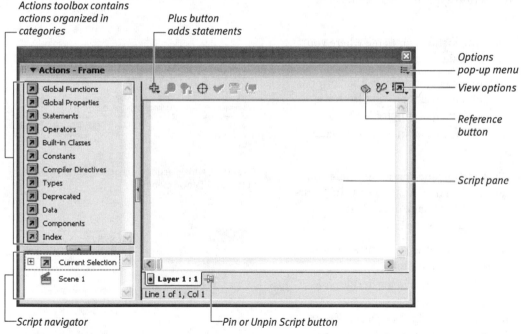

Actions toolbox contains actions organized in categories

Plus button adds statements

Options pop-up menu

View options

Reference button

Script pane

Script navigator

Pin or Unpin Script button

Figure 3.8 The Actions panel.

To add an action in the Script pane:

1. Select the instance or frame where you want to assign an action.

   In the Actions toolbox, expand an action category by clicking it.

2. Double-click the desired action.

   The action appears in the Script pane (**Figure 3.9**).

   or

1. Select the instance or frame where you want to assign an action.

   In the Actions toolbox, expand an action category by clicking it.

2. Select the action, and drag it into the Script pane (**Figure 3.10**).

   The action appears in the Script pane.

   or

1. Select the instance or frame where you want to assign an action.

2. Click the plus button above the Script pane, and choose the action from the pull-down menus (**Figure 3.11**).

   The action appears in the Script pane.

   or

1. Select the instance or frame where you want to assign an action, put your pointer in the Script pane of the Actions panel, and press the Esc key.

2. Type the two-letter code corresponding to the action you want.

   The action appears in the Script pane.

   Choose View Esc Shortcut Keys from the Actions panel's View Options button (**Figure 3.12**) to display them in the Actions toolbox.

Figure 3.9 Add an action by choosing a statement from the Actions toolbox. Here, the action stop() has been added to the Script pane.

Figure 3.10 Add an action by dragging it to the Script pane. The pointer changes temporarily to show you where you can drop the action.

Figure 3.11 Add an action by choosing it from the plus button's pull-down menus.

Figure 3.12 Choosing View Esc Shortcut Keys from the Actions panel's View Options button displays the shortcut keys for many actions in the Actions toolbox.

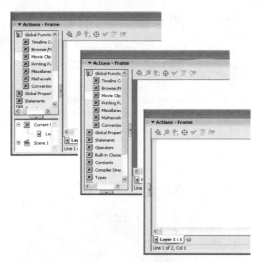

Figure 3.13 Resize the Actions panel by dragging or clicking the vertical or horizontal splitter bar that separates the Actions toolbox, the Script navigator, and the Script pane. The Script navigator can be completely collapsed (middle) and the Actions toolbox can be completely collapsed as well, leaving just the Script pane (bottom).

✔ Tip

■ While making your selection in the Actions toolbox, you can use the arrow keys, the Page Up and Page Down keys, or the Home and End keys to navigate through the list. Press Enter or the space-bar to open or close categories or to choose an action to put in the Script pane.

To edit actions in the Script pane:

◆ Highlight the action, and then simply click and drag it to a new position in the Script pane

◆ Highlight the action, and use the Delete key to remove it from the Script pane.

✔ Tip

■ You can still use familiar editing commands such as Copy, Cut, and Paste to create and rearrange ActionScripts.

To modify the Actions panel display:

◆ Drag or double-click the vertical splitter bar, or click the arrow button that divides the Actions toolbox and Script pane, to collapse or expand an area (**Figure 3.13**).

◆ Drag or double-click the horizontal splitter bar, or click the arrow button that divides the Actions toolbox and Script navigator, to collapse or expand an area (Figure 3.13).

THE ACTIONS PANEL

Actions panel options

The Actions panel provides many features that can help you write reliable code quickly and easily. Chapter 12 explains many of the debugging tools in detail.

When you're writing ActionScript in the Script pane, you'll be able to use code hints, which appear as you type. Code hints recognize what kind of action you are typing and offer choices and prompts on how to complete it. Flash makes it easy to be an expert! You can also customize the format options so that your code looks just the way you want it for ease of reading and understanding.

Coding help is always available in the Actions panel. The Reference button, for example, calls up the Help panel and sends you directly to the description and usage of any action selected in the Actions toolbox in case you have trouble remembering what a particular action does or how it is used. If you want to keep an ActionScript visible as you select other elements in your Flash movie, you can do so by pinning your script. *Pinning* makes your script "stick" in the Script pane until you unpin it. This technique is very useful if you've forgotten the name of a text box or a movie clip and need to reference it in an ActionScript statement. You can pin your current script and then go look for your text box or movie clip. Your script remains in place so that you can make the necessary edits.

To use code hints:

1. Enter an action in the Script pane and then type the opening parenthesis.

   Flash detects the action and anticipates that you will enter its parameters. A code hint appears to guide you (**Figure 3.14**). If an action has different ways of handling parameters, the tool tip shows those options (**Figure 3.15**).

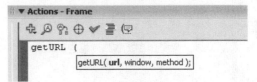

Figure 3.14 A code hint guides you as you enter ActionScript. The first required parameter for this action is the URL.

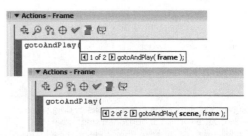

Figure 3.15 The action gotoAndPlay can be used with one or two parameters. The code hint shows you both ways, using only one parameter for frame (top) or using two parameters for scene and frame (bottom).

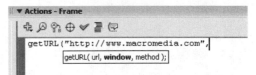

Figure 3.16 After you enter the first parameter, the code hint directs you to the next parameter. The next parameter for this action is the window.

Figure 3.17 When you enter the closing parenthesis, the code hint disappears. The getURL action shown here doesn't require the last parameter (the method).

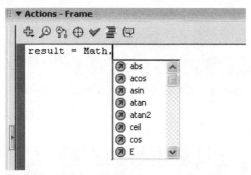

Figure 3.18 The code hint provides a scrolling list of methods and properties for each object. This list contains the methods and properties of the Math object.

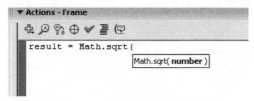

Figure 3.19 The sqrt() method of the Math object requires a number for its parameter.

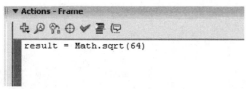

Figure 3.20 When you complete the method, the code hint disappears.

2. Enter the first parameter and then a comma.

   The bold in the code hint advances to highlight the next required parameter (**Figure 3.16**).

3. Continue entering the required parameters, and type a closing parenthesis to finish the action.

   The code hint disappears (**Figure 3.17**).

   or

1. Enter an object target path and then a period.

   Flash anticipates that you will enter a method or property of the particular object that appears before the period. A menu-style code hint appears to guide you (**Figure 3.18**).

2. Choose the appropriate method or property from the menu.

   The method or property appears in the Script pane after the dot. Another code hint appears to guide you, providing the parameters of the method (**Figure 3.19**).

3. Enter the parameters of the method, and type a closing parenthesis to finish.

   The code hint disappears (**Figure 3.20**).

   continues on next page

✔ Tips

- Code hints for object methods and properties appear only if your object name ends with a recognizable suffix. Flash provides code hints for a button, for example, only if the name of the button ends with _btn. Learn more about naming extensions later in this chapter and see Appendix A for a full list.

- Dismiss a code hint by pressing the Esc key or clicking a different place in your script.

- Navigate the menu-style code hints by using the arrow keys, the Page Up and Page Down keys, or the Home and End keys. You can also start typing and the entry that begins with the letter you type will appear in the code hint. Press Enter to choose the selection.

- You can call up code hints manually by pressing Ctrl-spacebar or by clicking the Show Code Hint button above the Script pane when your pointer is in a spot where code hints are appropriate (**Figure 3.21**).

- Change the delay time for code hints to appear or turn off code hints by choosing Preferences from the Actions panel's Options menu. When the Preferences dialog box appears, change your preferences in the ActionScript tab (**Figure 3.22**).

Show Code Hint button

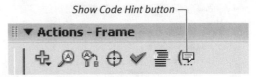

Figure 3.21 The Show Code Hint button is above the Script pane.

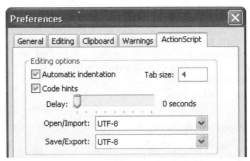

Figure 3.22 In the Preferences dialog box, you can change the time that it takes for code hints to appear.

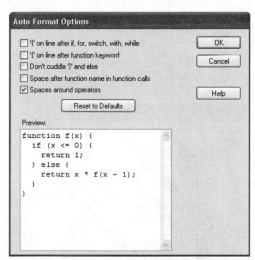

Figure 3.23 The Auto Format Options dialog box gives you a preview of how a typical block of code would look with the selections you made.

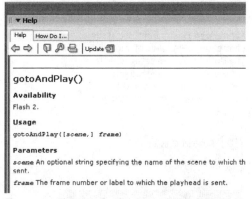

Figure 3.24 The entry for the gotoAndPlay action in the Help panel.

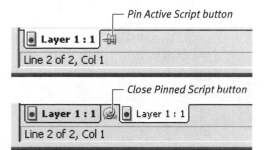

Figure 3.25 The Pin Active Script button (top) toggles to Close Pinned Script (bottom).

To set formatting options:

1. From the Actions panel's Options menu, choose Auto Format Options.

   The Auto Format Options dialog box appears.

2. Set the different formatting options and specify the way a typical block of code should appear (**Figure 3.23**); then click OK.

3. Choose Auto Format from the Actions panel's Options menu (Ctrl-Shift-F for Windows, Cmd-Shift-F for Mac), or click the Auto Format button above the Script pane.

   Flash formats your script in the Script pane according to the preferences you set in the Auto Format Options dialog box.

To look up actions in the Help panel:

◆ Select an ActionScript term in the Actions toolbox or in the Script pane, and click the Reference button above and to the right of the Script pane.

   or

◆ Right-click (Win) or Ctrl-Click (Mac) an action in the Actions toolbox or in the Script pane, and select View Help from the context menu that appears.

   The Help panel opens to the selected ActionScript term. The typical entry in the Help panel contains information about usage and syntax, lists parameters and their availability in various Flash versions, and shows sample code (**Figure 3.24**).

To pin or unpin a script in the Script pane:

◆ With ActionScript visible in the Script pane, click the Pin Active Script button at the bottom of the Actions panel (**Figure 3.25**).

   To unpin the script, click the button again.

Using Objects

Now that you know what objects are and how to operate the Actions panel, you can begin to script with objects and call their methods or evaluate and assign new properties.

Flash provides existing classes that reside in the Built-in Classes category in the Actions toolbox (**Figure 3.26**). These Flash classes have methods and properties that control different elements of your Flash movie, such as graphics, sound, data, time, and mathematical calculations. You can also build your own classes from scratch by combining some of the existing classes and actions with functions (see Chapter 11).

Creating objects

Before you can use one of the existing classes, you must create an instance of the class by giving it a name. The process is similar to creating an instance of, or *instantiating*, a symbol. You need to create an instance of the class to use it in ActionScript, and you do so by naming it. Use the keyword new to assign a unique name to a new instance of the class.

```
Adam = new Human ();

myColor_color = new Color ();
```

Where do you find the keyword new? In the Built-in Classes category of the Actions toolbox, the classes that require you to make new instances include the command new (**Figure 3.27**).

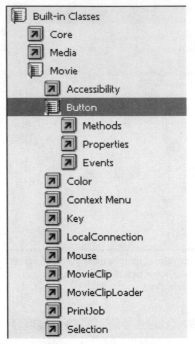

Figure 3.26 Flash's built-in classes control different kinds of information. The Built-in Classes category in the Actions toolbox is divided into more categories. Here, you see the Button class and the contents of its folder.

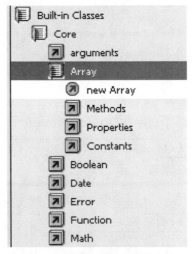

Figure 3.27 In the Array category, the action new Array will create a new instance from the Array class.

The previous two ActionScript statements create two new objects that you can manipulate. The first example is a hypothetical statement that makes a new human object called Adam from the Human class. The second is an actual ActionScript statement that makes a new color object called myColor_color from the Color class. The statement that contains the new operator in front of the class is called a *constructor function*. Constructor functions are specialized functions that create new instances from classes.

The Rules of Naming

Although you're free to make up descriptive names for your objects, you must adhere to certain simple rules. If you don't, Flash won't recognize your object's name and will ignore your commands to control the object with ActionScript.

1. Do not use spaces or punctuation (such as slashes, dots, and parentheses) because these characters often have a special meaning to Flash.

2. You can use letters, numbers, and underscore characters, but you must not begin the name with a number.

3. Do not use words that Flash uses for ActionScript. For example, var and new are reserved for commands and cannot be names.

That's it. Those are the only three rules. Some additional general naming strategies, however, can make your scripts easier to understand, debug, and share.

1. Use a consistent naming practice. A common method is to use multiple names to describe an object and to capitalize the first letter of every word except for the first. The names spinningSquare1, spinningSquare2, and leftPaddle, for example, are intuitive, descriptive, and easy to follow in a script.

2. Get in the habit of adding suffixes to your names to describe the object type. Using the standard suffix _mc for movie clips and _btn for buttons readily identifies the object. It also helps the ActionScript panel recognize the object type and will bring up the appropriate code hints. For example, if you begin typing leftPaddle_mc and then a dot, the code hint that appears will display a list of the movie-clip methods and events because it knows that leftPaddle_mc is a movie clip. In this book, all names will have the standard suffixes for objects found in Appendix A.

The following task demonstrates how to instantiate the date object, but the general method works for instantiation of all objects.

To instantiate an object:

1. Select the first frame on the main Timeline and open the Actions panel.

2. In the Script pane, enter a name for your new object, followed by an equals sign.

3. On the same line of the Script pane, choose Built-in Classes > Core > Date > new Date.

   The full statement creates a new date object with the name you entered. Your date object is instantiated and ready to use (**Figure 3.28**).

✔ Tip

■ Some of the Flash classes—such as Key, Math, and Mouse—do not need a constructor function to be instantiated. You can use their methods and properties immediately without having a named object. This practice makes sense because only one unique instance can exist for these special objects. (The Mouse class, for example, can have only one instance because there is only one mouse per computer.) You can tell which of the Flash objects don't require a constructor function by looking in the Built-in Classes category in the Actions toolbox. Objects that don't require a constructor function won't have the command new listed among their methods and properties.

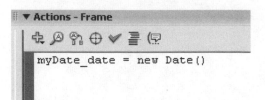

Figure 3.28 The finished statement creates an object called myDate_date from the Date class.

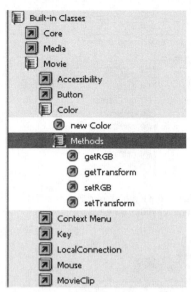

Figure 3.29 Below every class category, a Methods folder lists the methods you can choose to use. The methods of the color object are shown here.

Calling methods

The next step after creating a new object involves calling an object's methods. Recall that you can call a method by using an object's name followed by a period and then the method with its parameters within parentheses. All the methods of a particular class can be found in the Methods category of that class category in the Actions toolbox (**Figure 3.29**).

There are three ways to enter a method in the Script pane, but ultimately, your final ActionScript will look the same no matter which method you use. Your code in the Script pane will look something like this:

`myColor_color.setRGB(0x00CC33)`

This statement calls the method `setRGB()` to change the color associated with the `myColor_color` object. The parameter is the hex number 0x00CC33.

Your ActionScript could also look something like this:

`currentDate = myDate.getDate ()`

This statement calls the method `getDate()` from the myDate object and puts the information it retrieves into the variable called `currentDate`.

The following example continues the preceding task and calls a method of your newly created date object. Later chapters introduce specific classes, provide more information on the Date class, and show you how to use methods to control your Flash movie.

To call a method of an object:

1. Continuing with the preceding task, on the next line of the Script pane, enter the name of your date object, followed by a period.

   The code hint pull-down menu appears, displaying a list of choices available to the date object (**Figure 3.30**).

2. Select the method getDate.

   The completed statement, consisting of the object name followed by a dot and the method, appears in the Script pane (**Figure 3.31**).

   or

1. Continuing with the preceding task, on the next line of the Script pane, enter the name of your date object.

2. Choose Built-in Classes > Core > Date > getDate.

   The completed statement, consisting of the object name followed by a dot the method, appears in the Script pane (Figure 3.31).

   or

1. Continuing with the preceding task, on the next line of the Script pane, choose Built-in Classes > Core > Date > getDate.

   The getDate() method appears with a placeholder instanceName before it (**Figure 3.32**).

2. Replace the placeholder instanceName with the name of your date object.

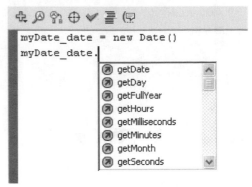

Figure 3.30 Select the method from the code hint pull-down menu for your date object.

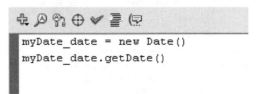

Figure 3.31 Your date object called myDate_date retrieves the current date from your computer's internal clock.

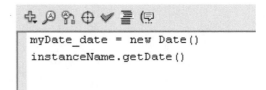

Figure 3.32 The placeholder instanceName that appears before the method should be replaced by the name of your date object.

USING OBJECTS

```
myDate_date = new Date();
myTextField_txt.text = myDate_date.getDate();
```

Figure 3.33 Assign the results of the getDate() method to the text property of a text field called myTextField_txt.

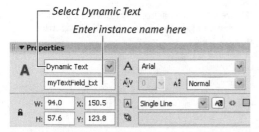

Select Dynamic Text
Enter instance name here

Figure 3.34 Your text field on the Stage should be set to Dynamic Text with myTextField_txt entered as the instance name.

In the previous task, Flash calls the getDate() method, which retrieves the current date. The information that a method gets is called the *returned value*. In order for the user to see the returned value and verify that the method works, you'll need to put that information in a variable and display it in a dynamic text field. You'll learn more about text fields in Chapter 10.

To display the results of the getDate method:

1. Continue with the previous task and insert myTextField_txt.text= in front of the myDate_date.getDate() statement (**Figure 3.33**).

   The returned value of the method will be displayed in the text field called myTextField_txt.

2. Select the Text tool, and drag out an empty selection on the Stage.

3. In the Property Inspector, choose Dynamic Text from the pull-down menu, and in the <Instance Name> field, enter myTextField_txt (**Figure 3.34**).

4. Test your movie by choosing Control > Test movie.

   Flash instantiates a date object and then calls the getDate() method. The returned value (the date) is put in the text property of your text field on the Stage.

USING OBJECTS

Assigning properties

Just as you have multiple ways to call a method, you have multiple ways to assign properties in the Actions panel. No matter which way you go, in the end, keep in mind that you want the Script pane to display your object name followed by a dot and then the property name. If you want to assign a value to a property, that value goes on the right side of an equals sign.

```
myTextField_txt.text = "hello";
```

This statement assigns the word *hello* to the `text` property of the object called `myTextField_txt`.

If you want to read the value of a property and put it in a variable to use later, the object–dot–property construction goes on the right side of an equals sign.

```
Var myCurrentText = myTextField_txt.text;
```

This statement puts the value of the `text` property of the object called `myTextField_txt` in the variable called `myCurrentText`.

When you're working with movie clips, you can use two more actions: `getProperty` and `setProperty`. Chapter 7 explains movie-clip properties.

To assign a value to a property:

1. In the Script pane, enter the name of your object, followed by a period.

   The code hint pull-down menu appears, displaying a list of choices available to the particular object (**Figure 3.35**).

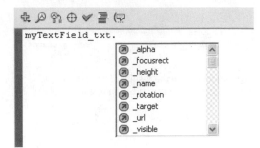

Figure 3.35 Select a property from the code hint pull-down menu for your object. Here, the properties of the TextField class appear.

USING OBJECTS

```
myTextField_txt.borderColor = 0x000000
```

Figure 3.36 The borderColor property takes a hex number as its value. The final statement makes the border color of the text field called myTextField_txt black.

```
instanceName.borderColor
```

Figure 3.37 The placeholder instanceName that appears before the property should be replaced by the name of your own object.

2. Select the desired property.

The statement consisting of the object name, a dot, and the property appears.

3. On the same line, enter an equals sign and then a value for the property.

A new value is assigned to the property (**Figure 3.36**).

or

1. In the Script pane, enter the name of your object.

2. Choose a property from the Actions toolbox.

Properties are located inside each class's folder in the Built-in Classes folder.

The statement consisting of the object name, a dot, and the property appears.

3. On the same line, enter an equals sign and then a value for the property.

A new value is assigned to the property (Figure 3.36).

or

1. Choose a property from the Actions toolbox.

Properties are located inside each class's folder in the Built-in Classes folder.

The statement consisting of a placeholder name, a dot, and the property appears (**Figure 3.37**).

2. Replace the placeholder instanceName with the name of your object.

3. On the same line, enter an equals sign and then a value for the property.

A new value is assigned to the property (Figure 3.36).

About Functions

If objects and classes are at the heart of ActionScript, functions must lie in the brain. Functions are the organizers of ActionScript. Functions group related ActionScript statements to perform a specific task. Often, you need to write code to do a certain thing over and over again. Functions eliminate the tedium of manually duplicating the code by putting it in one place where you can call on it to do its job from anywhere and at any time, as many times as you need.

As you learned earlier in this chapter, the objects Adam, Betty, and Zeke can perform certain tasks, called methods. If these objects were to put on a dinner party, they could organize themselves and do the following:

```
Adam.answerDoor();
Betty.serveDinner();
Zeke.chitChat();
```

But every Friday night when they have a dinner party, you would have to write the same three lines of code—not very efficient if these objects plan to entertain often. Instead, you can write a function that groups the code in one spot.

```
function dinnerParty () {
    Adam.answerDoor();
    Betty.serveDinner();
    Zeke.chitChat();
}
```

Now, every Friday night, you can just invoke the function by name and write the code `dinnerParty()`. The three statements inside the function's curly braces will be executed. You can add a function by choosing Statements > User-Defined Functions > function (Esc-fn).

You will also be using anonymous functions. As their name suggests, anonymous functions are not named.

Anonymous functions do not work alone and must be assigned to another object.

```
myButton_btn.onPress = function() {
    Adam.answerDoor();
    Betty.serveDinner();
    Zeke.chitChat();
}
```

Now your three friends perform their jobs when the object called myButton_btn is clicked.

You will learn much more about named functions and anonymous functions in the upcoming chapters, after you have a few more actions and concepts under your belt. Anonymous functions are important for handling events (Chapter 4) and for creating your own methods for objects (Chapter 11). Named functions are important for building reusable code (Chapter 11).

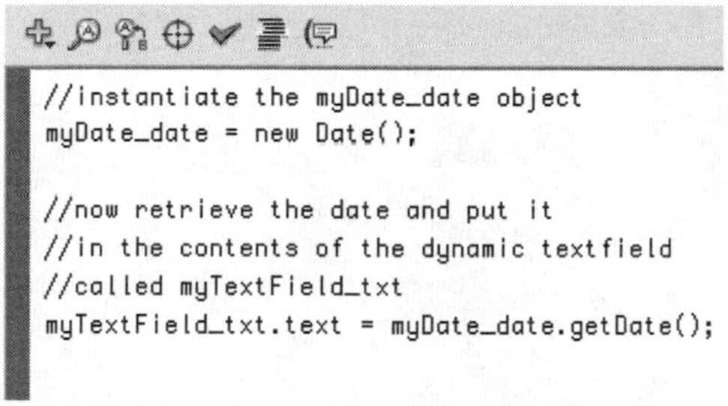

```
//instantiate the myDate_date object
myDate_date = new Date();

//now retrieve the date and put it
//in the contents of the dynamic textfield
//called myTextField_txt
myTextField_txt.text = myDate_date.getDate();
```

Figure 3.38 Comments interspersed with ActionScript statements help make sense of the code.

Using Comments

After you have built a strong vocabulary of Flash actions and are constructing complex statements in the Actions panel, you should include remarks in your scripts to remind yourself and your collaborators of the goals of the ActionScript. Comments help you keep things straight as you develop intricate interactivity and relationships among objects (**Figure 3.38**).

To create a comment:

◆ In the Script pane, type two slashes (//) and enter your comments after the slashes.

Comments appear in a different color from the rest of the script, making them easy to locate.

✔ Tips

■ If you have a long comment, break it up with multiple comment statements. That way, you'll have separate lines and you won't have to scroll the Script pane to see the end of a long remark.

■ If you have a long comment spanning multiple lines, you can use a slash and an asterisk (/*) to mark the beginning and an asterisk and a slash (*/) to mark the end of a comment block, as in the following examples:

/* This begins the comment. Even text in between is considered part of the comment.

This is the end of the comment.

*/

continues on next page

- Don't worry about creating too many comments. Comments are not compiled with the rest of the script, so they won't bog down performance. Also, because they aren't included in the exported .swf file, they don't increase the final file size.

- The slash convention for creating comments in ActionScript is the same for creating them in keyframes. When you choose Comment in the Label type pull-down menu in the Property Inspector, the name in the <Frame Label> field automatically begins with two slashes (//). You can also simply enter two slashes manually to begin a Comment in a frame label (**Figure 3.39**).

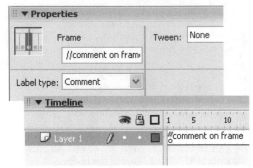

Figure 3.39 In the Property Inspector, double slashes indicate a comment in a Frame label.

ActionScript 2

Flash MX 2004 introduces a host of ActionScript terms that are new to the previous releases of Flash. There are two kinds of additions; the first are new built-in classes, methods, properties, and events that give you more control over your movie. The second are new language elements that give you a way to do object-oriented scripting that adheres more closely to established standards in other programming languages like JavaScript or Java. Since these new elements enable a significantly different way to code from earlier versions of Flash, they represent a new version of the ActionScript language, called ActionScript 2.

Flash MX 2004 supports both ActionScript and ActionScript 2, but don't worry too much about mixing up the two versions. ActionScript 2 is not a new language. Instead, think about it as ActionScript with a sprinkling of some new terms (something like "ActionScript Plus"). These new terms will most likely interest advanced Flash users familiar with other object-oriented languages and developers of applications. These new terms focus on creating your own custom classes, properties, and methods (we'll touch on these subjects in Chapter 11), as well as a way to handle specific kinds of data, and to keep track of errors when your code runs. There are also some specific requirements of ActionScript 2. An important one to keep in mind is that ActionScript 2 is case-sensitive, meaning Flash recognizes upper- and lowercase letters. Moreover, ActionScript 2 code for creating custom classes must be written and stored in a text file separate from your Flash movie—something that we will discuss in Chapter 11.

Part III: Navigating Timelines and Communicating

ADVANCED BUTTONS AND EVENT DETECTION

Creating graphics and animation in Flash is only half the story. You can incorporate interactivity via buttons, the keyboard, and the mouse to give the viewer control of those graphics and animation. Interactivity is essential for basic site navigation and e-commerce interfaces on the Web, as well as for game development, online tutorials, or anything else that requires the viewer to make choices.

What makes a movie interactive? Interactivity is the back-and-forth communication between the user and the movie. In a Flash movie, the user might react to something that's going on by moving the pointer, clicking the mouse button, or pressing a key on the keyboard. That reaction may trigger a response from the Flash movie, which in turn prompts the user to do something else. The things that the user does—mouse movements, button clicks, or keyboard presses—are part of things that happen, called *events*. Events form the basis of interactivity. There are many kinds of events, even events that happen without the user knowing about them. You will learn to detect these events and create the responses to events in statements conveniently known as *event handlers*.

This chapter first introduces events, event handlers, and anonymous functions used for event handling. Next, it explores the simplest class that handles events: the Button class. You'll learn how to extend its functionality by creating invisible buttons, tweening button instances, and creating fully animated buttons. You'll tackle the issues involved in creating a more complex button, such as a pull-down menu, which includes different button events, tracking options, and movie clips. You'll also learn about the Key class, the Mouse class, and the classes that control the contextual menu, as well as how to create actions that run continuously. Understanding these classes and event handling is essential to creating Flash interactivity because these elements are the scaffold on which you will hang virtually all your ActionScript.

Events and Event Handlers

Events are things that happen that Flash can recognize and respond to. A button click is an event, as are button rollovers, mouse movements, and key presses on the keyboard. Events can also be things that the user cannot control. The completion of a sound, for example, is also an event. Events can even occur regularly.

With all these events happening, you need a way to detect and respond to them. Event handlers are statements that perform this task. *Event handlers* perform certain actions as a response to events. You can create an event handler to detect a click of a button, for example. In response, you can make Flash go to another frame in a different scene.

Event handlers are associated with particular Flash classes. Button presses, rollovers, and releases are associated with the Button class. The pressing of a key is associated with the Key class. And the completion of a sound is associated with the Sound class. You will learn about all these events as you learn about the classes themselves. You'll begin with the Button class.

The Button Class

The Button class handles the events involving how the pointer interacts with a button; to a limited extent, it also handles keyboard presses. You can assign event handlers to buttons in one of two ways. First, you can assign an event handler to the button instance that sits on the Stage. When you assign an event handler to a button instance, use the ActionScript command

```
on (release) {

}
```

where `release` represents a specific kind of button event. Other kinds of button events are possible.

The second way to assign an event handler to a button requires that you give your button an instance name in the Property Inspector. Then you assign ActionScript to the main Timeline. In the Actions panel, you start by entering the instance name of your button followed by a dot and then an event that is assigned to an anonymous function. If your button were named `myButton_btn`, then your code would look similar to this:

```
myButton_btn.onRelease = function () {

}
```

In both cases, you then add ActionScript between the curly braces of the event handler. Those actions will be performed whenever the event happens.

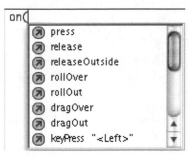

Figure 4.1 Use the on action to assign an event handler to a button instance.

The `release`/`onRelease` button event is the typical trigger for button interactivity. The event is triggered when the mouse button is released inside the `Hit` state of a button symbol. This setup allows viewers to change their minds and release the mouse button over a safe spot outside the hit area even after they've already clicked a button. Other types of button events make possible a range of interactions. **Table 4.1** lists all the button events.

To assign an event handler to a button instance:

1. Create a button symbol, and place an instance of the button on the Stage.

2. Select the button instance, and open the Actions panel.

3. In the Script pane, enter the ActionScript word on followed by an opening parenthesis.

   A code hint pull-down menu appears, providing you with all the events available to the button (**Figure 4.1**).

continues on next page

Table 4.1

Button Events	
BUTTON EVENT	**TRIGGERED WHEN**
on(press)/onPress	When the pointer is over the hit area and the mouse button is pressed.
on(release)/onRelease	When the pointer is over the hit area and the mouse button is pressed and released.
on(releaseOutside)/ onReleaseOutside	When the pointer is over the hit area and the mouse button is pressed and then released outside the hit area.
on(rollOver)/onRollover	When the pointer moves over the hit area.
on(rollOut)/onRollOut	When the pointer moves from the hit area off the hit area.
on(dragOver)/onDragOver	When the pointer is over the hit area and the mouse button is pressed; then the pointer is moved off the hit area and back over the hit area while the button remains pressed.
on(dragOut)/onDragOut	When the pointer is over the hit area and the mouse button is pressed; then the pointer is moved off the hit area while the button remains pressed.
on(keyPress"WhatKey")	When the key whatKey is pressed.
onSetFocus	When the button receives keyboard focus through the Tab key. (The button is highlighted by a yellow rectangle when the Tab key is used to select a button on the Stage.)
onKillFocus	When the button loses keyboard focus through the Tab key. (The button is highlighted by a yellow rectangle when the Tab key is used to select a button on the Stage.)

THE BUTTON CLASS

4. Choose an event from the code hint pull-down menu.

5. Enter a closing parenthesis and then an opening curly brace.

6. Choose another action as the response to the event.

7. On your last line of code, end your statement with a closing curly brace (**Figure 4.2**).

or

1. Create a button symbol, and place an instance of the button on the Stage.

2. Select the button instance, and open the Actions panel.

3. In the Actions toolbox, choose Global Functions > Movie Clip Control > on.

   A code hint pull-down menu appears, providing you with all the events available to the button (**Figure 4.3**).

4. Choose an event from the code hint pull-down menu.

5. In between the curly braces, choose another action as the response to the event.

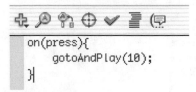

Figure 4.2 When the viewer presses and releases this button, Flash goes to Frame 10 and begins playing.

Figure 4.3 The code hint pull-down menu provides a list of available events.

THE BUTTON CLASS

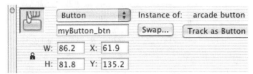

Figure 4.4 The button instance is called myButton_btn in the Property Inspector.

myButton_btn.

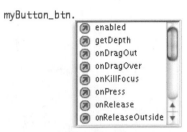

Figure 4.5 The code hint pull-down menu appears automatically because it recognizes _btn as the extension to the name of a button object.

```
myButton_btn.onRelease = function(){
    //Enter actions here
}
```

Figure 4.6 The response to the button click has not yet been added to the event handler.

To assign an event handler on the Timeline:

1. Create a button symbol, and place an instance of the button on the Stage.

2. Select the button instance, and enter a descriptive name in the Property Inspector. Make sure to add the suffix _btn to the name (**Figure 4.4**).

   This name is the name of your button object; you will use it to reference the button from ActionScript. This name is *not* the same one that appears in your Library.

3. Select the first frame of the main Timeline, and open the Actions panel.

4. In the Script pane, enter the instance name of your button followed by a dot.

   A code hint pull-down menu appears (**Figure 4.5**).

5. Choose an event from the pull-down menu.

6. Enter a closing parenthesis followed by =function(){}.

   An anonymous function is assigned to a particular event of your button instance (**Figure 4.6**).

continues on next page

THE BUTTON CLASS

7. With the pointer between the curly braces, choose an action as the response to the event (**Figure 4.7**).

or

1. Create a button symbol, and place an instance of the button on the Stage.

2. Select the button instance, and enter a descriptive name in the Property Inspector. Make sure to add the suffix **_btn** to the name.

3. Select the first frame of the main Timeline, and open the Actions panel.

4. In the Script pane, enter the name of your button.

5. In the Actions toolbox, choose an event from Built-in Classes > Movie > Buttons > Events. Complete the handler by adding **=function(){}**.

An anonymous function is assigned for the event.

6. With the pointer between the curly braces, choose an action as the response to the event.

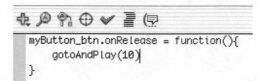

```
myButton_btn.onRelease = function(){
    gotoAndPlay(10)
}
```

Figure 4.7 When the viewer presses and releases the button called myButton_btn, Flash goes to Frame 10 and begins playing. Compare this script with the one in Figure 4.2.

✔ Tips

■ As described in Chapter 3, it is recommended that you end all instance names for buttons with **_btn** so that Flash can provide the appropriate code hints in the Script pane.

■ When you create your event handler on the main Timeline, your button must be present on the Stage at the same time to "receive" its instructions. If you create the event handler in keyframe 1, for example, but your button doesn't appear until keyframe 10, your button will not respond to the event handler.

THE BUTTON CLASS

```
on (release) {
}
```

```
myButton_btn.onRelease= function(){
}
```

Figure 4.8 Change the button event by highlighting it and choosing another. The event is in a different place, depending on whether your code is assigned to the button instance (top) or on the main Timeline (bottom).

```
on(press, release){
    gotoAndPlay(10);
}
```

Figure 4.9 If either the press or release event happens, Flash goes to Frame 10 and begins playing.

To select different button events:

1. Simply highlight the existing button event and press the Delete key (**Figure 4.8**).

2. Press the Show Code Hint button above the Script pane or press Ctrl-space (Windows) or Cmd-space (Mac) to bring up the code hint pull-down menu.

3. Choose a different event from the pull-down menu.

✔ Tips

- All the button events except `release` require that you choose Control > Test Movie to see the behavior of the button instance. These events don't work in the editing environment when you choose Control > Enable Simple Buttons.

- You can assign more than one event for a single `on` action. The action `on(press, release)`, for example, will detect when the mouse button is pressed as well as when the button is released and will execute any action within its curly braces if either of those two events occurs (**Figure 4.9**). After the first event, enter a comma and a second code hint pull-down menu will appear from which you can choose a second event.

- If you want to assign more than one event by using an anonymous function, you can create separate function statements or you can write the code in this form:
  myButton_btn.onPress = myButton_btn. onRelease = function () { }

continues on next page

THE BUTTON CLASS

■ Within one button instance, if you want one event to have a different consequence than another event has, you must create separate on action statements or separate anonymous function statements. To have the rollOver event make your movie play and the rollOut event make your movie stop, your actions would look like this:

```
on (rollOver) { play (); }
on (rollOut) { stop (); }
```

■ Don't confuse the rollover/onRollover button event with the Over keyframe of your button symbol. Both involve detecting when the pointer is over the hit area, but the Over state describes how your button looks when the mouse is over the hit area, whereas the rollover/onRollover event assigns an action when that event actually occurs. So the keyframes of a button symbol define how it looks, and the event handler defines what it does (**Figure 4.10**).

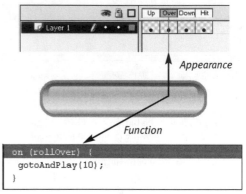

Figure 4.10 The Over state of the button symbol (top) defines how the button looks when the pointer is over the Hit state. A rollOver event handler (bottom) defines what the button does when the pointer is over the Hit state.

on(press) or onPress?

With two ways to assign event handlers to buttons, which one do you use? The answer partly depends on the complexity of your Flash project. Although it may be simpler to put event handlers directly on the button instance, in the long run, it's better practice to assign event handlers on the main Timeline. This method keeps all your ActionScript code in one place rather than scattered among individual buttons on the Stage. As your movie becomes more complex and you have more buttons to deal with, you'll find it easier to isolate and revise button events. Putting the event handler on the main Timeline also forces you to name your button instances so that you can target and control their properties with ActionScript.

Assigning event handlers directly to button instances, however, offers one distinct advantage: You can copy and paste button instances during author time and their event handlers will be pasted along with them. In this book, we will use both methods in examples because you should be comfortable using both on(press) and onPress.

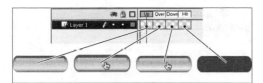

Figure 4.11 The four keyframes of a button symbol.

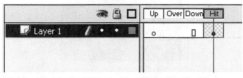

Figure 4.12 An invisible button has only the Hit keyframe defined.

Two instances of the same invisible-button symbol

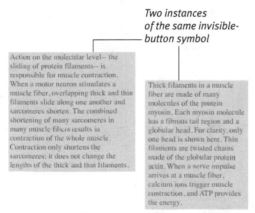

Figure 4.13 Invisible-button instances over text blocks.

Invisible Buttons

Flash lets you define four special keyframes of a button symbol that describe how the button looks and responds to the mouse: the Up, Over, Down, and Hit states. The Up state shows what the button looks like when the pointer is not over the button. Over shows what the button looks like when the pointer is over the button. Down shows what the button looks like when the pointer is over the button with the mouse button pressed. And Hit defines the actual active, or *hot*, area of the button (**Figure 4.11**).

You can exploit the flexibility of Flash buttons by defining only particular states. If you leave empty keyframes in all states except for the Hit state, you create an invisible button (**Figure 4.12**). Invisible buttons are extremely useful for creating multiple generic hotspots to which you can assign actions. By placing invisible button instances on top of graphics, you essentially have the power to make anything on the Stage react to the mouse pointer. If you have several blocks of text that you want the user to read in succession, you can have the user click each paragraph to advance to the next one. Instead of creating separate buttons out of each text block, make just one invisible button and stretch instances to fit each one. Assign actions to each invisible-button instance that covers the paragraphs (**Figure 4.13**).

When you drag an instance of an invisible button onto the Stage, you actually see the hit area as a transparent blue shape, which allows you to place the button precisely. When you choose Control > Enable Simple Buttons (Ctrl-Alt-B for Windows, Cmd-Option-B for Mac), the button disappears to show you its playback appearance.

INVISIBLE BUTTONS

To create an invisible button:

1. From the Insert menu, choose New Symbol.

   The Symbol Properties dialog box appears.

2. Type the symbol name of your button, choose Button as the behavior, and click OK.

   A new button symbol is created in the Library, and you enter symbol-editing mode.

3. Select the Hit keyframe.

4. Choose Insert > Keyframe.

   A new keyframe is created in the Hit state.

5. With the Hit keyframe selected, draw a generic shape that serves as the hotspot for your invisible button (**Figure 4.14**).

6. Return to the main Timeline.

7. Drag an instance of the symbol from the Library onto the Stage.

   A transparent blue shape appears on the Stage, indicating the Hit state of your invisible button.

8. Move, scale, and rotate the invisible-button instance to cover any graphic.

   When you enable simple buttons, the transparent blue area disappears but your pointer changes to a hand to indicate the presence of a button.

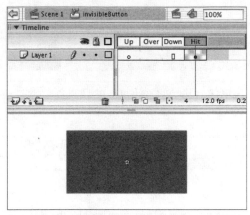

Figure 4.14 An invisible-button symbol. The rectangle in the Hit keyframe defines the active area of the button.

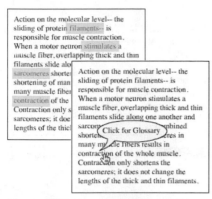

Figure 4.15 The Over state of this invisible button has a balloon with directions to go to a glossary. Multiple instances can cover different words.

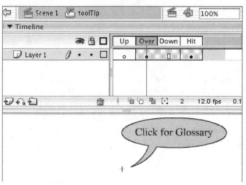

Figure 4.16 When only the Over state is defined in an invisible button, the graphics in the Over state will appear to pop up when the mouse rolls over the active area.

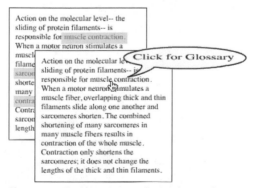

Figure 4.17 The instance over the words *muscle contraction* is stretched, making the Over state of the button stretch as much.

You can also create tool tips or helpful pop-up reminders by using invisible buttons. Create a short message in the Over state of an invisible button, and position these instances wherever the little messages apply (**Figure 4.15**).

To create pop-up tool tips with invisible buttons:

1. Create an invisible button, as described in the preceding task.

2. Select the Over state, and insert a new keyframe.

3. In the Over state, create a graphic that tells users about a particular feature that may be scattered through your Stage or movie (**Figure 4.16**).

4. Return to the main Timeline, and place instances of your invisible button over all the appropriate spots.

✔ Tips

■ Be careful about rotating and scaling your instance because it will affect the button's Over state (**Figure 4.17**).

■ Be conscious of the stacking order of invisible buttons and how they are placed in your layers. The topmost button will take precedence over any button underneath it, effectively disabling the action of the bottom button.

Tweening Buttons

You can tween buttons just as you do any other kind of symbol instance and create moving menus and interfaces that still respond to the pointer and carry out actions assigned to them.

To apply a motion tween to a button:

1. From the Insert menu, choose New Symbol, and create a button symbol.

2. Return to the main movie Timeline, and drag an instance of the button symbol onto the Stage. In the Property Inspector, give a name to your button instance.

3. Create a motion tween as you normally would for a graphic instance.

   Insert new keyframes, move or transform each instance, and then choose Motion Tween in the Property Inspector.

4. Create a new Layer, select the first keyframe and open the Actions panel.

5. Assign an event handler to the keyframe as previously described, coding in the form:

   myButton_btn.onRelease = function(){
   //some action
   }

6. Test your movie.

   Throughout its tween, the button instance is active and responds to your pointer (**Figure 4.18**). 🐾

✔ Tip

■ Assigning the event handler on the first keyframe of the Timeline is a better approach than assigning the event handler to the button instance in this case. Doing so keeps the ActionScript assigned to the button independent of its motion tween, so you can insert, delete, or modify keyframes or retween without losing the button's interactivity.

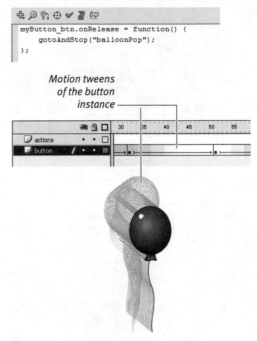

Figure 4.18 This balloon is a button that floats up and down in a motion tween. The event handler for this button is assigned on the main Timeline (top). When the user clicks the moving balloon, Flash will send the user to a frame label called "balloonPop" (not seen here).

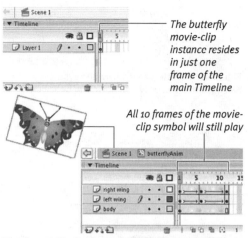

The butterfly movie-clip instance resides in just one frame of the main Timeline

All 10 frames of the movie-clip symbol will still play

Figure 4.19 Movie clips have independent Timelines.

Comparing a Movie-Clip Instance with a Graphic Instance

How does a movie-clip instance differ from a graphic instance? If you create the same animation in both a movie-clip symbol and a graphic symbol and then place both instances on the Stage, the differences become clear. The graphic instance shows its animation in the authoring environment, displaying however many frames are available in the main Timeline. If the graphic symbol contains an animation lasting ten frames and the instance occupies four frames of the main Timeline, you will see only four frames of the animation. Movie clips, on the other hand, do not work in the Flash authoring environment. You need to export the movie as a .swf file to see any movie-clip animation or functionality. When you export the movie (you can do so by choosing Control > Test Movie), Flash plays the movie-clip instance continuously, regardless of the number of frames the instance occupies and even when the movie itself has stopped.

Animated Buttons and the Movie-Clip Symbol

Animated buttons display an animation in any of the first three keyframes (Up, Over, and Down) of the button symbol. A button can spin when the pointer rolls over it, for example, because you have an animation of the spinning button in the Over state. How do you fit an animation into only one keyframe of the button symbol? The answer: Use a movie clip.

A movie clip is a special kind of symbol that allows you to have animations that run regardless of where they are or how many actual frames the instance occupies. This feature is possible because a movie clip's Timeline runs independently of any other Timeline, including other movie-clip Timelines and the main movie Timeline in which it may reside. This independence means that as long as you establish an instance on the Stage, a movie-clip animation will play all its frames regardless of where it is. Placing a movie-clip instance in a keyframe of a button symbol makes the movie clip play whenever that particular keyframe is displayed. That is the basis of an animated button.

An animation of a butterfly flapping its wings, for example, may take 10 frames in a movie-clip symbol. Placing an instance of that movie clip on the Stage in a movie that has only one frame will still allow you to see the butterfly flapping its wings (**Figure 4.19**). This functionality is useful for cyclical animations that play no matter what else may be going on in the current Timeline. Blinking eyes, for example, can be a movie clip placed on a character's face. No matter what the character does—whether it's moving or static in the current Timeline—the eyes will blink continuously.

To create a movie clip:

1. From the Insert menu, choose New Symbol.

   The Symbol Properties dialog box appears.

2. Type a descriptive name for your movie-clip symbol, choose Movie Clip as the behavior, and click OK (**Figure 4.20**).

   You will enter symbol-editing mode.

3. Create the graphics and animation on the movie-clip Timeline (**Figure 4.21**).

   Notice how the path above the Timeline tells you that you are currently editing a symbol.

4. Return to the main Stage.

   Your movie clip is stored in the Library as a symbol, available for you to bring onto the Stage as an instance (**Figure 4.22**).

✔ Tip

■ New instances of movie clips begin playing automatically from the first frame, as do instances in different scenes. Imagine that you build a movie-clip animation of a clock whose hand makes a full rotation starting at 12 o'clock. If you place an instance in scene 1 and continue your movie in scene 2, Flash will consider the instance in scene 2 to be new; it will reset the movie-clip animation and begin playing the clock animation at 12 o'clock.

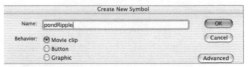

Figure 4.20 Create a new movie-clip symbol by naming it and selecting the Movie clip behavior.

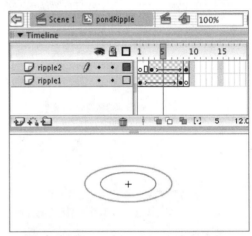

Figure 4.21 The pondRipple movie-clip symbol contains two tweens of an oval getting bigger and gradually fading.

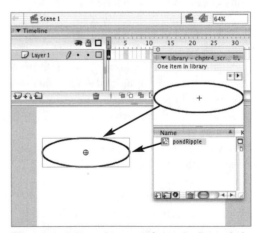

Figure 4.22 Bring an instance of a movie clip symbol onto the Stage by dragging it from the Library.

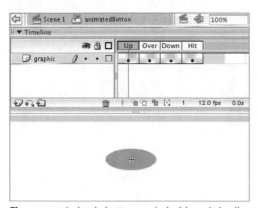

Figure 4.23 A simple button symbol with ovals in all four keyframes.

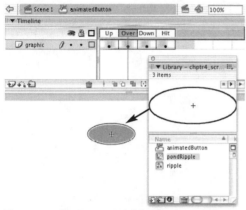

Figure 4.24 The Over state of the button symbol. Place an instance of the pondRipple movie clip in this keyframe to play the pond-ripple animation whenever the pointer moves over the button.

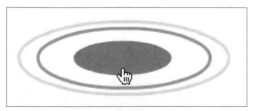

Figure 4.25 The completed animated button. When the pointer passes over the button, the pond-ripple movie clip plays.

To create an animated button:

1. Create a movie-clip symbol that contains an animation, as described in the preceding task.

2. Create a button symbol, and define the four keyframes for the Up, Over, Down, and Hit states (**Figure 4.23**).

3. In symbol-editing mode, select the Up, Over, or Down state for your button, depending on when you would like to see the animation.

4. Place an instance of your movie-clip symbol on the Stage inside your button symbol (**Figure 4.24**).

5. Return to the main movie Timeline, and drag an instance of your button to the Stage.

6. From the Control menu, choose Test Movie.

    Your button instance plays the movie-clip animation continuously as your pointer interacts with the button (**Figure 4.25**).

continues on next page

ANIMATED BUTTONS AND THE MOVIE-CLIP SYMBOL

✔ Tips

■ Stop the continuous cycling of your movie clip by placing a **stop** action in the last keyframe of your movie-clip symbol. Because movie clips have independent Timelines, they will respond to frame actions. Graphic symbols do not respond to any frame actions.

■ To better organize animated buttons, it's useful to create a new layer in the Timeline of your button symbol and reserve it specifically for the animation (**Figure 4.26**).

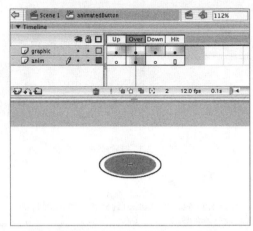

Figure 4.26 A new layer in the button symbol Timeline helps organize the animation.

Figure 4.27 Typical pull-down menus: the Mac OS File menu (left) and a Web menu from Netscape Navigator (right).

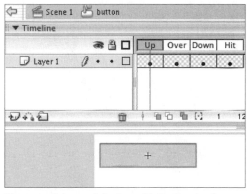

Figure 4.28 A generic button with the four keyframes defined.

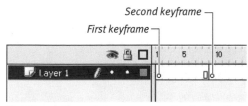

Figure 4.29 The pull-down menu movie-clip Timeline contains two keyframes: one at Frame 1 and another at Frame 9.

Complex Buttons

You can use a combination of invisible buttons, tweening buttons, animated buttons, and movie clips to create complex buttons such as pull-down menus. The pull-down (or pop-up) menu is a kind of button that is common in operating systems and Web interfaces and is useful for presenting several choices under a single heading. The functionality consists of a single button that expands to show more buttons and collapses when a selection has been made (**Figure 4.27**).

To build your own pull-down menu, the basic strategy is to place buttons inside a movie clip. The buttons specify which frames within the movie-clip Timeline to play. Whether the menu is expanded or collapsed is determined within the movie clip. Placing an instance of this movie clip on the Stage allows you to access either the expanded or collapsed state independently of what's happening in your main movie.

To create a simple pull-down menu:

1. Create a button symbol that will be used for the top menu button as well as the choices in the expanded list.

2. Add a filled rectangle to the Up, Over, Down, and Hit keyframes (**Figure 4.28**).

3. Create a new movie-clip symbol.
   Enter symbol-editing mode for the movie clip.

4. Insert a new keyframe at a later point in the movie-clip Timeline.
   You now have two keyframes. The first one will contain the collapsed state of your menu, and the second one will contain its expanded state (**Figure 4.29**).

continues on next page

COMPLEX BUTTONS

5. Drag one instance of your button symbol into the first keyframe, and add text over the instance to describe the button.

This is the collapsed state of your menu.

6. Drag several instances of your button symbol into the second keyframe, align them with one another, and add text over these instances to describe the buttons.

This is the expanded state of your menu (**Figure 4.30**).

7. Add a new layer, and place labels to mark the collapsed and expanded keyframes.

In the Frame Label field of the Property Inspector, enter collapsed for the first keyframe and expanded for the second keyframe.

The labels let you see clearly the collapsed and expanded states of your movie clip and let you use the gotoAndStop action with frame labels instead of frame numbers.

8. Select the button instance in the first keyframe and open the Actions panel.

9. In the Script pane, enter the event handler on (release) {}.

10. Place your pointer inside the curly braces of the event handler and select Global Functions > Timeline Control > gotoAndStop.

The gotoAndStop action appears inside the event handler.

11. In between the parentheses of the gotoAndStop action, enter "expanded" as the label of the frame at which you want Flash to stop. Be sure to include the quotation marks (**Figure 4.31**).

12. Select the first button instance on the last keyframe.

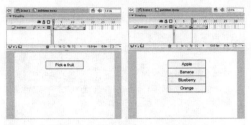

Figure 4.30 The two states of your pull-down menu. The collapsed state is in the first keyframe (left); the expanded state is in the second keyframe (right). The expanded state contains four button instances that represent the menu choices.

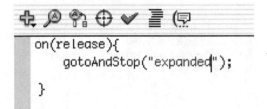

Figure 4.31 This button sends the Flash playhead to the frame labeled expanded and stops there.

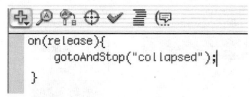

```
on(release){
    gotoAndStop("collapsed");
}
```

Figure 4.32 This button sends the Flash playhead to the frame labeled collapsed and stops there.

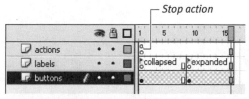

— Stop action

Figure 4.33 The completed movie-clip Timeline for the pull-down menu. A stop action is assigned to the first frame in the top layer.

13. In the Script pane of the Actions panel, enter the event handler on (release) {}.

14. Place your pointer inside the curly braces of the event handler and select Global Functions > Timeline Control > gotoAndStop.

The gotoAndStop action appears inside the event handler.

15. In between the parentheses of the gotoAndStop action, enter collapsed as the label of the frame at which you want Flash to stop. Be sure to include the quotation marks (**Figure 4.32**).

16. Repeat steps 13–15 on each of the remaining button instances on this keyframe.

17. While still in symbol editing mode for your movie clip, add a third layer, and in the first keyframe, assign the action stop.

Without this stop in the first frame of your movie clip, you would see the menu opening and closing repeatedly because of the automatic cycling of movie clips. The stop action ensures that the movie clip stays on Frame 1 until you click the menu button (**Figure 4.33**).

18. Return to the main movie Timeline, and place an instance of your movie clip on the Stage.

continues on next page

19. From the Control menu, choose Test Movie to see how your pull-down menu works.

When you click and release the first button, the buttons for your choices appear because you direct the playhead to go to the expanded keyframe on the movie-clip Timeline. When you click and release one of the buttons in the expanded state, the buttons disappear, returning you to the collapsed keyframe of the movie-clip Timeline. All this happens independently of the main movie Timeline, where the movie-clip instance resides (**Figure 4.34**).

At this point, you have created a complex button that behaves like a pull-down menu but still does not actually do anything (except modify itself). In Chapter 5, you'll learn how to make Timelines communicate with one another, which enables you to create complex navigation systems.

When you understand the concept behind the simple pull-down menu, you can create menus that are more elaborate by adding animation to the transition between the collapsed state and the expanded state. Instead of having the expanded state suddenly pop up, for example, you can create a tween that makes the buttons scroll down gently.

Movie clip in collapsed keyframe *Movie clip in expanded keyframe*

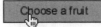 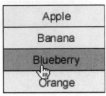

Figure 4.34 The two states of the pull-down menu work independently of the main Timeline.

COMPLEX BUTTONS

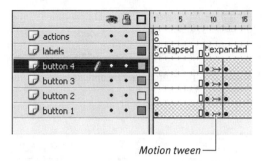

Motion tween

Figure 4.35 The pull-down-menu movie clip. The expanded-menu buttons are separated on different layers so you can motion-tween them.

To create an animated pull-down menu:

1. Create a simple pull-down menu, as described in the preceding task.

2. Enter symbol-editing mode for your movie clip.

3. Change the actions on the button in the first keyframe from gotoAndStop to gotoAndPlay.

   gotoAndPlay ("expanded");

   This action makes the playhead go to the label **expanded** and begin playing.

4. Create motion tweens for your button instances in the last keyframe (**Figure 4.35**).

5. In the last frame of the movie clip, insert a keyframe and assign a stop action (Global Functions > Timeline control > Stop).

6. Return to the main movie Timeline, and place an instance of your movie clip on the Stage.

7. From the Control menu, choose Test Movie to see how your pull-down menu works.

   When you click and release the first button, the playhead jumps to the label *expanded* in the movie clip and begins playing, showing the motion tweening of your button choices. 🖐

COMPLEX BUTTONS

123

Button-Tracking Options

You can define a button instance in the Property Inspector in one of two ways: Track as Button or Track as Menu Item (**Figure 4.36**). These two tracking options determine whether or not button instances can receive a button event even after the event has started on a different button instance. The Track as Menu Item option allows this to happen; the Track as Button option does not. The default option, Track as Button, is the typical behavior for buttons; it causes one button event to affect one button instance. More-complex cases, such as pull-down menus, require multiple button instances working together.

Imagine that you click and hold down the menu button to see the pop-up choices, drag your pointer to your selection, and then release the mouse button. You need Flash to recognize the `release` event in the expanded menu even though the `press` event occurred in the collapsed menu for a different button instance (in fact, in a different frame altogether). Choosing Track as Menu Item allows these buttons to receive these events and gives you more flexibility to work with combinations of button events.

To set Track as Menu Item with the press event:

1. Create a pull-down menu, as described in the preceding task.

2. Go to symbol-editing mode for the movie clip.

3. Select the button instance in the first keyframe, and change the mouse event to `press` (**Figure 4.37**).

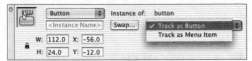

Figure 4.36 The button-tracking options in the Property Inspector.

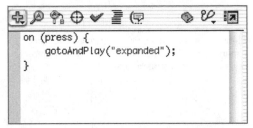

```
on (press) {
    gotoAndPlay("expanded");
}
```

Figure 4.37 The collapsed-menu button is assigned the `press` event.

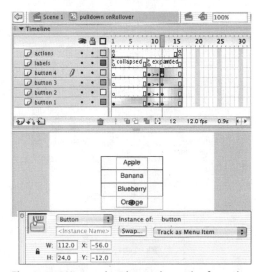

Figure 4.38 You need to change the setting for each button instance in the expanded section of the Timeline to Track as Menu Item, including buttons 1 through 4 in keyframes 9 and 12.

4. Select each button instance in the expanded keyframe.

5. In the Property Inspector, choose Track as Menu Item (**Figure 4.38**).

The button instances in the expanded menu will now accept a `release` event after the `press` event occurs on a different instance.

6. Return to the main Timeline, and test your movie.

You now click and hold down the mouse button to keep the menu open.

✔ Tip

■ When you set Track as Menu Item for this pull-down menu, the expanded button instances display their Down state as you move your pointer over them. This display occurs because your mouse button is, in fact, pressed, but that event occurred earlier on a different instance.

Refine the pull-down menu with a dragOver event so that the menu collapses even if no selection is made. This technique is important to keep pull-down menus expanded only when your viewer is making a choice from the menu.

To set Track as Menu Item with the dragOver event:

1. Continuing with the pull-down menu constructed in the preceding tasks, go to symbol-editing mode for the movie clip.

2. Add a new layer under the existing layers.

3. In the new layer, create an invisible button and place an instance in a new keyframe corresponding to the expanded keyframe.

   Your invisible-button instance should be slightly larger than the expanded menu (**Figure 4.39**).

4. Select the invisible-button instance.

5. In the Property Inspector, choose the Track as Menu Item option.

6. In the Actions panel, assign these actions:

   ```
   on (dragOver) {
       gotoAndStop ("collapsed");
   }
   ```

7. Return to the main Timeline, and test your movie.

   The invisible-button instance under the expanded menu detects whether the pointer leaves any of the other button instances. If it does, Flash sends the movie clip back to Frame 1 and collapses the menu.

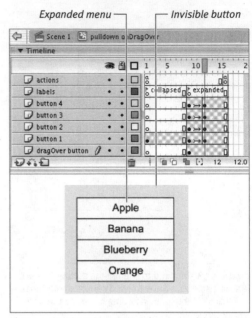

Expanded menu — Invisible button

Figure 4.39 When the pointer leaves one of the buttons in the expanded state of the menu, it is dragged over the invisible button that sits in the bottom layer. The dragOver event is detected in that button, signaling the playhead to jump to the keyframe labeled collapsed.

Button Properties

Because the buttons you create are objects of the Button class, you can control their properties by using dot syntax. Many button properties control the way a button looks (such as its width, height, and rotation), as well as the way a button behaves (such as its button tracking). **Table 4.2** summarizes the properties of the Button class. Many of these properties are also properties of the Movie Clip class (see Chapter 7).

Table 4.2

Button Properties

PROPERTY	VALUE	DESCRIPTION
_alpha	A number from 0 to 100	Specifies the alpha transparency; 0 is transparent, and 100 is opaque.
_visible	True or false	Specifies whether a button can be seen.
_name	A string-literal name	Gets the instance name of the button or sets a new instance name.
_rotation	A number	Specifies the degree of rotation in a clockwise direction from the 12 o'clock position. A value of 45, for example, tips the button to the right.
_width	A number, in pixels	Specifies the horizontal dimension.
_height	A number, in pixels	Specifies the vertical dimension.
_x	A number, in pixels	Specifies the horizontal position of the button's registration point.
_y	A number, in pixels	Specifies the vertical position of the button's registration point.
_xscale	A number	Specifies the percentage of the original button symbol's horizontal dimension.
_yscale	A number	Specifies the percentage of the original button symbol's vertical dimension.
_target	A string	Gets the target path of the button, using slash syntax.
useHandCursor	True or false	Determines whether the pointer changes to a hand icon when hovering over a button.
enabled	True or false	Determines whether the button can receive events.
menu	A ContextMenu object	Associates a button with a ContextMenu object.
trackAsMenu	True or false	Determines whether the button will track as a button or track as a menu item.
_focusRect	True or false	Determines whether a yellow rectangle appears around objects as you use the Tab key to select them.
tabEnabled	True or false	Determines whether the button can receive keyboard focus when you use the Tab key to select objects.
tabIndex	A number	Determines the order of focus when you use the Tab key to select objects. The tab order uses tabIndex in ascending order.

BUTTON PROPERTIES

To change a property of a button:

1. Create a button, and drag an instance of it to the Stage.

2. In the Property Inspector, give the button an instance name.

3. Select the first frame of the main Timeline, and open the Actions panel.

4. In the Script pane, enter the instance name of the button followed by a period.

   If your instance name ends with _btn, the code hint pull-down menu appears.

5. Select _alpha from the pull-down menu (**Figure 4.40**).

   or

   Choose Built-in Classes > Movie > Button > Properties > _alpha, and replace the placeholder instanceName with the name of your button instance.

6. Enter an equals sign after _alpha and a value for the property (**Figure 4.41**).

   The completed statement assigns a new value to the property of your button. 📶

To disable a button:

◆ Set the enabled property to false.

   If you name your button instance myButton_btn, enter the following statement:

   myButton_btn.enabled = false;

   Your button will no longer receive any events.

To disable the hand pointer:

◆ Set the useHandCursor property to false (**Figure 4.42**).

   If you name your button instance myButton_btn, enter the following statement:

   myButton.useHandCursor = false;

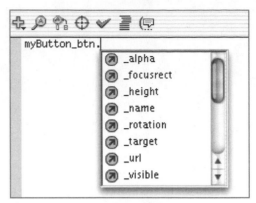

Figure 4.40 Use the code hint pull-down menu to select a property for your button called myButton_btn.

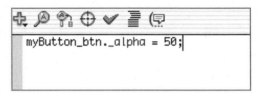

Figure 4.41 The value 50 is assigned to the _alpha property of the button called myButton_btn.

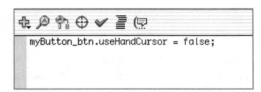

Figure 4.42 The hand pointer is disabled for the button called myButton_btn. Only the arrow pointer will show up.

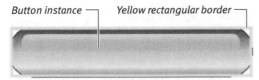

Button instance ⸏   Yellow rectangular border ⸏

Figure 4.43 When you use the Tab key, buttons show their focus with a yellow rectangular border in their Over state.

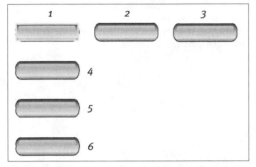

Figure 4.44 The automatic order of button focusing with the Tab key is by position. The numbers show the order in which the buttons will receive focus.

Changing button focus with the Tab key

The last several properties listed in Table 4.2—_focusRect, tabEnabled, and tabIndex— deal with controlling the button focus. The *button focus* is a way of selecting a button with the Tab key. When a Flash movie plays within a browser, you can press the Tab key and navigate between buttons, text boxes, and movie clips. The currently focused button displays its Over state with a yellow rectangular border (**Figure 4.43**). Pressing the Enter key (or Return key on the Mac) is equivalent to clicking the focused button. The button property _focusRect determines whether the yellow rectangular border is visible. If _focusRect is set to false, a focused button will display its Over state but will not display the yellow rectangular highlight. The property _tabEnabled, if set to false, will disable a button's capability to receive focus from the Tab key.

The order in which a button, movie clip, or text box receives its focus is determined by its position on the Stage. Objects focus from left to right and then from top to bottom. So if you had a row of buttons at the top of your movie and a column of buttons on the left side below it, the Tab key would focus each of the buttons in the top row first and then focus on each of the buttons in the column (**Figure 4.44**). After the last button receives the focus, the tab order begins again from the top row.

You can set your own tab order with the button property tabIndex. Assign a number to the tabIndex for each button instance, and Flash will organize the tab order, using the tabIndex in ascending order. Take control of the tab order to create more helpful forms, allowing the user to use the Tab and Enter keys to fill out multiple text boxes and click multiple buttons.

BUTTON PROPERTIES

129

To hide the yellow rectangular highlight over focused buttons:

◆ Set the _focusRect property to false.

If you name your button instance myButton_btn, for example, use the expression myButton_btn._focusRect = false.

✔ Tip

■ You can also hide the yellow rectangular highlight for all your buttons in one statement. Set the _focusRect property to false, and target the main Timeline by using the keyword _root. Use the expression _root._focusRect = false.

To disable focusing with the Tab key:

◆ Set the tabEnabled property to false.

If you name your button instance myButton_btn, for example, use the expression myButton_btn.tabEnabled = false.

To change the tab order of button focus:

1. Give each button instance a name in the Property Inspector.

2. Select the first frame of the main Timeline, and open the Actions panel.

3. Enter your first button instance name followed by a dot.

4. Select tabIndex from the code hint pull-down menu (**Figure 4.45**).

   or

   Choose Built-in Classes > Movie > Button > Properties > tabIndex and replace the placeholder instanceName with the name of your button instance.

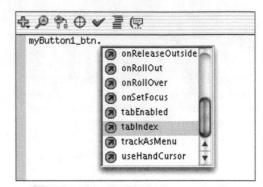

Figure 4.45 Use the code hint pull-down menu to select the tabIndex property.

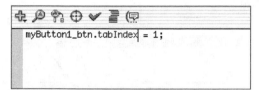

Figure 4.46 The button called myButton1_btn will receive the first focus with the Tab key.

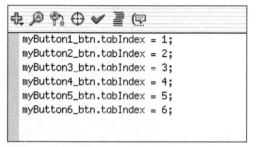

Figure 4.47 This block of code declares the tabIndex properties for myButton1_btn through myButton6_btn.

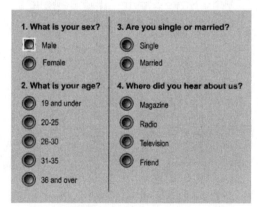

Figure 4.48 Control the order of button focusing to provide easier tab navigation through forms and questionnaires. This movie focuses buttons in columns to follow the question numbers rather than rely on Flash's automatic ordering.

5. After tabIndex, you must declare where in the tab order this object will be when the user presses the Tab key. Enter the equals sign (=) followed by a numerical value (**Figure 4.46**).

This button instance will be first in the tab order.

6. Continue to assign numbers in sequence to the tabIndex property of your button instances (**Figure 4.47**).

7. Choose Publish Preview > Default-(HTML) to view your movie in a browser.

When you press the Tab key, Flash follows the tabIndex in ascending order for button focusing (**Figure 4.48**).

✔ Tip

■ Some browsers intercept key presses, so you may have to click the Flash movie in your browser window before you can use the Tab key to focus on buttons.

The Movie Clip as a Button

Movie clips are objects that have their own Timeline in which animations play independently from the main Timeline. This fact lets you put movie clips inside button symbols to create animated buttons, as described earlier in this chapter. But movie clips can also behave like buttons all by themselves. You can assign many of the same event handlers to movie clips that you assign to buttons. Assign an on(release) or an onRelease event handler to a movie clip, for example, and the event will respond when the viewer clicks the movie-clip instance.

Within the movie-clip Timeline, you can assign the frame labels _up, _over, and _down, and those keyframes will behave like the Up, Over, and Down keyframes of a button symbol (**Figure 4.49**). The _up label identifies the state of the movie clip when the pointer is not over the hit area. The _over label identifies the state of the movie clip when the pointer is over the hit area. And the _down label identifies the state of the movie clip when the pointer is over the hit area and the mouse button is pressed. The hit area of a movie clip is, by default, the shape of the movie clip. You can define a different hit area by assigning another movie clip to the property hitArea.

Beware—actions assigned to movie clips behave quite differently from those assigned to buttons. An event handler on a movie clip belongs to that movie clip's Timeline, whereas an event handler on a button belongs to the Timeline on which it is sitting. Consider this simple code:

```
on(release){
    gotoAndStop(10);
}
```

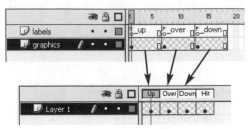

Figure 4.49 The _up, _over, and _down labels of a movie-clip symbol correspond to the Up, Over, and Down keyframes of a button symbol.

Why Have Movie Clips Behave Like Buttons?

Why would you want to use a movie clip as a button? Why not just use a regular button? Movie clips offer you more power and greater flexibility to deal with dynamic situations. Using movie clips as buttons lets you create more complex and sophisticated buttons. Because you can define the hit area of a movie clip yourself, you can shrink, grow, move, and change it dynamically by using ActionScript. You can't do that with buttons. Using movie clips as buttons also makes it easier to combine the methods of movie clips with the events of buttons. The startDrag() movie-clip method, for example, can be tied to the on(press) event handler on a single movie clip.

This doesn't mean that you shouldn't use buttons at all. It does mean you have more options for your creative toolkit.

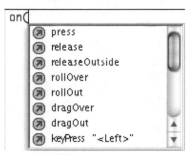

Figure 4.50 The on action can be assigned to a movie clip as well as a button. The code hint pull-down menu that appears for the on event handler looks identical for both.

```
on(press){
    //Enter actions here
}
```

Figure 4.51 The completed on (press) event handler assigned on a movie clip instance.

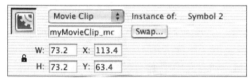

Figure 4.52 This movie clip instance has been named myMovieClip_mc in the Property Inspector.

When this action is assigned to a movie clip, Flash moves the playhead of the *movie clip's* Timeline to Frame 10. When the code is assigned to a regular button, Flash moves the playhead of the *main* Timeline to Frame 10. You will learn more about navigating different Timelines in Chapter 5.

To assign a button event handler to a movie clip:

1. Create a movie-clip symbol, and drag an instance of it to the Stage.

2. Select the instance, and open the Actions panel.

3. In the Script pane, enter the ActionScript word on followed by an opening parenthesis.

   A code hint pull-down menu appears, providing you with all the events available to the movie clip (**Figure 4.50**).

4. Choose an event from the code hint pull-down menu.

5. Enter a closing parenthesis and then an opening curly brace.

6. Choose another action as the response to the event.

7. On your last line of code, end your statement with a closing curly brace.

   The completed code is identical to an event handler that you would place on a button instance (**Figure 4.51**).

   or

1. Create a movie-clip symbol, drag an instance of it to the Stage, and give the instance a name in the Property Inspector (**Figure 4.52**).

2. Select the first frame of the main Timeline, and open the Actions panel.

continues on next page

3. In the Script pane, enter the instance name of the movie clip followed by a period.

   A code hint pull-down menu appears, providing you with all the events available to the button.

4. Select the event from the pull-down menu (**Figure 4.53**).

5. Complete the event handler by entering =function(){}.

6. Place the pointer between the curly braces of the function and choose an action as a response to the event (**Figure 4.54**).

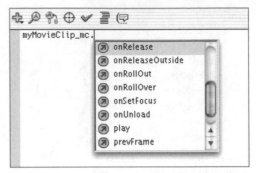

Figure 4.53 The onRelease event is assigned to the movie clip called myMovieClip_mc from the code hint pull-down menu.

To define the Up, Over, and Down keyframes of a movie clip:

1. Create a movie-clip symbol, and enter symbol-editing mode for it.

2. Insert a new layer.

3. Choose Insert > Keyframe twice along the Timeline.

   Two more keyframes are created in the movie-clip Timeline (**Figure 4.55**).

4. Select the first keyframe, and type _up as its label in the Property Inspector.

5. Select the second keyframe, and type _over as its label in the Property Inspector.

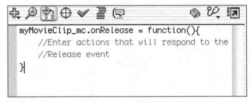

Figure 4.54 An anonymous function is created that responds to a click on the movie clip called myMovieClip_mc.

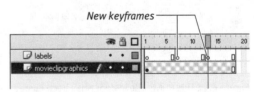

Figure 4.55 Two additional keyframes, at frames 7 and 13, are created in a new layer.

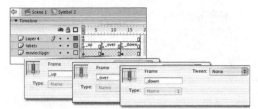

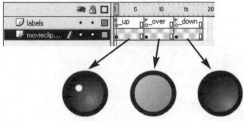

Figure 4.56 Label the three keyframes in the Property Inspector.

Figure 4.57 The three keyframes contain the Up, Over, and Down states of your movie clip.

6. Select the last keyframe, and type _down as its label in the Property Inspector.

The three keyframes define the Up, Over, and Down states of your movie clip (**Figure 4.56**).

7. In the layer containing your graphics, create keyframes corresponding to the labeled keyframes you just created, and alter your graphics for the Up, Over, and Down states (**Figure 4.57**).

8. Insert another new layer.

9. Select the first frame of the new layer, and open the Actions panel.

10. Choose Global Functions > Timeline Control > stop.

The **stop** action prevents the movie clip from playing automatically.

11. Exit symbol-editing mode.

12. Drag an instance of your movie-clip symbol to the main Stage.

13. Assign a button event handler to your movie-clip instance.

14. Test your movie.

Flash uses the _up, _over, and _down keyframes for the Up, Over, and Down states of the movie clip. You must have a button event handler assigned such as onPress or on(press) to the movie clip to make it behave like a button and recognize the labeled keyframes. 🔊

To create an animated button by using a movie clip:

1. Choose Insert > New Symbol.

2. Select Movie Clip, and click OK.

   A new movie-clip symbol is created in your Library, and you are put in symbol-editing mode.

3. Insert a new layer, and define the _up, _over, and _down labels for three separate keyframes, as described in the preceding task.

4. In the first layer, create keyframes corresponding to the labeled keyframes you just created.

5. For each keyframe in the first layer, create a motion or shape tween that you want to play for the Up, Over, and Down states of the button (**Figure 4.58**).

6. Insert another new layer, and create keyframes corresponding to the beginning and end of each labeled state.

7. Select each beginning keyframe and in the Actions panel, choose Global Functions > Timeline Control > Play.

8. Select each ending keyframe, and in the Actions panel, choose Global Functions > Timeline Control > gotoAndPlay.

9. Between the parentheses of each gotoAndPlay action, enter the frame label name to which each ending keyframe corresponds.

   For the Up, Over, and Down states, the ending keyframe sends the playhead back to the beginning keyframe, creating a loop for each of your tweens (**Figure 4.59**).

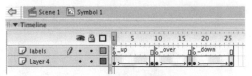

Figure 4.58 Create animations for the Up, Over, and Down states in the _up, _over, and _down keyframes.

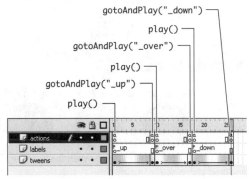

Figure 4.59 The actions in the top layer play and repeat the tweens in each labeled keyframe.

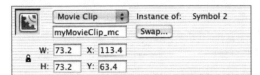

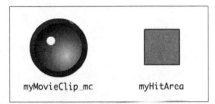

Figure 4.60 A new movie clip has been created and assigned an instance name of myMovieClip_mc.

Figure 4.61 The movie clip called myMovieClip_mc will use the movie clip called myHitArea as its hit area.

10. Exit symbol-editing mode.

11. Drag an instance of your movie clip to the Stage.

12. Assign a button event handler to your movie-clip instance.

13. Test your movie.

✔ Tip

- You can assign a `stop` action instead of a `gotoAndPlay` action to the end keyframes of the Up, Over, and Down states. Doing so makes the movie clip play the tween only once.

To define the hit area of a movie clip:

1. Create a movie-clip symbol, place an instance of it on the Stage, and name it in the Property Inspector (**Figure 4.60**). This instance is the movie clip to which you will assign a button event handler.

2. Create another movie-clip symbol, place an instance of it on the Stage, and name it in the Property Inspector. This instance is the movie clip that will act as the hit area for the first movie clip (**Figure 4.61**).

3. Assign a button event handler to the first movie-clip instance.

4. Select the first frame of the main Timeline, and open the Actions panel.

5. In the Script pane, enter the name for the first movie-clip instance followed by a period. The code hint pull-down menu appears.

6. Select `hitArea` from the code hint pull-down menu.

continues on next page

THE MOVIE CLIP AS A BUTTON

7. After `hitArea`, enter an equals sign (=) followed by the name of the second movie-clip instance (**Figure 4.62**).

The completed statement assigns the second movie clip as the hit area for the first movie clip.

8. Test your movie.

The `Up`, `Over`, and `Down` states of your first movie clip respond to the shape of the second movie clip. You can use any movie clip as the hit area for another movie clip, and you can place it any-where, even inside the movie clip that's acting as a button. As long as you name it, you can target it and assign it to the `hitArea` property of another.

```
myMovieClip_mc.hitArea = myHitArea;
```

Figure 4.62 The completed statement in the Script pane.

✔ Tip

■ The movie clip assigned to the `hitArea` property doesn't need to be visible to work. You can change its alpha trans-parency in the Property Inspector to be clear, or you can set its `_visible` property to `0`. See Chapter 7 for more information on modifying movie-clip properties.

Movie-clip properties that affect button behavior

Like buttons, movie clips have properties that affect their button behavior. **Table 4.3** summarizes these properties. Use these properties as you would for buttons to control whether a movie clip is enabled or whether the hand pointer is visible or to control the tab ordering for the focusing of movie clips. The following code will disable the hand pointer on a movie clip called myMovieClip_mc that is behaving as a button:

MyMovieClip_mc.useHandCursor = false

Table 4.3

Movie-Clip Properties That Affect Button Behavior		
PROPERTY	VALUE	DESCRIPTION
hitArea	Movie clip name	Defines the hit area of a movie clip.
useHandCursor	True or false	Determines whether the pointer changes to a hand icon when hovering over a movie clip.
enabled	True or false	Determines whether or not the movie clip can receive button events.
trackAsMenu	True or false	Determines whether the movie clip will track as a button or track as a menu item.
_focusrect	True or false	Determines whether a yellow rectangle appears around objects as you use the Tab key to select them.
tabEnabled	True or false	Determines whether the movie clip can receive keyboard focus when you use the Tab key to select objects. Movie clips (children) within a movie clip (parent) may still receive focus even if the parent cannot.
tabIndex	A number	Determines the order of focus when you use the Tab key to select objects. The tabIndex is in ascending order.
tabChilden	True or false	Determines whether movie clips inside movie clips can receive focus when you use the Tab key.
focusEnabled	True or false	Determines whether the movie clip can receive focus even when it is not acting as a button.

Keyboard Detection

The keyboard is just as important an inter-face device as the mouse, and Flash lets you detect events occurring from single key presses. This arrangement opens the possibility of having navigation based on the keyboard (using the arrow keys or the number keys, for example) or having keyboard shortcuts that duplicate mouse-based navigation schemes. Flash even lets you control live text the viewer types in empty text fields in a movie; these text fields merit a separate discussion in Chapter 10. This section focuses on single or combination keystrokes that trigger things to happen using the keyPress event and the Key class.

Key presses using buttons

The keyPress event is an option for the on event handler (**Figure 4.63**). The keyPress event happens when a single key on the keyboard is pressed. To use the keyPress event, you need to create a button symbol and place an instance of that button on the Stage. The button instance acts as a con-tainer for the event and associated actions, so you should make the button invisible or place the instance just off the Stage so that you can't see it in the final exported .swf file. The keyPress event is unusual in that it does not have a parallel event for an anonymous function. You must assign the keyPress event to the instance of a button.

To detect a key press with a button:

1. Create an invisible-button symbol, as described earlier in this chapter.

2. Place an instance of the button on or just off the Stage (**Figure 4.64**).

3. Select the instance, and open the Actions panel.

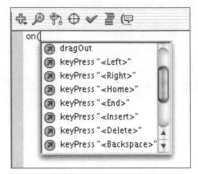

Figure 4.63 The code hint pull-down menu lists the keyPress events.

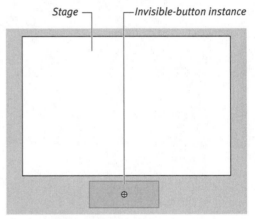

Figure 4.64 Placement of the button instance for a keyPress event, just off the Stage.

```
on(keyPress "<Left>"){
    nextFrame();
}
```

Figure 4.65 The keyPress key is set to the left arrow and the response is to advance to the next frame.

Stop action — Images on Stage in separate keyframes

Invisible-button instance with keyPress event

Figure 4.66 This movie has four successive images on the Stage. The on(keyPress "<right>") event handler with the response set to nextFrame allows you to advance to the next image simply by pressing the right arrow key.

```
on(keyPress "<Right>"){
    nextFrame();
}
on(keyPress "<Left>"){
    prevFrame();
}
```

Figure 4.67 Another keyPress event requires two separate on action statements. Here, the left and the right keys invoke two different responses.

4. In the Script pane, enter on and the opening parenthesis. The code hint pull-down menu appears.

5. Select a specific keypress event from the pull-down menu.

6. Complete the event handler, and choose an action as a response to the keyPress event (**Figure 4.65**).

7. From the Control menu, choose Test Movie to see how the keyPress event responds (**Figure 4.66**).

To detect multiple key presses with a button:

1. Select the button instance that contains the first keyPress event.

2. Open the Actions panel.

3. On a new line of the Script pane, enter another on and an opening parenthesis.

4. From the code hint pull-down menu, select a different keyPress event.

5. Complete the event handler and choose a different action as the response to the second key press (**Figure 4.67**).

Although multiple keystrokes can be handled with one button instance, each one requires a separate on statement.

141

To combine a keyPress event with another button event:

1. Create a button symbol that has its Up, Over, Down, and Hit states defined.

2. Place an instance of the button on the Stage.

3. Select the instance, and open the Actions panel.

4. Assign a keyPress event handler as described in the previous task and choose an action as the response to the event. For example, assign the following code:

   ```
   on (keyPress "<right>") {
       nextFrame();
   }
   ```

5. Place your pointer directly after the keyPress event and before the closing parenthesis.

6. Enter a comma.

   The code hint pull-down menu appears (**Figure 4.68**).

7. Choose another event.

8. Test your movie (**Figure 4.69**).

   Either clicking the button on the Stage or pressing the key on the keyboard will make your movie perform the action you selected.

✔ Tips

- When your Flash movie plays inside a browser, you must click the movie before any keyPress events can be detected because the window needs focus.

- The Esc and function keys are not valid keystrokes.

- The keyPress event does not recognize combination keystrokes, such as Option-A and Alt-A. Flash does distinguish between uppercase and lowercase letters, however.

Figure 4.68 Additional events can be added by inserting a comma.

Figure 4.69 The right arrow button is assigned two events: an on(release) event and an on(keyPress "<right>") event. Either event will advance the movie to the next frame.

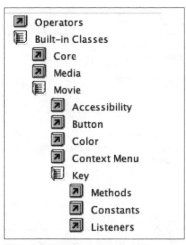

Figure 4.70 The Key class is under Built-in Classes > Movie.

The Key class

The Key class handles the detection of key presses on the keyboard (**Figure 4.70**). In Chapter 3, you learned that you must instantiate a class before you can use it. The Key class, however, is one of a few classes that don't require a constructor function to create an instance before you can use it. To call one of its methods, you use the class name itself (Key).

The Key class has methods that allow you to retrieve the key that was pressed last or to test whether a certain key was pressed. The most common method is isDown(), whose parameter is a specific key on the keyboard. This method checks whether that key has been pressed; if so, it returns a value of true.

All keys in Flash have a specific number associated with them; this number is known as the *key-code value* (see Appendix B). You use these codes in conjunction with the isDown() method to construct a conditional statement that detects the keyboard interaction. Key.isDown(32) for example, returns true or false, depending on whether the space-bar (whose key-code value is 32) is pressed.

Fortunately, you don't have to use clumsy numeric key codes all the time. The most common keys are conveniently assigned as properties of the Key class. These properties are constants that you can use in place of the key codes. The statement Key.isDown(32), for example, is the same as Key.isDown(Key.SPACE).

To detect a key press by using the Key class's isDown method:

1. Select the first keyframe in the Timeline, and open the Actions panel.

2. Choose Statements > Conditions/ Loops > if.

The incomplete if statement appears in the Script pane, with the condition parameter missing (**Figure 4.71**).

3. Choose Built-in Classes > Movie > Key > Methods > isDown.

The isDown() method appears as the condition parameter. The key-code parameter is required for this method (**Figure 4.72**).

4. Choose Built-in Classes > Movie > Key > Constants, and select a keyboard key from the list (**Figure 4.73**).

5. Choose a basic action as the response for this conditional statement (**Figure 4.74**).

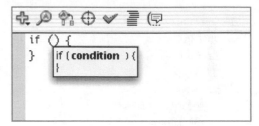

Figure 4.71 The if statement has a condition that it tests. If that condition is true, the actions within the curly braces will be carried out.

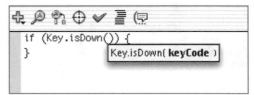

Figure 4.72 The method isDown() expects a key-code value, as suggested by the code hint.

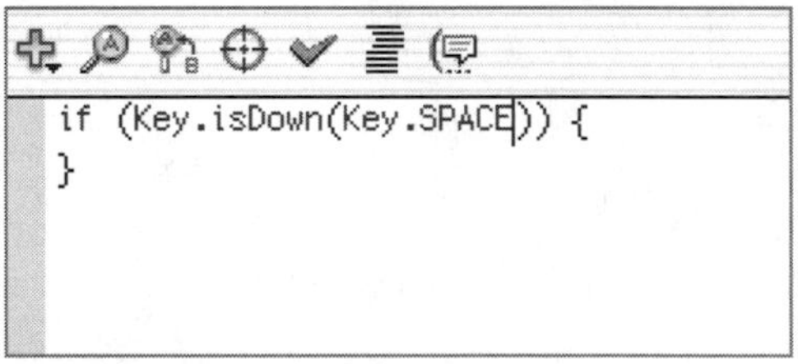

```
if (Key.isDown(Key.SPACE)) {
}
```

Figure 4.73 The property key.SPACE is in place as the key-code parameter for the method isDown().

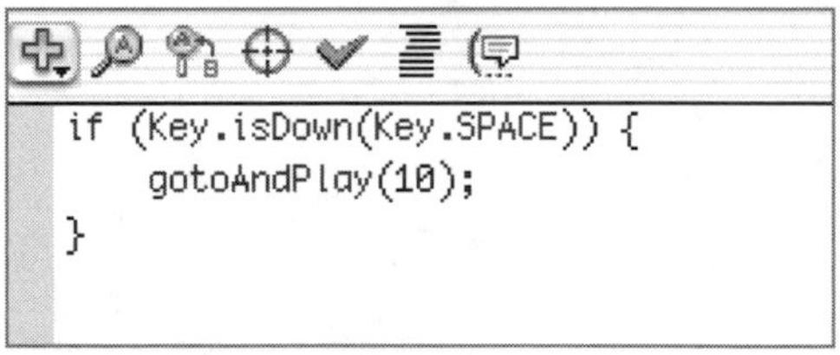

```
if (Key.isDown(Key.SPACE)) {
    gotoAndPlay(10);
}
```

Figure 4.74 If the spacebar is pressed, Flash goes to Frame 10.

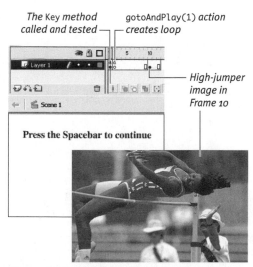

The Key *method called and tested* — *gotoAndPlay(1) action* — *creates loop*

— *High-jumper image in Frame 10*

Figure 4.75 This movie loops between Frames 1 and 2 until the spacebar is pressed.

```
if (Key.isDown(Key.SPACE) && Key.isDown(Key.CONTROL)) {
    gotoAndStop(10);
}
```

Figure 4.76 The operator && connects two statements.

6. Insert a new keyframe after the first one, and assign the frame action `gotoAndPlay(1)`.

This second keyframe loops back to the first so that the conditional statement is checked continuously. This method is the simplest way to have the `if` statement tested (**Figure 4.75**). ⊙

We'll explore more-refined ways of dealing with conditionals and action loops later in this chapter. For now, you can use this basic loop to test the `isDown()` method and different Key class properties.

To create key combinations with the Key class isDown method:

1. Select the first keyframe from the preceding task, and open the Actions panel.

2. Place your pointer directly after the condition parameter of the `if` statement.

3. Select Operators > Logical Operators > && or simply enter two ampersands (&&) manually.

The logical operator && joins two statements so that both must be true for the entire statement to be true. You can think of the operator as being the word *and*.

4. Select Built-in Classes > Movie > Key > Methods > isDown.

The `isDown()` method appears after the && operator. Another parameter is required for this method

5. Select Built-in Classes > Movie > Key > Constants > CONTROL.

The property `key.CONTROL` appears as the parameter for the second `isDown()` method (**Figure 4.76**). The `if` statement will perform the action within its curly braces only if both the spacebar and the Ctrl key are pressed together. ⊙

Creating listeners for key events

In the preceding section, you had to create a
two-frame loop on the main Timeline to test
the isDown() method. A way to eliminate
that loop and detect events of the Key class
is to create a listener. A *listener* is an object
that you create from the generic Object class.
You can create an object called myListener
with the statement myListener = new Object().
Then you use anonymous functions to assign
a key event to your listener. If you want your
listener to listen for the onKeyDown event and
respond by going to Frame 10, you create
the following function:

```
myListener.onKeyDown = function(){
    gotoAndStop(10);
}
```

When your event is assigned to your listener,
you must register your listener with the Key
class. Do so by using the addListener()
method of the Key class, as follows:

```
Key.addListener(myListener)
```

From that point on, whenever the key event
occurs, your listener object is notified. The
two events that your listener can detect are
onKeyDown and onKeyUp. The onKeyDown event
happens when a key on the keyboard is
pressed. The onKeyUp event happens when
a key is released.

Listeners are required for the events of the Key,
Selection, TextField, and Stage classes. They
are available for the Mouse class but are not
required except for the onMouseWheel event.

The keyPress Event, the Key Class, and Listeners

Why would you use the Key class and a
listener instead of a button with a keyPress
event? It's really a matter of sophistication
versus ease of use and simplicity. Using a
listener and the Key class to detect key
presses is much more powerful than
using a button instance because you can
construct ActionScript code that's more
complex around the Key class. You can
test for key combinations, for example,
by requiring two isDown() methods to be
true before performing certain actions as
a response. Using key-code values also
opens virtually the entire keyboard. The
function keys and the Esc key have key-
code values, so they are available to the
Key class.

The keyPress event is much easier to use,
however. If your Flash movie doesn't require
much in terms of keyboard interaction,
or if you simply want to have a keyboard
shortcut accompany a button event, use
the on(keyPress) action.

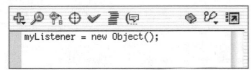

```
myListener = new Object();
```

Figure 4.77 The object called myListener will be your listener to detect events of the Key class. It is created from the Object class.

```
myListener = new Object();
myListener.onKeyDown = function() {

}
```

Figure 4.78 The onKeyDown event is assigned to your listener.

```
myListener = new Object();
myListener.onKeyDown = function() {
    gotoAndStop(5);
}
```

Figure 4.79 When the listener detects a key being pressed, Flash goes to Frame 5 and stops there.

```
stop();
myListener = new Object();
myListener.onKeyDown = function(){
    gotoAndStop(5);
}
Key.addListener(myListener);
```

Figure 4.80 The final step in using this listener is registering it to the Key class. The stop action in line 1 has been added here to keep the movie at Frame 1 until the key is pressed.

To create a listener for a key event:

1. Select the first frame of the main Timeline, and open the Actions panel.

2. In the Script pane, enter a name for your listener object followed by an equals sign

3. Select Built-in Classes > Core > Object > new Object.

   The completed statement creates a new, named object (**Figure 4.77**).

4. On a new line, enter the name of the listener object that you created in the last step followed by a period.

5. Select Built-in Classes > Movies > Key > Listeners > onKeyDown. Complete the handler by adding =function(){}.

   Flash creates an anonymous function to respond to the onKeyDown event (**Figure 4.78**).

6. With the pointer between the curly braces of the event handler, choose an action as the response to the onKeyDown event (**Figure 4.79**).

7. On the next line, choose Built-in Classes > Movie > Key > Methods > addListener.

   The addListener method appears. It requires a listener object as its parameter to be complete.

8. Enter the name of the listener object that you created.

   Your listener is registered to the Key class and will now respond to the onKeyDown event (**Figure 4.80**).

Combine a Key listener with the Key.isDown() method to make Flash respond only to certain key presses. First, your listener detects whether any key is pressed. Then you can use the if statement to test whether a certain key has been pressed.

To listen for a specific key press:

1. Continuing with the preceding task, select the first frame of the Timeline, and open the Actions panel.

2. Delete the gotoAndStop(5) action in the Script pane.

3. On the same line, Choose Statements > Conditions/Loops > if.

   The if statement appears within the onKeyDown event handler (**Figure 4.81**).

4. Select Built-in Classes > Movie > Key > Methods > isDown.

   The isDown() method appears as the condition parameter of the if statement.

5. Enter the key code for the specific key you want to detect, or select Built-in Classes > Movie > Key > Constants.

6. Add back the gotoAndStop(5) action within the if statement.

   The final script (**Figure 4.82**) creates and registers a listener to detect any key that is pressed with the onKeyDown event. The if statement within the event handler makes sure that there is a response only if a certain key is pressed.

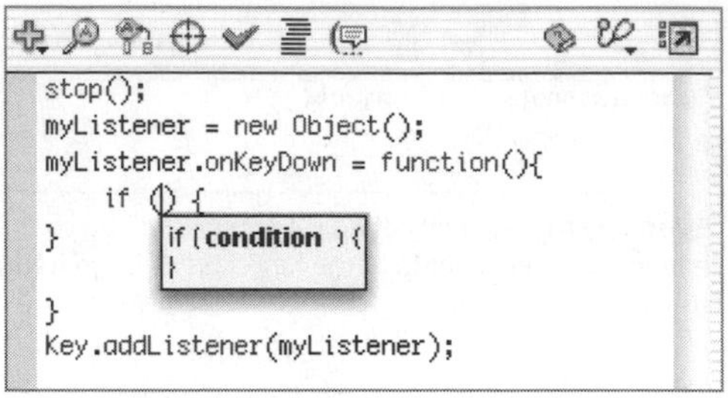

Figure 4.81 An if statement has been placed inside of the onKeyDown event handler.

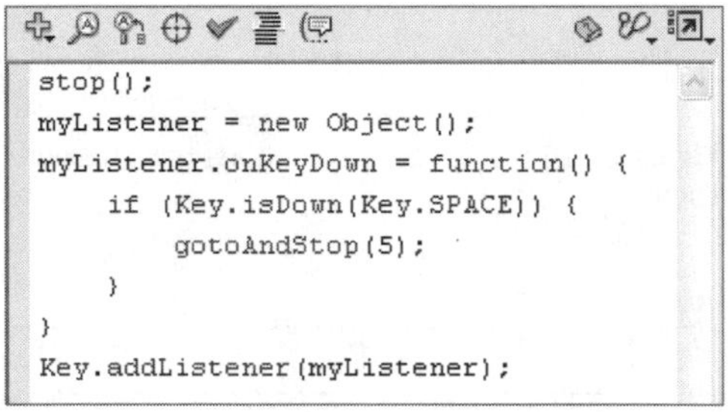

Figure 4.82 The completed script. The stop action has been added at the top to keep the movie at Frame 1 until the right arrow key is pressed.

Figure 4.83 An onMouseMove event handler.

Mouse Detection

The Mouse class, like the Key class, is one of the few ActionScript classes that do not need to be instantiated before you can use it. Its properties are available immediately, and its methods are called with the class name (**Mouse**). You will learn about its methods and properties in Chapter 7 when you learn more about the movie clip. Here, you'll learn about the mouse events and how to detect them.

You can detect four mouse events: onMouseMove, onMouseDown, onMouseUp, and onMouseWheel. The onMouseMove event happens whenever the user moves the mouse pointer, onMouseDown happens when the mouse button is pressed, onMouseUp happens when the mouse button is released, and onMouseWheel happens when the user scrolls the mouse wheel. To detect onMouseMove, onMouseDown, or onMouseUp, you can assign an anonymous function on the main Timeline, like this (**_root** is an ActionScript word that refers to the main Timeline):

`_root.onMouseMove = function(){ }`

Another way to detect any of the mouse events is to create a listener, just as you do to detect key events. Create a listener from the generic Object class. Assign a mouse-event handler to the listener and then register your listener with the Mouse class, using the method `Mouse.addListener()`.

To detect mouse movement:

1. Select the first frame of the main Timeline, and open the Actions panel.

2. Choose Built-in Classes > Movie > Mouse > Listeners > onMouseMove. Complete the handler by adding `=function(){}` (**Figure 4.83**).

continues on next page

3. Because no instance was defined, select and delete `instanceName` from the Script pane and replace it with `_root`, which refers to the main Timeline.

The `onMouseMove` event handler is assigned to the main Timeline.

4. Choose an action as a response to this event.

Whenever the mouse moves, Flash performs the actions listed within the `onMouseMove` event handler (**Figure 4.84**).

5. Choose Global Functions > Movie Clip Control > updateAfterEvent.

The `updateAfterEvent` action forces Flash to refresh the display. For certain events, such as `onMouseMove`, `updateAfterEvent` makes certain that the graphics are updated according to the event, not the frame rate.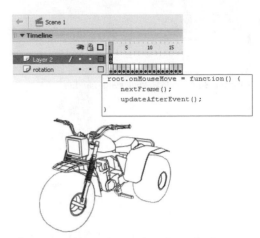

To create a listener to detect a mouse press:

1. Select the first frame of the main Timeline, and open the Actions panel.

2. Enter a name for your listener object, followed by the equals sign (=).

3. Choose Built-in Classes > Core > Object > new Object.

The constructor function `new Object()` appears. Flash instantiates a new generic object, using the name you entered for your listener (**Figure 4.85**).

4. On a new line, enter the name for the listener object that you just created.

5. Choose Built-in Classes> Movie > Mouse > Listeners > onMouseDown. Complete the handler by adding `=function(){}`.

The `onMouseDown` event handler for your listener is created (**Figure 4.86**).

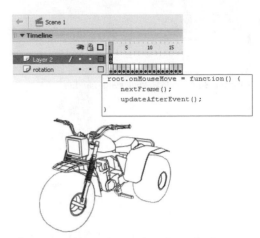

Figure 4.84 This movie contains a frame-by-frame animation of a three-wheeler that rotates. Anytime the mouse pointer moves, Flash advances to the next frame.

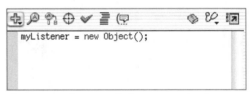

Figure 4.85 A listener called `myListener` has been created.

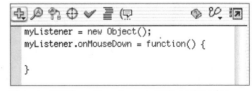

Figure 4.86 The `onMouseDown` event is assigned to your listener.

```
myListener = new Object();
myListener.onMouseDown = function() {
    nextFrame();
}
```

Figure 4.87 When the listener detects the mouse button being pressed, Flash goes to the next frame.

```
stop();
myListener = new Object();
myListener.onMouseDown = function() {
    nextFrame();
}
Mouse.addListener(myListener);
```

Figure 4.88 The final step in using this listener is registering it to the Mouse class. The stop action has been added here to keep the movie at Frame 1 until the event happens.

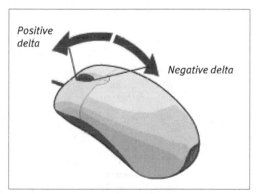

Figure 4.89 The mouse wheel returns a positive delta when it rolls forward and a negative delta when it rolls backward.

6. Now choose an action as the response to the onMouseDown event (**Figure 4.87**).

7. On a new line, choose Built-in Objects > Movie > Mouse > Methods > addListener.

8. Enter the name of your listener between the opening and closing parentheses (**Figure 4.88**).

Your listener is registered and will now listen and respond to the onMouseDown event. 🐭

The mouse wheel

Available only on Windows machines, the mouse wheel is a third button that is nestled between the left and right mouse buttons and spins forward or backward like a wheel. By assigning the mouse event onMouseWheel to a listener, you can detect and respond to the mouse wheel motion. For example, you can connect the forward or backward motion of the mouse wheel to the up or down scrolling of text or to the selection of items in a pull-down menu.

Two parameters are available when you define the function for the onMouseWheel event: delta and scrollTarget. The parameter delta is a number that indicates how quickly the user spins the mouse wheel. A positive (+) delta refers to a forward motion of the mouse wheel (**Figure 4.89**). A negative (–) delta refers to a backward motion. The parameter scrollTarget refers to the movie-clip instance over which the mouse wheel was scrolled. This parameter is useful to target only the object that lies under the mouse pointer.

MOUSE DETECTION

To detect mouse wheel motion:

1. Select the first frame of the main Timeline and open the Actions panel.

2. Enter a name for your listener object, followed by the equals sign (=).

3. Choose Built-in Classes > Core > Object > new Object.

   A listener object is instantiated.

4. On the next line, enter the name for the listener object that you just created.

5. Choose Built-in Classes> Movie > Mouse > Listeners > onMouseWheel. Complete the handler by adding =function before the parentheses and {} after the parentheses.

   The onMouseWheelevent handler for your listener is created (**Figure 4.90**).

6. Inside of the function (between the opening and closing curly braces), enter an action that will respond to the motion of the scroll wheel (**Figure 4.91**).

7. On the next line, select Built-in Classes > Movie > Mouse > Methods > addListener.

8. As the parameter of the addListener method, enter the name of the listener object you wish to register.

   Your listener is registered and will now listen and respond to the motion of the mouse wheel (**Figure 4.92**).

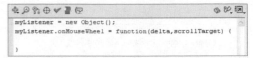

Figure 4.90 The onMouseWheel event is assigned to your listener called myListener.

Figure 4.91 For each notch that the user scrolls on the mouse wheel, Flash will move the movie clip called rocket_mc up or down on the y-axis.

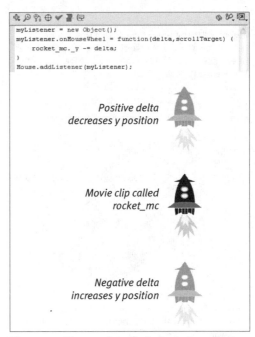

Positive delta decreases y position

Movie clip called rocket_mc

Negative delta increases y position

Figure 4.92 The completed code (top) allows the user to decrease the y position of the movie clip called rocket_mc by rolling the mouse wheel forward or increase the y position by rolling the mouse wheel backward.

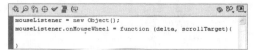

Figure 4.93 The onMouseWheel event is assigned to the listener called mouseListener.

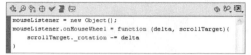

Figure 4.94 The scrollTarget returns the name of the movie clip directly under the mouse pointer. Line 3 in this Script pane allows the mouse wheel to change the rotation of any movie clip that is under the mouse pointer.

Often, there is more than one object on the Stage that can respond to the mouse wheel. In those cases, the object that is directly under the mouse pointer is usually the one that responds. For example, in a browser window, the mouse wheel controls text scrolling only in the frame that is under the pointer. The onMouseWheel event provides the parameter scrollTarget, which returns the name of the object that is under the mouse pointer. Knowing the name of the object lets you control it according to the motion of the mouse wheel.

To target an object to respond to mouse wheel motion:

1. Create multiple movie-clip symbols and place them on the main Stage.

2. Select the first frame of the main Timeline and open the Actions panel.

3. Enter a name for your listener object followed by the equals sign (=).

4. Choose Built-in Classes > Core > Object > new Object.
   Your listener object is instantiated.

5. On the next line, enter the name for the listener object that you just created.

6. Choose Built-in Classes> Movie > Mouse > Listeners > onMouseWheel. Complete the handler by adding =function before the parentheses and {} after the parentheses.
   The onMouseWheel event for your listener is created (**Figure 4.93**).

7. Inside the function (between the opening and closing curly braces), enter an action that tells the parameter scrollTarget to respond to the motion of the mouse wheel.
   In this example (**Figure 4.94**), the rotation property of the object directly under the mouse pointer changes according to the mouse wheel motion.

continues on next page

MOUSE DETECTION

8. On the next line, select Built-in Classes > Movie > Mouse > Methods > addListener.

9. As the parameter of the addListener method, enter the name of the listener object you created in step 3 (**Figure 4.95**).

Your listener is registered and will now listen and respond to the motion of the mouse wheel.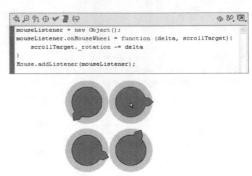

✔ Tip

■ Multiline textfields (discussed in Chapter 10) automatically scroll in response to the mouse wheel. You can, however, disable the mousewheel with the textfield property mouseWheelEnabled. Set the mouseWheelEnabled property of any textfield to false like so:

myTF_txt.mouseWheelEnabled = false

The textfield called myTF will no longer respond to the mouse wheel.

```
mouseListener = new Object();
mouseListener.onMouseWheel = function (delta, scrollTarget){
    scrollTarget._rotation -= delta
}
Mouse.addListener(mouseListener);
```

Figure 4.95 Here, the top-right dial is a movie clip whose rotation property can be currently affected by the mouse wheel.

Figure 4.96 The standard contextual menu (left) and the edit contextual menu that appears over dynamic or input text fields (right).

The Contextual Menu

In the playback of any Flash movie, a contextual menu appears when you right-click (Windows) or Ctrl-click (Mac) on the movie. There are three different types of contextual menus: a standard menu that appears over any part of the Stage, an edit menu that appears over text fields, and an error menu (**Figure 4.96**). You can customize, to a certain extent, the items that appear in the standard and edit menus through the ContextMenu class. You can disable certain items or create your own custom items with the related ContextMenuItem class. You can even make different contextual menus appear over different buttons, movie clips, or text fields.

Manipulating the contextual menu first requires that you instantiate a new object from the ContextMenu class, like so:

```
myMenu_cm = new ContextMenu()
```

After you have a new contextMenu object, you can call its methods or set its properties to customize the items that appear. All the default menu items are properties of the object builtInItems. Setting each property to true or false will enable or disable that particular item in the menu. For example, the following statement will disable the print item in the contextMenu object called myMenu_cm:

```
myMenu_cm.builtInItems.print = false
```

See **Table 4.4** for the properties of the builtInItems object of the ContextMenu class.

Finally, you must associate your contextMenu object with the menu property of another object, such as the _root Timeline, or a specific movie clip, like so:

```
_root.menu = myMenu_cm
```

Table 4.4

BuiltInItems Properties

PROPERTY	VALUE	MENU ITEMS
forward_back	True or false	Forward, Back
save	True or false	Save
zoom	True or false	Zoom in, Zoom out, 100%, Show all
quality	True or false	Quality
play	True or false	Play
loop	True or false	Loop
rewind	True or false	Rewind
print	True or false	Print

To disable the contextual menu:

1. Select the first frame of the main Timeline and open the Actions panel.

2. Enter a name for your new `contextMenu` object followed by an equals sign. Choose Built-in Classes > Movie > Context Menu > ContextMenu > new ContextMenu.

   A new contextMenu object is named and created (**Figure 4.97**).

3. On the next line of the Script pane, enter the name of the newly created contextMenu object, followed by a period.

4. From the code hint pull-down menu, select `hideBuiltInItems`.

   or

   Choose Built-in Classes > Movie > Context Menu > ContextMenu > Methods > hideBuiltInItems (**Figure 4.98**).

   This method sets all the properties of the `builtInItems` object of the ContextMenu class to `false`, which hides the items of the contextual menu.

5. On the third line of the Script pane, enter `_root.menu`, followed by an equals sign and the name of your contextMenu object.

   The contextMenu object now becomes associated with the `_root` Timeline, so the default items of the contextual menu of the main Timeline are hidden. The only items that remain are Settings and Debugger (**Figure 4.99**).

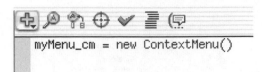

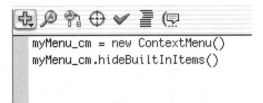

Figure 4.97 A new ContextMenu object called myMenu_cm is instantiated.

Figure 4.98 By using the hideBuiltInItems method, you disable all built-in (default) items of the contextual menu.

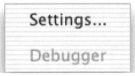

Figure 4.99 The final code (top) hides the all the default items except for the Settings and Debugger items (bottom).

```
myMenu_cm = new ContextMenu();
myMenu_cm.hideBuiltInItems();
_root.menu = myMenu_cm;
zoom_cm = new ContextMenu();
```

Figure 4.100 A new ContextMenu object named zoom_cm has been created.

Often when you create a movie, you may want to give the user different options in the contextual menu for different objects in your movie. For example, a particular movie clip of a map could have the zoom item in its contextual menu enabled, while other objects may have the zoom item in their contextual menu disabled. In this example, you will create two customized contextual menus: one for the main Timeline and another for a specific movie clip.

To associate custom contextual menus with different objects:

1. Continue with the preceding task. On the next available line in the Script pane, enter a new name for another contextMenu object followed by an equals sign and the constructor function, `new contextMenu()`.

   A second contextMenu object is named and created (**Figure 4.100**).

2. On the next available line, enter the name for the second contextMenu object that you just created, followed by a period.

3. Using the code hint pull-down menu, select `hideBuiltInItems`.

   or

   Choose Built-in Classes > Movie > Context Menu > ContextMenu > Methods > hideBuiltInItems.

   The items of your second contextMenu object, like the first, are disabled.

4. Enter the name for the second contextMenu object that you created, followed by a period.

   continues on next page

5. Select Built-in Classes > Movie > Context Menu > ContextMenu > Objects > builtInItems > Properties > zoom. Enter an equals sign and then the word true.

The completed statement, `zoom_cm.builtInItems.zoom = true`, tells Flash to enable the zoom item in the contextual menu.

6. On next line, enter `_root.` followed by the instance name of the object you wish to associate with your second contextual menu. Then enter a period, the property `menu,` and an equals sign. After the equals sign, enter the name of the second contextMenu item that you created in the beginning of this task.

The completed statement associates the second contextMenu object with the movie-clip instance only (**Figure 4.101**).

Creating new contextual menu items

You can add your own items in the contextual menu by creating new objects from the ContextMenuItem class. Each new item requires that you instantiate a separate contextMenuItem object, as in the following code:

```
myFirstItem_cmi = new
ContextMenuItem("First Item",
myFirstItemHandler);
```

The first parameter of the constructor function represents the text of the item in the contextual menu. Use quotation marks around the first parameter to display the enclosed text. The second parameter represents the name of a function that will be invoked when the user selects the item. Create the function to respond to the item selection, like so:

```
function myFirstItemHandler() {
    //place actions here
}
```

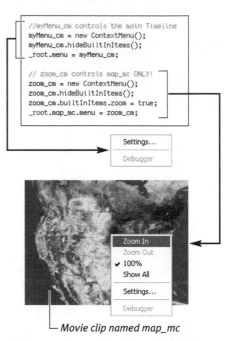

— *Movie clip named map_mc*

Figure 4.101 The completed script (top). The contextual menu that is attached to the main Timeline has its default items hidden (middle). The contextual menu that is attached to the movie clip called map_mc contains the Zoom In item (bottom).

Finally, you must add your new context-Menultem object to the `customItems` property of your contextMenu object. However, the `customItems` property is unlike the `builtInItems` property you learned about in the preceding section. The `customItems` property is really an array, which is an ordered list of values or objects. You can learn more about arrays in Chapter 11. In order to add your new context-Menultem object to the `customItems` array, use the array method `push()`, as in the following code:

`my_cm.customItems.push(myFirstItem_cmi);`

In this statement, `my_cm` is the name of the contextMenu object and `myFirstItem_cmi` is the name of the contextMenuItem object.

To create a new item for the contextual menu:

1. Select the first frame of the main Timeline and open the Actions panel.

2. In the Script pane, create a new `context-Menu` object, as in the following code:

   `my_cm = new ContextMenu();`

3. On the next line, enter a name for a contextMenuItem object followed by an equals sign; then choose Built-in Classes > Movie > Context Menu > ContextMenu-Item > new ContextMenuItem.

   A new `contextMenuItem` is instantiated.

4. In between the parentheses of the constructor function, enter an item name for the first parameter and a function name for the second parameter. Be sure to enclose the first parameter in quotation marks and to separate your parameters with a comma (**Figure 4.102**).

5. On the next line, enter the name of your contextMenu object, followed by a period.

6. In the code hint pull-down menu that appears, choose customItems.

   or

   Choose Built-in Classes > Movie > Context Menu > ContextMenu > Properties > customItems.

continues on next page

Figure 4.102 A new ContextMenuItem object called myFirstItem_cmi is created with two parameters; the name of the item ("First Item") and the name of a function that will be invoked when the item is selected (myFirstItemHandler).

THE CONTEXTUAL MENU

7. Add another period, and then choose Built-in Classes > Core > Array > Methods > push.

8. In between the parentheses of the push() method, enter the name of your contextMenuItem object.

   The completed statement adds your contextMenuItem object to the customItems array of your contextMenu object (**Figure 4.103**).

9. On a new line, create the function that will respond to the selection of your contextMenuItem (**Figure 4.104**).

```
my_cm = new ContextMenu();
myFirstItem_cmi = new ContextMenuItem("First Item", myFirstItemHandler);
my_cm.customItems.push(myFirstItem_cmi);
```

Figure 4.103 The ContextMenuItem called myFirstItem_cmi is put into the customItems array.

```
my_cm = new ContextMenu();
myFirstItem_cmi = new ContextMenuItem("First Item", myFirstItemHandler);
my_cm.customItems.push(myFirstItem_cmi);
function myFirstItemHandler() {
    //place actions here
}
```

Figure 4.104 The function that will respond to the selection of the item is defined in myFirstItemHandler.

10. On a new line, enter _root.menu, followed by an equals sign and the name of your contextMenu object.

The contextMenu object now becomes associated with the _root Timeline (**Figure 4.105**).

✔ **Tips**

- If you have multiple custom items in your contextual menu, you may want to organize them by separating them into groups. An optional third parameter in the contextMenuItem constructor function adds a horizontal separator above the item if it is set to true (**Figure 4.106**).

- The function that is defined as the second parameter of the new contextMenuItem is required. Without it, your item will not show up in the contextual menu.

```
my_cm = new ContextMenu();
myFirstItem_cmi = new ContextMenuItem("First Item", myFirstItemHandler);
my_cm.customItems.push(myFirstItem_cmi);
function myFirstItemHandler() {
    //place actions here
}
_root.menu = my_cm;
```

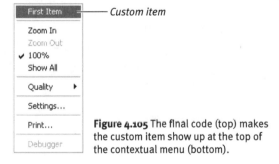

Custom item

Figure 4.105 The final code (top) makes the custom item show up at the top of the contextual menu (bottom).

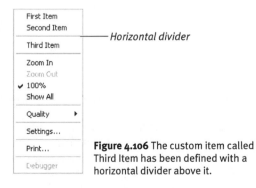

Horizontal divider

Figure 4.106 The custom item called Third Item has been defined with a horizontal divider above it.

Clip Events

The Movie Clip class, like the Mouse, Key, and Button classes, has its own set of events, which are referred to simply as *clip events*. Many clip events overlap the events of the Key class and the Mouse class; others are unique to the movie clip. You can assign clip event handlers to the movie-clip instance with the action onClipEvent (Global Functions > Movie Clip Control > onClipEvent).

The onClipEvent action for movie clips is analogous to the on action for buttons: The onClipEvent action assigns clip events to movie-clip instances, whereas the on action assigns button events to button instances. One notable difference, however, is that actions assigned to an onClipEvent pertain to the movie-clip Timeline, not to the main Timeline. You will learn more about navigating different Timelines in Chapter 5.

As you can with buttons, you can assign a clip event handler with anonymous functions on the main Timeline. Give your movie-clip instance a name in the Property Inspector and then assign a function to a clip event, as follows:

myMovieClip_mc.onMouseMove = function() { }

myMovieClip_mc is the name of your movie-clip instance, and onMouseMove is the clip event.

When you use anonymous functions to assign clip events, sometimes you can specify the main Timeline with the word _root as the name of the movie clip. You can assign the clip event onMouseMove to the main Timeline instead of a movie clip, as follows:

_root.onMouseMove = function() { }

Notice that this script is indistinguishable from the event handler for the Mouse class.

The clip events onKeyUp and onKeyDown are handled differently, depending on whether you assign them to a movie-clip instance or on the main Timeline with an anonymous function. When either of these events is assigned with an anonymous function, they must be assigned to a listener and registered to the Key class (see "Creating listeners for key events" earlier in this chapter). If events are assigned to a movie clip with the onClipEvent action, no listener is needed.

For easy reference, **Table 4.5** contains a list of clip events and some information about them.

Table 4.5

Clip Events	
CLIP EVENT	INTERACTION
onClipEvent (mouseDown)/onMouseDown	When the left mouse button is pressed
onClipEvent (mouseUp)/onMouseUp	When the left mouse button is released
onClipEvent (mouseMove)/onMouseMove	When the mouse is moved
onClipEvent (keyDown)/onKeyDown	When any key is pressed
onClipEvent (keyUp)/onKeyUp	When any key is released
onClipEvent (enterFrame)/onEnterFrame	When each frame of the movie clip is updated; triggered at the frame rate of the movie
onClipEvent (load)/onLoad	When the movie clip is instantiated and first appears in the Timeline
onClipEvent (unload)/onUnload	When the first frame after the movie-clip instance is removed from the Timeline
onClipEvent (data)/onData	When either external data or external .swf movies are loaded into the movie clip with the action loadVariables or loadMovie

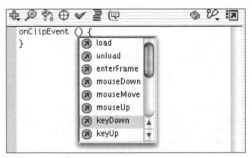

Figure 4.107 Some of the events of the onClipEvent handler. Mouse Down, Mouse Up, and Mouse Move are the same events as those for the Mouse class. Key Up and Key Down are the same events as those for the Key class, although they can be used in a slightly different manner.

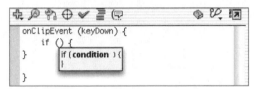

Figure 4.108 An if statement has been created.

```
onClipEvent (keyDown) {
    if (Key.getCode() == Key.SPACE) {
    }
}
```

Figure 4.109 When a key is pressed, Flash checks whether it was the spacebar.

Clip events are used in many ways. In this example, the keyDown clip event is coupled with a conditional statement that tests which key has been pressed.

To detect a key press with onClipEvent:

1. Create a movie-clip symbol, and drag an instance of it from the Library to the Stage.

2. Select the instance, and open the Actions panel.

3. Choose Global Functions > Movie Clip Control > onClipEvent.

   A drop-down list of all available events associated with onClipEvent appears. Select keyDown (**Figure 4.107**).

4. Insert a new line in between the curly braces of the onClipEvent handler and choose Statements > Conditions/Loops > if (**Figure 4.108**).

5. With your pointer between the opening and closing parentheses for the if statement, choose Built-in Classes > Movie > Key > Methods > getCode.

   The getCode() method appears as the condition parameter of the if statement.

6. After the getCode() method, enter two equals signs and the code key for the specific key you want to detect, or choose a Key property from Built-in Classes > Movie > Key > Constants.

   The getCode() method of the Key class retrieves the key code of the last key pressed. Flash checks to see whether that key matches the one you specify after the double equal signs. The double equal signs (==) tell Flash to compare equality (**Figure 4.109**).

continues on next page

CLIP EVENTS

7. Before selecting the action for the if statement, begin this line with _root. Now choose an action as the consequence for this if statement.

In this example, choose Global Functions > Timeline Control > gotoAndStop (**Figure 4.110**).

Because the onClipEvent action assigns code to the movie clip, all its actions pertain to the movie-clip Timeline, not the main Timeline. So you use the word _root to make the gotoAndStop action target the main Timeline. You'll learn more about targeting different Timelines in Chapter 5.

8. Test your movie.

The onClipEvent action assigned to your movie clip detects when a key is pressed. The if statement checks whether the key is the spacebar and makes Flash go to a different frame of the main Timeline.

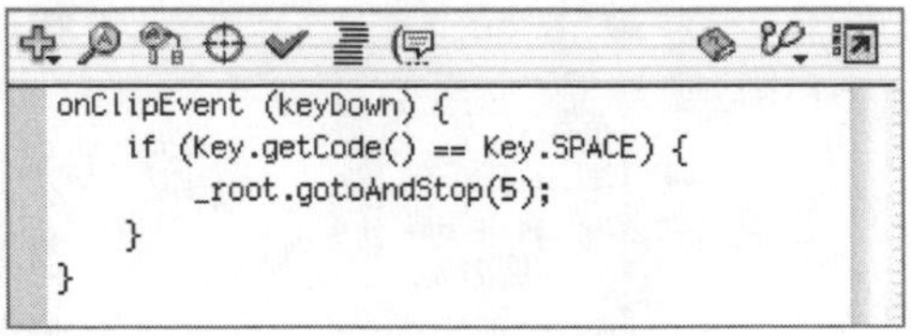

```
onClipEvent (keyDown) {
    if (Key.getCode() == Key.SPACE) {
        _root.gotoAndStop(5);
    }
}
```

Figure 4.110 Choose the gotoAndStop() method from Global Functions > Timeline Control. You can target the main Timeline with the word _root so that Flash moves the playhead of the main Timeline to Frame 5.

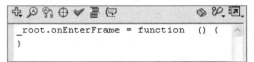

Figure 4.111 The enterFrame clip-event handler.

Creating Continuous Actions with enterFrame

So far, you have learned ways to execute an action in response to events that happen when the user does something. But on many occasions, you'll want to perform an action continuously. An if statement, for example, often needs to be performed continuously to check whether conditions in the movie have changed. And often, the command that changes the position of a movie clip needs to be performed continuously to animate it across the Stage.

The clip event enterFrame is an event that happens continuously. The clip event happens at the frame rate of the movie, so if the frame rate is set to 12 frames per second, the enterFrame event is triggered 12 times per second. Even when the enterFrame event is assigned to a movie clip whose Timeline is stopped, the event will continue to happen. This setup is an ideal way to make actions run on automatic pilot; they will run as soon as the enterFrame event handler is established and stop only when the movie clip to which the enterFrame is attached is removed.

To create continuous actions with enterFrame:

1. Select the first frame of the main Timeline, and open the Actions panel.

2. In the Script pane, enter _root. From the code hint pull-down menu that appears, select onEnterFrame.

   or

   Choose Built-in Classes > Movie > MovieClip > Events > onEnterFrame.

3. Directly to the right of the onEnterFrame event, enter an equals sign. Select Statements > User-Defined-Functions > function (**Figure 4.111**).

continues on next page

4. Insert a new line in between the curly braces of the function and choose Statements > Conditions/Loops > if.

5. For the condition parameter (between the opening and closing parentheses of the if statement), enter this statement:

Key.getCode()==Key.SPACE

This statement is the same conditional statement that you constructed in the preceding task. In this case, however, Flash does not wait for a **keyDown** event before testing this condition. Here, Flash tests the condition each time a frame in the main Timeline updates. This test happens continuously, even if the Timeline is stopped.

6. Choose an action as the consequence of this if statement (**Figure 4.112**).

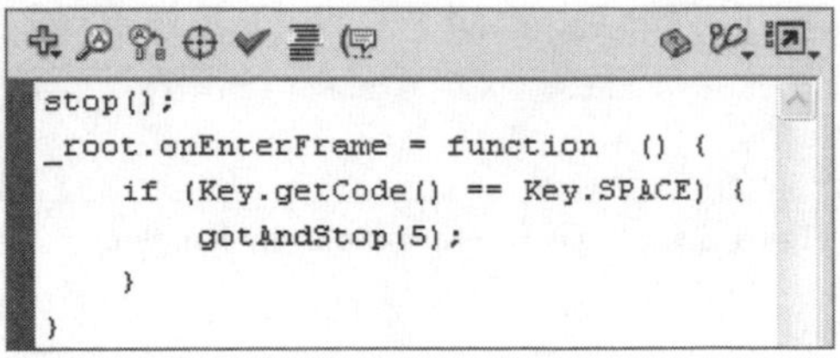

```
stop();
_root.onEnterFrame = function () {
    if (Key.getCode() == Key.SPACE) {
        gotAndStop(5);
    }
}
```

Figure 4.112 Flash continuously monitors whether the last key pressed was the spacebar. If so, it moves the playhead to Frame 5 and stops there.

✔ Tips

■ Here's a preview of the kind of dynamic updates you can do with the enterFrame clip event by combining it with movie-clip properties. Replace the if statement in the preceding task with the expression ball_mc._xscale += 1. Now add a movie-clip instance to the Stage, and name it ball_mc in the Property Inspector. The Script pane should look like this:

_root.onEnterFrame = function() {
ball_mc._xscale += 1; }

The statement ball_mc._xscale += 1 adds 1 percent to the horizontal width of your movie clip. Because the action is triggered continuously by the enterFrame event, the movie clip keeps growing.

■ Be careful of over-using the onEnterframe/onClipEvent(enterFrame) event handler because it can be processor-intensive. After you no longer need the event handler, it's good practice to delete the movie clip that is associated with it. This will prevent Flash from having to execute the event needlessly.

Creating Continuous Actions with setInterval

The enterFrame event, although easy to use and effective for creating most continuous actions, is limited to the frame rate of your Flash movie. If you want to perform an action on a continuous basis but do so at specific intervals, you should use the action setInterval instead.

You can use the setInterval action in two basic ways. In the first way, you provide two parameters. The first parameter is a function that is invoked on a continuous basis; the second parameter is the interval (in milliseconds) that separates the function invocation. So if you want the function called blinkingLight to be called every 5 seconds, you can write the statement setInterval (blinkingLight, 5000). Then you then must define the blinkingLight function.

The second way to use setInterval is to provide an object, its method, and an interval. Instead of calling a function at a periodic interval, Flash calls the method of the object at a periodic interval. This method can be one that already exists or one that you define yourself. You can call the nextFrame() method on the main Timeline every second with this statement:

setInterval (_root, "nextFrame", 1000)

Notice that the method name is in quotation marks.

To create continuous actions with setInterval (first way):

1. Select the first frame of the main Timeline, and open the Actions panel.

2. Choose Global Functions > Miscellaneous Functions > setInterval.

3. In between the parentheses, enter the name of a function followed by a comma and then an interval (in milliseconds) (**Figure 4.113**).

   The function will be called continuously at the specified interval.

continues on next page

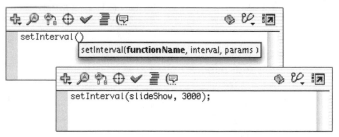

Figure 4.113 The function called slideshow will be called every 3 seconds.

4. On a new line, choose Statements > User-Defined Functions > function (Esc + fn).

5. Directly to the right of the function that was created in the preceding step, enter a name for the function (**Figure 4.114**). This name is the same one that you used in the setInterval action.

6. Choose actions for your function that you want to execute at the periodic interval (**Figure 4.115**).

✔ Tip

- Add the action **updateAfterEvent** (Global Functions > Movie Clip Control > updateAfterEvent) to your function if you are modifying graphics at a smaller interval than your movie frame rate. This method forces Flash to refresh the display, providing smoother results.

To create continuous actions with setInterval (second way):

1. Select the first frame of the main Timeline, and open the Actions panel.

2. Choose Global Functions > Miscellaneous Actions > setInterval.

3. In between the parentheses for setInterval(), enter the name of an object followed by the name of its method in quotation marks and then an interval (in milliseconds), separating your parameters with commas (**Figure 4.116**).

   The method will be called continuously at the specified interval. This example uses a method of the Movie Clip class, but you can define and use your own method. See Chapter 11 for more information about creating your own methods and objects.

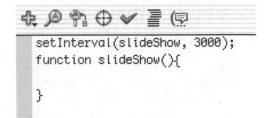

```
setInterval(slideShow, 3000);
function slideShow(){

}
```

Figure 4.114 A new function named slideshow() has been created.

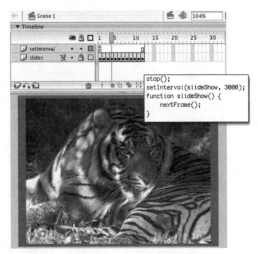

Figure 4.115 This movie contains images from your recent trip to the zoo. The images are in separate keyframes. The setInterval action advances to the next image every 3 seconds automatically. The stop action has been added to prevent the images from playing until setInterval calls the slideshow function.

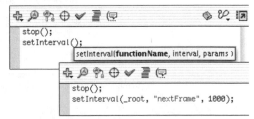

Figure 4.116 This setInterval does the same job as in the preceding example, except that it advances every second.

✔ Tips

- In both ways of using the `setInterval` action, you can pass parameters. In the first way, you can pass parameters to your function, and in the second way, you can pass parameters to your method. If the method you define in `setInterval` requires parameters, you must provide them at the end of the parameters for `setInterval`, as in this example:

  `setInterval (myObject, "myMethod", 1000, parameter1, parameter2)`

  This `setInterval` will call `myObject.myMethod(parameter1, parameter2)` every second.

- Although `setInterval` uses milliseconds to determine when to trigger a function or a method, it must do so during frame transitions set by the movie frame rate. This setup makes the interplay between `setInterval` and the frame rate a little tricky and makes exact timing less direct than you'd expect. At 10 frames per second, for example, a frame transition occurs every 100 milliseconds. If you define an interval of 200 milliseconds, Flash waits two frames (200 ms) until the interval passes; then it triggers the method or function on Frame 3. It waits two more frames (another 200 ms) and then triggers on Frame 6. Finally, after two more frames, it triggers on Frame 9.

  If you change your movie to play at 20 frames per second, a frame transition occurs every 50 milliseconds. Flash waits four frames (200 ms) and triggers the method or function on Frame 5. It waits another four frames and triggers on Frame 10. It continues to trigger on every fifth frame—at Frame 15 and Frame 20. If you compare the two movies, the one at 10 fps gets triggered three times in the first second (Frames 3, 6, and 9), whereas the one at 20 fps gets triggered four times in the first second (Frames 5, 10, 15, and 20). So even though they both have the same 200-ms interval defined in `setInterval`, frame rates can have significant effects.

The setInterval action continues to call the function or method at regular intervals until the movie ends or until you remove the setInterval action with clearInterval. The action clearInterval requires one parameter, which is the name you give the setInterval action. In the preceding examples, you didn't name the setInterval action because you had no intention of stopping it. In this next task, you will name your setInterval action. Then, you can clear it by using the clearInterval action.

To clear a setInterval action:

1. Continuing with the preceding example, select the first frame of the main Timeline, and open the Actions panel.

2. Place your pointer before the setInterval action, and insert a variable name and an equals sign (**Figure 4.117**).

3. At a later point in your Flash movie, when you want to stop the setInterval, choose Global Functions > Miscellaneous Functions > clearInterval.

   When Flash encounters the clearInterval action, it removes the setInterval and stops the continuous actions (**Figure 4.118**).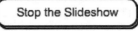

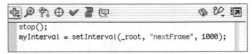

Figure 4.117 A variable name has now been assigned to the setInterval so that you can identify and clear the interval.

```
Stop the Slideshow
```

```
on (release) {
    clearInterval(myInterval);
}
```

Figure 4.118 When the clearInterval action is assigned to a button (top), it will remove the setInterval identified as myInterval. The movie will no longer advance to the next frame continuously, and the slide show will stop.

A Summary of Events and Event Handlers

Table 4.6 organizes and compares the many ways you can create event handlers to detect and respond to events.

Table 4.6

A Summary of Events and Event Handlers

OBJECT	EVENT HANDLER ASSIGNED ON INSTANCE	EVENT HANDLER ASSIGNED ON MAIN TIMELINE	ANONYMOUS FUNCTION ASSIGNED TO	LISTENER
Button	on(press)	onPress	button instance	No
	on(release)	onRelease		
	on(releaseOutside)	onReleaseOutside		
	on(rollOver)	onRollover		
	on(rollOut)	onRollOut		
	on(dragOver)	onDragOver		
	on(dragOut)	onDragOut		
	on(keyPress "whatkey")	-		
	-	onSetFocus		
	-	onKillFocus		
Mouse	No	onMouseUp	Listener or _root	Yes*
		onMouseDown		Yes*
		onMouseMove		Yes*
		onMouseWheel	Listener	Yes
Key	No	onKeyUp	Listener	Yes
		onKeyDown		Yes
Movie Clip (may also receive Button events)	onClipEvent(load)	onLoad	MC/_root	No
	onClipEvent(unload)	onUnload	MC/_root	No
	onClipEvent(data)	onData	MC/_root	No
	onClipEvent(enterFrame)	onEnterFrame	MC/_root	No
	onClipEvent(mouseDown)	onMouseDown	MC/_root/L	Yes*
	onClipEvent(mouseUp)	onMouseUp	MC/_root/L	Yes*
	onClipEvent(mouseMove)	onMouseMove	MC/_root/L	Yes*
	onClipEvent(keyUp)	onKeyUp	Listener	Yes
	onClipEvent(keyDown)	onKeyDown	Listener	Yes

not required
MC = movie-clip instance
_root = main Timeline
L = Listener

CONTROLLING
MULTIPLE TIMELINES

To create interactivity and direct your users to see, hear, and do exactly what you want, you have to know how to control the Flash playhead on different Timelines. The playhead displays what is on the Stage at any time, plays back any sound, and triggers any actions attached to the Timeline. Jumping from frame to frame on the main movie Timeline is simple enough; you use basic actions you should be familiar with, such as `gotoAndPlay`, `gotoAndStop`, `play`, and `stop`. But when you bring movie clips into your movie, you introduce other independent Timelines that can be controlled individually. Your main Timeline can control a movie clip's Timeline; a movie clip's Timeline can, in turn, control the main Timeline. You can even have the Timeline of one movie clip control the Timeline of another. Handling this complex interaction and navigation between Timelines is the subject of this chapter.

Navigating Timelines with Movie Clips

The independent Timelines of movie-clip symbols make complicated navigation schemes possible (**Figure 5.1**). While the main Timeline is playing, other Timelines of movie clips can be playing as well, interacting with one another and specifying which frames to play or when to stop. It's quite common, in fact, to have enough movie clips on the Stage all talking to one another that the main movie Timeline need be only a single frame for the entire movie to work. Driving all this navigation between Timelines is, of course, ActionScript. The basic actions used to navigate within the main Timeline (gotoAndStop, gotoAndPlay, stop, play, nextFrame, and prevFrame) can also be used to navigate the Timeline of any movie clip. This navigation is possible because you can give a name to every movie-clip instance on the Stage. You name a movie-clip instance in the Property Inspector. When an instance is named, you can identify its particular Timeline and give instructions on where you want to move its playhead.

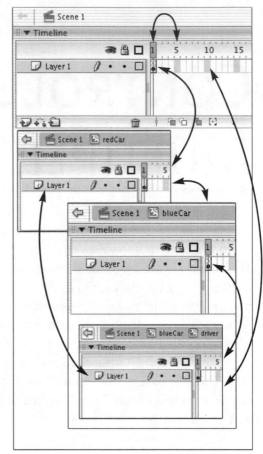

Figure 5.1 A movie can contain many Timelines that interact with one another. This example shows Scene 1 as the main Timeline; it contains two movie clips. One of the movie clips contains another movie clip. The arrows show just a few of the possible lines of communication.

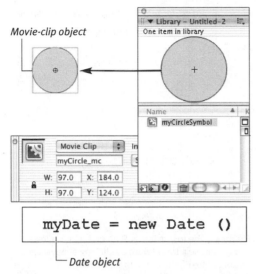

Movie-clip object

myDate = new Date ()

Date object

Figure 5.2 Instantiation of a movie-clip symbol (called myCircle_mc) versus instantiation of a date object (called myDate).

Figure 5.3 The Property Inspector for a selected movie clip. The name of this movie clip object is myCircle_mc.

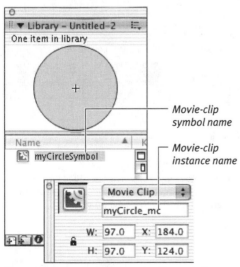

Movie-clip symbol name

Movie-clip instance name

Figure 5.4 The name of the movie-clip symbol appears in the Library (myCircleSymbol), and the name of the movie-clip instance appears in the Property Inspector (myCircle_mc).

Naming Instances

Instantiation of a Movie Clip object involves two steps: placing an instance on the Stage and naming that instance in the Property Inspector. You follow the same steps to instantiate the Button class and, as you'll learn in Chapter 10, the TextField class. These two steps accomplish the same task that the constructor function performs for other Flash classes (**Figure 5.2**). The result is the same; a named object is created from a class. You can use that object by calling its methods or evaluating its properties.

To name a movie-clip instance or a button instance:

1. Create a movie-clip symbol or a button symbol.

2. Drag an instance of the symbol from the Library to the Stage.

3. Select the instance.

4. In the Property Inspector, below the pull-down menu for the symbol type, enter a unique name for your instance (**Figure 5.3**).

    Now you can use this name to identify your movie-clip instance or your button instance with ActionScript.

✔ Tip

■ The name of your symbol (the one that appears in the Library) and the name you give it in the Property Inspector are two different identifiers (**Figure 5.4**). The name that appears in the Library is a symbol property and basically is just an organizational reminder. The name in the Property Inspector is more important because it is the actual name of the object and will be used in targeting paths. End your movie clip instance name with _mc so that the Actions panel can identify it as a movie clip.

Target Paths

A *target path* is essentially an object name, or a series of object names separated by dots, that tells Flash where to find a particular object. To control movie-clip Timelines, you specify both the target path for a particular movie clip and its method. The target path tells Flash which movie-clip instance to look at, and the method tells Flash what to do with that movie-clip instance. The methods that control the playhead are gotoAndStop(), gotoAndPlay(), play(), stop(), nextFrame(), and prevFrame(). If you name a movie-clip instance myClock_mc, for example, you can write the ActionScript statement myClock_mc.gotoAndStop(10) and the playhead within the movie-clip instance called myClock_mc will move to Frame 10 and stop there. myClock_mc is the target path, and gotoAndStop() is the method.

Above the Script pane of the Actions panel, the Insert Target Path button opens the Insert Target Path dialog box, which provides a visual way to insert a target path (**Figure 5.5**). All named movie-clip instances, button instances, and text fields are shown in a hierarchical fashion in the display window. You can select individual objects and the correct target paths appear in the Target field.

To target a movie-clip instance from the main Timeline:

1. Create a movie-clip symbol that contains an animation on its Timeline, and place an instance of it on the Stage.

2. In the Property Inspector, give the instance a name (**Figure 5.6**).

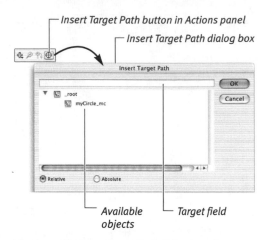

Insert Target Path button in Actions panel

Insert Target Path dialog box

Available objects

Target field

Figure 5.5 The Insert Target Path dialog box allows you to choose a target path by clicking a movie clip, button, or text field within the hierarchy.

Movie-clip instance called myClock_mc

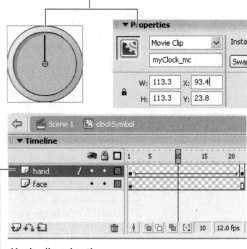

Movie-clip animation

Figure 5.6 The movie-clip instance called myClock_mc is on the main Timeline. The movie clip contains an animation (below) of the hand rotating.

Figure 5.7 A default placeholder named instanceName (selected) appears followed by a stop() action in the Script pane.

Figure 5.8 The target path is myClock_mc, and the method is stop(). The playhead of the myClock_mc Timeline stops when this action is triggered.

3. Select a keyframe of the main Timeline, and open the Actions panel.

You will assign an action to the main Timeline that will control the movie-clip instance.

4. Choose Built-in Classes > Movie > MovieClip > Methods > stop.

A default placeholder named instanceName appears followed by a stop() action in the Script pane (**Figure 5.7**).

5. Select the word instanceName inside the Actions panel and replace it with the instance name of the movie-clip symbol (**Figure 5.8**).

6. Test your movie (Control > Test movie).

Your movie clip would normally play its animation on the main Stage. The action you assign on the main Timeline, however, targets your movie clip and tells the playhead to stop.

You can have a movie clip within another movie clip. The first is the parent, and the second is the child. Any transformation you do to the parent will also affect the child. To control the Timeline of a child movie clip from the main Timeline, use both the parent and the child name in the target path. In the following example, the parent movie clip is a train (train_mc), and the child movie clip is its wheels (wheels_mc).

To target a child of a movie-clip instance from the main Timeline:

1. Create a movie-clip symbol that contains an animation on its Timeline, place an instance on the Stage, and name it in the Property inspector (**Figure 5.9**).

2. Create another movie-clip symbol that contains an animation on its Timeline.

3. Go to symbol-editing mode for the first movie clip, and drag an instance of your second movie clip to the Stage.

4. In the Property Inspector, give the second movie-clip instance a name (**Figure 5.10**).

   You now have a parent movie clip on the main Stage. The parent movie clip contains a child movie clip.

5. Exit symbol-editing mode, and return to the main Stage.

6. Select a keyframe in the main Timeline, and open the Actions panel.

7. Choose Built-in Classes > Movie > MovieClip > Methods > stop.

8. Select the placeholder instanceName and then click the Insert Target Path button. The Insert Target Path dialog box opens.

Figure 5.9 The movie-clip instance called train_mc is on the main Timeline. The movie clip contains an animation (below) of the train shaking back and forth.

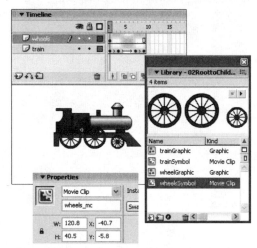

Figure 5.10 Place an instance of a movie clip inside the train movie clip. Name the child movie-clip instance wheels_mc.

Figure 5.11 The display window of the Insert Target Path dialog box. The hierarchy shows parent-child relationships.

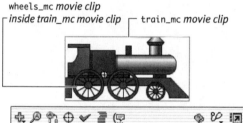

wheels_mc *movie clip*
inside train_mc movie clip — train_mc *movie clip*

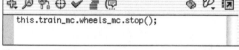

```
this.train_mc.wheels_mc.stop();
```

Figure 5.12 The ActionScript statement on the main Timeline tells the wheels_mc movie clip inside the train_mc movie clip to stop.

9. Choose Relative Mode from the radio buttons on the bottom of the Insert Target Path dialog box.

10. In the display window, click the triangle (Mac) or the plus sign (Windows) in front of the parent movie clip.

The hierarchy expands, showing the child movie clip within the parent (**Figure 5.11**).

11. Select the child movie clip as the target path, and click OK.

The target path, in the form `this.Parent.Child`, appears before the method.

12. Test your movie.

The animation of the wheels turning will play within the movie clip of the train, which is bobbing up and down. The action you assign on the main Timeline, however, targets the movie clip of the wheels that is inside the movie clip of the train and tells its playhead to stop. The animation of the train continues (**Figure 5.12**). Despite the parent-child relationship, the Timelines remain independent.

Absolute and Relative Paths

Flash gives you two mode options in the Insert Target Path dialog box: relative and absolute. In the preceding example, the method this.train_mc.wheels_mc.stop() originated from the main Timeline. When Flash executes that method, it looks within its own Timeline for the object called train_mc that contains another object called wheels_mc. This is an example of a path that uses relative mode. Everything is relative to where the ActionScript statement resides—in this case, the main Timeline. An alternative way of inserting a target path is to use absolute mode, which has no particular frame of reference. You can think of relative target paths as being directions given from your present location, as in "Go two blocks straight; then turn left." Absolute target paths, on the other hand, are directions that work no matter where you are, as in "Go to 555 University Avenue."

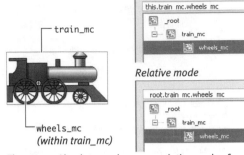

Figure 5.13 Absolute mode versus relative mode of target paths. This example shows the wheels_mc movie clip inside the train_mc movie clip. When you assign actions on the train Timeline, this in relative mode refers to _root in absolute mode.

Why Relative Paths?

Why use relative paths at all? Absolute paths seem to be a safer construction because they identify an object explicitly no matter where you are.

Relative paths, however, are useful in at least two cases:

◆ If you create a movie clip that contains actions that affect other movie clips relative to itself, you can move the entire ensemble and still have the target paths work by using relative terms. This method makes it easier to work with complex navigation schemes because you can copy, paste, and move the pieces without having to rewrite the target paths.

A direct parallel is managing a Web site and maintaining its links. If you were to create absolute paths to links to your résumé and then move your home page to a different server, you'd have to rewrite your links. The more practical method would be to establish relative links within your home page.

◆ Relative paths are also useful when you create movie clips dynamically. You will learn how to create movie-clip objects and name them on the fly with ActionScript. In these cases, movie clips are not static and relative target paths are required to follow them around.

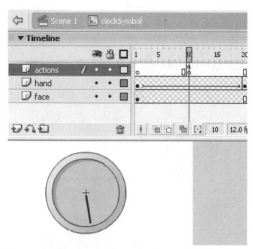

Figure 5.14 This movie clip contains an animation. At keyframe 10, you will assign an action to move the playhead of the main Timeline.

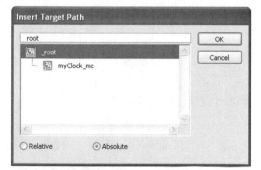

Figure 5.15 Absolute mode, selected in the Insert Target Path dialog box, shows a top-down view of all the Timelines.

Figure 5.16 The target _root inside the Script pane.

Why would you use one mode instead of the other? If you need to target a Timeline that sits at a higher level than the Timeline you're working in, you can use absolute mode. Imagine that a movie clip sits on the main Timeline. You want to have this movie clip control the main Timeline. In relative mode, you see only the Timelines that are inside the current one. In absolute mode, you see all the Timelines no matter where you are. Absolute mode is like having a bird's-eye view of all the movie clips on the Stage at the same time.

Using this and _root

In relative mode, the current Timeline is called this. The keyword this means *myself*. All other Timelines are relative to the this Timeline. In absolute mode, the main movie Timeline is called _root. All other Timelines are organized relative to the _root Timeline (**Figure 5.13**).

To target the main Timeline from a movie-clip instance:

1. Create a movie-clip symbol that contains an animation on its Timeline, place an instance of it on the Stage, and give the instance a name in the Property Inspector.

2. Go to symbol-editing mode for your movie clip.

3. Select a keyframe on the movie clip's Timeline, and open the Actions panel.

   You will assign ActionScript to the movie clip's Timeline to control the main Timeline (**Figure 5.14**).

4. Click the Insert Target Path button to open the Insert Target Path dialog box. Select Absolute as the mode.

5. Select _root and click OK (**Figure 5.15**).

   The target path _root appears in the Script pane (**Figure 5.16**).

continues on next page

ABSOLUTE AND RELATIVE PATHS

6. Enter a period directly following _root, and select gotoAndStop from the code hint pull-down menu.

or

Choose Global Functions > Timeline Control > gotoAndStop

7. With your pointer located in between the parentheses, enter a frame number as the main Timeline destination.

8. Test your movie.

When the ActionScript statement on the movie-clip Timeline is executed, Flash jumps outside that Timeline and looks up to the _root Timeline to perform the method there (**Figure 5.17**).

To target a movie-clip instance from another movie-clip instance:

1. Create a movie-clip symbol that contains an animation, place an instance of it on the Stage, and give the instance a name in the Property Inspector.

2. Create two more movie-clip symbols that contain animation.

3. Go to symbol-editing mode for the first movie clip, place instances of the second and third movie clips on the Stage, and give names to both instances in the Property Inspector (**Figure 5.18**).

You now have a parent movie clip on the main Timeline. The parent movie clip contains two child movie clips.

4. Go to symbol-editing mode for the wheels_mc movie clip.

5. Select a keyframe on the movie clip's Timeline and open the Actions panel.

You will assign ActionScript on the wheels_mc Timeline to control the smoke_mc Timeline.

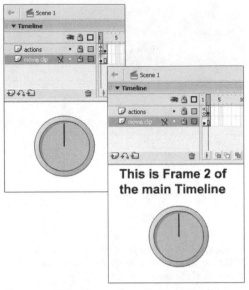

Figure 5.17 The action on the myClock_mc Timeline moves the playhead on the main Timeline to Frame 2. There is a stop action on the main Timeline at Frame 1.

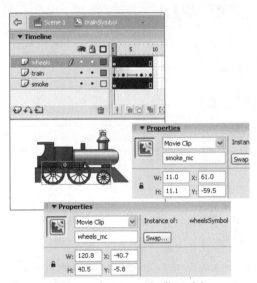

Figure 5.18 The smoke_mc movie clip and the wheels_mc movie clip are dragged into the movie-clip symbol called trainSymbol. The instance of trainSymbol on the Stage is called train_mc (not shown).

ABSOLUTE AND RELATIVE PATHS

Figure 5.19 Choosing the smoke_mc movie clip in the Insert Target Path dialog box and clicking OK replaces the placeholder named instanceName (top) with the full target path for the stop() method.

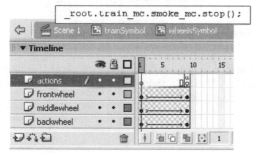

Figure 5.20 The animation in the wheels_mc movie clip plays. When the clip hits Frame 9 of its Timeline (bottom), the ActionScript there tells the smoke_mc movie clip to stop playing. The smoke animation has a chance to play only nine frames of itself.

6. Choose Built-in Classes > Movie > MovieClip > Methods > stop.

7. Select the placeholder named instanceName, and click the Insert Target Path button to open the Insert Target Path dialog box.

8. Select Absolute as the target path.

9. Select the smoke_mc movie-clip instance, and click OK.

   The target path _root.train_mc.smoke_mc appears in the Script pane (**Figure 5.19**).

10. Test your movie.

    When the ActionScript statement on the wheels_mc movie-clip Timeline is executed, Flash starts looking from the _root Timeline, drills down through the object called train_mc to the object called smoke_mc, and performs the method on that object (**Figure 5.20**).

ABSOLUTE AND RELATIVE PATHS

To target a movie clip's own Timeline:

1. Create a movie-clip symbol that contains an animation, place an instance of it on the Stage, and give the instance a name in the Property Inspector.

2. Go to symbol-editing mode for your movie clip.

3. Select a keyframe on the movie clip's Timeline, and open the Actions panel.

   You will assign ActionScript to the movie-clip Timeline that controls its own Timeline (**Figure 5.21**).

4. Choose Built-in Classes > Movie > MovieClip > Methods > stop.

5. Select the placeholder instanceName, and click the Insert Target Path button to open the Insert Target Path dialog box.

6. Select Absolute or Relative as the target path mode. In the Target Path dialog box, select the movie clip that you want to target.

   or

   Delete the placeholder instanceName and period entirely (**Figure 5.22**).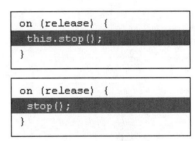

✔ Tip

■ Using this or an absolute path to target a movie clip's own Timeline is unnecessary, just as it is unnecessary to use this or _root when navigating within the main Timeline. It's understood that actions residing in one movie clip pertain, or are scoped, to that particular movie clip.

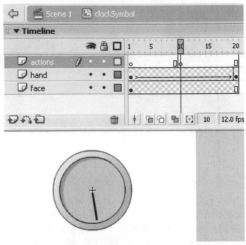

Figure 5.21 This movie clip contains an animation of the hand rotating. The action you'll assign on keyframe 10 will make it stop, so the hand barely makes it to 6 o'clock.

```
on (release) {
    this.stop();
}
```

```
on (release) {
    stop();
}
```

Figure 5.22 Two equivalent statements to target the myClock Timeline from within myClock itself.

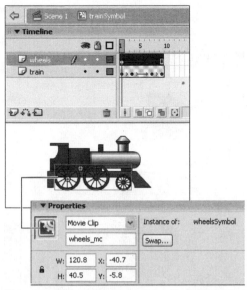

Figure 5.23 Place an instance of a movie clip inside the `train_mc` movie clip. This child movie clip is called `wheels_mc`.

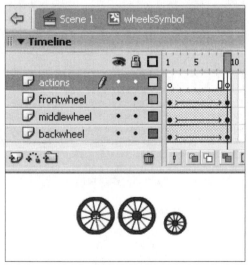

Figure 5.24 The wheels_mc movie clip contains an animation of the wheels rotating.

Figure 5.25 The completed code as seen in the Script pane.

Using _parent in target paths

Although it does not appear in the Insert Target Path dialog box, you can also use the relative term _parent. Use _parent to target the movie clip at the next-higher level from the current Timeline.

To target the parent of a movie clip:

1. Create a movie-clip symbol that contains an animation, place an instance of it on the Stage, and give the instance a name in the Property Inspector.

2. Create another movie-clip symbol that contains an animation.

3. Go to symbol-editing mode for the first movie clip, place an instance of the second movie clip on the Stage, and give the instance a name in the Property Inspector.

   You now have a parent movie clip on the main Timeline. The parent movie clip contains a child movie clip (**Figure 5.23**).

4. Go to symbol-editing mode for the child movie clip.

5. Select a keyframe on the child movie clip's Timeline, and open the Actions panel.

   You will assign ActionScript to the child movie clip's Timeline to control the parent movie clip's Timeline (**Figure 5.24**).

6. Choose Built-in Classes > Movie > MovieClip > Methods > stop.

7. Select the placeholder instanceName, and replace it with _parent (**Figure 5.25**).

continues on next page

ABSOLUTE AND RELATIVE PATHS

8. Test your movie.

When the ActionScript statement on the wheels_mc movie-clip Timeline is executed, Flash looks up to its parent—the train_mc movie-clip Timeline—and performs the method there (**Figure 5.26**). 🎧

Table 5.1 and **Figure 5.27** summarize the ways you can use absolute and relative paths to target different movie clips.

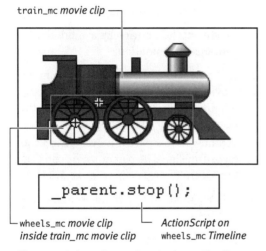

train_mc *movie clip*

```
_parent.stop();
```

wheels_mc *movie clip inside train_mc movie clip*

ActionScript on wheels_mc *Timeline*

Figure 5.26 The action on the wheels_mc Timeline targets its parent, which is the train_mc Timeline. The action makes the train stop shaking.

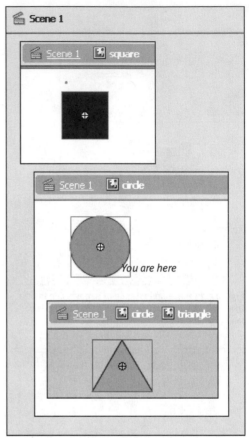

Figure 5.27 A representation of a movie with multiple movie clips. The main Timeline (Scene 1) contains the square movie clip and the circle movie clip. The circle movie clip contains the triangle movie clip. These names represent instances. Table 5.1 summarizes the absolute and relative target paths for calls made within the circle movie clip (you are here).

Table 5.1

Absolute versus Relative Target Paths

TO TARGET… (FROM CIRCLE)	ABSOLUTE PATH	RELATIVE PATH
Scene 1	_root	_parent
square	_root.square	_parent.square
circle	_root.circle	this
triangle	_root.circle.triangle	triangle

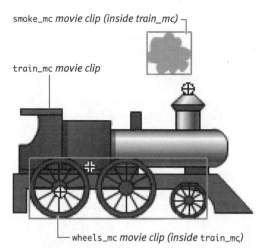

smoke_mc *movie clip (inside train_mc)*

train_mc *movie clip*

wheels_mc *movie clip (inside* train_mc)

Figure 5.28 Nested with statements are an alternative to multiple target paths.

Using the with Action to Target Movie Clips

An alternative way to target movie clips is to use the action with. Instead of creating multiple target paths to the same movie clip, you can use the with action to target the movie clip only once. Imagine creating these statements to make the wheels_mc movie clip inside a train movie clip stop and shrink 50 percent:

```
train_mc.wheels_mc.stop();
train_mc.wheels_mc._xscale = 50;
train_mc.wheels_mc._yscale = 50;
```

You can rewrite those statements with the with statement, like this:

```
with (train_mc.wheels_mc) {
    stop();
    _xscale = 50;
    _yscale = 50;
}
```

This with action temporarily sets the target path to train_mc.wheels_mc so that the method and properties between the curly braces affect that particular target path. When the with action ends, any subsequent statements refer to the current Timeline.

The with statement can even be nested to affect multiple targets simultaneously (**Figure 5.28**):

```
with (train_mc) {
    with (wheels_mc)
        { play();
    }
    with (smoke_mc) {
        stop();
    }
}
```

continues on next page

These nested with statements accomplish the same thing as the following statements:

```
train_mc.wheels_mc.play();
train_mc.smoke_mc.stop();
```

To use the with action:

1. In a keyframe or within an event handler, open the Actions panel.

2. Choose Statements > Variables > with (Esc + wt).

3. With your pointer between the parentheses, enter the target path or click the Insert Target Path button (**Figure 5.29**).

4. Between the curly braces of the with action, create your statements for the targeted object (**Figure 5.30**).

Figure 5.29 The with action in the Actions panel. The code hints help you determine the proper code to put between the parentheses.

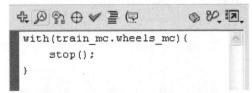

Figure 5.30 The action stop() and any other actions between the curly braces apply to the target path train_mc.wheels_mc.

```
with(train_mc){
    with(wheels_mc){
    }
}
```

Figure 5.31 The action with(wheels_mc) is nested within the action with(train_mc).

```
with(train_mc){
    with(wheels_mc){
        play();
    }

    |

}
```

Figure 5.32 Creating a new line after the closing curly brace ensures that your next statement will be inserted within the action with(train_mc) rather than within the action with(wheels_mc).

```
with(train_mc){
    with(wheels_mc){
        play();
    }
    with(smoke_mc){
        stop();
    }
}
```

Figure 5.33 The complete nested with action statements.

To use nested with actions:

1. In a keyframe or within an event handler, open the Actions panel.

2. Choose Statements > Variables > with.

3. With your pointer between the parentheses, enter the first target path.

4. On the next line, choose Statements > Variables > with.

5. With your pointer between the parentheses for the second with statement, enter the first nested target path (**Figure 5.31**).

6. Create statements for the first nested object.

7. Place your pointer after the closing curly brace of the first nested with statement, and press Enter to go to the next line (**Figure 5.32**).

   If you do not create a new line before proceeding with the next step, the second nested with statement will appear inside the first one.

8. Again, choose Statements > Variables > with.

9. With your pointer between the parentheses for the with statement, enter the second nested target path; then create a statement for this second nested object (**Figure 5.33**).

Scope

You've learned that to direct an ActionScript statement to affect a different Timeline, you need a target path that defines the *scope*. Without a target path, the ActionScript would affect its own Timeline. An ActionScript statement belongs, or is *scoped*, to a particular Timeline or a particular object where it resides. Everything you do in ActionScript has a scope, so you must be aware of it. You could be giving the correct ActionScript instructions, but if it isn't scoped correctly, nothing—or, worse, unexpected—things could happen.

When you assign ActionScript to a frame of the `_root` Timeline, the statement is scoped to the `_root` Timeline. When you assign ActionScript to a frame of a movie-clip Timeline, the statement is scoped to that movie-clip Timeline. When you create ActionScript objects by using the constructor function `new`, that object is scoped to the Timeline where it was created. If you create a date object (as you did in Chapter 3) on the main Timeline with the statement

`myDate = new Date();`

the object `myDate` is scoped to the `_root` Timeline. You can target the `myDate` object with the target path `_root.myDate`.

The scope of buttons, movie clips, and functions

Keeping track of the scope of ActionScript assigned to a Timeline is a straightforward matter. When you assign ActionScript to buttons, movie clips, and functions, however, you need to keep a few wrinkles in mind:

◆ ActionScript assigned to a button with the on action is scoped to the Timeline where the button lies. So if a button is on the main Timeline, the event handler

```
on(release){
    gotoAndStop(10);
}
```

will send the playhead of the main Timeline to Frame 10. The keyword `this` refers to the main Timeline, so `this.gotoAndStop(10)` is synonymous with the preceding statement, and `this._rotation = 45` will rotate the main Stage, *not* the button.

◆ ActionScript assigned to a movie clip with the onClipEvent action is scoped to the movie clip's Timeline. So if a movie clip is on the main Timeline, the event handler

```
onClipEvent(mouseDown){
    gotoAndStop(10);
}
```

will send the playhead of the movie-clip Timeline to Frame 10. The keyword `this` refers to the movie clip, so `this.goto AndStop(10)` affects the movie clip's Timeline. The statement `this._rotation = 45` will rotate the movie clip.

◆ ActionScript assigned to a movie clip with the on action (so that it behaves like a button) is scoped to the movie clip's Timeline. So if a movie clip is on the main Timeline, the event handler

```
on(release){
    gotoAndStop(10);
}
```

will send the playhead of the movie-clip Timeline to Frame 10. The keyword this refers to the movie clip, so this.goto AndStop(10) is synonymous with the preceding statement, and this._rotation = 45 will rotate the movie clip. Notice how the scope of the on action is different whether it is assigned to a button or to a movie clip.

◆ ActionScript assigned to a function is scoped to the Timeline on which it was created. So if this event handler is on the main Timeline for a movie clip or a button

```
myInstance.onRelease = function(){
    gotoAndStop(10);
}
```

the playhead on the main Timeline will move to Frame 10. The keyword this refers to the object of the function, however, so in this example, this refers to myInstance. The statement this._rotation = 45 will rotate myInstance whether it's a button or a movie clip. The statement this.gotoAndStop(10) will move the playhead of myInstance only if it is a movie clip. Buttons do not have Timelines that can be navigated.

Table 5.2 reviews the scope of different event handlers for buttons, movie clips, and functions.

Table 5.2

Scope of Event Handlers

ACTIONSCRIPT ASSIGNED TO	EVENT HANDLER	SCOPE
Button	on(event)	Timeline where button instance sits. Keyword this refers to Timeline where button instance sits.
Movie clip	onClipEvent(event) on(event)	Movie-clip Timeline. Keyword this refers to movie-clip instance.
Function on Timeline	myInstance.onEvent = function()	Timeline where function is created. Keyword this refers to the object of the function (myInstance).

Finding target paths

Sometimes, you'll want to target an object or a movie-clip Timeline but you don't know the target path. This happens when movie clips are generated dynamically and are given names automatically. If you want the target path of any movie clip, button, or other object at run-time, you can use the property _target or the function targetPath.

The property _target returns the absolute target path in slash notation. So if a movie clip called child_mc is inside a movie clip called parent_mc, the _target property of child is /parent_mc/child_mc.

Slash notation is considered a deprecated syntax, meaning that it is no longer supported. However, you can use the eval() function (Global Functions > Miscellaneous Functions > eval) to convert a target path written in slash notation to a target path written in dot syntax. So the statement, eval (this._target) returns the target path of the current Timeline in dot syntax.

The function targetPath returns the absolute target path in dot notation. It starts the target path with the Level designation. (Chapter 6 covers levels.) _level0, for example, refers to the _root Timeline in a movie that has no other loaded movies. So if a movie clip called child_mc is inside a movie clip called parent_mc, the targetPath function returns _level0.parent_mc.child_mc.

In the following examples, you'll use the trace command to display the target path in the Output window. This technique is useful for debugging code, but you can also integrate _target and targetPath into expressions when you need the absolute target path of an object.

To find the target path with _target:

1. Create a movie-clip symbol, place it on the main Stage, and give it a name in the Property Inspector.

2. Create another movie-clip symbol, place it inside the first movie clip, and give it a name in the Property Inspector.

   Now you have a parent movie clip that contains a child movie clip. The parent movie clip sits on the main Timeline.

3. Select the child movie clip inside the parent movie clip, and open the Actions panel.

4. Choose Global Functions > Movie Clip Control > on.

5. Select release as the event, and place your pointer on the next line between the curly braces.

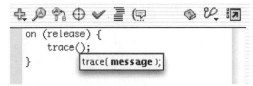

Figure 5.34 The trace action displays messages in the Output window.

Figure 5.35 This trace action will display the target path of the current movie clip in slash notation (which you see in Figure 5.36).

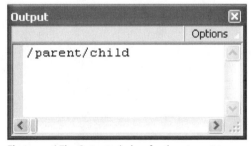

Figure 5.36 The Output window for the _target trace.

6. Choose Global Functions > Miscellaneous Functions > trace (**Figure 5.34**).

The trace command appears within the on(release) event handler. The trace command displays messages in an Output window when you test a movie for debugging purposes. You will display the target path in the Output window.

7. With your pointer between the parentheses of the trace command, type this, or choose it from the Insert Target Path button.

8. Enter a dot, and then choose Built-in Classes > Movie > MovieClip > Properties > _target (**Figure 5.35**).

9. Test your movie.

When you click the child movie clip, the Output window appears and displays its target path (**Figure 5.36**). (ℛ.))

SCOPE

To find the target path with targetPath:

1. Continue with the file you created in the preceding task.

2. Select the child movie clip, and open the Actions panel.

3. Place your pointer inside the parentheses for the **trace** statement in the Script pane.

4. Delete the current contents located between the parentheses.

5. Choose Global Functions > Movie Clip Control > targetPath.

6. Between the parentheses of the **targetPath** function, enter the keyword **this** (**Figure 5.37**).

7. Test your movie.

   When you click the child movie clip, the Output window appears and displays its target path (**Figure 5.38**).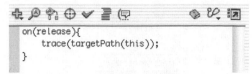

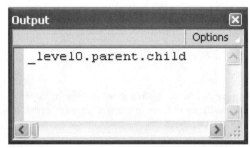

Figure 5.37 This trace action will display the target path of the current movie clip in dot notation (which you see in Figure 5.38).

Figure 5.38 The Output window for the targetPath trace.

stop action ─

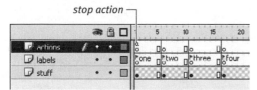

Figure 5.39 The movie clip as a container. This movie clip has a stop action in the first keyframe. The other labeled keyframes can contain buttons, graphics, animations, or any other kind of Flash information, which you can access simply by targeting the movie clip and moving its playhead to the appropriate keyframe.

stop action ─

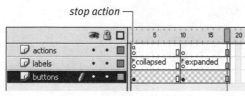

Figure 5.40 The pull-down-menu movie clip contains both collapsed and expanded states.

Movie Clips as Containers

So far in this chapter, you've learned how to name your movie-clip objects, target each one, and navigate within their Timelines from any other Timeline in your movie. But how does the ability to control movie-clip Timelines translate into meaningful interactivity for your Flash project? The key is to think of movie clips as containers that hold stuff: animation, graphics, sound, and even data. By moving the playhead back and forth or playing certain parts of a particular movie-clip Timeline, you can access that stuff whenever you want, independently of what else is going on (**Figure 5.39**).

Movie clips are commonly used, for example, to show objects with different states that toggle from one to the other; the different states are contained in the movie clip's Timeline. When you built pull-down menus in Chapter 4, you used movie clips to serve exactly that purpose. The pull-down menu is essentially a movie-clip object that toggles between a collapsed state and an expanded state. The buttons inside the movie clip control which of those two states you see while also providing navigation outside the movie clip's Timeline (**Figure 5.40**).

Another example is using different keyframes of a movie clip to hold different states of a main character in a game. Depending on the circumstances, you can tell the playhead to go to a certain frame of the movie clip to display the character in a sad state, in a happy state, or in a sleepy state.

The following example demonstrates how to create a radio button with a movie clip. Building a radio button is a matter of defining two different keyframes that toggle between an on state and an off state.

MOVIE CLIPS AS CONTAINERS

To create a radio button:

1. Create a movie-clip symbol.

2. Go to symbol-editing mode for the movie clip, and insert a new keyframe.

3. In the first keyframe, choose Global Functions > Timeline Control > stop.

4. Insert another keyframe, and in this second keyframe choose Global Functions > Timeline Control > stop.

   The stop action in both keyframes will prevent this movie clip from playing automatically and stop the playhead on each keyframe.

5. Insert another new layer.

6. Create graphics that correspond to the first keyframe and graphics that correspond to the second keyframe (**Figure 5.41**).

7. Exit symbol-editing mode, and return to the main Stage.

8. Place an instance of your movie clip on the Stage.

9. Select the movie clip, and open the Actions panel.

10. Choose Global Functions > Movie Clip Control > on.

11. From the code hint pull-down menu, select press as the event.

12. On the next line, choose Global Functions > Timeline Control > play.

13. Test your movie.

    When you click the movie clip, the playhead moves to the next keyframe and stops. Each click toggles between two different states, just like a radio button (**Figure 5.42**).

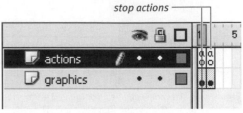

stop actions

Figure 5.41 The radio-button movie clip contains a stop action in both keyframes and two different states that toggle. The graphics will represent the two different states of the radio button.

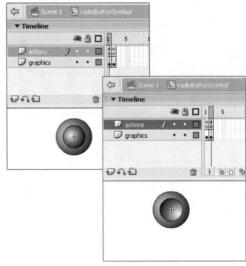

Figure 5.42 The movie clip in the first keyframe (top) sends the playhead to the second keyframe (bottom), and vice versa.

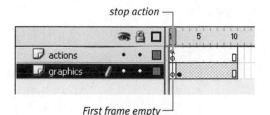

stop action —

First frame empty —

Figure 5.43 A movie clip with an empty first keyframe will be invisible on the Stage. This movie clip has a stop action in the top layer and graphics in the bottom layer starting in keyframe 2.

You can do the same thing to a movie clip that you do to a button to make it invisible—that is, leave the first keyframe that is visible to the user blank so that the instance is invisible on the Stage initially. If the first keyframe of a movie clip is blank and contains a stop frame action to keep it there, you can control when to expose the other frames inside that movie-clip Timeline. You could create a movie clip of an explosion but keep the first keyframe blank. Place this movie clip on a graphic of a submarine, and at the appropriate time, advance to the next frame to reveal the explosion.

Note that you have other ways of using ActionScript to hide or reveal the contents of a movie clip or to place a movie clip on the Stage dynamically; you'll learn about these possibilities in upcoming chapters. But being aware of both the simple (frame-based, as described here) and sophisticated (purely ActionScript-based) approaches will help you tackle a broader range of animation and interactivity challenges.

To create an "invisible" movie clip:

1. Create a movie-clip symbol.

2. Go to symbol-editing mode for the movie clip, and insert a new keyframe into its Timeline.

3. Select the first keyframe, and open the Actions panel.

4. Choose Global Functions > Timeline Control > stop.

5. Leave the first keyframe empty, and begin placing graphics and animations in the second keyframe (**Figure 5.43**).

continues on next page

MOVIE CLIPS AS CONTAINERS

6. Exit symbol-editing mode, and return to the main Timeline.

7. Drag an instance of the movie clip from the Library to the Stage.

The instance appears on the Stage as an empty circle (**Figure 5.44**). The empty circle represents the registration point of the instance, allowing you to place the instance exactly where you want it.

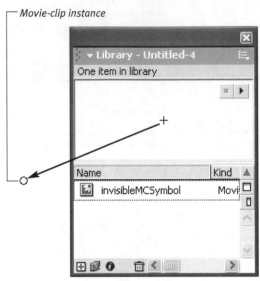

Movie-clip instance

Figure 5.44 An instance of a movie clip with an empty first frame appears as an empty circle.

MOVIE CLIPS AS CONTAINERS

MANAGING OUTSIDE COMMUNICATION

6

Flash provides powerful tools to communicate with other applications and external data, scripts, and files to extend its functionality. By using Flash to link to the Web, you can build sites that combine Flash animation and interactivity with non-Flash media supported by the browser. Use Flash to make your browser link to PDF documents, RealMedia files, or even Java applets. Use Flash to send email, communicate with JavaScript, or relay information to and from servers with the CGI GET and POST methods, as well as with Cold Fusion, PHP, ASP, and more. Flash also supports XML, allowing you to create customized code for data-driven e-commerce solutions. This chapter introduces you to some ways Flash can communicate with HTML, JavaScript, CGI, and XML.

You can also work with external images, video, and Flash movies. Load one or more Flash movies into another Flash movie to create modular projects that are easier to edit and have smaller file sizes. Your main Flash movie might serve simply as an interface that loads your portfolio of Flash animations when the viewer selects them. Learn to communicate from the main Flash movie to its loaded movie or even between two different Flash movies in separate browser windows.

In this chapter, you'll also learn about stand-alone Flash players, called *projectors*, and you'll see how specialized commands affect the way they appear, function, and interact with other programs. Because they don't require a browser to play, projectors are ideal for distributing Flash content on CD-ROM or other portable media.

Finally, you'll learn to communicate with your movie's playback environment. Learn to detect your viewers' system capabilities, Stage size, or Flash Player version so that you can better cater your content to them. Check on the amount of data that has downloaded to users' computers so you can tell them how much longer they have to wait before your movie begins. Keeping track of these external factors will help you provide a friendlier and customized user experience. Along with providing versatile and sophisticated communication options between Flash movies and between the browser and external files, Flash can serve as a key component of dynamic, commercial, and entertainment applications.

Communicating Through the Web Browser

Flash links to the Web browser through the action getURL in the Actions panel. This action is very similar to the HTML tag <A HREF>, in which the URL of a Web site is specified in the form http://www.domainname.com/directory. Use an *absolute URL* (a complete address to a specific file) to link to any Web site, or use a *relative URL* (a path to a file that's described in relation to the current directory) to link to local files contained on your hard drive or a CD-ROM. The getURL action also provides ways to target different frames you create within the browser window or in new browser windows. You can create Flash movies that navigate between these frames and windows and control what loads in each one.

Linking to the Web

Use the action getURL to link to the Web with the standard scheme http:// followed by the rest of the Web address. Use different schemes to request different protocols, such as mailto: for email.

If you test your Flash movie by choosing Control > Test Movie or play it in Flash Player, the action getURL automatically launches the default browser and loads the specified Web address in a new window.

To link to a Web site with the getURL action:

1. Create a button symbol, drag an instance from the Library to the Stage, and give it a name in the Property Inspector.

   You will assign the getURL action to this button.

2. Select the first frame of the main Timeline, and open the Actions panel.

3. Enter the name of your button followed by a period.

Figure 6.1 The getURL action has parameters for a URL, window name, and methods of sending variables.

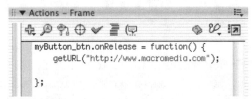

Figure 6.2 Enter a URL between the parentheses for the getURL action.

Figure 6.3 The Flash movie (top) links to the Macromedia site in the same browser window (bottom) when the Window field is left blank.

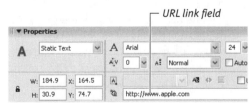

Figure 6.4 A Web address in the link field of the Property Inspector makes the entire static text link to the site.

4. Choose Built-in Classes > Movie > Button > Events > onRelease. Complete the event handler by entering =function(){}.

The onRelease event handler for your button is created.

5. On the next line of the onRelease event handler, choose Global Functions > Browser/Network > getURL (Esc + gu).

The getURL action is added to the onRelease event handler (**Figure 6.1**).

6. With your pointer between the parentheses, enter the full address of a Web site surrounded in quotation marks (**Figure 6.2**).

7. Export your Flash movie, and play it in either Flash Player or a browser.

When you click the button you created, the Web site loads in the same window as your Flash movie (**Figure 6.3**). Click the Back button in your browser to return to your Flash movie.

✔ Tips

- You can also link to the Web from a static horizontal text block. Create static text with the Text tool, and in the Property Inspector, enter the address of the Web site in the link field (**Figure 6.4**). Your static text will display a dotted underline to show that it is linked to a URL. When your viewers click the text, the Web site will load in the same browser window as your Flash movie.

- In addition to button instances, the getURL action can be assigned to a keyframe. If assigned to a keyframe, getURL will link to the URL when the playhead enters that particular frame. This method is effective for loading Web links automatically—perhaps after an introductory splash animation.

COMMUNICATING THROUGH THE WEB BROWSER

To preaddress an email:

1. Again, create a button symbol, drag an instance from the Library to the Stage, and give it a name in the Property Inspector.

2. Select the first frame of the main Timeline, and open the Actions panel.

3. Enter the name of your button followed by a period.

4. Choose Built-in Classes > Movie > Button > Events > onRelease. Complete the event handler by entering =function(){}.

The onRelease event handler for your button is created.

5. On the next line of the onRelease event, choose Global Functions > Browser/Network > getURL.

The getURL action is added to the onRelease event handler.

6. With your pointer between the parentheses, enter mailto: followed by the email address of the person who should receive the email (**Figure 6.5**).

The entire statement must be surrounded in quotation marks.

7. Export your Flash movie, and play it in either Flash Player or a browser.

When you click the button you created, an email form appears with the recipient's email address already filled in (**Figure 6.6**). The viewer then types a message and clicks Send. Use getURL to preaddress email that viewers can use to contact you about your Web site or to request more information.

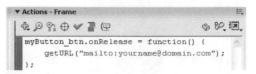

Figure 6.5 Enter email recipients after mailto: for the URL parameter. Separate additional email addresses with commas.

Figure 6.6 A new email message appears in your default mail program.

> Contact: yourname@yourdomain.com

Figure 6.7 This email address is also a button that links to the browser via mailto:.

✔ Tip

■ It's a good idea to spell out the email address of the getURL mailto: recipient in your Flash movie (**Figure 6.7**). If a person's browser isn't configured to send email, an error message will appear instead of an email form. By spelling out the address, you allow users to enter it in their email applications themselves.

Figure 6.8 This relative URL goes up one directory level and looks for a folder called images, which contains a file called photo.jpg.

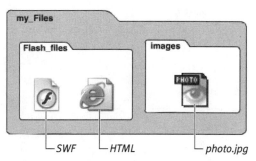

Figure 6.9 Your Flash movie (SWF) and its accompanying HTML file are in a directory that's at the same level as the directory that contains the file photo.jpg.

Linking to local files

Use relative paths rather than complete URLs to specify local files instead of files on the Web. This method allows you to distribute your Flash movie on a CD-ROM or floppy disk without requiring an Internet connection. Instead of using the complete URL http://www.myServer.com/images/photo.jpg, for example, you can specify just images/photo.jpg, and Flash will have to look only inside the folder called images to find the file called photo.jpg.

To link to a local file:

1. As before, create a button symbol, drag an instance from the Library to the Stage, and give it a name in the Property Inspector.

2. Select the first frame of the main Timeline, and open the Actions panel.

3. Enter the name of your button followed by a period.

4. Choose Built-in Classes > Movie > Button > Events > onRelease. Complete the event handler by entering =function(){}.

    The onRelease event handler for your button is created.

5. On the next line of the onRelease event, choose Global Functions > Browser/Network > getURL.

    The getURL action is added to the onRelease event handler.

6. With your pointer between the parentheses, enter the relative path to the desired file.

    Use a slash (/) to separate directories and two periods (..) to move up one directory (**Figure 6.8**).

7. Export your Flash movie, and place it and your linked file in the correct level in the folder hierarchy (**Figure 6.9**).

continues on next page

COMMUNICATING THROUGH THE WEB BROWSER

8. Play the movie in either Flash Player or a browser.

When you click the button you created, Flash looks for the file, using the relative path, and loads it into the same browser window (**Figure 6.10**).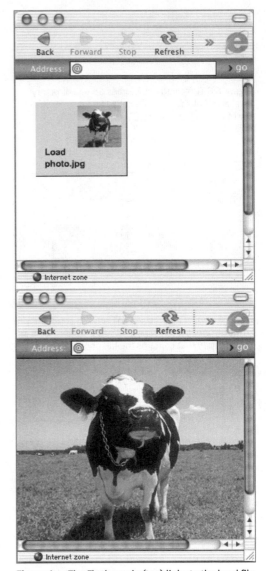

✔ Tip

■ Any file type can be targeted in the URL field of the getURL action. You can load HTML, JPEG, GIF, QuickTime, and PDF files and even other Flash movies. Just keep in mind that the viewer's browser must have the required plug-ins to display these different media types.

Figure 6.10 The Flash movie (top) links to the local file in the same browser window (bottom).

Table 6.1

Window Parameters for getURL	
WINDOW NAME	EXPLANATION
_self	Specifies the current frame of the current browser window; the default behavior when no Window parameter is specified.
_blank	Specifies a new browser window.
_parent	Specifies the frameset that contains the current frame.
_top	Specifies the top-level frameset in the current browser window.

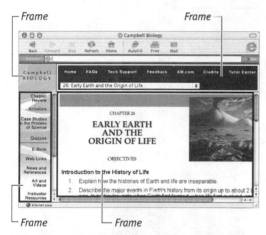

Figure 6.11 A Web site using frames to divide content. The window is divided horizontally into two frames. The bottom and top frames are divided vertically into two more frames. Ad banners, navigation bars, and content usually are separated in this way.

Working with browser framesets and windows

When you play your Flash movie in a browser window, the getURL action loads the new Web address in the same window, replacing your Flash movie. To make it load into a new window or a different frame of your window so that your original Flash movie isn't replaced, enter a second parameter in the getURL action for the Window, as defined in **Table 6.1.**

What's the difference between a window and a frame? Browser windows can be divided into separate areas, or *frames,* that contain individual Web pages. The collection of frames is called a *frameset,* and the frameset HTML file defines the frame proportions and the name of each frame (**Figure 6.11**).

The Flash Window parameter can use the name that the frameset HTML file assigns a frame to load a URL directly into that specific frame. This method is very similar to using the HTML <A HREF> tag attribute TARGET. If you divide a Web page into two frames, for example, you can call the left frame navigator and the right frame contents. Place a Flash movie in the navigator frame with buttons that are assigned the getURL action. By entering the frame name contents as the Window parameter of getURL, you target the right frame to load the URL.

Figure 6.12 depicts how each page will load into a frameset.

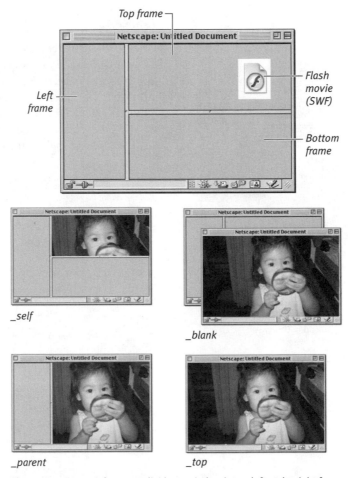

Figure 6.12 At top, a frameset divides a window into a left and a right frame. The right frame contains another frameset that divides itself into top and bottom frames. The Flash movie (SWF) plays in the top frame of the second frameset. The window names specify where the URL loads.

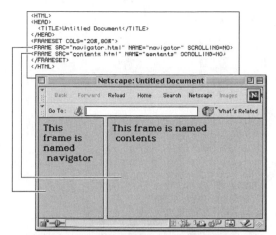

Figure 6.13 The frameset file (top) divides this window into a left column named navigator, which is 20 percent of the browser width, and a right column named contents, which is 80 percent of the browser width (bottom).

Figure 6.14 The parameters of the getURL action specifies the Google Web site to load in the contents frame (bottom). The code hints that appear after the opening parenthesis (top) remind you of the parameters that the action can take.

To open a Web site in a named frame:

1. In an HTML editor such as Dreamweaver or HomeSite, create an HTML frameset with two frames and unique names for both.

   Your Flash movie will play in one frame, and the Web site links will be loaded into the other frame (**Figure 6.13**).

2. In Flash, create a button symbol, drag an instance from the Library to the Stage as you did in the preceding tasks, and give it a name in the Property Inspector.

3. Select the first frame of the main Timeline, and open the Actions panel.

4. Enter the name of your button followed by a period.

5. Choose Built-in Classes > Movie > Button > Events > onRelease. Complete the event handler by entering =function(){}.

   The onRelease event handler for your button is created.

6. On the next line of the onRelease event, choose Global Functions > Browser/Network > getURL.

   The getURL action is added to the onRelease event handler.

7. In the URL field, enter http:// and then the address of a Web site; the http:// and the address must be surrounded by quotation marks.

8. After the closing quotation mark for the Web site address, enter a comma and then enter the name of the frame established in the HTML frameset (**Figure 6.14**).

   The second parameter, which tells Flash where to load the Web address, must also be surrounded by quotation marks.

continues on next page

COMMUNICATING THROUGH THE WEB BROWSER

9. Publish your Flash movie with its accompanying HTML file.

10. Create another HTML file for the other frame in the frameset.

11. Name both HTML files according to the <FRAME SRC> tags in the frameset document, and place all files within the same folder (**Figure 6.15**).

12. Open the frameset document in a browser.

Your Flash movie plays in one frame. The button loads a Web site in the other frame (**Figure 6.16**).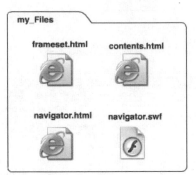

To open a Web site in a new window:

1. Create a button symbol, drag an instance from the Library to the Stage, and give it a name in the Property Inspector.

2. Select the first frame of the main Timeline, and open the Actions panel.

3. Enter the name of your button followed by a period.

4. Choose Built-in Classes > Movie > Button > Events > onRelease. Complete the event handler by entering =function(){}.

The onRelease event handler for your button is created.

5. On the next line of the onRelease event, choose Global Functions > Browser/Network > getURL.

The getURL action is added to the onRelease event handler.

6. With your pointer between the parentheses, enter a Web site address followed by a comma.

7. Enter _blank surrounded by quotation marks (**Figure 6.17**); then export your Flash movie and play it in Flash Player or a browser.

Figure 6.15 The frameset.html file puts the contents.html file in the contents frame and the navigator.html file in the navigator frame. The navigator.html file embeds the Flash movie (navigator.swf).

```
googleButton_btn.onRelease = function() {
    getURL("http://www.google.com", "contents");
};
yahooButton_btn.onRelease = function() {
    getURL("http://www.yahoo.com", "contents");
};
exciteButton_btn.onRelease = function() {
    getURL("http://www.excite.com", "contents");
};
```

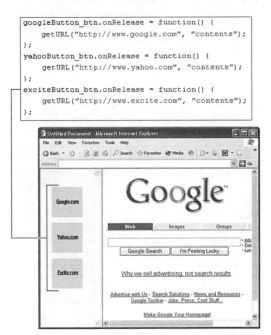

Figure 6.16 The ActionScript for the buttons in the navigator frame is shown. The Google, Yahoo, and Excite sites load in the other frame, keeping the left frame (which contains your Flash movie) intact.

Figure 6.17 When you enter _blank as the second parameter, the Peachpit Web site will load in a new, unnamed window.

Figure 6.18 Multiple getURL actions with the second parameter set to _blank (top) and set to a unique name (bottom). This behavior happens on all platforms except when Internet Explorer is used on Windows.

The first parameter for the getURL action is the Web address. The second parameter tells Flash to load that Web address in a new browser window. When you click the button you created, a new window appears and the Web site loads in it.

✔ Tips

- There is a crucial difference between opening a new window by using the term _blank and opening a new window by using a name that you enter yourself. If you use _blank, each time you click your button to link to a Web site, a new window will be created. If you use a name in the Window field, the first click will open a new window. Subsequent clicks actually find the newly created window you named, so Flash reloads the Web site into that existing window (**Figure 6.18**). Both methods are useful, depending on whether you want your Web links to be in separate windows or to replace each other in the first new window.

- Be careful when you create new browser windows, and keep track of where they are. Sometimes, windows may be hidden behind the active window, loading Web sites that the viewer cannot see.

Using JavaScript to control new window parameters

The Window parameter in the getURL action is useful for directing Web links to new browser windows, but the appearance and location of these new windows are set by the browser's preferences. If you play a Flash movie in a browser that shows the location bar and the toolbar, for example, and you open a new window, the new window will also have a location bar and a toolbar. You can't control these window parameters directly with Flash, but you can control them indirectly with JavaScript.

continues on next page

COMMUNICATING THROUGH THE WEB BROWSER

In the HTML page that holds your Flash movie, you can define JavaScript functions that control the opening and even closing of new browser windows. In your Flash movie, you can call on these JavaScript functions by using the getURL action. Instead of entering a Web address in the URL field, you enter javascript: followed by the name of the function. Flash finds the JavaScript in the HTML page, and the browser calls the function.

You can use JavaScript to control several window properties. These properties specify the way the window looks, how it works, and where it's located on the screen (**Figure 6.19**). These properties can be defined in the getURL action in your Flash movie and passed to the JavaScript function in the HTML page. When you define these window properties, use yes (1), no (0), or a number specifying pixel dimensions or coordinates. **Table 6.2** lists the most common window properties that are compatible with both Microsoft Internet Explorer and Netscape Navigator.

Table 6.2

JavaScript Window Properties

PROPERTY	DESCRIPTION
height	Vertical dimension, in pixels.
width	Horizontal dimension, in pixels.
left	X coordinate of left edge.
top	Y coordinate of top edge.
resizable	Resizable area in the bottom-right corner that allows the window to change dimensions (yes/no or 1/0).
scrollbars	The vertical and horizontal scroll bars (yes/no or 1/0).
directories	Also called links, where certain bookmarks are accessible (yes/no or 1/0).
location	Location bar, containing URL area (yes/no or 1/0).
menubar	Menu bar, containing drop-down menus such as File and Edit. Works only in the Windows operating system (yes/no or 1/0).
status	Status bar in the bottom-left corner, containing browser status and security (yes/no or 1/0).
toolbar	Toolbar, containing the back and forward buttons and other navigation aides (yes/no or 1/0).

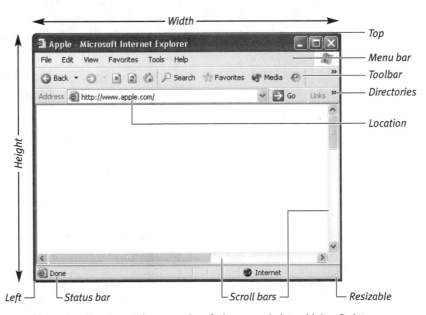

Figure 6.19 You can set the properties of a browser window with JavaScript.

To open a new window with JavaScript:

1. Create a button, name it, and attach the getURL action to an onRelease event handler as described in the preceding tasks.

   This button will communicate with a JavaScript function in the HTML page.

2. With your pointer between the parentheses for getURL, enter in the following:

   ```
   "javascript:openWindow('http://www.
   peachpit.com','mynewWindow','left=80,
   top=180,toolbar=0,scrollbars=0,
   |height=250,width=200')"
   ```

   The information that you enter in single quotation marks between the parentheses are parameters that get passed to the JavaScript function called openWindow. You don't have to define all the window properties (**Figure 6.20**).

3. Publish your Flash movie with its associated HTML file.

4. Open the HTML page in a text- or HTML-editing application such as Dreamweaver, BBEdit, or HomeSite.

   Now you must define the javaScript function in the HTML page.

   continues on next page

Figure 6.20 The javascript: statement calls the openWindow function in the HTML page that embeds the Flash movie. Note the use of single quotation marks inside of double quotation marks. You can also use escape sequences for the quotation marks. Use \" in place of the single quotation marks. Learn more about escape sequences in Chapter 9.

5. Add the following script to the head of the HTML page:

```
<script language="javaScript">
<!- Code for Flash JS Pop-up Window
function openWindow(URL, windowName, windowFeatures){
newWindow = window.open(URL, windowName, windowFeatures)
}
// End -->
</script>
```

This script defines a function called openWindow that has three parameters: URL, windowName, and windowFeatures. When this function is called, the object newWindow is created and receives the three parameters from the Flash movie. The HTML page should be similar to **Figure 6.21**.

6. Add the following statement inside the <EMBED> tag after the width and height parameters in the HTML code where your Flash movie (SWF) is referenced:

```
SwLiveConnect="true"
```

This parameter enables Netscape to launch the interface that allows your Flash movie to communicate with JavaScript when loading the Flash Player for the first time.

JavaScript

```
<!DOCTYPE html PUBLIC "-//W3C//DTD XHTML 1.0 Transitional//EN"
"http://www.w3.org/TR/xhtml1/DTD/xhtml1-transitional.dtd">
<html xmlns="http://www.w3.org/1999/xhtml" xml:lang="en" lang="en">
<head>

<script language="javaScript">

<!-- Code for Flash JS Pop-up Window

function openWindow(URL, windowName, windowFeatures){
        newWindow = window.open(URL, windowName, windowFeatures)
}

// End -->
</script>
```

Figure 6.21 JavaScript code in the header of an HTML document. The Flash movie embedded in this HTML document will call on the function openWindow.

7. Save the modified HTML page, and open it in a browser.

When you click the button that you created, Flash passes the Web address, the window name, and the window properties to the JavaScript function called `openWindow`. Then JavaScript creates a new window with the new properties (**Figure 6.22**).

✔ Tips

■ This method of using Flash to talk to JavaScript will not work with older versions of Internet Explorer (version 3 or earlier), Internet Explorer 4.5 or earlier for the Macintosh, or any beta versions of the Safari browser for the Apple.

■ More JavaScript window properties are available, but many of them work in only one of the two most popular browsers. The properties `innerHeight` and `innerWidth`, for example, define the dimensions of the actual window content area, but these properties are unique to Netscape Navigator. You are safe if you stick to the properties listed in Table 6.2.

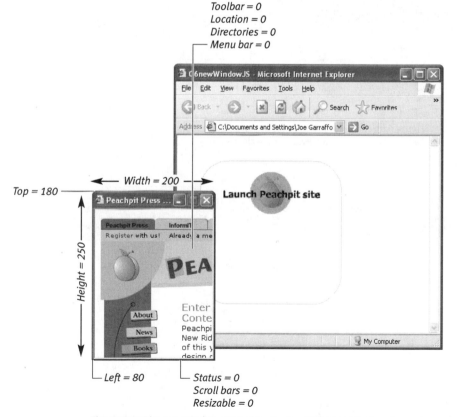

Figure 6.22 The new window created by the JavaScript function is a chromeless window, which is a customized window without any features. *Chrome* refers to all the interface features of a window.

After you open a window with JavaScript, you can use the same strategy to close it.

To close a window with JavaScript:

1. In your Flash movie, create a second button, and assign the `getURL` action to an `onRelease` event handler.

2. With your pointer between the parentheses for `getURL`, enter the following (**Figure 6.23**):

   `"javascript:closeWindow('mynewWindow')"`

3. Publish your Flash movie and modify its HTML page by adding JavaScript and the `SWLiveConnect` statement as you did in the preceding task.

   Next you must define the function called `closeWindow` in the JavaScript portion of your HTML page.

4. Add the new `closeWindow` function after the `openWindow` function, as follows:

   `function closeWindow(windowName) {`

   `newWindow.close(windowName)`

   `}`

   The function `closeWindow` calls the method `close()`. The parameter `windowName` is the name of the window you want to close (**Figure 6.24**).

5. Save your modified HTML page, and open it in a browser.

   When you click the first button, Flash tells JavaScript to create a new window called myNewWindow. When you click the second button, Flash tells JavaScript to close the window called myNewWindow.

```
closeButton_btn.onRelease = function() {
    getURL("javascript:closeWindow('mynewWindow')");
};
```

Figure 6.23 The `getURL` action calls the JavaScript `closeWindow` function. The window object called `mynewWindow` closes.

JavaScript

```
<!DOCTYPE html PUBLIC "-//W3C//DTD XHTML 1.0 Transitional//EN"
"http://www.w3.org/TR/xhtml1/DTD/xhtml1-transitional.dtd">
<html xmlns="http://www.w3.org/1999/xhtml" xml:lang="en" lang="en">
<meta http-equiv="Content-Type" content="text/html; charset=iso-8859-1">
<title>07CloseWindowJS</title>

<head>

<script language="javascript">

<!-- Code for Flash JS Pop-up Window

function openWindow(URL, windowName, windowFeatures){
newWindow = window.open(URL, windowName, windowFeatures)
}

function closeWindow(windowName){
newWindow.close(windowName)
}


// End -->
</script>

</head>
```

Figure 6.24 JavaScript code in the header of an HTML document. Both the `openWindow` and `closeWindow` functions are defined here.

Using CGI and the GET and POST methods

An optional third parameter for the getURL action allows you to send information via the GET and POST methods. These methods send variables that you define in your Flash movie to a server-side application (such as a CGI or PHP application) for processing. These methods are most commonly used to send information such as keywords to a search engine or a login name and password to enter a Web site.

The difference between GET and POST is very simple:

♦ GET appends the variables to the URL in the getURL action and is used for very few variables and for those that contain only a small amount of information. The variables term=CGI, category=All, and pref=all are put at the end of this URL as follows: http://search.domain.com/cgi-bin/ search?term=CGI&category=All&pref=all

You've probably seen this type of long URL after you've requested information from a search engine.

♦ POST sends the variables in the HTTP header of the user's browser. Use POST for more security or to send long strings of information in the getURL operation. A message board, for example, would do better with a POST method.

After the variables are sent to the Web server, they are processed by the CGI scripts in the URL or HTTP headers. These server-side scripts are handled by your Internet service provider or your Webmaster, so you should contact them for more information.

To send information by using GET:

1. Select the text tool, and drag out a text field on the Stage.

2. In the Property Inspector, choose Input Text from the pull-down menu.

   This option lets you use the text field you created to enter information.

3. In the Variable field of the Property Inspector, enter emailStr (**Figure 6.25**).

   Whatever you enter in that text field is assigned to the variable emailStr. This should ultimately match the variable in the CGI script so that the entered data can be sent.

4. Create a button, place an instance of it on the Stage, and name the button in the Property Inspector.

5. Assign the getURL action to the button's onRelease event handler.

6. With your pointer between the parentheses for the getURL statement, enter the address to the server-side script (such as "http: //www.myserver.com/ cgi-bin/list.cgi").

7. After the closing quotation mark for the URL, enter a comma followed by the window parameter of "_self" followed by a comma.

Variable field

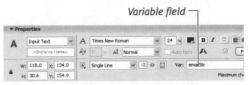

Figure 6.25 In the Variable field of the Property Inspector, enter emailStr as your input text.

Figure 6.26 Using the code hints inside of the getURL method (top), enter the URL, Window, and Method parameters (bottom).

8. Enter "GET" for the third parameter, as the Send method (**Figure 6.26**).

   Your Script pane should look like this:

   ```
   myButton_btn.onRelease = function {
   getURL ( "http://www.myserver.com/
   cgi-bin/list.cgi", "_self", "GET");
   }
   ```

   When a viewer enters an email address in the text field and then clicks the button, the email address is added to the end of the URL and is sent to the CGI script.

   You'll learn more about variables and input text in Part V.

Communicating with XML Objects

In addition to HTML and JavaScript, Flash supports XML. Although it's beyond the scope of this book to cover XML in depth, this short discussion will help you understand the exciting possibilities Flash brings to XML.

XML is very different from a traditional markup language such as HTML, which tells the browser how to lay out the content—put this text here, set it to this font, and put it next to this image. Instead, XML allows you to define content according to its meaning and its audience. Content is defined by tags that are easy to read and understand and not tied to the presentation layer (traditional HTML). A portion of XML could look something like this:

```
<invoice>
<vendorname>Big Tents</vendorname>
<vendorID>MYBDAY021570</vendorID>
<vendorLogo>03SUIRAUQA.GIF</vendorLogo>
<productdescription>
    <name>All-Weather Tent</name>
    <packageDimensions>
        <height>7.25"</height>
<width>7.25"</width>
<depth>48.5"</depth>
<weight>8lbs.</weight>
</packageDimensions>
    <wholesale>$75.43</wholesale>
<retail>$135.99</retail>
</productdescription>
</invoice>
```

In Flash, the XML and XMLSocket objects let you communicate with other applications and style sheets to manage media-rich content that can be unique to each user. Such industries as entertainment, automotive, banking, and e-commerce have recognized the benefits of combining Flash and XML. An example of a real-world application for

e-commerce would be one that provides an extensible interface between an online retailer and its partners, vendors, and suppliers in a Flash-enabled extranet. Using Flash as the tool for the interface (buttons, scroll bars, text-input fields, etc.), you could supply a merchant with a drag-and-drop interface for ordering products and placing them in a warehouse. The XML object could enable a vendor to change wholesale and retail prices while negotiating its product's placement in the retailer's Web site and email campaigns. Done traditionally, all of these different Web-based forms would take enormous amounts of time to create, and still there is the very difficult task of making sure the data matches on both sides. In the code example above, notice how easy it is to find the retail price.

XSL is the style sheet that is applied to XML, and you might need only one or two to supply Flash content to all the different types of users. The style sheet transforms the interface based on information it has received from the user's client (browser), Web server, or database. A merchant might see some streaming data of what's being purchased and sold daily and negotiate with a vendor in real time to further increase volume. A partner, on the other hand, may see how well a promotion is progressing with a retailer's customers and therefore can make the decision to extend the promotion through to the following year. Flash can expose that highly extensible layer between front-end, media-rich content and middle-/back-end negotiating and data. XML won't make your animations tween more smoothly, but it can make it easier to create unique and scalable user experiences. To learn more about Flash's XML and XMLSocket objects, refer to the Flash ActionScript Reference that comes with the software.

Using the browser to navigate Flash content

Most viewers are familiar, if not comfortable, with using their browser's Back and Forward buttons and adding frequently visited sites to their bookmarks (Netscape Navigator) or Favorites list (Internet Explorer). So when you have a Flash movie that is conveniently divided into navigable sections, you may want to let the browser handle much of the navigation. Labeling individual keyframes with named anchors provides a way for those keyframes to be accessed with a browser's Back and Forward buttons or to be saved in the browser's bookmarks or Favorites list.

You create named anchors in the Property Inspector using the same field you use for labels. A pull-down menu lets you choose a named anchor. When keyframes are identi-fied as named anchors, your browser adds them to its history list as they are played.

Named anchors come with restrictions: They can be applied only to the main Timeline, and they work only in Windows (Internet Explorer 5.6 and above, or Netscape Navigator 4.x). (You can still author them on the Mac.) Still, for the right audience (Windows users only), using named anchors is an effective way to take advantage of a browser's naviga-tion and bookmarking features to organize and move through your Flash content.

To create a named anchor:

1. In your Flash movie, add a new layer and insert keyframes where you want to add anchors.

2. Select the first keyframe.

3. In the Label field of the Property Inspector, enter a name for the anchor.

4. Select Anchor from the Label Type drop-down menu below the Label Type field (**Figure 6.27**).

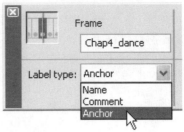

Figure 6.27 The anchor identifies this keyframe as a spot that can be added to Favorites (Internet Explorer) or bookmarks (Netscape Navigator) by the browser and allows the viewer to navigate to the keyframe with the Back and Forward buttons. In Internet Explorer, Chap4_dance will appear in the history list or in the Favorites list. In Netscape Navigator, the name of the Flash movie will appear in the history list or in the bookmarks list.

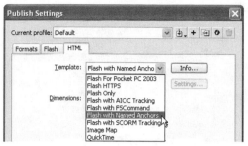

Figure 6.28 The Publish Settings dialog box.

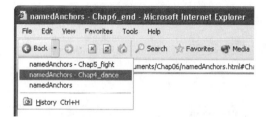

Figure 6.29 The Back button in Internet Explorer lists the named anchors as well as the Web sites you've visited.

5. Enter named anchors for the rest of the keyframes.

6. Choose File > Publish Settings.
The Publish Settings dialog box appears.

7. Click the HTML tab.

8. From the Template pull-down menu, choose Flash with Named Anchors (**Figure 6.28**).
This preference adds the necessary code to the HTML page so that both browsers recognize the named anchors in your Flash movie.

9. Publish your movie.

10. Open the HTML page in a browser on a Windows computer.
After your Flash movie plays through a named anchor, you can use the browser's Back button to navigate to it. Add the anchor to your Favorites list or bookmarks and you can return directly to that keyframe (**Figure 6.29**).

✔ Tip

■ Variables, functions, event handlers, and other information that is initialized in an earlier frame of a movie won't be available to a named anchor if the viewer returns later by using a bookmark or a Favorite. Because a bookmark or Favorite returns the viewer to the middle of your Flash movie, be sure that the anchor locations have no interactivity that depends on ActionScript on earlier frames.

COMMUNICATING THROUGH THE WEB BROWSER

To create automatic named anchors for scenes:

1. Choose Edit > Preferences (Windows) or Flash > Preferences (Mac).

   The Preferences dialog box appears.

2. Click the General tab.

3. Check the Named anchor on Scene check box (**Figure 6.30**), and click OK.

4. Insert a new scene.

   A named anchor automatically appears in the first frame of the new scene (**Figure 6.31**). Additional scenes will have named anchors added automatically in their first frames. (Scenes made before the preference is set will not have named anchors.) You can change the name of your scenes, but their named anchors will not change automatically. You must make that change manually in the Property Inspector.

5. Choose File > Publish Settings. Click the HTML tab and choose Flash with Named Anchors from the Template pull-down menu.

6. Publish your movie.

7. Open the HTML page in a browser.

   When your Flash movie plays through a named anchor in a scene, you can use the browser's Back button to navigate to it. Add the anchor to your browser's Favorites/bookmarks list, and you can return directly to that scene.

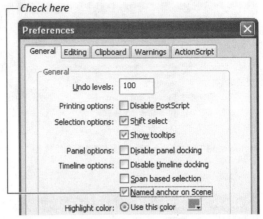

Check here

Figure 6.30 Checking Named anchor on Scene in the Preferences dialog box puts named anchors on additional scenes.

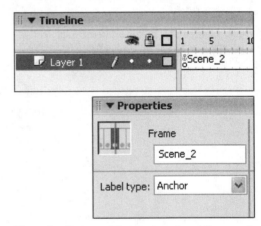

Figure 6.31 Frame 1 of Scene 2 is assigned the named anchor Scene_2 automatically.

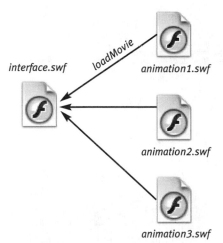

interface.swf   loadMovie   animation1.swf

animation2.swf

animation3.swf

Figure 6.32 A way to keep data-heavy content separate is to maintain external SWF files. Here, the interface.swf movie loads the animation files one by one as they're requested.

Communicating with External Flash Movies

You've learned how a Flash movie can use the action getURL to link to any file, including another Flash movie. This action loads the new SWF file into the same browser window, replacing the original movie, or into a new browser window.

Another way to communicate with external Flash movies and combine them with the original Flash movie is to use the actions loadMovie and loadMovieNum. Both actions allow you to bring in another SWF and integrate it with the current content. The original Flash movie establishes the frame rate, the Stage size, and the background color, but you can layer multiple external SWF files and even navigate within their Timelines. In Chapter 5, you learned to navigate the Timelines of movie clips within a single Flash movie. Now imagine the complexity of navigating multiple Timelines of multiple Flash movies!

One of the benefits of loading external Flash movies is that it allows you to keep your Flash project small and maintain quick download times. If you build a Web site to showcase your Flash animation work, for example, you can keep all your individual animations as separate SWF files. Build the main interface so that your potential clients can load each animation as they request it. That way, your viewers download only the content that's needed, as it's needed. The main interface doesn't become bloated with the inclusion of every one of your Flash animations (**Figure 6.32**).

You can load external SWF files into another Flash movie in two ways. One way is to load a SWF into a level with loadMovieNum; the other is to load a SWF into a movie clip with loadMovie.

Working with levels

Levels hold individual SWF files within a Flash movie. The original Flash movie is always at level 0, and subsequent Flash movies are kept at higher levels. You can have only one movie per level. Higher-level numbers will overlap lower-level numbers, so loaded movies will always appear above your original movie on the screen. To unload a movie, you simply specify the level number; the movie in that level is purged with the action unloadMovieNum. Another way to remove a movie in a particular level is to replace it with a new movie. If you load a new movie into a level already occupied by another movie, the old one is replaced.

To load an external movie:

1. Create the external movie you want to load.

   For this example, keep the animation at a relatively small Stage size (**Figure 6.33**).

2. Export your external movie as a SWF file.

3. Open a new Flash document to create the main movie that will load your external movie.

4. Create a button symbol, drag an instance of it from the Library to the Stage, and give it a name in the Property Inspector.

5. Select the first frame of the main Timeline, and create an onRelease event handler for your button.

6. Inside the onRelease event handler, choose Global Functions > Browser/Network > loadMovieNum (Esc + ln).

   The loadMovieNum action appears within the onRelease event handler.

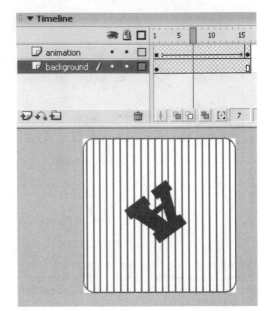

Figure 6.33 An animation of the letter *A* spins on a vertical grid.

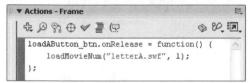

Figure 6.34 The loadMovieNum action has parameters for a URL (its target path), for level (its destination), and for method (for variables). The method parameter is not used in this example.

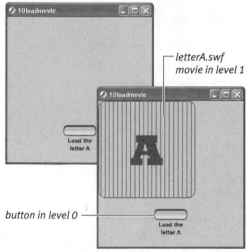

letterA.swf
movie in level 1

button in level 0

Figure 6.35 The original movie in level 0 (top) and the loaded movie in level 1 (bottom).

7. With your pointer between the parentheses, enter the name of your external SWF file surrounded by quotation marks and followed by a comma.

Here, you enter a relative path so Flash looks within the same directory for the SWF file. You can also change directories by using the slash (/) or double periods (..), or you can enter an absolute path if your SWF file resides on a Web site.

8. For the second parameter of the loadMovieNum action, enter a number higher than zero representing the level in which your movie will load (**Figure 6.34**). Ignore the optional third parameter.

9. Publish your movie.

10. Place the SWF file, its HTML file, and the external SWF file in the same directory.

11. Play the main movie in Flash Player or a browser.

When you click the button, Flash loads the external movie, which sits on top of your original movie and begins playing (**Figure 6.35**).

COMMUNICATING WITH EXTERNAL FLASH MOVIES

223

COMMUNICATING WITH EXTERNAL FLASH MOVIES

Characteristics of Loaded Movies

The following is a list of things to keep in mind when working with loaded movies:

◆ You can have only one movie per level.

◆ Loaded movies in higher levels will overlap loaded movies in lower levels.

◆ Loaded movies have transparent Stages. To have an opaque Stage, create a filled rectangle in the bottom layer of your loaded movie (**Figure 6.36**).

◆ Loaded movies are aligned with the Level 0 movie at their registration points. That means loaded movies are positioned from their top-left corner (x = 0, y = 0) to the top-left corner of the original movie (x = 0, y = 0). So loaded movies with smaller Stage sizes will still show objects that are off their Stage (**Figure 6.37**). Create a mask to block objects that may go beyond the Stage and that you don't want your audience to see. Likewise, loaded movies with larger Stage sizes will be cropped at the bottom and right boundaries (**Figure 6.38**).

◆ Movies loaded into level 0 replace the original movie, but the Stage size, frame rate, and background color are still set by the original movie. If the loaded movie has a different Stage size from the original, it is centered and scaled to fit.

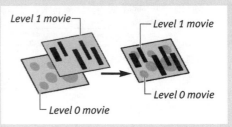

Figure 6.36 The Stage of an external SWF becomes transparent when the SWF is loaded on top of the level 0 movie.

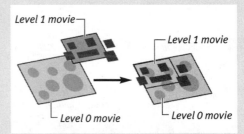

Figure 6.37 Smaller external SWFs are aligned at the top-left corner and display the work area off their Stages. Consider using masks or external SWFs with the same Stage dimensions.

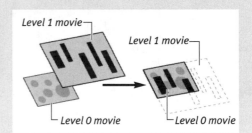

Figure 6.38 Larger external SWFs get cropped when they are loaded on top of the level 0 movie.

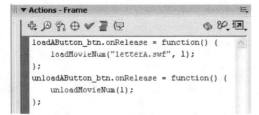

Figure 6.39 The unloadMovieNum action has only one parameter for Location. Any movie in level 1 will be removed.

To unload a movie:

1. Using the files from the preceding task, create another instance of the button in the original movie, and give it a name in the Property Inspector.

2. In the first frame of the main Timeline, create an **onRelease** event handler for the second button.

3. Within the **onRelease** event handler, choose Global Functions > Browser/Network > unloadMovieNum (Esc + un).

The **unloadMovieNum** action appears within the **onRelease** event handler.

4. With your pointer between the parentheses, enter the number that you entered for the **loadMovieNum** action (**Figure 6.39**).

5. Publish your movie, and place it in the same directory as your external SWF file.

6. Play your movie in Flash Player or in a browser.

The first button loads your external movie in the specified level. The second button unloads that movie from that level.

To replace a loaded movie:

1. Open a new Flash document, and create another small Flash animation to serve as a second external movie.

2. Using the Flash movie that you used as the original in the preceding tasks, add a third instance of your button, and give it a name in the Property Inspector.

3. In the first frame of the main Timeline, create an onRelease event handler for the third button.

4. Within the onRelease event handler, choose Global Functions > Browser/Network > loadMovieNum.

   The loadMovieNum action appears below the onRelease event handler.

5. With your pointer between the parentheses, enter the name of the second external movie surrounded by quotation marks and followed by a comma.

6. For the second parameter, enter the number that you used for the first loadMovieNum action (**Figure 6.40**).

7. Publish your movie, and place both this SWF file and the two external SWF files in the same directory.

8. In Flash Player or a browser, play the original movie, which contains the three buttons.

   When you click the first button, Flash loads the first external movie, which sits on top of your original movie. When you click your newly created third button, Flash loads the second external movie in the same level, replacing the first (**Figure 6.41**).

Figure 6.40 The loadMovieNum action assigned to the button called loadBButton_btn will load the movie letterB.swf into level 1, replacing anything currently occupying that level.

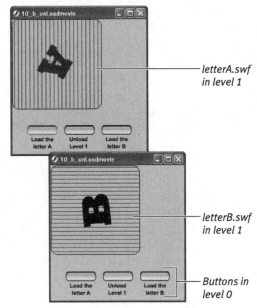

letterA.swf in level 1

letterB.swf in level 1

Buttons in level 0

Figure 6.41 Initially, the letterA.swf movie occupies level 1 (top). Loading another movie in the same level replaces letterA.swf.

Loading Flash movies into movie clips

Loading external movies into levels is somewhat restricting because the default placement of those movies is at the top-left corner of the original Stage. You can work with that positioning by shifting the elements in your external movie relative to where you know it will appear, or you can change all your external movies so that their Stage sizes correspond to the original Stage size.

A better solution is to load those movies into movie clips instead of levels with the action loadMovie. This action places the top-left corner of the loaded movie (x=0, y=0) at the registration point of the targeted movie clip (x=0, y=0) (**Figure 6.42**). Because you can place movie clips anywhere on the Stage, you effectively have a way to position your loaded movie where you want. However, the loaded movie takes over the movie clip; the Timeline of the movie clip is replaced by the Timeline of the loaded movie. Moreover, the movie clip maintains its instance name, and all the scaling, rotation, skewing, color effects, and alpha effects that have been applied to the movie-clip instance are also applied to the loaded movie (**Figure 6.43**).

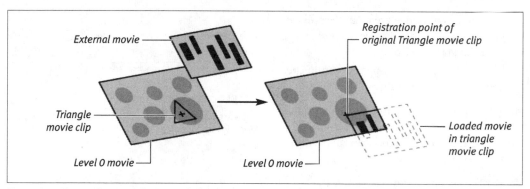

Figure 6.42 The movie's top-left corner is aligned with the registration point of the movie clip.

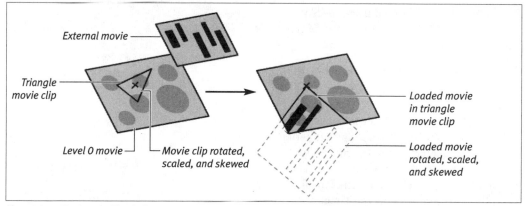

Figure 6.43 The external loaded movie inherits the movie-clip instance's name, position, scaling, skewing, rotation, color effects, and alpha effects.

To load an external Flash movie into a movie clip:

1. Create a movie-clip symbol with the registration point set to the upper-left corner, and drag an instance of it from the Library to the Stage (**Figure 6.44**).

2. Select the instance, and give it a name in the Property Inspector.

3. Create a button symbol, drag an instance of it from the Library to the Stage, and give it a name in the Property Inspector.

4. In the first frame of the main Timeline, create an `onRelease` event handler for the button.

5. Within the `onRelease` event handler, choose Global Functions > Browser/Network > loadMovie (Esc + lm).

    The `loadMovie` action appears within the `onRelease` event handler.

6. With your pointer between the parentheses, enter the name of an external SWF file surrounded by quotation marks and followed by a comma.

7. For the second parameter, enter the target path for the movie-clip instance on the Stage (**Figure 6.45**).

8. Publish your movie, and place the SWF file, its HTML file, and the external SWF file in the same directory.

9. Play the original movie in Flash Player or a browser.

    When you click the button that you created, Flash loads the external movie into the movie clip. The loaded movie inherits all the characteristics of the movie clip, such as position, scale, rotation, instance name, and color effect, but the Timeline of the movie clip is now the Timeline of the loaded movie (**Figure 6.46**). ⟨⟩

Registration point of this movie clip called tvScreen

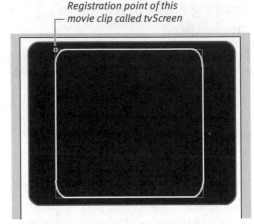

Figure 6.44 A movie-clip instance is the future destination for a loaded movie.

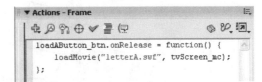

Figure 6.45 When the button called `loadAButton_btn` is clicked, letterA.swf will load into the movie clip called `tvScreen_mc`.

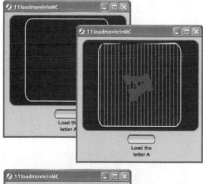

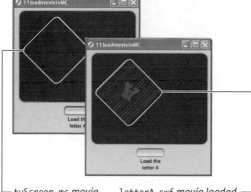

tvScreen_mc *movie clip rotated 45 degrees*   letterA.swf *movie loaded into* tvScreen_mc *movie clip*

Figure 6.46 The letterA.swf movie loads into the tvScreen_mc movie clip (top). When the tvScreen_mc movie clip rotates and shrinks, so does letterA.swf (bottom).

✔ Tips

- In the next chapter, you'll learn to dynamically create an empty movie clip with the movie-clip method `createEmptyMovieClip`. You can use this method to create a movie clip to act as your placeholder, load an external SWF into that movie clip, and then set its _x and _y properties to position it where you want.

- Another way that you could write the `loadMovie` statement is in dot syntax following the object-dot-method construction. First enter the movie clip's name followed by the `loadMovie` method. Inside the parentheses, you only need one parameter, the name of the external file that you want to load. This technique is especially helpful if the `loadMovie` statement is within a `with` statement or if multiple parent Timelines must be declared.

Flash Player Security

Loading external SWFs introduces data security issues and some restrictions that you should be aware of. Because SWFs published on the Internet can be loaded into any Flash movie, there is a potential that private information and sensitive data held in variables in the SWF can be accessed. To prevent this abuse, Flash movies operate within their own secure space, called a *sandbox*. Only movies playing in the same sandbox can access and/or control each other's variables and other Flash elements. The sandbox is defined by the domain in which the Flash movie resides. So, a movie on www.macromedia.com can access other movies on www.macromedia.com without restriction because they are in the same domain.

If you need to access data in SWFs that reside in different domains, you can call the ActionScript method `System.security.allowDomain ("domainName")` and other movies from the specified domain can access their variables. For more specific information and details on domain-based authentication and granting access, search the Macromedia tech notes on the Web site for Flash MX security.

COMMUNICATING WITH EXTERNAL FLASH MOVIES

Navigating Timelines of loaded movies

After external movies are loaded into your original movie, you can access their Timelines and control when and where the playback head moves. If you thought that navigation between movie-clip Timelines was complex, just think how intricate navigation can become with multiple movies, each containing its own movie clips!

Flash provides a straightforward way of targeting loaded movies and their Timelines to minimize confusion. Because loaded movies reside on different levels, Flash uses the term _level1 to refer to the movie in level 1, _level2 to refer to the movie in level 2, and so on. Movies that are loaded into movie clips simply take on their instance name, so targeting those loaded movies means just targeting movie clips. If loaded movies have movie clips themselves, use dot syntax to drill down the Timeline hierarchy as you do with movie clips on the root Timeline. For example, _level2.train_mc.wheels_mc is the target path for the movie clip named wheels_mc inside the movie clip named train_mc that resides in the loaded movie on level 2.

To target a loaded movie:

1. As in the preceding tasks, create an animation to serve as an external Flash movie, and export it as a SWF file.

2. Open a new Flash document.

3. Create a button, drag an instance of it from the Library to the Stage, and give it a name in the Property Inspector.

4. In the first frame of the main Timeline, create an onRelease event handler for the button.

5. Assign the action loadMovieNum to the button event handler, specifying the external SWF file and a number higher than zero for its level (**Figure 6.47**).

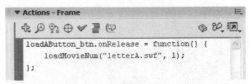

Figure 6.47 The loadMovieNum action assigned to the button called loadAButton_btn puts letterA.swf in level 1.

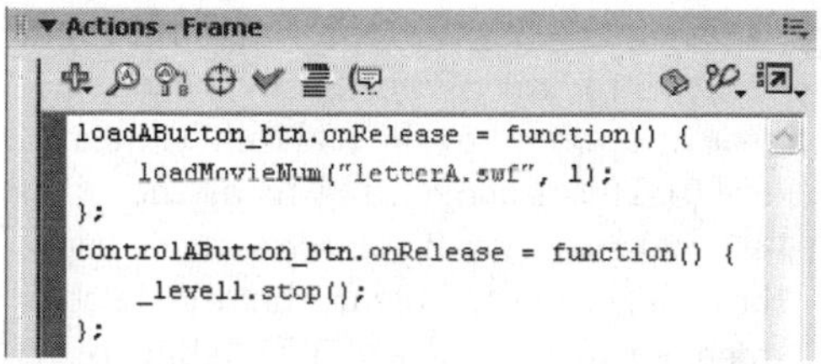

Figure 6.48 The stop() method acts on the movie in level 1.

6. Drag another instance of the button onto the Stage, and give it a name in the Property Inspector.

   This button will control the Timeline of the loaded movie.

7. In the first frame of the main Timeline, create an onRelease event handler for this second button.

8. On a new line within the onRelease event, enter _level and then the level number followed by a period.

9. Choose Built-in Classes > Movie > MovieClip > Methods > stop (**Figure 6.48**).

   The statement stops the playhead of the movie in the specified level.

10. Publish your movie, and place the SWF and its HTML in the same directory as the external SWF file.

11. Play the movie containing the buttons in Flash Player or a browser.

   The first button loads the external SWF in the specified level. The second button targets that level and stops the playback head. ✈

Defining the root Timeline for loaded movies

When working with loaded movies, understanding which Timeline the word _root refers to is crucial to constructing accurate target paths. In Chapter 5, you learned that if you wanted to target a movie clip on the main Timeline from within another movie clip on the main Timeline, you would write _root.instanceName. That target path tells Flash to jump out of the movie clip's Timeline to the root Timeline and find the instanceName instance. If this movie was played on its own, everything would work as you would expect. However, once you begin working with multiple movies using loadMovie or loadMovieNum, you may come across multiple _root references. Imagine that this movie is now loaded into a movie clip in a new file named main.swf. The _root in its target path now refers to the main Timeline of main.swf, and many of its actions that include _root in the target path will fail.

The answer to this problem is to force _root to refer to the main Timeline of the loaded movie as opposed to the real root Timeline (level 0). This is achieved by using the _lockroot property. If you set a movie clip's _lockroot property to true, that movie clip's Timeline will act as the root Timeline for any movies loaded into it.

In the following example, you will load an external movie into a movie clip. The external movie contains ActionScript that refers to the root Timeline, so you will use the _lockroot property to force the external movie to reference the movie clip as the root Timeline to preserve its functionality.

To identify a movie clip as the root for loaded external SWF files:

1. Create a new movie with multiple movie clips on the main Timeline. In this example, the movie clips contain animation (**Figure 6.49**).

   This movie will be your external SWF that you will load into another Flash movie.

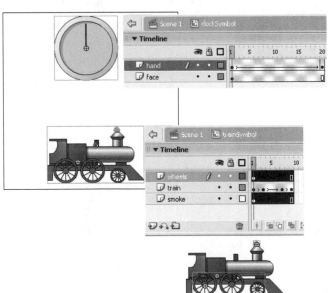

Figure 6.49 The clock_mc movie clip has an animation on its Timeline. The train_mc movie clip contains two nested movie clips, smoke_mc and wheels_mc.

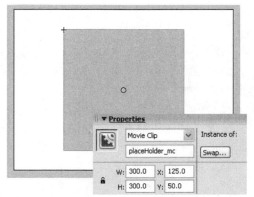

```
clock_mc.onRelease = function() {
    _root.train_mc.stop();
};
```

Figure 6.50 When you click on the clock_mc movie clip, the animation on the train_mc movie clip Timeline stops. Note that the target path before the stop action includes the _root keyword.

Figure 6.51 The registration point is at the upper-left corner for the movie clip named placeholder_mc.

```
loadButton_btn.onRelease = function(){
    loadMovie("anim.swf","placeHolder_mc");
}
```

Figure 6.52 When the loadButton_btn is clicked, the external SWF file called anim.swf will load into the movie clip called placeHolder_mc.

2. In the Property Inspector, give a name to each of your movie clips.

3. On the main Timeline, select the first frame and open the Actions panel.

4. Assign an onRelease event handler to one of your movie clips. Within the onRelease event handler, target the other movie clip to stop its animation, using _root in the target path (**Figure 6.50**).

5. Export your external movie as a SWF file.

6. In a new Flash document, create a movie clip with the registration point in the upper-left corner, place an instance of it on the Stage, and give it a name in the Property Inspector (**Figure 6.51**).
This movie clip will be your placeholder into which the external SWF will load.

7. Create a button symbol, drag an instance from the Library to the Stage, and give it a name in the Property Inspector.
This button will load the external SWF into your placeholder movie clip.

8. In the first frame of the main Timeline, create an onRelease event handler for the button.

9. Within the onRelease event handler, choose Global Functions > Browser/Network > loadMovie.

10. With your pointer between the parentheses, enter the name of the external SWF file followed by a comma and the target path of the movie-clip instance on the Stage (**Figure 6.52**).

11. Select the movie-clip instance on the Stage and open the Actions panel.

continues on next page

12. In the Actions panel, choose Global Functions > Movie Clip Control > onClipEvent.

13. Select load from the code hint drop-down menu.

14. On the next line, enter the keyword this followed by a period.

15. Choose Built-in Classes > Movie > MovieClip > Properties > _lockroot, and give it a Boolean value of true (**Figure 6.53**).

This movie clip will now act as the root Timeline for anything loaded into it.

16. Export your movie into the same directory as the external SWF that you created in step 1 and play it.

When you click the button, the external SWF loads into your placeholder movie clip. The functionality in the external SWF remains intact because you defined the placeholder movie clip to act as the root Timeline. (img)

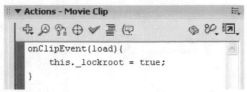

Figure 6.53 ActionScript assigned to the movie clip called placeholder_mc. Declaring _lockroot to be true forces it to be the _root Timeline for all movies loaded into it.

✔ Tip

■ In this task, you defined the placeholder movie clip to act as the root Timeline for loaded SWFs. If you have access to the FLA files of the loaded SWFs, you can also assign ActionScript to their main Timelines to force Flash to use them as the root Timelines. On the first keyframe, enter this._lockroot = true. The term _root will always refer to the main Timeline no matter what it is loaded into.

Communicating with External Images

Using the same actions that load external SWF files into your movie dynamically, you can load JPEG images dynamically. Use the action loadMovie or loadMovieNum to pull images into your movie at run time to reduce the size of your Flash movie and save download time. As is the case with external SWFs, keeping images separate from your Flash movie will make revisions quicker and easier because you can swap or change the images without messing with the actual Flash file.

Loaded images follow many of the same rules that loaded movies do, and those rules are worth repeating here:

◆ You can have only one image per level.

◆ Higher levels overlap lower levels.

◆ Images loaded into level 0 replace the original movie.

◆ The top-left corner of an image aligns with the top-left corner of the Stage or the registration point of a movie clip.

◆ An image loaded into a movie clip inherits its instance name and transformations.

To load an image in a level:

1. Create a button symbol, drag an instance to the Stage, and give it a name in the Property Inspector.

   This button will load a JPEG file into your movie dynamically.

2. Select the first frame of the main Timeline, and open the Actions panel.

3. Create an onRelease event handler for your button.

4. With your pointer within the onRelease event handler, choose Global Functions > Browser/Network > loadMovieNum.

   The loadMovieNum action appears within the onRelease event handler.

5. With your pointer between the parentheses, enter the path to the external JPEG file followed by a comma.

   The URL can be a relative path (such as /images/mypet/dog.jpg), so that Flash looks for the file relative to the current directory, or the URL can be an absolute path (such as http://www.mydomain.com/images/mypet/dog.jpg), so that Flash retrieves the file from any Web site.

   continues on next page

6. For the second parameter, enter a number higher than zero (**Figure 6.54**).

7. Publish your movie, and place your JPEG image in the correct directory so your Flash movie can find it.

When you click the button, Flash loads the external JPEG into a higher level. The top-left corner of the JPEG aligns with the top-left corner of the Stage (**Figure 6.55**).

To load an image in a movie clip:

1. Create a movie-clip symbol, drag an instance of it from the Library to the Stage, and give it a name in the Property Inspector.

2. Create a button symbol, drag an instance of it from the Library to the Stage, and give it a name in the Property Inspector.

This button will load a JPEG file into your movie clip dynamically.

3. In the first frame of the main Timeline, create an `onRelease` event handler for the button.

4. Choose Global Functions > Browser/Network > loadMovie.

The `loadMovie` action appears within the `onRelease` event handler.

5. With your pointer between the parentheses, enter the path to the external JPEG file followed by a comma.

6. For the second parameter, enter the target path for the movie-clip instance on the Stage (**Figure 6.56**).

```
▼ Actions - Frame
loadImageButton_btn.onRelease = function() {
    loadMovieNum("myPhoto.jpg", 1);
};
```

Figure 6.54 The loadMovieNum action can also be used to load JPEG files. Here, myPhoto.jpg is loaded in level 1 when the button is clicked.

Figure 6.55 The buttons on the bottom row load images that are kept external to your Flash movie. The top-left corner of each image aligns with the top-left corner of the Stage.

```
▼ Actions - Frame
loadImageButton_btn.onRelease = function() {
    loadMovie("myPhoto.jpg", "target");
};
```

Figure 6.56 The file myPhoto.jpg will be loaded into the movie clip called target when the button is clicked.

Target movie clip

myPhoto.JPG in
target movie clip

Figure 6.57 For precise placement of your loaded JPEG files, load them into movie clips, which you can position. This movie clip is empty, meaning that it contains no graphics or animation and simply acts as a shell to receive your loaded JPG files.

7. Publish your movie, and place your JPEG image in the correct directory so your Flash movie can find it.

When you click the button that you created, Flash loads the external JPEG into the movie clip. The top-left corner of the image aligns with the registration point of the movie clip. The image replaces all the movie-clip graphics and inherits all the characteristics of the movie clip, such as position, scale, rotation, instance name, and color effect (**Figure 6.57**).

To remove or replace a loaded image:

◆ To remove an image, use the action `unloadMovieNum` and choose a level, or use the action `unloadMovie` and choose a target.

◆ To replace an image, use the action `loadMovie` or `loadMovieNum` and load another JPEG file into the same level or movie clip. The new JPEG will replace the old one.

✔ Tip

■ Flash cannot load progressive JPEG files.

Communicating With External Video

In Chapter 2 you learned how to embed and play video from a variety of formats (AVI, MOV, MPEG) in Flash. However, embedded video has a length restriction (16,000 frames, or approximately 8.5 minutes of 30 fps video). Also, embedded video does not truly stream. It only streams because the main Timeline of a SWF streams. If an embedded video is inside a movie clip, the entire movie clip must download before playing. By dynamically loading external video, you can bypass these problems and make your Flash project more modular by separating download-on-demand content from interface elements (in the same way that loading external SWFs or JPGs can). Using external video is also free from the restriction that embedded video must have the same frame rate as its container Flash movie. So you can have a 12 fps Flash movie but still be able to show a 30 fps video.

Loading external video requires that your video be in the FLV (Flash Video) file format. The FLV format was previously used exclusively with communication applications, such as the Flash Communications Server. With Flash MX 2004, you now have the ability to progressively download an external FLV file without the Flash Communication Server.

To create an FLV file, you convert an existing video file to an FLV in one of three ways. You can do so from within Flash, from within Sorenson Squeeze, or from a third-party video application with Flash MX 2004 Professional.

Once you have an FLV file, use a Net-Connection and a NetStream object to load the video stream into Flash. The NetConnection object provides the measures to play back an FLV file from your local drive or Web address while the NetStream object makes the actual connection and tells Flash to play the video. In order to "receive" the streaming video, you must also create an Embedded Video symbol in your Library and place an instance on the Stage where you want the video to appear.

To create an FLV file from Flash:

1. In Flash, choose File > Import > Import to Library to open the Import dialog box.

2. Select the video file that you want to convert to the FLV format and click OK. The Video Import Wizard dialog box appears.

3. If you are importing a QuickTime MOV file, select Embed video and then click Next.

4. In the next set of options, choose Import the entire video, or if you wish, you can edit your video first (see Chapter 2 for a detailed discussion of the Video Import Wizard options). Click Next.

Figure 6.58
The imported video
is stored in your
Library.

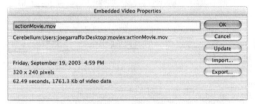

Figure 6.59 The Embedded Video Properties dialog box displays information about the embedded video and gives you options to update, import, and export.

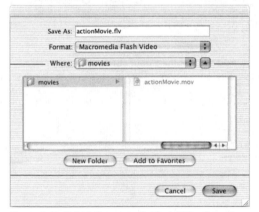

Figure 6.60 Select Macromedia Flash Video from the Format pull-down menu, and save your FLV file.

Figure 6.61 The original video (QuickTime format at right) is converted to an FLV format (at left). You can import FLV files into Flash without going through the Video Import Wizard, or you can load FLV files dynamically.

5. In the final set of options, choose a Compression profile and Advanced settings if you would like to modify your video (see Chapter 2). Click Finish.

   Flash imports your video file and stores it in the Library (**Figure 6.58**).

6. Open your Library and double-click the video icon or the preview window.

   or

   Select the video symbol in the Library; then, from the Library window's Options menu, choose Properties.

   The Embedded Video Properties dialog box appears, showing the symbol name, its properties, and the original file's location (**Figure 6.59**).

7. Click Export.

8. Choose a destination folder and name, and select Macromedia Flash Video (**Figure 6.60**).

9. Click Save.

   A new FLV file is created from your imported video file. The compression settings and all of the editing or modifications you chose in the Video Import Wizard are included in this FLV. You can import this FLV into another Flash document without having to go through the Video Import Wizard again, or you can use this FLV as an external file to be dynamically loaded into a Flash movie (**Figure 6.61**).

Creating FLV Files with Sorenson Squeeze

You can create FLV files in a variety of ways. Exporting embedded video files from Flash as described in the example task is the easiest, most basic method. However, a higher-quality professional-level compression is available when you create FLV files from within Sorenson Squeeze, a stand-alone application. The steps are straightforward, as outlined below:

1. In Squeeze, open the movie file that you want to convert to a Flash Video File (FLV).

2. From the preset menu, located above the preview window, select the Flash FLV Output icon (**Figure 6.62**).

3. Select a preset setting size, or you can customize an FLV by choosing one of the four icons above the Output Files window (**Figure 6.63**).

4. Click the Squeeze It button to create your FLV files.

For more information on Sorenson Squeeze, visit www.sorenson.com.

Figure 6.62 Select the Flash FLV Output button from the preset menu.

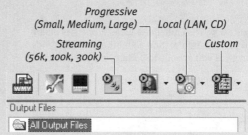

Figure 6.63 Select the output options that best meet your needs, or customize the file.

Creating FLV Files from QuickTime Pro (Flash MX 2004 Professional users only)

If you are using Flash MX 2004 Professional, you can use the Flash FLV Exporter, which enables many third-party video applications to export the FLV format. Avid Xpress/Media Composer, Adobe After Effects, Apple Final Cut Pro, Apple QuickTime Pro, Discreet Cleaner, and Anystream Agility are some of the applications that are supported. You can use the professional video editing tools in these applications to prepare your video and then export an FLV file for use as streaming video in a Flash movie. The following example demonstrates how easy it is to export an FLV from QuickTime Pro.

1. Open your video file in QuickTime Pro.

2. From the File menu, choose Export (**Figure 6.64**).

3. From the Export drop-down menu, select Movie to Macromedia Flash Video (FLV) (**Figure 6.65**).

4. To customize your FLV settings, click the Options button.

5. Adjust the Quality, Frames per second, Width, Height, and Audio Bitrate settings (**Figure 6.66**).

6. Click Save to export your FLV file.

Figure 6.64 Select File > Export while inside of the QuickTime Player.

Figure 6.65 From the Export drop-down menu, choose Movie to Macromedia Flash Video (FLV).

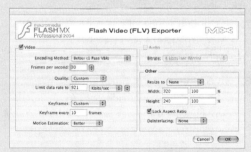

Figure 6.66 Flash MX 2004 Professional users can customize their export settings using their favorite video editing programs.

To dynamically load external video:

1. Convert your video file to an FLV file as described previously.

2. Open a new Flash document, with its Stage size large enough to accommodate the FLV file that you just created.

3. Open the Library. From the Options menu, choose New Video (**Figure 6.67**).

   A new Embedded Video symbol appears in your Library.

4. Place an instance of the embedded video on the Stage.

5. Modify its width and height to match the external FLV file that will be loaded in, and give it an instance name in the Property Inspector (**Figure 6.68**).

   Your external FLV will play inside this video instance.

6. Create a button symbol, drag an instance of it from the Library to the Stage, and give it a name in the Property Inspector.

   You will assign actions to this button to load the FLV during playback.

7. In the first frame of the main Timeline, create an onRelease event handler for the button.

8. On the next line of the onRelease event, enter a variable name followed by an equals sign; choose Built-in Classes > Media > NetConnection > new NetConnection (**Figure 6.69**).

   A new NetConnection object is instantiated.

9. On the next line, enter the name of the NetConnection object you just created followed by a period; choose Built-in Classes > Media > NetConnection > Methods > connect.

Figure 6.67 Choose New Video from the Options menu.

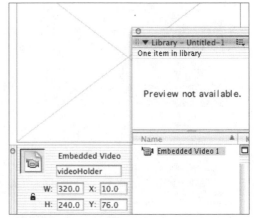

Figure 6.68 An Embedded Video "placeholder" named videoHolder is placed on the Stage. The instance looks like a square with an x inside of it.

```
vid_btn.onRelease = function() {
    myVideo_nc = new NetConnection();
}
```

Figure 6.69 A new NetConnection object named myVideo_nc is created.

10. With your pointer between the parentheses, enter the keyword null.

The parameter null tells Flash that it is not connecting through the Flash Communication Server but instead to expect a download from the local hard drive or a Web address.

11. On the next line, enter a new name variable followed by an equals sign; choose Built-in Classes > Media > NetStream > new NetStream.

12. With your pointer between the parentheses for the NetStream object, enter the name of your NetConnection object that you created in step 8 (**Figure 6.70**).

A new NetStream object is instantiated using your NetConnection object as its parameter.

13. Enter the instance name of the Embedded Video placeholder that you placed on the Stage followed by a period.

14. Choose Built-in Classes > Media > Video > Methods > attachVideo.

15. For the attachVideo parameter, enter the video source. In this case, enter the name of the new NetStream object that you created in step 12.

16. On the next line, enter the name of the NetStream object that you created in step 12 followed by a period.

17. Choose Built-in Classes > Media > NetStream > Methods > play.

18. As the parameter for the play() method, enter the name of the external FLV file that you wish to play on the Stage (**Figure 6.71**).

Make sure that the FLV filename is surrounded by quotation marks.

19. Publish your movie, and place the SWF file in the same directory as the FLV file you created earlier.

When you click the button, Flash attaches your external FLV file to the instance of the video symbol on the Stage and video will begin to stream. ⓐ

```
vid_btn.onRelease = function() {
    myVideo_nc = new NetConnection();
    myVideo_nc.connect(null);
    newStream_ns = new NetStream(myVideo_nc);
    videoHolder.attachVideo(newStream_ns);
    newStream_ns.play("kayak.flv");
};
```

Figure 6.71 The external FLV file named kayak.flv (top) loads into the videoHolder instance on the Stage and plays.

```
vid_btn.onRelease = function() {
    myVideo_nc = new NetConnection();
    myVideo_nc.connect(null);
    newStream_ns = new NetStream(myVideo_nc)
}
```

Figure 6.70 The NetConnection object is used as the parameter for the instantiation of a new NetStream object.

Communicating Between Two Movies

So far, you've learned how a single Flash movie can communicate outside itself—to retrieve a link on the Web, to incorporate another SWF, or to load an image or video. But can one Flash movie communicate with another entirely independent Flash movie? The answer is yes, with the help of a LocalConnection object. A LocalConnection object enables communication between two separate Flash movies as long as they are running from the same machine (server). Instructions from one movie can control the appearance, behavior, or interactivity of another. Imagine, for example, creating a frameset that contains a Flash movie in a top frame and a Flash movie in a bottom frame. The movie in the top frame could have buttons or pull-down menus that control the movie in the bottom frame. You could also build a Flash-based laboratory simulation in one browser window and keep a Flash lab notebook in another. Information from the simulation could be sent to the notebook and recorded automatically as the experiment progresses.

Using LocalConnection requires that you create a LocalConnection object in the sender movie as well as the receiver movie. Create the new object in both movies with the new constructor function, as follows:

```
myLocalConnection = new LocalConnection()
```

Next, in the sender movie, use the `send()` method to send the name of your message and the name of a function you want the receiver movie to perform:

```
myLocalConnection.send("incomingMessage",
"onReceive")
```

Finally, close the connection:

```
myLocalConnection.close()
```

In the receiver movie, you must define a function that will be performed when that movie receives the message from the sender movie. After the function is established, use the `connect()` method to listen for the name of the message. In the receiver movie, the code would look something like this:

```
myLocalConnection = new LocalConnection()
myLocalConnection.onReceive = function(){
animation_mc.play(); }
myLocalConnection.connect
("incomingMessage")
```

When this receiver movie receives the message called incomingMessage, the movie clip called *animation_mc* will play.

```
myButton_btn.onRelease = function() {
    myLocalConnection_lc = new LocalConnection();
};
```

Figure 6.72 The name of your LocalConnection object is myLocalConnection_lc.

```
myButton_btn.onRelease = function() {
    myLocalConnection_lc = new LocalConnection();
    myLocalConnection_lc.send("incomingMessage", "onReceive");
};
```

Figure 6.73 This send() method sends the message identified as incomingMessage and makes the receiver movie perform the function assigned to onReceive.

```
myButton_btn.onRelease = function() {
    myLocalConnection_lc = new LocalConnection();
    myLocalConnection_lc.send("incomingMessage", "onReceive");
    myLocalConnection_lc.close();
};
```

Figure 6.74 Close the connection.

To create the sender movie:

1. Create a button symbol, place an instance of it on the Stage, and give it a name in the Property Inspector.

2. In the first frame of the main Timeline, create an **onRelease** event handler for the button.

   This button will tell a movie clip in another Flash movie (the receiver movie) to play.

3. Create a new LocalConnection object by entering a name followed by an equals sign; choose Built-in Classes > Movie > LocalConnection > new LocalConnection (**Figure 6.72**).

4. On the next line, enter the name of your LocalConnection object followed by a period. Choose Built-in Classes > Movie > LocalConnection > Methods > send.

5. For the parameters of the **send()** method, enter "incomingMessage" and "onReceive". Put quotation marks around both parameters, and separate them with commas (**Figure 6.73**).

6. On the next line, enter the name of your LocalConnection object followed by a period. Choose Built-in Classes > Movie > LocalConnection > Methods > close (**Figure 6.74**).

   After sending a connection, you should close it, thereby disconnecting the LocalConnection object.

COMMUNICATING BETWEEN TWO MOVIES

245

To create the receiver movie:

1. In a new Flash document, create a movie clip that contains an animation.

   The movie clip should have a **stop** action in the first frame of its Timeline.

2. Drag an instance of the movie clip to the Stage, and name it in the Property Inspector.

   This movie clip will be the target of a function in this movie. When the incoming message is received, the function will instruct the movie clip to play.

3. Select the first frame of the main Timeline, and open the Actions panel.

4. In the Script pane, enter `myLocalConnection_lc = new LocalConnection()` to instantiate a new LocalConnection object.

5. Next, enter `myLocalConnection_lc`, then a period, and then the name of the incoming message from the sender movie. Enter an equals sign and then choose Statements > User-Defined Functions > function (Esc + fn) (**Figure 6.75**).

   You can think of the name of the incoming message as being similar to the name of an event. When the message is received, the function is executed. The final form of the function statement, in fact, is identical to an event handler.

6. Within the function statement curly braces, enter the name of your movie clip, a period, and then the method `play()`.

   This is the receiver movie's response to the incoming message (**Figure 6.76**).

```
myLocalConnection_lc = new LocalConnection();
myLocalConnection_lc.onReceive = function() {
};
```

Figure 6.75 Create the function that responds to the incoming message.

```
myLocalConnection_lc = new LocalConnection();
myLocalConnection_lc.onReceive = function() {
    animation_mc.play();
};
```

Figure 6.76 When this receiver movie gets the message from the sender, it will play its movie clip called animation_mc.

```
myLocalConnection_lc = new LocalConnection();
myLocalConnection_lc.onReceive = function() {
    animation_mc.play();
};
myLocalConnection_lc.connect("incomingMessage");
```

Figure 6.77 The connect() method opens the connection for the message called incomingMessage from the sender movie.

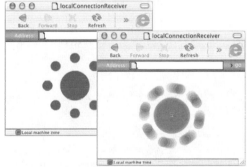

Figure 6.78 The sender movie (top) sends a message when the user clicks the button. The receiver movie in a separate browser window (bottom) responds by playing the animation.

7. On a new line outside the function statement, enter myLocalConnection_lc and then a period, and then choose Built-in Classes > Movie > LocalConnection > Methods > connect.

8. Between the parentheses of the method, enter the name of the incoming message within quotation marks as the parameter. In this example, the parameter is "incomingMessage" (**Figure 6.77**).

The connect() method opens the connection for your LocalConnection object. 🐾

To test communication between the sender and receiver movies:

◆ Publish both movies, and play them in separate browser windows.

When you click the button in the sender movie, a LocalConnection object is created and a message is sent. The receiver movie connects to the message and, as instructed by the sender movie, executes the function. As a result, the animation in the receiver movie plays (**Figure 6.78**).

Making a sender movie instruct a receiver movie to perform a function is useful, but it's even more useful to make the sender movie instruct a receiver movie to perform a function with certain parameters. Passing parameters between two independent movies is not only possible, but also allows customized communication. Parameters determine the way the function is performed, much as they determine the way methods are performed. (Learn more about functions and parameters in Chapter 11 and return here to see how they are used with the LocalConnection object.) Sending parameters from the sender movie can make the response in the receiver movie vary according to the interaction in the sender movie.

In this demonstration, you'll create an input text field in the sender movie and a dynamic text field in the receiver movie. You can make the sender movie pass text entered in its input text field to the receiver movie, which displays the text in its dynamic text field.

To pass parameters from the sender to the receiver movie:

1. Using the sender and receiver movies you created in the preceding tasks, delete the button in the sender movie and the movie clip in the receiver movie.

2. In both movies, select the Text tool and create a text field on the Stage.

3. In the Property Inspector, choose input text for the sender movie and dynamic text for the receiver movie, and give them names (**Figure 6.79**).

   The name of a text field, like the names of buttons and movie clips, lets you target the text field and control it.

4. In the sender movie, change the onRelease event handler to an onEnterFrame event handler scoped to the main Timeline (**Figure 6.80**).

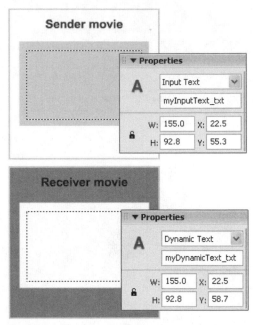

Figure 6.79 The input text field in the sender movie is called myInputText_txt. The dynamic text field in the receiver movie is called myDynamicText_txt.

```
_root.onEnterFrame = function() {
    mySender_lc = new LocalConnection();
    mySender_lc.send("incomingMessage", "onReceive");
    mySender_lc.close();
};
```

Figure 6.80 The onEnterFrame event is triggered continuously, so this message is sent to the receiver movie continuously.

```
_root.onEnterFrame = function() {
    mySender_lc = new LocalConnection();
    mySender_lc.send("incomingMessage", "onReceive", myInputText_txt.text);
    mySender_lc.close();
};
```

Figure 6.81 Flash passes the parameter myInputText_txt.text with its message.

```
myReceiver_lc = new LocalConnection();
myReceiver_lc.onReceive = function(myParameter) {
    myDynamicText_txt.text = myParameter;
};
myReceiver_lc.connect("incomingMessage");
```

Figure 6.82 In the receiver movie, the function's parameter is called myParameter.

Figure 6.83 The final scripts for the sender movie (top) and receiver movie (bottom). Text in the sender movie's input text field appears in the receiver movie's dynamic text field.

5. Place your cursor after the last parameter in the parentheses of the send() method. Add a comma; then enter myInputText_txt.text (**Figure 6.81**).

This parameter and any additional parameters in the send() method are sent to the receiver movie. Here, the contents of the text field called myInputText_txt are sent as a parameter to the receiver movie.

6. Open the receiver movie, and delete the action within the current function statement.

7. Within the parentheses of the function statement, enter myParameter as a name to identify the incoming parameter.

8. In a new line within the function's curly braces, enter the following:

myDynamicText_txt.text=myParameter;

myParameter is the name you entered in step 7, and myTextField_txt is the name of the dynamic text field on the Stage (**Figure 6.82**).

The receiver movie receives a single parameter, called myParameter, used in the actions within the function. Here, the parameter is assigned to the contents of the dynamic text field called myDynamicText_txt.

9. Test your movies by playing them in separate browser windows.

When you enter text in the sender movie, it is also displayed in the receiver movie because the text is being passed as a parameter (**Figure 6.83**).

Using Projectors and the fscommand Action

Most of the time, you'll play your Flash movie in a browser over the Web. Flash was conceived and developed to deliver content this way. But Flash also provides a way to create *projectors*—self-executable applications that don't require the browser or Flash Player for playback. On either a Windows or Mac system, you can publish projectors for either platform. In Windows, the file extension is .exe, and on the Mac, the word *projector* is appended to the filename. These projector files are larger than the normal exported SWF files, but they contain everything you need to play the content you create, including graphics, animation, sound, and interactivity. Use projectors to deliver your Flash content on transportable media such as CD-ROMs— an ideal scenario for portfolios, presentations, or marketing material.

Playback of Flash content through projectors is different in one respect: Projectors don't use an HTML page that contains tags or instructions to tell it how to be displayed. Will playback be full screen? Can the window be scalable? You have to give the projector answers to these playback questions rather than rely on an accompanying HTML page. To set or change these kinds of display parameters, use the fscommand action, which has just a few simple parameters for projectors, as detailed in **Table 6.3**.

Table 6.3

fscommand Parameters for Projectors

COMMAND	DESCRIPTION AND PARAMETERS
fullscreen	Allows playback at full screen and prevents resizing (true/false).
allowscale	Makes the graphics scale when the window is resized (true/false). The scaling mode is always set to showAll.
trapallkeys	Allows the movie, rather than Flash Player, to capture key presses (true/false)
showmenu	Displays the top menu bar. Also shows the control menu when you Control-click (Mac) or right-click (Windows) the movie (true/false).
exec	Opens an executable file (path to file). The target file must be in a folder called fscommand for security reasons.
quit	Quits the projector.

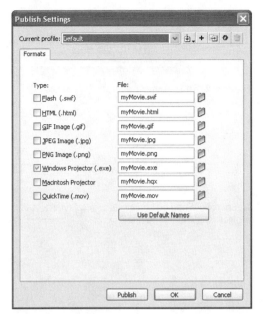

Figure 6.84 The Formats tab of the Publish Settings dialog box. Check the check boxes to choose the Windows and/or Macintosh projectors.

To publish a projector:

1. Open your Flash file.

2. Choose File > Publish Settings (Opt-Shift-F12 Mac, Shift-Ctrl-F12 Windows). The Publish Settings dialog box appears.

3. In the Formats tab, deselect all the check boxes except the Macintosh Projector and/or Windows Projector check boxes (**Figure 6.84**).

4. If you want to name your projector something other than the default name, change it in the field provided.

   Clicking the Use Default Names button at the bottom will restore all the file-names to their default names.

5. Click Publish.

   Your projector file is saved in the same folder as the Flash file.

   or

1. Open your SWF file in Flash Player.

2. Choose File > Create Projector.

3. Choose a filename and destination, and click Save.

   If you choose to create a projector from Flash Player, you can create projectors only for the operating system in which Flash Player is opened.

✔ Tips

■ The getURL action, when used in a projector, launches your default browser to open any Web link.

■ The preferred way to create projectors is through the Publish settings command (File > Publish Settings). Flash will not compress the projector if you make it from Flash Player. In larger files, you can see a big difference.

USING PROJECTORS AND THE FSCOMMAND ACTION

To use fscommand to define playback options in a projector:

1. Select the first keyframe of a Flash movie you want to publish as a projector, and open the Actions panel.

2. Choose Global Functions > Browser/Network > fscommand (Esc + fs).

   The fscommand action appears in the Script pane (**Figure 6.85**).

3. With your pointer between the parentheses, enter fullscreen surrounded by quotation marks; enter a comma and the value of true (**Figure 6.86**).

   The first parameter of the fscommand action is the command and the second parameter is its parameters. So this statement sets fullscreen to true.

4. On the next line, again choose Global Functions > Browser/Network > fscommand (Esc + fs).

5. With your pointer between the parentheses, enter showmenu surrounded by quotation marks; enter a comma and the value of false

   The showmenu command is set to false.

6. Create a button, place an instance of that button on the Stage, and give the instance a name in the Property Inspector.

7. Select the first frame of the main Timeline, and open the Actions panel.

8. Create an onRelease event handler for your button.

9. Within the onRelease event handler, choose Global Functions > Browser/Network > fscommand.

Figure 6.85 The parameters for the fscommand.

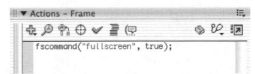

Figure 6.86 When fullscreen is true, playback of the projector fills the entire monitor.

USING PROJECTORS AND THE FSCOMMAND ACTION

```
fscommand("fullscreen", true);
fscommand("showmenu", false);
quitButton_btn.onRelease = function() {
    fscommand("quit");
};
```

Figure 6.87 The command fscommand ("quit") assigned to a button closes the projector.

10. With your pointer between the parentheses, enter quit surrounded by quotation marks (**Figure 6.87**).

   When you click this button, the projector will quit

11. Publish your movie as a projector.

12. Double-click your projector to play it.

   The Flash projector plays at full screen, effectively preventing the window from being scaled. The menu options are disabled when you right-click (Windows) or Control-click (Mac) the movie. When you click the button, the projector quits.

✔ Tip

■ You can also use the Stage properties (discussed later in this chapter) to define some of the ways a projector displays its Flash content. You can define the scale mode for your projector, for example, by setting the Stage.scaleMode property. The fscommand will always override the Stage properties if a conflict occurs, however.

Communicating with the Printer

Flash can send information directly to a printer to output text and graphics, circumventing the Web browser's print function. Printing Flash content is handled by the PrintJob class. With the PrintJob class, you can specify a level or movie clip to print, and you can also control which areas should be printed for the specific level or movie clip. The printable areas do not even have to be visible on the Stage. Graphics and text in any frame in the main Timeline of the movie or any frame of a movie clip's Timeline are available to the printer, making the PrintJob object more than a simple tool for making hard copies of what is visible on the computer screen.

Imagine, for example, that you have documents in external SWF files. You easily could load a particular movie into a movie clip or into another level with the action `loadMovie` and then print selected frames from that loaded movie.

In Chapter 10, you'll learn about input text and dynamic text; you can enter information on the keyboard and display text dynamically. You can combine this capability with order forms or receipts, resulting in customized documents that you can send to the printer.

The first step in printing requires that you instantiate a new PrintJob object. Then, you can call the `start()` method. The `start()` method spools the print job and opens the print dialog box. The "spooler" is simply the part of your computer's operating system that manages printing. The next step is to identify the content you wish to print with the method `addPage()`.

The `addPage()` method takes four parameters, but only the first is required. The parameters appear in the method as `addPage(target, printArea, options, frameNumber)`.

- `target` identifies the level or the movie clip to print.

- `printArea` defines the printable area.

- `options` specifies whether or not you want to print bitmaps.

- `frameNumber` identifies a specific frame to print.

Finally, you must call the `send()` method, which sends the spooled pages to the printer.

Figure 6.88 Content (this bicycle picture and label) is placed on Frame 1 of the root Timeline.

▼ Actions - Frame

```
printAll_btn.onRelease = function() {
    myPrintJob_pj = new PrintJob();
};
```

Figure 6.89 A new PrintJob object named myPrintJob_pj is created.

▼ Actions - Frame

```
printAll_btn.onRelease = function() {
    myPrintJob_pj = new PrintJob();
    myPrintJob_pj.start();
};
```

Figure 6.90 The start() method opens the printer dialog box.

Specifying the target to print

The first parameter of the addPage() method identifies the target to print. The target can be either a level or a movie clip. Enter a number to specify the level number, or enter the target path in quotation marks to specify a named movie clip on the Stage. In either case, if no other parameters of addPage() are defined, the entire Stage of the current frame will print.

To print all content in a specific level:

1. In a new Flash document, create the graphics you want to be available to the printer on keyframe 1 (**Figure 6.88**).

   You can use multiple layers and all layers will still print.

2. Create a button, drag an instance of this button to the Stage, and name it in the Property Inspector.

   You will assign ActionScript to this button to print the contents of the Stage.

3. Create an onRelease event handler for your button.

4. Within the onRelease event handler, enter a variable name followed by an equals sign. Choose Built-in Classes > Movie > PrintJob > new PrintJob (**Figure 6.89**).

   A new PrintJob object has been instantiated.

5. On the next line, enter the name of your PrintJob object followed by a period.

6. Choose Built-in Classes > Movie > PrintJob > Methods > start (**Figure 6.90**).

   This will spool the print job to the user's operating system and also open the print dialog box.

   continues on next page

COMMUNICATING WITH THE PRINTER

7. On the next line, enter the `PrintJob` object name followed by a period.

8. Choose Built-in Classes > Movie > PrintJob > Methods > addPage.

   Each printed page requires a separate `addPage()` method statement.

9. Between the parentheses for `addPage()`, enter a 0.

   The first parameter of the `addPage()` method identifies the target to print. The number 0 refers to the level, so this statement prints all the content on level 0.

10. On the next line, enter the name for the `PrintJob` object followed by a period. Choose Built-in Classes > Movie > PrintJob > Methods > send.

    The `send()` method sends the pages from the spooler to the printer.

11. On the next line, enter the keyword `delete` followed by a space and your `PrintJob` object name (**Figure 6.91**).

    As the last line of the script, make sure to delete the `PrintJob` object to free up memory.

12. Test your movie.

    When the button is clicked, Flash will spool everything that resides on level 0 and send it to the printer.

```
▼ Actions - Frame
⊕ ⌕ ⇆ ⊕ ✔ ☰ ⟨⟩
printAll_btn.onRelease = function() {
    myPrintJob_pj = new PrintJob();
    myPrintJob_pj.start();
    myPrintJob_pj.addPage(0);
    myPrintJob_pj.send();
    delete myPrintJob_pj;
};
```

Figure 6.91 After the PrintJob object spools the requested page and sends it to the printer, it will be deleted to free up memory.

✔ Tip

■ To calculate how the area of a graphic translates to the size of the printed piece, multiply the pixel dimensions by the screen resolution, which is 72 ppi (pixels per inch). So an 8.5-by-11-inch sheet of paper is equivalent to a Stage size of 612 pixels (8.5 inches x 72 ppi) by 792 pixels (11 inches x 72 ppi). Then you must take into account the margins for the actual printable area.

Specifying the printable area

The addPage() method can also control what areas of the Stage you want to print. While its first parameter controls the target, its second parameter, printArea, controls the x- and y-coordinates of the Stage to print. The second parameter for addPage() is in the form {xMin: value, xMax: value, yMin: value, yMax: value}. You provide coordinates for each of the values. For the printable area, xMin represents the left edge, xMax represents the right edge, yMin represents the top edge, and yMax represents the bottom edge. For example, the statement

myPrintJob_pj.addPage (0, {xMin: 50, xMax: 150, yMin: 10, yMax: 110})

identifies a 100-by-100-pixel area with the top-left corner at (50,10) at level 0 to print (**Figure 6.92**). If the printArea parameter isn't defined, then the default is to print the entire contents of the target.

✔ Tip

■ Any objects existing outside of the Stage will show up on print. To restrict the print area to the size of the default Stage, provide xMin, xMax, yMin, and yMax parameters similar to the following:

myPrintJob_pj.addPage(0, {xMin: 0, xMax: 550, yMin: 0, yMax: 400})

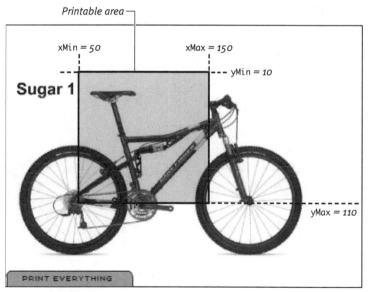

Figure 6.92 The gray square marks the printable area. This is defined in the second parameter for the addPage() method.

Printing bitmap graphics with transparencies or color effects

Graphics that contain bitmaps with alpha or color effects won't print properly unless you identify them to print as bitmaps. To do so, you must specify a third parameter for the addPage() method. The third parameter takes the form {printAsBitmap: Boolean}, where Boolean is either true or false. For example, the statement

myPrintJob_pj.addPage (0, {xMin: 50, xMax: 150, yMin: 10, yMax: 110}, {printAsBitmap:true})

identifies a specific area to print on level 0 as a bitmap. Bitmap printing preserves alpha and color effects but results in a lower quality of print.

Printing selected frames

If you specified a target path for the first parameter of the addPage() method instead of a level, then Flash would print the current frame of the targeted movie clip. So the statement, myPrintJob_pj.addPage(myMC_mc) would identify the current frame of the movie clip called myMC_mc to print. If you want to print only a selected frame of your movie clip, then you must specify a frame number as the fourth parameter of the addPage() method.

If you want to specify a frame number as the fourth parameter but not have to bother with specifying the second or third parameters (and leave them at their default settings), then you can use the keyword null. So the statement myPrintJob_pj.addPage(myMC_mc, null, null, 4) identifies Frame 4 of the movie clip myMC_mc to print.

To print a selected frame in a movie clip:

1. Continuing with the file from the preceding task, create a new movie clip that contains graphics and text in its second keyframe. Keep the first keyframe empty and add a stop() action to it (**Figure 6.93**).

   The movie clip's contents appear on its second frame, hidden from the viewer.

2. Return to the main Timeline, drag an instance of your movie clip to the Stage, and give the instance a name in the Property inspector.

3. Create another button, drag an instance of this button to the Stage, and name it in the Property inspector.

   This button will print the second (hidden) frame of your movie clip.

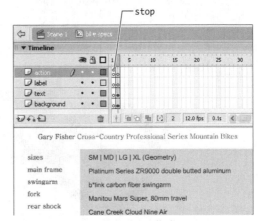

Figure 6.93 A new movie clip, called bikespecs_mc, contains the technical specs for the bike on its second keyframe. The stop action on the first frame of the Timeline keeps the contents hidden.

```
specsButton_btn.onRelease = function() {
    myPrintJob_pj = new PrintJob();
    myPrintJob_pj.start();
    myPrintJob_pj.addPage("bikespecs_mc", null, null, 2);
};
```

Figure 6.94 The addPage() method targets the second frame of the bikespecs_mc movie clip to print.

Figure 6.95 The bike specs are invisible to the user on the Stage (top) because the movie clip's first frame is empty. When the second button is clicked, the contents of the movie clip's second frame is sent to the printer (bottom).

4. Create an onRelease event handler for this button.

5. Within the onRelease event handler, add actions that instantiate a new PrintJob object, call the **start()** method, and call the addPage() method as described in the previous task.

6. For the parameters of the addPage() method, enter the target path of the movie clip in quotation marks, the keyword **null**, another keyword **null**, and finally the number 2. Separate the parameters by commas (**Figure 6.94**).

Flash identifies the second frame of the movie clip to print and uses default values for the second and third parameters.

7. Finally, call the **send()** method and then delete your PrintJob object as described in the previous task.

8. Test your movie.

When the button is clicked, Flash will retrieve the graphics, text, and any other information residing on the second keyframe of your movie clip and send it to the printer (**Figure 6.95**).

✔ Tips

■ If want to print more than one page, you can do so under a single print dialog box. Add a separate addPage() method for each page. The order that in which you list them in the Script pane is the order in which they will print.

■ You can use looping statements to easily print multiple frames of a Timeline. Substitute the frameNumber parameter in the addPage() method for a variable and increase its value each time you loop. You'll learn more about looping statements in Chapter 9.

COMMUNICATING WITH THE PRINTER

Printing in Flash Player 6

The PrintJob class offers many improvements over the older actions `print`, `printNum`, `printAsBitmap`, and `printAsBitmapNum`. However, if you are authoring for Flash Player 6, you must use those actions to print.

The actions `print` and `printNum` take two parameters. The first is the target path of a movie clip you wish to print (for `print`) or the level of the movie you wish to print (for `printNum`). The second is a modifier that determines how the content will print. The second parameter can be one of the following (be sure to include the quotation marks) (**Figure 6.96**):

♦ `"bmovie"` makes the bounding box of the frame marked with the label #B the print area.

♦ `"bframe"` scales each printable item to fit the maximum print area.

♦ `"bmax"` makes a composite bounding box of all the printable items and uses that area to print.

If you wish to print multiple frames of your Timeline, you can mark each keyframe to print by adding the label #P (**Figure 6.97**).

COMMUNICATING WITH THE PRINTER

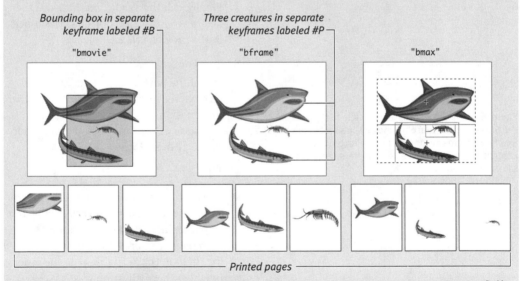

Figure 6.96 The three options for the second parameter of the `print` and `printAsBitMap` actions. `"bmovie"` (left) prints the marked frames within a defined bounding box in a frame labeled #B. `"bframe"` (center) prints the marked frames to fit the paper. `"bmax"` (right) prints the marked frames based on the composite sizes of all the objects.

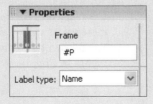

Figure 6.97 The #P label identifies individual keyframes to print.

Detecting the Movie's Playback Environment

Communicating with a movie's playback environment is important for knowing how your Flash movie will play and be seen by your audience. With that information, you can tailor the movie's display or provide warnings and recommendations to your viewers so they can better enjoy your movie. A viewer might have a lower screen resolution than you require to display the entire Stage of your movie, for example. You could load a different movie that fits, or you could modify the movie's display settings to allow

it to be scaled down. Detecting system capabilities and the kind of player hosting the movie is especially important as Flash content becomes more prevalent in devices such as cell phones, PDAs, and television set-top boxes.

Two classes can help you gather information about the playback environment: the System.capabilities class and the Stage class. The System.capabilities class can tell you about screen resolution, the operating system, the color capabilities, and many other useful properties. **Table 6.4** summarizes the System.capabilities properties.

Table 6.4

Properties of the System.capabilities Class	
PROPERTY	DESCRIPTION
language	Language that Flash Player supports, indicated by a two-letter code (en = English)
os	Operating system
manufacturer	Manufacturer of Flash Player
serverString	Information to send to a server containing the System.capabilities properties
isDebugger	Debugger capability
version	Flash Player version
playerType	The type of player playing the movie (e.g., standalone, plugIn, etc.)
hasAudio	Audio capability
hasMP3	MP3 decoder capability
hasAudioEncoder	Audio encoder capability
hasEmbeddedVideo	Embedded video support
hasPrinting	Printing support
hasVideoEncoder	Video encoder capability
screenResolutionX	Horizontal size of screen, in pixels
screenResolutionY	Vertical size of screen, in pixels
screenDPI	Screen resolution, in dots per inch
screenColor	Color capability (color, grayscale, or black and white)
pixelAspectRatio	Pixel aspect ratio of the screen
hasAccessibility	Accessibility capability

The Stage class can tell you about the display and layout of the movie, detect whether the Stage is resized, and modify the movie's properties in response. **Table 6.5** summarizes the properties of the Stage object.

Both the System.capabilities and the Stage classes can be used without a constructor function.

Figure 6.98 The `trace` statement returns the horizontal size of the computer screen in pixels.

To retrieve the properties of the user's system:

1. Select the first frame in the main Timeline of a new Flash document, and open the Actions panel.

2. Choose Global Functions > Miscellaneous Functions > trace.

   You will use the `trace` action to display information about your own system in the Output window in test mode.

3. Put your pointer between the parentheses, and choose Built-in Classes > Core > System > Objects > Capabilities > Properties > screenResolutionX (**Figure 6.98**).

   The `trace` action will display the horizontal resolution of your computer screen.

4. On the next line, create another `trace` action.

Table 6.5

Properties of the Stage Class	
PROPERTY	DESCRIPTION
align	Alignment of the Flash content ("T" = top, "B" = bottom, "R" = right, "L" = left, "TR" = top right, "TL" = top left, "BR" = bottom right, "BL" = bottom left, "C" = center)
height	Height of the Stage, in pixels (read-only)
width	Width of the Stage, in pixels (read-only)
scaleMode	Type of scaling display ("showAll", "noBorder", "exactFit", or "noScale")
showMenu	Shows the Control menu when you Control-click (Mac) or right-click (Windows) the movie (true/false)

Figure 6.99 The `trace` statement returns the vertical size of the computer screen in pixels.

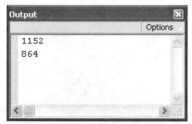

Figure 6.100 The Output window displays the `trace` actions. The monitor for this computer is 1152 x 864 pixels.

Figure 6.101 The `scaleMode` property controls how your Flash movie reacts to resizing. "showAll" displays all the content with no distortions or cropping.

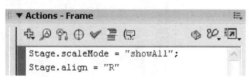

Figure 6.102 The `align` property controls where your Flash content appears in the window. "R" flushes the movie to the right edge.

5. Between the parentheses, choose Built-in Classes > Core > System > Objects > Capabilities > Properties > screenResolutionY (**Figure 6.99**).

The trace will display the vertical resolution of your computer screen.

6. Test your movie.

In the Output window that appears, the screen resolution of your monitor displays (**Figure 6.100**).

✔ Tip

■ Instead of `System.capabilities.version`, you can use the global variable `$version`. Both properties report the Flash Player version. The `$version` property is always listed in the Output window when you choose Debug > List Variables in test mode.

To modify the display mode of the movie:

1. Open an existing Flash movie that contains graphics on the Stage.

2. Select the main Timeline, and open the Actions panel.

3. Choose Built-in Classes > Movie > Stage > Properties > scaleMode.

The `Stage.scaleMode` property appears in the Script pane.

4. Place your pointer after `Stage.scaleMode`, and enter an equals sign followed by `"showAll"` (**Figure 6.101**).

5. Choose Built-in Classes > Movie > Stage > Properties > align.

The `Stage.align` property appears in the Script pane.

6. Place your pointer after `Stage.align` and enter an equals sign, followed by `"R"` (**Figure 6.102**).

continues on next page

7. Test your movie.

When you resize the test movie window, the graphics on the Stage resize so that one dimension (either height or width) always fills the window. This is the result of the `Stage.scaleMode = "showAll"` statement. The graphics are also aligned to the right side of the window as a result of the `Stage.align = "R"` statement. For a summary of the `scaleMode` property, see **Figure 6.103**.

✔ Tips

- Remember to include the quotation marks for the `align` and `scaleMode` properties, but don't include them for the `height`, `width`, and `showMenu` properties.

- The `width` and `height` properties of the Stage object will report different values depending on how `Stage.scaleMode` is defined. When `Stage.scaleMode = "noScale"`, `Stage.width` and `Stage.height` report the size of the window that contains the Flash movie. This result could be the size of the browser window, the projector, or the window in test movie mode. When `Stage.scaleMode` is set to `"exactFit"`, `"showAll"`, or `"noBorders"`, `Stage.width` and `Stage.height` report the size of the Flash Stage when it was created. The default scaling mode for all Flash movies is `"noScale"`.

- Avoid using the HTML page to hold your movie if you're going to modify the Stage properties to prevent conflicts with alignments and `scaleMode` settings.

"show all"

"noBorder"

"exactFit"

"noScale"

Figure 6.103 The `scaleMode` options. `"showAll"` (top) scales the movie to fit the window without any distortions or cropping to show all the content; this is the default mode. `"noBorder"` (top middle) scales the movie to fit the window without any distortions but will crop content to fill the window. In this mode, none of the background color shows. `"exactFit"` (bottom middle) scales the movie to fill the window on both the horizontal and vertical dimensions. In this mode, none of the background color shows but the content is distorted. `"noScale"` (bottom) keeps the movie at 100% no matter how big or small the window is. In this mode, the content is cropped if the window is too small and the background color shows if the window is too big.

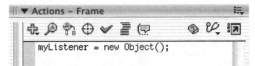

Figure 6.104 Create a new object called `myListener`.

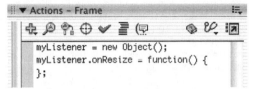

Figure 6.105 The onResize event handler.

Detection of the resizing of the Stage requires a listener object, just as the Key class does. Create a listener object from the generic Object category, and assign the event `onResize` with an anonymous function. After you register the listener with the Stage class with the method `addListener()`, you can detect and respond to Stage resizing.

To detect when the Stage is resized:

1. Select the first frame of the main Timeline, and open the Actions panel.

2. Enter the name of your listener object followed by an equals sign.

3. Choose Built-in Classes > Core > Object > new Object.

   A new object is instantiated for you to use as a listener (**Figure 6.104**).

4. On the next line, enter the name for your listener object followed by a period.

5. Choose Built-in Classes > Movie > Stage > Events > onResize, and add an equals sign.

6. Choose Statements > User-Defined Functions > function (**Figure 6.105**).

   The `onResize` event handler is completed and assigned to your listener object.

continues on next page

7. Assign actions that will be performed when the `onResize` event occurs (**Figure 6.106**).

In this example, when the viewer resizes the window, Flash checks whether the size is smaller than the default Stage size. If so, Flash scales the main Stage proportionally according to the smaller of the horizontal and vertical window dimensions. Resizing the window bigger, however, does not make the Flash content scale with the window. The result: You can shrink the window to accommodate smaller monitors and still see the content, but you can't enlarge the Stage more than its normal size.

8. On the next line outside the `onResize` event handler, choose Built-in Classes > Movie > Stage > Methods > addListener.

9. With your pointer between the parentheses, enter the name of your listener object.

The listener is registered with the Stage class to listen for the `onResize` event.

10. Test your movie.

11. Resize the movie window.

Resizing the window triggers the function defining the `onResize` event (**Figure 6.107**).

```
myListener = new Object();
myListener.onResize = function() {
  Stage.align = "C";
  if (Stage.height < 499 || Stage.width < 499) {
  Stage.align = "TL";
   _root._xscale = Math.min(Stage.width, Stage.height)/500*100;
   _root._yscale = Math.min(Stage.width, Stage.height)/500*100;
  }
};
Stage.addListener(myListener);
```

Figure 6.106 The full ActionScript for this example. The Stage for this movie is 500 x 500. If its window is resized smaller, the content is aligned to the top-left corner. The `Math.min()` method decides which dimension (horizontal or vertical) of the window is smaller and scales the movie proportionally according to that size.

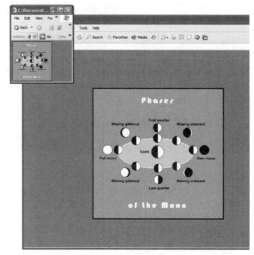

Figure 6.107 Decreasing the size of the window scales the movie so that all its content is still visible (top). Increasing the size of the window scales the movie only to 100%, at which point it maintains its size. This technique would be useful if you want viewers to be able to see your movie on smaller monitors but you want to prevent other users from enlarging your movie to the point where bitmaps and videos are jagged and lose resolution.

Detecting Download Progress: Preloaders

All the hard work you put into creating complex interactivity in your movie will be wasted if your viewer has to wait too long to download it over the Web and leaves. You can avoid losing viewers by creating short animations that entertain them while the rest of your movie downloads. These diversions, or *preloaders*, tell your viewer how much of the movie has downloaded and how much longer he or she still has to wait. When enough data has been delivered over the Web to the viewer's computer, you can trigger your movie to start. In effect, you hold back the playhead until you know that all the frames are available to play. Only then do you send the playhead to the starting frame of your movie.

Preloaders must be small because you want them to load almost immediately, and they should be informative, letting your viewers know what they're waiting for.

Flash provides many ways to monitor the state of the download progress. You can test for the number of frames that have downloaded with the Timeline properties `_framesloaded` and `_totalframes`. You can also test for the amount of data that has downloaded with the movie-clip methods `getBytesLoaded()` and `getBytesTotal()`. Testing the amount of data is a more accurate gauge of download progress because the frames of your movie most likely contain data that are not evenly spread.

If you are loading data-intensive images (JPGs) or movies (SWFs) into your Flash movie, then you can use the new MovieClipLoader class to detect their download progress. The MovieClipLoader class provides powerful events, such as `onLoadStart` and `onLoadProgress`, that give you a finer degree of control over the download progress.

All the approaches use the same basic concept. You tell Flash to compare the amount of frames or data loaded with the total amount of frames or data in the movie. As this ratio changes, you can display the percentage numerically with a dynamic text field or represent the changing ratio graphically as a growing progress bar. Because you often show the progress of the download, these preloaders are known as *progressive preloaders*.

To create a progressive preloader that detects data:

1. Create a long rectangular movie-clip symbol.

   Make sure that its registration point is at its far left edge (**Figure 6.108**).

2. Place an instance of the symbol on the Stage, and give it a name in the Property Inspector.

   Your preloader essentially is a rectangle that grows longer according to the percentage of downloaded frames. You will change the properties of the rectangular movie clip to stretch it dynamically. Because you'll want the bar to grow from left to right, the registration point is placed on the left edge.

3. Select the first frame of the main Timeline, and open the Actions panel.

4. Choose Global Functions > Timeline Control > stop.

   The **stop** action prevents your movie from playing until it has downloaded completely.

5. On the next line, enter a variable name followed by an equals sign.

6. Choose Global Functions > Miscellaneous Functions > setInterval.

7. For the parameters of the **setInterval** action, enter a name of a function followed by the interval 10 (**Figure 6.109**).

   The **setInterval** action calls this named function every 10 milliseconds.

   Now you need to create the function.

8. On a new line, choose Statements > User-Defined Functions > function.

9. Place your pointer before the opening parenthesis for the function and enter the name you gave your function in the **setInterval** action (**Figure 6.110**).

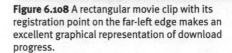

Figure 6.108 A rectangular movie clip with its registration point on the far-left edge makes an excellent graphical representation of download progress.

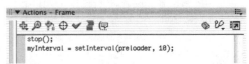

Figure 6.109 Create the setInterval action to monitor the download progress continuously

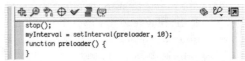

Figure 6.110 The function called preloader is invoked at regular intervals by the setInterval action. The function will contain the actions to test and display the download progress.

```
stop();
myInterval = setInterval(preloader, 10);
function preloader() {
    if (getBytesLoaded()>=getBytesTotal()) {
        play();
        clearInterval(myInterval);
    }
}
```

Figure 6.111 When the number of bytes downloaded is greater than or equal to the total number of bytes, the actions between the curly braces of the `if` statement are executed. Flash will begin playing the main Timeline and will remove the `setInterval` action.

```
stop();
myInterval = setInterval(preloader, 10);
function preloader() {
    if (getBytesLoaded()>=getBytesTotal()) {
        play();
        clearInterval(myInterval);
    }
    bar_mc._xscale = (getBytesLoaded()/getBytesTotal())*100;
}
```

Figure 6.112 The complete code (above) and the progress bar movie clip as it grows steadily during the download process (bottom).

10. With your pointer inside the curly braces of the function, choose Statements > Conditions/Loops > if.

11. For the condition of the if Statement, enter the following:

getBytesLoaded()>= getBytesTotal()

Flash checks whether the number of bytes (data) that have been loaded is greater than or equal to the total number of bytes in the main Timeline. You can find the getBytesLoaded() and getBytesTotal() methods by choosing Built-in Classes > Movie > MovieClip > Methods.

12. On the next line of the if statement, choose Global Functions > Timeline Control > play.

If the condition in the if statement is true, the movie begins to play.

13. On the next line, choose Global Functions > Miscellaneous Functions > clearInterval.

14. With your pointer between the parentheses for the clearInterval statement, enter the name you used to identify your setInterval action (**Figure 6.111**).

Once the download is complete, you no longer need to check its progress, so the clearInterval statement deletes the initial setInterval.

15. Place your pointer after the closing curly brace for the if statement and press Enter to make a new line.

16. Enter the following line of code (**Figure 6.112**):

bar_mc._xscale = (getBytesLoaded()/getBytesTotal())*100;.

The horizontal dimension of the movie clip called bar_mc now stretches based on the percentage of bytes loaded.

continues on next page

DETECTING DOWNLOAD PROGRESS: PRELOADERS

17. Begin creating your animation from keyframe 2 (**Figure 6.113**).

18. Test your movie with the Bandwidth Profiler and with Show Streaming on.

The Bandwidth Profiler is an information window above your movie in Test Movie mode; it displays the number of frames and the amount of data in each frame as vertical bars. If the vertical bars extend over the bottom of the red horizontal line, there is too much data to be downloaded at the bandwidth setting without causing a stutter during playback. The Show Streaming option simulates actual download performance (**Figure 6.114**). The green bar at the top shows the download progress. The triangle marks the current location of the playhead. The playhead remains in Frame 1 until the green progress bar reaches the end of the Timeline. Only then does the playhead begin moving.

✔ Tips

■ You won't see your preloader working unless you build an animation with many frames containing fairly large graphics that require lengthy download times. If your animation is small, you'll see your preloader whiz by because all the data will download quickly and begin playing almost immediately.

■ Explore other graphical treatments of the download progress. Stretching the length of a movie clip is just one way to animate the download process. With subtle changes to your ActionScript, you can apply a variety of animated effects to your preloader.

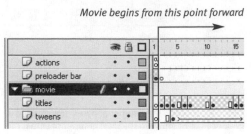

Movie begins from this point forward

Figure 6.113 The "real" movie begins at keyframe 2, after the rectangular movie clip is removed.

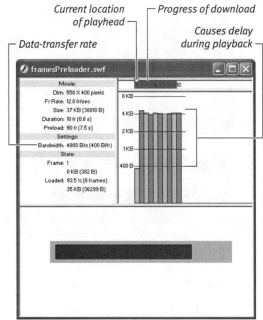

Figure 6.114 The Bandwidth Profiler shows the individual frames that cause pauses during playback because the amount of data exceeds the data-transfer rate. The alternating light and dark bars represent different frames. Notice how the progress of the download (about 8 out of 10 frames have loaded completely) affects the proportion of the movie clip (about 80%).

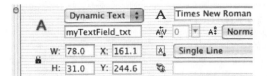

Figure 6.115 This dynamic text field is called `myTextField_txt`.

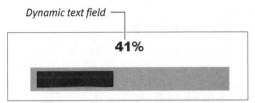

Dynamic text field

41%

Figure 6.116 The dynamic text field displays the percentage of the download progress along with the graphical representation.

Often, a preloader has an accompanying display of the percentage of download progress. This display is accomplished by a dynamic text field placed on the Stage. You will learn more about dynamic text in Chapter 10, but you can follow these steps now to add a simple numeric display.

To add a numeric display to the progressive preloader:

1. Continuing with the file from the preceding task, select the Text tool, and drag out a text field on the Stage.

2. In the Property Inspector, choose Dynamic Text and give the text field a name (**Figure 6.115**).

   The name of the text field, like the names of buttons and movie clips, lets you target the text field and control it.

3. Select the first frame of the main Timeline, and open the Actions panel.

4. Create a new line before the closing curly brace for the function.

5. Enter the following script:

   ```
   myTextField_txt.text = Math.round
   (getBytesLoaded()/getBytesTotal()
   *100)+"%"
   ```

   The percentage of download progress is rounded to a whole number by the `Math.round()` method. The percent (%) character is appended to the end, and the result is assigned to the `text` property of your text box, displaying it on the Stage (**Figure 6.116**).

The Bandwidth Profiler

The Bandwidth Profiler is a handy option to see how data is distributed throughout your Flash movie and how quickly (or slowly) it will download over the Web. In Test Movie mode, choose View > Bandwidth Profiler (Command-B for Mac, Ctrl-B for Windows) to see this information.

The left side of the Bandwidth Profiler shows movie information, such as Stage dimensions, frame rate, file size, total duration, and preload time in frames and seconds. It also shows the Bandwidth setting, which simulates actual download performance at a specified rate. You can change that rate in the Debug menu and choose the rate for a modem that your viewer is likely to have. Flash gives you options for 28.8 and 56 Kbyte modems, for example.

The bar graph on the right side of the Bandwidth Profiler shows the amount of data in each frame of your movie. You can view the graph as a streaming graph (choose View > Streaming Graph) or as a frame-by-frame graph (choose View > Frame by Frame Graph). The streaming graph indicates how the movie downloads over the Web by showing you how data streams from each frame, whereas the frame-by-frame graph simply indicates the amount of data in each frame. In Streaming Graph mode, you can tell which frames will cause hang-ups during playback by noting which bar exceeds the given Bandwidth setting.

To watch the actual download performance of your movie, choose View > Simulate Download. Flash simulates playback over the Web at the given Bandwidth setting. A green horizontal bar at the top of the window indicates which frames have been downloaded, and the triangular playhead marks the current frame that plays.

Detecting download progress of external images and movies

Using the MovieClipLoader class is an ideal way to monitor the loading of external images or movies into Flash. This class allows you to create listeners that return information on the download progress of loading SWF or JPG files, and it provides many events that are triggered at various points of the download process. Imagine that you have multiple JPG images on a Web server and you want to load them into a Flash photo album movie. Using the MovieClipLoader class, you can load each image into a movie clip and detect their initial download, progress, completion, or even errors in their loading. Similarly, this method can be used with external SWF files.

Creating a preloader for loaded JPGs or SWFs first requires that you instantiate a MovieClipLoader object and a listener object. Next, you create your event handlers for your listener. The following events take place in the order listed:

◆ listenerObject.onLoadStart: The listener is invoked when the first bytes of the downloaded file have been transferred to the movie.

◆ listenerObject.onLoadProgress: The listener is invoked during the loading process. This event handler can pass three important parameters, the movie clip target (the movie clip in which the JPG or SWF will load), the number of bytes loaded, and the total number of bytes.

◆ listenerObject.onLoadComplete: The listener is invoked when the entire file has been transferred to the movie.

◆ listenerObject.onLoadInit: The listener is invoked when the downloaded file's first frame actions have been executed.

It is not always necessary to use all four of the above listed events in every movie.

After your event handlers are created, register your listener to the MovieClipLoader object and then begin loading your external file with the method loadClip(). The loadClip() method is part of the MovieClipLoader class and functions much like the MovieClip method loadMovie(). However, you must use the loadClip() method in order to use the event handlers of the MovieClipLoader class.

To create a progressive preloader for external images or movies:

1. Create a small rectangular movie-clip symbol.

   Make sure that its registration point is at the far-left edge.

2. Place an instance of the symbol on the Stage, and give it a name in the Property Inspector (**Figure 6.117**).

   The properties of the rectangle will change in proportion to the amount of bytes that are downloaded. This will act as a visual indicator to the audience that the movie is loading.

3. Create a movie-clip symbol, and drag an instance of it from the Library to the Stage.

   This will act a placeholder into which external movies or images will load.

   continues on next page

Figure 6.117 A new rectangular movie clip is given an instance name of bar_mc.

4. Select the instance, and give it a name in the Property Inspector.

5. Select the Text tool, and drag out a text field on the Stage. In the Property Inspector, select Dynamic Text from the drop-down list, and give it an instance name (**Figure 6.118**).

The dynamic text box will display the percentage of download progress.

6. Select the first frame of the main Timeline, and open the Actions panel.

7. Enter a variable name followed by an equals sign. Choose Built-in Classes > Movie > MovieClipLoader > new MovieClipLoader.

A new MovieClipLoader object is instantiated.

8. On the next line, enter another name followed by an equals sign. Choose Built-in Classes > Core > Object > new Object (**Figure 6.119**).

A listener object is created.

9. On the next line, enter the name that you assigned to the MovieClipLoader object followed by a period. Choose Built-in Classes > Movie > MovieClipLoader > Methods > addListener.

10. With your pointer between the parentheses, enter the name that you assigned to the new listener object (**Figure 6.120**).

The new listener object is now registered to the MovieClipLoader object.

11. On the next line, enter the name that you assigned to the MovieClipObject followed by a period. Choose Built-in Classes > Movie > MovieClipLoader > Methods > loadClip.

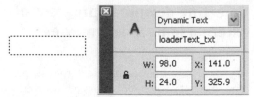

Figure 6.118 A dynamic text field is given an instance name of loaderText_txt.

Figure 6.119 A MovieClipLoader instance and a listener object is created.

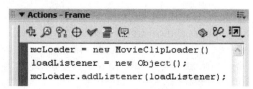

Figure 6.120 The new listener is registered to the MovieClipLoader.

12. With your pointer between the parentheses, enter the absolute or relative URL of the SWF file or JPG file you want to load. Make sure that the address is between quotation marks and followed by a comma.

Absolute URLs must include the protocol reference, such as http:// or file:///.

13. For the loadClip() method's second parameter, enter the target path of the movie clip into which you want the SWF or JPG to load. Separate the two parameters (the URL and the movie clip target) with commas (**Figure 6.121**).

14. On the next line, enter the name of your listener followed by a period. Choose Built-in Classes > Movie > MovieClipLoader > Listeners > onLoadStart.

15. Between the curly braces of this function, choose the **stop()** method for your movie clip placeholder (**Figure 6.122**).

As soon as the external movie begins to load, it will stop. This ensures that all its data is loaded before playing, preventing the stuttering that often happens when a movie is playing while downloading. If you are loading images, you won't need this step.

16. On the new line, enter the name of your listener followed by a period. Choose Built-in Classes > Movie > MovieClipLoader > Listeners > onLoadProgress.

continues on next page

```
mcLoader = new MovieClipLoader();
loadListener = new Object();
mcLoader.addListener(loadListener);
mcLoader.loadClip("http://www.someDomain.com/movie.swf", loader_mc);
```

Figure 6.121 The method loadClip() loads an external SWF file that resides at http://www.someDomain.com/movie.swf into the movie clip named loader_mc.

```
loadListener.onLoadStart = function() {
    loader_mc.stop();
};
```

Figure 6.122 When the movie begins to load the external SWF into the movie clip called loader_mc, the animation it contains stops.

17. Between the parentheses of the function, add variable names separated by commas (**Figure 6.123**).

The onLoadProgress event is triggered as data is downloaded. The three parameters that are passed to the function are the movie clip target, the bytes currently loaded, and the total bytes of the external file.

18. Enter the following code between the curly braces for the onLoadProgress handler:

```
preloaded= Math.floor
(loadedBytes/totalBytes*100)
loaderText_txt.text = preloaded + "%
loaded";
bar_mc._xscale = preloaded
```

Your script for the onLoadProgress handler should resemble **Figure 6.124**.

During the download progress, the percentage of total bytes downloaded is displayed in the text field on the Stage and the rectangular movie clip is stretched accordingly.

19. On a new line, enter the name of your listener followed by a period. Choose Built-in Classes > Movie > MovieClipLoader > Listeners > onLoadComplete.

20. Between the curly braces of the function, add the following code (**Figure 6.125**):

```
loaderText_txt._visible = false;
bar_mc._visible = false;
loader_mc.play();
```

The onLoadComplete event is triggered when all the data has downloaded. When this happens, the text field and rectangular movie clip disappears and the downloaded movie plays.

```
loadListener.onLoadProgress = function(mc, loadedBytes, totalBytes) {
};
```

Figure 6.123 The onLoadProgress handler passes a parameter for the target movie clip (called mc here), a parameter for the number of bytes loaded (called loadedBytes here), and a parameter for the number of total bytes (called totalBytes here).

```
loadListener.onLoadProgress = function(mc, loadedBytes, totalBytes) {
    preloaded = Math.floor(loadedBytes/totalBytes*100)
    loaderText_txt.text = preloaded + "% loaded";
    bar_mc._xscale = preloaded
};
```

Figure 6.124 During the loading progress, Flash updates the contents of the text field called loaderText_txt and stretches the rectangular movie clip called bar_mc in proportion to the percentage of downloaded bytes.

```
loadListener.onLoadComplete = function() {
    loaderText_txt._visible = false;
    bar_mc._visible = false;
    loader_mc.play();
};
```

Figure 6.125 When loading is complete, the text field and elongated rectangle disappears and the loaded movie plays.

DETECTING DOWNLOAD PROGRESS: PRELOADERS

21. Test your movie.

As your external movie or image loads into your placeholder movie clip, the text box displays the percentage of total bytes downloaded and the rectangular movie clip grows longer. When all the entire movie or image has loaded, the text box and elongated rectangular movie clip disappear (**Figure 6.126**).

✔ Tips

- If your audience's internet connection is fast enough or the movie you download is small enough, you may not need to stop the animation while it downloads (step 15). You may find that the external movie plays smoothly as it downloads, eliminating the need for the stop() action.

- The same security restrictions apply to external movies loaded with the method loadClip() as they do for loadMovie() and loadMovieNum(). See the sidebar "Flash Player Security" earlier in this chapter for details.

```
mcLoader = new MovieClipLoader();
loadListener = new Object();
mcLoader.addListener(loadListener);
mcLoader.loadClip("http://www.russellchun.com/bigMovie.swf", loader_mc);
loadListener.onLoadStart = function() {
    loader_mc.stop();
};
loadListener.onLoadProgress = function(loadTarget, loadedBytes, totalBytes) {
    preloaded = Math.floor(loadedBytes/totalBytes*100);
    loaderText_txt.text = preloaded+"% loaded into "+loadTarget;
    bar_mc._xscale = preloaded;
};
loadListener.onLoadComplete = function() {
    loaderText_txt._visible = false;
    bar_mc._visible = false;
    loader_mc.play();
};
```

62% loaded into _level0.loader_mc

Figure 6.126 The completed code (top) provides a progress bar and text updates (bottom left) until all the data for the external SWF (bottom right) loads.

Part IV: Transforming Graphics and Sound

CONTROLLING
THE MOVIE CLIP

7

The movie clip is a powerful object. Its power comes from the myriad of properties, methods, and events that are available to it. Essentially, Flash lets you control the way movie clips look and behave. Movie-clip properties such as position, scale, rotation, transparency, color, and even instance name can all be changed with ActionScript. As a result, you can create arcade-style interactivity, with characters changing in response to viewer input or conditions. Imagine a game of Tetris created entirely in Flash. Each geometric shape could be a movie clip, and the viewer would control its rotation and position with the keyboard. A game of Asteroids could feature an alien ship that moves in response to the viewer's position. This kind of animation isn't based on tweens you create while authoring the Flash movie. Rather, this is dynamic animation that is essentially "created" during playback.

Flash also gives you powerful methods to control a movie clip's behavior. You can make movie clips draggable so that viewers can actually pick up puzzle pieces and put them in their correct places, or you can develop a more immersive online shopping experience in which viewers can grab merchandise and drop it into their shopping carts. You'll learn how to detect where draggable movie clips are dropped on the Stage, as well as control collisions and overlaps with other movie clips. And you'll learn how to generate movie clips dynamically, so that new instances appear on the Stage during playback. You can use movie clips to create moving masks and even to create drawings—lines, curves, fills, and gradients.

Learning to control movie-clip properties, methods, and events is your first step in understanding how to animate entirely with ActionScript.

Dragging the Movie Clip

Drag-and-drop behavior gives the viewer one of the most direct interactions with the Flash movie. Nothing is more satisfying than grabbing a graphic on the screen, moving it around, and dropping it somewhere else. It's a natural way of interacting with objects, and it's easy to give your viewers this experience. Creating drag-and-drop behavior in Flash involves just two basic steps: creating the movie clip and then assigning ActionScript to an event handler that triggers the drag action.

The usual behavior for drag-and-drop interactivity is for the dragging to begin when the viewer presses the mouse button when the pointer is over the movie clip. Then, when the mouse button is released, the dragging stops. Hence, the action to start dragging is tied to an on (press) or an onPress event handler, and the action to stop dragging is tied to an on (release) or an onRelease event handler. If you use on (press), you assign ActionScript directly to the movie-clip instance. If you use onPress, you assign ActionScript to the root Timeline. Both ways are valid. As you learned in Chapter 4, although it may initially be simpler to assign scripts to the instance, in the long run, as you develop more complicated code, it is better practice to put all your code in one place on the main Timeline.

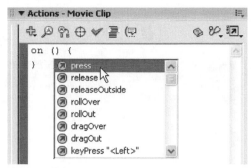

Figure 7.1 Select the press event for the on handler assigned to the movie clip.

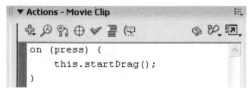

Figure 7.2 The target path this makes the startDrag method affect the current movie clip.

To start dragging a movie clip by using the on (press) event handler:

1. Create a movie-clip symbol, and place an instance of it on the Stage.

2. Select the movie-clip instance, and open the Actions panel.

3. Choose Global Functions > Movie Clip Control > on (Esc + on).

4. Select press as the event from the code hint pull-down menu (**Figure 7.1**).

5. On the next line, enter the target path this followed by a period.

6. Choose Global Functions > Movie Clip Control > startDrag (Esc + dr) (**Figure 7.2**).

7. Test your movie.

   When the pointer is over the movie clip and you press your mouse button, you can drag it around.

To start dragging a movie clip by using the onPress event handler:

1. Create a movie-clip symbol, place an instance of it on the Stage, and name it in the Property Inspector (**Figure 7.3**).

2. Select the first frame of the root Timeline, and open the Actions panel.

3. Enter the instance name for the movie clip that you just created followed by a period.

4. Choose Built-in Classes > Movie > MovieClip > Events > onPress. Complete the handler by entering =function(){ and a closing curly brace on the next line (**Figure 7.4**).

   The completed statement creates an onPress event handler for your movie clip.

5. On the next line, enter the keyword this, followed by a period.

   The keyword this refers to the current movie clip.

6. Choose Global Functions > Movie Clip Control > startDrag (Esc + dr) (**Figure 7.5**). The startDrag action appears between the function curly braces.

7. Test your movie.

   When your pointer is over the movie clip and you press your mouse button, you can drag it around.

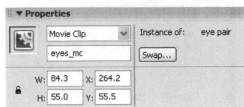

Figure 7.3 The movie-clip instance of these cartoon eyes is given the name eyes_mc in the Property Inspector.

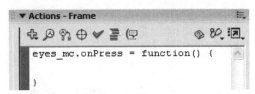

Figure 7.4 The onPress event handler is created with an anonymous function.

Figure 7.5 The target path this makes the startDrag method affect the movie clip called eyes_mc. Compare this figure with Figure 7.2.

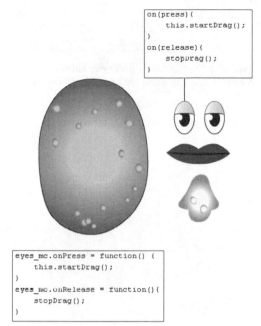

```
on(press){
    this.startDrag();
}
on(release){
    stopDrag();
}
```

```
eyes_mc.onPress = function() {
    this.startDrag();
}
eyes_mc.onRelease = function(){
    stopDrag();
}
```

Figure 7.6 Each of the three facial features are movie clips that can be dragged to the potato face and dropped into position. The ActionScript can be assigned to the movie-clip instance (top) or on the root Timeline (bottom).

To stop dragging a movie clip:

1. Using the file you created in the preceding task, create a new line after the closing curly brace for the onPress event.

2. If you are continuing with assigning actions to the movie instance, choose Global Functions > Movie Clip Control > on, and select release as the event

   or

   If you are continuing with assigning actions to the main Timeline, enter the instance name of the movie clip, choose Built-in Classes > Movie > MovieClip > Events > onRelease. Complete the handler by entering =function(){ and a closing curly brace on the next line.

   The onRelease event handler is completed for your movie clip.

3. Choose Global Functions > Movie Clip Control > stopDrag (Esc + sd).

   The stopDrag statement appears, with no parameters.

4. Test your movie.

   When your pointer is over the movie clip and you press your mouse button, you can drag it. When you release your mouse button, the dragging stops (**Figure 7.6**).

✔ Tip

■ Only one movie clip can be dragged at any one time. For this reason, the stopDrag action doesn't need any parameters; it will stop the drag action on whichever movie clip is currently draggable.

In many cases, you may want the movie clip to snap to the center of the user's pointer as it is being dragged rather than wherever the user happens to click.

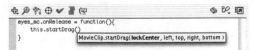

Figure 7.7 The lockCenter parameter forces the viewer to drag the movie clip by its registration point.

To center the draggable movie clip:

1. Place your pointer inside of the parentheses for the `startDrag` method, and click the Show Code Hint button (Cmd-spacebar for Mac, Ctrl-Space for Windows) (**Figure 7.7**).

   The code hints now become available to you.

2. Enter the Boolean value of `true`.

   The `startDrag` method's first parameter, called `lockCenter`, is set to `true`. After you press the mouse button when your pointer is over the movie clip to begin dragging, the registration point of your movie clip snaps to the mouse pointer.

✔ Tip

■ If you set the `lockCenter` parameter to `true`, make sure that the hit area of your movie clip covers its registration point. (By default, the hit area of your movie clip is the graphics it contains.) If it doesn't, after the movie clip snaps to your mouse pointer, your pointer will no longer be over any hit area and Flash won't be able to detect when to stop the drag action.

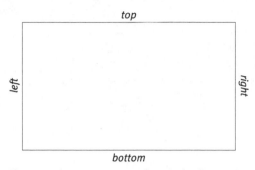

Figure 7.8 The parameters to constrain the drag motion define the left, right, top, and bottom boundaries.

✔ Tips

- You can use the left, right, top, bottom parameters to force a dragging motion along a horizontal or a vertical track, as in a scroll bar. Set the left and right parameters to the same number to restrict the motion to up and down, or set the top and the bottom parameters to the same number to restrict the motion to left and right.

- In order to define the left, right, top, and bottom parameters to constrain the draggable motion, you must also set the startDrag method's first parameter (lockCenter) to true or false.

You may also want to limit the area where viewers can drag movie clips.

To constrain the draggable movie clip:

1. Place your pointer inside of the parentheses for the startDrag method, and click the Show Code Hint button (Cmd-spacebar for Mac, Ctrl-spacebar for Windows).

   The code hints now become available to you.

2. Using the code hint to help guide you, enter pixel coordinates for each of the four fields representing the maximum and minimum limits for the registration point of your draggable movie clip (**Figure 7.8**).

   ▲ *Left:* the leftmost margin (minimum *x* position) where the registration point of the movie clip can go.

   ▲ *Right:* the rightmost margin (maximum *x* position) where the registration point of the movie clip can go.

   ▲ *Top:* the topmost margin (minimum *y* position) where the registration point of the movie clip can go.

   ▲ *Bottom:* the bottommost margin (maximum *y* position) where the registration point of the movie clip can go.

The pixel coordinates are relative to the Timeline in which the movie clip resides. If the draggable movie clip sits on the root Timeline, the pixel coordinates correspond to the Stage, so left=0, top=0 refers to the top-left corner. If the draggable movie clip is within another movie clip, left=0, top=0 refers to the registration point of the parent movie clip.

Setting the Movie-Clip Properties

Many movie-clip properties—size, transparency, position, rotation, and quality—define how the movie looks. By using dot syntax, you can target any movie clip and change any of those characteristics during playback. **Table 7.1** summarizes properties that are available. A few of these properties affect the entire movie, not just a single movie clip.

Table 7.1

Movie Clip Properties

PROPERTY	VALUE	DESCRIPTION
_alpha (Alpha)	A number from 0 to 100	Specifies the alpha transparency, where 0 is totally transparent and 100 is opaque.
_visible (Visibility)	true or false	Specifies whether a movie clip can be seen.
_name (Name)	A string-literal name	Specifies a new instance name of the movie clip.
_rotation (Rotation)	A number	Specifies the degree of rotation in a clockwise direction from the 12 o'clock position. A value of 45, for example, tips the movie clip to the right.
_width (Width)	A number in pixels	Specifies the horizontal dimension.
_height (Height)	A number in pixels	Specifies the vertical dimension.
_x (X Position)	A number in pixels	Specifies the horizontal position of the movie clip's registration point.
_y (Y Position)	A number in pixels	Specifies the vertical position of the movie clip's registration point.
_xscale (X Scale)	A number	Specifies the percentage of the original movie-clip symbol's horizontal dimension.
_yscale (Y Scale)	A number	Specifies the percentage of the original movie-clip symbol's vertical dimension.
_focusrect (Show focus rectangle)	true or false	Determines whether a yellow rectangle appears around objects as you use the Tab key to select objects.
_highquality (High quality)	A number 0, 1, or 2	Specifies the level of antialiasing for playback of the movie. 2 = best: antialiasing and bitmap smoothing. 1 = high: antialiasing and bitmap smoothing if there is no animation. 0 = low: no antialiasing. This property is a global property that affects the entire movie rather than a single movie clip. This property is also considered to be deprecated.
_quality (Quality)	LOW, MEDIUM, HIGH, or BEST	Specifies the level of antialiasing for playback of the movie. BEST = antialiasing and bitmap smoothing. HIGH = antialiasing and bitmap smoothing if there is no animation. MEDIUM = lower-quality antialiasing. LOW = no antialiasing. This property is a global property that affects the entire movie rather than a single movie clip.
_soundbuftime (Sound buffer time)	A number	Specifies the number of seconds before the movie begins to stream sound. The default value is 5. This property is a global property that affects the entire movie rather than a single movie clip.

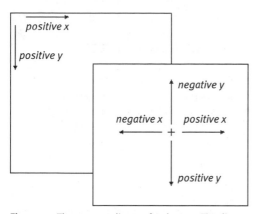

Figure 7.9 The *x, y* coordinates for the root Timeline (top) are centered at the top-left corner of the Stage. The *x, y* coordinates for movie clips (bottom) are centered at the registration point.

✔ Tips

■ There is a difference between an alpha of 0 and a visibility of false, although the result may look the same. When visibility is false, the movie clip literally cannot be seen. Mouse events in the movie clip and buttons within the movie clip aren't responsive because they are invisible. When alpha is 0, on the other hand, mouse events and buttons within the movie clip still function.

■ The *x* and *y* coordinate space for the root Timeline is different from movie-clip Timelines. In the root Timeline, the x-axis begins at the left edge and increases to the right; the y-axis begins at the top edge and increases to the bottom. Thus, x = 0, y = 0 corresponds to the top-left corner of the Stage. For movie clips, the coordinates x = 0, y = 0 correspond to the registration point (the crosshair). The value of *x* increases to the right of the registration point and decreases into negative values to the left of the registration point. The value of *y* increases to the bottom and decreases into negative values to the top (**Figure 7.9**).

■ The X Scale and Y Scale properties control the percentage of the original movie-clip symbol, which is different from what may be on the Stage. If, for example, you place an instance of a movie clip on the Stage and shrink it 50 percent and then you apply an X Scale setting of 100 and a Y Scale setting of 100 during playback, your movie clip will double in size.

In the following example, you will assign ActionScript to a button that changes a movie clip's property.

To change the position of a movie clip:

1. Create a movie-clip symbol, place an instance of it on the Stage, and name it in the Property Inspector.

2. Create a button symbol, place an instance of it on the Stage, and name it in the Property Inspector.

3. Select the first frame of the root Timeline, and open the Actions panel.

4. Enter the instance name of your button followed by a period.

5. Choose Built-in Classes > Movie > MovieClip > Events > onRelease. Complete the handler by entering =function(){ and a closing curly brace on the next line (**Figure 7.10**).

6. On the next line, choose Statements Variables > with.

   A with statement appears within the onRelease event handler.

7. Between the parentheses of the with statement, enter the instance name of the movie clip that you would like to assign actions to.

8. On the next line enter the property _x (X Position), followed by an equals sign and a number for the x position (**Figure 7.11**).

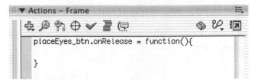

Figure 7.10 The onRelease event handler for the placeEyes_btn button is completed. In this example, this button will modify the x and y positions of a movie clip.

Figure 7.11 The x position of the movie clip eyes_mc on the root Timeline is set to 122.

```
Actions - Frame
placeEyes_btn.onRelease = function(){
    with(eyes_mc){
    _x = 122;
    _y = 93;
    }
}
```

Figure 7.12 The y position of the movie clip eyes_mc on the root Timeline is set to 93.

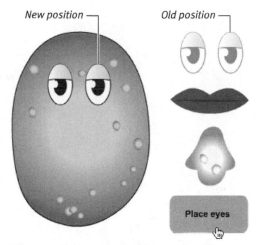

New position —

Old position —

Figure 7.13 The button sets the movie clip of the eyes_mc into its new position on the potato.

9. On the next line of the with statement, enter the property _y (Y Position) followed by an equals sign and a numerical value for its position on the Stage (**Figure 7.12**).

10. Test your movie.

   When you click the button that you created, your movie clip jumps to the new position defined by the two statements in your with statement (**Figure 7.13**).

✔ **Tips**

■ You can also change the position of the movie clip with the following statements:

   eyes_mc._x = 122;
   eyes_mc._y = 93;

   Notice, however, that there is less redundant coding when you use the with statement as described in the task.

■ The same results could also be achieved by using the setProperty action (Esc + sp). The setProperty action requires three parameters; the target, the property, and its new value. So you could change the x position of the movie clip called eyes_mc with the statement setProperty (eyes_mc, _x, 122). Dot syntax, however, is encouraged.

DRAGGING THE MOVIE CLIP

Getting the Movie-Clip Properties

Very often, you will want to change a movie clip's property relative to its current value. You may want to rotate a cannon 10 degrees each time your viewer clicks a button, for example. How do you find out the current value of a movie clip's property? You can get a property in two ways. The first way is to use the function getProperty. The second way is far simpler because it requires only that you write the target path and property in dot syntax. So if you want to change a movie clip's property based on its current value, you can write the expression

cannon_mc._rotation += 10;

This expression will add 10 degrees to the current angle of the movie clip called cannon.

To get a property of a movie clip:

1. Create a movie clip, place an instance on the Stage, and name it in the Property Inspector.

   In this example, you will get the rotation property of this movie clip and change it so that 10 degrees are added each time you click the movie clip.

2. Select the first frame of the root Timeline, and open the Actions panel.

3. Enter the instance name of the movie clip that you just created.

4. Choose Built-in Classes > Movie > MovieClip > Events > onPress. Complete the handler by entering =function(){ and a closing curly brace on the next line (**Figure 7.14**).

5. On the next line, enter the target path this followed by a period.

6. Choose Built-in Classes > Movie > MovieClip > Properties > _rotation.

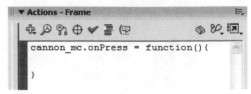

Figure 7.14 The onPress event handler for the cannon movie clip is completed.

```
▼ Actions - Frame
cannon_mc.onPress = function(){
    this._rotation += 10;
}
```

Figure 7.15 A numeric value of 10 is added to the current rotation of the movie clip named cannon_mc.

7. On the same line, choose Operators > Assignment > +=.

An addition assignment has been added to the _rotation property.

8. Enter the numeric value of 10 (**Figure 7.15**).

Each time the movie clip is clicked, Flash will get the current value of cannon_mc and rotate the cannon 10 pixels clockwise.

To get a property by using getProperty:

1. Continuing with the example in the preceding task, select the first frame of the root Timeline, and open the Actions panel.

2. Erase the statement within the onPress event handler, and change it as follows:

this._rotation =

While on the same line, choose Global Functions > Movie Clip Control > getProperty.

3. For the first parameter of the getProperty action, enter the target. For the second parameter, enter the property whose value you wish to retrieve (**Figure 7.16**).

Each time the movie clip is clicked, Flash gets the value of its rotation property and adds 10 to it.

✔ Tip

■ You can use shortcuts to add and subtract values by using combinations of the arithmetic operators. You learn about these combinations in Chapter 9.

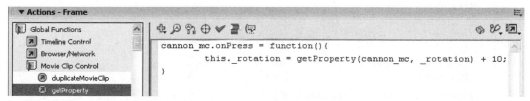

Figure 7.16 The getProperty function in this example retrieves the _rotation property of the cannon_mc movie clip and adds 10 to its current rotation.

GETTING THE MOVIE-CLIP PROPERTIES

Modifying the Movie-Clip Color

One conspicuous omission from the list of movie-clip properties is color. But you can use the Color class to change the color of movie clips.

The first step in modifying a movie clip's color is instantiating a new color object with a constructor function such as this:

```
nameofColorObject_color = new Color
(movieClipInstance_mc)
```

In this function, `nameofColorObject_color` is the name of your new color object and `movieClipInstance_mc` is the target path of the movie clip you want to control. Use the extension `_color` to identify objects of the Color class.

Next, you can use your new color object to set the RGB values of the movie clip by using the method `setRGB()`. To define your new color, use the hexadecimal equivalents of each color component (red, green, and blue) in the form of 0xRRGGBB. You may have seen this six-digit code in HTML to specify the background color of a Web page. You can find these values for a color in the Color Mixer panel. Choose a color in the color spectrum and the hexadecimal value for that color appears in the display to the left (**Figure 7.17**).

To set the color of a movie clip:

1. Create a movie-clip symbol whose color you want to modify, place an instance of it on the Stage, and name it in the Property Inspector.

2. Create a button symbol, place an instance of it on the Stage, and name it in the Property Inspector.

   You will use this button to call the `setRGB()` method of your new color object.

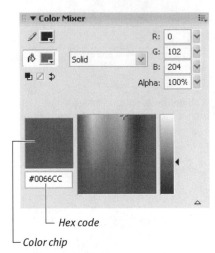

Hex code

Color chip

Figure 7.17 The Color Mixer panel has a display window to show the selected RGB color in hexadecimal code.

```
myColor_color = new Color();
                          new Color( target )
```

```
myColor_color = new Color(shirt_mc);
```

Figure 7.18 Use the code hints in the Script pane to help you create a new color object (top). The new color object is called myColor_color and is associated with the movie clip called shirt_mc (bottom).

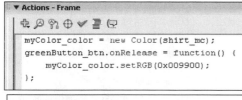
▼ Actions - Frame

```
myColor_color = new Color(shirt_mc);
greenButton_btn.onRelease = function() {
};
```

Figure 7.19 The onRelease event handler is completed for the greenButton_btn button.

▼ Actions - Frame

```
myColor_color = new Color(shirt_mc);
greenButton_btn.onRelease = function() {
    myColor_color.setRGB(0x009900);
};
```

Available colors:

Green

Orange

Purple

Figure 7.20 The setRGB() method takes the parameter oxRRGGBB, which is the hex code for a color. Use setRGB() with different hex codes to change the color of this movie clip, shirt_mc.

3. Select the first frame of the root Timeline, and open the Actions panel.

4. Enter a name for your new color object followed by an equals sign.

5. Choose Built-in Classes > Movie > Color > newColor.

   The expression new Color() appears. The new Color() constructor requires a target path to a movie clip as its parameter.

6. With your pointer between the parentheses for the new Color() constructor, enter your movie-clip name as the target, or use the Insert Target Path button (**Figure 7.18**).

   The completed statement instantiates a new color object and is ready to be used.

7. On the next line, enter the instance name of your button.

8. Choose Built-in Classes > Movie > Button > Events > onRelease. Complete the handler by entering =function(){ and a closing curly brace on the next line (**Figure 7.19**).

9. On the next line, Choose Built-in Classes > Movie > Color > Methods > setRGB.

   The setRGB() method appears within your button event handler with a placeholder named instanceName.

10. Replace instanceName with the name of your color object.

11. For the parameter of the setRGB() method, enter 0x followed by the six-digit hexadecimal code for the new color (**Figure 7.20**).

12. Test your movie.

    In the first frame, a color object is instantiated. When you click your button, that color object calls its setRGB() method. The movie clip associated with the color object is assigned a new RGB value.

Using the color-transform object

The method setRGB() lets you change only a movie clip's color. To change its brightness or its transparency, you must use the method setTransform(). This method allows you to define both the percentages and the offset values for each of the RGB components, as well as the alpha transparency. These parameters are the same as the ones in the Advanced Effect dialog box. This dialog box appears when you apply an advanced color effect to an instance (**Figure 7.21**).

To use the setTransform() method for your color object, you must first create another object that essentially holds the color-transformation information, which is in the parameters ra, rb, ga, gb, ba, bb, aa, and ab (**Table 7.2**). The color-transform object is created via the generic class called Object. After you define the color-transform object, you use it in the setTransform() method of your color object. This process may be a little confusing, but the basic idea is this: Where you normally would see numbers or strings as parameters for a method—the number 5 in the method gotoAndStop(5), for example—you now use an object such as setTransform (myColorTransformObject).

The baseline setTransform() parameters (the values that maintain the movie clip's color) are as follows:

ra=100   ba=100
rb=0   bb=0
ga=100   aa=100
gb=0   ab=0

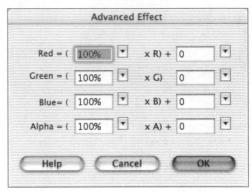

Figure 7.21 The options for advanced effects in the Property Inspector control the RGB and alpha percentages and the offset values for any instance.

Table 7.2

setTransform Parameters	
PARAMETER	VALUE
ra	Percentage (–100 to 100) of red component
rb	Offset (–255 to 255) of red component
ga	Percentage (–100 to 100) of green component
gb	Offset (–255 to 255) of green component
ba	Percentage (–100 to 100) of blue component
bb	Offset (–255 to 255) of blue component
aa	Percentage (–100 to 100) of alpha transparency
ab	Offset (–255 to 255) of alpha transparency

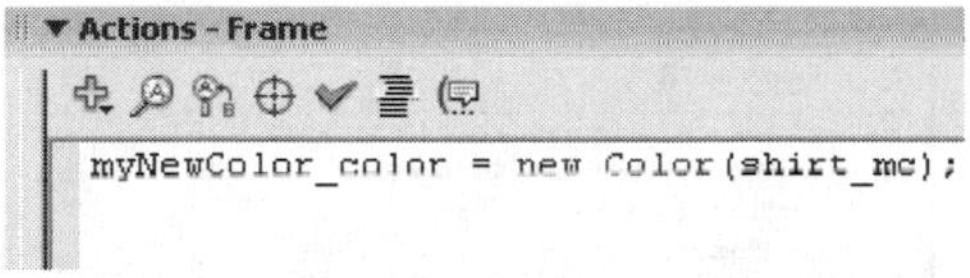

Figure 7.22 A new color object called myNewColor_color is created for the shirt_mc movie clip.

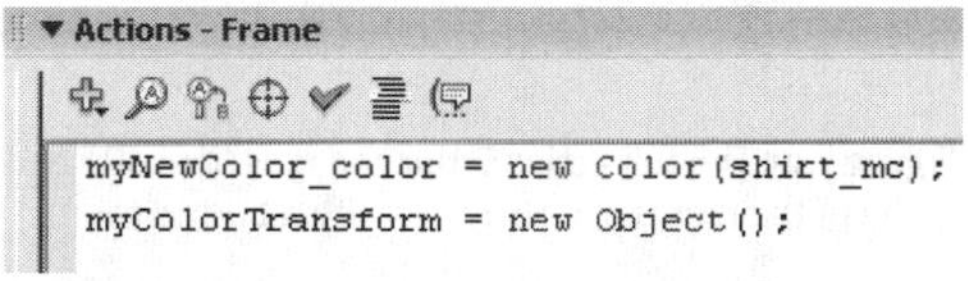

Figure 7.23 Create a new generic object called myColorTransform with the constructor function new Object. This object will hold the RGB and alpha information.

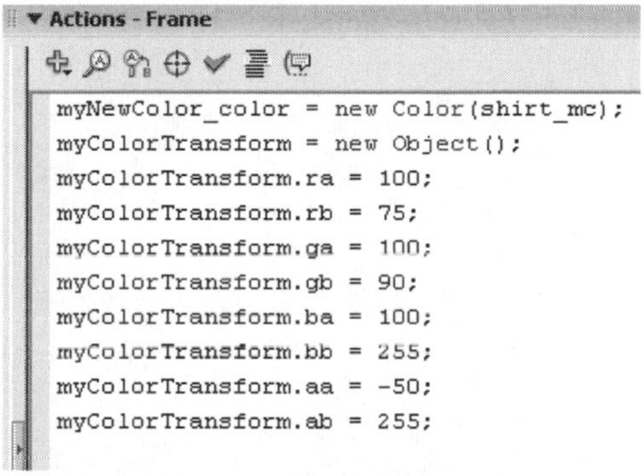

Figure 7.24 The red, green, blue, and alpha percentage and offset values are set with a series of statements. ra, rb, and so on are properties of the myColorTransform object.

To transform the color and alpha of a movie clip:

1. Create a movie-clip symbol whose color or transparency you want to modify, place an instance of it on the Stage, and name it in the Property Inspector.

2. Create a button symbol, place an instance of it on the Stage, and name it in the Property Inspector.

   You will use this button to call the setTransform() method of your color object.

3. Select the first frame of the root Timeline, and open the Actions panel.

4. Instantiate a new color object as described in "To set the color of a movie clip" earlier in this chapter (**Figure 7.22**).

5. On the next line, enter the name for a color-transform object followed by an equals sign.

6. Choose Built-in Classes > Core > Object > new Object.

   The new Object() constructor function appears. Your new color-transform object is instantiated (**Figure 7.23**). This object is a generic object that has no premade properties or methods.

7. On a new line, enter the name of your color-transform object, a period, and then one of the set transform parameters.

8. Repeat step 7 for all eight parameters (**Figure 7.24**).

   The parameters for the color transformation are defined in the properties of your color-transform object.

9. On the next line, enter the name of your button.

continues on next page

MODIFYING THE MOVIE-CLIP COLOR

10. Choose Built-in Classes > Movie > Button > Events > onRelease. Complete the handler by entering =function(){ and a closing curly brace on the next line.

11. In between the curly braces of your button handler, enter the name of your color-transform object followed by a period.

12. Choose Built-in Classes > Movie > Color > Methods > setTransform.

13. For the parameter of the setTransform method, enter the name of your color object.

The full script should look like the one in **Figure 7.25**.

14. Test your movie.

First, a color object and a color-transform object are instantiated. When you click the button that you created, the color object calls the setTransform() method, which uses the color-transform object as its parameter. The movie clip associated with the color object changes color and transparency. 🕹

✔ **Tip**

■ Instead of creating eight separate statements to define the parameters of your color-transform object, you can write just one statement that lists them all. You can use this syntax:

myColorTransform = { ra: '100', rb: '150', ga: '75', gb: '200', ba: '20', bb: '188', aa: '50', ab: '255'}

The parameters are separated from their values by colons, and the parameter/value pairs are separated by commas.

```
▼ Actions - Frame
⊕ ⊅ ⊕ ⊕ ✔ ≣ ⊕
myNewColor_color = new Color(shirt_mc);
myColorTransform = new Object();
myColorTransform.ra = 100;
myColorTransform.rb = 75;
myColorTransform.ga = 100;
myColorTransform.gb = 90;
myColorTransform.ba = 100;
myColorTransform.bb = 255;
myColorTransform.aa = -50;
myColorTransform.ab = 255;
transformButton_btn.onRelease = function() {
    myNewColor_color.setTransform(myColorTransform);
};
```

Figure 7.25 The full ActionScript changes the color and alpha of the movie clip shirt_mc with a button event.

To change the brightness of a movie clip:

◆ Increase the offset parameters for the red, green, and blue components equally, but leave the other parameters unchanged.

If your color-transform object is called `myColorTransform`, for example, set its properties as follows:

```
myColorTransform.ra=100
myColorTransform.rb=125
myColorTransform.ga=100
myColorTransform.gb=125
myColorTransform.ba=100
myColorTransform.bb=125
myColorTransform.aa=100
myColorTransform.ab=0
```

A color object using these parameters would increase the brightness of a movie clip to about 50 percent. Or you could set the offset parameters of red, green, and blue to their maximum (255), as follows:

```
myColorTransform.ra=100
myColorTransform.rb=255
myColorTransform.ga=100
myColorTransform.gb=255
myColorTransform.ba=100
myColorTransform.bb=255
myColorTransform.aa=100
myColorTransform.ab=0
```

A color object using these parameters would increase the brightness of a movie clip to 100 percent so that it would turn white.

To change the darkness of a movie clip:

◆ Decrease the offset parameters for the red, green, and blue components equally, but leave the other parameters unchanged.

To darken a movie clip about 50 percent, for example, set the color-transform properties as follows:

```
myColorTransform.ra=100
myColorTransform.rb=-125
myColorTransform.ga=100
myColorTransform.gb=-125
myColorTransform.ba=100
myColorTransform.bb=-125
myColorTransform.aa=100
myColorTransform.ab=0
```

To change the transparency of a movie clip:

◆ Decrease either the offset or the percentage parameter for the alpha component, and leave the other parameters unchanged.

Decrease *aa* to −100 or decrease *ab* to −255 for total transparency.

Controlling Movie Clip Depth Levels

When you have multiple draggable movie clips, you'll notice that the objects maintain their stacking order even while they're being dragged, which can seem a little odd. You would expect that the one you pick up would come to the top. You can make it do so by using the swapDepths() method to swap the stacking order of movie clips dynamically. swapDepths() can switch the stacking order of movie clips either by swapping two named movie clips or by swapping a named movie clip with whatever movie clip is in a designated depth level. The *depth level* is a number that refers to a movie clip's stacking order. Higher depth-level numbers will overlap lower ones, much like levels of loaded movies.

The amazing thing about swapDepths() is that it even works across layers, so a movie clip in the bottom layer can swap with a movie clip in the top layer.

Knowing where a movie clip lies in the stacking order can also be quite useful. The method getDepth(), which returns the depth level of any movie clip, is the logical counterpart to the swapDepths() method.

You can use swapDepths() anywhere, but in this example, you will link it to a startDrag() method to see the effects on depth levels.

To swap a movie clip with another movie clip:

1. Create two draggable movie clips on the Stage, as outlined earlier in this chapter.

   Your script should look similar to **Figure 7.26**.

2. In the Script pane, place your pointer after the first startDrag statement and press Enter to go to the next line.

```
puzzle1_mc.onPress = function() {
    this.startDrag();
};
puzzle1_mc.onRelease = function() {
    stopDrag();
};
puzzle2_mc.onPress = function() {
        this.startDrag();
};
puzzle2_mc.onRelease = function() {
    stopDrag();
};
```

Figure 7.26 The ActionScript to make the movie clips called puzzle1_mc and puzzle2_mc draggable.

```
puzzle1_mc.onPress = function() {
    this.startDrag();
    this.swapDepths(puzzle2_mc);
};
puzzle1_mc.onRelease = function() {
    stopDrag();
};
puzzle2_mc.onPress = function() {
        this.startDrag();
        this.swapDepths(puzzle1_mc);
};
puzzle2_mc.onRelease = function() {
    stopDrag();
};
```

Figure 7.27 Each swapDepths() method is associated with a startDrag() method. When you click puzzle1_mc, it swaps with puzzle2_mc. When you click puzzle2_mc, it swaps with puzzle1_mc.

3. Enter the keyword this followed by a period.

4. Choose Built-in Classes > Movie > MovieClip > Methods > swapDepths.

5. For the parameter of the swapDepths method, enter the target path for the second movie clip.

   When you click the first draggable movie clip, it will swap its stacking order with that of the other movie clip.

6. Place your pointer after the second startDrag statement, and add a similar swapDepths statement below it.

7. Between the parentheses for the second swapDepths statement, enter the target path of the first movie clip.

   The completed scripts should look like the one in **Figure 7.27**.

8. Test your movie.

   When you drag the first movie clip, it will swap its stacking order with that of the second movie clip and vice versa.

To swap the depth level of a movie clip:

1. Continuing with the same file you created in the preceding task, place your pointer inside of the parentheses for the first swapDepths statement.

2. Replace the target path with a number specifying the depth level (**Figure 7.28**).

3. Select the second swapDepths statement, and replace its Parameters field with the same depth-level number.

4. Test your movie.

   The first movie clip you drag is put into the specified depth level. The second movie clip you drag is swapped with whatever is currently in that depth level (**Figure 7.29**).

✔ Tip

- The difference between using a target path and using a depth number as the swapDepths() parameter depends on your needs. Use a target path simply to swap the two named movie clips so that the movie clip that is overlapping the other movie clip will be sent behind it. To keep a draggable movie clip above all other movie clips, use depth level to send it to the top of the stacking order.

```
puzzle1_mc.onPress = function() {
    this.startDrag();
    this.swapDepths(2);
};
puzzle1_mc.onRelease = function() {
    stopDrag();
};
puzzle2_mc.onPress = function() {
    this.startDrag();
    this.swapDepths(2);
};
puzzle2_mc.onRelease = function() {
    stopDrag();
};
```

Figure 7.28 The current movie clip swaps with the one in depth level 2.

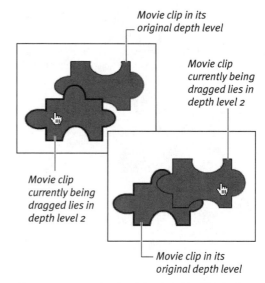

Movie clip in its original depth level

Movie clip currently being dragged lies in depth level 2

Movie clip currently being dragged lies in depth level 2

Movie clip in its original depth level

Figure 7.29 Swapping depth levels is ideal for dealing with multiple draggable movie clips, such as these puzzle pieces.

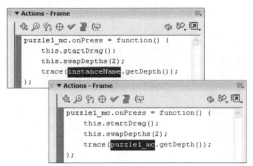

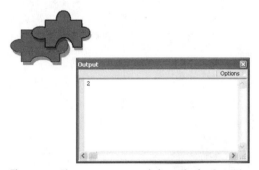

Figure 7.30 Replace the default placeholder named instanceName with the target path to the draggable movie clip, shown here as puzzle1_mc.

Figure 7.31 The trace command shows in the Output window that the currently dragged movie clip is in depth level 2. The Output window appears only when you test your Flash movie. It does not appear in your final SWF file.

To determine the depth level of a movie clip:

1. Using the file from the preceding task, place your pointer after the first swapDepths statement, and press Enter to go to the next line. Choose Global Functions > Miscellaneous Functions > trace.

   The trace command will display information in the Output window when you test your movie. You will add the getDepths() method to the trace command to see the depth level of your movie clip.

2. With your pointer between the parentheses for the trace statement, choose Built-in Classes > Movie > MovieClip > Methods > getDepth.

3. Select and replace the placeholder named instanceName with the target path to the first draggable movie clip (**Figure 7.30**).

4. Select the second swapDepths statement, and add another trace command with a getDepth() method for the second draggable movie clip.

5. Test your movie.

   When you drag the first movie clip, the Output window appears and displays the movie clip's depth level. When you drag the second movie clip, its depth level displays in the Output window (**Figure 7.31**).

✔ Tip

■ The method getDepth() is also a method of the Button class and the TextField class, so you can use it in the same way to determine the stacking order of those objects.

Detecting Movie-Clip Collisions

Now that you can make a movie clip that can be dragged around the Stage, you'll want to know where the user drops it. If the movie clips are puzzle pieces, for example, you need to know whether or not those pieces are dragged and dropped on the correct spots.

It's also valuable to check whether a movie clip intersects another movie clip. The game of Pong, for example, simply detects collisions between the ball, the paddles, and the wall, all of which are movie clips. Detecting movie-clip collisions can be useful on sophisticated e-commerce sites as well. Suppose that you develop an online shopping site that lets your customers drag merchandise into a shopping cart. You can detect when the object intersects with the shopping cart and provide interaction such as highlighting the shopping cart or displaying the product price before the user drops the object.

To detect dropped movie clips or colliding movie clips, use the movie-clip method hitTest(). You can use hitTest() in two ways. One way is to check whether the bounding boxes of any two movie clips intersect. The *bounding box* of a movie clip is the minimum rectangular area that contains the graphics. This method is ideal for graphics colliding with other graphics, such as a ball with a paddle, a ship with an asteroid, or a puzzle piece with its correct resting spot. In this case, you enter the target path of the movie clip as the parameter—for example, hitTest(_root.target).

The second way is to check whether a certain x-y coordinate intersects with a graphic. This method is point specific, which makes it ideal for checking whether only the registration point of a graphic or the mouse pointer intersects with a movie clip. In this case, the hitTest() parameters are an x value, a y value, and the shapeflag parameter, as in hitTest(x, y, shapeflag). The shapeflag parameter is either true or false. This parameter determines whether the bounding box of a movie clip is considered (false) or just the shape of the graphics is considered (true) (**Figure 7.32**).

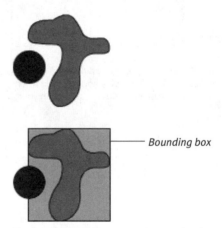

Bounding box

Figure 7.32 When the shapeflag parameter is true (top), the two objects won't intersect; only the shapes are considered. When the shapeflag parameter is false (bottom), the two objects will intersect; the bounding box is considered.

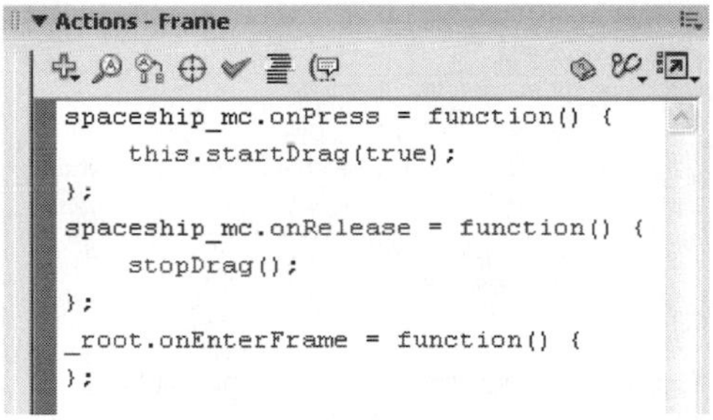

```
▼ Actions - Frame
🔆 🔎 ⊕ ✔ ☰ 🔲                    ◈ 🔏 📥
spaceship_mc.onPress = function() {
    this.startDrag(true);
};
spaceship_mc.onRelease = function() {
    stopDrag();
};
_root.onEnterFrame = function() {
};
```

Figure 7.33 The onEnterFrame event handler is an ideal handler for checking a condition continuously.

To detect an intersection between two movie clips:

1. Create a movie clip, place an instance of it on the Stage, and name it in the Property Inspector.

2. Create another movie clip, place an instance of it on the Stage, and name it in the Property Inspector. Then assign actions on the main Timeline to make it draggable.

3. Select the first frame of the root Timeline, and open the Actions panel.

4. Create a new line in the Script pane under the onRelease event handler, and choose Built-in Classes > Movie > MovieClip > Events > onEnterFrame.

5. Select and replace the placeholder named instanceName with _root. Complete the handler by entering =function(){ and a closing curly brace on the next line.

The onEnterFrame event handler for the root Timeline is established. This event occurs at the frame rate of the movie, which makes it ideal for checking the hitTest condition continuously (**Figure 7.33**).

6. On the next line for the onEnterFrame handler, choose Statements > Conditions/Loops > if.

7. For the condition parameter, enter the name of the draggable movie clip followed by a period.

8. Select hitTest from the code hint pull-down menu.

or

Choose Built-in Classes > Movie > MovieClip > Methods > hitTest.

9. Within the parentheses of the hitTest statement, enter the path of the stationary movie clip.

continues on next page

DETECTING MOVIE-CLIP COLLISIONS

305

10. Enter two equals signs followed by the Boolean value of `true` (**Figure 7.34**).

11. Choose an action to be performed when this condition is met.

The final script should look like **Figure 7.35**.

12. Test your movie (**Figure 7.36**). 🖱

✔ Tips

■ For true/false conditions (known as Booleans) like the one in this task, you can simply state the condition and leave out the last part, `== true`. Flash automatically returns a true or a false when you call the `hitTest()` method, and the `if` statement automatically tests whether the condition is true. You'll learn more about conditional statements in Part V.

■ It doesn't really matter whether you test the moving movie clip to the target or the target to the moving movie clip. The following two statements detect the same kind of collision:

```
spaceship_mc.hitTest(asteroid_mc)
asteroid_mc.hitTest(spaceship_mc)
```

■ To detect a dropped movie clip, you can set the alpha value of the stationary (target) movie clip to 0 so it is invisible. Assign the `hitTest()` method to an `if` statement immediately after the `stopDrag()` method like so:

```
eyes_mc.onPress = function(){
stopDrag();
if
(this.hitTest(invisibleTarget_mc)){
    //drop successful
}
```

In this example, when the draggable movie clip called `eyes_mc` is dropped, Flash checks to see whether or not it is dropped on the movie clip called `invisibleTarget_mc`.

Figure 7.34 This condition checks whether the `spaceship_mc` movie clip intersects the `asteroid_mc` movie clip.

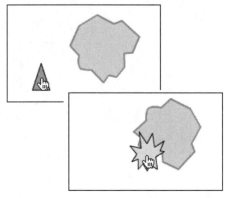

Figure 7.35 The consequence of an intersection is the `nextFrame` action.

Figure 7.36 Dragging the `spaceship_mc` movie clip into the bounding box of the `asteroid_mc` movie clip advances the spaceship movie clip to the next frame, which displays an explosion.

■ If the target of the `hitTest()` method is a movie clip that contains moving graphics, the bounding box of that movie clip will be the bounding box of the last keyframe in the animation.

To detect an intersection between a point and a movie clip:

1. Continuing with the same file you created in the preceding task, select the first frame of the root Timeline, and open the Actions panel.

2. Place your pointer within the parentheses of the if statement.

3. Change the condition so it reads as follows:

   asteroid_mc.hitTest(spaceship_mc._x, spaceship_mc._y, true)

   The hitTest() method now checks whether the *x* and *y* positions of the draggable movie clip called spaceship_mc intersect with the shape of the movie clip called asteroid_mc (**Figure 7.37**).

4. Test your movie.

✔ Tip

- The properties _xmouse and _ymouse are values of the current *x* and *y* positions of the pointer on the screen. You can use these properties in the parameters of the hitTest() method to check whether the pointer intersects a movie clip. This expression returns true if the pointer intersects the movie clip called asteroid:

  asteroid_mc.hitTest(_xmouse, _ymouse, true)

```
spaceship_mc.onPress = function() {
    this.startDrag(true);
};
spaceship_mc.onRelease = function() {
    stopDrag();
};
_root.onEnterFrame = function() {
    if (asteroid_mc.hitTest(spaceship_mc._x, spaceship_mc._y, true) == true) {
        spaceship_mc.nextFrame();
    }
};
```

Figure 7.37 The ActionScript (above) tests whether the registration point of the spaceship_mc movie clip intersects with any shape in the asteroid_mc movie clip. Notice that the spaceship is safe from collision because its registration point is still within the crevice and clear of the asteroid.

Detecting Dropped Movie Clips with _droptarget

Another way to detect whether or not one draggable movie clip has been dropped onto another is to use the movie-clip property _droptarget. This property retrieves the absolute target path of another movie clip where the draggable movie clip was dropped. The second movie clip essentially is the destination for the draggable movie clip. Use a conditional statement to compare whether the _droptarget value of the draggable movie clip is the same as the target path of the destination movie clip. Perform any actions based on whether the condition is true or false.

A word of caution here: The _droptarget property returns the absolute target path in slash syntax. This property originated in Flash 4, which supported only the slash syntax. (ActionScript 2.0 does *not* support slash syntax). So to test whether the _droptarget property matches the target path of a destination movie clip, you construct a conditional statement that looks like the following:

```
draggableMovieClip_mc._droptarget ==
"/destinationMovieClip_mc"
```

The backslash represents the root Timeline in slash syntax. Using the methods that you learned in the preceding task, create a draggable movie clip (**Figure 7.38**).

Test the _droptarget property in a conditional statement after the stopDrag() statement.

Figure 7.38 The hamburger disappears when it is dropped on the trash can.

Figure 7.39 is a completed script that will make burger_mc invisible when it is dropped on trashCan_mc.

```
burger_mc.onPress = function() {
    // begin dragging this movie clip
    this.startDrag();
};
burger_mc.onRelease = function() {
    // stop dragging this movie clip
    stopDrag();
    // check to see if this movie clip
    // is dropped on the destination movie clip
    if (this._droptarget == "/trashCan_mc") {
        // if it's true, then make it invisible
        this._visible = false;
    }
};
```

Figure 7.39 If the draggable movie clip is dropped on the movie clip called trashCan_mc, its visibility is set to false.

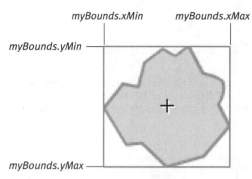

myBounds.xMin   *myBounds.xMax*

myBounds.yMin

myBounds.yMax

Figure 7.40 The xMin, xMax, yMin, and yMax properties of a boundary object refer to the edges of a movie clip whose boundaries have been retrieved.

Getting the Boundaries of Movie Clips

Often, when you are changing the dimensions and location of a movie clip dynamically, you'll need to know its boundaries to keep limitations on those changes. You could create a map that your viewer can move around or zoom in on for more details by setting the _x, _y, _xscale, and _yscale properties of the map. But you would also want to know where the edges of the map are so that you can make sure they are never exposed. The method you need to use is getBounds(). This method gets the minimum and maximum dimensions of the bounding box of a movie clip and puts the information in a generic object containing the properties xMin, xMax, yMin, and yMax. If you call your bounding-box object myBounds, the value of the movie clip's left edge would be myBounds.xMin, the right edge would be myBounds.xMax, the top edge would be myBounds.yMin, and the bottom edge would be myBounds.yMax (**Figure 7.40**).

To get the boundaries of a movie clip:

1. Create a movie-clip symbol, place an instance of it on the Stage, and give it a name in the Property Inspector.

   This clip will be the movie clip whose boundaries you will determine.

2. Select the first frame on the root Timeline, and open the Actions panel.

3. Enter a name for an object that will hold the boundary information followed by an equals sign.

4. Choose Built-in Classes > Movie > MovieClip > Methods > getBounds.

continues on next page

5. Replace the default placeholder named `instanceName` with the target path to the movie clip whose boundary box you want to retrieve (**Figure 7.41**).

The results of the `getBounds()` method will be assigned to the name of your object. The method, however, still needs a parameter for its `targetCoordinateSpace`.

Figure 7.41 myBounds is the name of the boundary object, and square_mc is the name of the movie clip whose boundaries you are interested in finding.

6. Between the parentheses of the `getBounds()` method, enter a target path to the Timeline whose *x-y* coordinate space you want to serve as the reference for the boundary information (**Figure 7.42**).

Flash gets the boundaries of the movie clip on the Stage. The boundaries are made relative to the root Timeline. All this information is put in an object whose properties contain the minimum and maximum *x* and *y* values.

Figure 7.42 getBounds() retrieves the minimum x (xMin), minimum y (yMin), maximum x (xMax), and maximum y (xMax) values of the movie clip called square_mc relative to the _root coordinates and stores that information in your boundary object called myBounds.

7. Test your movie.

Choose Debug > List Variables to verify the boundaries of the movie clip (**Figure 7.43**). Use the object properties xMin, yMin, xMax, and yMax as constraints on other interactivity. Use the boundary properties to constrain a draggable movie clip, for example (**Figure 7.44**).

```
Level #0:
Variable _level0.$version = "WIN 7,0,0,269"
Variable _level0.myBounds = [object #1] {
    xMin:47.9,
    xMax:268.05,
    yMin:28.4,
    yMax:178.6
}
Movie Clip: Target="_level0.square_mc"
```

Figure 7.43 The myBounds object and its properties are listed in the Output window when you choose List Variables in test mode.

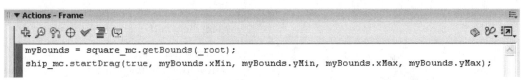

```
myBounds = square_mc.getBounds(_root);
ship_mc.startDrag(true, myBounds.xMin, myBounds.yMin, myBounds.xMax, myBounds.yMax);
```

Figure 7.44 Using the boundary information as the parameters for the startDrag() method will constrain a draggable movie clip to the edges of the square_mc movie clip.

Generating Movie Clips Dynamically

Creating movie clips on the fly—that is, during playback—opens a whole new world of exciting interactive possibilities. Imagine a game of Asteroids, in which enemy space-ships appear as the game progresses. You can store those enemy spaceships as movie-clip symbols in your Library and create instances on the Stage with ActionScript as you need them. Or, if you want an infinite supply of a certain draggable item (such as merchandise) to be pulled off the shelf of an online store, you can make duplicates of the movie clip each time the viewer drags it away from its original spot. Or create afterimages of a movie clip's motion, much like onion-skinning, by duplicating a movie clip and making it lag as it moves across the screen. All the while, you maintain the power to modify properties, control the position of the playhead in those Timelines, and use the clips as you would any other movie clips.

Flash has many methods that enable dynamically generated movie clips. Among them are `duplicateMovieClip()`, `attachMovie()`, and `createEmptyMovieClip()`.

Duplicating movie clips

When you use the method `duplicate MovieClip()`, an exact replica of an instance on the Stage is created in the same position as the original. Duplicate movie-clip instances are given their own unique names, as well as a specific depth level for each instance. This depth level determines stacking order, just as it does with the movie-clip method `swapDepths()`.

It's common practice to duplicate movie clips by using looping functions that append successive numbers to the instance name and assign depth levels automatically. For example, duplicating a movie clip named `asteroid_mc` in this manner would produce `asteroid_mc1` in depth level 1, `asteroid_mc2` in depth level 2, `asteroid_mc3` in depth level 3, and so on. Check out Chapter 9 to learn about the looping actions that complement the duplication of movie clips.

To duplicate a movie-clip instance:

1. Create a movie-clip symbol, place an instance of it on the Stage, and name it in the Property Inspector.

2. Create a button symbol, place an instance of it on the Stage, and name it in the Property Inspector.

continues on next page

GENERATING MOVIE CLIPS DYNAMICALLY

3. Select the first frame of the root Timeline, and open the Actions panel.

4. Enter the name of your button in the Script pane followed by a period.

5. Choose Built-in Classes > Movie > Button > Events > onRelease. Complete the handler by entering =function(){ and a closing curly brace on the next line (**Figure 7.45**).

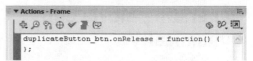

Figure 7.45 The onRelease event handler for the button called duplicateButton_btn is created.

6. On the next line, choose Global Functions > Movie Clip Control > duplicateMovieClip (Esc + dm).

   The duplicateMovieClip action appears within the onRelease event handler in the Script pane.

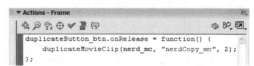

Figure 7.46 The duplicate movie clip called nerdCopy_mc is made in depth level 2 from the movie clip called nerd_mc.

7. With your pointer between the parentheses, enter the target path for the movie clip followed by a comma.

8. Enter the name for the new duplicate movie clip followed by a comma.

   Make sure the new name is surrounded by quotation marks.

9. Enter a number to specify the stacking order for your duplicate movie clip (**Figure 7.46**).

   At this point, when you play your movie, the actions assigned to your button duplicate the nerd_mc movie clip but the new instance appears right above the original, so you can't see whether anything happened. To see the duplicate, you need to move or change it in some way to make it stand out from the original.

10. On a new line, choose Statements > Variables > with.

11. As the object of the with statement, enter the name of the new duplicated movie clip that you created in step 6.

```
with (nerdCopy_mc) {
    _x += 40;
    _xscale = 75;
    _yscale = 110;
}
```

Figure 7.47 The with statement is used to temporarily change the scope to nerdCopy_mc.

```
duplicateMovieClip(nerd_mc, "nerdCopy_mc", 2);
with (nerdCopy_mc) {
    _x += 40;
    _xscale = 75;
    _yscale = 110;
}
```

Figure 7.48 The ActionScript (above) is assigned for the button instance at the bottom of the Stage. When the original movie clip (left) is duplicated, the copy can be targeted and controlled just like any other (right). This movie-clip copy, called nerdCopy_mc, has its x position, x scale, and y scale properties modified.

12. On the next line, enter an expression that adds 40 to the *x* position of the original movie clip. The assignment operator += tells Flash to move the object 40 pixels to the right.

13. Add more statements inside the with statement to transform the duplicate movie clip (**Figure 7.47**).

14. Test the movie (**Figure 7.48**).

✔ Tips

- You can have only one movie-clip instance per depth level. If you duplicate another instance in a level that's already occupied, that instance replaces the first one.

- Duplicate movie clips inherit the properties of the original instance. If the original instance has an alpha transparency of 50 percent, for example, the duplicate movie-clip instance will also have an alpha transparency of 50 percent. Duplicate instances will always start in Frame 1, however, even if the original movie-clip instance is in a different frame when it is duplicated.

- Duplicate movie clips also take on any ActionScript that may be assigned to the original instance. If the original instance contains ActionScript that makes it a draggable movie clip, for example, the duplicate will also be draggable.

- The depth level corresponds to the same depth level in the movie-clip method swapDepths(). Use swapDepths() to change the stacking order of duplicated movie clips.

GENERATING MOVIE CLIPS DYNAMICALLY

Attaching movie clips

The technique of duplicating movie clips is useful for existing movie clips, but what if you need to place a *new* movie clip on the Stage from the library dynamically? In this situation, you would turn to the `attachMovie()` method. This method lets you create new instances of movie clips from the library and attach them to existing movie-clip instances already on the Stage or to the root Timeline. The attached movie clip doesn't replace the original but actually becomes part of the movie-clip object in a parent/child relationship. If the original instance on the Stage is called `parentInstance_mc`, the target path for the attached movie clip would be something like:
`_root.parentInstance_mc.attachedInstance_mc`

If a movie clip attaches to the root Timeline, the target path is simply:
`_root.attachedInstance_mc`

To attach a movie clip from the library:

1. Create a movie-clip symbol, place an instance of it from the library on the Stage, and give it a name in the Property Inspector.

   This instance will be the original, parent instance to which you'll attach another movie clip.

2. Create another movie-clip symbol, and select it in the library.

3. From the Library Options menu, choose Linkage (**Figure 7.49**).

   The Linkage Properties dialog box appears.

4. In the Linkage section, select Export for ActionScript and leave Export in first frame checked; in the Identifier field, enter a unique name for your movie clip; then click OK (**Figure 7.50**).

   The identifier allows you to call on this movie clip by this name from ActionScript and attach it to an instance on the Stage.

5. Create a button, drag an instance of it to the Stage, and name it in the Property Inspector.

Figure 7.49 The Linkage option in the Library window.

Figure 7.50 The Linkage Properties dialog box.

6. Select the first frame of the root Timeline, and open the Actions panel.

7. Create an `onRelease` event handler for your button.

8. On the next line, enter the target path of the movie-clip instance on the Stage followed by a period.

This instance is the one to which you will attach the new instance.

9. Choose Built-in Classes > Movie > MovieClip > attachMovie.

10. With your pointer between the parentheses, enter the identifier of the movie clip in the Library window, a name for the newly attached instance, and a depth level, separating your parameters with commas (**Figure 7.51**).

The identifier and new name must be in quotation marks.

11. Test your movie.

When you click the button that you created, the movie clip identified in the library attaches to the instance on Stage and overlaps it. The registration point of the attached movie clip lines up with the registration point of the parent instance (**Figure 7.52**).

You need to keep several names straight when you use the `attachMovie()` method. In this example, the name of the movie-clip symbol in the library is apple movie clip. The name of the identifier is appleID. The name of the attached instance is `attachedApple_mc`.

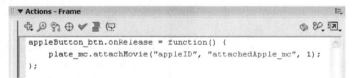

Figure 7.51 The `attachMovie()` method requires the parameters `idName`, `newName`, and `depth`. This `attachMovie()` method attaches the movie clip identified as appleID to the instance `plate_mc` in depth level 1 and names the attached instance `attachedApple_mc`.

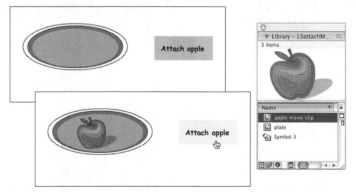

Figure 7.52 The movie-clip instance called `plate_mc` sits on the Stage (top). The actions assigned for the button attach an instance of the `apple_mc` movie clip from the library (right) to the `plate_mc` instance (bottom).

✔ Tips

- You can always attach movie clips to the root Timeline by entering `_root` as the object of the `attachMovie()` method. The registration point of the attached instance will be aligned with the top-left corner (x = 0, y = 0) of the Stage.

- An attached movie clip takes on the properties of the movie-clip instance to which it attaches. If the original movie clip instance is rotated 45 degrees, the attached movie clip will also be rotated 45 degrees.

- You can attach multiple movie clips to the same parent instance as long as you specify different depth levels. Each depth level can hold only one movie clip.

- You can also attach movie clips to a recently attached movie clip itself. The target path for the first attached movie clip becomes `_root.parentInstance_mc.attachedInstance1_mc`, the target path for another attached movie clip becomes `_root.parentInstance_mc.attachedInstance1_mc.attachedInstance2_mc`, and so on.

- You cannot attach a movie clip to another movie clip that has an external file loaded into it (see Chapter 6 for the `loadMovie` action and the files that can be dynamically loaded using `loadMovie`).

Creating empty movie clips

When you use `attachMovieClip()`, you need to prepare a movie-clip symbol in your Library by creating it at author time, assigning an identifier, and marking it to export for ActionScript. If you need just an empty movie clip—a movie clip without graphics, animations, or attached scripts—you can use the method `createEmptyMovieClip()`. This method is similar to `attach movieclip()` in that it attaches a movie clip dynamically to another movie clip already on the Stage. But instead of attaching a movie-clip symbol from the library, you attach an empty movie clip. You give each newly created empty movie clip a unique name and depth level.

Use empty movie clips as "shells" in preparation for additional content that may be loaded into your Flash movie. Create an empty movie clip on the root Timeline and modify its x and y properties to position it anywhere on the Stage. Now you can use `loadMovie()` to load external .swf files or JPEG images into your empty movie clip. Or you can use empty movie clips as the parent clip for the `attachMovieClip()` method.

Empty movie clips are also important for movie-clip drawing methods. You'll learn to draw lines, curves, fills, and gradients just by using ActionScript. An empty movie clip provides the anchor for all these drawing methods.

To create an empty movie clip on the root Timeline:

1. Select the first frame of the root Timeline, and open the Actions panel.

2. In the Script pane, enter **_root** followed by a period.

   An empty movie clip will be attached and scoped to the root Timeline.

3. Choose Built-in Classes > Movie > MovieClip > Methods > createEmptyMovieClip.

4. Between the parentheses, enter a unique name for your empty movie clip, as well as a unique depth level.

   Separate your parameters with commas, and make sure that your movie clip's name is in quotation marks (**Figure 7.53**).

   A movie clip with the name you've chosen is created on the root Timeline at the specified depth level.

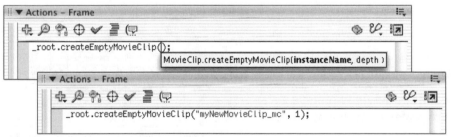

Figure 7.53 With the help of the code hints in the Script pane, a new empty movie clip called myNewMovieClip_mc is created on the root Timeline in depth level 1.

Removing Movie Clips Dynamically

Just as you can generate movie clips dynamically, you can remove them dynamically. You can delete movie-clip instances that have been duplicated or attached, delete empty movie clips, and even delete movie-clip instances that were put on the Stage at author time. **Table 7.3** lists the different ways to remove movie clips.

To remove a duplicated, attached, or empty movie clip by using removeMovieClip:

1. Choose Global Functions > Movie Clip Control > removeMovieClip (Esc + rm).

2. With your pointer between the parentheses, enter the target path of the movie clip (**Figure 7.54**).

To remove a duplicated, attached, or empty movie clip by using unloadMovie:

1. Choose Global Functions > Browser/ Network > unloadMovie (Esc + um).

2. Enter the target path of the movie clip (**Figure 7.55**).

To use unloadMovie to remove a movie clip placed on the Stage at author time:

1. Choose Global Functions > Browser/ Network > unloadMovie (Esc + um).

2. Enter the target path of the movie clip.

Table 7.3

Removing Movie Clips	
MOVIE CLIPS CREATED BY	REMOVE WITH
duplicateMovieClip	removeMovieClip, unloadMovie
attachMovie	removeMovieClip, unloadMovie
createEmptyMovieClip	removeMovieClip, unloadMovie
manual placement on Stage during author time	unloadMovie

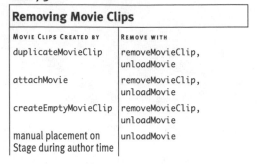

Figure 7.54 Use removeMovieClip to remove dynamically generated movie clips. This statement removes the myNewMovieClip_mc movie clip from the stage.

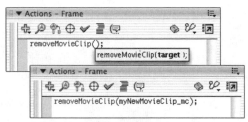

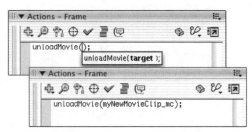

Figure 7.55 unloadMovie, which usually removes external SWF files, can be used to remove dynamically generated movie clips as well as movie clips placed on the Stage during author time.

Getting Movie Clip Depth Levels

When working with a movie clip, you may need to control the depth level at which an instance shows up at run time. As you have learned so far, every movie clip has an associated depth level, which determines whether it displays in front of or behind another object.

When you create a new movie clip using the `createEmptyMovieClip()` method, you are required to define the new object's depth level as a parameter. But how do you know what depth level to choose? After all, if you have already been generating movie clips dynamically, you may not know the depth levels for each of them. The method `getNextHighestDepth()` can tell you the next available depth value.

If, on the other hand, you want to know the name of the movie clip that is occupying a certain depth level, you can use the `getInstanceAtDepth()` method. You can use this method to help you target and manipulate particular movie clips that have been generated at run time.

To position dynamically attached movie clips:

1. Create two movie-clip symbols in the Library (Insert > New Symbol). Give each a unique ID name in the Linkage Properties Inspector.

    Leave these symbols in the Library.

2. Select the first frame of the root Timeline, and open the Actions panel.

3. Enter the target path _root followed by a period.

4. Choose Built-in Classes > Movie > MovieClip > createEmptyMovieClip.

5. Within the parentheses, enter an instance name and depth level for your new movie clip (**Figure 7.56**).

    An empty movie clip is generated on the main Stage.

6. On the next line, enter the instance name of your newly created movie clip followed by a period, the _x property and an equals sign, and a value for the x position.

7. Repeat step 6 for the y position of your movie clip (**Figure 7.57**).

    Your empty movie clip is positioned at the specified x and y coordinates.

    continues on next page

Figure 7.56 An empty movie clip named myClip_mc has been created and placed on level 1.

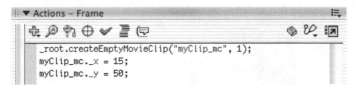

Figure 7.57 At run time, the empty movie clip named myClip_mc will position itself at the x position of 15 and the y position of 50.

8. On the next line, enter the instance name of your movie clip followed by a period.

9. Choose Built-in Classes > Movie > MovieClip > methods > attachMovie.

10. Enter the ID name for your first movie clip instance in your library followed by a new instance name and a depth level of 10.

The ID name and new instance name must be surrounded by quotation marks.

11. Repeat step 10 to attach the second movie clip at a depth level of 20.

12. On the next line, enter the instance name of your movie clip followed by a period.

13. Choose Built-in Classes > Movie > MovieClip > Methods > getInstanceAtDepth.

14. Enter a depth level of 20 inside of the parentheses. Place your pointer to the right of the closing parenthesis; enter a period followed by the _x property, an equals sign, and then a value for the x position.

Flash retrieves the name of the instance at depth level 20 and assigns a specific x position.

15. Repeat step 14 to define the y position for the attached movie clip in level 20 (**Figure 7.58**).

16. Test your movie.

At run time, Flash will initially attach the two movie-clip instances to the empty movie clip. The instance at depth level 20 is then placed at the exact x and y positions that you define (**Figure 7.59**).

▼ Actions – Frame

```
_root.createEmptyMovieClip("myClip_mc", 1);
myClip_mc._x = 15;
myClip_mc._y = 50;

myClip_mc.attachMovie("girl1", "girl1_mc", 10);
myClip_mc.attachMovie("girl2", "girl2_mc", 20);

myClip_mc.getInstanceAtDepth(20)._x = 134;
myClip_mc.getInstanceAtDepth(20)._y = 42;
```

Figure 7.58 The movie clip at depth level 20 is moved to the x position of 134 and the y position of 42.

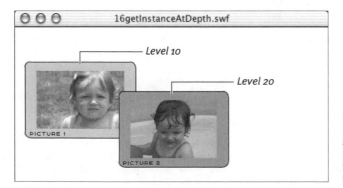

Level 10

Level 20

16getInstanceAtDepth.swf

PICTURE 1

PICTURE 2

Figure 7.59 At run time, Flash places girl1_mc at the x position of 15 and the y position of 50 and girl2_mc to the x position of 134 and the y position of 42.

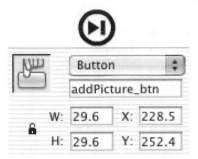

Figure 7.60 A new button is placed on the root Timeline and given an instance name of addPicture_btn in the Property Inspector.

```
▼ Actions - Frame

_root.createEmptyMovieClip("myClip_mc", 1);
myClip_mc._x = 15;
myClip_mc._y = 50;
myClip_mc.attachMovie("girl1", "girl1_mc", 10);
myClip_mc.attachMovie("girl2", "girl2_mc", 20);
myClip_mc.getInstanceAtDepth(20)._x = 134;
myClip_mc.getInstanceAtDepth(20)._y = 42;

addPicture_btn.onPress = function() {
    var newDepth = myClip_mc.getNextHighestDepth();
}
```

Figure 7.61 A variable named newDepth has been created within the onPress event, which will return the next highest depth for the empty movie clip.

A useful combination is to use getInstance AtDepth() and getNextHighestDepth() to control the placement of a movie clip at a specific depth level and even *x* and *y* positioning.

To control the depth level and positioning of a dynamically placed movie clip:

1. Continuing with the file you used in the preceding task, place a button instance on the root Timeline. In the Property Inspector, assign an instance name (**Figure 7.60**).

   This button will add a dynamically placed movie clip at a depth level it gets using the getNextHighestDepth() method.

2. Select the first frame of the main Timeline, and open the Actions panel.

3. Create a new line after your last line of code from the preceding task.

4. Assign an onRelease handler to the button.

5. Choose Statements > Variables > var.

6. Enter the variable name newDepth followed by an equals sign. Enter the name of the empty movie clip created in the preceding task followed by a period. Choose Built-in Classes > Movie > MovieClip > Methods > getNextHighestDepth (**Figure 7.61**).

   A new variable named newDepth is created and will store the next available depth level of movie clips attached to your empty movie clip.

   continues on next page

GETTING MOVIE CLIP DEPTH LEVELS

7. On the next line, enter the instance name of the empty movie clip followed by a period.

8. Choose Built-in Classes > Movie > MovieClip > Methods > attachMovie.

9. With your pointer between the parentheses, enter an ID name, a new name, and a depth level of newDepth.

A new movie clip with a depth level of newDepth is attached to the empty movie clip.

10. Using the getInstanceAtDepth() method, assign *x* and *y* values to the new movie clip (**Figure 7.62**).

11. On the next line, choose Global Functions > Miscellaneous Functions > trace.

12. Concatenate text and the variable newDepth to display a message in the Output window (**Figure 7.63**).

```
_root.createEmptyMovieClip("myClip_mc", 1);
myClip_mc._x = 15;
myClip_mc._y = 50;
myClip_mc.attachMovie("girl1", "girl1_mc", 10);
myClip_mc.attachMovie("girl2", "girl2_mc", 20);
myClip_mc.getInstanceAtDepth(20)._x = 134;
myClip_mc.getInstanceAtDepth(20)._y = 42;

addPicture_btn.onPress = function() {
    var newDepth = myClip_mc.getNextHighestDepth();
    myClip_mc.attachMovie("girl3", "girl3_mc", newDepth);
    myClip_mc.getInstanceAtDepth(newDepth)._x = 261;
    myClip_mc.getInstanceAtDepth(newDepth)._y = 91;
}
```

Figure 7.62 The movie clip girl3 is assigned an x position of 261 and a y position of 91.

```
_root.createEmptyMovieClip("myClip_mc", 1);
myClip_mc._x = 15;
myClip_mc._y = 50;
myClip_mc.attachMovie("girl1", "girl1_mc", 10);
myClip_mc.attachMovie("girl2", "girl2_mc", 20);
myClip_mc.getInstanceAtDepth(20)._x = 134;
myClip_mc.getInstanceAtDepth(20)._y = 42;

addPicture_btn.onPress = function() {
    var newDepth = myClip_mc.getNextHighestDepth();
    myClip_mc.attachMovie("girl3", "girl3_mc", newDepth);
    myClip_mc.getInstanceAtDepth(newDepth)._x = 261;
    myClip_mc.getInstanceAtDepth(newDepth)._y = 91;
    trace("A new movie clip was placed at level " + newDepth);
}
```

Figure 7.63 The trace statement is added to the onPress event and will display the current depth level of the new movie clip when the button is pressed.

13. Test your movie.

When you click your button, a new movie clip is attached to the next highest level. The Output window displays the depth level information (**Figure 7.64**).

Figure 7.64 When the button is clicked, a new movie clip will be placed at the next highest level. The output window displays the level at which the movie clip is placed.

Creating Shapes Dynamically

A special category of movie clip methods is reserved for creating lines, curves, fills, and gradients. These methods are the drawing methods of the movie clip. With these methods, you can create your own shapes and control their color, transparency, stroke width, and even the kind and placement of gradient fills. You could use the drawing methods to create your own simple paint and coloring application, or you could draw bar graphs or pie charts or connect data points to visualize numerical data that your viewer inputs.

To use the drawing methods, you must start with a movie clip. The movie clip acts as the point of reference for all your drawing coordinates. So if your movie clip is anchored at the top-left corner of the Stage (at x = 0, y = 0), all the drawing coordinates are relative to that registration point. The movie clip also acts as though it were a pen tip, anchoring the start of a line or curve and keeping track of its end point as you tell it to draw. The movie clip doesn't actually move, however. Think of the movie clip as being a virtual pen tip.

Although you can use any movie clip to begin drawing, the most common way is to use the method `createEmptyMovieClip()` to create an empty movie clip on the root Timeline. The new movie clip is positioned at the top-left corner of the Stage automatically, so its drawing coordinates are identical to the Stage coordinates. Use **Figure 7.65** to review the Stage coordinates.

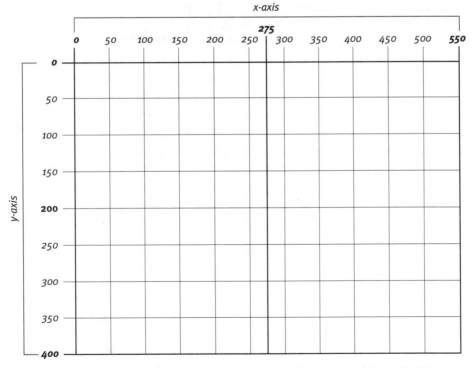

Figure 7.65 An overview of the default Stage size, 550 pixels in width by 400 pixels in height. The upper-left corner is x = 0 and y = 0, and the lower right corner is x = 550 and y = 400.

Creating lines and curves

Three methods draw lines and curves: the movcTo(), lineTo(), and curveTo() methods. The moveTo() method sets the beginning point of your line or curve. The lineTo() and curveTo() methods set the end point and, in the case of curves, determine its curvature.

The lineStyle() method changes the characteristics of your stroke, such as its point size, color, and transparency. The clear() method erases the drawings made with your movie clip.

To create lines:

1. Select the first frame of the root Timeline, and open the Actions panel.

2. Enter _root followed by a period.

3. Choose Built-in Classes > Movie > MovieClip > Methods > createEmptyMovieClip.

4. For its parameters, enter a name for this movie clip and a depth level, making sure that your instance name is in quotation marks (**Figure 7.66**).

   An empty movie clip is created on the root Timeline and registered at the top-left corner of the Stage.

5. On the next line, enter the target path to your movie clip followed by a period.

6. Choose Built-in Classes > Movie > MovieClip > Drawing Methods > lineStyle.

continues on next page

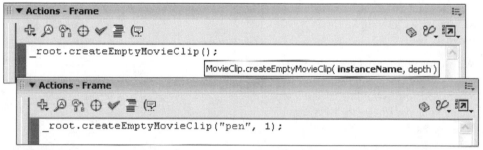

Figure 7.66 The empty movie clip called pen will be the coordinate space for the drawing and will act as a virtual pen.

CREATING SHAPES DYNAMICALLY

7. With your pointer between the parentheses, enter the thickness of the line, the RGB color in hex code, and its transparency, separating your parameters with commas (**Figure 7.67**).

The thickness is a number from 0 to 255; 0 is hairline thickness, and 255 is the maximum point thickness.

The RGB parameter is the hex code referring to the color of the line. You can find the hex code for any color in the Color Mixer panel below the color swatch. Red, for example, is 0xFF0000.

The transparency is a number from 0 to 100 for the line's alpha value; 0 is completely transparent, and 100 is completely opaque.

8. On the next line, enter the target path to your movie clip followed by a period.

9. Choose Built-in Classes > Movie > MovieClip > Drawing Methods > moveTo.

10. With your pointer between the parentheses, enter the *x* and *y* coordinates where you want your line to start, separating your parameters with commas (**Figure 7.68**).

11. On the next line, enter the target path to your movie clip followed by a period.

12. Choose Built-in Classes > Movie > MovieClip > Drawing Methods > lineTo.

Figure 7.67 Define the line style (stroke thickness, color, and transparency) before you begin drawing.

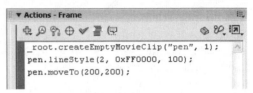

Figure 7.68 The beginning of this line is at x = 200, y = 200.

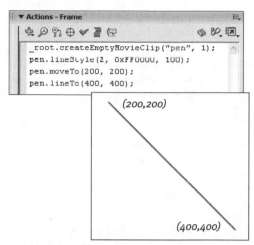

```
▼ Actions - Frame
_root.createEmptyMovieClip("pen", 1);
pen.lineStyle(2, 0xFF0000, 100);
pen.moveTo(200, 200);
pen.lineTo(400, 400);
```

(200,200)

(400,400)

Figure 7.69 This diagonal line is drawn with a 2-point red stroke. The virtual pen tip is now positioned at x = 400, y = 400 and ready for a new lineTo() method.

13. With your pointer between the parentheses, enter the *x* and *y* coordinates of the end point of your line, separating your parameters with commas (**Figure 7.69**).

The end point of your line segment automatically becomes the beginning point for the next, so you don't need to use the moveTo() method to move the coordinates.

14. Continue adding more lineTo() methods to continue drawing more line segments.

✔ **Tips**

■ You can change the line style at any time so multiple line segments can have different thicknesses, colors, or transparencies. Add a lineStyle() method before the lineTo() method whose line you want to modify.

■ After you finish your drawing, you can modify its properties by modifying the properties of the empty movie clip. Or you can affect the behavior of your drawing by calling a method of the empty movie clip. The drawing still "belongs" to the empty movie clip, so whatever you do to it will affect the drawing. You can duplicate your drawing, for example, by using the duplicateMovieClip action on the empty movie clip, or you can even make your drawing draggable by assigning a startDrag() method to the empty movie clip!

■ Instead of creating an empty movie clip to control the drawing methods, you could use the root Timeline. But you won't have as much control of the root Timeline as you would an empty movie clip.

To create curves:

1. Create an empty movie clip on the root Timeline as described in the preceding task.

2. Enter the target path to your empty movie clip, and then choose Built-in Classes > Movie > MovieClip > Drawing Methods > lineStyle.

3. Define the style of your curve as described in the preceding task.

4. On the next line, enter the target path to your empty movie clip, and then choose Built-in Classes > Movie > MovieClip > Drawing Methods > moveTo.

5. Move the starting point of your curve as described in the preceding task.

6. On the next line, enter the target path to your empty movie clip.

7. Choose Built-in Classes > Movie > MovieClip > Drawing Methods > curveTo.

8. With your pointer between the parentheses, enter *x* and *y* coordinates for the control point and *x* and *y* coordinates for the end of the curve (**Figure 7.70**).

   The *control point* is a point that determines the amount of curvature. If you were to extend a straight line from the control point to the end point of the

curve, you would see that it functions much like the handle of a curve (**Figure 7.71**). Check out the sample file in this section on the accompanying CD-ROM to see how the control point affects your curve in real time.

✔ Tip

■ To reduce the repetition of the target path, use a with statement to change the scope temporarily. For example, the statement

```
_root.createEmptyMovieClip("pen", 1);
with (pen) {
    lineStyle(5, 0xff0000, 100);
    moveTo(200, 100);
    curveTo(300, 100, 300, 200);
    curveTo(300, 300, 200, 300);
    curveTo(100, 300, 100, 200);
    curveTo(100, 100, 200, 100);
}
```

is the same as

```
_root.createEmptyMovieClip("pen", 1);
pen.lineStyle(5, 0xff0000, 100);
pen.moveTo(200, 100);
pen.curveTo(300, 100, 300, 200);
pen.curveTo(300, 300, 200, 300);
pen.curveTo(100, 300, 100, 200);
pen.curveTo(100, 100, 200, 100);
```

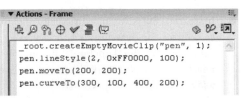

Figure 7.70 The curveTo() method requires x and y coordinates for its control point and for its end point. This curve starts at (200,200) and ends at (400,200) with the control point at (300,100) (see Figure 7.71).

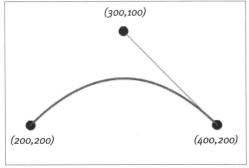

Figure 7.71 By drawing a straight line from the control point to the end point, you can visualize the curve's Bézier handle. The dots have been added to show the two anchor points and the control point.

Quadratic Bézier Curves

If you were to try to draw a circle with the curveTo() method using four segments, you might be surprised by the results. The following script does not produce a perfect circle, as you might expect (**Figure 7.72**):

```
_root.createEmptyMovieClip("pen", 1);
with (pen) {
    lineStyle(5, 0xff0000, 100);
    moveTo(200, 100);
    curveTo(300, 100, 300, 200);
    curveTo(300, 300, 200, 300);
    curveTo(100, 300, 100, 200);
    curveTo(100, 100, 200, 100);
}
```

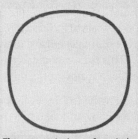

Figure 7.72 An imperfect circle drawn with four curveTo() statements.

The curveTo() method uses what are called quadratic Bézier curves—the same kind that it uses for the Oval tool in the Tools panel. Four segments don't produce a perfect circle because Flash needs eight (**Figure 7.73**). So how do you determine their anchor points and control points? The answer involves a fair bit of math and trigonometry (which you will explore in Chapter 11), but the code to produce a perfect circle in eight segments is presented here. Essentially, the start and end points of each curve lie on a circle of a certain radius (r). The *x* coordinate is r*cos(theta), and the *y* coordinate is r*sin(theta). *Theta* is the angle that one segment covers. So for eight segments, theta is 45 degrees. The control points lie exactly between the start and end anchor points at a distance of r/cos(0.5*theta).

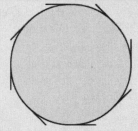

Figure 7.73 A perfect circle drawn with eight curveTo() statements. Line segments from the control points to the end points have been added to show the eight curves.

```
function radians(degrees) {
    return (Math.PI/180)*degrees;
}
theta = 45;
r = 100;
d = r/Math.cos(radians(0.5*theta));
this.lineStyle(1, 0x000000, 100);
this.moveTo(r, 0);
for (k=(theta/2); k<361; k=k+theta) {
    xControl = d*Math.cos(radians(k));
    yControl = d*Math.sin(radians(k));
    xAnchor = r*Math.cos(radians(k+(theta/2)));
    yAnchor = r*Math.sin(radians(k+(theta/2)));
    this.curveTo(xControl, yControl, xAnchor, yAnchor);
}
```

The clear() method erases the drawings made with the movie-clip drawing methods. In conjunction with an onEnterFrame event or a setInterval() function, you can make Flash continually erase a drawing and redraw itself. This is how you can create curves and lines that are not static, but change.

The following example shows the dynamic updates you can make in a drawing by moving their vertices with draggable movie clips.

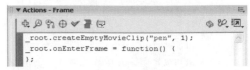

Figure 7.74 The onEnterFrame event handler is created for the root Timeline.

To use clear to update a drawing dynamically:

1. Create four small draggable movie clips with the code assigned to their instances.

   The code on the movie-clip instances should look like this:

   ```
   on (press) {
       this.startDrag();
   }
   on (release) {
       stopDrag();
   }
   ```

2. Give each draggable movie clip a unique name in the Property Inspector.

3. Select the first frame of the root Timeline, and open the Actions panel.

4. Create an empty movie clip on the root Timeline as described in the previous tasks.

5. On the next line, enter _root followed by a period.

6. Choose Built-in Classes > Movie > MovieClip > Events > onEnterFrame. Complete the handler by entering =function(){ and a closing curly brace on the next line (**Figure 7.74**).

   The onEnterFrame event handler is created. This event happens at the frame rate of the movie, providing a way to perform actions continuously.

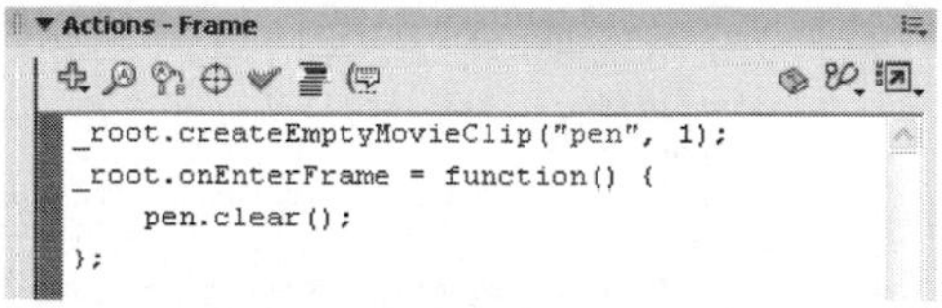

Figure 7.75 All drawings created with the pen movie clip are cleared continuously.

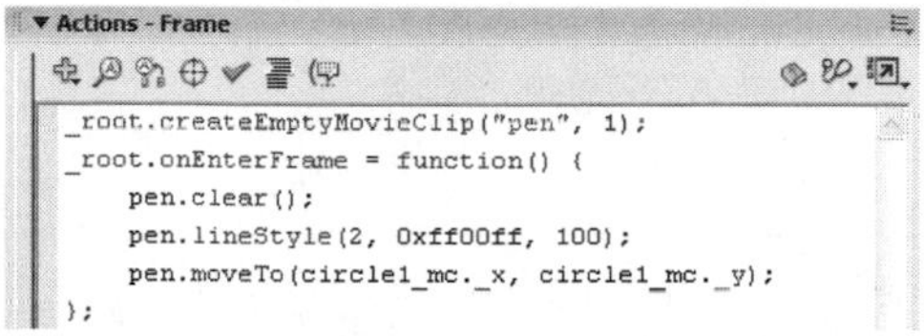

Figure 7.76 The first line segment will begin where the registration point of `circle1_mc` lies.

7. On the next line, enter the target path to your empty movie clip followed by a period.

8. Choose Built-in Classes > Movie > MovieClip > Drawing Methods > clear (**Figure 7.75**).

The `clear()` method erases the previous drawings made with your empty movie clip.

9. On the next line, enter the target path to the empty movie clip followed by a period.

10. Choose Built-in Classes > Movie > MovieClip > Drawing Methods > lineStyle.

11. With your pointer between the parentheses, enter the line thickness, hex code for its color, and its alpha value.

12. On the next line, enter the target path to the empty movie clip followed by a period.

13. Choose Built-in Classes > Movie > MovieClip > Drawing Methods > moveTo.

14. With your pointer between the parentheses, enter the _x property and the _y property for one of your draggable movie clips (**Figure 7.76**).

continues on next page

CREATING SHAPES DYNAMICALLY

15. Continue adding lineTo() methods whose *x* and *y* coordinates correspond to the *x* and *y* properties of the draggable movie clips.

The final script should look like **Figure 7.77**.

16. Test your movie.

Flash continuously erases the line segments with the clear() method and redraws them according to where the draggable movie clips lie. You can drag the movie clips around the Stage to change the shape dynamically (**Figure 7.78**).

✔ **Tip**

■ In this example, you could use onMouseMove instead of onEnterFrame because the only time the drawing needs to be updated is when the viewer is dragging one of the movie clips. If you do use onMouseMove, add the updateAfterEvent() statement (Global Functions > Movie Clip Control > updateAfterEvent) to force Flash to refresh the screen whenever the mouse pointer moves.

```
_root.createEmptyMovieClip("pen", 1);
_root.onEnterFrame = function() {
    pen.clear();
    pen.lineStyle(2, 0xff00ff, 100);
    pen.moveTo(circle1_mc._x, circle1_mc._y);
    pen.lineTo(circle2_mc._x, circle2_mc._y);
    pen.lineTo(circle3_mc._x, circle3_mc._y);
    pen.lineTo(circle4_mc._x, circle4_mc._y);
};
```

Figure 7.77 The line segments are drawn to where the draggable movie clips circle2_mc, circle3_mc, and circle4_mc are located.

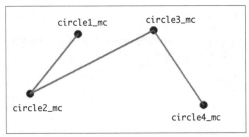

Figure 7.78 The three line segments between the four draggable movie-clip circles are redrawn continuously, creating a moveable, Tinker Toys–like shape that moves where you position the vertices.

Creating fills and gradients

You can fill shapes with solid colors, transparent colors, or radial or linear gradients by using the methods beginFill(), beginGradientFill(), and endFill(). You start the beginning of your shape to be filled by calling either the beginFill() or the beginGradientFill() method and mark the end of the shape with endFill(). If your path is not closed (the end points do not match the beginning points), Flash automatically closes it when the endFill() method is applied.

Applying solid or transparent fills with beginFill() is fairly straightforward; you specify a hex code for the color and a value from 0 to 100 for the transparency. Gradients are more complex. You control five parameters: gradient type, colors, alphas, ratios, and matrix type.

♦ **Gradient type** is either the string "radial" or the string "linear". You must include the quotation marks. Radial parameters define the gradient from the inside to the outside. Linear parameters define the gradient from the left to the right.

♦ **Colors** is a special object called an array object. An array holds information in an ordered way. You must create an array object and put the hex codes for the gradient colors into the array in the order in which you want them to appear. If you want blue on the left side of a linear gradient and red on the right side, for example, you create an array like this:

```
colors = new Array(0x0000FF, 0xFF0000)
```

continues on next page

◆ **Alphas** is also an array object and contains the alpha values (0 through 100) corresponding to the colors in the order in which you want them to appear. If you want your blue on one side to be 50 percent transparent, you create an array like this:

alphas = new Array (50,100)

◆ **Ratios** is an array object that contains values (0 through 255) corresponding to the colors that determine how they will mix. The ratio value defines the width where the color is at 100 percent. An array like ratios = new Array(0, 127) means that the blue is 100 percent at the left side and the red is 100 percent starting at the middle (**Figure 7.79**).

◆ **Matrix type** is a generic object whose properties you define. These properties determine the orientation of your gradient. You can use matrix type in two ways: box and matrix. The box way lets you set the orientation of the gradient with *x* and *y* coordinates, width and height properties (in pixels), and an angle property (in radians) (**Figure 7.80**). The matrix way uses a 3-by-3 matrix. Because matrices involve a high-level math background, we'll restrict the discussion of the matrix type to the box way.

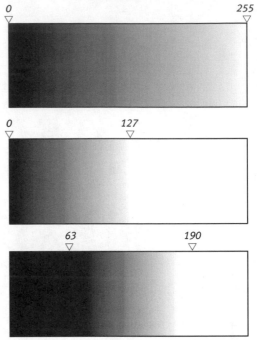

Figure 7.79 Ratios determine the mixing of colors for your gradient. The entire width of your gradient (or radius, for a radial gradient) is represented on a range from 0 through 255. Ratio values of (0,255) represent the typical gradient where each color is at one of the far sides (top). Ratio values of (0,127) create a tighter mixing in the first half of the gradient (middle). Ratio values of (63,190) would create a tighter mixing in the middle of the gradient (bottom).

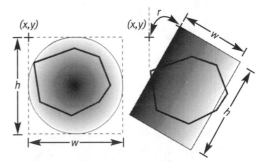

Figure 7.80 Parameters for the box matrix type. A radial gradient (left) and a linear gradient (right) are shown superimposed on a shape they would fill. x and y are the coordinates for the top-left corner of the gradient. w and h are its width and height. r is the clockwise angle that it makes from the vertical.

CREATING SHAPES DYNAMICALLY

▼ Actions – Frame

```
_root.createEmptyMovieClip("pen", 1);
pen.lineStyle(1, 0xFF0000, 100);
pen.beginFill(0x7E6AE3, 100);
```

Figure 7.81 This fill is light blue at 100 percent opacity.

▼ Actions – Frame

```
_root.createEmptyMovieClip("pen", 1);
pen.lineStyle(1, 0xFF0000, 100);
pen.beginFill(0x7E6AE3, 100);
pen.moveTo(100, 100);
pen.lineTo(100, 200);
pen.lineTo(200, 200);
pen.lineTo(200, 100);
pen.lineTo(100, 100);
```

Figure 7.82 The end point of the last `lineTo()` method (100,100) matches the beginning point (100,100), creating a closed shape that can be filled.

▼ Actions – Frame

```
_root.createEmptyMovieClip("pen", 1);
pen.lineStyle(1, 0xFF0000, 100);
pen.beginFill(0x7E6AE3, 100);
pen.moveTo(100, 100);
pen.lineTo(100, 200);
pen.lineTo(200, 200);
pen.lineTo(200, 100);
pen.lineTo(100, 100);
pen.endFill();
```

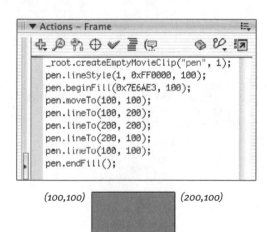

(100,100)   (200,100)

(100,200)   (200,200)

Figure 7.83 A blue box appears as a result of this code. The box was drawn counterclockwise from its top-left corner, but the order of line segments is irrelevant.

To fill a shape with a solid color:

1. Create an empty movie clip on the root Timeline.

2. On a new line, enter the target path of your empty movie clip and a period. Choose Built-in Classes > Movie > MovieClip > Drawing Methods > lineStyle, and define the style of your line.

3. On the next line, enter the target path of the empty movie clip followed by a period.

4. Choose Built-in Classes > Movie > MovieClip > Drawing Methods > beginFill.

5. With your pointer between the parentheses, enter the hex code for a color and a value for the alpha, separating your parameters with commas (**Figure 7.81**).

6. On a new line, enter the target path of the empty movie clip followed by a period. Choose Built-in Classes > Movie > MovieClip > Drawing Methods > moveTo, and move the starting point of your line.

7. Use the `lineTo()` or `curveTo()` method to draw a closed shape (**Figure 7.82**).

8. When the end points match the beginning points of your shape, enter the target path of the empty movie clip and a period, and then choose Built-in Classes > Movie > MovieClip > Drawing Methods > endFill.

   No parameters are required for the `endFill()` method. Flash fills the closed shape with the specified color (**Figure 7.83**).

CREATING SHAPES DYNAMICALLY

335

To fill a shape with a gradient:

1. Create an empty movie clip on the root Timeline.

2. On the next line, enter `colors` followed by an equals sign.

3. Choose Built-in Classes > Core > Array > new Array.

   The constructor function creates a new array object.

4. Between the parentheses of the `new Array()` statement, enter the colors of your gradient in hex code, separating your hex codes with commas (**Figure 7.84**).

   By adding parameters to the `new Array()` statement, you instantiate a new array object and populate the array at the same time. The first color refers to the left side of a linear gradient or the center of a radial gradient.

5. On the next line, enter `alphas` followed by an equals sign.

6. Choose Built-in Classes > Core > Array > new Array.

7. Between the parentheses of this `new Array()` statement, enter the alpha values that correspond to each color (**Figure 7.85**).

8. On the next line, enter `ratios` followed by an equals sign.

9. Choose Built-in Classes > Core > Array > new Array.

10. Between the parentheses of this `new Array()` statement, enter the ratio values that correspond to each color (**Figure 7.86**).

Figure 7.84 The colors array is created with blue on one side and red on the other. If this gradient is going to be a linear gradient, blue (0x0000FF) will be on the left. If it is going to be a radial gradient, blue will be in the center.

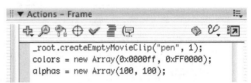

Figure 7.85 The alphas array is created with 100 percent opacity for both the blue and the red.

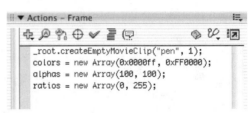

Figure 7.86 The ratios array is created with blue on the far left side (or the center, in the case of a radial gradient) and with red on the far right side (or the edge of a radial gradient).

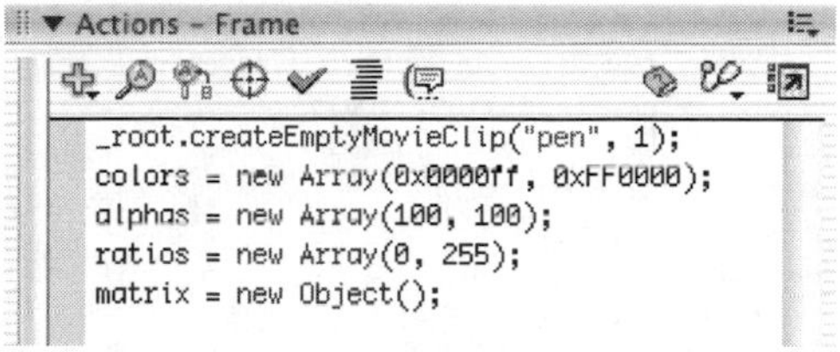

Figure 7.87 The matrix generic object is created.

```
_root.createEmptyMovieClip("pen", 1);
colors = new Array(0x0000FF, 0xFF0000);
alphas = new Array(100,100);
ratios = new Array(0, 255);
matrix = new Object();
matrix.matrixType = "box";
matrix.x = 100;
matrix.y = 100;
matrix.w = 100;
matrix.h = 100;
matrix.r = 0;
```

Figure 7.88 The *x, y* coordinates, width and height, and angle of the gradient are defined as properties of the matrix object.

11. On the next line, enter `matrix` followed by an equals sign.

12. Choose Built-in Classes > Core > Object > new Object.

Unlike the previous statements, which create arrays, your matrix object is created from the generic Object category (**Figure 7.87**).

13. In a series of statements, define the properties of your matrix object.

Enter the name of your matrix object followed by a period and then its property. Next, enter an equals sign and a value. Remember that the `matrixType` property is assigned the word "`box`" (in quotation marks).

The Script pane should look similar to **Figure 7.88**.

14. Enter the name of your empty movie clip followed by a period. Choose Built-in Classes > Movie > MovieClip > Drawing Methods > lineStyle, and define the style of your line.

15. On the next line, enter the name of your empty movie clip followed by a period. Choose Built-in Classes > Movie > MovieClip > beginGradientFill.

16. For the parameters of the `beginGradient Fill` method, enter the string "`linear`" or "`radial`" to choose your gradient type; then enter the name of your colors array, alphas array, ratios array, and matrix object.

Separate the parameters with commas.

All the information about your gradient that you defined in your arrays and matrix object is fed into the parameters of the `beginGradientFill()` method.

continues on next page

CREATING SHAPES DYNAMICALLY

17. On the next line, enter the name of your empty movie clip followed by a period.

18. Choose Built-in Classes > Movie > MovieClip > Drawing Methods > moveTo, and enter starting coordinates for your shape.

19. Create a series of lines or curves with lineTo() or curveTo() to create a closed path.

20. On a new line, enter the target path of your empty movie clip and a period, and then choose Built-in Classes > Movie > MovieClip > Drawing Methods > endFill. Flash fills your shape with the gradient (**Figure 7.89**). 🔊

✔ Tips

■ The colors array that you create for the beginGradientFill() method is not the same as an object you create from the Color class. The Color class controls a movie clip's color. The colors array discussed in this task is used as a parameter in the beginGradientFill() method.

■ The r property of the matrix-type object takes radians, not degrees. Using radians is way to measure angles using the mathematical constant pi. To convert degrees to radians, you must multiply by the number pi and then divide by 180. Using the Math class for pi (Math.PI), you can use the formula:

radians = degrees*(Math.PI/180)

■ The r property of the matrix-type object affects only linear gradients and has no effect on radial gradients.

```
_root.createEmptyMovieClip("pen", 1);
colors = new Array(0x0000FF, 0xFF0000);
alphas = new Array(100, 100);
ratios = new Array(0, 255);
matrix = new Object();
matrix.matrixType = "box";
matrix.x = 100;
matrix.y = 100;
matrix.w = 100;
matrix.h = 100;
matrix.r = 0;
pen.lineStyle(5, 0xFF0000, 100);
pen.beginGradientFill("linear", _root.colors,
    _root.alphas, _root.ratios, _root.matrix);
pen.moveTo(100, 100);
pen.lineTo(100, 200);
pen.lineTo(200, 200);
pen.lineTo(200, 100);
pen.lineTo(100, 100);
pen.endFill();
```

Figure 7.89 The complete ActionScript code creates a box with a linear gradient from blue to red.

Unwrap this Season's
Latest Looks

Figure 7.90 Combining draggable movie clips (the vertices), drawing methods (the lines connecting the vertices), and dynamic masking (uncovering the image "behind" the wrapping paper).

Figure 7.91 A movie clip containing a bitmap cityscape will be the masked movie clip.

Using Dynamic Masks

You can turn any movie clip into a mask and specify the movie clip to be masked with the method setMask(). To use the method, you define the movie clip you want to be masked as the target path before the method and then define the movie clip you want to act as a mask as its parameter: masked_mc.setMask(mask_mc). Because you can control all the properties of movie clips, you can make your mask move or grow and shrink in response to viewer interaction. You can even combine the setMask() method with the movie-clip drawing methods to create masks that change shape (**Figure 7.90**).

An effective combination is to assign startDrag() and stopDrag() methods to the movie-clip mask and create draggable masks. When you add startDrag() to an onPress handler and stopDrag() to an onRelease handler, your viewer can control the position of the movie clip mask.

To set a movie clip as a mask:

1. Create a movie clip, place an instance on the Stage, and name it in the Property Inspector (**Figure 7.91**).

   This movie clip will be masked.

   continues on next page

2. Create another movie clip, place an instance on the Stage, and name it in the Property Inspector (**Figure 7.92**). This movie clip will act as a mask.

3. Select the first frame of the root Timeline, and open the Actions panel.

4. Enter the target path to the movie clip you want to be masked followed by a period.

5. Choose Built-in Classes > Movie > MovieClip > Methods > setMask.

6. With your pointer between the parentheses for the **setMask** method, enter the name of the target path to the movie clip you want to use as a mask (**Figure 7.93**).

7. Test your movie.

   The opaque shapes of the mask movie clip reveal the masked movie clip (**Figure 7.94**).

Figure 7.92 A movie clip of vertical shapes will be the mask movie clip.

Figure 7.93 The mask_mc movie clip will mask the cityscape_mc movie clip.

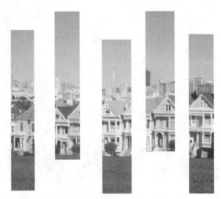

Figure 7.94 The result of the setMask() method.

Figure 7.95 If this shape were to be used in a movie clip for the setMask() method, Flash would recognize only a square for the mask.

Figure 7.96 You'll create a draggable mask to uncover this movie clip to make the viewer look for the monkey in the bush.

Figure 7.97 A simple circle will be the mask.

Figure 7.98 Create the mask of the circle over the masked image (the monkey in the bush).

✔ Tips

- You can specify the root Timeline as the movie clip to be masked and all the graphics on the main Timeline (including movie clips on the Stage) will be masked. To do so, enter _root as the target path before the setMask() method.

- Holes in the opaque shapes of your mask movie clip are not recognized and do not affect the mask (**Figure 7.95**).

- To undo a setMask() method, use the null keyword for its parameter as follows: masked.setMask(null).

To create a draggable mask:

1. Create a movie clip, put an instance of it on the Stage, and name it in the Property Inspector.

   This movie clip will be masked (**Figure 7.96**).

2. Create another movie clip, put an instance of it on the Stage, and name it in the Property Inspector.

   This movie clip will act as a mask (**Figure 7.97**).

3. Select the first frame of the root Timeline and open the Actions panel.

4. Enter the target path of the movie clip to be masked followed by a period.

5. Choose Built-in Classes > Movie > MovieClip > Methods > setMask.

6. With your pointer between the parentheses, enter the target path of the mask movie clip (**Figure 7.98**).

7. On the next line, enter the target path of the mask movie clip followed by a period.

continues on next page

USING DYNAMIC MASKS

8. Choose Built-in Classes > Movie > Button > Events > onPress. Complete the handler by entering =function(){ and a closing curly brace on the next line (**Figure 7.99**).

9. With your pointer between the curly braces for the onPress event, enter the target path of your mask movie clip followed by a period.

10. Choose Global Functions > Movie Clip Control > startDrag (**Figure 7.100**).

11. On the next line, after the closing curly brace of the onPress event handler, enter the target path of the mask movie clip followed by a period.

12. Choose Built-in Classes > Movie > Button > Events > onRelease. Complete the handler by entering =function(){ and a closing curly brace on the next line (**Figure 7.101**).

13. Choose Global Functions > Movie Clip Control > stopDrag.

14. Test your movie.

The movie clip acts as a mask while the onPress and onRelease handlers provide the drag-and-drop interactivity (**Figure 7.102**). 🕐

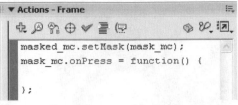

Figure 7.99 The onPress event handler is created for the movie clip called mask_mc.

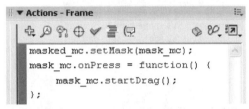

Figure 7.100 A new startDrag action has been created within the onPress event handler.

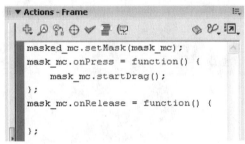

Figure 7.101 The onRelease event handler is created for the movie clip called mask_mc.

```
masked_mc.setMask(mask_mc);
mask_mc.onPress = function() {
    mask_mc.startDrag();
};
mask_mc.onRelease = function() {
    stopDrag();
};
```

Figure 7.102 The final ActionScript code (top) assigns interactivity to create a dynamic mask as well as a draggable movie clip.

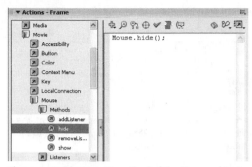

Figure 7.103 The hide() method of the Mouse object doesn't require previous instantiation.

Figure 7.104 The show() method of the Mouse object makes a hidden mouse visible again.

Customizing Your Pointer

When you understand how to control the movie clip, you can build your own custom pointer. Think about all the different pointers you use in Flash. As you choose different tools in the Tools palette—the Paint Bucket, the Eyedropper, the Pencil—your pointer changes to help you understand and apply them. Similarly, you can tailor the pointer's form to match its function.

Customizing the pointer involves first hiding the default mouse pointer. Then you must match the location of your new graphic to the location of the hidden (but still functional) mouse pointer. To do this, you set the X Position and Y Position properties of a movie clip to the x and y positions of the mouse pointer. The x and y positions of the mouse pointer are defined by the properties _xmouse and _ymouse.

To hide the mouse pointer:

1. Select the first frame, and open the Actions panel.

2. Choose Built-in Classes > Movie > Mouse > Methods > hide (**Figure 7.103**).

   When you test your movie, the mouse pointer becomes invisible.

To show the mouse pointer:

◆ From the Actions panel, choose Built-in Classes > Movie > Mouse > Methods > show (**Figure 7.104**).

To create your own mouse pointer:

1. Create a movie-clip symbol, place an instance of it on the Stage, and name it in the Property Inspector.

   This movie clip will become your pointer.

2. Select the first frame of the root Timeline, and open the Actions panel.

continues on next page

3. Choose Built-in Classes > Movie > Mouse > Methods > hide.

The `Mouse.hide()` method appears. When this movie begins, the mouse pointer disappears.

4. On the next line, enter the instance name for your movie clip.

5. Choose Built-in Classes > Movie > MovieClip > Events > onMouseMove. Complete the handler by entering =function(){ and a closing curly brace on the next line.

The onMouseMove event handler is completed.

6. On the next line of the onMouseMove handler, enter the target path to the movie clip followed by a period.

7. Choose Built-in Classes > Movie > MovieClip > Properties > _x, and add an equals sign.

8. Enter _root followed by a period. Choose Built-in Classes > Movie > MovieClip > Properties > _xmouse (**Figure 7.105**).

9. On the next line of the, enter the target path to the movie clip followed by a period.

10. Choose Built-in Classes > Movie > MovieClip > Properties > _y, and add an equals sign.

11. Enter _root followed by a period. Choose Built-in Classes > Movie > MovieClip > Properties > _ymouse (**Figure 7.106**).

12. Test your movie (**Figure 7.107**).

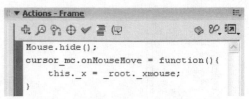

Figure 7.105 The mouse pointer disappears as soon as this movie begins. Using the onMouseMove event, the x value of the movie clip called cursor_mc is set to the mouse pointer's x position.

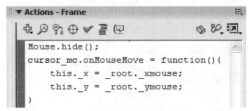

Figure 7.106 The y property for the movie clip called cursor_mc follows the mouse pointer's y position as well.

Figure 7.107 This magnifying glass is a movie clip that matches the x and y positions of the pointer. Create helpful pointers like this one with an appearance that matches function.

Use the function updateAfterEvent() to force Flash to redraw the screen independently of the movie's frame rate. This function eliminates the flicker associated with graphics moving around the screen faster than Flash can update the display and is especially important when you use a custom pointer. The action updateAfterEvent can be used only with the events mouseMove, mouseDown, mouseUp, keyDown, and keyUp.

To update the graphics onscreen:

1. Continuing with the file you created in the preceding task, create a new line inside of the onMouseMove event.

2. Choose Global Functions > Movie Clip Control > updateAfterEvent (**Figure 7.108**). (🖉)

   The updateAfterEvent function appears in the Script pane. Flash updates the graphics on the screen each time the pointer moves, creating smoother motions.

```
Mouse.hide();
cursor_mc.onMouseMove = function(){
    this._x = _root._xmouse;
    this._y = _root._ymouse;
    updateAfterEvent();
}
```

Figure 7.108 Add the updateAfterEvent function to force Flash to refresh the display and create smoother motion.

✔ Tips

■ Explore using multiple movie clips that track the location of your pointer. A vertical line that follows _xmouse and a horizontal line that follows _ymouse create a moving crosshair. (🖉)

■ To reactivate the hand cursor when rolling over buttons or movie clips, you will need to create new event handlers that set the visibility of your custom cursor to false for each button. The statement Mouse.show() can then reactivate the hand cursor. Use an onRollOut event handler to restore your original settings. For example, if you have a custom cursor called cursor_mc but still wanted the hand cursor to appear over a button called button1_btn, use the following code:

```
button1_btn.onRollOver = function(){
    cursor_mc._visible = false;
    Mouse.show()
}
button1_btn.onRollOut = function(){
    cursor_mc._visible = true;
    Mouse.hide()
}
```
(🖉)

Beginning to Animate with ActionScript

The actions and methods discussed so far in this chapter—scripts that let you control and test virtually all aspects of the movie clip (appearance, position, draggability, collisions, depth level, duplication and creation, drawing capability, and masking capability)—are the basic tools for animating entirely with ActionScript. Whereas motion tweens and shape tweens are created before playback, ActionScript animation is generated during playback, so it can respond to and change according to your viewer's actions. You can use the mouse properties _xmouse and _ymouse as parameters in movie-clip methods or to control movie-clip properties so that the location of your viewer's pointer determines the behavior and appearance of graphics onscreen.

The following examples show how to use the mouse properties _xmouse and _ymouse to create responsive animations. The first example is a simple game of tag. You create a movie clip that follows your pointer, and if the movie clip catches up to you, you lose the game. The second example combines _xmouse and _ymouse with the movie-clip drawing methods so you can draw with the pointer. The third example is a scrolling menu that moves according to where the pointer is located.

To create a mouse-tracking game:

1. Create a movie-clip symbol with two keyframes.

   The first keyframe contains a graphic and a **stop** action, and the second keyframe contains a "You lose!" message (**Figure 7.109**).

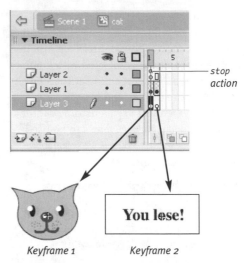

Keyframe 1   *Keyframe 2*

Figure 7.109 This cat movie clip displays a cat graphic in keyframe 1 when it chases your pointer and a different graphic in keyframe 2 when you lose the game.

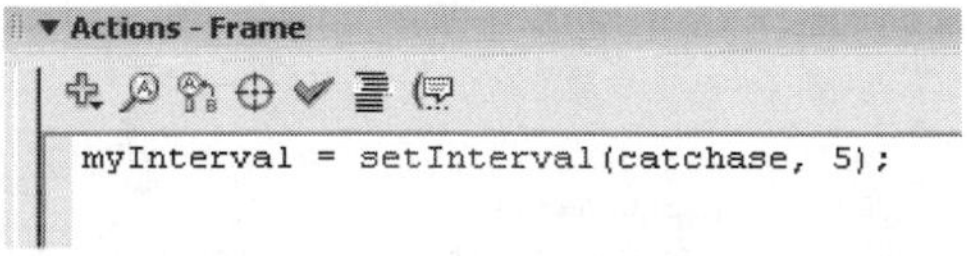

```
▼ Actions - Frame
⊕ 🔎 ⊕ ✔ ☰ ⊜
myInterval = setInterval(catchase, 5);
```

Figure 7.110 The action setInterval, like the event handler onEnterFrame, is a good way to execute ActionScript statements continuously. This setInterval is identified with the variable name myInterval.

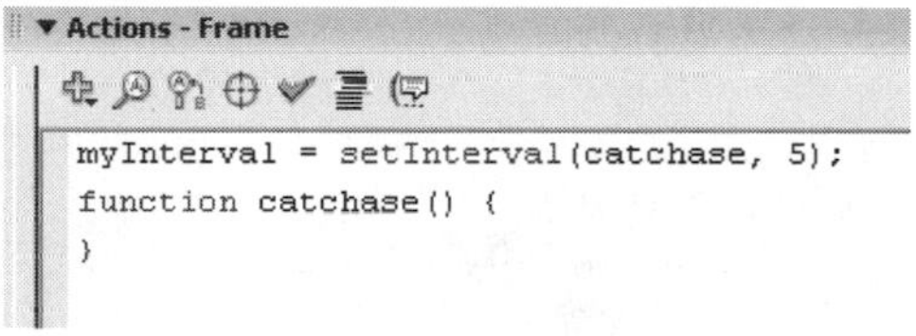

```
▼ Actions - Frame
⊕ 🔎 ⊕ ✔ ☰ ⊜
myInterval = setInterval(catchase, 5);
function catchase() {
}
```

Figure 7.111 The function called catchase will be called every 5 milliseconds.

2. Place an instance of the movie clip on the Stage, and name it in the Property Inspector.

In this example, the clip is called cat.

3. Select the first frame of the root Timeline, and open the Actions panel.

4. Enter a variable name and an equals sign, and then choose Global Functions > Miscellaneous Actions > setInterval.

5. With your pointer between the parentheses, enter the name of a function followed by a comma and then 5 (**Figure 7.110**).

The function you specify in the setInterval statement will be called every 5 milliseconds.

6. On a new line, choose Statements > User-Defined Functions > function.

7. Enter the name of your function that you used in step 5 (**Figure 7.111**).

8. On the next line, enter the target path of the movie clip followed by a period and the property _x. Then enter an equals sign.

The statement should look like the following:

cat._x =

continues on next page

9. On the same line, enter the following:

`cat._x + (_xmouse - cat._x)/100`

This statement starts with the *x* position of the cat movie clip and adds the difference between the mouse position and the cat position. If the mouse is to the right of the cat, the statement adds a positive value. If the mouse is to the left of the cat, the statement adds a negative value. In either case, the cat gets closer to the mouse. The division by 100 makes sure that the cat doesn't jump on the mouse immediately. The increment is small (one-hundredth of the distance), so the cat lags behind the position of the mouse.

10. On the next line, enter the same information for the *y* coordinate (**Figure 7.112**).

11. On a new line, choose Statements > Conditions/Loops > if.

12. For the condition, enter the following:

`cat.hitTest(_xmouse,_ymouse, true)`

This statement uses the `hitTest()` method to test whether the *x* and *y* positions of the mouse intersect the cat movie clip. The `shapeflag` parameter (the third parameter) is set to `true` so that only the graphics of the cat movie clip are considered rather than the entire bounding box (**Figure 7.113**).

13. In between the curly braces of the `if` statement, enter the target path for the cat movie clip followed by a period.

14. Choose Built-in Classes > Movie > MovieClip > Methods > nextFrame.

When the `hitTest()` returns true, the cat movie clip advances to the next frame, displaying the "You lose!" message (**Figure 7.114**).

Figure 7.112 The x and y positions of the cat movie-clip instance change according to the position of the pointer.

Figure 7.113 The condition checks whether the pointer intersects the cat movie-clip instance.

Figure 7.114 The cat movie clip advances to the next frame in its Timeline.

▼ Actions - Frame

```
myInterval = setInterval(catchase, 5);
function catchase() {
    cat._x = cat._x+(_xmouse-cat._x)/100;
    cat._y = cat._y+(_ymouse-cat._y)/100;
    if (cat.hitTest(_xmouse, _ymouse, true)) {
        cat.nextFrame();
        clearInterval(myInterval);
    }
}
```

Figure 7.115 The setInterval is cleared.

```
myInterval = setInterval(catchase, 5);
function catchase() {
    cat._x = cat._x+(_xmouse-cat._x)/100;
    cat._y = cat._y+(_ymouse-cat._y)/100;
    if (cat.hitTest(_xmouse, _ymouse, true)) {
        cat.nextFrame();
        clearInterval(myInterval);
    }
    updateAfterEvent();
}
```

You lose!

Figure 7.116 The ActionScript assigned to the catchase function (top) provides all the interactivity for the mouse-chasing game. The cat movie clip chases the pointer (left) and displays a message that was hidden on Frame 2 of its Timeline when it intersects with the pointer (right).

15. On the next line, choose Global Functions > Miscellaneous Functions > clearInterval.

16. For the parameter of the clearInterval() action, enter the name you gave to your setInterval statement in step 4 (**Figure 7.115**).

The setInterval is cleared, preventing the catChase function from being invoked, which stops the cat movie clip from following the mouse pointer.

17. Create a new line after the closing brace of the if statement, and choose Global Functions > Movie Clip Control > updateAfterEvent.

18. Test your movie (**Figure 7.116**).

To draw with the pointer:

1. Select the first frame of the root Timeline, and open the Actions panel.

2. Enter _root followed by a period.

3. Choose Built-in Classes > Movie > MovieClip > Events > onMouseMove. Complete the handler by entering =function(){ and a closing curly brace on the next line (**Figure 7.117**).

4. On the next line, inside of the onMouseMove event, enter _root followed by a period.

5. Choose Built-in Classes > Movie > MovieClip > Drawing Methods > lineStyle.

6. With your pointer between the parentheses, enter a thickness, a hex-code value, and an alpha value (**Figure 7.118**).

7. On the next line, enter _root followed by a period.

8. Choose Built-in Classes > Movie > MovieClip > Drawing Methods > lineTo.

9. With your pointer between the parentheses, enter _xmouse, a comma, and _ymouse (**Figure 7.119**).

    Whenever the pointer moves, Flash draws a line segment from the previous position to the current position of the pointer.

10. On a new line but still within the onMouseMove event handler, choose Global Functions > Movie Clip Control > updateAfterEvent.

11. Test your movie (**Figure 7.120**).

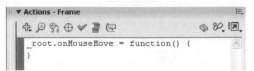

Figure 7.117 The onMouseMove event handler is created for the root Timeline.

Figure 7.118 This line style is defined as a 1-point red line.

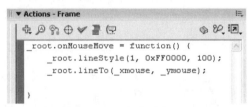

Figure 7.119 The lineTo() method draws a segment to the *x, y* position of the mouse pointer.

```
_root.onMouseMove = function() {
  _root.lineStyle(1, 0xFF0000, 100);
  _root.lineTo(_xmouse, _ymouse);
  updateAfterEvent();
};
```

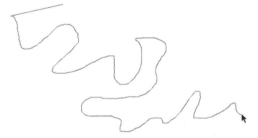

Figure 7.120 Whenever your mouse pointer moves, a new line segment is drawn, creating a simple drawing program.

Figure 7.121 A movie clip with a long row of buttons extends off the Stage. To provide access to the buttons, the movie clip will scroll to the right or to the left, depending on where the mouse pointer is located.

Figure 7.122 The onEnterFrame event handler is created on the root Timeline.

To create a scrolling menu that responds to the mouse pointer:

1. Create a movie clip that contains a long row of buttons or graphics (**Figure 7.121**), put it on the Stage, and name it in the Property Inspector.

2. Select the first frame of the root Timeline, and open the Actions panel.

3. Enter _root followed by a period.

4. Choose Objects > Movie > MovieClip > Events > onEnterFrame. Complete the handler by entering =function(){ and a closing curly brace on the next line (**Figure 7.122**).

5. On the next line of the onEnterFrame event, enter the name of your movie clip followed by a period and then _x for its *x* property.

continues on next page

6. Enter an equals sign, the name of your movie clip, a period, and _x; then add this expression:

`(.5 * Stage.width - _xmouse)/10`

When you subtract the horizontal position of the mouse pointer from half of the Stage width, you get a number that is positive if the pointer is on the left or negative if the pointer is on the right. Use this value to move the x position of your movie clip. The division by 10 makes the increments smaller and, hence, the movement of the movie clip slower (**Figure 7.123**).

7. Test your movie.

✔ Tip

■ The next step for this scrolling menu would be to script boundaries so that the movie clip can't scroll off the screen. You'll learn about creating `if` statements in Chapter 9.

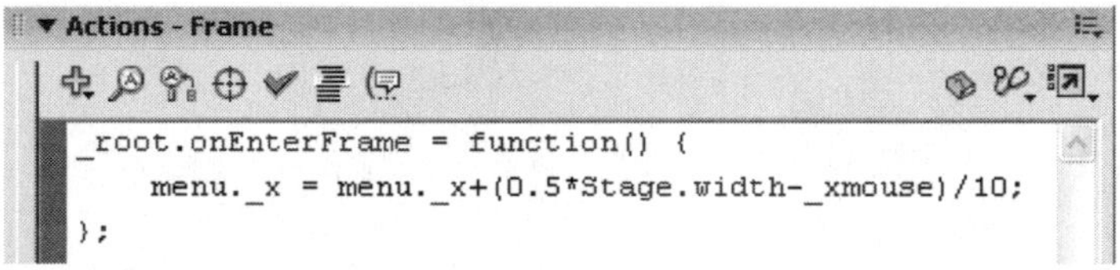

```
▼ Actions - Frame

_root.onEnterFrame = function() {
    menu._x = menu._x+(0.5*Stage.width-_xmouse)/10;
};
```

Figure 7.123 The horizontal position of the mouse pointer is used to calculate the new position of the movie clip called menu.

CONTROLLING SOUND

Incorporating sound into your Flash movie can enhance the animation and interactivity and add excitement to even the simplest project by engaging more of the user's senses. You can play background music to establish the mood of your movie, use narration to accompany a story, or give audible feedback to interactions such as button clicks and drag-and-drop actions. Flash supports several audio formats for import, including WAV, AIF, and MP3, which enables you to work with a broad spectrum of sounds. Flash also gives you many options for sound export, from speech-quality compression to high-quality MP3 compression, to help keep your Flash file size to a minimum.

This chapter explores the Sound class—the Flash class that lets you control sound with ActionScript. You should already be familiar with basic sound handling in Flash, such as importing sounds and assigning them to keyframes with the Event, Start, Stop, and Stream Sync options. If you are unsure about some of these techniques, review the tutorials and the Help files that accompany Flash for additional information. Moving forward, you'll learn how to use the Sound class to play sounds from the Library dynamically without having to assign them to keyframes. You'll learn how to load sounds that reside outside your movie, enabling efficient management of your Flash and sound content. Using ActionScript, you can start, stop, and adjust the sound volume or its stereo effect, giving you control based on user interactions or movie conditions. You'll learn to use the Sound class's properties and events to time your sounds with animations or with other sounds. You'll also learn how to retrieve and display information about an MP3 file using its ID3 tag, which can tell you file information like song title, artist, or genre.

All these methods, properties, and events of the Sound class give you the flexibility and power to integrate sounds into your movies creatively. You can create a slider bar that lets your viewers change the volume, for example, or add sounds to an arcade game that are customized to the game play. Develop dynamic slide shows synchronized to music or narration, or even make your own jukebox to play MP3 tunes.

Using the Sound Class

Attaching a sound file to a keyframe in the Timeline is an easy way to incorporate sounds into your movie. Two common ways to integrate sound on the Timeline are to use the Event Sync option to play a clicking sound in the Down state of a button symbol and to use the Stream Sync option to synchronize dialogue with an animation. But if you need to control when a sound plays at run-time, change its volume and playback through the left and right speakers dynamically, or retrieve information about the number of seconds it has been playing, turn to the Sound class.

The methods of the Sound class control a sound's playback behavior, and the properties of the Sound class can help you control its timing and gather MP3 file information. You need to instantiate the Sound class by using a constructor function to give it a name, just as you did with the Color class in Chapter 7. When a sound object is named, you'll be able to use it to play and modify sound files that you associate with it.

To create a global sound object:

1. Select the first frame of the main Timeline, and open the Actions panel.

2. Enter a name for your new sound object followed by an equals sign.

3. Choose Built-in Classes > Media > Sound > new Sound (**Figure 8.1**).

   The new Sound() constructor function appears in the Script pane. The constructor takes an optional parameter that specifies a movie clip. This movie clip contains the sounds that would be controlled by the sound object. By not specifying a movie clip, you create a sound object that controls all the sounds in the Timeline.

Figure 8.1 The completed statement in the Script pane creates the sound object called mySound_sound.

Figure 8.2 Choose the Linkage option from the Library for each sound you want to attach.

Attaching Sounds

After your new sound object is instantiated, you must associate a sound with it. You can load an external MP3 file into your sound object (which is covered later in this chapter), or you can attach a sound from the Library. When you have multiple imported sounds in your Library, you have to convey to the sound object which one to play and control. You identify sounds in the Library by using the Linkage option, just as you did in Chapter 7 when you attached a movie clip from the Library to a movie-clip instance on the Stage. In addition to identifying your sound, the Linkage option exports it with the SWF file so that it will be available when called by the sound object. When the sound is identified with the Linkage option, you attach it to the sound object by using the method attachSound().

To attach a sound to the sound object:

1. Continuing with the file you created in the preceding task, import a sound file by choosing File > Import > Import to Library.

   Your selected sound file appears in the Library. You may import these sound formats: AIF (Mac), WAV (Windows), and MP3 (Mac and Win). More formats may be available if QuickTime is installed on your system.

2. Select the sound symbol in your Library.

3. From the Options menu, choose Linkage (**Figure 8.2**).

   The Linkage Properties dialog box appears.

4. In the Linkage section, check the Export for ActionScript check box. Leave Export in first frame checked.

   continues on next page

5. In the Identifier field, enter a name to identify your sound (**Figure 8.3**).

6. Click OK.

   Flash exports the selected sound in the SWF file with the unique identifier so that it is available to play when called by the sound object.

7. Select the first frame of the main Timeline, and open the Actions panel.

8. On the next line,' after the new sound object constructor function, enter the name of your sound object followed by a period.

9. Choose Built-in Classes > Media > Sound > Methods > attachSound.

   or

   From the code hint drop-down menu, double-click on **attachSound**.

10. With your pointer between the parentheses, enter the identifier name of your sound file within quotation marks (**Figure 8.4**).

    Your sound file is attached to the sound object.

    It's very important that you specify the sound-file identifier within quotation marks. They tell Flash that the word is the literal name of the identifier and not an expression that it must evaluate to determine the name of the identifier.

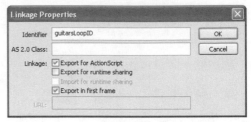

Figure 8.3 This sound is called guitarsLoopID and will be included in the exported SWF file.

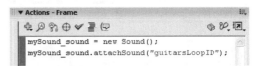

Figure 8.4 The attachSound() method attaches a sound from the Library ("guitarsLoopID") to the sound object (mySound_sound).

Playing Sounds

After you have created a new sound object and attached a sound to it from the Library, you can play the sound. Use the start() method to play a sound from your sound object. The start() method takes two parameters: secondOffset and loops.

The secondOffset parameter is a number that determines how many seconds into the sound it should begin playing. You can set the sound to start from the beginning or at some later point. If you have a 20-second sound attached to your sound object, for example, a secondOffset setting of 10 makes the sound play from the middle. It doesn't delay the sound for 10 seconds but begins immediately at the 10-second mark.

The loops parameter is a number that determines how many times the sound will play. A loops setting of 2 plays the entire sound two times with no delay in between.

If no parameters are defined for the start() method, Flash plays the sound from the beginning and plays one loop.

To play a sound:

1. Continuing with the file you used in the preceding task, create a button symbol, place an instance of it on the Stage, and give it a name in the Property Inspector. You will assign actions to this button to start playing your sound.

2. Select the first frame of the main Timeline, and open the Actions panel.

3. Assign an onRelease event handler to your button.

4. Enter the name of your sound object followed by a period.

continues on next page

5. Choose Built-in Classes > Media > Sound > Methods > start.

6. With your pointer between the parentheses, enter 0 followed by a comma and then 5 (**Figure 8.5**).

   The secondOffset parameter is set to 0, and the loops parameter is set to 5.

7. Test your movie.

   When your viewer clicks the button, the sound plays from the beginning and loops five times. 🔊

✔ Tips

■ Unfortunately, you have no way of telling the start() method to loop a sound indefinitely. Simply set the loops parameter to a ridiculously high number, such as 99999.

■ The start() method plays the attached sound whenever it's called, even when the sound is already playing. This situation can produce multiple, overlapping sounds. For example, when the viewer clicks the button created in the preceding task multiple times, the sounds play over one another. To prevent overlaps of this type, insert a stop() method (as outlined in the following task) right before the start() method. This technique ensures that a sound always stops before it plays again.

■ The start() method always plays the latest sound attached to the sound object. This means you can attach more sounds from the Library to the same sound object and the start() method will play the most current sound. You could create three buttons and assign the following script:

```
mySound_sound = new Sound ();
firstButton_btn.onRelease =
function() {
    mySound_sound.attachSound
    ("Hawaiian");
}
secondButton_btn.onRelease =
function() {
    mySound_sound.attachSound
    ("Jazz");
}
startButton_btn.onRelease =
function() {
    mySound_sound.start(0,1)
}
```

When you click firstButton_btn and then startButton_btn, you'll hear the Hawaiian sound. When you click second Button_btn and then startButton_btn, you'll hear the Jazz sound. If you begin playing the Jazz sound before the Hawaiian sound finishes, you'll hear overlapping sounds.

```
startButton_btn.onRelease = function() {
    mySound_sound.start(0, 5);
};
```

Figure 8.5 A portion of the Script pane shows just the onRelease handler for the button called startButton_btn. This start() method plays the sound that is attached to mySound_sound 5 times.

```
stopButton_btn.onRelease = function() {
    mySound_sound.stop();
};
```

Figure 8.6 A portion of the Script pane shows just the onRelease handler for the button called stopButton_btn. This stop() method stops playing any sounds attached to the mySound_sound sound object. The stop() method has no parameters.

To stop a sound:

1. Continuing with the file you used in the preceding task, place another instance of the button symbol on the Stage, and give it a name in the Property Inspector.

2. Select the first frame of the main Timeline, and open the Actions panel.

3. Assign an onRelease event handler to your new button instance.

4. Enter the name of your sound object followed by a period.

5. Choose Built-in Classes > Media > Sound > Methods > stop (**Figure 8.6**).

6. Test your movie.

   When your viewer clicks this button, any sound attached to the sound object that is playing stops. 🔊

You can have all sounds stop indiscriminately by using the action **stopAllSounds**.

To stop all sounds:

◆ Choose Global Functions > Timeline Control > stopAllSounds (Esc + ss).

   When this action is performed, Flash stops all sounds whether they are attached to a sound object or playing from the Timeline.

Modifying Sounds

When you use the Sound class, Flash gives you full control of its volume and its output through either the left or right speaker, known as *pan control*. With this level of sound control, you can let your users set the volume to their own preferences, and you can create environments that are more realistic. In a car game, for example, you can vary the volume of the sound of cars as they approach or pass you. Playing with the pan controls, you can embellish the classic Pong game by making the sounds of the ball hitting the paddles and the walls play from the appropriate sides.

The two methods for modifying sounds are setVolume() and setPan(). The method setVolume() takes a number from 0 to 100 as its parameter, representing the percentage of full volume. So 100 represents the maximum volume, and 0 is silence. The method setPan() takes a number from –100 to 100. The setting –100 plays the sound completely through the left speaker, 100 plays the sound completely through the right speaker, and 0 plays the sound through both speakers equally.

To set the volume of a sound:

1. Continuing with the file you used in the preceding task, place another instance of the button symbol on the Stage, and give it a name in the Property Inspector.

2. Select the first frame of the main Timeline, and open the Actions panel.

3. Assign an onRelease event handler to your button.

4. Enter the name of your sound object followed by a period.

5. Choose Built-in Classes > Media > Sound > Methods > setVolume.

6. With your pointer between the parentheses, enter a number from 0 to 100 (**Figure 8.7**).

7. Test your movie.

    First, play your sound. When you click this button, the volume changes according to the volume parameter.

```
volUp_btn.onRelease = function() {
    mySound_sound.setVolume(100);
};
volDown_btn.onRelease = function(){
    mySound_sound.setVolume(20);
}
```

Figure 8.7 A portion of the Script pane shows just the onRelease handler for a button called volUp_btn. This setVolume() method restores the volume for the mySound_sound sound object to 100 percent. Also listed in the Script pane is an onRelease handler for a button called volDown_btn. This setVolume() method reduces the volume for the mySound_sound sound object to 20 percent.

```
leftSpeaker_btn.onRelease = function(){
    mySound_sound.setPan(-100);
}
rightSpeaker_btn.onRelease = function(){
    mySound_sound.setPan(100);
}
bothSpeakers_btn.onRelease = function(){
    mySound_sound.setPan(0);
}
```

Figure 8.8 A portion of the Script pane shows just the onRelease handlers for rightSpeaker_btn, leftSpeaker_btn, and bothSpeakers_btn.

To set the right and left balance of a sound:

1. Continuing with the file you used in the preceding task, place another instance of the button symbol on the Stage, and give it a name in the Property Inspector.

2. Select the first frame of the main Timeline, and open the Actions panel.

3. Assign an onRelease event handler to your button.

4. Enter the name of your sound object followed by a period.

5. Choose Built-in Classes > Media > Sound > Methods > setPan.

6. With your pointer between the parentheses, enter a number from −100 to 100 (**Figure 8.8**).

   This single number controls the balance between the left and right speakers.

7. Test your movie.

   First, play your sound. When you click this button, the left-right balance changes according to the pan parameter.

Modifying Independent Sounds

When you instantiate your sound object and do not specify a movie clip for its parameter, such as mySound_sound = new Sound (), the setVolume() and setPan() methods will have a global effect, controlling all the sounds in the root Timeline. Even if you create two separate sound objects like the following

mySound1_sound = new Sound ();

mySound2_sound = new Sound ();

you cannot use the setPan() method to play mySound1_sound through the left speaker and mySound2_sound through the right speaker.

To modify sounds independently, you must create your sound objects with parameters that target specific movie clips. Thereafter, sound objects will be applied to different movie clips and you can use the setVolume() and setPan() methods to control the two sounds separately.

To modify two sounds independently:

1. Import two sound files into Flash.

2. From the Options menu in the Library window, choose Linkage.
   The Linkage Properties dialog box opens.

3. Check the Export for ActionScript box, and give both sounds unique identifiers (**Figure 8.9**).

4. Select the first frame of the main Timeline, and open the Actions panel.

5. Using the method createEmptyMovieClip() (Built-in Classes > Movie > MovieClip > Methods > createEmptyMovieClip), create two movie-clip instances on the root Timeline, using unique names in different depth levels (**Figure 8.10**).

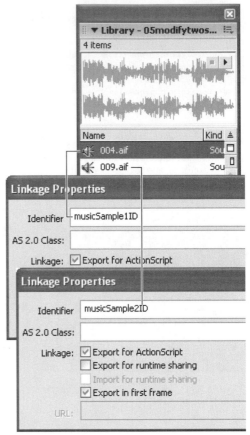

Figure 8.9 Give each imported sound a different identifier in the Linkage Properties dialog box.

Figure 8.10 Create two empty movie-clip instances on the main Timeline to act as targets for the new sound objects. The two movie-clip instances here are called movieClip1_mc and movieClip2_mc.

```
▼ Actions - Frame
╬ ♪ ╣ ⊕ ✔ 彗 (♀               ⊛ 80 函
  _root.createEmptyMovieClip("movieClip1_mc", 1);
  _root.createEmptyMovieClip("movieClip2_mc", 2);
  mySound1_sound = new Sound(movieClip1_mc);
  mySound2_sound = new Sound(movieClip2_mc);
```

Figure 8.11 The mySound1_sound sound object is created; it targets movieClip1_mc. The mySound2_sound sound object is created; it targets movieClip2_mc.

```
▼ Actions - Frame
╬ ♪ ╣ ⊕ ✔ 彗 (♀               ⊛ 80 函
  _root.createEmptyMovieClip("movieClip1_mc", 1);
  _root.createEmptyMovieClip("movieClip2_mc", 2);
  mySound1_sound = new Sound(movieClip1_mc);
  mySound2_sound = new Sound(movieClip2_mc);
  mySound1_sound.attachSound("musicSample1ID");
  mySound2_sound.attachSound("musicSample2ID");
```

Figure 8.12 Attach the two sounds from the Library to the two sound objects.

```
start1Button_btn.onRelease = function() {
    mySound1_sound.start(0, 1);
};
```

Figure 8.13 A portion of the Script pane shows just the onRelease handler for the button called start1Button_btn. This start() method plays the mySound1_sound object. Notice that although mySound1_sound targets movieClip1_mc, movieClip1_mc need not be referenced at all in the target paths of mySound1_mc's methods. The methods attachSound() and start() refer to the sound object, not to the targeted movie-clip instance.

Flash creates two movie clips dynamically. You will use these movie clips as targets for your sound objects. (See Chapter 7 for more information about the createEmptyMovieClip() method.)

6. On the next lines, instantiate two new sound objects as you did earlier in this chapter.

7. Between the parentheses of each constructor function, enter the names of the empty movie clips (**Figure 8.11**). Now each sound object is associated with its own movie clip (its own independent Timeline).

8. Use the attachSound() method to attach the two sounds from the Library to each of your sound objects (**Figure 8.12**).

9. Create a button symbol, place an instance of it on the Stage, and name it in the Property Inspector.

10. Select the first frame of the main Timeline, and open the Actions panel.

11. Assign an onRelease event handler to the button.

12. Assign the start() method for the first sound object (**Figure 8.13**).

continues on next page

MODIFYING INDEPENDENT SOUNDS

13. Repeat steps 9 through 12 to create a button that starts to play the second sound object (**Figure 8.14**).

14. Place two more instances of button symbols on the Stage, and name them in the Property Inspector.

15. For the first button instance, assign the setPan() method to the first sound object with a pan parameter of –100 (**Figure 8.15**).

This button plays the first sound object in the left speaker.

16. For the second button instance, assign the setPan() method to the second sound object with a pan parameter of 100 (**Figure 8.16**).

This button plays the second sound object in the right speaker.

17. Test your movie.

When this movie starts, two empty movie clips are created. Then two sound objects are created, targeting the newly created movie clips. Finally, a different sound is attached to each sound object. This technique enables you to control the left-right balance of each sound separately with the buttons called leftButton_btn and rightButton_btn. ((·))

```
start2Button_btn.onRelease = function() {
    mySound2_sound.start(0, 1);
};
```

Figure 8.14 A portion of the Script pane shows just the onRelease handler for the button called start2Button_btn. This start() method plays the mySound2 object.

```
leftButton_btn.onRelease = function() {
    mySound1_sound.setPan(-100);
};
```

Figure 8.15 A portion of the Script pane shows just the onRelease handler for the button called leftButton_btn. The setPan() method for mySound1_sound plays it in the left speaker.

```
rightButton_btn.onRelease = function() {
    mySound2_sound.setPan(100);
};
```

Figure 8.16 A portion of the Script pane shows just the onRelease handler for the button called rightButton_btn. The setPan() method for mySound2_sound plays it in the right speaker.

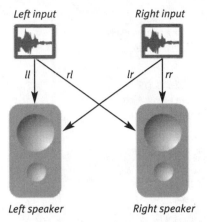

Left input   Right input

ll   rl   lr   rr

Left speaker   Right speaker

Figure 8.17 The parameters of setTransform() determine distribution of sounds between the left and right speakers. The first letter refers to the output speaker; the second letter refers to the input sound.

Transforming Sounds

For advanced users who want more precise control of how a sound is playing through the left and right speakers, Flash provides the method setTransform(). This method allows you to set percentages that determine how much of the right or left channel plays through the right and left speakers. Using this method, you can make your sound switch speakers from left to right dynamically or switch from stereo to mono.

The setTransform() method of the Sound class is very similar to the setTransform() method of the Color class discussed in Chapter 7. As with the Color class, using setTransform() with the Sound class requires that you create a generic object to hold the information specifying the distribution of left and right sounds. The properties of the sound-transformation object are ll, lr, rr, and rl (**Figure 8.17**). **Table 8.1** summarizes the functions of these properties.

Table 8.1

setTransform Parameters for the Sound Object	
PARAMETER	VALUE
ll	Percentage value specifying how much of the left input plays in the left speaker
lr	Percentage value specifying how much of the right input plays in the left speaker
rr	Percentage value specifying how much of the right input plays in the right speaker
rl	Percentage value specifying how much of the left input plays in the right speaker.

To switch the left and right speakers:

1. Import a sound file into Flash.

2. From the Options menu in the Library window, choose Linkage.
   The Linkage Properties dialog box opens.

3. Check the Export for ActionScript box, and give the sound an identifier (**Figure 8.18**).

4. Create a button symbol, place an instance of it on the Stage, and give it a name in the Property Inspector.

5. Select the first frame of the main Timeline, and open the Actions panel.

6. Instantiate a new sound object, as you did earlier in this chapter (**Figure 8.19**).
   Don't specify a target movie clip for the parameter.

7. Attach the sound to this sound object with the method attachSound().

8. Assign an onRelease event handler to your button.

9. Choose the start() method for your sound object (**Figure 8.20**).
   This button plays your sound.

10. Place another instance of the button symbol on the Stage, and give it a name in the Property Inspector.

11. In the Actions panel, assign an onRelease event handler to the second button.

12. On the next line, enter a name for your transformation object followed by an equals sign.

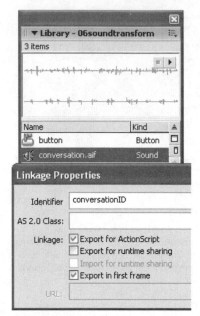

Figure 8.18 This sound is identified in the Library as conversationID.

Figure 8.19 The mySound_sound sound object is created.

Figure 8.20 The sound called conversationID plays five times when the button called startButton_btn is clicked.

```
transformButton_btn.onRelease = function() {
    mySoundTransform = new Object();
};
```

Figure 8.21 A portion of the Script pane shows just the onRelease handler for the button called transformButton_btn. The mySoundTransform object is created from the generic Object class.

```
transformButton_btn.onRelease = function() {
    mySoundTransform = new Object();
    mySoundTransform.ll = 0;
    mySoundTransform.lr = 100;
    mySoundTransform.rl = 100;
    mySoundTransform.rr = 0;
};
```

Figure 8.22 A portion of the Script pane shows just the onRelease handler for the button called transformButton_btn. The four parameters of the setTransform() method are defined as properties of the mySoundTransform object.

```
transformButton_btn.onRelease = function() {
    mySoundTransform = new Object();
    mySoundTransform.ll = 0;
    mySoundTransform.lr = 100;
    mySoundTransform.rl = 100;
    mySoundTransform.rr = 0;
    mySound_sound.setTransform(mySoundTransform);
};
```

Figure 8.23 A portion of the Script pane shows just the onRelease handler for the button called transformButton_btn. The setTransform() method uses the object called mySoundTransform as its parameter. The four properties of the mySoundTransform object supply the method with the information required to distribute the sounds to the left and right speakers.

13. Choose Built-in Classes > Core > Object > new Object.

Your new sound-transformation object is instantiated (**Figure 8.21**).

14. On the next line of the onRelease event, enter the name of your sound-transformation object followed by a period and then one of the parameters. Enter an equals sign and then a percentage. Do this for all four parameters (**Figure 8.22**).

The properties of your sound-transformation object are defined. These properties will be used as the parameters of the setTransform() method.

15. On the next line, still inside of the onRelease event, enter the name of your sound object followed by a period.

16. Choose Built-in Classes > Media > Sound > Methods > setTransform.

17. With your pointer between the parentheses, enter the name of your sound-transformation object (**Figure 8.23**).

18. Test your movie.

When you click the second button, Flash creates a generic object whose properties (mySoundTransform.ll, mySoundTransform.lr, and so on) hold the sound-transformation information. Then this information is passed to the sound object by the setTransform() method. The distribution of sound in the left and right speakers changes. 🎧

TRANSFORMING SOUNDS

Creating Dynamic Sound Controls

One of the most effective uses of the Sound class and its methods is to create dynamic controls that allow the user to set the desired volume level or speaker balance. A common strategy is to create a draggable movie clip that acts as a sliding controller. By correlating the position of the draggable movie clip with the volume parameter of the setVolume() method, you can make the volume change dynamically as the viewer moves the movie clip.

For a vertical slider bar that controls volume, you can create two elements: the actual handle or slider and the track or groove that it runs along (**Figure 8.24**). First, you create a movie clip called groove_mc. To make things easy, make the groove_mc movie clip 100 pixels high with its center point at the bottom of the rectangle. Making the groove_mc 100 pixels high will make it simpler to correlate the position of the slider on the groove_mc with the setVolume() parameter. To create the draggable slider, create a movie clip called slider_mc and assign the startDrag() action with constraints on the motion relative to the groove_mc movie clip.

To constrain a slider over a groove for a volume-control interface:

1. Create a movie clip of a tall rectangle that is 100 pixels high and whose registration point lies at the bottom edge.

2. Place an instance of the clip on the Stage, and name it groove_mc in the Property Inspector.

3. Create another movie clip of a slider.

4. Place the clip on the groove_mc movie clip, and name it slider_mc in the Property Inspector (**Figure 8.25**).

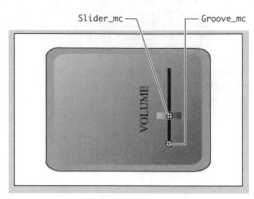

Figure 8.24 The components of a volume control are the slider that moves up and down and the groove.

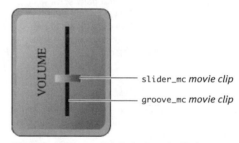

Figure 8.25 The movie-clip instance called groove_mc will limit the motion of the draggable movie clip called slider_mc. Make sure that the registration point of the groove_mc movie clip lies at its bottom edge.

```
▼ Actions - Frame
slider_mc.onPress = function() {
        this.startDrag(true,
        _root.groove_mc._x,
        _root.groove_mc._y-100,
        _root.groove_mc._x,
        _root.groove_mc._y);
};
```

Figure 8.26 A portion of the Script pane shows just the onPress handler for the slider movie clip. The startDrag() method has been broken into four lines to fit the page only. The second through fifth parameters constrain the slider_mc movie clip from the center point to 100 pixels above the center point of the groove_mc movie clip.

```
slider_mc.onPress = function() {
        this.startDrag(true,
        _root.groove_mc._x,
        _root.groove_mc._y-100,
        _root.groove_mc._x,
        _root.groove_mc._y);
};
slider_mc.onRelease = function() {
        stopDrag();
};
```

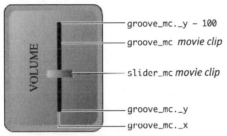

Figure 8.27 The full script. The startDrag() method has been broken into three lines to fit the page only. The slider movie clip can be dragged along the groove movie clip.

5. Select the first frame of the main Timeline, and open the Actions panel.

6. Assign an onPress event handler to the slider_mc movie clip.

7. Enter the keyword this followed by a period.

8. Choose Global Functions > Movie Clip Control > startDrag.

9. With your pointer between the parentheses, enter the Boolean value of true followed by a comma.

   The lockCenter parameter tells Flash to move the object so the center of the movie clip is on the tip of the pointer.

10. Enter the following parameters for the left, top, right, and bottom constraints:

    _root.groove_mc._x

    _root.groove_mc._y-100

    _root.groove_mc._x

    _root.groove._y

    The actions assigned to the slider movie clip constrain the left and right sides to the center of the groove movie clip. The top is constrained to 100 pixels above the lower edge of the groove movie clip, and the bottom is constrained to the lower edge of the groove movie clip (**Figure 8.26**).

11. Assign an onRelease event handler to the slider movie clip.

12. Choose Global Functions > Movie Clip Control > stopDrag.

13. Test your movie (**Figure 8.27**). 🎧

CREATING DYNAMIC SOUND CONTROLS

The GlobaltoLocal movie-clip method

The second part of creating a dynamic sound control for volume is correlating the *y* position of the slider bar with the parameter for the setVolume() method. You want the top of the groove to correspond to a volume of 100 and the bottom of the groove_mc to correspond to a volume of 0 (**Figure 8.28**).

But how do you get the *y*-coordinates of the moving slider to match up with a number from 0 to 100? One way is to use the movie-clip method globaltoLocal(), which can convert the coordinates of the slider bar to coordinates that are relative to the groove movie clip. Because the groove movie clip is 100 pixels high and the slider bar is constrained to the groove movie clip's height, the groove movie clip's local coordinates provide a convenient correlation with the volume settings (**Figure 8.29**).

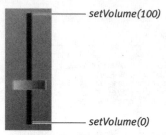

setVolume(100)

setVolume(0)

Figure 8.28 The setVolume() parameters need to correspond with the position of the slider_mc movie clip on top of the groove_mc movie clip.

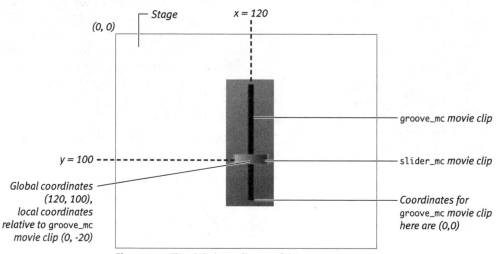

Stage

x = 120

(0, 0)

y = 100

Global coordinates (120, 100), local coordinates relative to groove_mc movie clip (0, -20)

groove_mc *movie clip*

slider_mc *movie clip*

Coordinates for groove_mc *movie clip here are (0,0)*

Figure 8.29 The global coordinates of the slider_mc movie clip are determined by the root Timeline's Stage. The local coordinates are relative to the groove_mc movie clip.

```
slider_mc.onMouseMove = function() {
    myPoint = new Object();
};
```

Figure 8.30 A portion of the Script pane shows just the onMouseMove handler for the slider_mc movie clip. The myPoint object is created from the generic Object class.

```
slider_mc.onMouseMove = function() {
    myPoint = new Object();
    myPoint.x = this._x;
};
```

Figure 8.31 A portion of the Script pane shows just the onMouseMove handler for the slider_mc movie clip. The current *x* position of the slider movie clip is assigned to myPoint.x.

To transform global coordinates to local coordinates:

1. Continuing with the file you used in the preceding task, select the first frame of the main Timeline, and open the Actions panel.

2. On a new line, enter the name of your slider movie clip followed by a period.

3. Choose Built-in Classes > Movie > MovieClip > Events > onMouseMove. Complete the event handler by entering =function(){ and a closing curly brace on the next line.

   The slider moves whenever the pointer moves, so the onMouseMove event provides a good way to trigger a volume change based on the slider position.

4. Enter a name for the generic object that will hold the *x* and *y* information to be transformed from global to local coordinates.

5. Enter an equals sign, and then choose Built-in Classes > Core > Object > new Object.

   This object is your point object (**Figure 8.30**).

6. Enter the name of your point object followed by a period, the property x, and an equals sign.

7. Enter this._x (**Figure 8.31**).

   This step sets the x property of your point object to the *x* position of the draggable movie clip.

   continues on next page

8. On the next line, enter the name of your point object followed by a period, the property y, and an equals sign.

9. Enter this._y.

This step sets the y property of your point object to the *y* position of the draggable movie clip.

10. On the next line, enter the target path of the movie clip whose coordinate system you want to use followed by a period.

11. Choose Built-in Classes > Movie > MovieClip > Methods > globalToLocal.

12. With your pointer between the parentheses, enter the name of your point object (**Figure 8.32**).

Flash transforms the coordinates of your point object (relative to the root Timeline) to the coordinates of the targeted movie clip (relative to the groove movie clip's Timeline). 🎧

To link the slider position to the volume setting:

1. Continuing with the file you used in the preceding task, import a sound file into Flash.

2. From the Options menu in the Library window, choose Linkage.

The Linkage Properties dialog box opens.

3. Check the Export for ActionScript box, and give the sound an identifier.

4. Create a button symbol, place an instance of it on the Stage, and give it a name in the Property Inspector.

5. Select the first frame of the main Timeline, and open the Actions panel.

```
slider_mc.onMouseMove = function() {
    myPoint = new Object();
    myPoint.x = this._x;
    myPoint.y = this._y;
    _root.groove_mc.globalToLocal(myPoint);
};
```

Figure 8.32 A portion of the Script pane shows just the onMouseMove handler for the slider_mc movie clip. The global coordinates of myPoint (myPoint.x and myPoint.y) change to the local coordinates of the groove_mc movie clip.

```
startButton_btn.onRelease = function() {
    myMusic_sound = new Sound();
    myMusic_sound.attachSound("musicSampleID");
    myMusic_sound.start(0, 10);
};
```

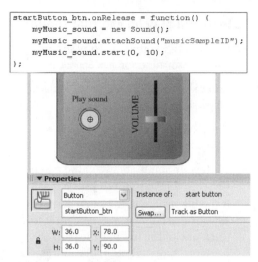

Figure 8.33 The event handler of the startButton_btn creates a sound object, attaches a sound from the Library, and plays it.

```
slider_mc.onMouseMove = function() {
    myPoint = new Object();
    myPoint.x = this._x;
    myPoint.y = this._y;
    _root.groove_mc.globalToLocal(myPoint);
    _root.myMusic_sound.setVolume(-1*myPoint.y);
};
```

Figure 8.34 A portion of the Script pane shows just the onMouseMove handler for the slider_mc movie clip. The groove_mc movie-clip symbol is 100 pixels tall, with its center point at the bottom edge. Hence, the local coordinates of the groove_mc movie clip range from −100 to 0. To change this range, multiply by (−1). The result is a range from 100 at the top to 0 at the bottom that can feed into the setVolume() parameter.

6. Assign an onRelease event handler to your button and actions as you did in the preceding tasks to create a new sound object.

7. Attach the sound from the Library to the sound object; then assign the method that starts the sound (**Figure 8.33**).

8. Create a new line within the onMouseMove event handler and enter the target path of your sound object followed by a period.

9. Choose Built-in Classes > Media > Sound > Methods > setVolume.

10. With your pointer between the parentheses, enter -1*myPoint.y.

    The *y* position of your slider moves from −100 to 0. By multiplying the point object by −1, you convert the range of values from 100 to 0 (**Figure 8.34**).

11. Choose Global Functions > Movie Clip Control > updateAfterEvent.

12. Test your movie.

    When you drag the slider up or down in the groove, you change the sound volume dynamically.

CREATING DYNAMIC SOUND CONTROLS

Loading External Sounds

Each time you use the Linkage Properties dialog box to identify a sound in the Library and mark it for export, that sound is added to your SWF file, increasing its size. Sounds take up an enormous amount of space, even with MP3 compression, so you have to be judicious with your inclusion of sounds. One way to manage sounds so that your file stays small is to keep sounds as separate files outside your Flash movie. Use the method loadSound() to bring MP3 sounds into Flash and associate them with a sound object only when you need them. (MP3 is the only allowable format.) This method also allows you to change the sound file easily without having to edit your Flash movie. You can maintain several background-music tracks that users can choose among, for example. To turn the music on, you use the method loadSound(). To choose a different track, you call the method again and load a different sound file.

The method loadSound() requires two parameters. The first parameter is the path to the MP3 file. The second parameter determines whether you want the sound to be a streaming or an event sound. Enter true for streaming or false for not streaming (event). Streaming sounds will begin to play as soon as enough data downloads. For this reason, streaming sounds do not need the start() method. Event sounds, however, must download in their entirety and do require the start() method to begin playing.

To load and play an external sound:

1. Instantiate a sound object with the constructor function new Sound().

2. Enter the name of your sound object followed by a period.

3. Choose Built-in Classes > Media > Sound > Methods > loadSound.

4. With your pointer between the parentheses, enter the path to your MP3 file.

   If the file resides in the same directory as your Flash movie, you can enter just the name of the file. Put the path or filename in quotation marks. Enter a comma; then enter true for a streaming sound (**Figure 8.35**).

5. Test your movie.

   As soon as your movie begins, it creates a sound object, then loads an MP3 file into it, and plays.

✔ Tip

- There is a bug in the Flash Player that prevents you from loading a local MP3 file from Internet Explorer on Windows. Use Control > Test Movie from Flash or upload your files to a server to make your movie play correctly. Check the Macromedia site for updates to the Flash Player; this problem may have been fixed after the printing of this book.

Figure 8.35 The loadSound() method streams the MP3 file called kennedy.mp3 that resides in the same directory as the Flash movie. The sound plays as soon as enough data has downloaded.

LOADING EXTERNAL SOUNDS

To stop a loaded sound:

◆ Use the stop() method.

The loaded sound associated with your sound object will stop playing.

✔ Tip

■ After you stop a loaded sound, you have two ways to make it play again, depending on whether your sound is a streaming sound or an event sound. If your sound is a streaming sound, you must reload it with loadSound() to begin playing it again. If your sound is an event sound, you must use the start() method.

Event or Streaming: Sound-Sync Options

Sounds behave differently depending on their sync options. The method loadSound() requires that a sound have a Stream or an Event sync option. (Two additional sync options, Start and Stop, are available only to sounds that are assigned to a keyframe.) Understanding the differences between the two sync options will help you decide when to use one or the other.

◆ Streaming sounds begin playing before they have downloaded completely. You can have only one stream per sound object, so overlapping sounds are not possible (unless you instantiate more sound objects). Streaming sounds are ideal for long passages of music or narration. To stop a streaming sound, call the stop() method; to start a streaming sound, call the loadSound() method again.

◆ Event sounds must be downloaded completely before they can play. Event sounds play when you call the start() method. If you call the start() method again before the first sound has finished, another instance begins, creating overlapping sounds. To stop an event sound, call the stop() method. Event sounds are appropriate for short sounds and sound effects for user-interface elements such as button rollovers and mouse clicks.

Reading Sound Properties

The Sound class provides two properties that you can use to find out more about the lengths of sounds. position is a property that measures the number of milliseconds a sound has been playing. duration is a property that measures the total number of milliseconds of the sound. Both properties are read-only (**Table 8.2**).

Use position and duration to time your animations to your sounds. In the following task, you'll modify an image according to the length of time a sound has been playing. As the sound plays, the image slowly reveals itself. When the sound ends, the image is revealed completely.

To use the position and duration properties:

1. Continuing with the file you used in the preceding task, import an image, convert it to a movie clip, place the movie-clip instance on the Stage, and name it in the Property Inspector.

   You will modify the scale and the alpha of this movie clip according to the length of time your sound plays.

2. Select the first frame of the main Timeline, and open the Actions panel.

3. Enter _root followed by a period.

Table 8.2

Sound Properties	
PROPERTY	DESCRIPTION
position	Length of time a sound has been playing (in milliseconds)
duration	Total length of a sound (in milliseconds)

4. Choose Built-in Classes > Movie > MovieClip > Events > onEnterFrame. Complete the event handler by entering =function(){ and a closing curly brace on the next line.

The onEnterFrame event handler is created (**Figure 8.36**).

5. Enter the name of your movie clip followed by a period, the property _alpha, and an equals sign.

6. Enter the following after the equals sign:

(mySound_sound.position/
mySound_sound.duration)*100

mySound_sound is the name of your sound object. mySound_sound.position is the number of milliseconds that the sound has been playing. mySound_sound.duration is the total duration of the sound, in milliseconds. So when you carry out the division and multiply by 100, you get a value that represents the percentage of the sound that has downloaded (**Figure 8.37**).

The complete statement increases the alpha value of the movie clip as the sound plays so that the movie clip begins completely transparent and ends completely opaque when the sound stops.

7. Create two more statements that use the duration and position properties of the sound object to modify the _xscale and _yscale properties of the movie clip.

The statements should look like the following:

image_mc._xscale = 50+((mySound_sound.position/
mySound_sound.duration)*50);

image_mc._yscale = 50+((mySound_sound.position/
mySound_sound.duration)*50);

The movie clip called image_mc slowly increases from 50 percent of its size to 100 percent of its size.

continues on next page

```
▼ Actions - Frame
mySound_sound = new Sound();
mySound_sound.loadSound("kennedy.mp3", true);
_root.onEnterFrame = function() {
};
```

Figure 8.36 Assign the onEnterFrame event handler to the root Timeline.

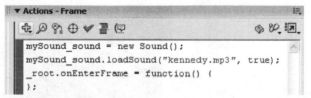

```
_root.onEnterFrame = function() {
    image_mc._alpha = (mySound_sound.position/mySound_sound.duration)*100;
};
```

Figure 8.37 The position and duration properties of the mySound_sound object modify the _alpha property of the movie clip called image_mc. As the value of position reaches duration, the opacity of the image increases.

8. Test your movie.

As you hear the words spoken by Senator Ted Kennedy at his brother's funeral, an image of Robert Kennedy slowly appears. The duration and position properties of the sound object enable you to synchronize the sound to the transparency and size of the image (**Figure 8.38**).

✔ Tip

■ The position property behaves a little differently when you use loadSound() set to streaming. When you load several streaming sounds, the sound object does not recognize the start of each new sound, so the position property does not reset. In this case, the position measures the cumulative length of time your sounds have played.

```
mySound_sound = new Sound();
mySound_sound.loadSound("kennedy.mp3", true);
_root.onEnterFrame = function() {
    image_mc._alpha = (mySound_sound.position/mySound_sound.duration)*100;
    image_mc._xscale = 50+((mySound_sound.position/mySound_sound.duration)*50);
    image_mc._yscale = 50+((mySound_sound.position/mySound_sound.duration)*50);
};
```

Figure 8.38 The full script (above). As the sound progresses, the image slowly appears (middle). When the sound is complete (position equals duration), the image is opaque and full-size. (Photo courtesy of the U.S. Senate.)

Detecting Sound Events

You can detect when a sound loads with the event onLoad or detect when a sound ends with onSoundComplete. Assign an anonymous function to the event to build the event handler. For example, consider the following script:

```
mySound_sound.onSoundComplete = function(){
    gotoAndStop(10);
}
```

In this script, when the sound assigned to mySound_sound is complete, Flash goes to Frame 10.

The onSoundComplete event lets you control and integrate your sounds in several powerful ways. Imagine creating a jukebox that randomly plays selections from a bank of songs. When one song finishes, Flash knows to load a new song. Or you could build a business

presentation in which the slides are timed to the end of the narration. In the following example, the completion of the sound triggers a graphic to appear on the Stage, providing a visual cue for the end of the sound.

To detect the completion of a sound:

1. Continuing with the file you used in the preceding task, select the first frame of the main Timeline, and open the Actions panel.

2. Enter the name of your sound object followed by a period.

3. Choose Built-in Classes > Media > Sound > Events > onSoundComplete. Complete the event handler by entering =function(){ and a closing curly brace on the next line (**Figure 8.39**).

continues on next page

```
mySound_sound_sound = new Sound();
mySound_sound.loadSound("kennedy.mp3", true);
_root.onEnterFrame = function() {
    image_mc._alpha = (mySound_sound.position/mySound_sound.duration)*100;
    image_mc._xscale = 50+((mySound_sound.position/mySound_sound.duration)*50);
    image_mc._yscale = 50+((mySound_sound.position/mySound_sound.duration)*50);
};
mySound_sound.onSoundComplete = function() {
};
```

Figure 8.39 Create the onSoundComplete event handler for your sound object called mySound_sound.

DETECTING SOUND EVENTS

Your onSoundComplete event handler detects when the sound associated with the sound object ends. When that happens, the function is triggered.

4. Within the event handler, add actions to be performed when the sound ends (**Figure 8.40**).

5. Test your movie (**Figure 8.41**).

✔ **Tip**

■ If a sound is looping, the onSoundComplete event is triggered when all the loops have finished.

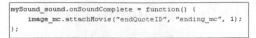

```
mySound_sound.onSoundComplete = function() {
    image_mc.attachMovie("endQuoteID", "ending_mc", 1);
};
```

Figure 8.40 The statement within the onSoundComplete event handler (above) attaches a movie clip from the Library to the image_mc movie clip.

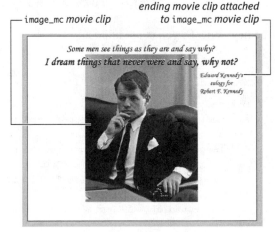

Figure 8.41 When the onSoundComplete event is triggered, a movie clip containing a quote from the sound attaches to the image_mc movie clip. The registration point of the attached movie clip was modified so that when it appears, it is positioned correctly. (Photo courtesy of the U.S. Senate)

Table 8.3

ID3v2 Sound Properties	
PROPERTY	DESCRIPTION
id3.COMM	Comment
id3.TALB	Album/movie/show title
id3.TBPM	Beats per minute
id3.TCOM	Composer
id3.TCOP	Copyright message
id3.TDAT	Date
id3.TDLY	Playlist delay
id3.TENC	Encoded by
id3.TEXT	Lyricist/text writer
id3.TFLT	File type
id3.TIME	Time
id3.TIT1	Content group description
id3.TIT2	Title/song name/description
id3.TIT3	Subtitle/description refinement
id3.TKEY	Initial key
id3.TLAN	Languages
id3.TLEN	Length
id3.TMED	Media type
id3.TOAL	Original album/movie/show Title
id3.TOFN	Original filename
id3.TOLY	Original lyricists/text writer
id3.TOPE	Original artists/performers
id3.TORY	Original release year
id3.TOWN	File owner/licensee
id3.TPE1	Lead performers/soloists
id3.TPE2	Band/orchestra/accompaniment
id3.TPE3	Conductor/performer refinement
id3.TPE4	Interpreted, remixed, or otherwise modified by
id3.TPOS	Part of a set
id3.TPUB	Publisher
id3.TRCK	Track number/position in set
id3.TRDA	Recording dates
id3.TRSN	Internet radio station name
id3.TRSO	Internet radio station owner
id3.TSIZ	Size
id3.TSRC	International Standard Recording Code (ISRC)
id3.TSSE	Software/hardware and settings used for encoding
id3.TYER	Year
id3.WXXX	URL link frame

Working with MP3 Song Information

MP3 files are the most popular format for storing and playing digital music. The MP3 compression is dramatic, and yet the quality is maintained at near-CD levels. Another virtue of MP3 files is that they are capable of carrying simple information about the audio file itself. This *metadata* (data about data) tag was originally appended to the end of an MP3 file and called ID3 version 1. Information about the music file (such as song title, artist, album, year, comment, and genre) could be stored at the end of the song file in the ID3 tag and then detected and read by decoders.

Over time and slight version upgrades, ID3 is currently at version 2. One of the more notable improvements was moving the data to the beginning of the song file to better support streaming. It now also supports several new fields, such as composer, conductor, media type, copyright message, and recording date.

Flash can read the ID3v2 data of an MP3 file. Each bit of information about the song, or tag, corresponds to a property of the id3 object of the sound object. So, for example, mySound_sound.id3.TALB refers to the album name of the MP3 file. **Table 8.3** covers all of the ID3 version 2 Sound properties.

How do you retrieve these ID3 properties? First, you must create an event handler that is triggered when available ID3 tags are present after a `loadSound()` or an `attachSound()` method is called. Using the event handler `onID3` is the only way you can access the ID3 data.

Sometimes an MP3 file may contain both ID3v1 and ID3v2 tags. The older Flash player, Flash Player 6, supports a few of the version 1 tags. **Table 8.4** covers the supported ID3v2 properties for the Flash Player 6 and their corresponding ID3v1 properties.

In the following example, you will load an external MP3 file and display the track information in the Output window.

To retrieve ID3 information about an MP3 file:

1. Instantiate a new sound object with the constructor function `new Sound()`.

2. On the next line, enter the name for your new sound object followed by a period.

3. Choose Built-in Classes > Media > Sound > Methods > loadSound.

4. With your pointer between the parentheses, enter the path to your MP3 file, and then enter `true` (**Figure 8.42**).

   Make sure that the MP3 path and name are surrounded by quotation marks and a comma separates the two parameters.

5. On a new line, enter the name of your sound object followed by a period.

6. Choose Built-in Classes > Media > Sound > Events > onID3. Complete the event handler by entering `=function(){` and a closing curly brace on the next line.

   An anonymous function is created with `onID3` as the event handler (**Figure 8.43**).

Table 8.4

Flash Player 6 Supported ID3 Tags

ID3V2 PROPERTY	CORRESPONDING ID3V1 PROPERTY
id3.COMM	id3.comment
id3.TALB	id3.album
id3.TCON	id3.genre
id3.TIT2	id3.songname
id3.TPE1	id3.artist
id3.TRCK	id3.track
id3.TYER	id3.year

Figure 8.42 The `loadSound()` method streams the MP3 files named dontknowwhy.mp3 that resides in the same directory as the Flash movie. The sound plays as soon as enough data has downloaded.

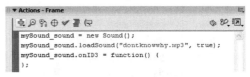

Figure 8.43 The `onID3` event handler is attached to the sound object named `mySound_sound`. The `onID3` event handler is triggered when ID3 tags are available from an attached or loaded MP3.

WORKING WITH MP3 SONG INFORMATION

```
mySound_sound = new Sound();
mySound_sound.loadSound("jazz1.mp3", true);
mySound_sound.onID3 = function() {
    trace("Artist: "+mySound_sound.id3.TPE1);
    trace("Album: "+mySound_sound.id3.TALB);
    trace("SongName: "+mySound_sound.id3.TIT2);
    trace("Released: "+mySound_sound.id3.TYER);
};
```

Figure 8.44 Use the trace statement to display the ID3 information in the Output window.

Figure 8.45 The Output window displays the ID3 information about the MP3 file that has been loaded into Flash.

7. On a new line inside the event handler, choose Global Functions > Miscellaneous Functions > trace.

8. With your pointer between the parentheses, enter the name of your sound object followed by a period.

9. Choose Built-in Classes > Media > Sound > Objects > id3 > Properties > TPE1.

The performer's name will appear in the Output window during testing mode in Flash.

10. Repeat steps 6 through 8 to retrieve all the ID3 information you want (**Figure 8.44**).

11. Save your FLA file in the location where it can find your MP3 file based on the target path you entered in step 4.

When you test your movie in the Flash authoring environment, the Output window will display the ID3 information (**Figure 8.45**). 🎧

✔ **Tips**

■ Using dynamic text fields, you can have Flash dynamically populate text fields and display the ID3 information on the Stage (rather than in the Output window). You will learn more about dynamic text fields in Chapter 10. 🎧

■ When an MP3 file contains a mix of ID3v2 and ID3v1 tags, the event handler onID3 is triggered twice.

■ To view the ID3 files of your MP3 files outside of Flash:

In *Windows XP*: Right-click the MP3 file and select Properties > Summary > Advanced.

Using *Mac OS X*: In iTunes, select the song in your playlist, and press command I.

WORKING WITH MP3 SONG INFORMATION

Part V: Working with Information

CONTROLLING INFORMATION FLOW

As your Flash movie displays graphics and animation and plays sounds, a lot can be happening behind the scenes, unapparent to the viewer. Your Flash document may be tracking many bits of information, such as the number of lives a player has left in a game, a user's login name and password, or the items a customer has placed in a shopping cart. Getting and storing this information requires *variables*, which are containers for information. Variables are essential in any Flash movie that involves complex interactivity because they let you create scenarios based on information that changes. You can modify variables and use them in *expressions*—formulas that can combine variables with other variables and values—and then test the information against certain conditions to determine how the Flash movie will unfold. This testing is done in *conditional statements*, which control the flow of information. Conditional statements are the decision makers of your Flash movie; they evaluate information that comes in and then tell Flash what to do based on that information. You would use conditional statements to make a ball bounce back if it collides with a wall, for example, or to increase the speed of the ball if the game time exceeds 1 minute.

This chapter is about managing information by using variables, expressions, and conditional statements. You've dealt with all three in limited ways in earlier chapters, but here, you'll learn how to work with them in more detail. When you understand how to get, modify, and evaluate information, you can truly direct your Flash movie and change the graphics, animation, and sound in dynamic fashion.

Initializing Information

Variables hold information. You can create, change the contents of, and discard variables at any time. When you put information into a variable the first time, it's called *initialization*. Initializing a variable in the Actions panel involves using the equals sign (=), which assigns a value to a variable. The variable name goes on the left side of the equals sign and a value goes on the right side. This point is crucial because a = b is *not* the same as b = a. To help identify variables at the time of initializing, you can use the identifier var. When you put the term var in front of the name of your variable, it becomes clear which part is the variable and which part is the new value, as in the following example:

```
var myPassword = "hocusPocus";
```

You've initialized variables before; you just didn't call it that. When you create new objects, as in the statement myColor_color = new Color (myMovieClip), you initialize the variable myColor. This could have also been written var myColor_color = new Color (myMovieClip). In this case, the variable called myColor_color contains a color object, but a variable can hold any kind of information, such as a number, letters, a true or false value, or even a reference to another variable. The different kinds of information that variables can contain are known as *data types*.

Variables, data types, and strict typing

Examples of typical types of variables are a user's score (number data type), an Internet address (string data type), a date object (object data type), and the on/off state of a radio button (Boolean data type). You can easily change the data type that a variable holds. A variable that was initialized with a number data type can be changed later in the movie to hold a string data type by simply reassigning a value to it. It's good practice to keep the data type of variables constant, however, so that when you manipulate them, you don't get unexpected results (trying to multiply a string by a string, for example). In ActionScript 2, however, you can specify the data type of your variable when you create it and Flash will allow only that data type in the variable. This is called *strict typing*. Strict data-typing prevents you from accidentally assigning the wrong type of data to a variable, which can cause problems during the playback of your movie. Strict data-typing involves adding a colon (:) and the data type after the name of your variable—for example, var myScore: Number = 20. In this statement, the variable called myScore is strictly typed for a numerical value. **Table 9.1** lists the data types that variables can hold.

Variable names should describe the information that variables hold. The variable names playerScore and spaceshipVelocity, for example, are appropriate and will cause fewer headaches than something like xyz or myVariable. Use the same rules to name variables as you would to name movie clips, buttons, and other objects: Do not use special characters or spaces, and always begin your variable name with a letter. The common practice, known as Hungarian notation, is to string together multiple words to describe a variable and capitalize every word except the first. Moreover, when naming a variable for an object, use the standard suffixes listed in Appendix A so that the object type can be easily identified.

Table 9.1

Variable Data Types

DATA TYPE	DESCRIPTION	EXAMPLE
Number	A numeric value.	var myScore:Number = 24
String	A sequence of characters, numbers, or symbols. A string is always contained within quotation marks.	var yourEmail:String = "johndoe@domain.com"
Boolean	A value of either true or false. The words are not enclosed in quotation marks. Alternatively, you can use 1 for true and 0 for false.	var radiobutton:Boolean = true
Object	The name of an object that you create from a constructor function.	var myColor_color:Object = new Color(myMovie_mc)
Null	A value representing no data.	A variable that hasn't yet been assigned a value or no longer contains a value
Undefined	A value representing a variable that hasn't yet been assigned a value.	An empty input text field

To initialize a variable:

1. Select the first frame of the root Timeline, and open the Actions panel.

2. In the Script pane, enter var (or choose Statements > Variables > var) followed by a descriptive name.

3. On the same line, enter an equals sign followed by a value. If the value is a string, remember to put quotation marks around it.

   The value on the right side of the equals sign is assigned to the variable on the left side (**Figure 9.1**).

✔ Tips

- You cannot use certain words for variable names because they are reserved for special functions or for use as keywords in ActionScript. You will just confuse Flash by trying to use them as variables. These words are break, else, instanceof, typeof, case, for, new, var, continue, function, return, void, default, if, switch, while, delete, in, this, and with.

- It's good practice to initialize your variables in the first frame of your Timeline. That way, you keep them all in the same place and can edit their initial values easily.

- When you assign a property to a variable, or assign to one variable a reference to another, Flash determines the value and puts it in your variable at that moment. If the property or the referenced variable subsequently changes, the value of your variable will not change unless you reassign it. Consider this example:

  var xPosition = _xmouse

  When you initialize the variable called xPosition in the first frame of your movie, it holds the x-coordinate of the pointer. As you move the pointer around the screen, the property _xmouse changes but the variable xPosition does not. The variable xPosition still holds the original x-coordinate from when it was initialized. To have a variable updated continually, you must put it within an event handler that is triggered continuously (such as onEnterFrame) or within a function call of a setInterval action.

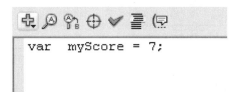

Figure 9.1 Variables can be initialized to hold different kinds of information. The word var indicates that myScore is a variable and the equals sign assigns the numerical value 7 to the variable.

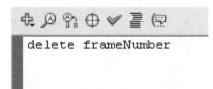

Figure 9.2 This statement deletes the variable called *frameNumber*.

If you no longer need a variable, it's a good idea to delete it so you can free memory. To remove a variable, use the `delete` action.

To delete a variable:

◆ In the Script pane, enter `delete` (or choose Statements > Variables > delete) followed by the name of the variable you want to remove.

  When this statement is executed, the variable is deleted (**Figure 9.2**).

Expressions and strings

Using expressions and using strings are two important ways to describe data. An *expression* is a statement that may include variables, properties, and objects and must be resolved (figured out) before Flash can determine its value. Think of an expression as being an algebraic formula, like $a^2 + b^2$. The value of the expression has to be calculated before it can be used (**Figure 9.3**).

A *string,* on the other hand, is a statement that Flash uses *as is* and considers simply to be a collection of characters. The string $a^2 + b^2$ is literally a sequence of seven characters (counting the spaces around the plus sign). When you initialize a variable with a string data type, you must enclose the characters in quotation marks.

```
myVolume = myLength*myWidth;
dogYears = 7*Age;
downloadProgress = _root._framesloaded/_root._totalframes;
```

Figure 9.3 Some examples of expressions. The variable names are on the left side of the equals signs, and the expressions are on the right.

Expressions and strings aren't mutually exclusive—that is, sometimes you can have an expression that includes strings! For example, the statement `"Current frame is "` `+ _root._currentframe` is an expression that puts together a string and the frame number of the main Timeline. You'll learn more about this kind of operation, called concatenation, later in this chapter.

✔ Tip

■ If quotation marks always surround a string, how do you include quotation marks in the actual string? You use the backslash (\) character before including a quotation mark. This technique is called *escaping* a character. The string `"The line \"Call me Shane\" is from a 1953 movie Western"` produces the following result: The line "Call me Shane" is from a 1953 movie Western. **Table 9.2** lists a few common escape sequences for special characters.

Table 9.2

Common Escape Sequences	
SEQUENCE	CHARACTER
\b	Backspace
\r	Return
\t	Tab
\"	Quotation mark
\'	Single quotation mark
\\	Backslash

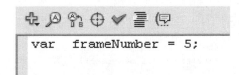

Figure 9.4 The variable `frameNumber` is initialized to 5.

Using Variables and Expressions

Use variables and expressions as placeholders for parameters within your ActionScript. In virtually every action or method that requires you to enter a parameter, you can place a variable or an expression instead of a fixed value. For example, you can enter an expression instead of a frame number for the parameter for the basic action **gotoAndStop**. This expression might be a variable called **myCard** that holds a number from 1 to 52. Frames 1 through 52 in the Timeline could contain graphics of the 52 playing cards, so changing the variable **myCard** in the **gotoAndStop** action would make Flash display different cards.

The parameter in the action **getURL** can be an expression rather than a fixed Internet address. The expression might be a string concatenated with a variable such as **"http://"+yourWebSite**. Changing the variable called **yourWebSite** makes Flash load different URLs with the **getURL** action.

You can also use a variable as a simple counter. Rather than taking the place of a parameter, a counter variable keeps track of how many times certain things occur for later retrieval and testing. A player's score can be stored in a variable so that Flash knows when the player reaches enough points to win the game. Or a variable could keep track of a certain state. You can set the variable **myShield=true** if a character's force field is turned on, for example, and change the variable to **myShield=false** if the force field is turned off.

To use a variable:

1. In the first keyframe of the root Timeline, initialize a variable as described in the previous section. Assign a numerical value to your variable (**Figure 9.4**).

continues on next page

2. Create a button symbol, drag an instance of it to the Stage, and give it a name in the Property Inspector.

3. Select the first frame of the root Timeline again, and open the Actions panel.

4. Assign an onRelease event handler to your button.

5. Between the curly braces of the event handler, enter the action, gotoAndStop(). For its parameter, enter the name of the variable you initialized in the root Timeline (**Figure 9.5**).

6. Provide additional frames so that the playhead has somewhere to go.

7. Test your movie (**Figure 9.6**).

   Your variable contains a number. When Flash performs the gotoAndStop action, it uses the information contained in your variable as the frame to go to. If you change the value of your variable, Flash will go to a different frame. This strategy lets you change parameters in code that may be spread throughout your movie by just changing variables initialized on the first keyframe.

✔ Tip

■ If you want to use a frame label instead of a frame number to identify the frame you want Flash to go to, you must define a string data type for your variable. Assign the string "Conclusion" to the variable myFrameLabel, for example. By using myFrameLabel as the parameter in the gotoAndPlay action, you can have Flash go to the frame labeled Conclusion.

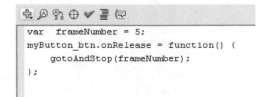

```
var  frameNumber = 5;
myButton_btn.onRelease = function() {
    gotoAndStop(frameNumber);
};
```

Figure 9.5 The variable called frameNumber is the parameter for the gotoAndStop() action. Instead of a static number, the gotoAndStop() action will use the value of the variable.

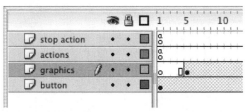

Figure 9.6 When the user clicks the button in the bottom layer, Flash goes to the value of frameNumber, which is 5.

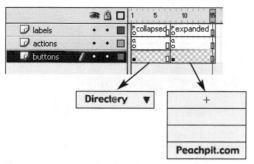

Figure 9.7 A movie clip of a pull-down menu has two states—collapsed and expanded—that toggle back and forth.

The scope of variables

When you initialize variables, they belong to the Timeline where you create them. This is known as the *scope* of a variable. Variables have their own scope, just as you learned in Chapter 5 that functions and event handlers have a scope. If you initialize a variable on the root Timeline, the variable is scoped to the root Timeline. If you initialize a variable inside a clip event handler, the variable is scoped to that movie clip.

Think of a variable's scope as being its home. Variables live on certain timelines, and if you want to use the information inside a variable, first you must find it with a target path. This process is analogous to targeting movie clips and other objects. To access either a movie clip or a variable, you identify it with a target path. When you construct a target path for a variable, you can use the absolute term _root or the relative terms this and _parent.

In the following task, you will build a pull-down menu that loads a Web site by using the getURL action. The URL for the action is stored in a variable that is initialized and scoped to the main Timeline. Because the getURL action resides in a movie clip, the variable and the action that uses the variable have different scopes. Use a target path to tell Flash how to get from the movie clip's Timeline to the main Timeline to identify the variable.

To target a variable with a different scope:

1. Create a movie clip of a pull-down menu, as demonstrated in Chapter 4 in the section "Complex Buttons."

2. Drag an instance of the movie clip from the Library to the Stage (**Figure 9.7**), and give the instance a name in the Property Inspector.

continues on next page

USING VARIABLES AND EXPRESSIONS

3. Select the first frame of the root Timeline, and open the Actions panel.

4. Initialize a variable, and assign an Internet address as its value, such as:

var myURL = "http://www.peachpit.com"

This variable is initialized in the root Timeline and holds a string data type.

5. Enter symbol-editing mode for your movie clip, and choose one of the buttons from the expanded pull-down menu.

6. Add to the on(release) event handler by choosing Global Functions > Browser/ Network > getURL.

7. As the parameter for the getURL action, enter _root followed by a dot and then the name of the variable you initialized in the root Timeline (**Figure 9.8**).

8. Test your movie.

When you click your pull-down menu to expand it and then choose the button to which you assigned the getURL action, Flash retrieves the information stored in the variable on the root Timeline. If you had not specified the root Timeline in the URL field of the getURL action, Flash would look within the movie clip for that variable and would not be able to find it.

The variable myURL is scoped to the root Timeline.

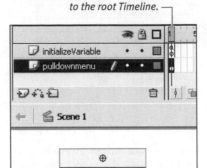

The getURL action assigned to the button inside this movie clip targets _root.myURL.

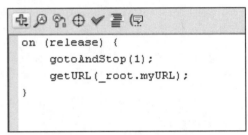

```
on (release) {
    gotoAndStop(1);
    getURL(_root.myURL);
}
```

Figure 9.8 For the last button of the pull-down menu, assign _root.myURL as the parameter of the getURL action. Because this action is inside the movie clip of the pull-down menu, _root is necessary to target the variable myURL in the root Timeline.

Global variables

If you want to have access to a variable no matter where you are, you can initialize a global variable. A global variable does not have a specific scope but is scoped to all timelines. A global variable is like the Key or the Mouse class in that you can access it from any Timeline simply by referencing its name.

You can initialize a global variable by preceding it with the identifier _global. Do not use the ActionScript term var because it applies only to local variables. After the variable is initialized, you can read its contents from anywhere in your Flash movie with just the variable name. If you want to modify the contents of your global variable, use the _global identifier with the variable name and assign new values.

To initialize a variable with a global scope:

1. Select the first frame of the main Timeline, and open the Actions panel.

2. In the Script pane, enter _global (or choose Global Properties > Identifiers > global).

3. Enter a dot following the _global identifier; then enter a name for your variable.

4. Complete the statement by entering an equals sign followed by a value (**Figure 9.9**).

   Your global variable is established. Although the variable is initialized in the root Timeline, you can access its contents from anywhere in your Flash movie without having to specify a target path (**Figure 9.10**).

```
_global.gravityConstant = 9.8
```

Figure 9.9 The global variable called gravityConstant contains the value 9.8. You can use this variable from any Timeline in the movie just by referencing its name, gravityConstant.

```
        _global.gravityConstant = 9.8;

VFinal = _root.rocket.VInital + (gravityConstant * _root.myTime)
```

Figure 9.10 After a global variable is initialized (top), you can use it anywhere. Notice that in the example statement (bottom), which calculates the final velocity (VFinal) based on gravityConstant and two more variables (called VInitial and myTime), target paths are unnecessary for gravityConstant.

Loading External Variables

You don't actually have to initialize variables inside your movie. Flash lets you keep variables outside your Flash movie in a text document that you can load whenever you need the variables. This way, you can change the variables in the text document easily and thereby change the Flash movie without even having to edit the movie. Build a quiz, for example, with variables holding the questions and answers. Keep the variables in a text document, and when you want to change the quiz, simply edit the text document. You can also set up the variables in the text document to be generated automatically with server-side scripts based on other external data. Then your Flash movie can read the variables in the text document with only the most recent or user-customized values.

The external text document can contain as many variables as you want, but it needs to be in Multipurpose Internet Mail Extensions (MIME) format, which is a standard format that CGI scripts use. The variables are written in the following form:

```
variable1=value1&variable2=
value2&variable3=value3
```

The variable/value pairs are separated by a single ampersand (&) symbol.

Variables can be loaded into either a specified level with the action `loadVariablesNum()` or a specified movie clip with `loadVariables()`. In both cases, you must remember the variables' scope when you want to retrieve their values.

To load external variables in a level:

1. Launch a simple text editor, and open a new document.

2. Write your variable names and their values in the standard MIME format (**Figure 9.11**).

```
myRotation=45&mySize=150
```

Figure 9.11 Two variables and their values written in MIME format. In this example, the variables are saved in a text document called data.txt.

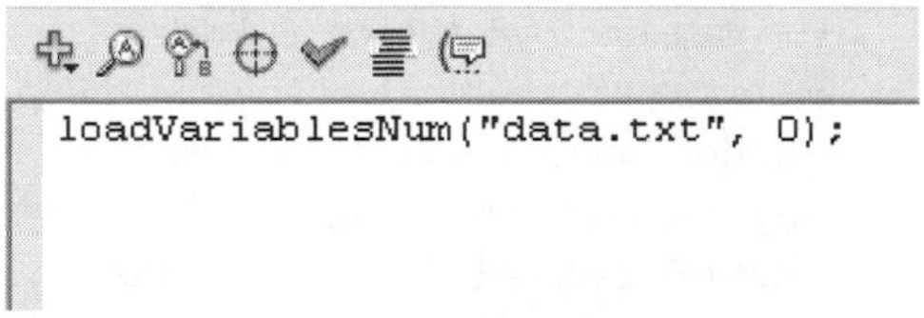

```
loadVariablesNum("data.txt", 0);
```

Figure 9.12 The LoadVariablesNum statement loads the variables from the data.txt file into level 0.

3. Save your text document in the same directory where your Flash movie will be saved.

It doesn't matter what you name your file, but it helps to keep the name simple and to stick to a standard three-letter extension.

4. In Flash, open a new document.

5. Select the first keyframe of the root Timeline, and open the Actions panel.

6. Choose Global Functions > Browser/ Network > loadVariablesNum (Esc + vn).

7. For the first parameter of the loadVariablesNum action, enter the path to your text file.

Because your SWF file and the text file will be in the same directory, you can simply enter the text file's name within quotation marks.

8. For the second parameter of the loadVariablesNum action, enter the number 0 (**Figure 9.12**).

The second parameter tells Flash where to load the variables. The number 0 corresponds to level 0. Flash loads the variables from your text file into level 0, or the root Timeline. Now your variables are available and scoped to _root.

To test your loaded variables:

1. Continuing the preceding task, create a movie-clip symbol, drag an instance of it to the Stage, and give it a name in the Property Inspector.

2. Select the first frame of the main Timeline, and open the Actions panel.

3. Assign an onRelease event handler to your movie-clip instance.

4. Between the curly braces of your event handler, assign the loaded variables to different properties of your movie clip as in the following:

   ```
   this._rotation = _root.myRotation
   this._xscale = _root.mySize
   this._yscale = _root.mySize
   ```

The variables myRotation and mySize are external variables loaded from the text document. Because the variables are loaded into level 0, you need to enter _root or _level0 before the variable name.

5. Save your FLA in the same directory as your text file and test your movie.

   When you click your movie clip, Flash uses the externally loaded variables as the values of this movie clip's rotation and scaling (**Figure 9.13**). 🔊

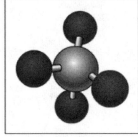

```
loadVariablesNum("data.txt", 0);
molecule_mc.onRelease = function() {
    this._rotation = _root.myRotation;
    this._xscale = _root.mySize;
    this._yscale = _root.mySize;
};
```

Figure 9.13 The values of myRotation and mySize from the text file are used to set the rotation property and the xscale and yscale properties of the movie clip called molecule_mc.

✔ Tips

- The variables you specify in an external text file are loaded into Flash as strings, making quotation marks around string values unnecessary. Flash automatically converts strings to numbers for certain operations and actions. In the preceding example, Flash knows to use a number for the _rotation, _xscale, and _yscale properties. So the string values "45" and "150" are used as number values 45 and 150. If you want to tell Flash explicitly to use a number, you can apply the Number function. Choose Global Functions > Conversion Functions > Number, and enter your variable name for its parameter (**Figure 9.14**).

- Write your variable and value pairs in an external text file without any line breaks, spaces, or other punctuation except the ampersand. Although you may have a harder time reading the file, Flash will have an easier time understanding it.

```
loadVariablesNum("data.txt", 0);
molecule_mc.onRelease = function() {
    this._rotation = Number (_root.myRotation);
    this._xscale = Number (_root.mySize);
    this._yscale = Number (_root.mySize);
};
```

Figure 9.14 Use the Number function to convert the contents of a variable to a number data type. If the value of the variable called mySize is "150", the Number function converts it to 150.

The LoadVars class

When you want to have more control over the loading of external variables and other data, you can use the LoadVars class instead of the loadVariablesNum action. The LoadVars class provides its own properties, methods, and events to handle and manage incoming (and outgoing) data. You can test how much of the external data has loaded with the method getBytesLoaded(), for example, or you can test the success or failure of a load with the event onLoad.

Using the LoadVars class requires that you first create an instance with a constructor function. After the instance is instantiated, use the load() method to bring external variables from a text file into the object. As is the case with the loadVariablesNum action, the variables must be in MIME format.

To load external variables with the LoadVars class:

1. Create a text document containing the names of variables and their values in MIME format, just as you did in the preceding section.

2. In a new Flash document, select the first frame of the main Timeline, and open the Actions panel.

3. In the Script pane, instantiate a new LoadVars object with the constructor function new LoadVars () (choose Built-in Classes > Client/Server > LoadVars > new LoadVars) (**Figure 9.15**).
   An instance of the LoadVars class is created.

4. On a new line of the Script pane, enter the name of the new LoadVars object you just created followed by a period.

5. In the code hint pull-down menu that appears, select load (or choose Built-in Classes > Client/Server > LoadVars > Methods > load).

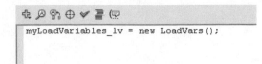

```
myLoadVariables_lv = new LoadVars();
```

Figure 9.15 The new instance called myLoadVariables_lv is created from the LoadVars class.

```
myLoadVariables_lv = new LoadVars();
myLoadVariables_lv.load("data.txt");
```

Figure 9.16 The load() method loads the data.txt file from the same directory as the Flash movie and puts the variables in the myLoadVariables_lv object.

```
myLoadVariables_lv = new LoadVars();
myLoadVariables_lv.load("data.txt");
molecule_mc.onRelease = function() {
    this._rotation = myLoadVariables_lv.myRotation;
    this._xscale = myLoadVariables_lv.mySize;
    this._yscale = myLoadVariables_lv.mySize;
};
```

Figure 9.17 The variables in the myLoadVariables_lv object change the rotation and scale of the movie clip called molecule_mc.

6. For the parameter of the load() method, enter the path to the text file that contains your variables.

If your SWF file and the text file will reside in the same directory, you can enter just the text file's name. Enclose the path- or filename in quotation marks (**Figure 9.16**).

Flash calls the load() method, which loads the variable and value pairs from the external text file into the LoadVars object.

7. Use the loaded external variables within your Flash movie.

The variables are scoped to the LoadVars object, so you must remember to include that object in your target path (**Figure 9.17**).

After you call the load() method for your LoadVars object, you can check and respond to the success or failure of the load. Use the onLoad event handler for this purpose. In this handler, you specify a parameter—the word **success** or **fail**—that determines whether the handler responds to a successful load or a failed load. Here is one example:

```
myLoadVars_lv.onLoad = function(success){
    trace("data loaded okay!");
};
```

Here is another example:

```
myLoadVars.onLoad = function(fail) {
    trace("data failed to load!");
};
```

Once you are done with loaded data, it's good practice to delete the LoadVars object using the **delete** command. For example:

```
delete myLoadVars;
```

Otherwise, the data will persist and take up memory until the movie ends.

LOADING EXTERNAL VARIABLES

To detect the completion of loaded data:

1. Continuing with the file you used in the preceding task, select the first frame of the main Timeline, and open the Actions panel.

2. On a new line of the Script pane, enter the name of your LoadVars object followed by a period.

3. In the code hint pull-down menu that appears, select the onLoad event (or choose Built-in Classes > Client/Server > LoadVars > Events > onLoad).

   Your onLoad event handler appears after the load() call.

4. For the parameter of the onLoad event handler, enter the word fail. Complete the handler with a closing parenthesis and a set of curly braces (**Figure 9.18**).

   This event handler is triggered when an attempt to load data occurs and is unsuccessful. If you want to detect a successful load, enter success as the parameter.

5. Choose actions to be performed between the curly braces of the event handler when the load() call is unsuccessful. (✎)

```
myLoadVariables_lv = new LoadVars();
myLoadVariables_lv.load("data.txt");
molecule_mc.onRelease = function() {
    this._rotation = myLoadVariables_lv.myRotation;
    this._xscale = myLoadVariables_lv.mySize;
    this._yscale = myLoadVariables_lv.mySize;
};
myLoadVariables_lv.onLoad = function(fail) {
    // add actions here to be performed
    // when the variables fail to load
};
```

Figure 9.18 The onLoad event handler for the myLoadVariables_lv object will be triggered when the load() method fails. Nothing is written inside the event handler yet.

Loading variables from HTML tags

Via the `loadVariablesNum` action and the LoadVars object, you can load variables from external text files in MIME format into your movie. But you can also access variables that are placed in the HTML page accompanying your SWF file. Those variables are integrated with the `<OBJECT>` and `<EMBED>` tags and are loaded into the SWF automatically. By putting variables in the HTML, you eliminate the need to use a `loadVariablesNum` action or the LoadVars object.

To load a variable from the HTML `<OBJECT>` and `<EMBED>` tags:

1. Open the HTML document that gets created with your SWF file when you publish your movie.

2. Find the `<OBJECT>` tag, which should be followed by a series of `<PARAM NAME VALUE>` tags that tell the browser how to display the movie.

3. Insert your variable as follows:
   `<PARAM NAME=FlashVars VALUE= "myRotationVariable=45">`

`FlashVars` is the name of the parameter, and the value is a string of variable name/value pairs in MIME format. If you have multiple variables, use ampersands to connect them like this `"myRotationVariable= 45&mySizeVariable=150"`.

4. Find the `<EMBED>` tag, which should be followed by a series of parameters that tell the browser how to display the movie.

5. Insert your variable as follows:
   `FlashVars="myRotationVariable=45"`
   Inserting the `FlashVars` parameter into both the `<OBJECT>` and `<EMBED>` tags is required for cross-browser compatibility (**Figure 9.19**).

6. Save the modified HTML document, and open it in a browser.
   The HTML page provides the variables to its SWF file; no action within the SWF file is necessary to load them. The variables are scoped to the `_root` Timeline.

✔ Tip

■ Variables loaded from the `<OBJECT>` and `<EMBED>` tags have a size limit of 64k.

```
<OBJECT classid="clsid:D27CDB6E-AE6D-11cf-96B8-444553540000"
  codebase="http://download.macromedia.com/pub/shockwave/cabs/flash/swflas
  WIDTH="550" HEIGHT="400" id="myMovie" ALIGN="">
      <PARAM NAME=movie VALUE="myMovie.swf">
      <PARAM NAME=FlashVars VALUE="myRotationVariable=45">
      <PARAM NAME=quality VALUE=high>
      <PARAM NAME=bgcolor VALUE=#FFFFFF>
<EMBED src="myMovie.swf"
      quality=high bgcolor=#FFFFFF
      FlashVars="myRotationVariable=45"
      WIDTH="550"
      HEIGHT="400"
      NAME="myMovie"
      ALIGN=""
      TYPE="application/x-shockwave-flash"
      PLUGINSPAGE="http://www.macromedia.com/go/getflashplayer">
</EMBED>
</OBJECT>
```

Figure 9.19 A portion of the HTML page shows where the `FlashVars` parameters are inserted.

Storing and Sharing Information

Although variables enable you to keep track of information, they do so only within a single playing of a Flash movie. When your viewer quits the movie, all the information in variables is lost. When the viewer returns to the movie, the variables are again initialized to their starting values or are loaded from external sources.

You can have Flash remember the current values of your variables even after a viewer quits the movie, however. The solution is to use the SharedObject class. SharedObjects save information on a viewer's computer, much like browsers save information in cookies. When a viewer returns to a movie that has saved a SharedObject, that object can be loaded back in and the variables from the previous visit can be used.

You can use SharedObjects in a variety of ways to make your Flash site much more convenient for repeat visitors. You can store visitors' high scores in a game, or you can store their login names so that they don't have to type them again. If you have created a complex puzzle game, you could store the positions of the pieces for completion at a later date; for a long animated story, you could store the user's current location.

Using SharedObjects requires you to put information that you want to keep in the `data` property of a named SharedObject. The statement `mySharedObject_so.data .highscore=200` would store the high-score information in the `mySharedObject_so` object. The method `getLocal()` creates or retrieves a SharedObject, and the method `flush()` stores the `data` properties. In the following example, you will save a login name from a text field (you will learn more about text fields in the next chapter). When you quit and then return to the movie, your login name is retrieved and displayed.

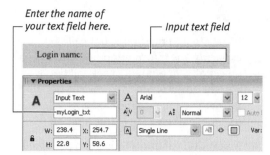

*Enter the name of
your text field here.*

Input text field

Login name:

▼ Properties

A | Input Text | A | Arial | 12
| -myLogin_txt | | 0 | Normal | Auto
W: 238.4 | X: 254.7 | Single Line | Var:
H: 22.8 | Y: 58.6

Figure 9.20 Create an input text field with the Text tool and give it a name in the Property Inspector.

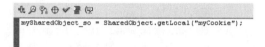

```
mySharedObject_so = SharedObject.getLocal("myCookie");
```

Figure 9.21 The getLocal() method creates a SharedObject that is stored on the user's computer.

To store information on a user's computer:

1. Select the Text tool and drag a text box onto the Stage.

2. In the Property Inspector, select Input Text and in the <Instance Name> field, enter the name loginData_txt (**Figure 9.20**).

   This input text field allows users to enter information via the keyboard.

3. Create a button, place an instance of it on the Stage, and give it a name in the Property Inspector.

   You will assign actions to this button to save the information in your text field in a SharedObject.

4. Select the first frame of the main Timeline, and open the Actions panel.

5. In the Script pane, enter mySharedObject_so as a name for your SharedObject followed by an equals sign.

6. On the right side of the equals sign, enter SharedObject.getLocal("myCookie") (**Figure 9.21**).

   Flash creates a SharedObject on the user's local hard drive. You can reference this object with the name mySharedObject_so. If the SharedObject already exists from a previous visit, Flash retrieves the object instead of creating one.

continues on next page

7. On the next line, create an OnRelease event handler for your button. Between the curly braces of the event handler, enter the following:

mySharedObject_so.data.loginData = myLogin_txt.text.

The contents of your text field on the Stage is saved in the data object of your SharedObject.

8. On a new line, enter mySharedObject_so.flush() (**Figure 9.22**).

Calling the flush() method saves all the information in the data property of your SharedObject on the viewer's computer.

✔ Tips

■ If the flush() method is not called explicitly, the information in the data object of your SharedObject will be saved automatically when the viewer quits the movie. The flush() method enables you to choose when to save information.

■ Many kinds of information can be stored in the data object of a SharedObject, such as numbers, strings, and even objects such as an array (see the accompanying CD-ROM for another example of SharedObjects). ⊚

Just remember to assign the information to the data object of a SharedObject, as in

mySharedObject_so.data.name="Russell"

rather than

mySharedObject_so.data="Russell".

```
mySharedObject_so = SharedObject.getLocal("myCookie");
saveButton.onRelease = function() {
    mySharedObject_so.data.myLoginData = myLogin_txt.text;
    mySharedObject_so.flush();
};
```

Figure 9.22 The onRelease handler for the button called saveButton puts the contents of the input text field in the myLoginData property of the data object of your SharedObject and saves it on the user's computer.

To retrieve information from a user's computer:

1. Continuing with the file you used in the preceding task, create a second button, place an instance of it on the Stage, and give it a name in the Property Inspector.

   You will assign actions to this second button, which will retrieve mySharedObject_so.data and the most recently saved contents of your text field.

2. Select the main Timeline, and in the Actions panel, assign an onRelease handler to this second button.

3. Between the curly braces of the event handler, enter the following statement:

   myLogin_txt.text = mySharedObject_so.data.myLoginData

   This statement retrieves the information in myLoginData that was saved on the viewer's computer in a SharedObject. That information is used to change the contents of your text field (**Figure 9.23**).

4. Test your movie.

   Enter your name in the text field on the Stage and then click the button to save the information into a SharedObject. Quit the movie. When you open up the movie again and click the second button, your name appears in the text field because Flash retrieved the information from your previous session (**Figure 9.24**).

```
mySharedObject_so = SharedObject.getLocal("myCookie");
saveButton.onRelease = function() {
    mySharedObject_so.data.myLoginData = myLogin_txt.text;
    mySharedObject_so.flush();
};
loadButton.onRelease = function() {
    myLogin_txt.text = mySharedObject_so.data.myLoginData;
};
```

Figure 9.23 The onRelease handler for the button called loadButton puts the saved data into the input text field.

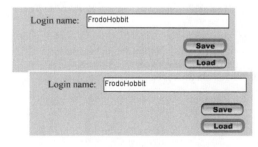

Figure 9.24 Enter your login name in the input text field and click the button called saveButton (top). Close the movie and then return to it. When you click the button called loadButton, your login name appears again (bottom) so you don't have to retype it.

To clear information on a user's computer:

◆ Use the keyword Null or Undefined to clear information that you've saved in a SharedObject.

Consider the following statement:

mySharedObject_so.data.myLoginData=Null

This statement removes the myLoginData property.

Flash keeps track of a SharedObject that is saved on the viewer's computer by remembering the name of the object as well as the location of the movie in which it was created. The location of the movie is known as the SharedObject's *local path*. By default, the local path is the relative path from the domain name to the filename. So if your movie is at www.myDomain.com/ flash/myMovie.swf, the local path is "/flash/ myMovie.swf". Flash lets you specify a different local path when you use the getLocal() method so that you can store a SharedObject in a different place. Why would you do this? If you have multiple movies, you can define one SharedObject and a common local path, allowing all the movies to access the same SharedObject and share its information.

Valid local paths for a SharedObject include all the directories in which your movie sits. Do not include the domain name, and do not specify any other directories in the domain. Remember, you are not telling Flash to store information on the server; you are telling Flash to store information locally on the viewer's computer (the host), and the local path helps Flash keep track of the SharedObject. Because local paths are relative to a single domain, a SharedObject can be shared only with multiple movies in the same domain.

To store information that multiple movies can share:

1. Continuing with the file that you created in the preceding task, in the Actions panel, add a forward slash as the second parameter to the getLocal() method. Make sure the forward slash is between quotation marks (**Figure 9.25**).

   Flash will save the SharedObject called mySharedObject_so with the local path "/". This entry represents the top-level directory.

```
mySharedObject_so = SharedObject.getLocal("myCookie", "/");
saveButton.onRelease = function() {
    mySharedObject_so.data.myLoginData = myLogin_txt.text;
    mySharedObject_so.flush();
};
loadButton.onRelease = function() {
    myLogin_txt.text = mySharedObject_so.data.myLoginData;
};
```

Figure 9.25 The second parameter of the getLocal() method determines the local path of the SharedObject and its location on the viewer's computer. The single slash indicates the top-level directory of the domain where the Flash movie resides.

2. In a new Flash document, create an input text field on the Stage, and give it the name myLogin2_txt in the Property Inspector.

This input text field will display information determined by the SharedObject you created in your first movie.

3. Select the first frame of the main Timeline, and open the Actions panel.

4. In the Script pane, enter the following statement:

mySharedObject2_so = SharedObject.getLocal ("myCookie", "/")

Flash retrieves the SharedObject with the local path "/" from the viewer's computer. Notice that the parameter "myCookie" is identical to the first Flash movie, but that mySharedObject2_so can be different (**Figure 9.26**).

5. On a new line of the Script pane, assign the property myLoginData in the **data** object of the SharedObject to the contents of your input text field with the following statement:

myLogin2_txt.text = mySharedObject2_so.data.myLoginData;

This statement retrieves the myLoginData information from the SharedObject and displays it in the text field.

6. Test your movies.

Play the first movie, enter your name in the text field, click the first button to save its position in a SharedObject, and close the movie. Now open your second movie. Flash reads the information in the SharedObject created by the first movie and displays your name (**Figure 9.27**).

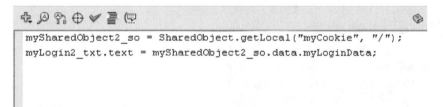

```
mySharedObject2_so = SharedObject.getLocal("myCookie", "/");
myLogin2_txt.text = mySharedObject2_so.data.myLoginData;
```

Figure 9.26 In this second Flash movie, the getLocal() method retrieves the same SharedObject that was saved in the first Flash movie. (The getLocal() method uses the same name and local path in its parameters for both movies.)

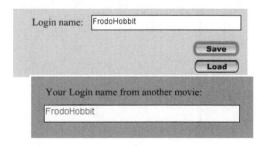

Figure 9.27 When the login name in the first Flash movie (top) is saved, you can open the second Flash movie (bottom) and its input text field displays the same login name. Both movies use the same SharedObject.

SharedObjects, Permission, and Local Disk Space

The default amount of information that Flash Player allows you to store on a viewer's computer is set at 100 KB. If you create a SharedObject that exceeds this amount, a dialog box appears over the Stage asking the viewer for permission to store information (**Figure 9.28**). Viewers can allow the request or deny it. If they deny the request, the SharedObject is not saved and the method flush() returns a value of false. If users allow the request, the SharedObject is saved and the method flush() returns true. When the dialog box is open, the method flush() returns the string "pending".

Viewers can change their local storage settings at any time by right-clicking (Windows) or Ctrl-clicking (Mac) the movie and then choosing Settings from the contextual menu (**Figure 9.29**). They can choose never to accept information from a particular domain or to accept varying amounts (10 KB, 100 KB, 1 MB, 10 MB, or unlimited). Local storage permission is specific to the domain (which appears in the dialog box), so future movies from the same domain can save SharedObjects according to the same settings.

If you know that the information you save to a viewer's computer will grow, you can allow more space initially by defining a minimum disk space for the flush() method. Calling the method mySharedObject.flush(1000000) saves the SharedObject and reserves 1,000,000 bytes (1 MB) for the information. If Flash asks the viewer to allow disk space for the SharedObject, it will ask for 1 MB. After the permission is given, Flash won't ask for more space until the SharedObject exceeds 1 MB or the viewer changes his or her local storage settings.

Figure 9.28 Flash asks to store more information than the viewer currently allows. This request comes from local, which is the viewer's own computer.

Figure 9.29 From the Flash Player menu (top), access the Settings dialog box. You can decide how much information a particular domain can save on your computer. This setting is for local, which is the viewer's computer.

Table 9.3

Common Operators	
SYMBOL	DESCRIPTION
+	Addition
-	Subtraction
*	Multiplication
/	Division
%	Modulo; calculates the remainder of the first number divided by the second number. 7%2 results in 1.
++	Increases the value by one increment. x ++ is equivalent to x = x + 1.
-	Decreases the value by one increment. x — is equivalent to x = x - 1.
+=	Adds a value and assigns it to the variable. x += 5 is equivalent to x = x + 5.
-=	Subtracts a value and assigns it to the variable. x -= 5 is equivalent to x = x - 5.
*=	Multiplies by a value and assigns it to the variable. x *= 5 is equivalent to x = x * 5.
/=	Divides by a value and assigns it to the variable. x /= 5 is equivalent to x = x / 5.

Modifying Variables

Variables are useful because you can always change their contents with updated information about the status of the movie or your viewer. Sometimes, this change involves assigning a new value to the variable. At other times, the change means adding, subtracting, multiplying, or dividing the variable's numeric values or modifying a string by adding characters. The variable myScore, for example, could be initialized at 0. Then, for every goal a player makes, the myScore variable changes in increments of 1. The job of modifying information contained in variables falls upon *operators*—symbols that "operate" on data.

Assignment and arithmetic operators

The assignment operator (=) is a single equals sign that assigns a value to a variable. You've already used this operator in initializing variables and creating new objects. **Table 9.3** lists the other common operators.

Operators are the workhorses of Flash interactivity. You will use them often to perform calculations behind the scenes—adding the value of one variable to another or changing the property of one object by adding or subtracting the value of a variable, for example. The following task is a simple example of how you can use operators to modify a variable that affects the graphics in a movie. You will create a button that increases the value of a variable each time the button is clicked. That variable is used to set the rotation of a movie clip.

To incrementally change a variable that affects a movie-clip property:

1. Create a movie clip, place an instance of it on the Stage, and give it a name in the Property Inspector.

2. In the first keyframe of the root Timeline, initialize a variable called myRotation to 0.

3. Create a button symbol, and place an instance of it on the Stage.

4. Select the button, and in the Actions panel, create an event handler with the on event.

5. Between the curly braces of the event handler, enter myRotation += 10 (**Figure 9.30**).

   The statement adds 10 to the current value and reassigns the sum to the variable called myRotation.

6. Select the first frame of the main Timeline and in a new line on the Script pane, enter an onEnterFrame event handler for the main Timeline.

7. Between the curly braces of the event handler, enter the name of your movie clip, a period, and then _rotation.

8. On the same line, enter an equals sign and then the name of your variable, myRotation (**Figure 9.31**).

   The onEnterFrame event handler makes the statement on line 3 run continuously. This code assigns the rotation of the movie clip to the value of the myRotation variable, which the user can increase by clicking the button.

```
on (release) {
    myRotation += 10;
}
```

Figure 9.30 Each time the button is clicked, its actions increase the myRotation variable by 10.

```
var myRotation = 0;
_root.onEnterFrame = function(){
    cannon_mc._rotation = myRotation;
}
```

Figure 9.31 The rotation of the cannon_mc movie clip is updated continually to the value of the myRotation variable in the root Timeline.

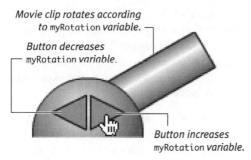

Movie clip rotates according
to myRotation *variable.*

Button decreases
myRotation *variable.*

Button increases
myRotation *variable.*

Figure 9.32 The turret of this cannon is the movie clip whose rotation property changes according to the myRotation variable.

9. Place another instance of the button on the Stage.

10. Assign a decrement assignment operator (-=) to the myRotation variable to decrease its value each time the button is clicked.

This code will control the rotation of the movie clip in the opposite direction (**Figure 9.32**).

✔ Tips

■ To perform more-complicated mathematical calculations (such as square root, sine, and cosine) or string manipulations on your variables and values, you must use the Math class or the String class. You'll learn about these objects in Chapters 10 and 11.

■ The same arithmetic rules of associativity (remember them from math class?) apply when Flash evaluates expressions, which means that certain operators take precedence over others. The most important rule is that multiplication and division will be performed before addition and subtraction. 3 + 4 * 2, for example, gives a very different result than 3 * 4 + 2 does.

■ Use parentheses to group variables and operators so that they are calculated before other parts of the expression are evaluated. (3 + 2) * 4 will return a value of 20, but without the parentheses, 3 + 2 * 4 will return a value of 11.

■ Use the modulo operator (%) to check whether a variable is an even or an odd number. The statement myNumber%2 returns 0 if myNumber is even and 1 if myNumber is odd. Use this logic to create toggling functionality. You can count the number of times a viewer clicks a light switch, for example. If the count is even, you could turn the light on; if the count is odd, you could turn the light off.

Concatenating Variables and Dynamic Referencing

The addition operator (+) adds the values of numeric data types. But it can also put together string data types. The expression "Hello" + "world", for example, results in the string "Hello world". This kind of operation is called *concatenation.* You can even mix strings, numbers, and variables to create expressions that create new objects or variables dynamically. For example, a common practice for naming duplicate movie-clip instances is to concatenate a variable with the name of the original movie clip. The variable is simply a counter that increases by 1 each time a duplicate is made. If the movie-clip name is mushroom_mc and the variable name is counter, you can concatenate a new name with the following expression:

"mushroom_mc" + counter

The result will be something like mushroom_mc1 or mushroom_mc2, depending on the value of counter. The new names of the duplicated movie clips are assigned dynamically with a concatenated expression (**Figure 9.33**).

This kind of concatenation to reference an object dynamically works because it happens to be a parameter of a method. Flash knows to resolve the expression before using it as the parameter. What happens in other cases? Consider this statement in the Script pane of the Actions panel:

var "myVariable" + counter = 5

This statement doesn't make sense to Flash and causes an error. You must instruct Flash to resolve the left side first and then treat it as one concatenated variable name before you can assign a value to it. The way to do that is to use the array access operators.

```
on (release) {
    duplicateMovieClip("mushroom_mc", "mushroom_mc"+counter, counter);
    counter ++;
}
```

Figure 9.33 The duplicateMovieClip action makes a copy of the movie clip called mushroom_mc. The name of the copy is assigned dynamically, based on the concatenation of "mushroom_mc" and the value of the variable called counter. The first click creates a movie clip called mushroom_mc1, the second click creates mushroom_mc2, and so on.

Array access operators

When you want to reference a variable or an object dynamically, use the array access operators. The array access operators are the square brackets (located on the same keys as the curly braces). They are called array access operators because they are usually used to access the contents of an array object, but they are just as useful for accessing the contents of other objects.

What does this capability mean? Think of the main Timeline as being a _root or a _level0 movie-clip object; variables and objects sitting in the main Timeline are its contents. So a variable called myVariable initialized in the main Timeline can be targeted with the array access operators as follows:

_root[myVariable]

Notice that there is no dot between the object (_root) and the square brackets. The array access operators automatically resolve concatenated expressions within the square brackets. So, the statement

_root["myVariable" + counter] = 5

puts together a single variable name based on the value of counter and then assigns the numeric value of 5 to that dynamically created name.

Using the array access operators also enables you to call methods and change the properties of dynamically referenced objects with dot syntax. If you want to modify an object's transparency, for example, you can do so this way:

_root["mushroom_mc" + counter]._alpha = 50

Depending on the value of counter, a particular movie clip in the root Timeline will become 50 percent transparent. If you want to make a movie clip play, you can call its method like this:

_root["myClip_mc" + counter].play()

To reference a variable dynamically and assign a value:

◆ In the Script pane of the Actions panel, enter the parent of the variable followed by an opening square bracket, an expression, a closing square bracket, an equals sign, and a value.

Flash resolves the expression within the square brackets and assigns the value to it (**Figure 9.34**).

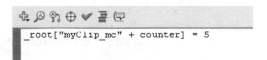

Figure 9.34 Use the square brackets (array access operators) to dynamically reference a variable. In this example, if counter = 1, the result of this assignment will be to initialize a variable called myClip_mc1 to the value 5. The parent object here is _root, or the main Timeline.

To reference an object dynamically and call its method:

1. In Script pane of the Actions panel, enter the parent of the object followed by an opening square bracket, an expression, and a closing square bracket.

2. On the same line, enter a period, and then choose a method (**Figure 9.35**).

   Flash resolves the expression between the square brackets and calls the method for that object.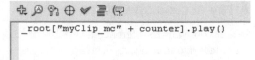

```
_root["myClip_mc" + counter].play()
```

Figure 9.35 Use the array access operators to dynamically reference an object and then call one of its methods. If counter = 1, this statement targets the movie clip called myClip_mc1 in the main Timeline and then makes it play.

To reference an object dynamically and change its property:

◆ In the Script pane of the Actions panel, enter the parent of the object followed by an opening square bracket, an expression, a closing square bracket, a dot, a property, an equals sign, and finally, a value (**Figure 9.36**).

   Flash resolves the expression between the square brackets and assigns the value on the right of the equals sign to the object.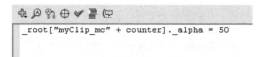

```
_root["myClip_mc" + counter]._alpha = 50
```

Figure 9.36 Use the array access operators to dynamically reference an object and then evaluate or modify one of its properties. If counter = 1, this statement targets the movie clip called myClip_mc1 in the main Timeline and changes its transparency to 50 percent.

Dynamic Referencing with the eval Function

You can also resolve an expression for dynamic referencing by using the eval function, which reads an expression and returns the value as a single string. You can modify an object's transparency with the following statement:

```
eval ("mushroom_mc" + counter)._alpha = 50
```

Or you can call a method of an object like this:

```
eval ("mushroom_mc" + counter).play()
```

Notice that the eval function accomplishes the same task as the array access operators. Which technique should you use? You should learn and use the array access operators for dynamic referencing. The eval function is an older function that was useful before recent ActionScript objects and syntax made it redundant. The array access operators are preferable because they are less taxing on the processor and result in more compact code that's easier to read.

In addition, in some cases the eval function fails to give predictable results. You cannot use eval to assign values directly to variables, for example. The statement eval("myVariable" + counter) = 5 will fail.

Table 9.4

Comparison Operators	
SYMBOL	DESCRIPTION
==	Equality
===	Strict equality (value and data type must be equal)
<	Less than
>	Greater than
<=	Less than or equal to
>=	Greater than or equal to
!=	Not equal to
!==	Strict inequality

```
if (condition) {
  consequence1;
  consequence2;
  consequence3;
}
```

Figure 9.37 If, and only if, the condition within the parentheses is true, consequence1, consequence2, and consequence3 are all performed. If the condition is false, all three consequences are ignored.

Testing Information with Conditional Statements

Variables and expressions go hand in hand with conditional statements. The information you retrieve, store in variables, and modify in expressions will be useful to you only when you can compare it with other pieces of information. Conditional statements let you do this kind of comparison and carry out instructions based on the results. The logic of conditional statements is the same as the logic in the sentence "If abc is true, then do xyz," and in Flash, you define abc (the condition) and xyz (the consequence).

Conditional statements begin with the statement if(). The parameter that goes between the parentheses is the *condition*—a statement that compares one thing with another. Is the variable myScore greater than the variable alltimeHighScore? Does the _currentFrame property of the root Timeline equal 10? These are typical examples of the types of things that are compared in conditions.

How do you construct conditions? You use comparison operators.

Comparison operators

A *comparison operator* evaluates the expressions on both sides of itself and returns a value of true or false. **Table 9.4** summarizes the comparison operators.

When the condition is evaluated and the condition holds true, Flash performs the consequences within the if statement's curly braces. If the condition turns out to be false, all the actions within the curly braces are ignored (**Figure 9.37**).

continues on next page

In the following task, you will use the same file that you created to rotate a cannon turret in the section "Modifying Variables" earlier in this chapter. You want to constrain the rotation of the turret to a maximum of 90 degrees, so you will construct a conditional statement to have Flash test whether the value of its rotation is greater than 90. If it is, you will keep its rotation at 90, preventing the turret from rotating past the horizontal plane.

To create a conditional statement:

1. Continuing with the task that demonstrates the rotation of a movie clip (see "Modifying Variables" earlier in this chapter), select the button, and open the Actions panel.

2. After the variable incrementally increases by 10, add a conditional statement by choosing Statements > Conditions/ Loops > if (Esc + if).

3. For the condition, enter the variable name followed by the > symbol and then 90 (**Figure 9.38**).

   Flash tests to see whether the variable is greater than 90.

4. Between the curly braces of the if statement, enter your variable name and then an equals sign followed by the number 90 (**Figure 9.39**).

   If the variable exceeds 90, Flash resets it to 90. This setting prevents the cannon turret from rotating past the horizontal plane.

5. Choose the other button that decreases the rotation variable, and create a similar conditional statement to test whether the variable is less than –90.

6. If the condition is true, set the variable to –90.

```
on (release) {
    myRotation += 10;
    if (myRotation > 90) {
    }
}
```

Figure 9.38 Add a condition that tests the myRotation variable to see if it exceeds 90.

Movie-clip rotation at 90 —

```
on (release) {
    myRotation += 10;
    if (myRotation > 90) {
        myRotation = 90;
    }
}
```

Figure 9.39 The cannon turret can't rotate past 90 degrees because the if statement won't allow the variable myRotation to increase beyond 90.

✔ Tips

- Any action residing outside the `if` statement will be performed regardless of whether the condition in the `if` statement is true or false. Consider the following script:

```
if (myVariable == 10) {
    myVariable = 20;
}
myVariable = 30;
```

After Flash runs this block of code, `myVariable` will always be set to 30, even if the condition `myVariable == 10` is true. The last statement is executed no matter what.

- A common mistake is to mix up the assignment operator (=) and the comparison operator for equality (==). The single equals sign assigns whatever is on the right side of it to whatever is on the left side. Use the single equals sign when you are setting and modifying properties and variables. The double equals signs compare the equality of two things; use them in conditional statements.

A simple but powerful and widely applicable use of the `if` statement is to monitor the state of a button click and provide continuous actions as long as the button is held down. A button that provides this kind of functionality is sometimes called a *continuous-feedback button*. A continuous-feedback button causes change even when it's held down at a constant state. When you click and hold down a button, for example, you can increase the sound volume (like a television remote control) until you let go. A simple button event cannot accomplish this functionality.

The solution requires you to toggle the value of a variable based on the state of the button. When the button is depressed, a variable called `pressing` is set to `true`. When the button is released or the pointer is moved away from the button, the variable `pressing` is set to `false`. Within an `onEnterFrame` handler, you can monitor the status of the variable continuously with an `if` statement. If `pressing` is `true`, you can perform an action. As long as `pressing` remains `true`, those actions will continue to be executed.

When you build your continuous-feedback button, you will actually use a movie clip. This procedure allows you to assign both button events (`onPress` and `onRelease`) as well as clip events (`onEnterFrame`) to the instance.

To create a continuous-feedback button:

1. Create a movie-clip symbol, place an instance of it on the Stage, and give it a name in the Property Inspector.

2. Select the first frame of the main Timeline, and open the Actions panel.

3. Choose Built-in Classes > Movie > MovieClip > Events > onPress. Complete the handler by entering =function(){ and a closing curly brace on the next line.

4. Replace the placeholder instanceName with the name of your movie-clip instance.

5. Between the curly braces of your onPress event handler, enter the name of a variable, an equals sign, and then the word true (**Figure 9.40**).

   The variable is set to true whenever the button is pressed. Note that there are no quotation marks around the word true, so true is treated correctly as a Boolean data type, not a string data type.

6. On a new line of the Script pane, choose Built-in Classes > Movie > MovieClip > Events > onRelease. Complete the handler by entering =function(){ and a closing curly brace on the next line.

7. Replace the placeholder instanceName with the name of your movie-clip instance.

8. Between the curly braces of your onRelease event handler, enter the name of the variable you used in the previous event handler, an equals sign, and then the word false (**Figure 9.41**).

   The variable is set to false whenever the button is released.

9. On a new line of the Script pane, choose Built-in Classes > Movie > MovieClip > Events > onEnterFrame. Complete the handler by entering =function(){ and a closing curly brace on the next line.

```
continuousFeedback.onPress = function() {
    pressing = true;
};
```

Figure 9.40 The variable called pressing keeps track of whether the movie clip called continuousFeedback is being pressed or released. When the movie clip is pressed, pressing is set to true.

```
continuousFeedback.onPress = function() {
    pressing = true;
};
continuousFeedback.onRelease = function() {
    pressing = false;
};
```

Figure 9.41 The variable called pressing keeps track of whether the movie clip called continuousFeedback is being pressed or released. When the movie clip is released, pressing is set to false.

```
continuousFeedback.onPress = function() {
    pressing = true;
};
continuousFeedback.onRelease = function() {
    pressing = false;
};
continuousFeedback.onEnterFrame = function() {
    if (pressing == true) {
        // put actions that you want to be performed
        // continuously, as long as the movie clip is
        // being pressed
    }
};
```

Figure 9.42 The status of the pressing variable can be monitored continuously by an if statement inside an onEnterFrame handler.

```
continuousFeedback.onEnterFrame = function() {
    if (pressing == true) {
        _root.gotoAndPlay(_root._currentframe-3);
    }
};
```

```
continuousFeedback.onEnterFrame = function() {
    if (pressing == true) {
        _root.myScrollbar._y += 5;
    }
};
```

```
continuousFeedback.onEnterFrame = function() {
    if (pressing == true) {
        currentVolume = _root.mySound.getVolume() - 5;
        _root.mySound.setVolume(currentVolume);
    }
};
```

Figure 9.43 Three examples of how a continuous-feedback button can affect a movie. At top, when the button is held down, Flash moves the playhead three frames behind the current frame, creating a rewind button like the one shown here that controls a snowboard video. In the middle, when the button is held down, a movie clip called myScrollbar moves down the Stage like a regular scroll bar. At the bottom, when the button is held down, the volume of the sound object called mySound decreases.

10. Replace the placeholder instanceName with the name of your movie-clip instance.

11. Between the curly braces of the onEnterFrame event handler, choose Statements > Conditions/Loops > if.

12. For the condition, enter the variable name followed by two equals signs and then true (**Figure 9.42**).

The condition tests whether the button is being pressed.

13. Choose an action as a consequence that you want to be performed as long as the button is held down (**Figure 9.43**).

✔ Tips

■ To refine the continuous-feedback interaction, you can add an onDragOut event to your onRelease handler, as follows:

```
continuousFeedback.onRelease =
continuousFeedback.onDragOut =
function(){ }
```

Now if your viewer releases the movie clip or if the pointer wanders off the movie clip, the continuous actions will stop.

■ You can use a shorthand way of testing whether a variable is true or false by eliminating the comparison operator (==) altogether. The if statement automatically tests whether its condition is true, so you can test whether a variable is true simply by entering the variable name within the parentheses of the if statement, like so:

```
if (myVariable) {
// myVariable is true
}
```

You can test whether a variable is false by preceding the variable name with an exclamation point, which means "not," like so:

```
if (!myVariable) {
// myVariable is not true
}
```

Providing Alternatives to Conditions

In many cases, you'll need to provide an alternative response to the conditional statement. The else statement lets you create consequences when the condition in the if statement is false. The else statement takes care of any condition that the if statement doesn't cover.

The else statement has to be used in conjunction with the if statement and follows the syntax and logic of this hypothetical example:

```
if (daytime) {
    goToWork;
    } else {
    goToSleep;
}
```

Use else for either-or conditions—something that can be just one of two options. In the preceding example, there are only two possibilities: It is either daytime or nighttime. Situations in which the else statement can be useful include collision detection, true/false or right/wrong answer checking, and password verification.

For this task, you will build an if-else statement to detect the keyboard input given to the question, Is the earth round? The answer can be only right or wrong—there are no other alternatives.

To use else for the false condition:

1. Select the first frame of the main Timeline and open the Actions panel. In the Script pane, create a listener object (see Chapter 4 for listeners).

2. On the next line, create an onKeyDown event handler for your listener object (**Figure 9.44**).

3. On a new line after your completed event handler, register your listener to the Key class (**Figure 9.45**).

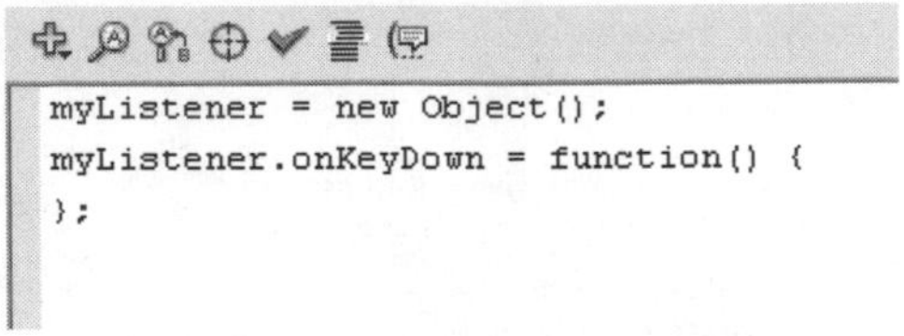

```
myListener = new Object();
myListener.onKeyDown = function() {
};
```

Figure 9.44 The onKeyDown event handler will detect a key press on the keyboard.

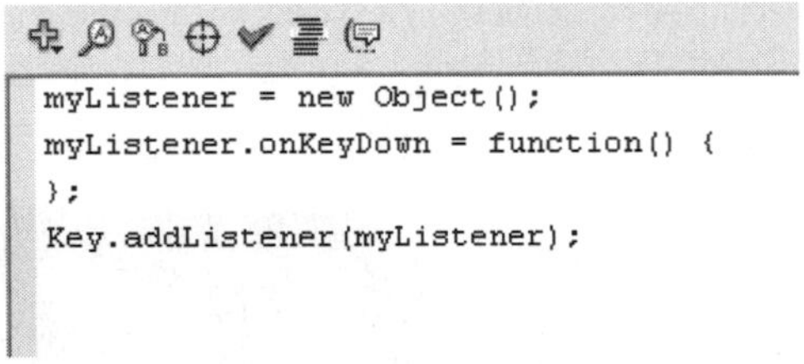

```
myListener = new Object();
myListener.onKeyDown = function() {
};
Key.addListener(myListener);
```

Figure 9.45 Register your listener object to the Key class.

```
myListener = new Object();
myListener.onKeyDown = function() {
    if (Key.isDown(89)) {
    }
};
Key.addListener(myListener);
```

Figure 9.46 The if statement within the onKeyDown event handler checks whether the Y key, which corresponds to the key code value of 89, has been depressed.

Is the Earth round? (Y/N)

```
myListener = new Object();
myListener.onKeyDown = function() {
    if (Key.isDown(89)) {
        trace("Yes, you're correct!");
    } else {
        trace("No, you're wrong!");
    }
};
Key.addListener(myListener);
```

Figure 9.47 The else statement triggers the "No, you're wrong" trace if any key other than the Y key has been depressed. Note how the else statement is part of the if statement and how it begins on the same line as the ending curly brace of the if statement.

4. Between the curly braces of the onKeyDown event handler, create the if statement by choosing Statements > Conditions/Loops > if.

5. As the condition, enter Key.isDown (89) to test whether the Y key is depressed (**Figure 9.46**).

6. Choose an action as a response to this condition.

7. On the same line as the closing curly brace of the if statement, enter else followed by a opening curly brace.

8. On the next line, choose another action as a response to the false condition, and then close the else statement with a closing curly brace (**Figure 9.47**).

In this example, Flash listens for a key being depressed. If the key is the Y key, then the correct message is sent. Otherwise, the error message is sent. The else statement covers any other key other than the Y key.

✔ Tips

- You can add an else statement by choosing Statements > Conditions/Loops > else or by pressing Esc+el, but doing so will add a closing brace behind the else statement.

- By convention, the else statement "cuddles" the closing brace of the if statement to show that they belong together. In the Auto Format options, however, you can change the Script pane's formatting to put the else statement on its own line.

- The conditions for this task did not include the comparison operator for equality (==). For Boolean data types and methods that return Boolean values, you don't need to compare them explicitly to the value true. So the following two conditions are identical:

```
if (Key.isDown(89))
if (Key.isDown(89)==true)
```

Branching Conditional Statements

If you have multiple possible conditions and just as many consequences, you need to use more-complicated branching conditional statements that can provide functionality that a single else statement can't. If you create an interface to a Web site or a game that requires keyboard input, for example, you would want to test which keys are pressed and respond appropriately to each key press. Flash gives you the else if statement, which lets you construct multiple responses, as in the following hypothetical example:

```
if (sunny) {
    bringSunglasses;
} else if (raining) {
    bringUmbrella;
} else if (snowing) {
    bringSkis;
}
```

Each else if statement has its own condition that it evaluates and its own set of consequences to perform if that condition returns true. Only one condition in the entire if-else if code block can be true. If more than one condition is true, Flash performs the consequences for the first true condition it encounters and ignores the rest. In the preceding example, even if it is both sunny *and* snowing, Flash can perform the consequence only for the sunny condition (bringSunglasses) because it appears before the snowing condition. If you want the possibility of multiple conditions to be true, you must construct separate if statements that are independent, like the following:

```
if (sunny) {
    bringSunglasses;
}
if (raining) {
    bringUmbrella;
}
if (snowing) {
    bringSkis;
}
```

The following example uses the Key class and branching conditional statements to move and rotate a movie clip according to different key presses.

To use else if for branching alternatives:

1. Create a movie-clip symbol, place an instance of it on the Stage, and give it a name in the Property Inspector.

2. Select the first frame of the main Timeline, and open the Actions panel.

3. Choose Built-in Classes > Movie > MovieClip > Events > onEnterFrame. Complete the handler by entering =function(){ and a closing curly brace on the next line.

4. Replace the placeholder instanceName with the name of the movie-clip instance.

5. Between the curly braces of the event handler, choose Statements > Conditions/ Loops > if.

6. As the condition, enter Key.isDown(Key.UP).

   The first condition uses the isDown() method of the Key class to test whether the up arrow key is pressed.

```
beetle_mc.onEnterFrame = function() {
    if (Key.isDown(Key.UP)) {
        this._rotation = 0;
        this._y -= 30;
    }
};
```

Figure 9.48 If the up arrow key is pressed, this movie clip is rotated to 0 degrees and is repositioned 30 pixels up the Stage.

```
beetle_mc.onEnterFrame = function() {
    if (Key.isDown(Key.UP)) {
        this._rotation = 0;
        this._y -= 30;
    } else if (Key.isDown(Key.LEFT)) {
        this._rotation = -90;
        this._x -= 30;
    }
};
```

Figure 9.49 The else if statement provides another alternative to the first condition. Either the up arrow key or the left arrow key is possible.

7. On the next line between the curly braces of the if statement, enter this followed by a dot, the property _rotation, an equals sign, and 0.

8. On the next line, enter this followed by a dot, the property _y, a minus sign and equals sign (-=), and 30.

   The two statements within the if statement rotate the movie clip so that the head faces the top and subtract 30 pixels from its current *y* position, making it move up the Stage. Recall that the operator -= means "subtract this amount and assign the result to myself" (**Figure 9.48**).

9. On the same line as the closing curly brace of the if statement, enter else if and an opening parenthesis. Enter Key.isDown(Key.RIGHT) and then a closing parenthesis.

10. On the same line, enter an opening curly brace.

11. On the next line, create two more statements to set the rotation of the movie clip to 90 and add 30 pixels to its *x* position, and then close the else if statement with a closing curly brace (**Figure 9.49**).

continues on next page

BRANCHING CONDITIONAL STATEMENTS

12. Continue adding two more `else if` statements in the manner described earlier to test whether `Key.DOWN` has been depressed or whether `Key.LEFT` has been depressed. Change the rotation and position of the movie clip accordingly.

13. Test your movie.

Your series of `if` and `else if` statements tests whether the user presses the arrow keys and moves the movie clip accordingly (**Figure 9.50**). Now you have the beginnings of a game of Frogger!

The switch, case, and default actions

Another way to create alternatives to conditions is to use the `switch`, `case`, and `default` actions instead of the `if` statement. These actions provide a different way to test the equality of an expression. The syntax and logic follow this hypothetical example:

```
switch (weather) {
    case sun :
        bringSunglasses
        break;
    case rain :
        bringUmbrella
        break;
    case snow :
        bringSkis
        break;
    default:
        stayHome
}
```

```
beetle_mc.onEnterFrame = function() {
    if (Key.isDown(Key.UP)) {
        this._rotation = 0;
        this._y -=30;
    } else if (Key.isDown(Key.LEFT)) {
        this._rotation = -90;
        this._x -=30;
    } else if (Key.isDown(Key.RIGHT)) {
        this._rotation = 90;
        this._x += 30;
    } else if (Key.isDown(Key.DOWN)) {
        this._rotation = 180;
        this._y += 30;
    }
};
```

Figure 9.50 The complete script (bottom) has four conditions that use `if` and `else if` to test whether the up, left, right, or down arrow key is pressed. The rotation and position of the movie clip (this beetle, top) change depending on which condition holds true.

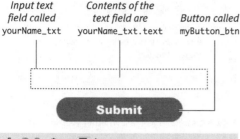

Figure 9.51 Enter yourName_txt.text as the condition parameter of the switch statement.

Flash compares the expression in the switch parentheses to each of the expressions in the case statements. If the two expressions are equal, the actions after the colon are performed (for example, if weather is equal to sun, bringSunglasses will happen). The break action is necessary to break out of the switch code block after a case has matched. Without it, Flash will run through all the actions. The default action, which is optional, provides the case statement if no other cases match the switch expression.

A subtlety to keep in mind is that the switch and case statements test for a *strict equality*. A strict equality is represented by three equals signs (===); it compares both the value and the data type of two expressions.

In the following example, you'll create an input text field for your viewers to enter their names. When viewers click the Submit button, the switch and case statements will compare what they typed in the text field with some known users.

To use switch and case for branching alternatives:

1. Select the Text tool, and drag a text field onto the Stage.

2. In the Property Inspector, select Input Text, and give the text field a name.

3. Create a button, place an instance below the text field, and give your button instance a name in the Property Inspector.

4. Select the first frame of the main Timeline, and open the Actions panel.

5. Assign an onRelease event handler to your button.

6. Choose Statements > Conditions/Loops > switch (Esc + sw).

7. As the condition for the switch statement, enter the name of your input text field followed by a dot and then text (**Figure 9.51**).

continues on next page

BRANCHING CONDITIONAL STATEMENTS

429

The switch statement will check the equality of the contents of the input text field with the expressions in the case statements.

8. In a new line between the curly braces of the switch statement, choose Statements > Conditions/Loops > case (Esc + ce).

9. Replace the placeholder condition with the string "Adam" (**Figure 9.52**).

10. On a new line after the colon, choose an action to be performed when the contents of the text field match "Adam" (**Figure 9.53**).

11. On a new line choose Statements > Conditions/Loops > break (Esc + br).

    The break action discontinues the current code block and makes Flash go on to any ActionScript after the switch statement.

12. Repeat steps 8 through 11, but replace "Adam" with a different user's name (**Figure 9.54**).

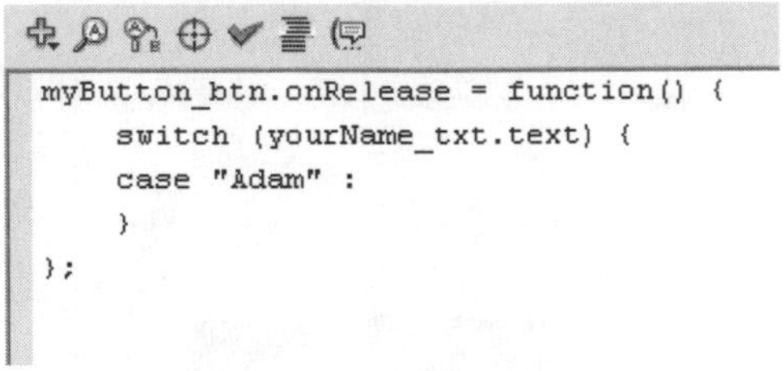

```
myButton_btn.onRelease = function() {
    switch (yourName_txt.text) {
    case "Adam" :
    }
};
```

Figure 9.52 Flash will test whether yourName_txt.text is equal to the string "Adam".

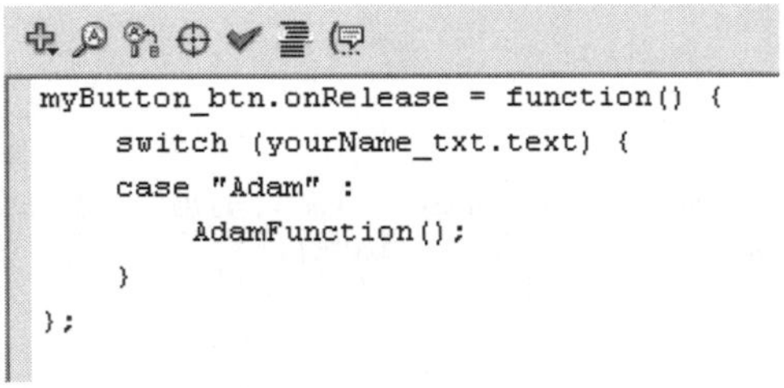

```
myButton_btn.onRelease = function() {
    switch (yourName_txt.text) {
    case "Adam" :
        AdamFunction();
    }
};
```

Figure 9.53 If yourName_txt.text==="Adam", the function called AdamFunction is triggered.

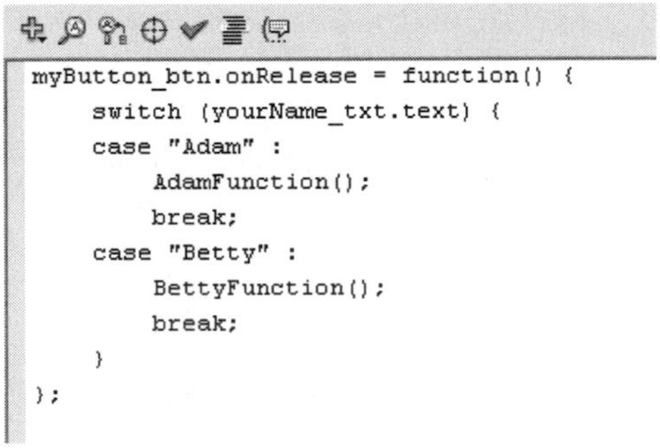

```
myButton_btn.onRelease = function() {
    switch (yourName_txt.text) {
    case "Adam" :
        AdamFunction();
        break;
    case "Betty" :
        BettyFunction();
        break;
    }
};
```

Figure 9.54 Create additional cases to test their equality against the switch expression.

```
myButton_btn.onRelease = function() {
    switch (yourName_txt.text) {
    case "Adam" :
        AdamFunction();
        break;
    case "Betty" :
        BettyFunction();
        break;
    default :
        errorFunction();
    }
};
```

Figure 9.55 If the expression in the switch statement doesn't match either "Adam" or "Betty", the default action will be performed. It's helpful if you think of the default action as being like the else action. Both actions define the consequences when the condition fails.

```
beetle.onEnterFrame = function() {
  switch (true) {
  case Key.isDown(Key.UP) :
   this._y -= 30;
   this._rotation = 0;
   break;
  case Key.isDown(Key.LEFT) :
   this._x -= 30;
   this._rotation = -90;
   break;
  case Key.isDown(Key.RIGHT) :
   this._x += 30;
   this._rotation = 90;
   break;
  case Key.isDown(Key.DOWN) :
   this._y += 30;
   this._rotation = 180;
  }
};
```

Figure 9.56 The full script to move a beetle movie clip with the arrow keys, using switch and case instead of the if statement.

13. On a new line, choose Statements > Conditions/Loops > default (Esc + dt).

14. Choose an action to be performed when the contents of the text field don't match any of the case statements (**Figure 9.55**).

15. Test your movie.

✔ **Tip**

■ What would the switch and case statements look like for the keyboard-controlled beetle in the preceding example? To create identical interactivity, you can enter the value true for the switch parameter and test it against each key press in separate case statements (**Figure 9.56**). It may look backward, but it works!

Combining Conditions with Logical Operators

You can create compound conditions with the logical operators && (AND), | | (OR), and ! (NOT). The operators combine two or more conditions in one if statement to test for more-complicated scenarios. You could test whether the up arrow key and the right arrow key are pressed together to make a movie clip move diagonally, for example. Or you could test whether a draggable movie clip is dropped on one valid target or another. You could use the NOT operator to test whether a variable contains a valid email address whose domain is not restricted.

The following task uses the same file that you created to move a movie clip from the keyboard. You will combine conditions to have Flash test for combination key presses to move the movie clip diagonally.

To combine conditions:

1. Continuing with the file that moves a movie clip with the keyboard arrow keys, select the first frame of the main Timeline, and open the Actions panel.

2. Select the first if statement.

3. Place your pointer at the end of the existing condition.

4. Choose Operators > Logical Operators > &&.

5. Enter your second condition after the two ampersands (**Figure 9.57**).

   Both conditions appear within the parentheses of the if statement separated by the && operator.

6. Change the actions within the if statement to rotate and move the movie clip diagonally (**Figure 9.58**).

```
if (Key.isDown(Key.UP) && Key.isDown(Key.RIGHT))
```

Figure 9.57 The logical && operator joins these two expressions so that both the up and right arrow keys must be pressed for the whole condition to be true.

```
if (Key.isDown(Key.UP) && Key.isDown(Key.RIGHT)) {
    this._rotation = 45;
    this._y -=15;
    this._x +=15;
}
```

Figure 9.58 The first portion of the script shows that when both up and right arrow keys are pressed, the beetle rotates 45 degrees and moves diagonally top and right.

7. Continue to add else if statements with combined conditions for the other three diagonal key presses while keeping the four conditions for the cardinal directions (**Figure 9.59**).

Using the && logical operator to combine two conditions, Flash checks whether the user presses two key combinations.

✔ **Tip**

■ You can nest if statements within other if statements, which is equivalent to using the logical && operator in a single if statement. These two scripts test whether both conditions are true before setting a new variable:

```
if (yourAge >= 12) {
    if (yourAge <=20) {
        sstatus = "teenager";
    }
}
```
or
```
if (yourAge >= 12 && yourAge <=20) {
    status = "teenager";
}
```

```
beetle_mc.onEnterFrame = function() {
    if (Key.isDown(Key.UP) && Key.isDown(Key.RIGHT)) {
        this._rotation = 45;
        this._y -=15;
        this._x +=15;
    } else if (Key.isDown(Key.DOWN) && Key.isDown(Key.RIGHT)) {
        this._rotation = 135;
        this._y +=15;
        this._x +=15;
    } else if (Key.isDown(Key.UP) && Key.isDown(Key.LEFT)) {
        this._rotation = -45;
        this._y -=15;
        this._x -=15;
    } else if (Key.isDown(Key.DOWN) && Key.isDown(Key.LEFT)) {
        this._rotation = -135;
        this._y +=15;
        this._x -=15;
    } else if (Key.isDown(Key.UP)) {
        this._rotation = 0;
        this._y -= 30;
    } else if (Key.isDown(Key.LEFT)) {
        this._rotation = -90;
        this._x -=30;
    } else if (Key.isDown(Key.RIGHT)) {
        this._rotation = 90;
        this._x += 30;
    } else if (Key.isDown(Key.DOWN)) {
        this._rotation = 180;
        this._y += 30;
    }
};
```

Figure 9.59 The complete script contains combined conditions for two key presses as well as conditions for a single key press.

COMBINING CONDITIONS WITH LOGICAL OPERATORS

Looping Statements

With looping statements, you can create an action or set of actions that repeat a certain number of times or while a certain condition holds true. Repeating actions are often used to build *arrays*, which are special kinds of variables that hold data in a structured, easily accessible way. The looping action makes sure that each piece of data is put in a particular order or retrieved in a particular order. You'll learn more about arrays in Chapter 11.

In general, use looping statements to execute actions automatically a specific number of times by using an incremental variable. The incremental variable modifies the parameters of each successive method in the loop or modifies certain properties of objects that are created. You can generate intricate patterns by duplicating movie clips or dynamically drawing lines and shapes with looping statements. Use looping statements to change the properties of a whole series of movie clips, modify multiple sound settings, or alter the values of a set of variables.

There are three kinds of looping statements—the while, do while, and for actions—but they all accomplish the same task. The first two statements perform loops while a certain condition holds true. The third statement performs loops by using a built-in counter and condition.

To use the while statement to duplicate movie clips:

1. Create a movie-clip symbol, place an instance of it on the Stage, and give it a name in the Property Inspector.

2. Select the first frame of the main Timeline, and open the Actions panel.

3. Initialize the variable i to 0.
   The variables i, j, and k is often used as loop counters.

4. On the next line, choose Statements > Conditions/Loops > while (Esc + wh).

5. As the condition, enter i<361 (**Figure 9.60**).

```
var i = 0;
while (i<361) {

}
```

Figure 9.60 Initialize the variable i, and create the condition that must be true for the loop to continue. As long as the variable i is less than 361, this loop will run.

```
var i = 0;
while (i<361) {
    duplicateMovieClip(oval_mc, "oval_mc"+i, i);
    _root["oval_mc" + i]._rotation = i;
    _root["oval_mc" + i]._alpha = (i/360)*100;
}
```

Figure 9.61 The oval_mc movie clip is duplicated, and its duplicate is rotated and changed in transparency.

```
var i = 0;
while (i<361) {
    duplicateMovieClip(oval_mc, "oval_mc"+i, i);
    _root["oval_mc" + i]._rotation = i;
    _root["oval_mc" + i]._alpha = (i/360)*100;
    i += 10;
}
```

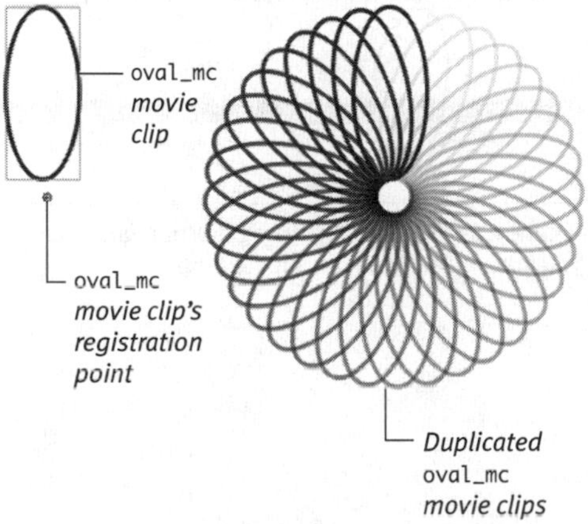

Figure 9.62 At the end of each loop, the variable i increases by 10. This loop will run 37 times. The oval_mc movie clip (left) is the basis for the pattern (right) made with the looping statement.

6. Assign any actions that you want to run while the condition remains true (i is less than 361).

   For this example, add a `duplicate MovieClip` action and two statements that rotate and modify the transparency of the duplicates (**Figure 9.61**).

7. On a new line, enter i += 10, or use the equivalent statement i = i + 10.

   Each time the loop runs, the variable i increases by an increment of 10. When it exceeds 361, the condition that the `while` statement checks at each pass becomes `false`. Flash ends the loop (**Figure 9.62**).

The do while statement

The do while (Esc + do) statement is similar to the while statement, except that the condition is checked at the end of the loop rather than the beginning. This means that the actions in the loop are executed at least once. The same script in the preceding task could be written with the do while statement, as shown in **Figure 9.63**.

The for statement

The for (Esc + fr) statement provides a built-in counter and parameters for increments or decrements to the counter, so you don't have to write separate statements. The parameter fields for the for statement are Init, which initializes the counter variable; Condition, which is the expression that is tested; and Next, which determines the amount of increment or decrement of the counter variable. The preceding task could be written with a for statement, as shown in **Figure 9.64**.

✔ Tips

■ Do not use looping statements to build continuous routines to check a certain condition. Real-time testing should be done with the if statement in an enterFrame event handler or from a setInterval function call. When Flash executes looping statements, the display remains frozen and no mouse or keyboard events can be detected.

■ Make sure that the increments to your variables are inside the curly braces of the while or do while statements. If they aren't, the condition will never be met and Flash will be stuck executing the loop infinitely. Fortunately, Flash warns you about this problem when it detects a problem in your script that causes it to stall (**Figure 9.65**).

```
var i = 0;
do {
    duplicateMovieClip(oval_mc, "oval_mc"+i, i);
    _root["oval_mc" + i]._rotation = i;
    _root["oval_mc" + i]._alpha = (i/360)*100;
    i += 10;
} while (i < 361);
```

Figure 9.63 The equivalent do while statement.

```
for (i = 0; i < 361; i += 10) {
    duplicateMovieClip(oval_mc, "oval_mc"+i, i);
    _root["oval_mc" + i]._rotation = i;
    _root["oval_mc" + i]._alpha = (i/360)*100;
}
```

Figure 9.64 The equivalent for statement. You can read the parameters this way: Start my counter at 0. As long as it is smaller than 361, perform the following actions. Then add 10 to my counter and repeat.

Figure 9.65 This warning dialog box appears when you inadvertently run an infinite loop.

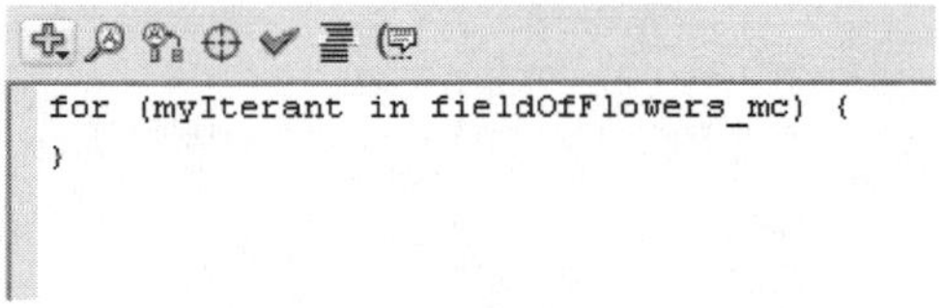

```
for (myIterant in fieldOfFlowers_mc) {
}
```

Figure 9.66 The variable called myIterant will loop through the objects inside the movie clip called fieldOfFlowers_mc.

The for..in loop

Another kind of loop, called the for..in loop, is used specifically to look through the properties or elements of an object. You don't use a counter variable as you do for the other kinds of loops. Instead, you use a variable called an *iterant* (or *iterator*), which references each property or element in an object. You can use the iterant in expressions within the for..in loop to modify each of the object's properties. If you had a movie clip called parentMovieClip_mc that contained many child movie clips, you could use the for..in loop to reference each child this way:

```
for (myIterant in parentMovieClip_mc) {
parentMovieClip_mc[myIterant]._rotation = 90;
}
```

This for..in statement would look inside parentMovieClip_mc, using the variable myIterant to reference each child movie clip. The expression within the curly braces rotates every child movie clip inside the parent movie clip.

To use the for..in loop to reference elements inside a movie clip:

1. Create a movie-clip symbol that contains many child movie clips.

2. Drag an instance of the parent movie clip to the main Stage, and give it a name in the Property Inspector.

3. Select the first frame of the main Timeline, and open the Actions panel.

4. Choose Statements > Conditions/Loops > for.in (Esc + fi).

5. For the iterant, enter a variable name, then enter in, and then enter the name of your parent movie-clip instance (**Figure 9.66**).

continues on next page

6. Between the curly braces of the for..in loop, enter an expression that references each child movie clip with the iterant and modifies its property (**Figure 9.67**).

In this example, all the child movie clips rotate the same amount. 🔗

✔ Tip

■ Enter _root as the target object for the for..in statement and you can reference all the objects (buttons, text fields, and movie clips) that sit on the main Stage.

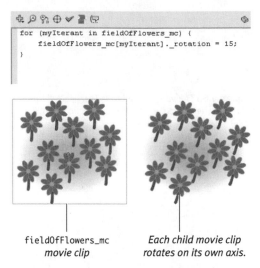

```
for (myIterant in fieldOfFlowers_mc) {
    fieldOfFlowers_mc[myIterant]._rotation = 15;
}
```

fieldOfFlowers_mc
movie clip

Each child movie clip rotates on its own axis.

Figure 9.67 Using the array access operators, dynamically reference each child movie clip within fieldOfFlowers_mc and modify the rotation of those clips.

CONTROLLING TEXT

You know that Flash lets you create visually engaging text elements—such as titles, labels, and descriptions—to accompany your graphics, animation, and sound. But did you know that you can do more with text than just set the style, color, and size? Flash text can be *live*, meaning that your viewers can enter text in the Flash movie as it plays, as well as select and edit the text. And Flash text can be dynamic, so it can update during playback. The text that viewers can enter is called *input text,* and the text that you can update during playback is called *dynamic text.* Both input and dynamic text are part of the class called the TextField class. Input and dynamic text provide a way to receive complex information from the viewer and tailor your Flash movie by using that information.

During author time, you use the Text tool and the Property Inspector to create your text fields. But you can also create text fields at run time, dynamically defining their properties (such as background color) or formatting (such as font size and style, set with the TextFormat class). This control of text fields' content and appearance lets you animate text purely through ActionScript, making it responsive to the viewer and to different events. With the TextExtent class, you can determine the exact dimensions of your text and its formatting so your layouts appear just the way you want them.

Two additional classes—the Selection class and the String class—help control the information within text fields. You will use these classes to analyze and manipulate the text or the placement of the insertion point within the text. You can catch a viewer's misspellings or incorrectly entered information, for example, before using the text in your Flash movie or passing it on to an outside application for processing.

This chapter explores some of the many possibilities of the TextField, TextFormat, TextExtent, Selection, and String classes and introduces the tools you can use to integrate text and control the information exchange between your Flash movie and your audience.

Input Text

You can build your Flash project to gather information directly from the viewer—information such as a login name and password, personal information for a survey, answers to quiz questions, requests for an online purchase, or responses in an Internet chat room. These user inputs, which Flash calls *input text*, are assigned to the `text` property of a text field so that they can be passed along to other parts of the Flash movie for further processing or sent to a server-side application through the CGI `GET` or `POST` method.

The following task demonstrates how you can use input text to let your user control the parameters of an action. In this case, you will accept information from the viewer in an input text field and use that information to load a URL.

To use input text to request a URL:

1. Choose the Text tool in the Tools palette, and drag out a text field on the Stage (**Figure 10.1**).

2. In the Property Inspector, choose Input Text from the pull-down menu.

   Your selected text field becomes input text, allowing text entry during playback.

3. In the Instance Name field of the Property Inspector, enter the name for your text field. Use the extension `_txt` for text field objects.

4. Click the Show Border button in the Property Inspector.

   Your text box is drawn with a black border and a white background (**Figure 10.2**).

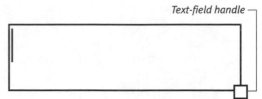

Text-field handle

Figure 10.1 A text field is created with the Text tool. You can resize the text field with the handle in the bottom-right corner.

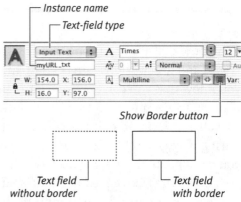

Instance name

Text-field type

Show Border button

Text field without border

Text field with border

Figure 10.2 The Property Inspector defines the text field as input text. The instance name is `myURL_txt`, and the Show Border button is selected. A text field without a border (bottom left) appears on your Stage in authoring mode with a dotted border. A text field with a border (bottom right) appears with a solid black border and a white background.

Figure 10.3 The code hint pull-down menu will help guide you in entering the proper code.

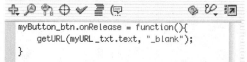

Figure 10.4 The actions assigned to the button called myButton_btn load the URL entered in the text field called myURL_txt in a new browser window.

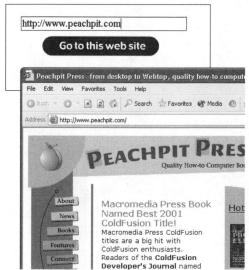

Figure 10.5 The contents of the input text field are used as the URL for the getURL action. Note that the viewer must include the protocol http:// in the input text field.

5. Create a button symbol, place an instance of the button on the Stage below the text field, and name the button instance in the Property Inspector.

6. Select the first frame of the main Timeline, and open the Actions panel.

7. On the first line of the Script pane, create an onRelease event handler for your button.

8. Place your cursor on the second line (between the opening and closing curly braces) and choose Global Functions > Browser/Network > getURL (**Figure 10.3**).

9. Enter the instance name of your input text field followed by a period (.) and the word text for the parameter of getURL. Enter a comma and then "_blank" for the second parameter (**Figure 10.4**).

10. Test your movie.

    When your viewer enters a URL in the text field, the URL is put into the text property of the text field. Then, when the viewer clicks the button, Flash opens a new browser window and loads the specified Web site (**Figure 10.5**).

✔ Tip

■ You can put initial text in an input text field to instruct viewers on what to enter. Put "Enter Web site address here" in your text field, for example, so that viewers know to replace that text with their Web site address. Or you could start them off by putting "http://" in the text field so that it's there already.

INPUT TEXT

Dynamic Text

For text that you control—such as scores in an arcade game, the display of a calculator, or the percentage-of-download progress of your Flash movie—take advantage of Flash's dynamic text option. Whereas input text fields accept information from the viewer, dynamic text fields output information to the viewer. As is the case with input text, the contents of the text field are assigned to its text property.

In the following task, you will create an input text field and a dynamic text field. When viewers enter the temperature, in Celsius, in the input text field, Flash will convert the value to Fahrenheit and display it in the dynamic text field.

To use dynamic text to output expressions:

1. Choose the Text tool in the Tools palette, and drag out a text field onto the Stage.

2. In the Property Inspector, choose Input Text from the pull-down menu.

3. In the Instance Name field, enter the name of your input text field. Use the extension _txt for text field objects (**Figure 10.6**).

   Your selected text field becomes an input text field, allowing text entry during playback.

4. Again, choose the Text tool, and drag out another text field on the Stage.

5. In the Property Inspector, this time choose Dynamic Text from the pull-down menu.

   Your selected text field becomes a dynamic text field, allowing you to display and update text in that field.

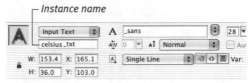

Instance name

Figure 10.6 Enter celsius_txt as the instance name for your input field.

Figure 10.7 Enter fahrenheit_txt as the instance name for your dynamic text field.

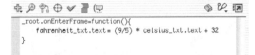

Figure 10.8 This statement calculates the Fahrenheit value from the expression on the right side of the equals sign.

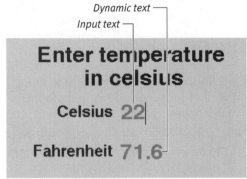

Figure 10.9 The contents of the dynamic text field (fahrenheit_txt.text) updates itself when new input text (celsius_txt.text) is entered.

6. In the Instance Name field of the Property Inspector, enter the name for the dynamic text field (**Figure 10.7**).

7. Select the first frame of the main Timeline, and open the Actions panel.

8. In the Script Pane, enter _root. Choose Built-in Classes > Movie > Movie Clip > Events > onEnterFrame. Complete the event handler by entering =function(){ on the same line and a closing curly brace on the next line.

   The onEnterFrame event is triggered continuously, providing a way to do the conversion of Celsius to Fahrenheit in real time.

9. In between the curly braces of the onEnterFrame event handler, enter the name of your dynamic text field followed by a period, the word text, and an equals sign. Continue by entering a formula that incorporates the input text field's text property (**Figure 10.8**).

10. Test your movie.

    Flash displays the contents of the dynamic text field based on the information that the viewer enters in the input text field (**Figure 10.9**). The calculation is done in real time, and the display is updated any time the input text changes.

✔ **Tip**

■ Use dynamic text as a debugging tool to show the contents of variables. If you are developing a complicated Flash movie involving multiple variables, you can create a dynamic text field to display the variables' current values so that you know how Flash is processing the information. In Chapter 12, you'll learn other ways to track variables, but this way you can integrate the display of variables into your movie.

DYNAMIC TEXT

Selecting Text-Field Options

The Property Inspector offers many options for an input or dynamic text field (**Figure 10.10**). The most important field to fill is Instance Name. The Instance Name field contains the instance name of your text field, letting you target it to modify its properties and call its methods. The Variable field contains a variable name that holds any information currently in the text field. The other options let you modify the way text appears:

◆ The Line Type pull-down menu defines how text will fit into the text field. Single Line forces entered text to stay on one row in the text field. If text goes beyond the limits of the text field, the text begins to scroll horizontally. Multiline No Wrap allows entered text to appear on more than one row in the text field if the viewer presses the Return key for a carriage return. Multiline automatically puts line breaks in text that goes beyond the text field. Password disguises the letters entered in the text box with asterisks; use this option to hide sensitive information such as a password from people looking over your viewer's shoulder.

◆ The Selectable button allows your viewers to select the text inside the text field. (This button is not available for input text because input text is—by nature—always selectable.)

◆ The Render As HTML button allows text formatted with HTML 1.0 tags to be displayed correctly.

◆ The Show Border button draws a black border and white background around your text field. Deselect this option to leave the text field invisible, but be sure to draw your own background or border if you want your viewers to find your text field on the Stage.

◆ The Maximum Characters field puts a limit on the amount of text your viewer can enter. If you want the viewer to enter their home state by using only the two-digit abbreviation, for example, enter 2 in this field. (This option is available only for input text.)

◆ The Character button brings up the Character Options dialog box, where you can choose to embed font outlines with your exported SWF so that your text field displays anti-aliased type in the font of your choice. Keep in mind that this option increases your file size.

◆ The Format button brings up the Format Options dialog box, where you can choose paragraph spacing and alignment options.

◆ Alias Text creates crisp and legible text optimized for small size representation.

✔ Tip

■ Unfortunately, dynamic and input text fields do not support vertical text. Vertical text is allowed only for static text.

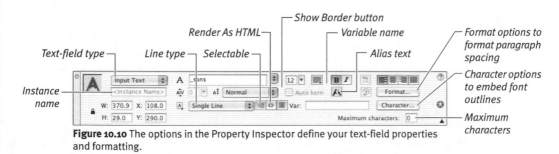

Figure 10.10 The options in the Property Inspector define your text-field properties and formatting.

Embedding Fonts and Device Fonts

Embedding font outlines via the Character Options dialog box ensures that the font you use in the authoring environment is the same one that your audience sees during playback. This operation is done by default for static text, but you must choose the option when you create input text or dynamic text. When you don't embed fonts in your movie, Flash uses the closest font available on your viewer's computer and displays it as aliased text (**Figure 10.11**).

Why wouldn't you choose to embed font outlines all the time? Embedding fonts dramatically increases the size of your exported SWF file because the information needed to render the fonts is included. You can keep the file size down by embedding only the characters that your viewers will use in the text field. If you ask viewers to enter numeric information in an input text field, for example, you can embed just the numbers of the font outline. All the numbers would be available during movie playback; the other characters would be disabled and would not display at all.

Another way to maintain small file sizes and eliminate the problem caused by viewers not having the matching font is to use device fonts. Device fonts appear at the beginning (Windows) or end (Mac) of your Font Style pull-down menu. The three device fonts are _sans, _serif, and _typewriter. This option finds the fonts on a viewer's system that most closely resemble the specified device font. Following are the corresponding fonts for the device fonts:

On the Mac

- u _sans maps to Helvetica.
- u _serif maps to Times.
- u _typewriter maps to Courier.

In Windows

- u _sans maps to Arial.
- u _serif maps to Times New Roman.
- u _typewriter maps to Courier New.

When you use device fonts, you can be assured that your viewer sees text that is very similar to the text you see in the authoring environment. Be aware of two warnings about device fonts, however: They do not display anti-aliased, and they cannot be tweened or masked on the Timeline (device fonts can, however, be masked if you use ActionScript to set your mask).

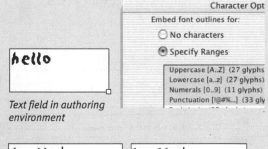

Text field in authoring environment

Text field during playback with font outline embedded

Text field during playback without font outline embedded

Figure 10.11 A text field using a font in authoring mode (top) displays differently during playback on a computer that doesn't have the font, depending on whether the font outlines are embedded (bottom).

Concatenating Text

Using dynamic text to *concatenate*, or connect, input text with other variables and strings lets you work with expressions in more flexible ways and also allows you to create more-personalized Flash interactions with your viewers. You can have viewers first enter their names in an input text field called yourName_txt, and in a dynamic text field, you can set its text property to this:

"Hello, "+yourName_txt.text+", welcome to Flash!"

Your viewers will see their own names concatenated with your message.

In an earlier task in this chapter, you created a Flash movie that loaded a URL based on input text. By concatenating the contents of the input text called myURL_txt in the expression "http://"+myURL_txt.text, you eliminate the requirement that your viewer type the Internet protocol scheme before the actual Web site address.

Use this strategy in combination with other Flash actions to develop flexible, customizable functions and interfaces. In the following example, you concatenate input text from a customer to compile the information in the correct layout automatically and then use the print action to print a complete receipt or order form.

To concatenate text fields for custom printing:

1. Choose the Text tool in the Tools palette, create several input text fields, and give each of them a unique instance name in the Property Inspector (**Figure 10.12**).

2. Create a movie-clip symbol, and enter symbol-editing mode for that movie clip.

3. In the first keyframe of the movie clip, create a large dynamic text field.

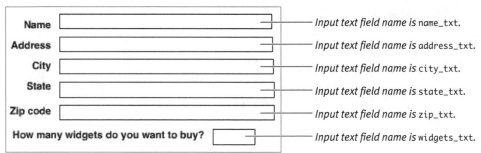

Figure 10.12 Define six input text fields with unique instance names.

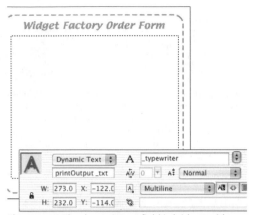

Figure 10.13 The dynamic text field is laid out with surrounding graphics ready to print.

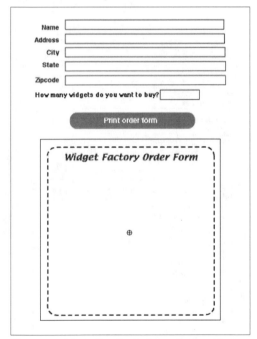

Figure 10.14 The button lies between the input text fields above and the dynamic text field below.

4. In the Property Inspector, choose Multiline from the Line Type pull-down menu, enter an instance name, embed the entire font outline through the Character Options dialog box, and add graphics you want to include in the printed piece (**Figure 10.13**).

   The dynamic text field will display concatenated information.

5. Return to the root Timeline, drag an instance of the movie clip you just created to the Stage, and give the instance a name in the Property Inspector.

6. Create a button symbol, and drag an instance of it to the Stage. Place it between your input text fields and the movie clip that contains your dynamic text field (**Figure 10.14**).

7. Select the button instance, and open the Actions panel.

8. Choose Global Functions > Movie Clip Control > on.

9. Select release as the event handler. Place your cursor after the opening curly brace and hit Return to go to the next line.

10. Enter the target path to the dynamic text field's text property followed by an equals sign.

continues on next page

CONCATENATING TEXT

11. Directly following the equals sign, enter a combination of strings and the input text field's `text` properties to concatenate the user-entered information into a compact, printable form (**Figure 10.15**). Use escape sequences such as \r for carriage returns.

12. On a new line, choose Global Functions > Printing Functions > print (**Figure 10.16**).

13. Enter the name of your movie-clip instance followed by a comma.

This represents the target parameter for your print object. The comma separates the target from the location.

14. For the second parameter, enter `"bframe"` to make Flash print the contents of the movie clip.

15. Test your movie.

When your viewer enters information into the input text fields and then clicks the button, the dynamic text in the movie clip concatenates the input text and displays the information. Then the `print` action prints the movie clip (**Figure 10.17**). 🎯

✔ Tips

- You can also hide a movie clip that's on the Stage from the viewer but still have it available for printing by setting the `_visible` property to false. Changing the visibility property of a movie clip doesn't affect how it prints.

- For long lines of code like the one in this task, choose Word Wrap from the Actions panel Options menu to see all the code within the Script pane.

- It's important that you embed fonts for dynamic text fields sent to the printer. Embedding fonts for a text field results in a much better-quality print, but it also will increase the file size of your exported movie.

```
on (release) {
    orderform.printOutput_txt.text = "Hello, "+name_txt.text+
" thanks for your order! \rDelivery to: \r"+name_txt.text+
"\r"+address_txt.text+"\r"+city_txt.text+", "+state_txt.text+
" "+zip_txt.text+"\r\rWidgets: "+widgets_txt.text+"\rTOTAL
COST: $ "+widgets_txt.text*5;
}
```

Figure 10.15 The target path to the dynamic text field called `printOutput_txt` includes the movie clip called orderform. The dynamic text field displays a string that concatenates the contents of the input text fields and totals the cost of ordered widgets by multiplying each of them by 5.

```
print(orderform, "bframe");
```

Figure 10.16 The `print` statement sends the contents of the movie clip to the printer.

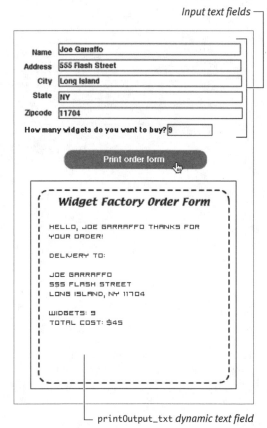

Input text fields

printOutput_txt dynamic text field

Figure 10.17 The Flash movie (top) provides input text fields that compile the entered information in a dynamic text field and prints it (bottom).

Displaying HTML

Flash can display HTML 1.0–formatted text in dynamic text fields. When you mark up text with HTML tags and assign the text to a dynamic text field, Flash will interpret the tags and preserve the formatting. This means that you can integrate HTML pages inside your Flash movie, maintaining the styles and functional HREF anchors.

Common HTML Tags Supported by Text Fields

◆ <A HREF> Anchor tag to create hot links

◆ <B> Bold style

◆ <FONT COLOR> Font-color style

◆ <FONT FACE> Font-face style

◆ <FONT SIZE> Font-size style

◆ <I> Italics style

◆ <P> Paragraph

◆ <U> Underline style

A useful combination is to load HTML-formatted text into dynamic text fields with the action loadVariablesNum. Simply by changing the HTML that resides outside the Flash file, you can update the information that displays during playback of your movie. This feature can be very convenient because you don't have to open the Flash file to make periodic edits and a server-side script or even a user who's unfamiliar with Flash can make the necessary updates.

To load and display HTML in a dynamic text field:

1. Open a text-editing application or a WYSIWYG HTML editor, and create your HTML document.

2. At the very beginning of the HTML text, add a variable name and the assignment operator (the equals sign).

3. Save the text file (**Figure 10.18**).

continues on next page

```
HTMLpage=<HTML><BODY>
<B>This is an HTML page</B></P>
This contains <I>simple</I> HTML 1.0 tags that <FONT FACE="ARIAL">Flash</FONT> can
understand. Flash will display HTML formatted text when the HTML option is checked in
Dynamic Text in the Text Options panel.</P>
</P>
A HREF will also work to create links to Web sites! For example, if you <FONT
COLOR="#0000FF"><u><A HREF="http://www.macromedia.com">click here</A></u></FONT>, you
will be sent to Macromedia's Web site.</BODY></HTML>
```

Figure 10.18 The HTML text is assigned to the variable called HTMLpage and saved as a separate document.

4. In Flash, select the first keyframe in the root Timeline, and open the Actions panel.

5. Choose Global Functions > Browser/Network > loadVariablesNum.

6. For the loadVariablesNum parameters, enter the name of the text file you just created followed by a comma and the number zero. Place the name of the text file in quotation marks (**Figure 10.19**).

Flash loads the text file that contains the variable into level 0.

7. Choose the Text tool, and drag out a large text field that nearly covers the Stage.

8. In the Property Inspector, choose Dynamic Text and Multiline, and click the Render As HTML button.

The Render As HTML button lets Flash know to treat the contents of the text field as HTML-formatted text.

9. Give the text field an instance name (**Figure 10.20**).

10. Create a button symbol, and place an instance of it on the Stage.

11. In the Property Inspector, give your button an instance name.

12. Select the first frame of the main Timeline and open the Actions panel.

13. On the next available line, create an onRelease event handler for your button.

14. Within the onRelease event handler, enter the instance name of your Dynamic Text Field followed by a period.

15. From the code hint pull-down menu, select htmlText. Enter an equals sign followed by the variable you assigned in the text file (**Figure 10.21**).

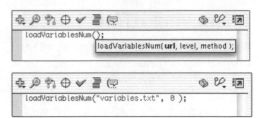

Figure 10.19 With the help of code hints, enter code that loads the file variables.txt, which contains the variable holding HTML text.

Figure 10.20 Enter display_txt as the instance name for your dynamic text field, and click the Render As HTML button.

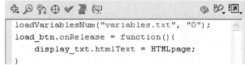

Figure 10.21 The dynamic text field instance called display_txt shows the contents of the variable HTMLpage.

Dynamic text field

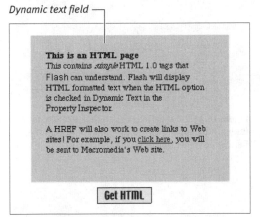

This is an HTML page
This contains *simple* HTML 1.0 tags that Flash can understand. Flash will display HTML formatted text when the HTML option is checked in Dynamic Text in the Property Inspector.

A HREF will also work to create links to Web sites! For example, if you <u>click here</u>, you will be sent to Macromedia's Web site.

Get HTML

Figure 10.22 The dynamic text field displays the HTML-formatted text.

The contents of the external variable are put into the htmlText property of your dynamic text field. The htmlText property displays HTML-tagged text correctly, as would a browser.

16. Export a SWF file to the same directory that contains your text file.

17. Play the SWF in either Flash Player or a browser.

First, the variable in the external text file is loaded into level 0. When your viewer clicks the button, Flash sets the htmlText property of the dynamic text to the variable, which holds HTML-formatted text. The dynamic text field displays the information, preserving all the style and format tags (**Figure 10.22**).

✔ Tips

■ Because only a limited number of HTML tags are supported by dynamic text, you should do a fair amount of testing to see how the information displays. When Flash doesn't understand a tag, it simply ignores it.

■ The anchor tag (<A>) normally appears underlined and in a different color in browser environments. In Flash, however, the hot link is indicated only by the pointer changing to a finger. To create the underline and color style for hot links manually, apply the underline tag (<U>) and the font-color tag (<FONT COLOR="#0000FF">).

■ The HTML tags override any style settings you assign in the Property Inspector for your dynamic text. If you choose red for your dynamic text, when you display HTML text in the field, the <FONT COLOR> tag would modify the text to a different color.

DISPLAYING HTML

In the preceding task you learned how to populate a dynamic text field by loading HTML-formatted contents from an external document. Flash also allows you to write your HTML code directly into the Script pane for display in a dynamic text field. For this approach, it is not necessary for you to include the <HTML>, <HEAD>, or <BODY> tag.

To populate a dynamic text field with HTML code from the Script pane.

1. Choose the Text tool, and drag out a large text field that nearly covers the stage.

2. In the Property Inspector, choose Dynamic Text and Multiline, and check the Render As HTML button.

   The Render As HTML button lets Flash know to treat the contents of the text field as HTML-formatted text.

3. Give your text field an instance name (**Figure 10.23**).

4. Select the first keyframe in the root Timeline, and open the Actions panel.

5. Enter the instance name you assigned to your text field followed by a period, and then select htmlText from the code hint pull-down menu.

   The htmlText property displays HTML-formatted code in the contents of the dynamic text field correctly.

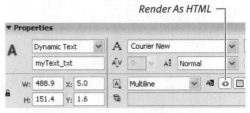

Render As HTML

Figure 10.23 Enter myText_txt as the instance name for your dynamic text field and be sure to click the Render As HTML button.

6. Enter an equals sign followed by your HTML code in quotation marks (**Figure 10.24**).

7. Test your movie.

All the HTML-formatted text assigned to your text field will display correctly as it would in a browser (**Figure 10.25**).

✔ Tip

■ You can also set your dynamic text field to support HTML-formatted text with ActionScript instead of clicking the Render As HTML button in the Property Inspector (as you did in step 2). Set the html property of your text field to true, and your text field will display HTML code correctly. For example, enter the statement myText_txt.html = true.

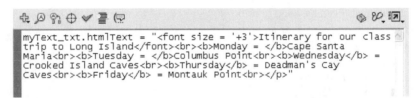

```
myText_txt.htmlText = "<font size = '+3'>Itinerary for our class
trip to Long Island</font><br><b>Monday = </b>Cape Santa
Maria<br><b>Tuesday = </b>Columbus Point<br><b>Wednesday</b> =
Crooked Island Caves<br><b>Thursday</b> = Deadman's Cay
Caves<br><b>Friday</b> = Montauk Point<br></p>"
```

Figure 10.24 The completed code.

```
Itinerary for our class trip to Long Island
Monday = Cape Santa Maria
Tuesday = Columbus Point
Wednesday = Crooked Island Caves
Thursday = Deadman's Cay Caves
Friday = Montauk Point
```

Figure 10.25 At run time Flash displays all HTML code In the dynamic text field named myText_txt.

DISPLAYING HTML

Tweening Text Fields

If you place text fields in movie-clip symbols, you can apply motion tweens to them just as you can with other symbol instances. This technique lets you create titles and banners that not only can be updated dynamically, but also can move across the screen, rotate, and shrink or grow. Imagine a blimp traveling across the Stage with a giant scoreboard attached to its side. By using a dynamic text field as the scoreboard on the blimp graphic, you can update scores or have messages appear as the blimp floats. You could use the same method to create a stock ticker-tape monitor, with the stock prices moving across the screen. Or you could create a game that displays the current status of an individual player right next to the player's icon as it moves around the Stage.

Eventually, you'll learn to animate text fields just with ActionScript. Even so, keep in mind that you will still rely on tweens, or a combination of tweens and ActionScript, for many kinds of motions. Making text follow a path, for example, is a challenge better solved with tweens than with ActionScript alone.

To create a moving dynamic text field:

1. Select the Text tool, and drag out a text field on the Stage.

2. In the Property Inspector, choose Dynamic Text and Single Line, give the text field an instance name, and embed the entire font outline through the Character Options dialog box (**Figure 10.26**).

3. Select your text field, and choose Insert > Convert to Symbol (F8) from the main toolbar.

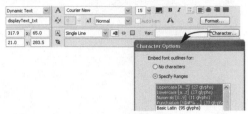

Figure 10.26 Enter displayText_txt as the instance name for your dynamic text field, and embed all font outlines by clicking the Character button in the Property Inspector and shift-selecting the range of characters in the dialog box that appears.

Movie -clip instance containing the dynamic text field — Mask in the screen layer — Background graphic

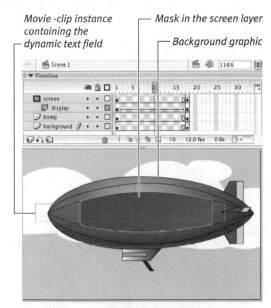

Figure 10.27 On the main Timeline, tween the movie-clip instance that contains the dynamic text field. This movie-clip instance (the dotted-line rectangle) moves across the Stage behind a mask of the scoreboard on the blimp.

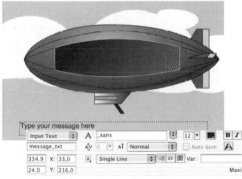

Figure 10.28 Enter message_txt as the instance name for the input text field.

4. In the dialog box that appears, name your symbol and choose Movie Clip as the behavior; then click OK.

Flash puts your dynamic text field inside a movie-clip symbol and places an instance of it on the Stage.

5. In the Property Inspector, name the movie-clip instance.

6. Create a motion tween of the movie-clip instance moving across the Stage (**Figure 10.27**).

7. Select the Text tool, and drag out another text field below the tween of the movie-clip instance in a separate layer.

8. In the Property Inspector, choose Input Text and Single Line, and give this text field a instance name (**Figure 10.28**).

9. Select the main Timeline, and open the Actions panel.

10. Enter _root followed by a period, select onEnterFrame from the code hint pull-down menu, and enter an equals sign.

11. Choose Statements > User-Defined Functions > function

12. On the second line within the onEnterFrame event handler, enter the instance name of your movie clip followed by a period. Enter the instance name of your dynamic text field followed by a period.

13. Select text from the code hint pull-down menu, and enter an equals sign.

Flash now understands that whatever follows the equals sign will be what is displayed in the dynamic text field inside of your movie clip.

continues on next page

14. After the equals sign, enter the name of your input text field, a period, and then the word text (**Figure 10.29**).

The dynamic text field inside of the movie clip is updated continuously with the contents of the input text field.

15. Test your movie.

When your viewer enters information in the input text field, that information is assigned to the dynamic text field inside the movie clip and the updated text moves across the screen (**Figure 10.30**).

✔ Tip

■ It's important to include the entire font outline in a dynamic text field when you tween it (change its rotation and alpha, especially) or when it's part of a masked layer. If the font outline is not included, the text field won't tween properly or show up behind the mask.

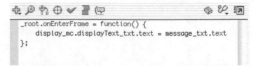

```
_root.onEnterFrame = function() {
    display_mc.displayText_txt.text = message_txt.text
};
```

Figure 10.29 Assign the text property of the input text-field called message_txt to the text property of the dynamic text-field called displayText_txt. Because the dynamic text field is inside a movie clip, the target path is display_mc.displayText_txt.

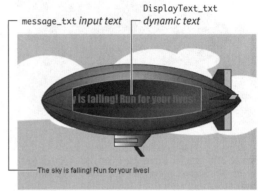

Figure 10.30 Flash tweens the dynamic text field (top) containing any message your viewer enters in the input text field (bottom).

TWEENING TEXT FIELDS

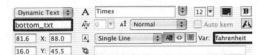

Figure 10.31 The instance name and variable name (highlighted with bold rectangles) of a text field are different identifiers and must be unique.

TextField Properties

When you drag an input or dynamic text field on the Stage with the Text tool, you are creating an instance of the TextField class. Before you can have access to its methods and properties, however, you must name your text field in the Property Inspector so that you can identify it with ActionScript.

The instance name of a text field is very different from its variable name (**Figure 10.31**). The variable name simply holds the contents of the text field. The instance name, on the other hand, identifies the text field for targeting purposes. When you can target the text field, you can evaluate or modify its many properties. These properties determine the kind and display of the text field. You've already used the `text` property, to get and set the contents of text fields. The `text` property holds the current contents of a text field. So the statement `myTextField_txt.text = "Congratulations!"` would display the string `Congratulations!` in the text field called `myTextField_txt`. There are many other properties. For example, you've encountered the `htmlText` and `html` properties as well. Other properties include `type`, which defines an input or dynamic text field; `border`, which determines whether the text field has one; and `_rotation`, which controls the angle of the text field.

Table 10.1 summarizes many of the properties of the TextField class. Many of these properties are identical to the ones you can set in authoring mode in the Property Inspector. In addition, you can use the properties common to the Movie Clip and the Button classes, such as `_rotation`, `_alpha`, `_x`, `_y`, `_width`, `_height`, `_xscale`, `_yscale`, `_name`, `_visible`, `tabEnabled`, and `tabIndex`.

Table 10.1

TextField Properties		
PROPERTY	**VALUE**	**DESCRIPTION**
text	A string	The contents of the text field.
type	"dynamic" or "input"	Specifies a dynamic or input text field.
autosize	"none", "left", "center", or "right"	Controls automatic alignment and sizing so that a text field shrinks or grows to accommodate text.
background	true or false	Specifies whether the text field has a background fill.
backgroundColor	A hex code	Specifies the color of the background (visible only when border = true).
border	true or false	Specifies whether the text field has a border.
borderColor	A hex code	Specifies the color of the border.
textColor	A hex code	Specifies the color of the text.
textWidth	A number, in pixels	Specifies the width of the text (read-only).
textHeight	A number, in pixels	Specifies the height of the text (read-only).
length	A number	Specifies the number of characters in a text field (read-only).
scroll	A number	Specifies the top line visible in the text field.
bottomscroll	A number	Specifies the bottom line visible in the text field (read-only).
hscroll	A number	Specifies the horizontal scrolling position of a text field. 0 defines the position where there is no scrolling. Values are in 1/20-pixel units.
maxscroll	A number	Specifies the maximum value for the scroll property (read-only).
maxhscroll	A number	Specifies the maximum value for the hscroll property (read-only).
mouseWheelEnabled	true or false	Specifies whether the user's mouse wheel can scroll multiline text fields.
restrict	A string	Specifies the allowable characters in the text field.
maxChars	A number	Specifies the maximum number of characters allowable.
variable	A string	Specifies the name of the text-field variable.
embedFonts	true or false	Specifies whether fonts are embedded. You must create a font symbol and export it for ActionScript in its Linkage properties.
html	true or false	Specifies whether the text field renders HTML tags.
htmlText	A string	Specifies the contents of a text field when html = true.
condenseWhite	true or false	Specifies whether extra white space in an HTML text field should be removed.
multiline	true or false	Specifies whether the text field can display more than one line.
wordWrap	true or false	Specifies whether the text field breaks lines automatically.
selectable	true or false	Specifies whether the contents of the text field are selectable.
password	true or false	Specifies whether input text is disguised.
tabEnabled	true or false	Specifies whether the text field can receive focus when the Tab key is used.
tabIndex	A number	Specifies the order of focus when the Tab key is used.

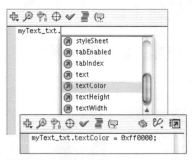

Figure 10.32 The dynamic text field is called myText_txt.

Figure 10.33 Select the property textColor from the code hint pull-down menu for the text field named myText_txt (top). The textColor property of the text field called myText_txt is set to red (bottom).

```
┌─ Black border                    Embedded font ─┐
│─ (x = 100, y = 350)    Light-green background ─│
│  ┌─────────────────────────────────────────┐  │
│  │ myText_txt.textColor = 0xff0000;         │  │
│  │ myText_txt.text = "Customizing Dynamic Text"; │  │
│  │ myText_txt.embedFonts = true;            │  │
│  │ myText_txt.background = true;            │  │
│  │ myText_txt.backgroundColor = 0xdffcb8;   │  │
│  │ myText_txt.border = true;                │  │
│  │ myText_txt.borderColor = 0x0000ff;       │  │
│  │ myText_txt._x = 100;                     │  │
│  │ myText_txt._y = 350;                     │  │
│  └─────────────────────────────────────────┘  │
│           Customizing Dynamic Text              │
```

```
with(myText_txt){
    textColor = 0xff0000;
    text = "Customizing Dynamic Text";
    embedFonts = true;
    background = true;
    backgroundColor = 0xdffcb8;
    border = true;
    borderColor = 0x0000ff;
    _x = 100;
    _y = 350;
}
```

Figure 10.34 The script (above) modifies many properties of the text field called myTextField_txt, resulting in the text in the middle. If you have many properties to change, use the with action to alter the scope temporarily, as shown in the bottom script.

To modify the properties of the text field:

1. Select the Text tool in the Tools palette, and drag out a text field on the Stage.

2. In the Property Inspector, select Dynamic Text, give the text field a name in the Instance Name field, and leave all other options at their default settings (**Figure 10.32**).

3. Select the first frame of the main Timeline, and open the Actions panel.

4. In the Script Pane, enter the instance name for your Dynamic text field followed by a period.

5. From the code hint pull-down menu, select a property. For this example, choose textColor and enter an equals sign.

6. After the equals sign, enter 0xff0000. The completed statement changes the color of the text to red (**Figure 10.33**).

7. Repeat steps 5 and 6, choosing different properties and values to modify your text field (**Figure 10.34**).

✔ Tips

■ To modify the font, font size, and other characteristics of the text, you must use the TextFormat class, which we discuss later in this chapter.

■ If you modify the properties _alpha and _rotation, you must embed the font outlines for your text field. If you don't, the text won't be modified correctly.

■ The properties _x and _y refer to the top-left corner of the text field.

■ The properties _width and _height change the pixel dimensions of the text field but do not change the size of the text inside the text field. The properties _xscale and _yscale, on the other hand, will scale the text.

Embedding Fonts: Creating Font Symbols for ActionScript Export

When you set the embedFonts property of a text field to true, you must provide the font outline in the exported SWF. This process involves creating a font symbol in the Library and marking it for ActionScript export. If you don't, Flash won't know to make the font available when it publishes your movie. In the Library, choose New Font from the Options menu. In the Font Symbol Properties dialog box that appears, select the font in the list (**Figure 10.35**). Click OK, and you'll have a new font symbol in your Library. Select the symbol, and choose Linkage from the Options menu. In the Linkage Properties dialog box that appears, select Export for ActionScript and choose an identifier for your font symbol (**Figure 10.36**). Click OK. Your font symbol will be exported to the SWF. When you set the embedFonts property to true via ActionScript, the font symbol will be available.

Figure 10.35 Choose New Font from the Library window's Options menu (top) to create a font symbol. Choose your font in the Font Symbol Properties dialog box (below). The Name field contains the name of the symbol that will appear in the Library.

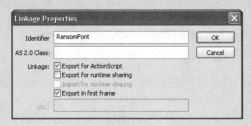

Figure 10.36 The Linkage Properties dialog box enables you to export your font symbol for use in ActionScript. The Identifier field contains the name that you will use in ActionScript to refer to this font.

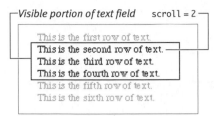

Figure 10.37 The scroll property is the first visible row of text within a text field.

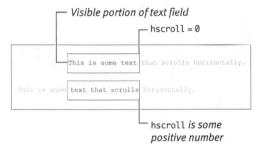

Figure 10.38 The hscroll property is relative to the point at which there is no scrolling. The value of hscroll increases as horizontal scrolling occurs.

Controlling text-field scrolling

The TextField properties scroll, maxscroll, hscroll, maxhscroll, and bottomscroll all give information about the position of text within a text field that may be too small to fit in its borders.

When the information in a multiline text field exceeds its defined boundaries, Flash displays only the current text (unless you set the autosize property to fit the information). Text that can't fit within the text field is hidden from view but still accessible if the viewer clicks inside the text field and drags up or down. You can display different portions of the hidden text dynamically by defining the properties scroll and hscroll.

Think of the text field as being a window that shows only a portion of a larger piece of text. Each row of text has an index value. The top row is 1, the second row is 2, and so on. The scroll property refers to the topmost visible row. The bottomScroll property refers to the bottommost visible row. So the visible portion of a text field is the rows from scroll to bottomscroll, and as new lines of text scroll up or down, those properties change (**Figure 10.37**).

If a line of text exceeds the width of its text field, you can use hscroll to display different portions of its horizontal scrolling. The point on the right edge of the text field where the initial text is visible has an hscroll value of 0. The value of hscroll is measured in 1/20-pixel units, and as hscroll increases, the text scrolls to reveal more of itself (**Figure 10.38**).

You can retrieve the value of `scroll` and `hscroll` so that you know exactly which portion of the text your viewer is currently looking at, or you can modify their values to force your viewer to look at a particular portion. It is common to provide interface controls so that viewers themselves can control the scrolling of text, just as they control the scroll bars in a Web browser or any window on the computer screen. In the following task, you'll create interface controls of this kind.

Figure 10.39 Enter `scrollwindow_txt` as the instance name of your text field.

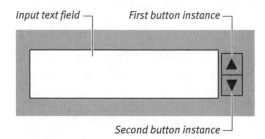

Figure 10.40 Place two buttons next to the input text field.

To create a vertical scrolling text field:

1. Select the Text tool in the Tools palette, and drag out a text field onto the Stage.

2. In the Property Inspector, choose Input Text, enter an instance name, choose Multiline from the pull-down menu, and click the Show Border button (**Figure 10.39**).

3. Create a button symbol of an arrow pointing up, place an instance of the button on the Stage, and give it a name in the Property Inspector.

4. Place a second instance of the button on the Stage, choose Modify > Transform > Flip Vertical to make the second button point down, and give the down arrow button a name in the Property Inspector.

5. Align both buttons vertically next to the input text field (**Figure 10.40**).

6. Select the first frame of the main Timeline, and open the Actions panel.

7. Assign an `onPress` event handler to the up arrow button.

TEXTFIELD PROPERTIES

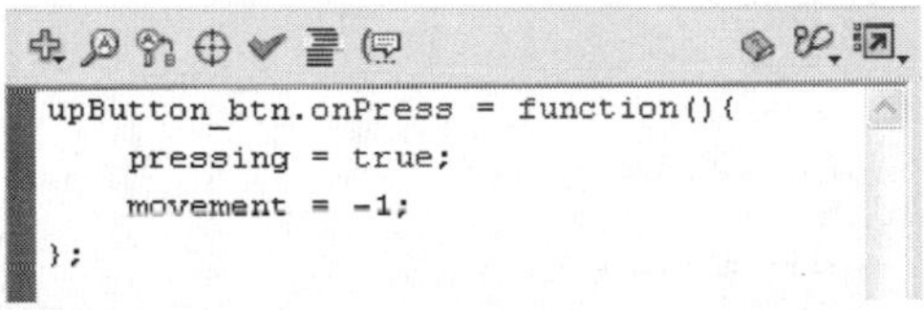

```
upButton_btn.onPress = function(){
    pressing = true;
    movement = -1;
};
```

Figure 10.41 Pressing the upButton_btn button sets the variable pressing to true and the variable movement to –1.

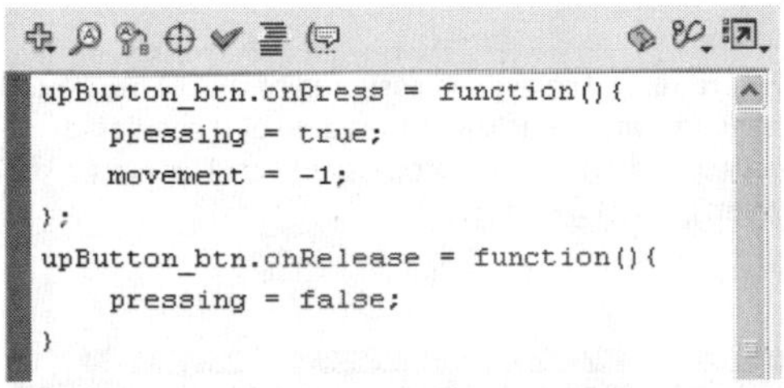

```
upButton_btn.onPress = function(){
    pressing = true;
    movement = -1;
};
upButton_btn.onRelease = function(){
    pressing = false;
}
```

Figure 10.42 Releasing the upButton_btn button sets the variable pressing to false.

```
upButton_btn.onPress = function() {
    pressing = true;
    movement = -1;
}
upButton_btn.onRelease = function() {
    pressing = false;
}
downButton_btn.onPress = function() {
    pressing = true;
    movement = 1;
}
downButton_btn.onRelease = function() {
    pressing = false;
}
```

Figure 10.43 The script so far, as shown in the Script pane of the Actions panel.

8. On a new line inside the onPress event handler, create a variable named press-ing, enter an equals sign, and enter the Boolean value true.

9. On the next line, create a variable named movement and give it a value of –1 (**Figure 10.41**).

When the mouse button is pressed, the variable pressing is set to true, and the variable movement is set to –1.

10. Assign an onRelease event handler to the up arrow button.

11. On a new line inside the onRelease event handler, create a variable named pressing and give it a Boolean value of false (**Figure 10.42**).

12. Create similar onPress and onRelease event handlers for your down arrow button, and enter the same statements in the Script pane of the Actions panel, except assign the variable movement to change to 1 when the mouse button is pressed (**Figure 10.43**).

13. Assign an onEnterFrame event handler to the root Timeline.

14. On a new line inside the onEnterFrame event handler, choose Statements > Conditions/Loops > if.

continues on next page

TextField Properties

15. For the condition of the if statement, enter pressing == true.

16. With your cursor between the opening and closing curly braces of the if statement, enter the name of the input text field followed by a period. Select the property scroll from the code hint pull-down menu, and enter an equals sign.

17. Directly following the equals sign, enter the name of your input text field followed by a period and then the property scroll; add the value of the variable movement (**Figure 10.44**).

Flash continuously checks to see whether one of the buttons is pressed. If so, Flash adds the value of movement to the current scroll property. If the up arrow button is pressed, the scroll value is decreased by 1. If the down arrow button is pressed, the scroll value is increased by 1 (**Figure 10.45**).

```
upButton_btn.onPress = function() {
    pressing = true;
    movement = -1;
}
upButton_btn.onRelease = function() {
    pressing = false;
}
downButton_btn.onPress = function() {
    pressing = true;
    movement = 1;
}
downButton_btn.onRelease = function() {
    pressing = false;
}
_root.onEnterFrame = function(){
    if (pressing ==true){
        scrollWindow_txt.scroll = scrollWindow_txt.scroll + movement
    }
}
```

Figure 10.44 The actions assigned to the onEnterFrame handler continuously add the value of the variable movement to the scroll property of scrollwindow_txt when pressing is true.

> Enter text in this input text
> box. Use the up and down
> buttons on the right to

Figure 10.45 The buttons on the right increase or decrease the value of the scroll property of the input text field.

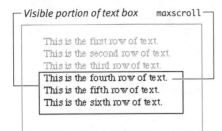

Visible portion of text box   maxscroll

This is the first row of text.
This is the second row of text.
This is the third row of text.
This is the fourth row of text.
This is the fifth row of text.
This is the sixth row of text.

Figure 10.46 The `maxscroll` property refers to the maximum value of the `scroll` property. This value is the value of `scroll` when the last line of text is visible. In this example, `maxscroll = 4`.

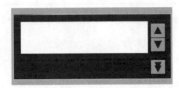

```
skipToEndButton_btn.onRelease = function() {
    scrollWindow_txt.scroll = scrollWindow_txt.maxscroll;
};
```

Figure 10.47 A portion of the Script pane shows the `onRelease` handler for a button called `skipToEndButton_btn`. The property `maxscroll` is assigned to the `scroll` property of `scrollwindow_txt` (bottom).

Whereas the `scroll` property defines the first visible text row in a text field, the `maxscroll` property defines the maximum allowable value for `scroll` in that text field. This row appears at the top of the text field when the last line of text is visible (**Figure 10.46**). You can't change the value of `maxscroll`, because it's defined by the amount of text and the size of the text field itself, but you can read its value. Assign the value of `maxscroll` to `scroll`, and you can scroll the text to the bottom of the text field automatically. Or you can calculate the value of `scroll` proportionally to `maxscroll` and build a draggable scroll bar that reflects and controls the text's position within the text field.

To scroll to the end of a text field:

1. Continuing with the preceding task, create a new button symbol, drag an instance of it to the Stage, and give it a name in the Property Inspector.

2. Select the first frame of the main Timeline, and open the Actions panel.

3. Assign an `onRelease` event handler to your latest button.

4. Enter the name of the text field followed by a period and then the property `scroll`.

5. After the `scroll` property, enter an equals sign, the name of the text field, a period, and then the property `maxscroll` (**Figure 10.47**).

    When the viewer clicks this button, the current value of `maxscroll` for the text field is assigned to `scroll`. The text automatically moves so that the last line is visible. (⚷)

To create a horizontal scrolling text field:

1. Select the Text tool in the Tools palette, and drag out a text box onto the Stage.

2. In the Property Inspector, choose Input Text, enter an instance name, choose Single Line from the pull-down menu, and click the Show Border button (**Figure 10.48**).

3. Create a button symbol of a right-pointing arrow, place an instance of the button on the Stage, and give it a name in the Property Inspector.

4. Place a second instance of the button on the Stage, choose Modify > Transform > Flip Horizontal to make the second button point left, and give the left arrow button a name in the Property Inspector.

5. Align both buttons horizontally above the input text field (**Figure 10.49**).

6. Select the first frame of the main Timeline, and open the Actions panel.

7. Assign code to the right and left arrow buttons as you did to the down and up arrow buttons in the preceding task.

   Your code should look similar to this:

```
rightButton_btn.onPress = function() {
    pressing = true;
    movement = 20;
}
rightButton_btn.onRelease = function() {
    pressing = false;
}
leftButton_btn.onPress = function() {
    pressing = true;
    movement = -20;
}
leftButton_btn.onRelease = function() {
    pressing = false;
```

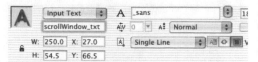

Figure 10.48 Enter scrollWindow_txt as the instance name of your input text field.

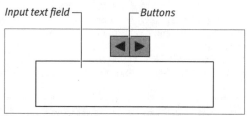

Figure 10.49 Align two buttons above your input text field.

```
rightButton_btn.onPress = function() {
    pressing = true;
    movement = 20;
}
rightButton_btn.onRelease = function() {
    pressing = false;
}
leftButton_btn.onPress = function() {
    pressing = true;
    movement = -20;
}
leftButton_btn.onRelease = function() {
    pressing = false;
}
_root.onEnterFrame = function(){
    if (pressing ==true){
        scrollWindow_txt.hscroll = scrollWindow_txt.hscroll + movement
    }
}
```

Figure 10.50 The actions assigned to the onEnterFrame handler continuously add the value of the variable movement to the hscroll property of scrollwindow_txt when pressing is true.

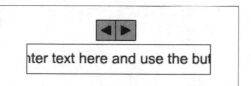

Figure 10.51 The buttons above the input text field increase or decrease the value of the hscroll property of the input text field.

8. Assign an onEnterFrame event handler to the root Timeline.

9. On a new line within the onEnterFrame event handler, choose Statements > Conditions/Loops > if.

10. For the condition of the if statement, enter pressing == true.

11. Within the curly braces of the if statement, enter the name of the input text field followed by a period and then the property hscroll; add the value of the variable movement (**Figure 10.50**).

Flash continuously checks to see whether one of the buttons is pressed. If so, Flash adds the value of movement to the current hscroll property. If the right arrow button is pressed, the hscroll value increases by 20, moving the text to the left by 1 pixel. If the down arrow button is pressed, the hscroll value decreases by 20, moving the text to the right by 1 pixel (**Figure 10.51**).

TEXTFIELD PROPERTIES

Sometimes in authoring mode, you'll want to restrict the size of your text field so that its contents are scrollable. By defining your text field as scrollable, you can keep much of the text it contains hidden from view.

To define a scrollable text field in authoring mode:

1. Select the Text tool in the Tools palette, and drag out a text field on the Stage.

2. Choose Text > Scrollable from the main menu's toolbar.

   The resizing handle at the bottom-right corner of your text field fills in with black, indicating that the text field is scrollable. Although your text field remains resizable, any text that does not fit in the text field will begin to scroll (**Figure 10.52**).

   or

   Shift-double-click the resizing handle of the text field.

   The handle turns black, and the text field becomes scrollable.

A text field
defined as
scrollable will

keep its size
and allow text to
scroll

Figure 10.52 When you define a text field as scrollable in authoring mode, the resizing handle turns black (top). You can enter text in authoring mode, but the size of the text field will remain constant, hiding text that can't fit and allowing scrolling (bottom).

Figure 10.53 Use the code hints to help you define a text field called myText that is 300 pixels wide by 100 pixels tall and will be created on the root Timeline at x = 50, y = 50, in depth level 1.

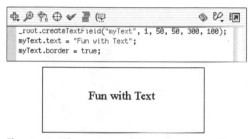

Figure 10.54 The contents of the text property of myText appear on the Stage. The default format for a dynamically created text field is black 12-point Times New Roman (Windows) or Times (Mac).

Generating Text Fields Dynamically

If you need to have text appear in your movie based on a viewer's interaction, you have to be able to create a text field during run time. You can generate text fields dynamically with the movie-clip method createTextField(). The method creates a new text field, which you must attach to a movie clip. You can choose the root Timeline as the movie clip to which it is attached, and your text field will be placed on the main Stage. You also must specify the text field's depth level, its *x* and *y* positions, and its width and height in pixels, as in this example:

```
_root.createTextField("newTF_txt", 1, 100,100,200,50)
```

This statement creates a new text field called newTF_txt on the main Stage in depth level 1. Its top-left corner is positioned at x = 100, y = 100, and it is 200 pixels wide by 50 pixels tall.

To create a text field on the main Stage:

1. Select the first frame of the main Timeline, and open the Actions panel.

2. Enter _root, and choose Built-in Classes > Movie > MovieClip > Methods > createTextField.

   The new text field will be created in the root Timeline (the main Stage).

3. Enter a name (in quotation marks), depth level, *x* position, *y* position, width, and height, separating the parameters with commas (**Figure 10.53**).

   A text field is created on the main Stage. To see it, assign text to it with the text property (**Figure 10.54**).

To remove a text field that was created dynamically:

1. In the Script pane of the Actions panel, enter the instance name of the text field you want to remove.

2. Choose Built-in Classes > Movie > TextField > Methods > removeTextField (**Figure 10.55**).

   The text field deletes itself when this method is performed. You can use this method to remove only text fields created by the movie-clip method createTextField().

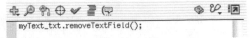

```
myText_txt.removeTextField();
```

Figure 10.55 The dynamically generated text field called myText_txt is removed.

The Default Text Field Appearance

When you create a text field dynamically with the createTextField() method, it has the following default properties:

type = dynamic	html = false
selectable = true	embedFonts = false
multiline = false	restrict = null
password = false	maxChars = null
wordWrap = false	variable = null
background = false	autoSize = none
border = false	

The text field also has the following default format properties (which you can change with a TextFormat object):

font = Times New Roman (Windows)	leftMargin = 0
font = Times (Mac)	rightMargin = 0
size = 12	indent = 0
textColor = 0x000000	leading = 0
bold = false	URL = ""
italic = false	Target = ""
underline = false	bullet = false
align = "left"	

Options controlled by TextFormat properties

Options controlled by TextField properties

Figure 10.56 The Property Inspector can be divided into sections of options controlled by TextFormat properties and options controlled by TextField properties.

Modifying Text in Text Fields

Although the properties of a text field can define the way text behaves and the way the text field itself appears, the properties don't control the formatting of the text that it contains. For that task, you need to use the TextFormat class. The TextFormat class controls character and paragraph formatting, which are also options available in authoring mode in the Property Inspector. Notice that the Property Inspector is divided into sections of options that are controlled by the TextField class and those that are controlled by the TextFormat class (**Figure 10.56**). **Table 10.2** summarizes the properties of the TextFormat class.

Table 10.2

TextFormat Properties

PROPERTY	VALUE	DESCRIPTION
size	A number	Specifies the point size of the text.
font	A string	Specifies the font of the text. You must create a font symbol and export it for ActionScript in its Linkage properties. Use the Linkage Identifier for the font value. Works only when embedFonts = true.
color	A hex number	Specifies the color of the text.
underline	true or false	Specifies whether the text is underlined.
italic	true or false	Specifies whether the text is italicized.
bold	true or false	Specifies whether the text is bold.
bullet	true or false	Specifies whether text is in a bulleted list.
leading	A positive number	Specifies the space between lines, in points.
align	"left", "center", or "right"	Specifies the alignment of text within the text field.
indent	A number	Specifies the point indentation of new paragraphs.
blockIndent	A number	Specifies the point indentation of the entire text.
rightMargin	A number	Specifies the space between the text and the right edge, in points.
leftMargin	A number	Specifies the space between the text and the left edge, in points.
tabStops	An array of numbers	Specifies the point distances of custom tab stops.
URL	A string	Specifies the URL that the text links to.
target	A string	Specifies the target window where a hyperlink is displayed.

To change the formatting of text in a text field, first create a new instance of the TextFormat class, like so:

mmyFormat_fmt = new TextFormat()

Then assign new values to the property of your TextFormat object:

myFormat_fmt.size = 48

Finally, call the setTextFormat() method for your text field. This method is a method of the TextField class, not of the TextFormat class:

myTextField_txt.setTextFormat
(myFormat_fmt)

This statement will change the text size in the text field called myTextField_txt to 48 points.

To modify the text formatting of a text field:

1. Create a new font symbol in the Library, and export it for ActionScript in the Linkage Properties dialog box (**Figure 10.57**).

2. Select the Text tool, and drag out a text field on the Stage.

3. In the Property Inspector, choose Input Text or Dynamic Text, enter an instance name, choose a different font from the one you marked for export in step 1, and embed its font outline.

4. Enter some text in the text field (**Figure 10.58**).

    You will use a TextFormat object to modify this text field.

5. Select the first frame of the main Timeline, and open the Actions panel.

6. Enter a name for your new TextFormat object followed by an equals sign.

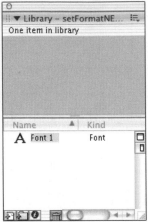

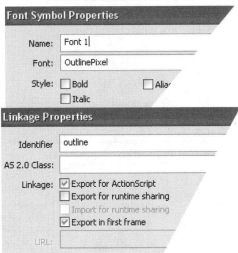

Figure 10.57 Create a font symbol, and export it for ActionScript. This font is identified as outline.

Figure 10.58 Create a text field called myText_txt. The outline for this text field's font (RamseyNote) is embedded.

MODIFYING TEXT IN TEXT FIELDS

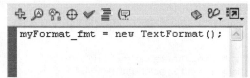

```
myFormat_fmt = new TextFormat();
```

Figure 10.59 Instantiate a TextFormat object called myFormat_fmt. Using the suffix _fmt will give you access to the code hint pull-down menus for this class.

```
myFormat_fmt = new TextFormat();
myFormat_fmt.font = "outline"
```

Figure 10.60 Assign the outline font that you have marked for export.

```
myFormat_fmt = new TextFormat();
myFormat_fmt.font = "outline";
myFormat_fmt.size = 24;
myFormat_fmt.color = 0xFF0000;
myText_txt.setTextFormat(myFormat_fmt);
```

Figure 10.61 Assign the new format to your text field called myText_txt.

7. Choose Built-in Classes > Movie > TextFormat > newTextFormat (**Figure 10.59**).

   A new TextFormat object is instantiated.

8. On the next line, enter the name of your TextFormat object followed by a period. In the code hint pull-down menu that appears, choose font.

   or

   Choose Built-in Classes > Movie > TextFormat > Properties > font.

9. Enter a value for the property font by entering an equals sign followed by the identifier of the exported font symbol (**Figure 10.60**).

10. Continue creating statements to assign values to the properties of your TextFormat object.

11. On a new line, enter the name of your input or dynamic text field followed by a period. Choose setTextFormat from the code hint pull-down menu.

    or

    Choose Built-in Classes > Movie > TextField > Methods > setTextFormat.

12. For the parameter of the setTextFormat method, enter the name of your TextFormat object (**Figure 10.61**).

    The TextFormat object is used as the parameter for the setTextFormat() method and changes the formatting of the text field.

continues on next page

MODIFYING TEXT IN TEXT FIELDS

13. Test your movie.

Flash creates a TextFormat object. The properties of the object are passed through the setTextFormat() method and modify the existing contents of the text field (**Figure 10.62**). 🎧

✔ Tips

- The setTextFormat() modifies only existing text in the text field. If you add more text after the setTextFormat() method is called, that text will have its original formatting.

- You can also use a variant: the setNewTextFormat() method. This method modifies any new text that appears in the text field. Existing text is unaffected. Use setNewTextFormat() when you want to distinguish existing text from new text with different formatting.

Figure 10.62 The original text (in Figure 10.58) changes to red 24-point OutlinePixel.

```
myFormat_fmt = new TextFormat();
myFormat_fmt.font = "outline";
myFormat_fmt.size = 24;
myFormat_fmt.color = 0xFF0000;
myText_txt.setTextFormat(9, myFormat_fmt);
```

Figure 10.63 The character at the index 9 position will change formats.

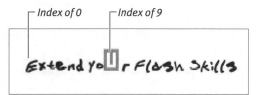

Figure 10.64 While the rest of the text stays the same, the *u* character at index 9 changes to red 24-point OutlinePixel.

The setTextFormat() method enables you to format the entire text field, a single character, or a span of characters. In order to do so, you must specify the position in the string that's in your text field. The position is known as the *index*. The index of the first character is 0, the index of the second character is 1, and so on. If you use an index as the first parameter of the setTextFormat() method, that single character will be affected. If you use a beginning index and an ending index as the first and second parameters, the span of characters between the two indexes, including the beginning index, will be affected.

To modify the text formatting of a single character:

1. Continuing with the file you created in the preceding example, select the first frame of the main Timeline, and open the Actions panel.

2. Place your pointer inside of the parentheses of the setTextFormat method.

3. Before the TextFormat object's name, enter an index followed by a comma, to separate the two parameters (**Figure 10.63**).

4. Test your movie.

   Flash modifies the format of a single character (**Figure 10.64**).

To modify the text formatting of a span of characters:

1. Continuing with the file you used in the preceding example, select the first frame of the main Timeline, and open the Actions panel.

2. Place your pointer inside of the parentheses of the setTextFormat method.

3. Before the TextFormat object's name, enter a beginning index and an ending index, separating the three parameters with commas (**Figure 10.65**).

4. Test your movie.

   Flash modifies the format of the span of characters (**Figure 10.66**). (꙰)

Creating dynamic text animations

Using a combination of TextFormat properties and TextField properties, you can animate text entirely with ActionScript to make its motion respond dynamically to run-time events or to viewer interaction. You can also use ActionScript to do things to text that are difficult, if not impossible, to do with normal tweens, such as swapping characters' styles or animating the color of the text independently of the color of its background.

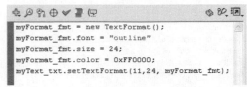

```
myFormat_fmt = new TextFormat();
myFormat_fmt.font = "outline"
myFormat_fmt.size = 24;
myFormat_fmt.color = 0xFF0000;
myText_txt.setTextFormat(11,24, myFormat_fmt);
```

Figure 10.65 The characters beginning at index 11 and up to, but not including, index 24 will change formats.

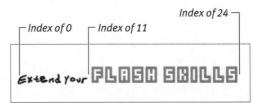

Figure 10.66 While the rest of the text stays the same, the words *Flash Skills*, from index 11 to index 24, changes to red 24-point OutlinePixel. Although the method specifies the indexes 11 and 24, the last index is not included in the selection.

```
_root.createTextField("blinkingSign_txt", 1, 200, 150, 10, 10);
blinkingSign_txt.text = "Open 24 hours! Visit us!";
blinkingSign_txt.autoSize = "center";
blinkingSign_txt.embedFonts = true;
```

Figure 10.67 Create the text field called blinkingSign_txt, and set its text, autosize, and embedFonts properties.

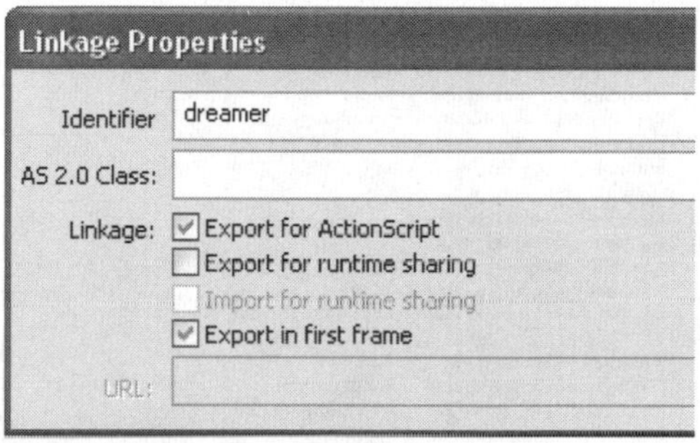

Linkage Properties

Identifier   dreamer

AS 2.0 Class:

Linkage: ☑ Export for ActionScript
           ☐ Export for runtime sharing
           ☐ Import for runtime sharing
           ☑ Export in first frame

URL:

Figure 10.68 This font symbol is marked for export and identified as dreamer.

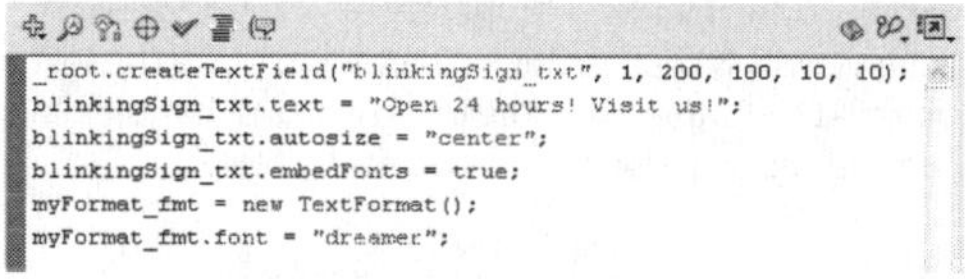

```
_root.createTextField("blinkingSign_txt", 1, 200, 100, 10, 10);
blinkingSign_txt.text = "Open 24 hours! Visit us!";
blinkingSign_txt.autoSize = "center";
blinkingSign_txt.embedFonts = true;
myFormat_fmt = new TextFormat();
myFormat_fmt.font = "dreamer";
```

Figure 10.69 A new TextFormat object is created, and dreamer is used as the new font.

In the following demonstration, a text field is generated and animated dynamically by being modified with setInterval statements and an onEnterFrame event handler.

To animate text:

1. Create a text field on the root Timeline with the method createTextField(), and place it in depth level 1 on the center of the Stage. The size of the text field doesn't matter.

2. Assign text to the text field's text property, set autosize to "center", and set embedFonts to true.

   The code should look like **Figure 10.67**.

3. Because you are embedding the font, make sure that you create a font symbol in the Library.

4. Select your newly created font symbol in the Library and choose Linkage from the Options menu. In the Linkage Properties dialog box, mark the font symbol for export for ActionScript, and give it a name in the Identifier field (**Figure 10.68**).

5. On a new line in the Script pane of the Actions panel, create a new TextFormat object with the constructor function, and set the font property of the object to the font that you marked for export (**Figure 10.69**).

6. On a new line, choose Global Functions > Miscellaneous Functions > setInterval.

7. For the parameters of the setInterval statement, enter makeRed followed by a comma and then 100.

   The function called makeRed will be invoked every 100 milliseconds.

8. On a new line again, choose Global Functions > Miscellaneous Functions > setInterval.

continues on next page

9. For the parameters of this `setInterval` statement, enter `makeBlue` followed by a comma and then 200.

    The function called `makeBlue` will be invoked every 200 milliseconds.

10. On a new line, choose Statements > User-Defined Functions > function. Enter the name `makeRed`.

    Your `makeRed` function is created.

11. Within the function, assign the value `0xff0000` to the `color` property of your TextFormat object.

12. On the next line within the function, enter the name of your text field followed by a period. In the code hint pull-down menu, select setTextFormat.

    For the parameter of the `setTextFormat()` method, enter the name of your TextFormat object.

    When the `makeRed` function is invoked, your text field turns red (**Figure 10.70**).

13. Repeat steps 10 through 12 to create a function called `makeBlue`. For the `color` property of the TextFormat object, use the hex code `0x0000FF`.

    When the `makeBlue` function is invoked, your text field turns blue.

14. On a new line, enter `_root`. Choose Built-in Classes > Movie > MovieClip > Exents > onEnterFrame. Complete the event handler by entering `=function(){}`.

15. Within the curly braces of the `onEnterFrame` event handler, increase the `size` property of the TextFormat object by 1 and then call the `setTextFormat()` method again (**Figure 10.71**).

    The `onEnterFrame` handler continuously increases the font size of your text field.

16. Test your movie (**Figure 10.72**). 🎧

```
function makeRed() {
    myFormat_fmt.color = 0xff0000;
    blinkingSign_txt.setTextFormat(myFormat_fmt);
}
```

Figure 10.70 The function called `makeRed`, which changes the text field called `blinkingSign_txt` to a red Dreamer font.

```
_root.createTextField("blinkingSign_txt", 1, 200, 100, 10, 10);
blinkingSign_txt.text = "Open 24 hours! Visit us!";
blinkingSign_txt.autosize = "center";
blinkingSign_txt.embedFonts = true;
myFormat_fmt = new TextFormat();
myFormat_fmt.font = "dreamer";
setInterval(makeRed, 100);
setInterval(makeBlue, 200);
function makeRed() {
    myFormat_fmt.color = 0xff0000;
    blinkingSign_txt.setTextFormat(myFormat_fmt);
}
function makeBlue() {
    myFormat_fmt.color = 0x0000ff;
    blinkingSign_txt.setTextFormat(myFormat_fmt);
}
_root.onEnterFrame = function() {
    myFormat_fmt.size++;
    blinkingSign_txt.setTextFormat(myFormat_fmt);
}
```

Figure 10.71 The full script. The functions `makeRed` and `makeBlue` are invoked alternately by the `setInterval` actions, which change the formatting to make the text blink. At the same time, the `onEnterFrame` handler continuously increases the size of the text.

Open 24 hours! Visit us!

Open 24 hours! Visit us!

Figure 10.72 The text field animates by growing and blinking red and blue.

Determining the Dimensions of Text

When creating dynamic text fields with specific text and formatting at run time, you'll likely need to know the exact size of your text for layout purposes. For example, if you want to display a user's name on the screen, you'll need to know the size of the text so you can create a text field big enough to accommodate it. A particular bit of text can be measured by six properties: ascent, descent, width, height, textFieldWidth, and textFieldHeight (**Figure 10.73**). Knowing these measurements will allow you to create a text field that can display all the text without cropping.

Flash allows you to retrieve this information with getTextExtent, a method of the TextFormat class. To retrieve information about a text field, you must already have a textFormat object and a string of text.

The getTextExtent method retrieves the various measurements of a specific string of text and puts that information in a generic object containing the properties ascent, descent, width, height, textFieldWidth, and textFieldHeight. **Table 10.3** summarizes these properties.

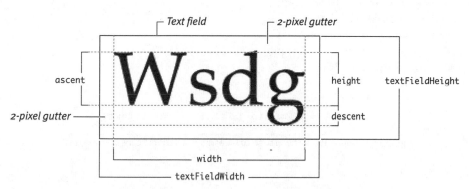

Figure 10.73 Text fields have six measurements that can be retrieved through the getTextExtent method: ascent, descent, width, height, textFieldWidth, and textFieldHeight.

Table 10.3

Properties Returned by the getTextExtent Method	
METHOD	**DESCRIPTION**
ascent	Represents the distance from the baseline to the top of the text in pixels
descent	Represents the distance from the baseline to bottom of the text in pixels
width	Represents the width of the text in pixels
height	Represents the height of the text in pixels
textFieldHeight	Represents the height of the text field in pixels
textFieldWidth	Represents the width of the text field in pixels

In the next task, you will define a string of text and create a new textFormat object for it. You will then call the getTextExtent method to retrieve the properties width, height, textFieldWidth, and textFieldHeight. You will use these measurements as parameters for the createTextField method to create a text field of sufficient size to display the text.

To retrieve exact dimensions for a dynamic text field:

1. Select the first frame of the main Timeline, and open the Actions panel.

2. Create a new textFormat object, as defined in the preceding tasks.

3. Assign various properties to your textFormat object (**Figure 10.74**).

4. On a new line, enter a variable name followed by an equals sign. Enter the text that you would like to measure. Make sure that the text is surrounded by quotation marks (**Figure 10.75**).

```
myFormat_fmt = new TextFormat();
myFormat_fmt.font = "Arial";
myFormat_fmt.size = 18;
myFormat_fmt.leading = 4;
myFormat_fmt.align = "right";
```

Figure 10.74 Create a new textFormat object and define several of its properties.

```
myText_str = "How big is this piece of text?";
```

Figure 10.75 Define the text you wish to measure in a variable called myText_str.

Text Field Properties vs. the getTextExtent Return Properties

How do the properties of a text field (_height, _width, textHeight, and textWidth) relate to the properties returned by the getTextExtent method (ascent, descent, width, height, textFieldWidth, and textFieldHeight)? Although the names of the properties are quite similar, their usage is very different. The properties of a text field affect the dimensions of an existing text field on the Stage. The properties returned by the getTextExtent method, on the other hand, are measurements of a particular string of text with a particular formatting. The properties returned by the getTextExtent method give you the information you need to create a text field with the correct proportions to fit the text.

DETERMINING THE DIMENSIONS OF TEXT

5. On the next line, create a new variable name followed by an equals sign. Enter the name of your TextFormat object followed by a period. Select `getTextExtent` from the code hint pull-down menu.

or

Choose Built-in Classes > Movie > TextFormat > Methods > getTextExtent.

6. For the parameters of the `getTextExtent` method, enter the name of the variable that holds your string of text (**Figure 10.76**).

Flash makes measurements of your string with the formatting applied. The six measurements are put into the `ascent`, `descent`, `width`, `height`, `textFieldWidth`, and `textFieldHeight` properties.

7. On the next line, enter _root, and then choose Built-in Classes > Movie > MovieClip > Methods > createTextField.

8. For the parameters of the `createTextField` method, enter an instance name in quotation marks, a depth level, a value for its *x* position, and a value for its *y* position. For the last two required parameters, enter the variable name you entered for step 5 followed by a period and the `textFieldWidth` or `textFieldHeight` measurements that were returned by the `getTextExtent` method (**Figure 10.77**).

A new dynamic text field is created on the root Timeline. The text field's width and height are set to be the exact width and height required for your formatted string of text.

9. Using a `with` statement, assign your text and set various properties to the newly created dynamic text field (**Figure 10.78**).

continues on next page

```
obj1 = myFormat_fmt.getTextExtent(myText_str);
```

Figure 10.76 Call the `getTextExtent` method of your textFormat object and use the variable that holds your text as the parameter. The measurements will be returned as properties of the object called `obj1`.

```
_root.createTextField("titleText_txt", 1, 20, 20, obj1.textFieldWidth, obj1.textFieldHeight);
```

Figure 10.77 Use the `textFieldWidth` property and the `textFieldHeight` property as the last two parameters to define your new text field.

```
with (titleText_txt) {
    border = true;
    wordWrap = true;
    text = myText_str;
}
```

Figure 10.78 Set the `border` and `wordWrap` properties of your newly created dynamic text field to true, and assign your variable `myText_str` to its contents.

DETERMINING THE DIMENSIONS OF TEXT

10. On a new line outside the with state-ment, call the setTextFormat method to assign the textFormat object for your dynamic text field. The full script is shown in **Figure 10.79**.

11. Test your movie.

    Flash measures your text and creates a dynamic text field just large enough to accommodate it (Figure 10.79).

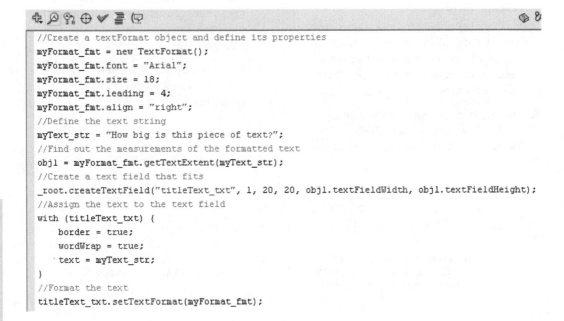

```
//Create a textFormat object and define its properties
myFormat_fmt = new TextFormat();
myFormat_fmt.font = "Arial";
myFormat_fmt.size = 18;
myFormat_fmt.leading = 4;
myFormat_fmt.align = "right";
//Define the text string
myText_str = "How big is this piece of text?";
//Find out the measurements of the formatted text
obj1 = myFormat_fmt.getTextExtent(myText_str);
//Create a text field that fits
_root.createTextField("titleText_txt", 1, 20, 20, obj1.textFieldWidth, obj1.textFieldHeight);
//Assign the text to the text field
with (titleText_txt) {
    border = true;
    wordWrap = true;
    text = myText_str;
}
//Format the text
titleText_txt.setTextFormat(myFormat_fmt);
```

How big is this piece of text?

Figure 10.79 The full script (top) creates a dynamic text field that just fits the formatted text (bottom).

How big
is this
piece of
text?

Figure 10.80 You can define the horizontal length (in pixels), at which point the text will wrap to the next line. The getTextExtent method will return the height and textFieldHeight at which all the content shows.

- If you want your text to wrap at a certain pixel width, you can enter that value as the second parameter of the getTextExtent method. For example, in the preceding task, you can change the getTextExtent statement to the following:

  obj1 = myFormat_fmt.getTextExtent
  (myText_str, 100);

  Flash will return the six measurements based on the text wrapping at 100 pixels (**Figure 10.80**).

- Input and dynamic text fields have a 2-pixel gutter surrounding the text. Thus, textFieldWidth will always be width+4, and textFieldHeight will always be height+4 (2 pixels on both sides).

- The getTextExtent will not work properly with HTML-formatted text.

DETERMINING THE DIMENSIONS OF TEXT

Formatting Text Fields from an External Style Sheet

External Cascading Style Sheets (CSS) help designers and developers maintain consistency across multiple HTML documents. Flash now gives you the opportunity to tap into this resource to help you maintain the same formatting rules—such as font size, color, and other formatting styles—across all associated dynamic or input text fields. You can even apply styles defined by the style sheet to a text field that contains HTML or XML formatted text.

First, you must create a new style sheet object from the StyleSheet class, which is part of the TextField class:

```
myStyle = new TextField.styleSheet()
```

Next, you can load an external CSS document that defines your style with the load() method:

```
myStyle.load("mystyles.css");
```

Finally, you apply those styles to your text field by assigning your style sheet object to the text field's styleSheet property:

```
myTextField_txt.styleSheet = myStyle;
```

Common CSS tags supported by text fields

- ◆ font-family specifies font to be used.

- ◆ font-size sets the size of the font.

- ◆ font-weight sets the weight of a font.

- ◆ font-style sets the style of the font (normal, italic, oblique).

- ◆ text-align aligns the text.

- ◆ text-indent indents the first line of text in a text field.

By writing HTML-formatted text inside of the Script pane and assigning a style sheet object to the styleSheet property of the textfield object, you can control its format options through an external CSS document. This feature can be very convenient; you will not have to open the Flash file to make text style changes because it can all be done inside of one CSS document. In addition, the CSS document can maintain the same style in both your HTML pages and your Flash movies.

To display HTML text with CSS formatting:

1. Open a text-editing application or a WYSIWYG HTML editor, and create your CSS document.

2. Save the text file (**Figure 10.81**).

   For external Cascading Style Sheets, use a .css extension.

3. In Flash, choose the Text tool, and drag out a large text field.

4. In the Property Inspector, choose Dynamic Text, and enter an instance name (**Figure 10.82**).

5. Select the first keyframe in the root Timeline, and open the Actions panel.

6. Enter a variable name followed by an equals sign. Choose Built-in Classes > Movie > TextField > StyleSheet > new StyleSheet.

   A new style sheet object is instantiated.

7. On the next line, enter the name of your style sheet object and then choose Built-in Classes > Movie > TextField > StyleSheet > Methods > load.

continues on next page

Figure 10.81 In an external cascading style sheet, a selector is defined with the name of headingInfo.

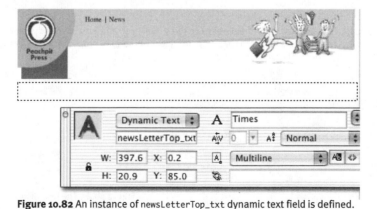

Figure 10.82 An instance of newsLetterTop_txt dynamic text field is defined.

8. For the parameter of the `load` method, enter the path to the filename of your external CSS document. Make sure that the path is surrounded by quotation marks (**Figure 10.83**).

The external cascading style sheet loads into the style sheet object.

9. On the next line, enter a `with` statement. Between its parentheses, enter the name of your dynamic text field.

10. Between the curly braces of the `with` statement, assign your style object to the `styleSheet` property, assign the value `true` to the `html` property, and assign HTML-formatted text to the `text` property (**Figure 10.84**).

11. Test your movie.

Flash loads and applies the style defined in the external cascading style sheet to the HTML-formatted text in your dynamic text (**Figure 10.85**).

✔ Tip

- In order to utilize the formatting that was created in the external style sheet, you must begin and end your HTML-formatted text with the selector name that was used in the style sheet. In this task, the selector name is `headingInfo` (see Figures 10.81 and 10.84).

```
myStyle = new TextField.StyleSheet();
myStyle.load("mystyles.css");
```

Figure 10.83 Load the external style sheet document called mystyles.css into the new style sheet object. The mystyles.css document in this example must reside in the same folder as the Flash movie.

```
myStyle = new TextField.StyleSheet();
myStyle.load("mystyles.css");
with (newsLetterTop_txt) {
    styleSheet = myStyle;
    html = true;
    text = "<headingInfo>Welcome to the PeachPit Press Newsletter</headingInfo>";
}
```

Figure 10.84 Assign the myStyle style sheet object to the `styleSheet` property of your dynamic text field. Set the `html` property to `true` and assign HTML-formatted text to the `text` property. Make sure you reference the selector; here it is called headingInfo.

Figure 10.85 The text displays in the style defined in the external cascading style sheet.

FORMATTING FROM EXTERNAL STYLE SHEETS

Manipulating Text-Field Contents

When you define a text field as an input text field, you give your viewers the freedom to enter and edit information. You've seen how this information can be used in expressions with other actions or concatenated and displayed in dynamic text fields. Often, however, you need to analyze the text entered by the viewer before using it. You may want to tease out certain words or identify the location of a particular character or sequence of characters. If you require viewers to enter an email address in an input field, for example, you can check to see whether that address is in the correct format by looking for the @ symbol. Or you could check a customer's telephone number, find out the area code based on the first three digits, and personalize a directory or news listing with local interests.

This kind of parsing, manipulation, and control of the information within text fields is done with a combination of the Selection class and the String class. The Selection class lets you control the focus of multiple text fields and the position of the insertion point within a focused text field. The String class lets you retrieve and change the characters inside a text field.

The Selection Class

The Selection class controls the selection of characters in text fields. Unlike most classes, the Selection class doesn't need a constructor function to be instantiated before you can use it because there can be only one insertion-point position or selection in a Flash movie at a time. So the Selection class will always refer to that one position or selection.

The methods of the Selection class affect a text field in two ways: It can control which text field is currently active, or *focused*, and it can control where the insertion point is positioned within that text field. **Table 10.4** summarizes important methods of the Selection class.

Table 10.4

Methods of the Selection Class	
METHOD	DESCRIPTION
getBeginIndex()	Retrieves the index at the beginning of the selection
getEndIndex()	Retrieves the index at the end of the selection
getCaretIndex()	Retrieves the index of the insertion-point position
setSelection (beginIndex, endIndex)	Positions the selection at a specified beginIndex and endIndex
getFocus()	Retrieves the instance name of the active text field
setFocus (instanceName)	Sets the focus of the text field specified by the instance name

Controlling the Focus of Text Fields

You can have only one focused object on the Stage at any time. If you have multiple text fields on the Stage, you need to be able to control which one is focused before you can retrieve or assign the insertion-point location or selection. The getFocus() and setFocus() methods of the Selection class let you do this.

The method getFocus() returns a string of the absolute path to the text field by using the _level0 term. If the selected text field called yourName_txt is on the root Timeline, for example, and you call the getFocus() method, the returned value is "_level0.yourName_txt".

It's important to remember that the returned value is a string and that the _level0 term is used. If you compare the getFocus() method with a pathname using _root or this, or if you forget the quotation marks, then Flash won't recognize the path. The getFocus() method returns a value of null if there is no focused text field on the Stage.

The setFocus() method takes one parameter, which is the text field you want to give focus to. You must use a string for the path to specify the text field, although you can use either an absolute or relative path. setFocus("scoreboard_txt"), for example, will make the text field called scoreboard_txt active.

To set the focus of a text field:

1. Select the Text tool in the Tools palette, and drag out two separate text fields on the Stage.

2. In the Property Inspector, choose Input Text, give each field an instance name, and click the Show Border button for both text fields.

3. Select the first frame of the main Timeline, and open the Actions panel.

4. Create a new listener object from the generic Object class (**Figure 10.86**).

5. Assign the onKeyDown event handler to your listener.

6. Within the onKeyDown event handler, choose Statements > Conditions/ Loops > if.

7. For the condition of the if statement, enter Key.isDown(Key.LEFT).

8. With your pointer between the curly braces of the if statement, choose Built-in Classes > Movie > Selection > Methods > setFocus.

```
myListener = new Object();
```

Figure 10.86 Create the listener called myListener.

```
myListener = new Object();
myListener.onKeyDown = function() {
    if (Key.isDown(Key.LEFT)) {
        Selection.setFocus("displayLeft");
    }
}
```

Figure 10.87 When the left key is pressed, Flash focuses the first input text field, called displayLeft.

```
myListener = new Object();
myListener.onKeyDown = function() {
    if (Key.isDown(Key.LEFT)) {
        Selection.setFocus("displayLeft");
    }
    if (Key.isDown(Key.RIGHT)) {
        Selection.setFocus("displayRight");
    }
}
```

Figure 10.88 When the right key is pressed, Flash focuses the second input text field, called displayRight.

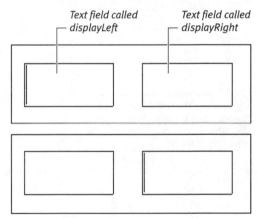

Text field called displayLeft   Text field called displayRight

Figure 10.89 The focus of text fields is controlled by the left and right keys. At top, the left text field is focused (the blinking insertion point is visible inside the text field). At bottom, the right text field is focused.

9. For the parameter of the setFocus method, enter the name of the first input text field in quotation marks (**Figure 10.87**).

When the left key is pressed, Flash focuses the first input text field.

10. Place your pointer on a new line outside the closing brace of your if statement, and choose Statements > Conditions/Loops > if.

11. For the condition of your second if statement, enter Key.isDown(Key.RIGHT).

12. In between the curly braces of the second if statement, choose Built-in Classes > Movie > Selection > Methods > setFocus.

13. For the parameter of the second setFocus method, enter the name of the second input text field in quotation marks (**Figure 10.88**).

When the right key is pressed, Flash focuses the second input text field.

14. Register your listener to the Key class with the method addListener().

15. Test your movie.

Flash detects when the right or the left key is pressed on the keyboard and changes the selected text field (**Figure 10.89**). If you disable the automatic focusing with the Tab key, you can build your own way to navigate and select multiple text fields.

In the next task, you will display the name of the focused text field in the Output window by using the method getFocus(). (The Output window appears only in authoring mode; it is used for testing and verification purposes.)

To get the focus of a text field:

1. Continuing with the file you created in the preceding task, place your pointer on a new line after the closing brace of the last if statement.

2. Choose Global Functions > Miscellaneous Functions > trace.

3. With your pointer between the parentheses of the trace statement, choose Built-in Classes > Movie > Selection > Methods > getFocus (**Figure 10.90**).

4. Test your movie.

   When you use the right and left keys to change the focus of the text fields, Flash displays their target paths in the Output window (**Figure 10.91**).

Figure 10.90 Add a trace statement to display the name of the focused text field.

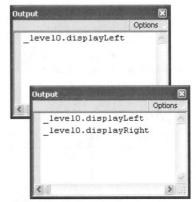

Figure 10.91 The Output window when the left key is pressed (top) and when the right key is pressed immediately afterward (bottom).

Figure 10.92 Enter mySelection_txt as the instance name for your input text field.

Controlling the Selection Within Text Fields

When you have a focused text field, either by using ActionScript or by a viewer's clicking it with the pointer, you can control the selection or insertion-point position inside it. This technique lets you direct your viewers' attention to particular characters or words they've entered, perhaps to point out errors or misspellings. It also lets you keep track of the insertion-point position, much the way that the _xmouse and _ymouse properties let you keep track of the location of the viewer's mouse pointer. You can also select certain parts of the text field and replace just those portions with different text.

The position of each character in a string is numbered and used as the index for the methods of the Selection class, just as the index for the setTextFormat() method is used. The first character is assigned the index of 0, the second character is 1, and so on. If an insertion point isn't positioned within a text field when Flash retrieves the selection index, it returns a value of –1.

The following task demonstrates how the getCaretIndex() method of the Selection class retrieves the position of the user's cursor within a text field.

To identify the position of the insertion point in a text field:

1. Select the Text tool, and drag out a text field on the Stage.

2. In the Property Inspector, choose Input Text and Multiline from the pull-down menus, give the input text field an instance name, and click the Show Border button (**Figure 10.92**).

continues on next page

3. Select the Text tool, and drag out a second text field on the Stage.

4. In the Property Inspector, choose Dynamic Text and Multiline from the pull-down menus, give the dynamic text field an instance name, and click the Show Border button (**Figure 10.93**).

5. Select the first frame of the main Timeline, and open the Actions panel.

6. Enter _root, and choose Built-in Classes > Movie > MovieClip > Events > onEnterFrame. Complete the event handler by entering =function(){ and a closing curly brace on the next line.

7. Within the onEnterFrame event handler, enter the instance name of your dynamic text field followed by a period and the property text.

8. On the same line, enter an equals sign, and then choose Built-in Classes > Movie > Selection > Methods > getCaretIndex (**Figure 10.94**).

9. Test your movie.

Initially, the dynamic text field displays −1 because the input text field is not focused. When your viewer begins to type in the input text field, Flash updates the dynamic text field to display the insertion point's position (**Figure 10.95**).

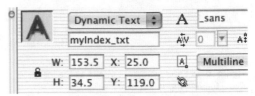

Figure 10.93 Enter myIndex_txt as the instance name for your dynamic text field.

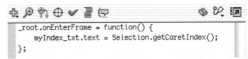

```
_root.onEnterFrame = function() {
    myIndex_txt.text = Selection.getCaretIndex();
};
```

Figure 10.94 Flash assigns the position of the insertion point, or caret, to the contents of the text field called myIndex_txt.

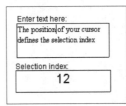

Figure 10.95 The current index of the insertion point is 12. The first letter, *T*, is 0. The space between *position* and *of* is 12.

Figure 10.96 Create the text field called `myPhrase_txt`.

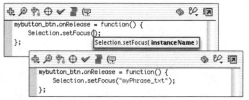

Figure 10.97 Set the focus to the text field called `myPhrase_txt`.

You can choose a portion of the text field's contents with `Selection.setSelection()` and then replace it with the TextField method `replaceSel()`. In the next example, you will replace a portion of the text field with different text when you click a button.

To change the selection in a text field:

1. Select the Text tool in the Tools palette, and drag out a text field on the Stage.

2. Enter the text *Carrots are good to eat.*

3. In the Property Inspector, choose Input Text and Multiline, enter an instance name, and embed the font that you want to use (**Figure 10.96**).

4. Create a button symbol, place an instance on the Stage, and give it a name in the Property Inspector.

5. Select the first frame of the main Timeline, and open the Actions panel.

6. Assign an `onRelease` event handler to your button.

7. Within the `onRelease` event handler, choose Built-in Classes > Movie > Selection > Methods > setFocus.

8. For the parameter of the `setFocus` method, enter the name of your text field in quotation marks (**Figure 10.97**).

   When you click this button, Flash focuses the text field. (The focus moves from your button to the text field.)

9. On a new line, choose Built-in Classes > Movie > Selection > Methods > setSelection.

continues on next page

10. For the parameter of the `setSelection` method, enter 0 followed by a comma and then 7 (**Figure 10.98**).

The `setSelection()` method selects all the characters between its first parameter and its second parameter, inclusive of the first parameter. So this `setSelection()`selects the first seven characters (index 0 to index 6) of the text field.

11. On the next line, enter the name of your text field followed by a period. Choose Built-in Classes > Movie > TextField > Methods > replaceSel.

12. For the parameter of the `replaceSel` method, enter a replacement for the selection (**Figure 10.99**).

In this example, the replacement word is *Burritos*. Make sure that the replacement word is in quotation marks.

13. Test your movie.

When you click the button, the `setSelection()` method selects the word *Carrots* and the `replaceSel()` method replaces it with the word *Burritos* (**Figure 10.100**). 🐭

```
mybutton_btn.onRelease = function() {
    Selection.setFocus("myPhrase_txt");
    Selection.setSelection(0, 7);
};
```

Figure 10.98 Select everything between index 0 (inclusive) and index 7. The word *Carrots* is selected.

```
mybutton_btn.onRelease = function() {
    Selection.setFocus("myPhrase_txt");
    Selection.setSelection(0, 7);
    myPhrase_txt.replaceSel("Burritos");
};
```

Figure 10.99 Replace the selection with the word *Burritos*.

Figure 10.100 The original text field (top) and the text field after the selection is replaced (bottom). Notice that the insertion point is positioned just after the new selection.

Table 10.5

EVENT	DESCRIPTION
Selection and TextField Events	
onSetFocus	Happens when a new text field receives focus. When onSetFocus is used as a TextField event, the handler can take one parameter: oldFocus. When onSetFocus is used as a Selection event, the handler can take two parameters—oldFocus and newFocus—and requires a listener.
onChanged	Happens when the contents of a text field change. This TextField event can also be assigned to a listener.
onScroller	Happens when one of the text-field properties—scroll or hscroll—changes. This TextField event can also be assigned to a listener.
onKillFocus	Happens when a text field loses focus. The handler for this TextField event can take one parameter: newFocus.

Detecting Changes in the Text Field

Often, you'll want to capture information from a text field only when the viewer has entered something new. Or you'll want to respond when a viewer has selected a particular text field. You can detect these changes in text fields with event handlers and listeners. Flash provides a variety of them through the Selection class and the TextField class (**Table 10.5**).

In this section, you'll look at two important TextField events: onSetFocus and onChanged.

The onSetFocus event happens when a text field receives focus because a viewer clicked inside the text field or pressed the Tab key in a browser or because you used the setFocus() ActionScript command. Each text field has its own onSetFocus event. You can use an optional parameter in an onSetFocus event handler that can tell you what the previously focused text field was, as in this example:

```
myTF_txt.onSetFocus = function(oldFocus){
    trace ("you came from" + oldFocus)
}
```

In this handler, when you focus the text field called myTF_txt, the Output window displays a message telling you where the previous focus was. If the previous focus was not a text field, oldFocus = null.

The onChanged event happens when the viewer changes the contents of a text field. A viewer can click inside a text field and select portions of the text, but the onChanged event is triggered only when the viewer adds to, deletes, or changes its contents.

In the following task, you will create multiple input text fields. You will detect which text field your viewer selects and display a customized message in a dynamic text field.

To detect the focus of a text field:

1. Select the Text tool, and drag out three text fields on the Stage.

2. In the Property Inspector, choose Input Text and Single Line from the pull-down menus, and enter an instance name for each of the input text fields.

3. Select the Text tool, and drag out a fourth text field on the Stage.

4. In the Property Inspector, choose Dynamic Text and Multiline from the pull-down menus, and enter an instance name for this dynamic text field (**Figure 10.101**).

5. Select the first frame of the main Timeline, and open the Actions panel.

6. Enter the name of your first input text field. Choose Built-in Classes > Movie > TextField > Events > onSetFocus.

7. Complete the event handler by adding =function before the parentheses, adding an opening and closing curly brace after the parentheses, and deleting the term oldFocus that appears inside of the parentheses. Your code will look similar to this:

```
name_txt.onSetFocus=function(){
}
```

8. Within the onSetFocus event handler, assign a message to the text property of your dynamic text field that gives instructions to the viewer for the text field that he or she selected (**Figure 10.102**).

    Make sure the message to be displayed is in quotation marks.

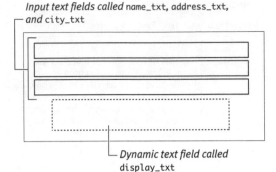

Input text fields called name_txt, address_txt, *and* city_txt

Dynamic text field called display_txt

Figure 10.101 Create three input text fields (top) and one dynamic text field (bottom).

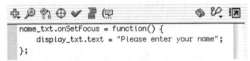

Figure 10.102 When the input text field called name_txt is focused, the bottom dynamic text field tells the viewer to enter his or her name.

```
name_txt.onSetFocus = function() {
    display_txt.text = "Please enter your name";
};
address_txt.onSetFocus = function() {
    display_txt.text = "Please enter your address"
};
```

Figure 10.103 When the input text field called `address_txt` is focused, the bottom dynamic text field tells the viewer to enter his or her address.

```
name_txt.onSetFocus = function() {
    display_txt.text = "Please enter your name";
};
address_txt.onSetFocus = function() {
    display_txt.text = "Please enter your address"
};
city_txt.onSetFocus = function() {
    display_txt.text = "Please enter your city";
};
display_txt.text = "Please select a text field";
```

Figure 10.104 The full script. A different message appears for each focused input text field and another message appears when no text field is selected.

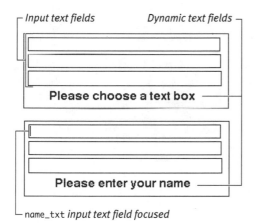

Input text fields   *Dynamic text fields*

Please choose a text box

Please enter your name

`name_txt` *input text field focused*

Figure 10.105 This example shows the start of this movie (top) and the top field focused (bottom).

9. On a new line, create another `onSetFocus` event handler for your second input text field as you did in steps 6 and 7.

10. Within the second `onSetFocus` event handler, assign a message to the `text` property of the dynamic text field, giving instructions to the viewer (**Figure 10.103**).

11. Add a third `onSetFocus` handler to detect when the third input text field has received focus, and have the dynamic text field change in response.

12. Add a statement outside all the `onSetFocus` handlers that gives initial instructions to the viewer before any of the text fields receive focus.

    The final script should look like **Figure 10.104**.

13. Test your movie.

    When your viewer first sees your Flash movie, none of the text fields is focused, so the message in the dynamic text field tells the viewer what to do. When the viewer selects a text field, Flash detects which one it is and displays a custom message (**Figure 10.105**).

To detect a change in the contents of a text field:

1. Select the Text tool, and drag out a text field on the Stage.

2. In the Property Inspector, choose Input Text and Single Line from the pull-down menus, and enter an instance name for this input text field.

3. Select the first frame of the main Timeline, and open the Actions panel.

4. Enter the name of your text field followed by a period.

5. Choose Built-in Classes > Movie > TextField > Events > onChanged. Complete the event handler by adding =function(){ and a closing curly brace on the next line.

    Your onChanged handler is created.

6. Assign actions within the curly braces of the onChanged handler (**Figure 10.106**).

    Any additions, deletions, or changes in the contents of this text field will trigger the actions within this handler.

✔ Tip

- The onChanged event does not detect changes in a text field via ActionScript. Only user-entered changes trigger the event.

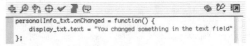

Figure 10.106 When the contents of the text field called personalInfo_txt change, this event handler will be triggered.

The String Class

You can apply the methods and properties of the String class to analyze and manipulate string data types. The String class can tell you the position of a certain character, for example, or what character occupies a certain position. You can also dissect just a portion of the string and put that part, called a *substring*, into a new string, or you can concatenate substrings and strings. You can even change the lowercase and uppercase styles of different parts of the string. **Table 10.6** summarizes several methods and properties of the String class.

You can perform all this parsing and shuffling of strings without first having to create an instance of the String class. Flash does this automatically by creating a temporary String instance that it discards after the work of the method is completed.

Like those of the Selection and TextField class, the indices of the String class are based on the positions of the characters in the string; the first character is assigned an index of 0.

✔ Tip

■ You can use the String function to convert the value of any variable, expression, or object to a string before applying the methods of the String class. If your variable `radioButton` is a Boolean data type, the statement `String (radioButton)` returns the string `"true"` or `"false"`. Now you can manipulate the actual characters with the methods of the String class.

Table 10.6

Methods and Properties of the String Class

METHOD OR PROPERTY	DESCRIPTION
`indexOf(searchString, fromIndex)`	Searches the string and returns the index of the first occurrence of a substring specified in the parameter `searchString`. The optional `fromIndex` parameter sets the starting position of the search.
`lastIndexOf(searchString, fromIndex)`	Searches the string and returns the index of the last occurrence of a substring specified in the parameter `searchString`. The optional `fromIndex` parameter sets the starting position of the search.
`charAt(index)`	Returns the character at the specified index position.
`substring(indexA, indexB)`	Returns the string between the `indexA` and `indexB` parameters.
`substr(start, length)`	Returns the string with the specified length from the start index.
`concat(string1,…,stringN)`	Concatenates the specified strings.
`toLowerCase()`	Returns a string that contains all lowercase characters.
`toUpperCase()`	Returns a string that contains all uppercase characters.
`length`	A property that returns the length of the string.

Analyzing Strings

Use the methods of the String class to identify a character or characters in a string. The following tasks analyze input text fields to verify that the viewer has entered the required information.

To identify the position of a character:

1. Select the Text tool in the Tools palette, and drag out a text field on the Stage.

2. In the Property Inspector, choose Input Text and Single Line from the pull-down menu, and enter an instance name for this input text field.

3. Create a button symbol, place an instance of it on the Stage, and give it a name in the Property Inspector.

4. Select the first frame of the main Timeline, and open the Actions panel.

5. Assign an onRelease event handler to your button.

6. Within the onRelease event handler, enter a variable name followed by an equals sign.

7. On the same line, enter the name of your input text field followed by a period and then the text property.

8. With your pointer next to the text property, choose Built-in Classes > Core > String > Methods > indexOf.

   The indexOf() method appears after the text property. This method takes two parameters: searchString and fromIndex. The parameter searchString is the specific character you want to identify in the string. The parameter fromIndex, which is optional, is the starting position in the string.

9. Between the parentheses of the indexOf() method, enter the character you want to find (**Figure 10.107**).

   When your viewer enters information in the input text field and clicks the button you created, Flash searches the contents of the input text field for the specified character and assigns its position to your variable. Use this variable in the methods of the Selection, TextField, and String objects to modify the information further.

```
myButton_btn.onRelease = function(){
    charPosition = myString_txt.text.indexOf("%")
}
```

Figure 10.107 Assign the indexOf("%") method to myString_txt.text to search its contents for the % sign. If that character is found, the index of its position within the text is assigned to the variable charPosition. If that character is not found, -1 is assigned to the variable.

✔ Tips

- The flip side of the method `indexOf()` is `charAt()`. This method returns the character that occupies the index position you specify for a string. You could use this method to verify that the first, second, and third characters correspond to numbers for a certain area code of a telephone number, for example.

- If the character you search for with `indexOf()` occurs more than once in the string, Flash returns the index of only the first occurrence. Use the method `lastIndexOf()` to retrieve the last occurrence of the character.

- If you want to retrieve all the occurrences of a certain character, you must use several iterations of the method `indexOf()`. Use its optional second parameter, `fromIndex`, which begins the search at a specific index. Imagine that the text field called `my_txt` contains the string `"home/ images/vacation"`. Then assign this script:

```
slash1 = my_txt.text.indexOf ("/")

slash2 = my_txt.text.indexOf ("/",
slash1+1)
```

The first statement assigns the variable `slash1` to the first occurrence of the slash symbol in the string input (`slash1` = 4). The second statement searches for the slash symbol again but starts the search at the next character after the first slash (at index 5, or the *i* in *images*). By constructing a `while` or a `do while` loop, you can make Flash march down the string, starting new searches as it finds occurrences of the character. Do this until the returned value of the `indexOf()` method equals the value of the `lastIndexOf()` method.

ANALYZING STRINGS

If Flash searches a string with the indexOf() or lastIndexOf() method and doesn't find the specified character, it returns a value of −1. You can use this fact to check for missing characters within a string. If indexOf("%") == −1, for example, you know that the percentage symbol is missing from the string. In the next task, you'll search an input text field for the @ symbol and the period to check whether an email address has been entered correctly.

To check for a missing character:

1. Select the Text tool, and drag out a text field on the Stage.

2. In the Property Inspector, choose Input Text and Single Line from the pull-down menus, and enter an instance name for this input text field.

3. Select the Text tool again, and drag out another text field on the Stage.

4. In the Property Inspector, choose Dynamic Text and Multiline from the pull-down menus, and enter an instance name for this dynamic text field (**Figure 10.108**).

5. Create a button symbol, place an instance of the button on the Stage between the input text field and the dynamic text field, and give the button a name in the Property Inspector (**Figure 10.109**).

6. Select the first frame of the main Timeline, and open the Actions panel.

7. Assign an onRelease handler to the button.

8. Within the onRelease event handler, choose Statements > Conditions/Loops > if.

9. For the condition of the if statement, enter the name of the input text field followed by a period and then the property text.

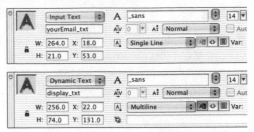

Figure 10.108 Enter yourEmail_txt as the instance name for your input text field, and enter display_txt as the instance name for your dynamic text field.

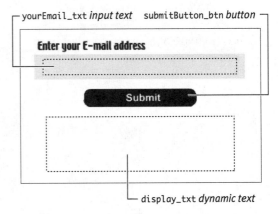

Figure 10.109 Place the input text field at the top, the button in the middle, and the dynamic text field at the bottom.

10. With your insertion point immediately after the word **text**, choose Built-in Classes > Core > String > Methods > indexOf.

The indexOf() method appears after the **text** property of your text field.

11. Between the parentheses of the indexOf() method, enter "@".

Make sure that you include the quotation marks.

Flash searches the input text field for the @ symbol.

12. Complete the rest of the condition so that the whole statement looks like the following:

yourEmail_txt.text.indexOf ("@") == -1

This condition checks to see whether the @ symbol in the string within yourEmail_txt.text is not present (**Figure 10.110**).

13. After the conditional statement, enter the logical OR operator, ||.

14. Add a second condition that checks whether a period (.) is not present in this string:

yourEmail_txt.text.indexOf (".") == -1

15. In between the curly braces of the if statement, enter the name of your dynamic text field followed by a period and then the **text** property.

16. Following the **text** property, enter an equals sign and a message that notifies your viewer of a problem with the input (**Figure 10.111**).

17. With your pointer positioned after the closing curly brace for the if statement, enter else{}.

continues on next page

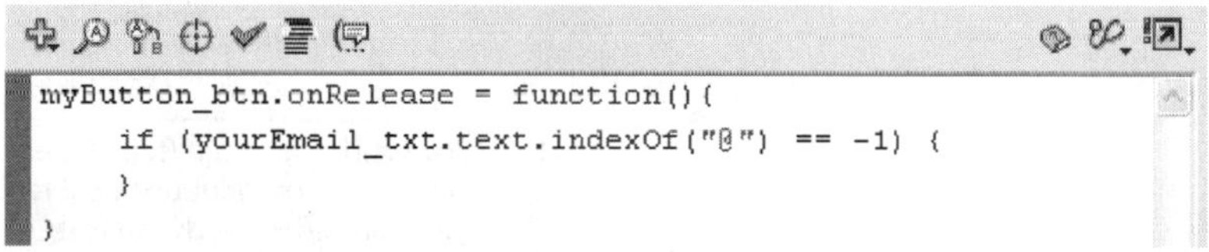

```
myButton_btn.onRelease = function(){
    if (yourEmail_txt.text.indexOf("@") == -1) {
    }
}
```

Figure 10.110 If the @ symbol is missing from the string inside yourEmail_txt.text, this condition will hold true.

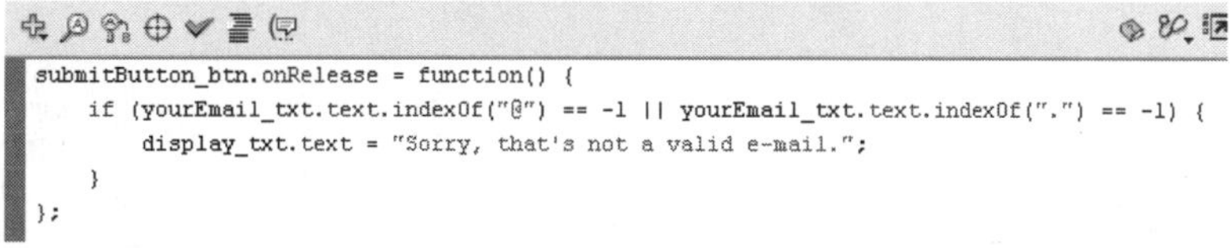

```
submitButton_btn.onRelease = function() {
    if (yourEmail_txt.text.indexOf("@") == -1 || yourEmail_txt.text.indexOf(".") == -1) {
        display_txt.text = "Sorry, that's not a valid e-mail.";
    }
};
```

Figure 10.111 The message in quotation marks appears in the dynamic text field called display_txt.

18. Between the curly braces of the `else` statement, send an alternative message to the contents of the dynamic text field that thanks your viewer for submitting an email address (**Figure 10.112**).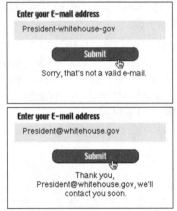

19. Test your movie.

When the viewer clicks the button after entering an email address in the input text field, Flash checks the string for both the @ symbol and a period and returns the indexes of those symbols. If either index is −1, the viewer receives a message that the input is incorrect. Otherwise, the viewer receives a thank-you message (**Figure 10.113**).

✔ Tip

■ Use the `indexOf()` or `lastIndexOf()` method to check for a character or sequence of characters. If you specify a string as the parameter, such as `indexOf(".org")`, Flash returns the index of the first occurrence of the sequence .org that appears in the string.

```
} else {
    display_txt.text = "Thank you, "+yourEmail_txt.text+
    " we'll contact you soon";
}
```

Figure 10.112 This message appears in the dynamic text field called `display_txt` when the condition is false.

```
submitButton_btn.onRelease = function() {
    if (yourEmail_txt.text.indexOf("@") == -1 ||
    yourEmail_txt.text.indexOf(".") == -1) {
        display_txt.text = "Sorry, that's not a
        valid e-mail.";
    } else {
        display_txt.text = "Thank you, "+
        yourEmail_txt.text+", we'll contact you soon.";
    }
};
```

Enter your E-mail address

President-whitehouse-gov

Submit

Sorry, that's not a valid e-mail.

Enter your E-mail address

President@whitehouse.gov

Submit

Thank you,
President@whitehouse.gov, we'll
contact you soon.

Figure 10.113 The full script (top). Entering an incorrect email address in the input text field results in a warning displayed in the dynamic text field (middle). Entering an email address with an @ sign and a period results in a thank-you message displayed in the dynamic text field (bottom).

ANALYZING STRINGS

```
if (yourEmail_txt.text.length == 0) {
  display_txt.text = "Please enter something";
}
```

Figure 10.114 Flash checks whether the string inside yourEmail_txt.text is empty and displays an appropriate message.

The String class has one property, length, that tells you value of the number of characters in a string. This property is a read-only property that is useful for checking the relative positions of characters. If you are building an online purchasing interface with input text fields for prices, you can check the input text to see whether a period character is three positions before the length of the input string in the following expression:

input.text.indexOf (".") == input.text.length – 3

If this condition is true, you could treat the last two digits as a decimal.

The following task refines the preceding example of verifying an email address. You will have Flash make sure that the length of the input isn't 0 (meaning that the viewer hasn't entered anything).

To check the length of a string:

1. Continuing with the file you used in the preceding task, select the main Timeline, and open the Actions panel.

2. On a new line after the closing curly brace of the else statement, add another if statement.

3. For the condition, check the length of the string.

   The expression should look like the following:

   yourEmail_txt.text.length == 0

4. Within the curly braces of the if statement, assign text to the dynamic text field to notify the viewer that the input text field is empty.

   When your viewer clicks the button, Flash also checks the length of the input text field to see whether anything has been entered (**Figure 10.114**).

Rearranging Strings

When you have information about the position of certain characters and the length of a string, you can select a portion of the string and put it in a new variable. Flash provides tools to get specific selections from a string and put them together with other strings via methods such as concat(), fromCharCode(), slice(), split(), substr(), and substring(). Many of these methods are similar. In this section, we will discuss only substring(), to get a specific portion of a string, and concat(), to put several strings together. You can use a combination of these two methods to control the information that flows from input text fields into the rest of your Flash movie and back out into dynamic text fields.

The following task uses several of these methods to copy the current selection that the viewer has made and paste it into a dynamic text field.

To get selected portions of strings:

1. Select the Text tool, and drag out a text field on the Stage.

2. In the Property Inspector, choose Input Text and Multiline from the pull-down menus, and enter an instance name for this input text field (**Figure 10.115**).

3. Drag out another text field on the Stage.

4. In the Property Inspector, choose Dynamic Text and Multiline from the pull-down menus, and enter an instance name for this dynamic text field (**Figure 10.116**).

5. Create a button symbol, and place an instance of it on the Stage between the input text field and the dynamic text field (**Figure 10.117**).

Figure 10.115 Enter inputBox_txt as the instance name for your input text field.

Figure 10.116 Enter outputBox_txt as the instance name for your dynamic text field.

Figure 10.117 Place the input text field at the top, the button in the middle, and the dynamic text field at the bottom.

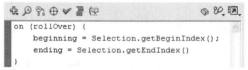

```
on (rollOver) {
    beginning = Selection.getBeginIndex()
}
```

Figure 10.118 The variable called beginning contains the position of the start of the selection.

```
on (rollOver) {
    beginning = Selection.getBeginIndex();
    ending = Selection.getEndIndex()
}
```

Figure 10.119 The variable called ending contains the position of the end of the selection.

6. Select the button, and open the Actions panel.

7. Choose Global Functions > Movie Clip Control > on. Select the rollOver event from the code hint pull-down menu.

8. Within the on curly braces of the on (rollOver) event handler, enter a variable name, followed by an equal sign.

9. Choose Built-in Classes > Movie > Selection > Methods > getBeginIndex

The position of the start of the selection is assigned to this variable (**Figure 10.118**).

10. On the next line, enter another variable name followed by an equals sign.

11. Choose Built-in Classes > Movie > Selection > Methods > getEndIndex (**Figure 10.119**).

The position of the end of the selection is assigned to this variable.

12. On the next line, enter another variable name followed by an equals sign.

13. For its value, enter the name of the input text field followed by a period and then the text property.

14. Choose Built-in Classes > Core > String > Methods > substring.

The substring() method appears after your text property. This method takes two parameters: indexA and indexB. indexA defines the start of the sequence of characters you want to grab, and indexB defines the end of the sequence.

continues on next page

REARRANGING STRINGS

15. Between the parentheses of the **sub-string()** method, enter your variable for the beginning of the selection and then your variable for the end of the selection, separating them with commas (**Figure 10.120**).

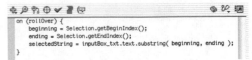

Figure 10.120 The substring() method creates a substring out of the string inside inputBox_txt.text between indexes beginning and ending.

16. On a new line outside the **on(rollOver)** event handler, create a new event handler by choosing Global Functions > Movie Clip Control > on.

17. Select the **Release** event.

18. Within the **on(Release)** event handler, assign the variable holding the selected substring to the **text** property of the dynamic text field (**Figure 10.121**).

Figure 10.121 The contents of outputBox_txt display the contents of the variable called selectedString.

Your viewer can enter information in the input text field and select portions of the text. When the viewer's mouse rolls over the button that you created, Flash captures the position of the selection and puts the substring into another variable. When your viewer clicks the button, the substring appears in the dynamic text field (**Figure 10.122**).

✔ Tip

■ You might wonder why the Selection methods are assigned to the Roll Over event rather than the Release event. That's because Flash must maintain the focus of a text field to capture information about the position of the insertion point or the selection. When the viewer clicks a button, the text field loses focus and the selection disappears. Assigning the information about the selections to the Roll Over event ensures that you have it before it is lost.

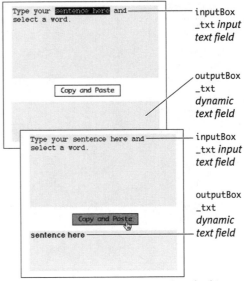

Figure 10.122 The selection *sentence here* (top) is put in a substring and displayed in the dynamic text field below the button (bottom).

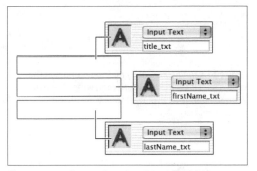

Figure 10.123 Create three input text fields.

With the method concat(), you can put together strings you've dissected in an order that's more useful. The parameters of the concat() method are individual expressions, separated by commas, that you want to combine. The concat() method accomplishes the same thing as the addition operator (+), which is discussed in Chapter 9. The following two statements are equivalent:

```
"Hello, ".concat (firstName, " ",
lastName);
```

```
"Hello, " + firstName + " " + lastName;
```

To combine two separate strings:

1. Select the Text tool, and drag out a text field on the Stage.

2. In the Property Inspector, choose Input Text and Multiline from the pull-down menus, and enter an instance name for this input text field.

3. Select the Text tool again, and drag out two more input text fields with the same settings as the first.

4. In the Property Inspector, give these input text fields different instance names (**Figure 10.123**).

5. Select the Text tool, and drag out a fourth text box on the Stage.

6. In the Property Inspector, choose Dynamic Text and Multiline from the pull-down menus, and enter an instance name for this dynamic text field.

7. Create a button symbol, and place an instance of it on the Stage.

8. Select the button symbol, and open the Actions panel.

9. Choose Global Functions > Movie Clip Control > on.

continues on next page

10. Select `release` from the code hint pull-down menu.

11. Within your on(`release`) event handler, enter the name of your dynamic text field followed by a period and then the `text` property.

12. On the same line, enter an equals sign. Enter the name of your first input text field followed by a period and the `text` property. Choose Built-in Classes > Core > String > Methods > concat.

The concat() method appears. You still need to supply the parameters of the concat() method, which are values that will be concatenated (**Figure 10.124**).

13. For the parameters of the concat() method, enter the `text` properties of the second and third input text fields, separating all your parameters with commas.

14. Test your movie.

When the viewer enters information in the input text fields and then clicks the button, Flash concatenates the contents of the three input text fields and displays them in the dynamic text field (**Figure 10.125**).

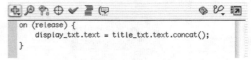

Figure 10.124 The concat() method combines the values specified in its parameters, which have not yet been defined here, with the string inside `title_txt.text`.

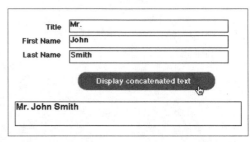

Figure 10.125 Flash concatenates the top three input text fields into one string in the bottom dynamic text field.

Modifying Strings

You can perform two simple methods on a string to modify its characters: toUpperCase() and toLowerCase(). Both methods return a string with all uppercase letters or all lowercase letters. If you want to modify only certain letters to uppercase or lowercase, first you'll need to create substrings of those specific characters, as discussed in the preceding section. Modify the substrings to uppercase or lowercase; then put the string back together with concat().

To change the case of characters in strings:

1. Select the Text tool, and drag out a text field on the Stage.

2. In the Property Inspector, choose Input Text and Single Line from the pull-down menus, and enter an instance name for this input text field.

3. Select the Text tool, and drag out another text field on the Stage.

4. In the Property Inspector, choose Dynamic Text and Single line from the pull-down menus, and enter an instance name for this dynamic text field.

5. Create a button symbol, and place an instance of it on the Stage.

6. Select the button symbol, and open the Actions panel.

7. Choose Global Functions > Movie Clip Control > on.

8. Select release from the code hint pull-down menu.

9. Within the on(release) event handler, enter the name of your dynamic text field followed by a period and the text property.

continues on next page

10. Enter an equals sign followed by the name of your input text field, a period, and the **text** property.

11. Choose Built-in Classes > Core > String > Methods > toUpperCase.

The **toUpperCase()** method requires no parameters (**Figure 10.126**).

12. Test your movie.

When your viewer enters text in the input text field and clicks the button you created, Flash converts the entire string to uppercase and displays the results in the dynamic text field (**Figure 10.127**). Note that the method does not change the original string that calls it. In this example, the contents of myInput_txt remain as they were originally.

```
on (release) {
    display_txt.text = myInput_txt.text.toUpperCase();
}
```

Figure 10.126 The toUpperCase() method returns the contents of myInput_txt in all uppercase letters.

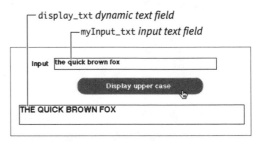

display_txt *dynamic text field*

myInput_txt *input text field*

Input | the quick brown fox

Display upper case

THE QUICK BROWN FOX

Figure 10.127 The results of the toUpperCase() method shown in the dynamic text field called display_txt.

MANIPULATING INFORMATION

The information that you store in variables, modify in expressions, and test with conditional statements often needs to be processed and manipulated by mathematical functions such as square roots, sines, cosines, and exponents. Flash can perform these calculations with the Math class, which lets you create formulas for complicated interactions between the objects in your movie and your viewer or for sophisticated geometry in your graphics. The Math class, for example, allows you to model the correct trajectory of colliding objects or the effects of gravity for a physics tutorial, calculate probabilities for a card game, or generate random numbers to add unpredictable elements to your movie. Much of the information you manipulate sometimes needs to be stored in arrays to give you better control of your data and a more efficient way to retrieve it. You can use the Array class to keep track of ordered data such as shopping lists, color tables, and scorecards.

When the information you need depends on the time or the date, you can use the Date class to retrieve the current year, month, or even millisecond. Build clocks and timers to use inside your Flash movie, or send the time information (along with a viewer's profile) to a server-side script.

All this information handling and processing is easier when you use functions. Build functions that string together separate actions and methods to accomplish many tasks at the same time. Build a single function, for example, that automatically attaches a sound, plays it, and adjusts the volume level and pan settings based on the parameters you provide. You can even build functions to customize your own classes. Extend the capabilities of predefined Flash classes by creating your own methods and properties for your customized classes. This chapter explores the variety of ways you can manipulate information with added complexity and flexibility and shows you how to integrate the predefined classes you've learned about in previous chapters.

Calculating with the Math Class

The Math class lets you access trigonometric functions such as sine, cosine, and tangent; logarithmic functions; rounding functions; and mathematical constants such as pi and e. **Table 11.1** summarizes the methods and properties of the Math class. As with the Key, Mouse, Selection, and Stage classes, you don't need to instantiate the Math class to call on its methods or properties, and all the Math class's properties are read-only values that are written in all uppercase letters. You precede the method with the class name, Math.

To calculate the square root of 10, for example, you write

var myAnswer = Math.sqrt (10)

The calculated value is put in the variable myAnswer. To use a constant, use similar syntax:

var myCircum = Math.PI * 2 * myRadius

The mathematical constant pi is multiplied by 2 and the variable myRadius, and the result is put into the variable myCircum.

Table 11.1

Methods and Properties of the Math Class	
METHOD OR PROPERTY	**DESCRIPTION**
abs(number)	Calculates the absolute value. Math.abs(-4) returns 4.
acos(number)	Calculates the arc cosine.
asin(number)	Calculates the arc sine.
atan(number)	Calculates the arc tangent.
atan2(y, x)	Calculates the angle (in radians) from the x-axis to a point on the y-axis.
ceil(number)	Rounds the number up to the nearest integer. Math.ceil (2.34) returns 3.
cos(number)	Calculates the cosine of an angle, in radians.
exp(number)	Calculates the exponent of the constant e.
floor(number)	Rounds the number down to the nearest integer. Math.floor (2.34) returns 2.
log(number)	Calculates the natural logarithm.
max(x, y)	Returns the larger of two values. Math.max (2, 7) returns 7.
min(x, y)	Returns the smaller of two values. Math.min (2, 7) returns 2.
pow(base, exponent)	Calculates the exponent of a number.
random()	Returns a random number between 0 and 1 (including 0 but not including 1).
round(number)	Rounds the number to the nearest integer. Math.round (2.34) returns 2.
sin(number)	Calculates the sine of an angle, in radians.
sqrt(number)	Calculates the square root.
tan(number)	Calculates the tangent of an angle, in radians.
E	Euler's constant; the base of natural logarithms.
LN2	The natural logarithm of 2.
LOG2E	The base-2 logarithm of e.
LN10	The natural logarithm of 10.
LOG10E	The base-10 logarithm of e.
PI	The circumference of a circle divided by its diameter.
SQRT1_2	The square root of 1/2.
SQRT2	The square root of 2.

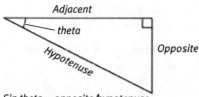

Sin theta = opposite/hypotenuse
Cos theta = adjacent/hypotenuse
Tan theta = opposite/adjacent

Figure 11.1 The angle, theta, of a right triangle is defined by sin, cos, and tan and by the length of the three sides.

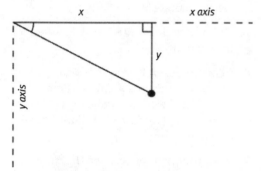

Figure 11.2 A point on the Stage makes a right triangle with *x* (adjacent side) and *y* (opposite side).

Calculating Angles with the Math Class

The angle that an object makes relative to the Stage or to another object is useful information for creating many game interactions, as well as for creating dynamic animations and interfaces based purely in ActionScript. To create a dial that controls the sound volume, for example, you need to compute the angle at which your viewer drags the dial relative to the horizontal or vertical axis and then change the dial's rotation and the sound's volume accordingly. Calculating the angle also requires that you brush up on some of your high-school trigonometry, so a review of some basic principles related to sine, cosine, and tangent is in order.

The mnemonic device SOH CAH TOA can help you keep the trigonometric functions straight. This acronym stands for Sine = Opposite over Hypotenuse, Cosine = Adjacent over Hypotenuse, and Tangent = Opposite over Adjacent (**Figure 11.1**). Knowing the length of any two sides of a right triangle is enough information for you to calculate the other two angles. You will most likely know the lengths of the opposite and adjacent sides of the triangle because they represent the *y* and *x* coordinates of a point (**Figure 11.2**). When you have the *x* and *y* coordinates, you can calculate the angle (theta) by using the following mathematical formulas:

Tan theta = opposite/adjacent

or

Tan theta = y/x

or

theta = ArcTan (y/x)

In Flash, you can write this expression by using the Math class this way:

```
myTheta = Math.atan(this._y/this._x)
```

Alternatively, Flash provides an even easier method that lets you define the y and x positions without having to do the division. The atan2() method accepts the y and x positions as two parameters, so you can write the equivalent statement:

myTheta = Math.atan2(this._y, this._x)

Unfortunately, the trigonometric methods of the Math class require and return values in radians, which describe angles in terms of the constant pi—easier mathematically, but not so convenient if you want to use the values to modify the _rotation property of an object. You can convert an angle from radians to degrees, and vice versa, by using the following formulas:

Radian = Math.PI/180 * degrees
Degrees = radian * 180/Math.PI

The following tasks calculate the angles of a draggable movie clip and display the angles (in degrees) in a dynamic text field.

To calculate the angle relative to the Stage:

1. Create a movie-clip symbol, place an instance of it on the Stage, and give the movie-clip instance a name in the Property Inspector.

   In this example, the movie-clip instance is called circle_mc.

2. Create a dynamic text field on the Stage, choose Single Line in the Property Inspector, and give the dynamic text field an instance name.

   In this example, the text field is called myDegrees_txt.

3. Select the first frame of the main Timeline, and open the Actions panel.

4. Enter the instance name of the movie clip followed by a period.

5. Choose Global Functions > Movie Clip Control > startDrag.

6. With your pointer between the parentheses, enter the Boolean value of true for the lockcenter parameter (**Figure 11.3**).

   The center of the movie clip follows your viewer's pointer.

7. On the next line, enter _root followed by a period.

8. Choose Built-in Classes > Movie > MovieClip > Events > onEnterFrame. Complete the event handler by entering =function(){ and a closing curly brace on the next line.

9. With your pointer between the curly braces of the onEnterFrame event handler, enter a name for a variable that will hold the angle in radians followed by an equals sign.

Figure 11.3 This startDrag action makes the movie clip follow the pointer and centers it on the pointer.

```
circle_mc.startDrag(true);
_root.onEnterFrame = function() {
    myRadians = Math.atan2(circle_mc._y, circle_mc._x);
);
```

Figure 11.4 The Math.atan2() method calculates the angle that the movie clip called circle_mc makes with the origin (top-left corner of the Stage).

```
circle_mc.startDrag(true);
_root.onEnterFrame = function() {
    myRadians = Math.atan2(circle_mc._y, circle_mc._x);
    myDegrees_txt.text = myRadians*180/Math.PI+" degrees";
);
```

Figure 11.5 The dynamic text field called myDegrees_txt displays the angle in degrees.

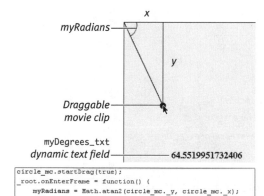

```
circle_mc.startDrag(true);
_root.onEnterFrame = function() {
    myRadians = Math.atan2(circle_mc._y, circle_mc._x);
    myDegrees_txt.text = myRadians*180/Math.PI+" degrees";
);
```

Figure 11.6 The full script as it appears in the Script pane (below). The movie clip makes an angle of approximately 65 degrees below the x-axis. The lines have been drawn in to show the right triangle.

10. Choose Built-in Classes > Core > Math > Methods > atan2.

11. With your pointer between the parentheses of the atan2() method, enter circle_mc._y followed by a comma and then circle_mc._x (**Figure 11.4**).

Flash calculates the arc tangent of the *y* position of the movie clip divided by the *x* position of the movie clip and returns the value in radians.

12. On the next line within the onEnterFrame event handler, enter myDegrees_txt.text followed by an equals sign.

13. Enter an expression that multiplies by 180 your variable that holds the radian angle and divides it by the constant pi:

myRadians * 180/Math.PI

14. Continuing on the same line, concatenate the string "degrees" to the end of the expression.

The angle is converted from radians to degrees and assigned to the contents of the dynamic text field (**Figure 11.5**).

15. Test your movie.

As the viewer moves the pointer around the Stage, the movie clip follows the pointer. Flash calculates the angle that the movie clip makes with the x-axis of the root Timeline and displays the angle (in degrees) in the dynamic text field (**Figure 11.6**).

To calculate the angle relative to another point:

1. Continuing with the file you used in the preceding task, create another movie-clip symbol, place an instance of it on the Stage, and give it a name in the Property Inspector.

   In this example, the name is myReferencePoint_mc.

2. Select first frame of the main Timeline, and open the Actions panel.

3. Select the statement that calculates the angle from the atan2() method, and change the expression to read as follows:

   Math.atan2 ((circle_mc._y –myReferencePoint_mc._y), (circle_mc._x –myReferencePoint_mc._x))

By subtracting the *y* and *x* positions of the reference point from the draggable movie clip's position, Flash calculates the *y* and *x* distances between the two points (**Figure 11.7**).

4. Test your movie.

   As the viewer moves the pointer around the Stage, the movie clip follows the pointer. Flash calculates the angle that the draggable movie clip makes with the stationary movie clip and displays the angle (in degrees) in the dynamic text field.

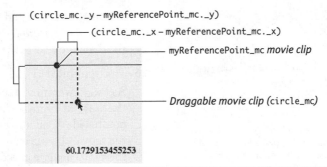

(circle_mc._y – myReferencePoint_mc._y)

(circle_mc._x – myReferencePoint_mc._x)

myReferencePoint_mc *movie clip*

Draggable movie clip (circle_mc)

60.1729153455253

```
circle_mc.startDrag(true);
_root.onEnterFrame = function() {
    myRadians = Math.atan2((circle_mc._y - myReferencePoint_mc._y), (circle_mc._x - myReferencePoint_mc._x));
    myDegrees_txt.text = myRadians*180/Math.PI+" degrees";
};
```

Figure 11.7 The difference between the *y* positions of the circle_mc movie clip and the myReferencePoint_mc movie clip is the *y* parameter for Math.atan2(). The difference between the *x* positions of the circle_mc movie clip and the myReferencePoint_mc movie clip is the *x* parameter for Math.atan2().

So far, the returned values for your angles have had many decimal places. Often, you will need to round those values to the nearest whole number (or integer) so that you can use those values as parameters in methods and properties. Use `Math.round()` to round values to the nearest integer, `Math.ceil()` to round to the closest integer greater than or equal to the value, and `Math.floor()` to round to the closest integer less than or equal to the value.

To round a number to an integer:

1. Continuing with the file you used in the preceding task, select the first frame of the main Timeline, and open the Actions panel.

2. Select the statement that converts the angle from radians to degrees.

3. Place your pointer in front of the expression, and enter the method `Math.round`.

   Use parentheses to group the expression that converts radians to degrees (**Figure 11.8**).

   Flash converts the angle from radians to degrees and then applies the `Math.round()` method to that value, returning an integer.

```
circle_mc.startDrag(true);
_root.onEnterFrame = function() {
    myRadians = Math.atan2((circle_mc._y - myReferencePoint_mc._y), (circle_mc._x - myReferencePoint_mc._x));
    myDegrees_txt.text = Math.round(myRadians*180/Math.PI)+" degrees";
};
```

Figure 11.8 The expression within the parentheses is rounded to the nearest integer and displayed in the dynamic text field called `myDegrees_txt`.

You can apply the methods that calculate angles and round values to create a draggable rotating dial. The approach is to calculate the angle of the mouse's position to the center point of the dial and then set the _rotation property of the dial to the angle.

To create a draggable rotating dial:

1. Create a movie-clip symbol of a dial, place an instance of it on the Stage, and give it a name in the Property Inspector. In this example, the name is myDial_mc (**Figure 11.9**).

2. Select the first frame of the main Timeline, and open the Actions panel.

3. Assign an onPress handler for your movie clip.

4. Within the onPress handler, enter a new variable name called pressing followed by an equals sign.

5. Enter the Boolean value of true (**Figure 11.10**).

6. Assign event handlers for both the onRelease event and the onReleaseOutside event for your movie clip.

7. Within the onRelease and onReleaseOutside handlers, enter pressing followed by an equals sign.

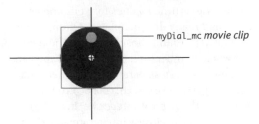

Figure 11.9 Place a circular movie clip called myDial_mc on the Stage.

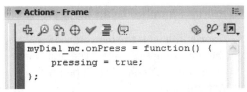

Figure 11.10 Set pressing to true when the button is pressed.

8. Enter the Boolean value of `false` (**Figure 11.11**).

   The variable called **pressing** keeps track of whether your viewer is pressing or not pressing this movie clip.

9. On a new line outside the event handlers, enter **_root** followed by a period.

10. Choose Built-in Classes > Movie > MovieClip > Events > onEnterFrame. Complete the event handler by entering =function(){ and a closing curly brace on the next line.

11. Within the **onEnterFrame** handler, choose Statements > Conditions/Loops > if.

12. For the condition of the `if` statement, enter **pressing == true**.

13. In between the curly braces of the `if` statement, enter a new variable name followed by an equals sign.

14. Enter the following expression:

    `Math.atan2((_ymouse-myDial_mc._y), (_xmouse-myDial_mc._x))`

    Flash calculates the angle between the viewer's pointer and the center of the movie clip (**Figure 11.12**).

15. On the next line, enter a new variable name followed by an equals sign.

continues on next page

```
myDial_mc.onPress = function() {
    pressing = true;
};
myDial_mc.onRelease = myDial_mc.onReleaseOutside=function () {
    pressing = false;
};
```

Figure 11.11 Set pressing to false when the button is either released or released outside the button's hit area.

```
▼ Actions - Frame
myDial_mc.onPress = function() {
    pressing = true;
};
myDial_mc.onRelease = myDial_mc.onReleaseOutside=function () {
    pressing = false;
};
_root.onEnterFrame = function() {
    if (pressing == true) {
        myRadians = Math.atan2((_ymouse-myDial_mc._y), (_xmouse-myDial_mc._x));
    }
};
```

Figure 11.12 The variable myRadians contains the calculated angle between the pointer and the movie clip.

16. Enter an expression to convert radians to degrees and round the result to an integer (**Figure 11.13**).

17. On the next line, enter myDial_mc._rotation followed by an equals sign.

18. Enter your variable that holds the angle in degrees, and add 90.

The rotation of the movie clip is assigned to the calculated angle. The 90 is added to compensate for the difference between the calculated angle and the movie-clip

rotation property. A value of 0 for _rotation corresponds to the 12 o'clock position of a movie clip, but a value of 0 corresponds to the 3 o'clock position of the calculated arcTangent angle, so adding 90 equalizes them (**Figure 11.14**).

19. Test your movie.

When viewers press the button in the dial, they can rotate it by dragging it around its centerpoint. When they release the button, the dial stops rotating. 🕹

```
myDial_mc.onPress = function() {
    pressing = true;
};
myDial_mc.onRelease = myDial_mc.onReleaseOutside=function () {
    pressing = false;
};
_root.onEnterFrame = function() {
    if (pressing == true) {
        myRadians = Math.atan2((_ymouse-myDial_mc._y), (_xmouse-myDial_mc._x));
        myDegrees = Math.round(myRadians*180/Math.PI);
    }
};
```

Figure 11.13 The angle is converted from radians to degrees, rounded to the nearest integer, and assigned to the variable called myDegrees.

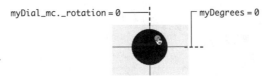

myDial_mc._rotation = 0 ———   ┌ myDegrees = 0

```
myDial_mc.onPress = function() {
    pressing = true;
};
myDial_mc.onRelease = myDial_mc.onReleaseOutside=function () {
    pressing = false;
};
_root.onEnterFrame = function() {
    if (pressing == true) {
        myRadians = Math.atan2((_ymouse-myDial_mc._y), (_xmouse-myDial_mc._x));
        myDegrees = Math.round(myRadians*180/Math.PI);
        myDial_mc._rotation = myDegrees+90;
    }
};
```

Figure 11.14 The final statement within the if statement modifies the rotation of the myDial_mc movie clip. The rotation of myDial_mc is set at myDegrees+90 to account for the difference between the reference point of the trigonometric functions and Flash's _rotation property.

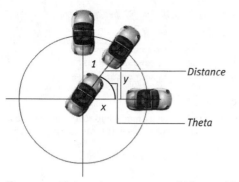

Figure 11.15 The *x* and *y* components of this car, which moves a certain distance, are determined by the cosine and sine of its angle, theta.

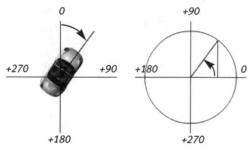

Figure 11.16 The rotation property of a movie clip begins from the vertical axis and increases in the clockwise direction (left). Values for sine and cosine angles begin from the horizontal axis and increase in the counterclockwise direction (right).

Using Sine and Cosine for Directional Movement

When you want to control how far an object on the Stage travels based on its angle, you can use the sine and cosine trigonometric functions. Suppose that you want to create a racing game featuring a car that your viewer moves around a track. The car travels at a certain speed, and it moves according to where the front of the car is pointed.

Calculating just how far the car moves in any direction requires the `Math.sin()` and `Math.cos()` methods of the Math class. The new location of the car is determined by the *x* and *y* components of the triangle that is formed by the angle of the car. When the car is angled up, the *y* component is 1 and the *x* component is 0. When the car is angled to the right, the *y* component is 0 and the *x* component is 1. When the car is angled somewhere between up and right, the sine and cosine of the angle give you the *x* and *y* contributions (**Figure 11.15**). The sine of the angle determines the magnitude of the *y* component, and the cosine of the angle determines the magnitude of the *x* component. Sine and cosine, however, are based on angles that begin at 0 degrees from the horizontal axis. The rotation property, on the other hand, is based on angles that begin at 0 degrees from the vertical axis (**Figure 11.16**). Moreover, the *y* component for the sine function is positive above the origin of the circle and negative below it. When you deal with a movie clip's coordinate space, you must do two transformations: Subtract the rotation property from 90 to get the angle for sine and cosine, and then use the negative value of sine for the change in the *y* direction:

```
myCar_mc._x += Math.cos(90-rotation);
myCar_mc._y += -Math.sin(90-rotation);
```

In the following task, you will create a movie clip whose rotation can be controlled by the viewer. The movie clip has a constant velocity, so it will travel in the direction in which it is pointed, just as a car moves according to where it is steered.

To create a controllable object with directional movement:

1. Create a movie-clip symbol, place an instance of it on the Stage, and name it in the Property Inspector.

   In this example, the name is car_mc.

2. Select the first frame of the main Timeline, and open the Actions panel.

3. Enter _root followed by a period.

4. Choose Built-in Classes > Movie > MovieClip > Events > onEnterFrame. Complete the event handler by entering =function(){ and a closing curly brace on the next line.

5. On the next line, choose Statements > Conditions/Loops > if.

6. For the condition of the if statement, enter the following:

   Key.isDown (Key.LEFT)

   Flash checks to see whether the left arrow key is pressed.

7. On the next line of the if statement, enter car_mc._rotation -= 10;

   Flash subtracts 10 from the current rotation property of the movie-clip car when the left arrow key is pressed (**Figure 11.17**).

8. With your pointer after the closing curly brace for the if statement, choose Statements > Conditions/Loops > else if. Delete the extra opening curly brace that's inserted before the else if statement.

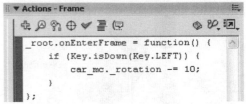

Figure 11.17 The car_mc movie clip rotates 10 degrees counterclockwise when the left arrow key is pressed.

```
▼ Actions - Frame
⊹ ⌗ ↻ ⊕ ✔ ☰ ⟨₽          ◈ ಐ ⃢
_root.onEnterFrame = function() {
    if (Key.isDown(Key.LEFT)) {
        car_mc._rotation -= 10;
    } else if (Key.isDown(Key.RIGHT)) {
        car_mc._rotation += 10;
    }
};
```
Figure 11.18 The car_mc movie clip rotates 10 degrees clockwise when the right arrow key is pressed.

```
▼ Actions - Frame
⊹ ⌗ ↻ ⊕ ✔ ☰ ⟨₽          ◈ ಐ ⃢
_root.onEnterFrame = function() {
    if (Key.isDown(Key.LEFT)) {
        car_mc._rotation -= 10;
    } else if (Key.isDown(Key.RIGHT)) {
        car_mc._rotation += 10;
    }
    myAngle = 90 - car_mc._rotation;
};
```
Figure 11.19 The variable myAngle will be used as the angle for sine and cosine.

```
▼ Actions - Frame
⊹ ⌗ ↻ ⊕ ✔ ☰ ⟨₽          ◈ ಐ ⃢
_root.onEnterFrame = function() {
    if (Key.isDown(Key.LEFT)) {
        car_mc._rotation -= 10;
    } else if (Key.isDown(Key.RIGHT)) {
        car_mc._rotation += 10;
    }
    myAngle = 90 - car_mc._rotation;
    xchange = Math.cos(Math.PI/180*myAngle)*5;
};
```
Figure 11.20 The cosine of the movie clip's angle is calculated and assigned to xchange.

9. Between the parentheses of the else if statement, enter the following:

Key.isDown (Key.RIGHT)

Flash checks to see whether the right arrow key is pressed.

10. On the next line of the else if statement, enter car_mc._rotation += 10.

Flash adds 10 to the current rotation property of the movie-clip car when the right arrow key is pressed (**Figure 11.18**).

11. On a new line, after the closing brace of the else if action, create a new variable called myAngle, and then add an equals sign.

12. Enter the following expression: 90 – car_mc._rotation (**Figure 11.19**).

When you subtract the rotation property of the movie clip from 90, you get the equivalent angle for use in the sine and cosine functions.

13. On the next line, enter the variable name xchange followed by an equals sign.

14. Choose Built-in Classes > Core > Math > Methods > cos.

The Math.cos() method appears.

15. Between the parentheses of the Math.cos() method, enter an expression to convert myAngle from degrees to radians; multiply the entire expression by 5 (**Figure 11.20**).

The variable xchange represents the magnitude of the x component. Multiplying by 5 increases the magnitude of the change so that the movie clip moves a little faster in the x direction.

continues on next page

SINE AND COSINE FOR DIRECTIONAL MOVEMENT

16. On a new line, enter the variable name ychange followed by an equals sign.

17. Choose Built-in Classes > Core > Math > Methods > sin.

The Math.sin() method appears.

18. Between the parentheses of the Math.sin() method, enter an expression to convert myAngle from degrees to radians; multiply the entire expression by 5 and make it negative by placing a minus sign in front of the expression (**Figure 11.21**).

The variable ychange represents the magnitude of the *y* component. Multiplying by 5 increases the magnitude of the change so that the movie clip moves a little faster in the *y* direction. You must use the negative value for the change in the *y* direction to compensate for the discrepancy between the coordinate space for sine and the coordinate space for the movie clip.

19. On the next line, enter car_mc._x += xchange.

Flash adds the value of xchange to the current *x* position of the movie clip.

20. On the next line, enter car_mc._y += ychange.

Flash adds the value of ychange to the current *y* position of the movie clip.

21. Test your movie.

When your viewer presses the left or right arrow key, the rotation of the movie clip changes. The *x* and *y* positions change as well, calculated from the angle of the movie clip. The movie clip moves according to where the nose of the car is pointed (**Figure 11.22**).

```
▼ Actions - Frame
_root.onEnterFrame = function() {
    if (Key.isDown(Key.LEFT)) {
        car_mc._rotation -= 10;
    } else if (Key.isDown(Key.RIGHT)) {
        car_mc._rotation += 10;
    }
    myAngle = 90 - car_mc._rotation;
    xchange = Math.cos(Math.PI/180*myAngle)*5;
    ychange = -Math.sin(Math.PI/180*myAngle)*5;
};
```

Figure 11.21 The negative sine of the movie clip's angle is calculated and assigned to ychange.

```
_root.onEnterFrame = function() {
    if (Key.isDown(Key.LEFT)) {
        car_mc._rotation -= 10;
    } else if (Key.isDown(Key.RIGHT)) {
        car_mc._rotation += 10;
    }
    myAngle = 90 - car_mc._rotation;
    xchange = Math.cos(Math.PI/180*myAngle)*5;
    ychange = -Math.sin(Math.PI/180*myAngle)*5;
    car_mc._x += xchange;
    car_mc._y += ychange;
};
```

Figure 11.22 The final script is shown at the bottom. As the movie clip of the car rotates, the *x* and *y* components are calculated from cosine and sine and the car's new position is defined.

SINE AND COSINE FOR DIRECTIONAL MOVEMENT

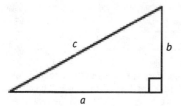

Figure 11.23 This right triangle has sides a, b, and c.

Calculating Distances with the Math Class

Using the Pythagorean theorem, Flash makes it possible for you to calculate the distance between two objects. This technique can be useful for creating novel interactions among interface elements—graphics, buttons, or sounds whose reactions depend on their distance from the viewer's pointer, for example. You can also create games that have interaction based on the distance between objects and the player. A game in which the player uses a net to catch goldfish in an aquarium, for example, can use the distance between the goldfish and the net to model the behavior of the goldfish. Perhaps the closer the net comes to a goldfish, the quicker the goldfish swims away.

The distance between any two points is defined by the equation

$$a^2 + b^2 = c^2$$

or

c = square root $(a^2 + b^2)$

The variables a and b are the lengths of the sides of a right triangle, and c is the length of the hypotenuse (**Figure 11.23**). Using Flash's Math.sqrt() and Math.pow() methods, you can calculate the distance between the points on the hypotenuse with the following expression:

c = Math.sqrt ((Math.pow (a, 2)) + (Math.pow (b, 2)))

To calculate the distance between the pointer and another point:

1. Create a movie clip, place an instance of it on the Stage, and give it a name in the Property Inspector.

   In this example, the name is myReference_mc.

2. Select the first frame of the main Timeline, and open the Actions panel.

3. Enter _root followed by a period.

4. Choose Built-in Classes > Movie > Mouse > Listeners > onMouseMove.

5. Within the onMouseMove handler, enter xDistance followed by an equals sign.

6. Enter the following:

   _xmouse – myReference_mc._x

   The distance between the *x* position of the pointer and the *x* position of the movie clip is assigned to the variable xDistance (**Figure 11.24**).

7. On a new line, enter yDistance followed by an equals sign.

8. Enter the following:

   _ymouse – myReference._y

   The distance between the *y* position of the pointer and the *y* position of the movie clip is assigned to the variable yDistance (**Figure 11.25**).

9. On the next line, enter the name myDistance followed by an equals sign.

10. Choose Built-in Classes > Core > Math > Methods > sqrt.

    The Math.sqrt() method appears.

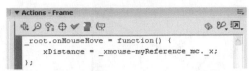

Figure 11.24 The difference between the *x* position of the pointer and the *x* position of the movie clip called myReference_mc is the distance between them on the x-axis.

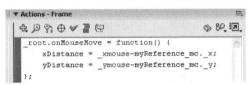

Figure 11.25 The difference between the *y* position of the pointer and the *y* position of the movie clip called myReference_mc is the distance between them on the y-axis.

11. With your pointer between the parentheses of the `Math.sqrt()` method, choose Built-in Classes > Core > Math > Methods > pow.

12. Enter `xDistance` and 2 as the parameters of the `Math.pow()` method.

13. Add another `Math.pow()` method with the parameters `yDistance` and 2 (**Figure 11.26**).

    Flash calculates the square of `xDistance` and adds it to the square of `yDistance`; then it calculates the square root of that sum.

14. Create a dynamic text field on the Stage, and give it an instance name.

15. On the next available line within the `onMouseMove` event handler, assign the value of `myDistance` to the `text` property of the dynamic text field on the Stage (**Figure 11.27**).

16. Test your movie.

    As the pointer moves around the movie clip, Flash calculates the distance between points in pixels.

```
▼ Actions - Frame
_root.onMouseMove = function() {
    xDistance = _xmouse-myReference_mc._x;
    yDistance = _ymouse-myReference_mc._y;
    myDistance = Math.sqrt(Math.pow(xDistance, 2) + Math.pow(yDistance, 2));
};
```

Figure 11.26 The distance between the two points is calculated from the variables `xDistance` and `yDistance`.

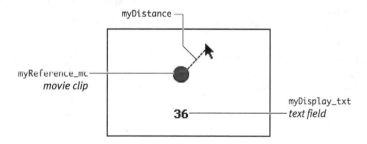

```
_root.onMouseMove = function() {
    xDistance = _xmouse-myReference_mc._x;
    yDistance = _ymouse-myReference_mc._y;
    myDistance = Math.sqrt(Math.pow(xDistance, 2) + Math.pow(yDistance, 2));
    myDisplay_txt.text = Math.round(myDistance);
};
```

Figure 11.27 The full script is shown at the bottom. The dynamic text field called `myDisplay_txt` displays an integer of `myDistance`.

Generating Random Numbers

When you need to incorporate random elements into your Flash movie, either for a design effect or for game play, you can use the Math class's `Math.random()` method. The `Math.random()` method generates random numbers between 0 and 1 (including 0 but not including 1) with up to 15 decimal places in between. Typical return values are

`0.242343544598273`

`0.043628738493829`

`0.7567833408654`

You can modify the random number by multiplying it or adding to it to get the span of numbers you need. If you need random numbers between 1 and 10, for example, multiply the return value of `Math.random()` by 9 and then add 1, as in the following statement:

`Math.random() * 9 + 1`

You will always multiply `Math.random()` by a number to get your desired range and then add or subtract a number to change the minimum and maximum values of that range. If you need an integer, apply the `Math.round()` method to round the number to the nearest integer.

To generate a random number:

1. Create a button symbol, and place an instance of it on the Stage. In the Property Inspector, give it an instance name.

2. Create a dynamic text field, and give it an instance name in the Property Inspector.

3. Select the first frame of the main Timeline, and open the Actions panel.

4. Assign an `onRelease` event handler to your button.

5. With your pointer between the curly braces of the `onRelease` event handler, enter the name of your text field followed by a period, the `text` property, and an equals sign.

6. Choose Built-in Classes > Core > Math > Methods > random.

   The `Math.random()` method appears (**Figure 11.28**).

   When you click the button, a new random number between 0 and 1 is generated and displayed in the dynamic text field.

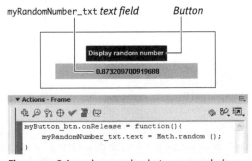

Figure 11.28 A random number between 0 and 1 is displayed in the text field called myRandomNumber_txt when the button is clicked.

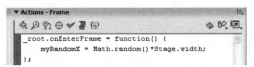

Figure 11.29 A random number between 0 and the width of the Stage is assigned to the variable myRandomX.

Use randomly generated numbers to add unpredictable animated elements to your movie. Enemy ships in an arcade game could appear anywhere to attack the player. You can make Flash deal random cards from a deck of cards so that every hand is different. Or for a test, you can shuffle the order in which the questions appear. The following task demonstrates how random numbers can modify property values by setting the *x* and *y* properties of a movie clip.

To use random numbers as property values:

1. Create a movie-clip symbol, place an instance of it on the Stage, and give it a name in the Property Inspector.

2. Select the first frame of the main Timeline, and open the Actions panel.

3. Enter _root followed by a period.

4. Choose Built-in Classes > Movie > MovieClip > Events > onEnterFrame. Complete the event handler by entering =function(){ and a closing curly brace on the next line.

5. On the next line of the onEnterFrame event handler, enter a variable name followed by an equals sign.

6. Enter Math.random () * Stage.width.

   Flash generates a random number between 0 and the width of the current Stage (**Figure 11.29**).

7. On the next line, assign a second variable to a random number between 0 and the height of the Stage.

   continues on next page

8. On a new line, enter the *x* position of your movie clip followed by an equals sign and the first randomly generated number (**Figure 11.30**).

The movie clip's *x* position is set to the first random number.

9. On the next line, enter the *y* position of your movie clip followed by an equals sign.

10. Enter the variable name for the second randomly generated number.

The movie clip's *y* position is set to the second random number (**Figure 11.31**).

11. Test your movie.

The *x* and *y* positions of your movie clip are set randomly, making your movie clip jump around the Stage. 🐭

✔ Tips

■ The Math.random() method replaces the random action used in earlier versions of Flash. Although the random action still works, it is deprecated, so you should stick to using the Math class to generate your random numbers.

■ Although most properties, such as _x and _y, can accept noninteger values that are generated from the Math.random() method (as in the preceding example), some properties require integers (or whole numbers—that is, numbers without fractions or decimals). The _currentFrame property, which determines the current frame number of a Timeline, must be given as an integer. Use the Math.round() method to convert a fraction to an integer and then apply it to the _currentFrame property.

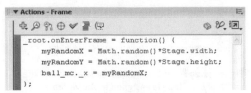

Figure 11.30 The *x* position of the movie clip is set to *myRandomX*.

ball_mc *movie clip*

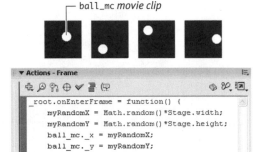

Figure 11.31 The *y* position of the movie clip is set to *myRandomY*. The movie clip changes its position on the Stage randomly (top).

Index	Value
0	"monitor"
1	"mouse"
2	"keyboard"
3	"CPU"
4	"modem"
5	"speakers"

Figure 11.32 An array is like a two-column table with an Index column and a corresponding Value column.

Ordering Information with Arrays

When you have many pieces of related information that you want to store, you may need to use the Array class to help arrange it. *Arrays* are containers that hold data, just as variables do, except that arrays hold data in a specific sequence. The position of each piece of data is called its *index*. Indexes are numbered sequentially, beginning at 0, so that each piece of data corresponds to an index, as in a two-column table (**Figure 11.32**). Because each piece of data is ordered numerically, you can retrieve and modify the information easily—and, most important, automatically—just by referencing its index. Suppose that you're building an address book of a list of your important contacts. You can store names in an array so that index 0 holds your first contact, index 1 holds your second contact, and so on. By using a looping statement, you can quickly check every entry in the array automatically.

The indexes of an array are referenced with the square bracket, as in the following:

`myArray[4]`

The square brackets are known as *array access operators*. This statement accesses the data in index 4 of the array called `myArray`. The number of entries defines the length of an array, so the length of the array in Figure 11.32 is 6. You can think of an array as being a sequence of ordered variables. You could convert the variables `myScores0`, `myScores1`, `myScores2`, and `myScores3` to a single array called `myScores` of length 4 with indices from 0 to 3. Because you have to handle only one array object instead of four separate variables, using arrays makes information easier to manage.

The data that arrays hold can be mixed. So you could have a number in index 0, a string in index 1, and a Boolean value in index 2. You can change the data in any index in an array at any time, just as you can with variables. The length of arrays is not fixed, either, so arrays can grow or shrink to accommodate new information as needed.

Creating an array involves two steps. The first is to use a constructor function to instantiate a new array from the Array class, as in this example:

```
myArray_array = new Array()
```

The second step is to fill, or *populate*, your array with data. One way to populate your array is to assign the data to each index in separate statements, like this:

```
myArray_array[0] = "Russell";
myArray_array[1] = "Rebecca";
myArray_array[2] = "Clint";
myArray_array[3] = "Kathy";
```

Another way to assign the data is to put the information as parameters within the constructor function:

```
myArray_array = new Array ("Russell",
"Rebecca", "Clint", "Kathy")
```

The second way is a more compact way of populating your array, but you are restricted to entering data in sequence.

To create an array:

1. Select the first keyframe of the Timeline, and open the Actions panel.

2. Enter a name for your array followed by an equals sign.

3. Choose Built-in Classes > Core > Array > new Array.

   Flash instantiates a new array (**Figure 11.33**).

4. On the next line, enter the name of your new array, with an index number between its square brackets, followed by an equals sign.

5. Enter the data you want to store in the array at that index position (**Figure 11.34**).

6. Continue to assign more data to the array.

```
▼ Actions - Frame
my_array = new Array();
```

Figure 11.33 A new array called my_array is instantiated.

```
▼ Actions - Frame
my_array = new Array();
my_array[0] = 10;
my_array[1] = 15;
my_array[2] = 35;
```

Figure 11.34 This array contains three entries.

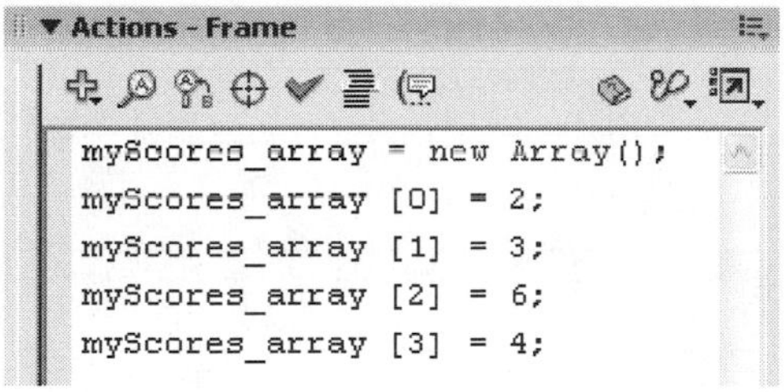

Figure 11.35 This array, called `myScores_array`, has four entries.

Because the entries contained in arrays are indexed numerically, they lend themselves nicely to looping actions. By using looping actions such as `while`, `do while`, and `for`, you can have Flash go through each index and retrieve or assign new data quickly and automatically. To average the scores of many players in an array without a looping action, for example, you would have to total all their scores and divide by the number of players, like this:

```
mySum = myScores[0] + myScores[1] +
myScores[2] + ...
myAverage = mySum/myScores.length;
```

The property `length` defines the number of entries in the array.

Using a looping action, however, you can calculate the `mySum` value this way:

```
for (i=0; i<myScores.length; i++) {
    mySum = mySum + myScores[i];
}
myAverage = mySum/myScores.length;
```

Flash starts at index 0 and adds each indexed entry in the array to the variable `mySum` until it reaches the end of the array.

To loop through an array:

1. Select the first keyframe of the Timeline, and open the Actions panel.

2. Instantiate a new array called `myScores_array`.

3. Populate your `myScores_array` array with numbers representing scores (**Figure 11.35**).

4. Create a button symbol, and place an instance of the button on the Stage. In the Property Inspector, give the button an instance name.

5. Select the first keyframe of the Timeline. On the next available line in the Actions panel, create an `onRelease` event handler.

continues on next page

ORDERING INFORMATION WITH ARRAYS

6. Within the `onRelease` event handler, initialize a variable called mySum to 0.

7. On the next line, choose Statements > Conditions/Loops > for.

8. With your pointer between the parentheses, enter the following:

    i=0; i<myScores_array.length; i++

    Flash begins with the counter variable i set at the value 0. It increases the variable by increments of 1 until the variable reaches the length of the array called myScores_array (**Figure 11.36**).

9. As the action for the `for` loop, enter mySum followed by an equals sign.

10. Enter mySum+myScores_array[i].

    Flash adds the value in each index of the mySCore array to mySum. When the value of i reaches the value of myScores_array.length, Flash jumps out of the `for` loop and stops adding any more index values. Therefore, the last addition is myScores_array[myScores_array.length-1], which corresponds to the last index of the array (**Figure 11.37**).

11. On the next line after the ending curly brace of the `for` statement, enter myAverage_txt.text =.

12. Enter the expression mySum/myScores_array.length (**Figure 11.38**).

13. Create a dynamic text field on the Stage with the instance name myAverage_txt.

14. Test your movie.

    When you click the button on the Stage, Flash loops through the myScores_array array to add all the data entries and divides the total by the number of entries. The average is displayed in the dynamic text field on the Stage. (⬤)

Figure 11.36 This `for` action loops the same number of times as there are entries in the array myScore_array.

```
scores_btn.onRelease = function() {
    var mySum = 0;
    for (i=0; i<myScores_array.length; i++) {
        mySum = mySum+myScores_array[i];
    }
};
```

Figure 11.37 The value of each entry in the array is added to the variable mySum.

```
scores_btn.onRelease = function() {
    var mySum = 0;
    for (i=0; i<myScores_array.length; i++) {
        mySum = mySum+myScores_array[i];
    }
    myAverage_txt.text = mySum/myScores_array.length;
};
```

Figure 11.38 Outside the `for` loop, the average value of the entries in the array is calculated and displayed in the text field called myAverage_txt.

ORDERING INFORMATION WITH ARRAYS

The methods of the Array class let you sort, delete, add, and manipulate the data in an array. **Table 11.2** summarizes the methods of the Array class. It's convenient to think of the methods in pairs: shift() and unshift(), for example, both modify the beginning of an array; push() and pop() both modify the end of an array; and slice() and splice() both modify the middle of an array.

Table 11.2

Methods of the Array Object

METHOD	DESCRIPTION
concat(array1,…,arrayN)	Concatenates the specified values and returns a new array.
join(separator)	Concatenates the elements of the array, inserts the separator between the elements, and returns a string. The default separator is a comma.
pop()	Removes the last element in the array and returns the value of that element.
push(value)	Adds elements to the end of the array and returns the new length.
shift()	Removes the first element in the array and returns the value of that element.
unshift(value)	Adds elements to the beginning of the array and returns the new length.
slice(indexA,indexB)	Returns a new array beginning with indexA and ending with (indexB-1).
splice(index,count,elem1,…,elemN)	Inserts or deletes elements. Set count to o to insert specified values starting at index. Set count > o to delete the number of elements starting at and including index.
reverse()	Reverses the order of elements in the array.
sort()	Sorts an array by using the < operator. Numbers are sorted in ascending order, and strings are sorted alphabetically.
sortOn(fieldName)	Sorts an array based on the fieldName parameter.
toString()	Returns a string with every element concatenated and separated by a comma.

Following is an example of how some of these methods operate:

STATEMENT	VALUE OF MYARRAY
myArray = new Array(2,4,6,8)	2, 4, 6, 8
myArray.pop()	2, 4, 6
myArray.push(1,3)	2, 4, 6, 1, 3
myArray.shift()	4, 6, 1, 3
myArray.unshift(5,7)	5, 7, 4, 6, 1, 3
myArray.splice(2,0,8,9)	5, 7, 8, 9, 4, 6, 1, 3
myArray.splice(3,2)	5, 7, 8, 6, 1, 3
myArray.reverse()	3, 1, 6, 8, 7, 5
myArray.sort()	1, 3, 5, 6, 7, 8

✔ Tips

- It's important to note which methods of the Array class modify the original array and which ones return a new array. concat(), join(), slice(), and toString() return a new array or string and do not alter the original array. new_array = original_array.concat(8), for example, puts 8 at the end of original_array and assigns the resulting array to new_array. original_array is not affected. Also note that some methods modify the array as well as return a specific value. These two things are not the same. The statement my_array.pop(), for example, modifies my_array by removing the last element and also returns the value of that last element. So in the example

  my_array = new Array (2, 4, 6, 8);
  myPop_array = my_array.pop();

  the value of myPop_array is 8, and the value of my_array is now 2, 4, 6.

- An easy way to remember the duties of some of these methods is to think of the elements of your array as being components of a stack. (In fact, *stack* is the programmer's term.) An array is often thought of as being like a stack of books or a stack of cafeteria trays on a spring-loaded holder. The bottom of the stack is the first element in an array. When you push an array, imagine that you literally push a new tray on top of the stack to add a new element. When you pop an array, you "pop," or remove, the top tray from the stack (the last element). When you shift an array, you take out the bottom tray (the first element) so that all the other trays shift down into new positions.

Two-Dimensional Arrays

We've compared an array with a two-column table, in which the index is in one column and its contents are in a second column. What if you need to keep track of information stored in more than one row in a table, as you would in a traditional spreadsheet? The solution is to nest an array inside another one to create what's known as a two-dimensional array. This type of array creates two indexes for every piece of information. To keep track of a checker piece on a checkerboard, for example, you can use a two-dimensional array to reference its row and its column (**Figure 11.39**).

For the three rows, create three separate arrays and populate them with numbers:

```
Row0_array = new Array(1,2,3)
Row1_array = new Array(4,5,6)
Row2_array = new Array(7,8,9)
```

Now you can put those three arrays inside another array, like so:

```
gameBoard_array = new Array()
gameBoard_array[0] = Row0_array
gameBoard_array[1] = Row1_array
gameBoard_array[2] = Row2_array
```

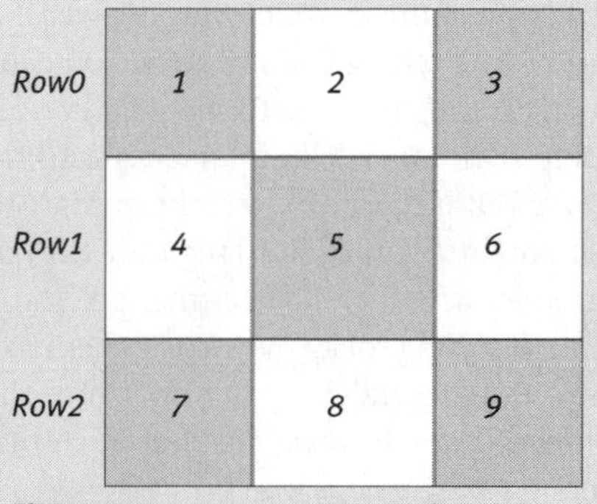

Row0	1	2	3
Row1	4	5	6
Row2	7	8	9

Figure 11.39 You can use a two-dimensional array to map a simple checkerboard and keep track of what's inside individual squares. Each row is an array. The rows are put inside another array.

To access or modify the information of a checkerboard square, first use one set of square brackets that references the row. The statement `gameBoard_array[2]` references the array called Row2_array. Then, by using another set of square brackets, you can reference the column within that row. So the statement `gameBoard_array[2][0]` accesses the number 7.

Keeping Track of Movie Clips with Arrays

Sometimes, you'll have to deal with many movie clips on the Stage at the same time. Keeping track of them all and performing actions to modify, test, or evaluate each one can be a nightmare unless you use arrays to help manage them all. Imagine that you are creating a game in which your viewer has to avoid rocks falling from the sky. You can use the `hitTest()` method to see whether each falling-rock movie clip intersects with the viewer. But if there are 10 rocks on the Stage, that potentially means 10 separate `hitTest()` statements. You can better manage the multiple falling rocks by putting them in an array. Doing so allows you to perform the `hitTest()` on one array instead of on many separate movie clips.

Put a movie clip into an array by referencing its name with array access operators, like so:

```
rock_array[0]=_root["fallingRock0_mc"]
rock_array[1]=_root["fallingRock1_mc"]
rock_array[2]=_root["fallingRock2_mc"]
```

These statements put the movie clip called `fallingRock0_mc` in index 0 of the array called `rock_array`, the movie clip called `fallingRock1_mc` in index 1, and the movie clip called `fallingRock2_mc` in index2. Now you can reference the movie clips through the array. This statement changes the transparency of the movie clip `fallingRock2_mc`:

```
rock_array[2]._alpha = 40
```

You can even call methods this way:

```
rock_array[2].hitTest(_xmouse, _ymouse, true)
```

This statement checks to see whether the `fallingRock2_mc` movie clip intersects with the mouse pointer.

The following examples combine looping statements to populate an array with movie clips automatically. When the array is full of movie clips, you can perform the same action, such as modifying a property or calling the `hitTest()`, on all the movie clips by referencing the array.

To populate an array with duplicate movie clips:

1. Create a movie-clip symbol, place an instance of it on the Stage, and give it a name in the Property Inspector.

   In this example, the name is `block_mc`.

2. Select the first frame of the main Timeline, and open the Actions panel.

3. Enter a name for your array followed by an equals sign.

4. Choose Built-in Classes > Core > Array > new Array.

   Your array object is instantiated (**Figure 11.40**).

5. On the next line, choose Statements > Conditions/Loops > for.

Figure 11.40 A new array called `blockArray_array` is instantiated.

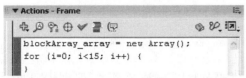

Figure 11.41 Create a for statement that uses a counter that begins at 0 and ends at 14, increasing by 1 with each loop.

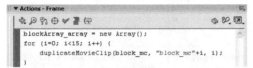

Figure 11.42 The movie clip called block_mc on the Stage is duplicated and automatically given a new name based on the loop variable i.

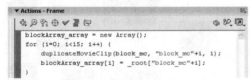

Figure 11.43 Each duplicate is referenced dynamically with the square brackets (on the right-hand side of the equals sign) and put in blockArray_array. The movie clip block_mc0 is in blockArray_array[0], the movie clip block_mc1 is in blockArray_array[1], and so on.

6. With your pointer between the parentheses, enter i=0; i<15; i++ (**Figure 11.41**).

This loop will occur 15 times, starting when i=0 and ending when i=14.

7. Inside the for statement, choose Global Functions > Movie Clip Control > duplicateMovieClip.

8. For the parameters of duplicateMovieClip, enter block_mc (the name of your movie clip), "block_mc"+i, and finally, i (**Figure 11.42**).

Flash duplicates the block_mc movie clip and gives each duplicate a unique name based on the variable i. The first duplicate is called block_mc0, the second is called block_mc1, and so on.

9. On the next line, enter the following:

blockArray_array[i] = _root.["block_mc"+i]

Each new duplicate is put inside a different index of your array (**Figure 11.43**).

Now that your array is populated with movie clips, you can reference them easily with just the array's index value to change their property.

To reference movie clips inside an array (part 1, modify properties):

1. Continuing with the file you created in the preceding task, select the main Timeline, and open the Actions panel.

2. Create a new line within the `for` statement.

   Your next statement will still appear within the `for` statement, but after the duplicates are made and placed inside your array.

3. Enter `blockArray_array[i]._x = Math.random()*Stage.width` (**Figure 11.44**).

   A random number from 0 to the width of the current Stage is generated and assigned to the x position of every movie clip inside `blockArray_array`.

4. On a new line, enter `blockArray[i]._y = Math.random()*Stage.height` (**Figure 11.45**).

   A random number from 0 to the height of the current Stage is generated and assigned to the y position of every movie clip inside `blockArray_array`.

5. Test your movie.

   The `for` loop generates duplicate movie clips automatically and puts them inside your array. At the same time, it references the movie clips inside the array and changes their x and y positions based on a random number (**Figure 11.46**).

```
for (i=0; i<15; i++) {
    duplicateMovieClip(block_mc, "block_mc"+i, i);
    blockArray_array[i] = _root["block_mc"+i];
    blockArray_array[i]._x = Math.random()*Stage.width;
}
```

Figure 11.44 The x position of each movie clip inside `blockArray_array` is randomized.

```
for (i=0; i<15; i++) {
    duplicateMovieClip(block_mc, "block_mc"+i, i);
    blockArray_array[i] = _root["block_mc"+i];
    blockArray_array[i]._x = Math.random()*Stage.width;
    blockArray_array[i]._y = Math.random()*Stage.height;
}
```

Figure 11.45 The y position of each movie clip inside `blockArray_array` is randomized.

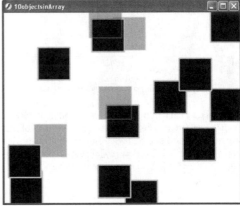

```
blockArray_array = new Array();
for (i=0; i<15; i++) {
    duplicateMovieClip(block_mc, "block_mc"+i, i);
    blockArray_array[i] = _root["block_mc"+i];
    blockArray_array[i]._x = Math.random()*Stage.width;
    blockArray_array[i]._y = Math.random()*Stage.height;
}
```

Figure 11.46 The full script is shown at the bottom. The duplicate movie clips scatter randomly within the boundaries of your Stage.

```
_root.onEnterFrame = function() {
    for (i=0; i<15; i++) {
    }
};
```

Figure 11.47 Enter the same loop parameters for the `for` loop as you did for the first loop that generated your duplicates.

Now you'll check to see whether the viewer's pointer touches any of the movie-clip duplicates. Instead of checking each duplicate separately, you loop through the array again and check all the duplicates at the same time.

To reference movie clips inside an array (part 2, call a method):

1. Continuing with the file you used in the preceding task, select the main Timeline, and open the Actions panel.

2. On a new line after the `for` statement, enter _root.and create an `onEnterFrame` handler.

3. On for a new line inside the `onEnterFrame` event handler, choose Statements > Conditions/Loops > for.

4. With your pointer between the parentheses, enter i=0; i<15; i++ (**Figure 11.47**).

5. On the next line, choose Statements > Conditions/Loops > if.

6. For the condition, enter `blockArray_array[i]` to reference each movie clip inside the array.

7. Choose Built-in Classes > Movie > MovieClip > Methods > hitTest.

8. Between the parentheses of the `hitTest()` method, enter the parameters _xmouse, _ymouse, and `true` (**Figure 11.48**).

continues on next page

```
_root.onEnterFrame = function() {
    for (i=0; i<15; i++) {
        if (blockArray_array[i].hitTest(_xmouse, _ymouse, true)) {
        }
    }
};
```

Figure 11.48 Flash checks every movie clip inside blockArray_array to see whether the clips intersect with the mouse pointer.

9. Choose a consequence for the if statement.

For this example, enter blockArray_array[i]._alpha = 30 (**Figure 11.49**).

10. Test your movie.

When the for loop is performed, all the movie clips inside blockArray_array are tested to see whether they intersect with the pointer. Because the for loop is within an onEnterFrame handler, this checking is done continuously. If a positive intersection occurs, that particular movie clip turns 30 percent transparent (**Figure 11.50**).

```
blockArray_array = new Array();
for (i=0; i<15; i++) {
    duplicateMovieClip(block_mc, "block_mc"+i, i);
    blockArray_array[i] = _root["block_mc"+i];
    blockArray_array[i]._x = Math.random()*Stage.width;
    blockArray_array[i]._y = Math.random()*Stage.height;
}
_root.onEnterFrame = function() {
    for (i=0; i<15; i++) {
        if (blockArray_array[i].hitTest(_xmouse, _ymouse, true)) {
            blockArray_array[i]._alpha = 30;
        }
    }
};
```

Figure 11.49 The full script. If Flash detects an intersection between a movie clip and your pointer, that particular movie clip changes transparency.

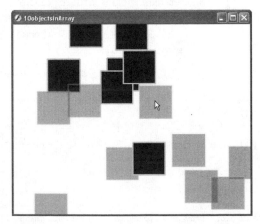

Figure 11.50 The pointer has passed over many of the movie clips, which have turned semi-transparent. Use this technique to manage multiple movie clips for game interactivity.

Table 11.3

Methods of the Date Class	
METHOD	DESCRIPTION
getDate()	Returns the day of the month as a number from 1 to 31.
getDay()	Returns the day of the week as a number from 0 (Sunday) to 6 (Saturday).
getFullYear()	Returns the year as a four-digit number.
getHours()	Returns the hour of the day as a number from 0 to 23.
getMilliseconds()	Returns the milliseconds.
getMinutes()	Returns the minutes as a number from 0 to 59.
getMonth()	Returns the month as a number from 0 (January) to 11 (December).
getSeconds()	Returns the seconds as a number from 0 to 59.

Using the Date and Time

The Date class lets you retrieve the local or universal (GMT) date and time information from the clock in your viewer's computer system. Using a date object, you can retrieve the year, month, date, day of the week, hour, minute, second, and millisecond. Use a date object and its methods to create accurate clocks in your movie or to find information about certain days and dates in the past. You can create a date object for your birthday, for example, by specifying the month, date, and year. Using methods of the Date class, you can retrieve the day of the week for your date object that tells you what day you were born.

First, you need to instantiate the Date class with the constructor function new Date(). Then you can call on its methods to retrieve specific time information. **Table 11.3** summarizes the common methods for retrieving the dates and times.

To create a clock:

1. Create a dynamic text field on the Stage, and give it an instance name in the Property Inspector.

   The dynamic text field will display the time.

2. Select the first frame of the main Timeline, and open the Actions panel.

3. Enter _root and create an onEnterFrame handler.

4. Within the onEnterFrame event handler, enter the name of a new date object followed by an equals sign.

continues on next page

5. Choose Built-in Classes > Core > Date > new Date.

The new Date() constructor function appears. Your date object is instantiated (**Figure 11.51**). If you don't specify any parameters of the date object, you create a generic date object that you can use to retrieve current date and time information. If you specify the parameters of the date object, you create an object that references a specific date or time.

6. On a new line, enter currentHour followed by an equal sign.

7. Enter the name of your date object followed by a period.

8. With your pointer next to your date object, choose Built-in Classes > Core > Date > Methods > getHours.

The getHours() method appears after the name of your date object. Flash retrieves the current hour and puts the returned value in your variable called currentHour (**Figure 11.52**).

9. Repeat step 8 to retrieve the current minute with the getMinutes() method and the current second with the getSeconds() method, and assign the returned values to variables (**Figure 11.53**).

10. On a new line, choose Statements > Conditions/Loops > if.

11. For the condition, enter currentHour > 12.

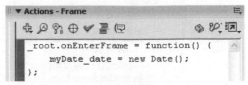

```
_root.onEnterFrame = function() {
    myDate_date = new Date();
};
```

Figure 11.51 The myDate_date date object is instantiated inside an onEnterFrame handler.

```
_root.onEnterFrame = function() {
    myDate_date = new Date();
    currentHour = myDate_date.getHours();
};
```

Figure 11.52 The current hour is assigned to the variable currentHour.

```
_root.onEnterFrame = function() {
    myDate_date = new Date();
    currentHour = myDate_date.getHours();
    currentMinute = myDate_date.getMinutes();
    currentSecond = myDate_date.getSeconds();
};
```

Figure 11.53 The current hour, minute, and second are retrieved from the computer's clock and assigned to different variables.

```
▼ Actions - Frame
_root.onEnterFrame = function() {
    myDate_date = new Date();
    currentHour = myDate_date.getHours();
    currentMinute = myDate_date.getMinutes();
    currentSecond = myDate_date.getSeconds();
    if (currentHour>12) {
        currentHour = currentHour-12;
    }
};
```

Figure 11.54 The returned value for the method getHours() is a number from 0 to 23. To convert the hour to the standard 12-hour cycle, subtract 12 from values greater than 12.

```
▼ Actions - Frame
_root.onEnterFrame = function() {
    myDate_date = new Date();
    currentHour = myDate_date.getHours();
    currentMinute = myDate_date.getMinutes();
    currentSecond = myDate_date.getSeconds();
    if (currentHour>12) {
        currentHour = currentHour-12;
    } else if (currentHour == 0) {
        currentHour = 12;
    }
};
```

Figure 11.55 Because there is no 0 on our clocks, have Flash assign 12 to any hour that has the value 0.

12. On the next line of the if statement, enter currentHour = currentHour–12 (**Figure 11.54**).

13. Place your pointer after the closing curly brace for the if statement, and choose Statements > Conditions/Loops > else if. Delete the extra opening curly brace that's inserted before the else if statement.

14. For the condition of the else if statement, enter currentHour == 0.

15. On the next line, enter currentHour = 12 (**Figure 11.55**).

16. On a new line after the closing curly brace of your else if statement, enter the name of your text field followed by a period, the text property, and an equals sign.

17. After the equals sign, create an expression that concatenates the variable names for the hour, the minute, and the second with appropriate spacers between them (**Figure 11.56**).

18. Test your movie.

The dynamic text field displays the current hour, minute, and second in the 12-hour format.

✔ Tip

■ Note that minutes and seconds that are less than 10 display as single digits, such as 1 and 2, rather than as 01 and 02. Refine your clock by adding conditional statements to check the value of the current minutes and seconds and add the appropriate 0 digit.

Using the Date and Time

myDisplay_txt *dynamic text field*

```
myDisplay_txt.text = "The time is now: \r"+currentHour+":"+currentMinute+":"+currentSecond;
```

Figure 11.56 The dynamic text field (top) displays the concatenated values for the hour, minute, and second.

The returned values for the getMonth() and getDays() methods of a date object are numbers instead of string data types. The getMonth() method returns values from 0 to 11 (0 = January), and the getDays() method returns values from 0 to 6 (0 = Sunday). To correlate these numeric values with the names of the months or days of the week, you can create arrays that contain this information. You can create an array that contains the days of the week with the following statements:

daysofWeek_array = new Array ();

daysofWeek_array[0] = "Sunday";

daysofWeek_array[1] = "Monday";

daysofWeek_array[2] = "Tuesday";

daysofWeek_array[3] = "Wednesday";

daysofWeek_array[4] = "Thursday";

daysofWeek_array[5] = "Friday";

daysofWeek_array[6] = "Saturday";

To create a calendar:

1. Create a dynamic text field on the Stage, and give it an instance name in the Property Inspector.

   The dynamic text field will display the date.

2. Select the first keyframe of the Timeline, and open the Actions panel.

3. Enter a name for a new array that will hold the days of the week followed by an equals sign.

4. Enter the constructor function new Array().

5. In a series of statements, assign to each index of your new array a string representing the names of the days of the week (**Figure 11.57**).

6. On a new line, enter a name for a second new array followed by an equals sign.

```
daysofWeek_array = new Array();
daysofWeek_array[0] = "Sunday";
daysofWeek_array[1] = "Monday";
daysofWeek_array[2] = "Tuesday";
daysofWeek_array[3] = "Wednesday";
daysofWeek_array[4] = "Thursday";
daysofWeek_array[5] = "Friday";
daysofWeek_array[6] = "Saturday";
```

Figure 11.57 The array daysofWeek_array contains strings of all the days of the week.

```
daysofMonth_array = new Array();
daysofMonth_array[0] = "January";
daysofMonth_array[1] = "February";
daysofMonth_array[2] = "March";
daysofMonth_array[3] = "April";
daysofMonth_array[4] = "May";
daysofMonth_array[5] = "June";
daysofMonth_array[6] = "July";
daysofMonth_array[7] = "August";
daysofMonth_array[8] = "September";
daysofMonth_array[9] = "October";
daysofMonth_array[10] = "November";
daysofMonth_array[11] = "December";
```

Figure 11.58 The array daysofMonth_array contains strings of all the months.

```
myDate_date = new Date();
currentYear = myDate_date.getFullYear();
currentMonth = myDate_date.getMonth();
currentDate = myDate_date.getDate();
currentDay = myDate_date.getDay();
```

Figure 11.59 The current year, month, date, and day are retrieved from the computer's clock and assigned to new variables.

7. Enter the constructor function new Array().
This array will hold the months of the year.

8. In a series of statements, assign to each index of your second new array a string representing the names of the months of the year (**Figure 11.58**).

9. On a new line, enter the name of your new date object followed by an equal sign.

10. Enter the constructor function new Date() without any parameters.

11. In a series of statements, call the getFullYear(), getMonth(), getDate(), and getDay() methods, and assign their values to new variables (**Figure 11.59**).

12. Enter the name of your dynamic text field followed by a period, the text property, and an equals sign.

13. Enter the name of your array that contains the days of the week, and put in the variable containing the getDay() returned value as its index.
The value of the variable currentDay is a number from 0 to 6. This number is used to retrieve the correct string in the array corresponding to the current day.

14. Concatenate the array that contains the days of the month, and put the variable containing the getMonth() returned value as its index.

continues on next page

USING THE DATE AND TIME

15. Concatenate the other variables that hold the current date and year (**Figure 11.60**).

16. Test your movie.

Flash gets the day, month, date, and year from the system clock. The names of the specific day and month are retrieved from the array objects you initialize in the first keyframe, and the information is displayed in the dynamic text field. 🖋

Another way to provide time information to your viewer is to use the Flash function getTimer. This function returns the number of milliseconds that have elapsed since the Flash movie started playing. You can compare the returned value of getTimer at one instant with the returned value of it at another instant and the difference gives you the elapsed time between those two instants. Use the elapsed time to create timers for games and activities in your Flash movie. You can time how long it takes for your viewer to answer questions correctly in a

test or give your viewer only a certain amount of time to complete the test. Or you can award more points in a game if the player successfully completes a mission within an allotted time.

Because getTimer is a function and not an object, you don't need to use a constructor function to instantiate it, which makes using it a very simple and convenient way to get elapsed times.

To create a timer:

1. Create a dynamic text field on the Stage, and give it an instance name in the Property Inspector.

2. Select the first frame of the main Timeline, and open the Actions panel.

3. Enter _root, and create an onMouseDown handler.

4. Within the onMouseDown event handler, enter startTime followed by an equals sign.

┌─myDisplay_txt *dynamic text field*

TODAY IS
MONDAY, SEPTEMBER 29, 2003

```
myDisplay_txt.text = "Today is \r"+daysofWeek_array[currentDay]+", "+daysofMonth_array[currentMonth]+" "+currentDate+", "+currentYear;
```

Figure 11.60 The day, month, date, and year information is concatenated and displayed in the myDisplay text field (top).

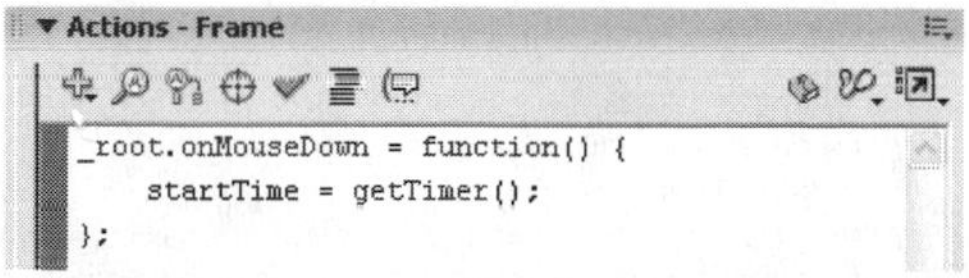

Figure 11.61 When the viewer presses the mouse button, the getTimer function retrieves the time elapsed since the start of the Flash movie. That time is put in the variable startTime.

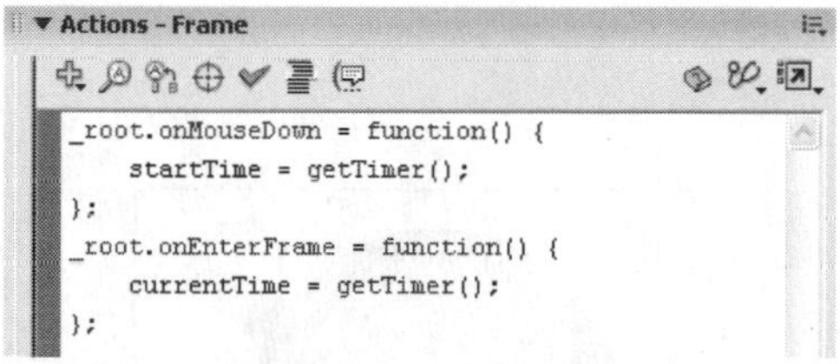

Figure 11.62 On an ongoing basis, the getTimer function retrieves the time elapsed since the start of the Flash movie. That time is put in the variable currentTime.

5. Choose Global Functions > Miscellaneous Functions > getTimer (**Figure 11.61**).

Whenever the mouse button is pressed, the time that has passed since the movie started playing is assigned to the variable called startTime.

6. On a new line, enter _root and create an onEnterFrame handler.

7. Within the onEnterFrame event handler, enter currentTime followed by an equals sign.

8. Choose Global Functions > Miscellaneous Functions > getTimer.

The getTimer function appears (**Figure 11.62**).

9. On the next line, enter elapsedTime followed by an equals sign.

continues on next page

10. Enter (currentTime-startTime)/1000.

Flash calculates the difference between the current timer and the timer at the instant a mouse button is clicked. The result is divided by 1,000 to give seconds (**Figure 11.63**).

11. On a new line, assign the variable elapsedTime to the text property of your dynamic text field (**Figure 11.64**).

12. Test your movie.

Flash displays the time elapsed since the last instant the viewer pressed the mouse button. Experiment with different event handlers to build a stopwatch with Start, Stop, and Lap buttons.

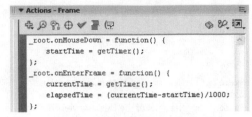

Figure 11.63 The variable elapsedTime is the time between the two instances of time recorded in the variables startTime and currentTime.

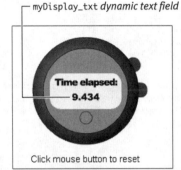

Click mouse button to reset

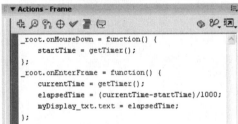

Figure 11.64 The value of elapsedTime is displayed in the text field called myDisplay_txt (top).

Building Reusable Scripts

When you need to perform the same kind of manipulation of information multiple times, you can save time and reduce code clutter by building your own functions. You used functions in previous chapters, mostly as event handlers. When you assign an anonymous function to an event, for example, that function is triggered whenever the event happens. But whether they are anonymous or named, functions have the same job: They group related statements to perform a task that you can invoke from anywhere, at any time. You decide how to mix and match ActionScript statements as needed.

To create a function, use the function command in the Actions toolbox (Statements > User-Defined Functions > function), and give your function a name. Your statement could look something like this:

```
function doExplosion () {

}
```

Any actions within the curly braces of the function are performed when the function is called. You call this function by name, just like this: doExplosion().

The following task builds a function that creates a sound object, attaches a sound, starts it, and sets the volume. By consolidating all these methods, you can play the sound with just one call to a single function—and do so multiple times from different places in your movie.

To build and call a function:

1. Select the first keyframe of the main Timeline, and open the Actions panel.

2. Choose Statements > User-Defined Functions > function (Esc + fn).

3. Immediately after the word function, enter a name for your function.

   The function statement appears in the Script pane with a set of curly braces. All statements included within the curly braces become part of the function; they will be performed when the function is called (**Figure 11.65**).

4. On the next line inside the function, enter the name of a new sound object followed by an equals sign.

continues on next page

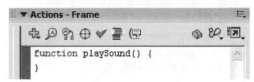

Figure 11.65 This function is called playSound and contains no parameters.

5. Enter the constructor function new Sound() (**Figure 11.66**).

6. Assign the three following methods, which attach the sound, start playing it, and set its volume (**Figure 11.67**):

```
mySound_sound.attachSound ("musicID")
mySound_sound.start (0,2)
mySound_sound.setVolume (50)
```

Alternatively, you can place the three statements within a with action:

```
with (mySound_sound) {
    attachSound ("musicID");
    start (0, 2);
    setVolume (50);
}
```

7. Create a button symbol, and place an instance of the button on the Stage. In the Property Inspector, give your button an instance name.

8. Select the first keyframe of the main Timeline, and open the Actions panel.

9. Create an onRelease event handler for your button.

10. With your pointer between the curly braces of the onRelease event handler, enter the name of your function (**Figure 11.68**).

    The function that you created is called when this button is clicked.

11. Import a sound clip.

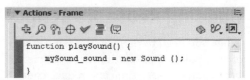

Figure 11.66 The new sound object called mySound_sound is instantiated.

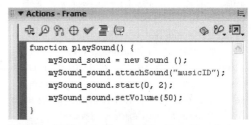

Figure 11.67 When the function playSound is called, the three methods of the sound object are performed.

```
myButton_btn.onRelease = function(){
    playSound();
}
```

Figure 11.68 Call your function by entering its name and the opening and closing parentheses.

BUILDING REUSABLE SCRIPTS

Figure 11.69 The Linkage Properties dialog box for an imported sound. Select Export for ActionScript, and enter a name in the Identifier field.

12. In the Linkage Properties dialog box (accessed from the Library Options pull-down menu), check the Export for ActionScript check box and enter a name in the Identifier field (**Figure 11.69**). The name in the Identifier field should be the same name you used in the attachSound method in step 6.

13. Test your movie.

Your function is defined in the first keyframe of the main Timeline. When your viewer clicks the button on the Stage, Flash calls the function, which creates a new sound object, attaches the sound, and starts playing it at a specified volume level. 🔊

✔ Tips

■ You can initialize variables that are called local variables, which are scoped only within the function. Local variables expire at the end of the function and won't conflict with variables you've initialized elsewhere. You initialize local variables in the Actions panel by choosing Statements > Variables > var (Esc + vr). Use local variables to keep your functions independent and self-contained. That way, you can copy and paste functions from one project to another easily, without having to worry about conflicts with duplicate variable names.

■ Remember that the scope of a function is defined in the Timeline on which it is created. If you call a function that was created on the main Timeline from within a movie clip, the actions from the function still pertain to the main Timeline.

Parameters and returned values

When you define a function, you can tell it to perform a certain task based on parameters that you provide, or *pass*, to the function at the time you call on it. This arrangement makes functions more flexible because the work they do is tailored to particular contexts. In the preceding task, for example, you can define the function to accept a parameter for the sound volume. When you call the function, you also provide a value for the sound volume and the function incorporates that value in the `setVolume()` method.

To build a function that accepts parameters:

1. Continuing with file you used in the preceding task, select the first keyframe, and open the Actions panel.

2. With your pointer between the parentheses of the function statement, enter sndLoop and sndVolume, separated by a comma.

   These names are the parameters for your function. You can name your parameters whatever you like (as long as they conform to the standard naming rules for variables and objects), and you can have as many parameters as you like (**Figure 11.70**).

3. Select the `start()` method within your function, and replace the loop parameter with sndLoop.

4. Select the `setVolume()` method, and replace the volume parameter with sndVolume.

   The parameters sndLoop and sndVolume will be used to play the sound for a certain number of loops and at a certain volume (**Figure 11.71**).

5. Select your function call.

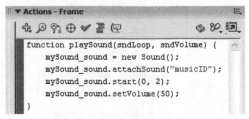

Figure 11.70 The function playSound accepts the parameters sndLoop and sndVolume and then passes them to the statements within its curly braces (which are not yet defined).

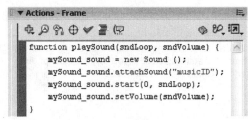

Figure 11.71 The final script for a function that accepts and passes parameters. The parameters of the function playSound modify the start() method and the setVolume() method.

```
function playSound(sndLoop, sndVolume) {
    mySound_sound = new Sound();
    mySound_sound.attachSound("musicID");
    mySound_sound.start(0, sndLoop);
    mySound_sound.setVolume(sndVolume);
}
myButton_btn.onRelease = function() {
    playSound(2, 50);
};
```

Figure 11.72 The function playSound is called, passing the parameters 2 and 50. The sound "musicID" starts playing and loops twice at a volume of 50.

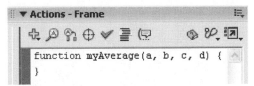

Figure 11.73 The function myAverage accepts the parameters a, b, c, and d.

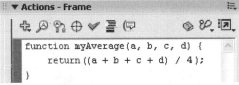

Figure 11.74 The return action evaluates the expression and makes the result available to the statement that called the function.

6. With your pointer between the parentheses of your function, enter a value for the sndLoop parameter and a value for the sndVolume parameter. Separate the two values with a comma (**Figure 11.72**).

7. Test your movie.

The actual values of the parameters that pass to the function are defined when you call the function. Another button may call the same function with different values for the parameters.

When you pass parameters to a function, you often want to know the results of a particular calculation. To make your function report a resulting calculation, use the return action. The return action, defined in your function statement, returns the value of any expression that you want to know when you call a function.

To build a function that returns values:

1. Select the first keyframe of the main Timeline, and open the Actions panel.

2. Choose Statements > User-Defined Functions > function.

3. Immediately after the word function, enter a name for your function.

4. Between the parentheses of the function, enter a, b, c, d (**Figure 11.73**).

5. Between the curly braces for the function, choose Statements > User-Defined Functions > return (Esc + rt).

6. Between the parentheses of the return action, enter an expression to average the four parameters.

This function returns the value of the expression (**Figure 11.74**).

continues on next page

BUILDING REUSABLE SCRIPTS

7. Select the Text tool in the Tools palette, create a dynamic text field on the Stage, and give the text field an instance name in the Property Inspector.

8. Create a button symbol, place an instance of it on the Stage, and give the button an instance name in the Property Inspector.

9. On a new line, create an `onRelease` event handler for your button.

10. Enter the name of your text field, a period, and then the `text` property followed by an equals sign.

11. Enter the name of your function and four values for its parameters, separating the values with commas (**Figure 11.75**).

    These four values pass to the function, where they are processed. The function returns a value back to where it was called. The returned value is assigned to the dynamic text field, where it is displayed. Use the `return` command whenever you need to receive a value after a function has been called.

12. Test your movie. 🎞

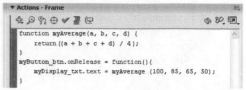

Figure 11.75 The function `myAverage` is called, and the returned value appears in the `myDisplay_txt` dynamic text field.

The Arguments class

Sometimes, you want to build a function that can accept a variable number of parameters. Building a function that calculates a mathematical average, for example, is much more useful when you can input as many or as few numbers as you want. The Arguments class can help solve this problem. The Arguments class is an array that contains the number of parameters that are passed to a function, as well as their values. Every function has an arguments object (arguments), which you can use without instantiation.

In the preceding task, you defined a function with the following script:

```
function myAverage(a, b, c, d) {
    return ((a + b + c + d)/4)
}
```

You called the function like so:

```
myAverage (3, 54, 4, 6);
```

The arguments object for this function would be an array with four elements:

```
arguments[0]=3
arguments[1]=54
arguments[2]=4
arguments[3]=6
```

The length property of the arguments object returns the number of entries in the array. So for this function, arguments.length = 4.

The following task builds a function that can accept any number of parameters and calculates their average with the arguments object. Note that you *must* refer to the arguments object with a lowercase *a*.

To use the arguments object to handle a variable number of parameters passed to a function:

1. Select the first frame of the main Timeline, and open the Actions panel.

2. Choose Statements > User-Defined Functions > function.

3. Immediately after the word function, enter a name for your function (**Figure 11.76**).

4. On the next line, enter var total= 0.
   The variable called total will hold the sum of the numbers you will pass to this function. Each time this function is called, total will be reset to 0.

5. Choose Statements > Conditions/ Loops > for.

6. Between the parentheses of the for loop, enter i=0; i<arguments.length; i++.
   This loop statement will be performed as many times as there are elements in the arguments array.

continues on next page

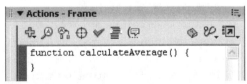

Figure 11.76 Create the function called calculateAverage, and do not define any parameters.

7. On the next line within the `for` loop, enter `total += arguments[i]`.

The variable `total` adds the value of each element in the `arguments` array to itself. This adds up all the parameters that are passed to the function (**Figure 11.77**).

8. On a new line after the closing brace of the `for` statement, choose Statements > User-Defined Functions > return.

9. Enter `total/(arguments.length)`.

The function returns the average of all the parameters that are passed to it (**Figure 11.78**).

10. Create a dynamic text field on the Stage, and give it an instance name in the Property Inspector.

In this example, the instance name is `outputResult_txt`.

11. Create a button symbol, place an instance on the Stage, and give it an instance name in the Property Inspector.

12. Select the first frame on the main Timeline, and open the Actions panel.

13. On the next line after the closing curly brace for the function, create an `onRelease` handler for the button.

14. On the next line of the `onRelease` event, enter the following:

`outputResult_txt.text = calculateAverage(10, 40, 100);`

When this button is clicked, the numbers 10, 40, and 100 are passed to the function. The average is calculated and returned, where it is displayed in the dynamic text field called `outputResult_txt` (**Figure 11.79**). You can pass any number of parameters to the `calculateAverage` function and still get a mathematical average.

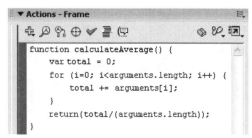

Figure 11.77 All the parameters that are passed to this function are stored in the `arguments` array, and the variable called `total` adds them up.

```
function calculateAverage() {
    var total = 0;
    for (i=0; i<arguments.length; i++) {
        total += arguments[i];
    }
    return(total/(arguments.length));
}
```

Figure 11.78 The sum of all the parameters is divided by the number of parameters. The result is returned to the statement that called the function.

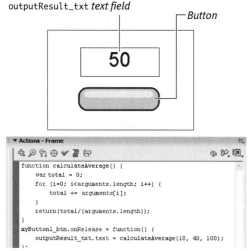

`outputResult_txt` *text field* — Button

50

Figure 11.79 Three parameters are passed to the `calculateAverage` function, and the average is displayed in the `outputResult_txt` text field.

BUILDING REUSABLE SCRIPTS

Building Custom Classes with ActionScript 2

While Flash provides a wealth of built-in classes to help you create interactivity, you may need to build a unique class especially suited for your project. Building your own class lets you organize and customize information to create functionality that Flash doesn't provide.

In ActionScript 2, creating a custom class involves writing and saving the code in an external ActionScript file with the file extension .as. An external ActionScript class file is simply a text file that you can compose in any number of text editing applications or within the Actions Script pane. Usually you will want to save the ActionScript class file in the same directory as your Flash movie. This is the usual place, called the *classPath*, that Flash expects to find the ActionScript class file. However, in the Publish Settings dialog box, you can change the classPath and direct Flash to look in a different folder for your ActionScript class file.

Creating a class definition

The class definition is the "container" that will hold all the ActionScript pertaining to your customized class. You define a new class with the keyword `class` followed by a name of your choosing and the opening and closing curly braces:

```
class ClassName {

}
```

By convention, a class name begins with an uppercase letter. Although this isn't required, it makes sharing and reading code much easier. Of particular importance is that ActionScript 2 is case sensitive (whereas ActionScript 1 is not). Therefore, `ClassName` and `className` are no longer identical.

Within the class declaration, it is customary to add the properties and methods of the class (**Figure 11.80**).

```
//Class definition
class ClassName {
    // Properties
    var myName:String;
    var myAge:Number;
    // Method
    function doSomething(val:String):Boolean {
        if (val == "bingo") {
            return true;
        } else {
            return false;
        }
    }
    //Constructor function
    function ClassName(v1:String, v2:Number) {
        myName = v1;
        myAge = v2;
    }
}
```

Figure 11.80 The ActionScript code to create a new custom class called ClassName. This ActionScript code must be saved in an external file called ClassName.as. The class properties, methods, and constructor function are defined within the curly braces.

Creating properties and methods

As you learned in Chapter 3, all classes have properties, which describe their objects, and methods, which are things that their objects do. You will initialize variables to act as your properties and create functions to establish your methods, as shown in this example:

```
class ClassName {
    // Properties
    var name:String;
    var age:Number;

    // Method
    function doSomething(val:String):
     Boolean {
        if (val == "bingo"){
            return true;
        } else {
            return false;
        }
    }
}
```

Recall from Chapter 9 that in ActionScript 2, Flash supports strict data typing, which defines each variable with the kind of data that it holds. Strict data typing introduces a way of telling Flash to mind its variables. The idea is to tell Flash at the outset that your variable is designed to contain a specific data type. The following declares a strictly typed variable to hold a number (rather than a string or Boolean). Notice that when applying strict data typing, the syntax requires that the variable be preceded by the `var` keyword followed by a colon and data type:

```
var height:Number;
```

Or you may declare and initialize a variable simultaneously as follows:

```
var height:Number = 10;
```

Returning to our example class definition, you should now be able to understand the syntax that establishes its properties. This class has two properties; `name` can hold a string, and `age` can hold a number.

Now consider the function statement that defines the class's method. The method called `doSomething` is defined and requires one parameter, `val`. Strict data typing can be applied to function parameters and function return values as well. Bearing that in mind, the following becomes clear. First, the parameter, `val`, is strictly typed as a string. This means that this method expects to receive text. If not, an error will be generated. Second, the `:Boolean` appended to the function tells Flash that it should expect this method to return a Boolean value. So in practice, the method must receive a string. If a string is passed to the method, it tests the value of the string (referred to as `val`). A `true` or `false` (a Boolean data type) is returned from the method.

Defining a constructor function

The purpose of the constructor function is to instantiate a class (i.e., create an object based on the class). You define how new instances are created from your class by defining the constructor function's parameters like so:

```
function ClassName (v1:String, v2:Number){
    name = v1;
    age = v2;
}
```

There are a few key points to keep in mind: The constructor function's name must be identical to the class definition name (ClassName). In your Flash movie (not from the external ActionScript file), you will instantiate ClassName like so:

```
myObject = new ClassName("Elvis", 4)
```

This statement invokes the constructor function called ClassName. The variables v1 and v2 are used within the constructor function to set the properties of your instance. In this example, we have created a new instance called myObject, which is an instance of the ClassName class. The instance called myObject was created with two properties: name = "Elvis", and age = 4. This object can call its method as follows: myObject.doSomething ("bingo"). The final hypothetical class definition is shown in Figure 11.80.

In the following task, you will create a new class that allows you to make circles of varying radii (these are hypothetical circles, not actual graphics on the Stage). You will build a method that calculates and returns the area of your circle.

To build a custom class:

1. Open the Actions panel in a new Flash document.

2. On the first line, enter class Circle{}.
   The new class called Circle is created.

3. On the first line, in between the curly braces, enter var radius:Number.
   The Circle class has one property, called radius.

4. On the next line, enter the following:
   ```
   function getArea():Number {
       return (Math.PI*radius*radius);
   }
   ```
   This function statement establishes the method called getArea(). When called, it calculates the area based on the value of the radius property and returns a number.

continues on next page

CUSTOM CLASSES WITH ACTIONSCRIPT 2

5. On a new line outside the previous function, enter the following:

```
function Circle(rad:Number) {

    radius = rad;

}
```

This function statement establishes the constructor function so you can create new instances of this class. When you instantiate this class, you also provide a number for the new object's radius property. The final script should look like **Figure 11.81**.

6. In the Actions panel Options menu, choose Export Script (Ctrl-Shift-X for Windows, Cmd-Shift-X for Mac) (**Figure 11.82**).

Save your script using the *exact* name as your class name with the .as extension (Circle.as). Choose as its destination the same folder that holds your future FLA file that will use this class.

Your custom class is ready to be used by a Flash movie.

To instantiate and use your custom class:

1. Open a new Flash document, select the first keyframe of the main Timeline, and open the Actions panel.

2. Enter the following in the Script pane:

   `var myCircle:Circle = new Circle(5);`

   The Circle class that was created in the external document (Circle.as) is called upon from this statement. A new instance of the Circle class is created. Its name is myCircle, and it has a radius of 5.

3. On the next line, choose Global Functions > Miscellaneous Functions > trace.

4. Between the parentheses of the trace statement, enter the name you assigned to the new circle object followed by a period and the custom function getArea() (**Figure 11.83**).

```
class Circle {
    // Property
    var radius:Number;
    // Method
    function getArea():Number {
        return (Math.PI*radius*radius);
    }
    // Constructor function
    function Circle(rad:Number) {
        radius = rad;
    }
}
```

Figure 11.81 The Circle class contains one property, called radius. It will be defined when you instantiate an object and pass the parameter rad through the constructor function. The method called getArea() is also defined in this Class file.

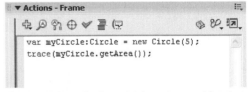

Figure 11.82 Choose Export Script to save your external ActionScript class file. You can also use a simple text editor.

```
var myCircle:Circle = new Circle(5);
trace(myCircle.getArea());
```

Figure 11.83 In a Flash movie, the myCircle object is instantiated with a radius of 5. The method called getArea() returns the area of a object based on its radius property.

Figure 11.84 The returned value of the getArea() method is displayed in the Output window in testing mode.

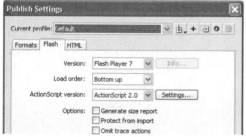

Figure 11.85 Make sure ActionScript 2.0 is selected and click the Settings button to change the classPath.

— Browse to Path button

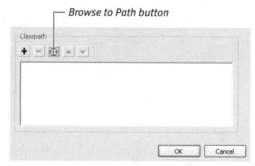

Figure 11.86 Click the Browse to Path button to choose a different directory to keep your external ActionScript class file.

5. Save the Flash document in the same folder as your external ActionScript class file.

6. Choose Control > Test Movie.

   The Output window opens and displays the area of myCircle (**Figure 11.84**). 🕸

To change the classPath:

1. Choose File > Publish Settings.

   The Publish Settings dialog box appears.

2. Click the Flash tab.

3. Click the Settings button next to the ActionScript version pull-down menu. Make sure that ActionScript 2.0 is selected (**Figure 11.85**).

   The ActionScript settings dialog box appears.

4. Click the Browse to Path button and select the folder where your external ActionScript class file is located (**Figure 11.86**). Click OK.

   Flash redirects the classPath in order to find the external ActionScript file that defines your custom class.

MANAGING CONTENT AND TROUBLESHOOTING

12

As the complexity of your Flash movie increases with the addition of bitmaps, videos, sounds, and animations, as well as the ActionScript that integrates them, you'll need to keep close track of all the elements so you can make necessary revisions and bug fixes. After all, the most elaborate Flash movie is useless if you can't pinpoint the one variable that's keeping the whole thing from working. Fortunately, Flash provides several tools for troubleshooting and managing Library symbols and code.

This chapter shows you how to create shared Library symbols and external ActionScripts that supply common elements—symbols and code—to a team of Flash developers working on a project. You'll learn about components, which are specialized movie clips that contain prescripted code that makes common interactivity easy to apply. For example, using components that Flash provides, you can quickly build a progressive preloader or a check box and specify parameters to customize it for your own project without having to build your own from scratch. You'll learn about behaviors, which are prepackaged ActionScript code that can make applying interactivity easier. This chapter also delves into the Movie Explorer, Output window, and Debugger panel, which offer information about the organization and status of your movie. These three windows let you review your ActionScript in context with the other components in your movie, receive error and warning messages, and monitor the changing values of variables and properties as your movie plays.

Finally, you'll learn some strategies for making your Flash movie leaner and faster—optimizing graphics and code, organizing your work environment, and avoiding some common mistakes—guidelines to help you become a better Flash animator and developer.

Sharing Library Symbols

Flash makes it possible for teams of animators and developers to share common symbols of a complex project. Each animator might be working on a separate movie that uses the same symbol—the main character in an animated comic book, for example. An identical symbol of this main character needs to reside in the Library of each movie, and if the art director decides to change this character's face, a new symbol has to be copied to all the Libraries—that is, unless you create a shared Library symbol. There are two kinds of shared symbols: runtime shared symbols and author-time shared symbols.

Runtime sharing of symbols

In runtime sharing, one movie provides a symbol for multiple movies to use during runtime. This simplifies the editing process and ensures consistency throughout a Flash project (**Figure 12.1**).

Your viewers also benefit from the shared symbols because they have to download them only once. For example, a main character would be downloaded just once—for the first movie and all subsequent movies using that character.

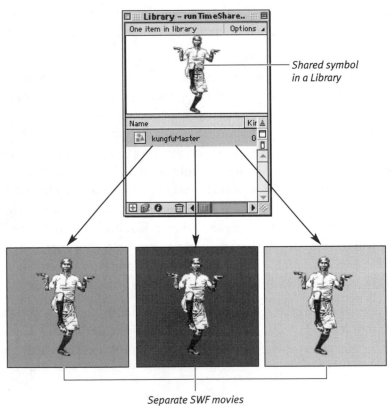

Shared symbol in a Library

Separate SWF movies

Figure 12.1 A runtime shared symbol (top) can be used by multiple SWF files.

Figure 12.2 Choose Options > Linkage from the Library window's Options menu.

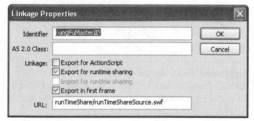

Figure 12.3 To mark a symbol as a shared symbol, it is given an identifier in the Linkage Properties dialog box, selected for export, and given a URL where it can be found. This shared symbol is located in the directory called runTimeShare in the file called runTimeShareSource.swf.

To create a runtime shared Library symbol, you mark the symbol for Export for runtime sharing in the Linkage Properties dialog box. When you export the SWF file, the symbol you identified will be available to other SWF movies.

To create a runtime shared symbol:

1. In a new Flash document, create a symbol you want to share. The symbol can be a graphic, button, movie clip, font symbol, sound, or bitmap.

2. In the Library window, select your symbol. From the Options menu, choose Linkage (**Figure 12.2**).

   The Linkage Properties dialog box appears.

3. From the Linkage choices, select Export for runtime sharing. In the Identifier field, enter a unique name for your symbol. In the URL field, enter the relative or absolute path to the source movie that will share this symbol. Keep the Export in first frame box checked. Click OK (**Figure 12.3**).

   Your selected symbol is now marked for export and available to be shared by other movies.

4. Export your Flash movie as a SWF file with the name and in the location you specified in the URL field of the Linkage Properties dialog box.

   This is your source movie that shares its symbol.

Once you create a movie that shares a
Library symbol, you can create other movies
that use it. You do this by opening a new
Flash document and creating a symbol. In
its Linkage Properties dialog box, mark the
symbol to import for runtime sharing and
enter the name and location of the source
symbol as it appears in the Identifier field of
its own Linkage Properties dialog box. At
runtime, your new movie finds, imports, and
uses the source symbol.

To use a runtime shared symbol:

1. Open a new Flash document and create
a new symbol.

   It doesn't matter what kind of symbol you
create (movie clip, graphic, or button) or
what content is inside it because it will
be replaced by the shared symbol from
the source movie at runtime. This symbol
is simply a placeholder.

2. In the Library window, select your symbol.
From the Options menu, choose Linkage.

   The Linkage Properties dialog box
appears.

3. From the Linkage choices, select Import
for runtime sharing. In the Identifier field,
enter the name for the shared symbol
in the source movie (as it appears in
the Identifier field of its own Linkage
Properties dialog box). In the URL field,
enter the path to the source movie. Click
OK (**Figure 12.4**).

   Your selected symbol is now marked to
find the shared symbol in the source
movie and import it.

4. Drag an instance of the symbol onto the
Stage and use it in your movie.

5. Export your Flash movie as a SWF file
and place it in a location where it can
find the source movie (**Figure 12.5**).

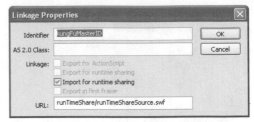

Figure 12.4 In the Linkage Properties dialog box,
check the Import for runtime sharing box and enter
the Identifier and location of the shared symbol you
wish to use.

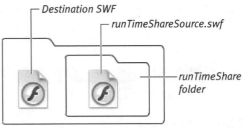

Figure 12.5 The destination SWF imports the shared
symbol from the source SWF. The URL field in Figures
12.3 and 12.4 specify where the source SWF is located
relative to the destination SWF.

SHARING LIBRARY SYMBOLS

When you play the SWF, it imports the shared symbol from the source movie. The shared symbol takes over the current symbol (**Figure 12.6**).

✔ Tips

- When you make changes and revisions to the shared symbol in the source movie, all the destination movies that use the shared symbol will be automatically updated to reflect the change.

- You can also drag the shared symbol from the source movie's Library into the destination movie. The shared symbol will be automatically imported into your destination movie with the correct Linkage Properties options checked and field values entered.

- Unfortunately, you can't assign ActionScript that affects runtime shared symbols. For example, you can't use the methods `attachMovieClip()` or `attachSound()` to dynamically place a shared symbol from the Library into your movie. The reason is that a symbol can't be marked for both import for runtime sharing and export for ActionScript at the same time.

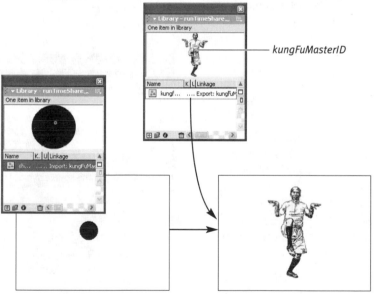

kungFuMasterID

Destination file at author-time   Destination file at runtime

Figure 12.6 The black circle symbol in the destination movie (left) imports the kungFuMasterID shared symbol from the runTimeShareSource.swf at runtime. As a result, the shared symbol appears in the destination SWF (right).

Author-time sharing of symbols

When you want to share symbols among FLA files instead of SWF files, turn to author-time sharing. Author-time sharing lets you choose a source symbol in a particular FLA file so that another FLA file can reference it and keep its symbol up-to-date. You only have to worry about modifying one FLA file containing the source symbol instead of multiple FLA files that contain the same symbol. Each movie stores its own copy of the common symbol. You can update the symbol to the source symbol whenever you want, or even make automatic updates before you publish a SWF file.

To update a symbol with another from a different Flash file:

1. Select the symbol you wish to update in the Library window. From the Options menu, choose Properties.

   The Symbol Properties dialog box appears.

2. Click Advanced.

   The Symbol Properties dialog box expands to display more options (**Figure 12.7**).

3. In the Source section of the dialog box, click Browse. Select the Flash file that contains the symbol you wish to use to update your currently selected symbol. Click OK (Windows) or Open (Mac).

   The Select Source Symbol dialog box appears, showing a list of all the symbols in the selected Flash file's Library.

4. Select a symbol and click OK (**Figure 12.8**).

   The Select Source Symbol dialog box closes.

5. In the Symbol Properties dialog box that is still open, note the new source for your symbol (**Figure 12.9**). Click OK.

   The Symbol Properties dialog box closes and your symbol is updated with the symbol you just chose for its new source. Your symbol retains its name, but its content is updated to the source symbol.

SHARING LIBRARY SYMBOLS

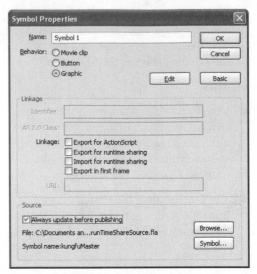

Figure 12.7 The Advanced button in the Symbol Properties dialog box displays more options under Linkage and Source.

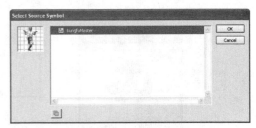

Figure 12.8 Select the source symbol for author-time sharing.

Figure 12.9 The Source area of the Symbol Properties dialog box displays the path to the author-time source symbol and the name of the source symbol.

To make automatic updates to a symbol:

◆ In the Symbol Properties dialog box, check the Always update before publishing box.

Whenever you export a SWF from your Flash file, whether by publishing it or by using the Control > Test Movie command, Flash will locate the source symbol and update your symbol.

Runtime Sharing or Author-time Sharing?

Although they may seem similar, runtime and author-time sharing are two very different ways to work with symbols. Each approach is better suited for different types of projects. Runtime sharing is useful when multiple SWF movies can share common assets, decreasing symbol redundancy, file size, and download times. Publish a single SWF file holding all the common symbols that multiple SWF files can access. Author-time sharing, on the other hand, is useful for organizing your workflow before you publish your SWF movie. You can use author-time sharing to keep different symbols in separate FLA files. A "master" FLA file can reference all of the symbols in the separate files and compile them into a single SWF. Working this way, you can have different members of a Flash development team work on different symbols and rely on author-time sharing to ensure that the final published movie will contain the updated symbols. Compare these two ways of sharing Library symbols in **Figure 12.10**.

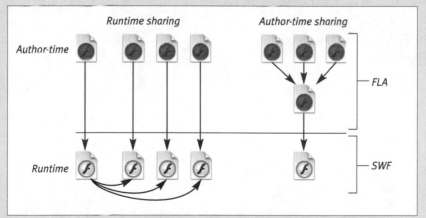

Figure 12.10 During runtime sharing (left), multiple SWF files can share symbols from a single common SWF file. During author-time sharing (right), multiple FLA files can provide updated symbols to a single FLA file that publishes a SWF file to play during runtime.

Sharing Fonts

Just as you can create symbols to share between movies, you can create font symbols and share them. After creating a font symbol, you identify it to be exported using the Linkage identifier in a process identical to the one used to create runtime shared symbols. Use shared fonts to reduce the need to embed the same font outline for multiple movies. When multiple movies share a common font, the font has to be downloaded only once for the first movie, reducing file size and download times for the subsequent movies.

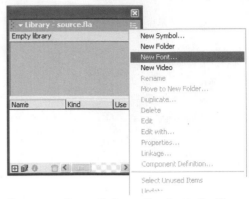

Figure 12.11 Choose Options > New Font in the Library window.

To create a font symbol to share:

1. Open the Library window. From the Options menu, choose New Font (**Figure 12.11**).

   The Font Symbol Properties dialog box appears.

2. Enter a name for your new font symbol in the Name field. From the Font pull-down menu, select the font you wish to include in your Library as a font symbol. Check the optional boxes for Style. Click OK (**Figure 12.12**).

   The font symbol appears in your Library.

3. Select your font symbol in the Library window. From the Options menu, choose Linkage.

   The Linkage Properties dialog box appears.

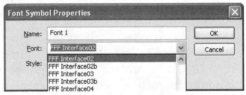

Figure 12.12 Create a font symbol by choosing a font and giving it a name in the Font Symbol Properties dialog box. Here the symbol called Font 1 is created for FFF Interface02.

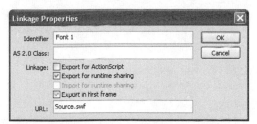

Figure 12.13 In the Linkage Properties dialog box, mark your symbol font for runtime sharing, give it an identifier, and specify its location relative to the destination file that will use the shared font. If the destination and source file will reside in the same directory, you can simply enter the name of the source file in the URL field, as is shown here.

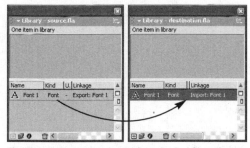

Figure 12.14 Drag the shared font symbol from the source Library (left) to the destination Library (right).

4. From the Linkage choices, select Export for runtime sharing. In the Identifier field, enter a unique name for your symbol. In the URL field, enter the path for the source movie that will share this font. Click OK (**Figure 12.13**).

Your selected font symbol is now marked for export and available to be shared by other movies.

5. Export your Flash movie as a SWF file with the name and in the location you specified in the URL field of the Linkage Properties dialog box.

Your selected font symbol resides in the SWF file. This SWF file provides the shared font to other movies.

To use a shared font symbol:

1. Open a new Flash file (the destination file) where you want to use a shared font symbol.

2. Open the Library of the source file that contains your shared font symbol by choosing File > Import > Open External Library. Drag the shared font symbol from its Library to the Library of the destination Flash file.

The font symbol appears in the Library of the destination Flash file. The font symbol is automatically marked as Import for runtime sharing (**Figure 12.14**).

3. In the destination Flash file, select the font symbol in the Library window. From the Options menu, choose Linkage.

The Linkage Properties dialog box appears.

continues on next page

4. Confirm that Import for runtime sharing is checked, the Identifier field contains the name of the shared font symbol in the source movie, and the URL field contains the path to the source movie (**Figure 12.15**). Click OK.

Your font symbol in the destination movie is now set to share the font symbol in the source movie.

5. Select the Text tool in the Tools window. In the Property Inspector, choose the shared font symbol from the pull-down list of available fonts (**Figure 12.16**). Create input text or dynamic text, and be sure to embed all the font outlines in the Character Options.

6. Publish the destination SWF file and the source SWF file.

The source SWF shares its font with the destination SWF. The destination SWF displays the shared font correctly and with anti-aliasing, but its file size remains small (**Figure 12.17**).

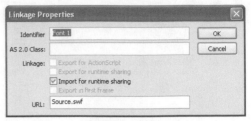

Figure 12.15 The Linkage Properties dialog box for the font symbol in the destination file. This font symbol will import the font called Font 1 from the file called Source.swf.

Figure 12.16 Shared fonts are available in the Property Inspector and are distinguished by an asterisk after their names.

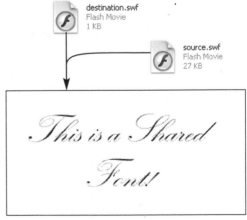

Figure 12.17 The destination SWF file displays the shared font correctly because the font is supplied by the source SWF file. Notice the difference in file size between destination.swf (1 KB) and source.swf (27 KB).

Using Components

There are times when you'll create an interface element, like a check box or a pull-down menu, which you'll want to use in multiple projects but in slightly varying ways. For one movie, you may want your pull-down menu to have three choices, but for another movie, you may want it to have four. Or you may want to hand off your pull-down menu to a designer or animator for their own use, but you want to provide them with easy guidelines so they can customize the pull-down menu without recoding any of your ActionScript. How do you develop this modular piece of interactivity that can be easily customized, even by non-ActionScript coders? The solution is to use components. Components are a special kind of symbol called a compiled clip that have been programmed by one developer to be used by other developers who can easily modify some of the component's functionality or appearance.

If this sounds very general, it's because components are meant to tackle any sort of task—not just the creation of pull-down menus, check boxes, and other user-interface elements, but data handling, graphics behaviors, sound manipulation, and many other kinds of interactivity as well. Components are like templates. They provide the general functionality as well as the parameters to help you make them fit your particular needs.

Flash UI components

Flash provides a set of components of common user interface elements, located in the Components panel (Window > Development Panels > Components). They are the Button, CheckBox, ComboBox, Label, List, Loader, NumericStepper, ProgressBar, RadioButton, ScrollPane, TextArea, TextInput, and Window (**Figure 12.18**). (Flash MX 2004 Professional provides additional components for advanced interactivity and data and media handling.) Each of these components comes with its own parameters that you define in the Component Inspector (Window > Development Panels > Component Inspector), or in the Property Inspector. For example, the ComboBox, which works like a pull-down menu, lets you define the number of menu items, their labels, the data to pass when one of the choices is selected, and even an event handler.

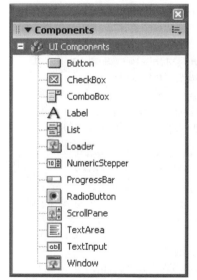

Figure 12.18 The Components panel shows the user-interface components Flash provides to quickly and easily add interactivity to your movie.

You can use the Flash UI components to varying degrees, depending on how much you want to modify them and how willing you are to dig into the custom methods and properties that each component provides. For example, you can change their appearance by calling the custom method setStyle(). Consult the ActionScript dictionary (Help > ActionScript Dictionary > Using Components) to learn more about each component's unique methods and properties.

If you don't need anything more than the standard functionality and basic design that the Flash UI components give, they are great resources to use. Look for more exciting components from Macromedia and from third-party developers. In the following example, you'll use the Loader component to quickly create a placeholder in which an external JPG or SWF file can load at run time.

To use the Flash Loader component:

1. Choose Window > Development Panels > Components (Ctrl-F7 for Windows, Command-F7 for Mac). Double-click the UI Components to expand the list of available components.

   The Components panel opens and displays the user-interface components that Flash provides (Figure 12.18).

2. Select the Loader component, and drag it to the Stage (**Figure 12.19**).

   A completely transparent placeholder is placed on the stage. The default size is 100 pixels by 100 pixels, but it can be adjusted to whatever size you require. By default, the contents of the external image or SWF movie that will load are scaled to fit the Loader.

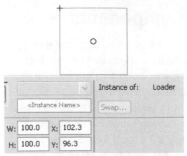

Figure 12.19 The Loader component acts as the placeholder to load external images or SWF movies. By default, the Loader component is 100 x 100 pixels in width and height.

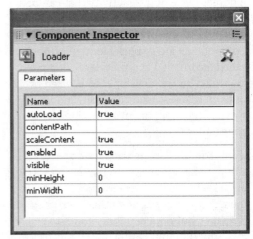

Figure 12.20 The Component Inspector displays the parameters and values for the Loader component.

Name	Value
autoLoad	true
contentPath	images/ranch.jpg
scaleContent	true
enabled	true
visible	true
minHeight	0
minWidth	0

Parameters

Figure 12.21 The Loader component on the Stage will load the image from the target path next to the contentPath parameter. A relative or absolute URL can be used as the contentPath.

Figure 12.22 The Stage has four Loader components (top). During playback, external images load in the Flash movie (bottom).

3. With the component selected, choose Window > Development Panels > Component Inspector and click on the Parameters tab.

The Component Inspector opens. The Parameters tab lists the various parameters that you can set to customize your Loader component (**Figure 12.20**). You can also view and set your component's parameters from the Parameters tab of the Property Inspector.

4. In the Value column, click in the field next to the contentPath parameter and enter an absolute or relative path to your SWF or JPG file (**Figure 12.21**).

5. Test your movie.

At run time, your external movie or image will load into the Loader component (**Figure 12.22**). By default, the contents are scaled to fit the Loader rectangle, but you can change this behavior by changing its parameters in the Component Inspector or in the Parameters tab of the Property Inspector.

✔ Tips

- A Loader component cannot receive focus, meaning that you cannot assign a startDrag method or an onPress event handler to it. In spite of this, content loaded into the Loader component can receive focus and handle its own interactivity. For more information about controlling focus, check the Loader Components section in the Component Dictionary.

- You can use the Free Transform tool (Q) to adjust the width and height or even skew the Loader component bounding box.

- If you load an external SWF into a Loader component and the scale parameter is set to true, off-Stage elements in the external SWF will be visible.

USING COMPONENTS

579

Using Behaviors

Behaviors are prepackaged ActionScript code that are categorized so you can easily apply them to your movie without having to write the code yourself. Users of previous versions of Flash will find some similarities between the Behaviors panel and the no-longer-used Normal mode feature of the Actions pane. Both let you create and modify ActionScript through a simple, accessible menu-driven approach. You can use the Behaviors panel to assign common interactivity (including navigation, sound and movie clip control, and loading of external media) to movie clips, buttons, and frames.

Add a behavior by first selecting an instance on the Stage or a keyframe on the Timeline. Then, select a behavior from the plus button pull-down menu. The behaviors are organized in six sections (**Figure 12.23**), with the contents of each section changing depending on whether a keyframe or an instance is selected. For example, if you select a keyframe and then look in the Movieclip category, you will see a set of actions that are relevant only to controlling Timelines.

In the following tasks, you will assign simple actions using the Behaviors panel to a movie clip or a keyframe.

To assign a behavior to a movie clip:

1. Create a movie clip symbol, and drag an instance from the Library on to the Stage.

2. In the Property Inspector, give your movie clip an instance name.

3. Choose Window > Development Panels > Behaviors.
   The Behaviors panel opens.

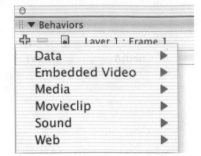

Figure 12.23 Six default categories in the Behaviors panel are always present when you click the plus sign. Their contents change, depending on what Flash element you have selected.

4. Click the plus sign, choose Movieclip, and then choose an action for your movie clip.

In some cases, additional dialog boxes will appear prompting you to provide additional parameters for the behavior. With the movie clip selected, open the Actions panel to view the source code that Flash assigned to this movie clip (**Figure 12.24**).

5. Test your movie.

✔ Tip

■ You can change the event handler for the movie clip or button by clicking on the event listed in the Behaviors panel and selecting a new event handler (**Figure 12.25**).

```
on (release) {
    //Duplicate Movieclip Behavior
    //Requires Flash Player 7 or later
    var newdepth = this._parent.getNextHighestDepth();
    var newname = "copy"+newdepth;
    var prevname = "copy"+(newdepth-1);
    if (this._parent[prevname] == undefined) {
        this._parent[prevname] = this;
    }
    this.duplicateMovieClip(newname, newdepth);
    this._parent[newname]._x = this._parent[prevname]._x+10;
    this._parent[newname]._y = this._parent[prevname]._y+10;
    //End Behavior
}
```

Figure 12.24 A behavior for duplicating a movie clip is added to a movie-clip instance. Use the Behaviors panel to quickly add complex ActionScript like this.

Figure 12.25 You can change the event associated with a button or movie clip by choosing the event in the Behaviors panel.

To assign a behavior to a keyframe:

1. Select the first frame of the main Timeline.

2. Choose Window > Development Panels > Behaviors.

   The Behaviors panel opens.

3. Click the plus sign, and select an action for your keyframe.

   Depending on the behavior you select, additional dialog boxes may appear prompting you to provide additional parameters for the behavior (**Figure 12.26**).

4. Test your movie.

To modify a behavior:

◆ Double-click either the event or the action.

   A dialog box appears where you can change the parameters of the behavior.

To delete a behavior:

◆ Select the behavior in the Behaviors panel and press the Delete key or click the minus button (**Figure 12.27**).

To rearrange behaviors:

◆ Select the behavior in the Behaviors panel and press the Up or Down arrow to move the selected behavior up or down the list (Figure 12.27).

   The behaviors will execute in order from the top of the list to the bottom.

Figure 12.26 Another dialog box opens, allowing you to define additional parameters for your behavior. For the Go to Webpage behavior, you must enter the URL and the location where it will open.

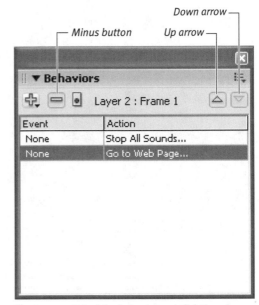

Figure 12.27 Select the behavior and click the minus button to delete or the Up or Down arrows to rearrange the order.

USING BEHAVIORS

Editing ActionScript

When the code in the Script pane of the Actions panel becomes long and complex, you can check, edit, and manage it using the Options menu of the Actions panel. There are menu options for searching and replacing words, importing and exporting scripts, and printing your scripts as well as for different ways to display your script such as using word wrap (**Figure 12.28**).

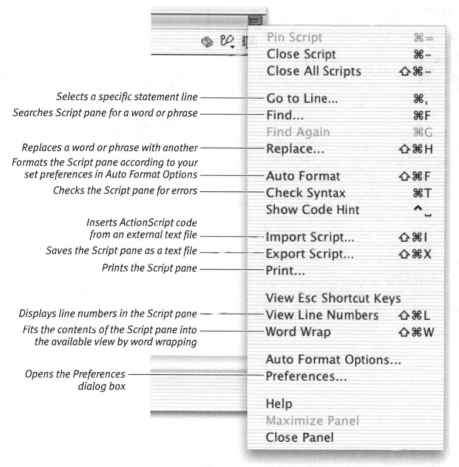

Pin Script	⌘=
Close Script	⌘–
Close All Scripts	⇧⌘–
Selects a specific statement line — Go to Line...	⌘,
Searches Script pane for a word or phrase — Find...	⌘F
Find Again	⌘G
Replaces a word or phrase with another — Replace...	⇧⌘H
Formats the Script pane according to your set preferences in Auto Format Options — Auto Format	⇧⌘F
Checks the Script pane for errors — Check Syntax	⌘T
Show Code Hint	^_
Inserts ActionScript code from an external text file — Import Script...	⇧⌘I
Saves the Script pane as a text file — Export Script...	⇧⌘X
Prints the Script pane — Print...	
View Esc Shortcut Keys	
Displays line numbers in the Script pane — View Line Numbers	⇧⌘L
Fits the contents of the Script pane into the available view by word wrapping — Word Wrap	⇧⌘W
Auto Format Options...	
Opens the Preferences dialog box — Preferences...	
Help	
Maximize Panel	
Close Panel	

Figure 12.28 The Options menu of the Actions panel contains editing functions for the Script pane.

To check the syntax in the Script pane:

◆ In the Actions panel, choose Check Syntax from the Options menu (Command-T for Mac, Ctrl-T for Windows). You can also click the Check Syntax button above the Script pane (**Figure 12.29**).

Flash checks the script in the Script pane for errors in syntax. If it finds an error, it displays a warning dialog box and reports any errors in an Output window (**Figure 12.30**). Use the information provided in the Output window to locate the error and correct the syntax.

✔ Tip

■ Check Syntax reports just the errors in the current Script pane, not for the entire movie.

Use the Find and Replace functions in the Actions panel to quickly change variable names, properties, or even actions. For example, if you created a lengthy script involving the variable redTeamStatus but change your mind and want to change the variable name, you can replace all instances of redTeamStatus with blueTeamStatus. You could find all the occurrences of the property _x and replace them with _y, or you could find all the occurrences of the action gotoAndStop and replace them with gotoAndPlay.

Check Syntax button ―

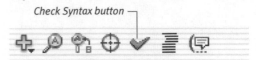

Figure 12.29 The Check Syntax button is the check mark icon above the Script pane.

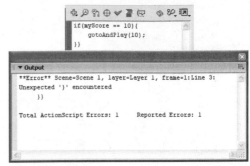

Figure 12.30 The Script pane (above) contains an extra closing curly brace. Flash notifies you of the nature and location of the error in the Output window (below).

EDITING ACTIONSCRIPT

To find and replace ActionScript terms in the Script pane:

1. In the Actions panel, choose Replace from the Options menu (Command-H for Mac, Ctrl-H for Windows). The Replace dialog box appears.

2. In the Find what field, enter a word or words that you want Flash to find. In the Replace with field, enter a word or words that you want the found words to be replaced with. Check the Match case box to make Flash recognize upper- and lowercase letters (**Figure 12.31**).

3. Click Replace to replace the first instance of the found word, or click Replace All to replace all instances of the found word.

✔ Tip

- The Replace dialog box replaces all the occurrences of a particular word or phrase only in the current Script pane of the Actions panel. To replace every occurrence of a certain word in the whole movie, you need to go to each script and repeat this process.

Figure 12.31 Every occurrence of _root.myPaddle._x will be replaced with _root.myPaddle._y.

The Import Script, Export Script, and Print functions of the Actions panel let you work with external text editors or print the contents of the Script pane.

To import an ActionScript:

◆ Select Import Script from the Options menu (Command-Shift-I for Mac, Ctrl-Shift-I for Windows). From the dialog box that appears, choose the text file that contains the ActionScript you wish to import. Click Open.

Flash inserts the ActionScript contained in the text file into the current Script pane at the insertion point. (Note that this works differently from previous versions of Flash, where the entire contents of the Script pane would be replaced.)

To export an ActionScript:

◆ Select Export Script from the Options menu (Command-Shift-X for Mac, Ctrl-Shift-X for Windows). Enter a destination filename. Click Save.

Flash saves a text file that contains the entire contents of the current Script pane. The recommended extension for external ActionScript files is *.as*, as in myCode.as.

Including External ActionScript

In Chapter 11, you learned how to create an external ActionScript file to define a custom class. You can also create external ActionScript files to simply share common code among multiple movies. Create the ActionScript code that appears many times in different movies, and keep that code in a text file outside the Flash movies. If you need to change the code, you only need to change it in one place.

External code can be incorporated into a Flash movie with the action #include. This action pulls in an external text file containing ActionScript and includes it in the existing script in the Script pane.

It's important to point out that the #include action to share external ActionScript code is performed when the SWF is published and not dynamically during run time. You must re-export your Flash movie in order for Flash to include the most current ActionScript. This means that the #include action, although useful, is limited to authoring mode as author-time shared symbols are (**Figure 12.32**).

In the following task, the #include action is assigned to the first frame of the main Timeline. A text document contains ActionScript. When you export the SWF file, the code in the external text document is incorporated into the script.

To include external ActionScript with the #include action:

1. Open a text-editing application such as SimpleText for Mac or Notepad for Windows.

2. Write your ActionScript code, and save it as a text document. Do not include any quotation marks around your script. Use the extension *.as* to identify it as an ActionScript file (**Figure 12.33**).

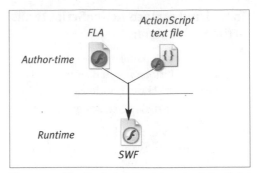

Figure 12.32 The #include action integrates ActionScript from an external text file when the FLA exports a SWF. The #include action does not work at run time.

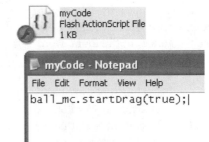

Figure 12.33 This is the ActionScript in a text file saved as myCode.as.

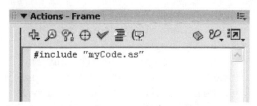

Figure 12.34 When this movie is published, the external text file called myCode.as is included in this Script pane.

3. Open a new document in Flash. Create a movie-clip symbol, and place an instance of it on the Stage. In the Property Inspector, give it a name. In this example, call it ball_mc.

4. Select the first frame of the main Timeline, and open the Actions panel.

5. Enter #include (Esc + in).

6. On the same line, after the #include action and surrounded by quotation marks, enter the name of the text file that contains ActionScript (**Figure 12.34**).

7. Save your FLA file in the same directory as your ActionScript text file.

8. Export a SWF from your FLA file.
   Flash integrates the code from the text document. If you change the code in the text file, you must re-export the SWF so that Flash can include the latest changes.

✔ Tips

- Do not include a semicolon at the end of a #include statement. Although ActionScript statements are usually separated by semicolons, the #include statement is an exception.

- If you want to store your external ActionScript text file separately from you FLA file, you can include a relative or absolute path before the filename.

- If you use the Check Syntax button on a script that contains an #include statement, the syntax of the external ActionScript is also checked.

INCLUDING EXTERNAL ACTIONSCRIPT

Using the Movie Explorer

In order to get a bird's-eye view of your whole Flash movie, you can use the Movie Explorer panel (Option-F3 for Mac, Alt-F3 for Windows). You will notice that the Movie Explorer is very similar to the Script Navigator, which is included in the bottom-left side of the Actions panel. While the Script Navigator allows you to jump from one piece of ActionScript code to another, the Movie Explorer can display all the code in your movie at once. Moreover, the Movie Explorer tracks all the elements of your movie, not just ActionScript code, and it will take you directly to a particular ActionScript, graphic, or frame you want to modify. The Movie Explorer panel can selectively represent the graphical components of a movie and provide information about frames and layers, as well as show ActionScript assigned to buttons, movie clips, and keyframes. The display list is organized hierarchically, letting you see the relationships between various elements (**Figure 12.35**).

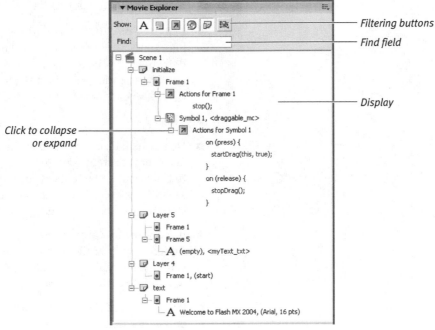

Figure 12.35 A typical display in the Movie Explorer shows various elements of the movie in an expandable hierarchy.

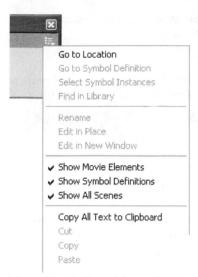

Go to Location
Go to Symbol Definition
Select Symbol Instances
Find in Library

Rename
Edit in Place
Edit in New Window

✓ Show Movie Elements
✓ Show Symbol Definitions
✓ Show All Scenes

Copy All Text to Clipboard
Cut
Copy
Paste

Figure 12.36 The Options menu of the Movie Explorer panel.

The Movie Explorer even updates itself in real time, so as you're authoring a Flash movie, the panel displays the latest modifications. Use the Movie Explorer to find particular elements in your movie. For example, if you want to find all the instances of a movie clip, you can search for them and have Flash display the exact scene, layer, and frame where each instance resides. You can then quickly go to those spots on the Timeline to edit the instances. You can also edit various elements within the Movie Explorer panel itself, such as the names of symbols or the contents of a text selection. The customized display and quick navigation capabilities of the Movie Explorer make it much easier to find your way around a complex movie.

To display different categories of elements:

From the Options menu at the right of the Movie Explorer panel, select one or more of the following (**Figure 12.36**):

◆ Show Movie Elements displays all the elements in your movie and organizes them by scene. Only the current scene is displayed.

◆ Show Symbol Definitions displays all the elements associated with symbol instances that are on the Stage.

◆ Show All Scenes displays all the elements in your movie in all scenes.

To filter the categories of elements that are displayed:

From the row of filtering buttons at the top of the panel, select one or more to add categories of elements to display (**Figure 12.37**).

◆ Show Text displays the actual string in a text selection, the font name and font size, and the instance name and variable name for input and dynamic text.

◆ Show Buttons, Movie Clips, and Graphics displays the symbol names of buttons, movie clips, and graphics on the Stage, as well as the instance names of movie clips and buttons.

◆ Show ActionScript displays the actions assigned to buttons, movie clips, and frames.

◆ Show Video, Sounds, and Bitmaps displays the symbol names of imported video, sounds, and bitmaps on the Stage.

◆ Show Frames and Layers displays the names of layers, keyframes, and frame labels in the movie.

◆ Customize which Items to Show displays a dialog box from which you can choose individual elements to display.

To find and edit elements in the display:

1. Enter the name of the element you wish to find in the Find field at the top of the Movie Explorer panel (**Figure 12.38**).

   All the elements of the movie that contain that name appear in the display list automatically as you type in the field.

2. Click the desired element to select it.

   The element will also be selected on the Timeline and on the Stage. If a scene or keyframe is selected, Flash takes you to that scene or keyframe.

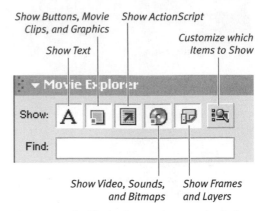

Show Buttons, Movie Clips, and Graphics — Show ActionScript — Show Text — Customize which Items to Show — Show Video, Sounds, and Bitmaps — Show Frames and Layers

Figure 12.37 The filtering buttons let you selectively display elements.

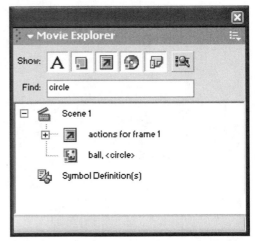

Figure 12.38 Entering a word or phrase in the Find field displays all occurrences of that word or phrase in the Display window. Here, the instance named *circle* of the movie-clip symbol called *ball* has been found.

USING THE MOVIE EXPLORER

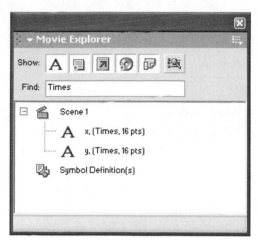

Figure 12.39 All the occurrences of the Times font appear in the Display window.

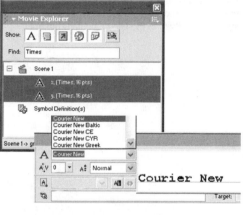

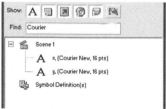

Figure 12.40 With the Times text elements selected, choose a different font, such as Courier New (top) from the Property Inspector. Flash changes those text elements from Times to Courier New (bottom).

3. From the Options menu of the Movie Explorer panel, choose Edit in Place or Edit in New Window to go to symbol-editing mode for a selected symbol.

or

Choose Rename from the Options menu. The name of the element becomes selectable so that you can edit it.

or

Double-click the desired element to modify it. Flash makes the element editable or opens an appropriate window, depending on what type of element it is.

Double-clicking a symbol (except for sound, video, and bitmaps) opens symbol-editing mode.

Double-clicking ActionScript opens the script in the Actions panel.

Double-clicking a scene or layer lets you rename it.

Double-clicking a text selection lets you edit its contents.

To replace all occurrences of a particular font:

1. In the Find field of the Movie Explorer panel, enter the name of the font you wish to replace.

All occurrences of that font appear in the display (**Figure 12.39**).

2. Select all the text elements, using Shift-click to make multiple selections.

3. In the Property Inspector, choose a different font and style for all text elements.

All the selected text elements change according to your choices in the Property Inspector (**Figure 12.40**).

USING THE MOVIE EXPLORER

To find all instances of a movie-clip symbol:

◆ In the Find field of the Movie Explorer panel, enter the name of the movie-clip symbol whose instances you want to find.

All instances of that movie-clip symbol appear in the display (**Figure 12.41**).

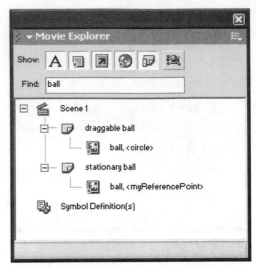

Figure 12.41 Entering the symbol name *ball* in the Find field displays all the instances of the ball symbol. There are two instances listed: one called *circle* in the layer called draggable ball, and another called *myReferencePoint* in the layer called stationary ball.

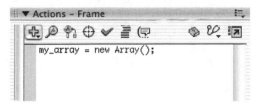

Figure 12.42 The object my_array is created from the new Array constructor function.

Listing Variables and Objects in the Output Window

While the Movie Explorer represents many of a movie's graphic elements and ActionScript, it doesn't display variables or object target paths. For this you use the Output window. Often, while your movie is playing, you will want to know the values of your variables and the target paths of movie clips to determine whether Flash is handling the information correctly. This is especially important when your movie is very complicated, perhaps involving many parameters passing between functions or having dynamically allocated variables. For example, say you want to initialize and populate an array object in the first frame of the Timeline. After assigning to the frame the ActionScript that does the job, you can test your movie, but you won't really know if Flash has correctly populated the array because there's nothing visual on the Stage. In order to see if the array is indeed filled up with the correct values, you can list the variables in the Output window in testing mode. The List Variables command displays all the variables in a movie with their scopes and values.

In the following task, you first create a simple array object, and then assign values to it using a looping statement. In testing mode, you list the movie's variables in the Output window to see the array's final values.

To list variables in the Output window:

1. Select the first frame of the main Timeline, and open the Actions panel.

2. Instantiate a new array object called my_array, as described in Chapter 11 (**Figure 12.42**).

continues on next page

VARIABLES & OBJECTS IN THE OUTPUT WINDOW

3. Choose Statements > Conditions/Loops > for. Between the parentheses, enter i=0; i<5; i++ (**Figure 12.43**).

4. On the next line, enter my_array[i] = i*5. Each time the for statement loops, the value of i increases by 1. Flash assigns each entry in the my_array array the value of its index multiplied by 5. This loop populates the my_array array (**Figure 12.44**).

5. Test your movie (Control > Test Movie). In testing mode, from the top menu, choose Debug > List Variables (Command-Option-V for Mac, Ctrl-Alt-V for Windows). The Output window opens, displaying all the variables in the movie. The first variable listed is $version, which contains information about the version of Flash Player and the system platform. The second variable is the my_array object. Flash lists its location (_level0.my_array), its data type (object of the Array class), and all of its values in each index (0, 5, 10, 15, 20). The third variable is the counter variable, called i, that was used in the for looping statement (**Figure 12.45**).

✔ Tip

- The List Variables command displays all the variables in a movie at the instant you choose the command from the menu. If the variables change as the movie plays, you need to choose List Variables again in order to see the latest values. For real-time display of variables, use the Debugger panel, described later in this chapter.

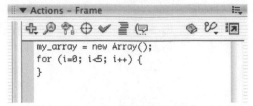

Figure 12.43 Create a loop that begins with i=0 and increases by 1 until it reaches 4.

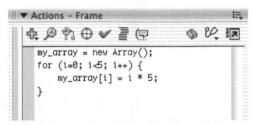

Figure 12.44 The object my_array is automatically filled with the values determined by the looping statement.

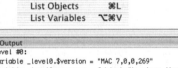

Figure 12.45 Choose Debug > List Variables in testing mode to see all the current variables. The my_array object and its values are listed, verifying the results of the looping statement.

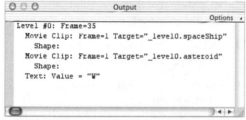

Figure 12.46 Information about the same movie is displayed in the Movie Explorer (top) and the Output window (bottom). The Movie Explorer visually displays the hierarchy of objects. The Output window lists the target path of objects and other graphic elements. Note that the Output window shows only the first letter of a static text field.

Figure 12.47 Choose Debug > List Objects in testing mode.

You can also use the Output window to display a list of the objects in the movie. While the Output window's display is not as graphically appealing as the display in the Movie Explorer, it gives you information about objects that you can't get from the Movie Explorer. The object information listed in the Output window includes the object's level, type of symbol (Movie Clip, Button, Edit Text) or type of graphic (Text, Shape), and the absolute target path of the objects. The target path of objects is the most important bit of information the Output window can tell you directly, although the Movie Explorer can give that to you indirectly. A comparison of the typical information display for the same movie in the Movie Explorer and in the Output window is shown in **Figure 12.46**.

To list objects in the Output window:

◆ In testing mode, choose Debug > List Objects (Command-L for Mac, Ctrl-L for Windows) (**Figure 12.47**).

All the objects in the current state of the movie are displayed in the Output window.

✔ Tip

■ As with the command List Variables, the command List Objects displays only the movie's current status. If a movie clip disappears from the Timeline as the movie plays, you need to select List Objects again to update the display of objects in the Output window.

Tracing Variables in the Output Window

Sometimes you'll want to know the status of a variable or expression at a particular point during the playback of your movie. For example, imagine that you've created a game of Pong in which a movie clip of a ball bounces between two other movie clips of paddles. You want to find out, for testing purposes, the position of the paddle at the instant of a collision with the ball. The command List Variables would be very little help because of the rapidly changing variables for the paddle positions. The solution is to use the action trace. You can place the action trace at any point in the movie to have Flash send a custom message to the Output window during testing mode. The custom message is an expression you create that gives you tailored information at just the right moment. In the Pong example, you would use the trace action as follows:

```
trace ("paddle X-position is " +
myPaddle_mc._x);
trace ("paddle Y-position is " +
myPaddle_mc._y);
```

Place these two trace statements in the if statement that detects the collision. At the moment of collision, Flash will send a message to the Output window, and it would look something like this:

```
paddle X-position is 25
paddle Y-position is 89
```

You can also use trace to monitor the condition of an expression so you can understand the circumstances that change its value. For example, in the following task, you'll create a simple draggable movie clip and another movie clip that remains stationary. You'll assign a trace action to display the value of the draggable movie clip's hitTest() method, letting you see when and where the value becomes true or false.

To display an expression in the Output window:

1. Create a movie-clip symbol, place an instance of it on the Stage, and name the instance myMovieClip_mc.

2. Create another movie-clip symbol, place an instance of it on the Stage, and name the instance rock_mc.

3. Select the first frame of the main Timeline, and open the Actions panel.

4. Enter _root, and then create an onEnterFrame handler.

5. On the next line within the onEnterFrame handler, enter myMovieClip_mc followed by a period.

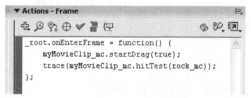

Figure 12.48 The startDrag action will make the movie clip called myMovieClip_mc follow the pointer.

```
_root.onEnterFrame = function() {
    myMovieClip_mc.startDrag(true);
    trace(myMovieClip_mc.hitTest(rock_mc));
};
```

Figure 12.49 The trace action evaluates the expression within its parentheses and displays the value in the Output window.

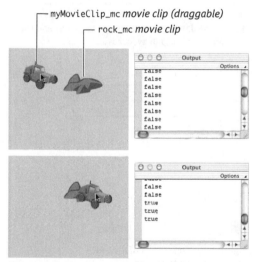

myMovieClip_mc *movie clip (draggable)*
rock_mc *movie clip*

Figure 12.50 The Output window displays false when myMovieClip_mc is clear of the rock_mc movie clip (top). It displays true when there is a collision (bottom).

6. Choose Global Functions > Movie Clip Control > startDrag. Enter true for its parameter (**Figure 12.48**).

7. On the next line, choose Global Functions > Miscellaneous Functions > trace (Esc + tr).

8. Between the parentheses, enter the following expression (**Figure 12.49**):

    myMovieClip_mc.hitTest(rock_mc).

    Flash evaluates the hitTest() method to see if the draggable movie clip collides with the movie clip called rock_mc. The returned value is displayed in the Output window in testing mode.

9. Test your movie.

    The Output window opens, displaying the result of the trace action (**Figure 12.50**).

The typeof operator can be used in conjunction with the trace action to display the data type of a certain variable. This information is very useful when you begin to encounter problems with unexpected values in your variables. If you suspect that the problem stems from using a variable in ways that are incompatible with its data type, placing a trace action to display the data type will confirm or disprove your suspicions.

To determine the data type of a variable:

1. Open the file you created in the section, "Listing Variables and Objects in the Output Window" earlier in this chapter.

    This is the file in which you created an array and populated the array with a looping statement.

    Select the first frame, and open the Actions panel.

continues on next page

2. Create a new line after the ending curly brace of the last statement in the Script pane.

3. Choose Global Functions > Miscellaneous Functions > trace.

4. With your pointer between the parentheses, choose Operators > Miscellaneous Operators > typeof.

The typeof operator appears between the parentheses of the trace statement.

5. Between the parentheses of the typeof operator, enter my_array (**Figure 12.51**).

Flash evaluates my_array and displays its data type in the Output window in testing mode.

6. Add two more trace actions with the typeof operator (**Figure 12.52**).

7. Test your movie.

Flash displays the results of the three trace statements in the Output window in testing mode. The first trace displays the data type of my_array as an object. The second trace displays my_array[3] as a number, and the third trace displays my_array.toString() as a string (**Figure 12.53**).

```
my_array = new Array();
for (i=0; i<5; i++) {
    my_array[i] = i*5;
}
trace(typeof (my_array));
```

Figure 12.51 The data type of my_array will be evaluated and displayed in the Output window.

```
my_array = new Array();
for (i=0; i<5; i++) {
    my_array[i] = i*5;
}
trace(typeof (my_array));
trace(typeof (my_array[3]));
trace(typeof (my_array.toString()));
```

Figure 12.52 Add trace actions to evaluate and display the data type of index 3 of my_array and the method toString() of my_array.

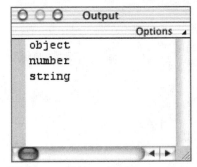

Figure 12.53 The results of the trace action in the Output window.

Debugging

The Debugger panel lets you monitor and modify the values of all the variables and properties in your movie as it plays. You can also examine the values of objects that hold data, such as instances of the Date or Sound class. Use the Debugger to verify that Flash is manipulating the information in variables the way you want it to and to test certain conditions or the effects of certain variables quickly. For example, imagine that you created an animation with the variable myVelocity controlling the speed of a spaceship. In the Debugger panel, you can modify the variable myVelocity as the movie plays to see how it affects the motion of your spaceship. Increase or decrease the value of myVelocity until you are satisfied with the results.

The Debugger panel opens and is active in testing mode when you select Control > Debug Movie. Once open and active, the Debugger displays information in several separate parts: a Display list at the top left; Properties, Variables, and Watch lists below it; a call stack window at the bottom left; and a Code view on the right (**Figure 12.54**). The Display list shows the root Timeline and the hierarchy of movie clips in that Timeline. You can select the root Timeline or the other movie clips to see the properties belonging to that particular Timeline or to see all the variables within that particular scope. The Code view lets you define breakpoints in your ActionScript so that you can step through the movie line by line to determine where and when some piece of interactivity in your movie is going awry. The call stack at the bottom left displays the names of your function calls as you step through the code.

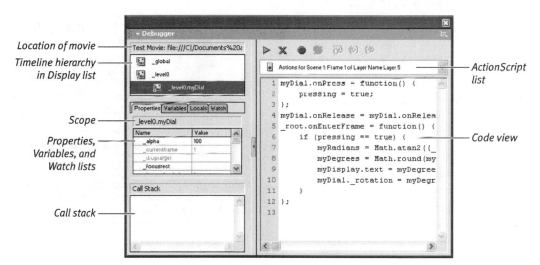

Figure 12.54 The Debugger panel displays a hierarchy of Timelines and their properties and variables on the left side. ActionScript can be displayed on the right side for you to step through the code line by line.

Use the Control menu to rewind, play, and step forward or backward through your movie, frame by frame, as necessary, to scrutinize the movie's properties and variables (**Figure 12.55**).

To access the debugger:

◆ From the Flash authoring environment, choose Control > Debug Movie (Command-Shift-Return for Mac, Ctrl-Shift-Enter for Windows).

Flash exports a SWF and enters testing mode. The Debugger panel opens and is activated. Your movie is initially paused so you can set breakpoints in your code. Click the continue button (the green right-pointing arrow) to start your movie.

To modify a property or a variable in the Debugger panel:

1. In the Display list of the Debugger panel, select the movie clip whose properties or variables you wish to modify.

2. Click the Properties or the Variables tab. You may have to adjust the moveable divider that separates the Call stack to see the full list of variables or properties.

3. Double-click the field in the Value column next to the property or variable you wish to modify.

4. Enter a new value.

   The new value must be a constant (a string, number, or Boolean value) rather than an expression that refers to another variable or property. For example, it must be 35 instead of 35 + myAlpha. The movie reflects the new value immediately (**Figure 12.56**).

Figure 12.55 Use the Control menu to control the playback of your movie in testing mode.

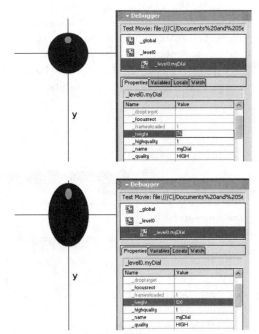

Figure 12.56 The values of properties can be selected (top) and modified (bottom); your movie will reflect changes even while it plays.

✔ Tip

■ Certain properties are read-only and are grayed out, indicating that they cannot be modified. For example, the property _totalframes is a fixed value determined by the number of frames in your movie.

Figure 12.57 The selected variable (myRadians) is added to the Watch list by using the pull-down menu.

Figure 12.58 The selected variable (myRadians) is added to the Watch list by using the display menu.

Figure 12.59 Choose Add from the display menu on the Watch list to enter a variable by hand.

The Variables tab in the Debugger panel lets you watch only the variables within the same scope. If you want to watch variables belonging to different scopes, you can use the Watch tab to choose the variables you would like to observe. This lets you create a set of critical variables that are culled in one place for you to watch and modify. The variables in your Watch list are displayed with their absolute target paths.

To add variables to the Watch list:

1. In the Debugger panel, select the root Timeline or a movie clip from the Display list.

2. Select the variable from the Variables tab. From the Options menu at the top-right corner of the Debugger panel, choose Add Watch (**Figure 12.57**).

   A blue dot appears next to the variable, marking it to be displayed on the Watch list.

   or

   Select the variable from the Variables tab. Control-click (Mac) or right-click (Windows) the variable. Choose Watch from the display menu that appears (**Figure 12.58**).

   A blue dot appears next to the variable, marking it to be displayed on the Watch list.

   or

   From the Watch tab, Control-click (Mac) or right-click (Windows) in the empty list. Choose Add from the display menu that appears (**Figure 12.59**). Enter the absolute target path of the variable.

DEBUGGING

601

To remove variables from the Watch list:

◆ In the Watch list, Control-click (Mac) or right-click (Windows) the variable, and choose Remove from the display menu.

◆ In the Variables list, Control-click (Mac) or right-click (Windows) the variable, and choose the check-marked Watch.

◆ In the Variables or Watch list, select the variable and then choose Remove Watch from the Options menu at the top-right corner of the Debugger panel.

Breakpoints and Stepping through Code

Breakpoints are places in a particular script where you tell Flash to pause so you can more easily inspect the condition of variables and properties and the status of your movie. You can have multiple breakpoints, and you can set them either in the Debugger panel or in the Actions panel. Once set, you can step through the code, line by line if you need to. Various options let you play through the code or skip function statements as desired.

To set breakpoints in your code:

1. In the active Debugger panel, choose a script from the ActionScript list.

ActionScript appears in the Code view on the right side of the Debugger panel.

2. Select a line of code where you want to set a breakpoint. Click the Toggle Breakpoint button.

or

Place your pointer to the left of the line number and click once.

Flash adds a red stop sign next to the line number (**Figure 12.60**). When the movie plays in the Debugger, it will stop when it reaches the breakpoint so you can inspect the state of the movie and its variables and properties.

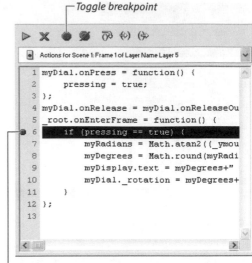

Toggle breakpoint

Breakpoint

Figure 12.60 A breakpoint is set at line 6 of this ActionScript.

DEBUGGING

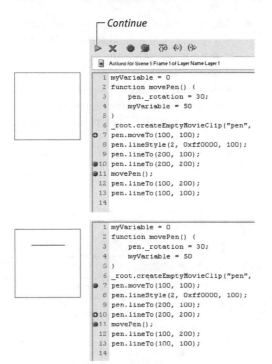

Figure 12.61 The yellow arrow marks the current line where the Debugger is paused. At top, the Debugger is paused at line 7 and the Stage is empty. When you click the Continue button, the Debugger proceeds to the next breakpoint and pauses at line 10 (bottom). The horizontal line segment from (100,100) to (200,100) is drawn. The code at line 10 is not yet performed.

To remove a breakpoint:

◆ In the Debugger panel, select the breakpoint. Click the Toggle Breakpoint button, or Control-click (Mac) or right-click (Windows) the line of code and select Remove Breakpoint.

The breakpoint is removed.

or

In the Actions panel, select the breakpoint.

The breakpoint is removed.

To remove all breakpoints:

◆ In the Debugger panel, click the Remove All Breakpoints button, or Control-click (Mac) or right-click (Windows) and select Remove All Breakpoints.

All breakpoint are removed.

To step through code:

◆ Click the Continue button to advance the Debugger through ActionScript code until the next breakpoint is encountered (**Figure 12.61**).

A yellow arrow marks the line of code where the Debugger is paused.

continues on next page

DEBUGGING

- ◆ Click the Step Over button to skip over a function that you have defined. The debugger continues to the next line after the function call (**Figure 12.62**).

  Although the Debugger steps over a function, the statements inside the function are still performed.

- ◆ Click the Step In button to perform the statements inside a function (**Figure 12.63**).

- ◆ Click the Step Out button to break out of a function. The debugger continues to the next line after the function call (**Figure 12.64**).

  Although the Debugger steps out of a function, the rest of the statements inside the function are still performed.

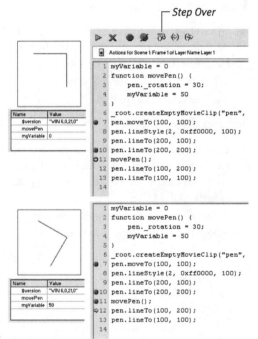

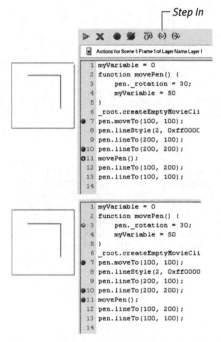

Figure 12.62 At top, the Debugger is paused at line 11 and the Stage shows two line segments. When you click the Step Over button, the Debugger steps over the function called movePen and stops at the first statement after the function call at line 12 (bottom). The statements inside the function are still performed, as you can see by the rotation and the new value for myVariable.

Figure 12.63 At top, the Debugger is paused at line 11 and the Stage shows two line segments. When you click the Step In button, the Debugger proceeds to the next line inside the function called movePen (bottom).

Step Out

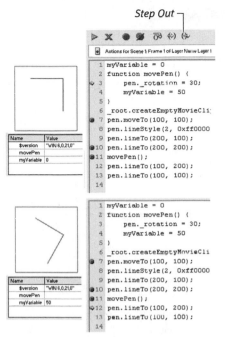

Figure 12.64 At top, the Debugger is paused at line 3 and the Stage shows two line segments. When you click the Step Out button, the Debugger steps out of the function called movePen and stops at the first statement after the function call at line 12 (bottom). The statements inside the function are still performed, as you can see by the rotation and the new value for myVariable.

Figure 12.65 To enable remote debugging, check the Debugging Permitted option in the Flash tab of the Publish Settings dialog box. The password (in this case mySecretWord) will give you access to the debugger.

Remote Debugging

You can also access the Debugger panel of a SWF movie remotely (outside testing mode). This lets you watch variables and properties and check interactivity when your movie is in a "real-life" setting, such as when it's uploaded to a Web site.

To enable remote debugging, you must select the Debugging Permitted option in the Flash tab of the Publish Settings dialog box. When you publish your movie, an SWD (Shockwave Debugging) file is also exported. This file contains debugging information that allows you to set breakpoints and step through your code. Keep both the SWF and SWD files together in the same directory and upload them to your Web site. You'll now be able to debug your movie remotely.

To debug remotely:

1. Open the Flash file you want to debug. Choose File > Publish Settings.

2. Click the Flash tab. In the list of options, check the Debugging Permitted box. If you wish to protect your movie by limiting debugging access, enter a password in the Password field (**Figure 12.65**).

3. Publish your Flash movie.

   Flash exports an HTML, SWF, and SWD file. Although the SWD file is not required for remote debugging, it is required to set breakpoints and step through code.

4. Keep all three files together and upload them to your Web site, or place them in a desired directory locally on your hard drive.

5. In Flash, choose Window > Debugger.

   The Debugger panel opens.

continues on next page

DEBUGGING

6. From the Options menu, choose Enable Remote Debugging (**Figure 12.66**).

7. From your browser or from the Flash stand-alone player, open the SWF file that you've kept either on your computer or uploaded to the Web.

The Remote Debug dialog box appears requesting information on where the Flash application is running.

8. Select Localhost because Flash and the Debugger are on the same (local) computer. Click OK. Enter your password if you entered one in the Publish Settings dialog box (**Figure 12.67**).

The SWF movie opens in the stand-alone player or a Web browser. The Debugger opens in the Flash authoring tool in a paused state with information about the Flash movie you are remotely debugging.

✔ Tip

■ If you don't get the Remote Debug dialog box, or if you've closed the Debugger panel, you can open it by right-clicking (Windows) or Control-clicking (Mac) inside the movie. From the menu that appears, choose Debugger (**Figure 12.68**).

Figure 12.66 Choose Options > Enable Remote Debugging in the Debugger panel.

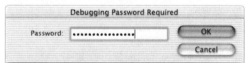

Figure 12.67 When remote debugging has been enabled and the SWD file is in the same directory as the SWF file, the Remote Debug dialog box appears, letting you access the Debugger for the remote movie. If you selected a password in the Publish Settings dialog box when you published your movie, enter it in the second dialog box that appears (bottom).

Figure 12.68 You can access the Debugger from the contextual display menu.

Optimizing Your Movie

Understanding the tools you use to create graphics, animation, sound, and ActionScript is important, but it's equally important to know how best to use them to create streamlined Flash movies. After all, the best-laid designs and animations won't be appreciated if poor construction and clunky code make them too large to download or too inefficient to play easily. To streamline a Flash movie, you use optimizations that keep the file size small, the animations smooth, and the revisions simple. Many different factors affect the file size and performance of the final exported SWF. Bitmaps, sounds, complicated shapes, color gradients, alpha transparencies, and embedded fonts all increase the Flash file size and slow down the movie's performance. Only you can weigh the trade-offs between the quality and quantity of Flash content and the size and performance of the movie. Keep in mind the audience to whom you're delivering your Flash movies. Does your audience have Internet connections with DSL or cable lines, or does your audience rely on 56K modems? Knowing the answer to this question helps you make more informed choices about what to include in your movie and how to build it.

The following strategies can help you work more efficiently and help you create smaller, more manageable, better performing Flash movies.

To optimize your authoring environment:

◆ Use layers to separate and organize your content. For example, place all your actions on one layer, all your frame labels on another layer, and all your sounds in still another layer. By using layers, you'll be able to understand and change different elements of your movie quickly (**Figure 12.69**). Having many layers does not increase the size of the final exported SWF file. Use comments in keyframes as well, to explain the different parts of the Timeline.

◆ Use dynamic text fields in addition to the **trace** action, Output window, and Debugger panel to observe variables in your movie. Dynamic text fields and the **trace** action let you display expressions and variables in the context of your movie.

◆ Avoid using scenes in your movie. Although scenes are a good organizational feature for simple movies, Timelines that contain scenes are more difficult to navigate from movie clips. Also, movie-clip instances are not continuous between scenes. Use labels to mark different areas of the Timeline instead, or use movie clips to hold different parts of your animation.

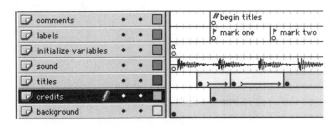

Figure 12.69 Well-organized layers like these are easy to understand and change.

To optimize bitmaps and sounds for playback performance:

◆ Avoid animating large bitmaps. Keep bitmaps as static background elements if they are large, or make them small for tweening.

◆ Place streaming sounds on the root Timeline instead of within a movie clip. A movie clip needs to be downloaded in its entirety before playing. A streaming sound on the root Timeline, however, will begin playing as the frames download.

◆ Use the maximum amount of compression tolerable for bitmaps and sounds. You can adjust the JPEG quality level for your exported SWF file in Publish Settings. You can also adjust the compression settings for the stream sync and event sync sounds separately, so you can keep a higher-quality streaming sound for music and narration and a lower-quality event sound for button clicks (**Figure 12.70**).

◆ Avoid using the Trace Bitmap command to create an overly complex vector image of an imported bitmap. The complexity of a traced bitmap can make the file size larger and the performance significantly slower than if you use the bitmap itself.

◆ Import bitmaps and sounds at the exact size or length that you want to use them in Flash. Although editing within Flash is possible, you want to import just the information you need to keep the file size small. For example, do not import a bitmap and then reduce it 50 percent to use in your movie. Instead, reduce the bitmap 50 percent first and then import it into Flash.

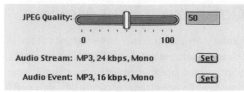

Figure 12.70 The JPEG quality and audio-compression options in the Publish Settings dialog box.

To optimize graphics, text, and tweening for playback performance:

◆ Use tweening wherever you can instead of frame-by-frame animation. In an animation, Flash only has to remember the keyframes, making tweening a far less memory-intensive task.

◆ Tween symbols instead of groups. Each group in the keyframes of a tween must be downloaded, whereas only the single symbol in a tween must be downloaded. Moreover, groups don't allow you to apply instance effects like tint, brightness, or alpha. Using groups in tweens makes editing difficult because you have to apply the same edit on every single group in the keyframes of the tween.

◆ Avoid creating animations that have multiple objects moving at the same time or that have large areas of change. Both of these kinds of animations will tax a computer's CPU and slow the movie's performance.

◆ Break apart groups within symbols to simplify them. Once you're satisfied with an illustration in a symbol, break apart the groups into shapes to "flatten" the illustration out. Flash will have fewer curves to remember and thus have an easier time tweening the symbol instance. Alpha effects on the instance will also affect the symbol as a whole instead of the individual groups within the symbol (**Figure 12.71**).

continues on next page

Figure 12.71 A symbol defined as separate groups (top left) contains more information (top middle) and can produce undesirable transparency effects (top right). A symbol defined as a shape (bottom left) contains less information (bottom middle) and will become transparent as one unit (bottom right).

- Use color gradients and alpha transparencies sparingly.

- Use the Properties Inspector to change the color, tint, and brightness of instances instead of creating separate symbols of different colors.

- Optimize curves by avoiding special line styles (such as dotted lines) and using the Pencil tool rather than the Brush tool and by reducing the complexity of curves with Modify > Shape > Optimize or Command-Shift-Option-C for Mac, Ctrl-Alt-Shift-C for Windows (**Figure 12.72**).

- Use fewer font styles, and embed only the essential font outlines.

Figure 12.72 Complex curves and shapes can be simplified without losing their detail.

To optimize ActionScript code:

- Try to keep all your code in one place, preferably on the main Timeline, and keep code in just one layer.

- Use a consistent naming practice for variables, movie clips, objects, and other elements that need to be identified. Consistent and simple names make the job that the variable performs more apparent.

- Use comments within your ActionScript to explain the code to yourself and to other developers who may look at your Flash file for future revisions.

- Think about modularity. This means use smaller, separate components to build your interactivity. For example, use functions to define frequently accessed tasks, use the external scripts when and if possible, and keep large or common assets outside your movie but available through shared symbols, loadMovie(), and loadSound(). You'll reduce redundancy, save memory, and make revisions easier.

Avoiding Common Mistakes

When troubleshooting your Flash movie, there are a few obvious places where you should look first to locate what might be common mistakes. These usually involve some simple but critical element, such as overlooking quotation marks or a relative path term or forgetting to name an instance. Pay close attention to the following warning list to ensure that all your Flash movies are free of bugs.

To avoid common mistakes:

◆ Be mindful of uppercase and lowercase letters. ActionScript 2 is case-sensitive so make sure the names of your variables and objects exactly match. Flash keywords must also match in case. For example, Key.isDown() is not the same as key.isDown().

◆ Double-check the data type of your values. Review the Script pane to make sure that quotation marks are only around string data types. The keyword this should not be within quotation marks. Movie-clip target paths can be within quotation marks, but it's good practice to keep them as expressions.

◆ Double-check the target paths for your movie clips, variables, and objects.

◆ Remember to name your movie-clip, button, and text-field instances in the Property Inspector.

◆ Check to see if ActionScript statements are within the correct parentheses or curly braces in the Script pane. For example, verify that statements belonging to an if statement or to a function statement are contained within their curly braces.

◆ Place a stop action in the first keyframe of a movie clip to prevent it from playing automatically and looping.

◆ To test simple actions and simple buttons, remember to choose Enable Simple Frame Actions and Enable Simple Buttons from the Control menu. For more complex button events, you must choose Test Movie from the Control menu.

◆ Remember that the default setting for your Flash movie in the testing mode is to loop.

◆ For additional help and advice on debugging your movie, check out the vast Flash resources on the Web. Begin your search from Macromedia's Web site, where there is a searchable archive of tech notes, documentation, tutorials, case studies, and more. You'll also find links to other Web sites with articles, FLA source files, bulletin boards, and mailing lists. Check out the CD that accompanies this book for more Flash links and resources.

NAMING SUFFIXES FOR OBJECT TYPES

Naming Suffixes for Object Types	
OBJECT	**SUFFIX**
Array	_array
Button	_btn
Camera	_cam
Color	_color
ContextMenu	_cm
ContextMenuItem	_cmi
Date	_date
Error	_err
LoadVars	_lv
LocalConnection	_lc
Microphone	_mic
MovieClip	_mc
MovieClipLoader	_mcl
NetConnection	_nc
NetStream	_ns
PrintJob	_pj
SharedObject	_so
Sound	_sound
String	_str
TextField	_txt
TextFormat	_fmt
Video	_video
XML	_xml
XMLNode	_xmlnode
XMLSocket	_xmlsocket

KEYBOARD KEYS AND MATCHING KEY CODES

B

Letters	
LETTER KEY	KEY CODE
A	65
B	66
C	67
D	68
E	69
F	70
G	71
H	72
I	73
J	74
K	75
L	76
M	77
N	78
O	79
P	80
Q	81
R	82
S	83
T	84
U	85
V	86
W	87
X	88
Y	89
Z	90

Numbers and Symbols

KEY	KEY CODE	KEY CLASS PROPERTY
0	48	
1	49	
2	50	
3	51	
4	52	
5	53	
6	54	
7	55	
8	56	
9	57	
Numbpad 0	96	
Numbpad 1	97	
Numbpad 2	98	
Numbpad 3	99	
Numbpad 4	100	
Numbpad 5	101	
Numbpad 6	102	
Numbpad 7	103	
Numbpad 8	104	
Numbpad 9	105	
Numbpad *	106	
Numbpad +	107	
Numbpad Enter	108	
Numbpad -	109	
Numbpad .	110	
Numbpad /	111	
Backspace	8	BACKSPACE
Tab	9	TAB
Clear	12	
Enter	13	ENTER
Shift	16	SHIFT
Control	17	CONTROL
Alt	18	
Caps Lock	20	CAPSLOCK
Esc	27	ESCAPE
Spacebar	32	SPACE
Page Up	33	PGUP
Page Down	34	PGDN
End	35	END
Home	36	HOME
Left arrow	37	LEFT
Up arrow	38	UP

Numbers and Symbols

Right arrow	39	RIGHT
Down arrow	40	DOWN
Insert	45	INSERT
Delete	46	DELETEKEY
Help	47	
Num Lock	144	
;:	186	
=+	187	
-_	189	
/?	191	
`~	192	
[{	219	
|	220	
]}	221	
'"	222	

Function Keys

FUNCTION KEY	KEY CODE
F1	112
F2	113
F3	114
F4	115
F5	116
F6	117
F7	118
F8	119
F9	120
F10	121
F11	122
F12	123

KEYBOARD KEYS AND MATCHING KEY CODES

INDEX

Symbols

, (comma), 80
; (semicolon), 80
& (ampersand), 398
{} (curly braces), 80
.. (double periods), 223
\ (backslash), 392
/ (forward slash), 223
// (double forward slash), 99–100
&& (AND operator), 145, 432
|| (OR operator), 432
! (NOT operator), 432
% (modulo operator), 415
+ (addition operator), 416
= (assignment operator), 388, 413, 421
== (comparison operator), 419–420, 421, 423, 425
=== (strict equality operator), 429

A

absolute paths, 180–186
absolute URLs, 200
actions
    adding in the Script pane, 84–85
    creating continuous, 165–170
    editing in the Script pane, 85
    See also specific actions
Actions panel, 81–89
    code hints, 86–88
    display options, 85
    formatting options, 89
    Help panel, 89
    layout of, 83
    opening, 81
    Options menu, 583
    undocking/redocking, 82

ActionScript, 75–100
    Actions panel, 81–89
    animation, 346–352
    breakpoints in, 602–603
    checking syntax, 584
    classes, 76
    code hints, 86–88
    comments, 99–100
    debugging, 599–606
    dot syntax, 78–79
    editing, 583–585
    external, 586–587
    finding/replacing terms, 585
    font symbols, 460
    functions, 98
    importing/exporting, 585
    methods, 77, 93–95
    new terms, 100
    objects, 76, 90–92
    optimizing, 610
    properties, 77, 96–97
    punctuation, 80
    scope of, 190–191
    stepping through code, 603–604
ActionScript 2, 100, 561–565
    building custom classes, 563–564
    changing the classPath, 565
    class definitions, 561
    constructor functions, 563
    instantiating/using custom classes, 564–565
    properties and methods, 562
addition operator, 416
addListener() method, 146, 147, 489
addPage() method, 254–259
Advanced Effect dialog box, 296
align property, 263, 264
alpha
    gradient fills and, 334, 336
    movie clips and, 289, 297–298
    printing bitmaps with, 258

C

syntax
    checking, 584
    dot, 78–79, 192
    slash, 79, 192, 308
System.capabilities class, 261
system properties, 262–263

T

tabEnabled property, 130
tabIndex property, 130–131
target paths, 176
    absolute, 180–186
    finding, 192–194
    loaded movies and, 230–231
    movie-clip instances and, 176–177
    parent/child movie clips and, 178–179, 185–186
    relative, 180–186
targetPath function, 192, 194
_target property, 192–193
temporal compression, 47
text, 439–512
    animating, 476–478
    concatenating, 446–448
    dimensions of, 479–483
    dynamic, 439, 442–443
    fonts and, 445, 460
    formatting, 472–476
    HTML, 449–453
    input, 439, 440–441
    optimizing, 610
    strings, 499–512
    vertical, 444
    wrapping, 483
text fields
    analyzing, 500–505
    changing selections in, 493–494
    concatenating for printing, 446–448
    creating on the main Stage, 469–470
    CSS formatting of, 484–486
    cursor position in, 491–492
    default appearance of, 470
    detecting changes in, 495–498
    displaying HTML in, 449–453
    dynamically generating, 469
    focus of, 488–490, 496–497
    manipulating content of, 487
    modifying text in, 471–478
    options for, 444
    properties of, 457–459, 480
    removing, 470
    retrieving dimensions for, 479, 480–483
    scrolling, 461–468
    strings and, 499–512
    tweening, 454–456

text property, 457
Text tool, 439, 440
TextExtent class, 439, 479–483
    properties list, 479
TextField class, 439, 457–458
    events list, 495
    properties list, 458
    StyleSheet class, 484
TextFormat class, 439, 471–478
    properties list, 471
this keyword, 181, 184
time information
    clock creation, 545–547
    timer creation, 550–552
    See also date and time information
Timelines, 173–198
    absolute paths and, 180–186
    defining for loaded movies, 232–234
    event handlers assigned on, 107
    loaded movies and, 230–234
    navigating with movie clips, 174
    relative paths and, 180–186
    scope and, 190–191
    target paths and, 176–179, 184, 192–194
    See also root Timeline
timers, creating, 550–552
title animation, 13–14
toLowerCase() method, 511
_totalframes property, 267
toUpperCase() method, 511, 512
trace action, 193, 262–263, 596, 597, 598
Trace Bitmap dialog box, 70
traced animations, 72
tracing variables, 596–598
Track as Button option, 124
Track as Menu Item option, 124–126
transitions
    blur, 22
    gradient, 20–21
transparency
    changing in movie clips, 299
    printing bitmaps with, 258
troubleshooting, 611
    See also debugging
tweening
    buttons, 114
    mask layer, 26–28
    masked layers, 29–30
    motion, 4–14
    optimizing, 609
    shape, 15–21
    text field, 454–456
two-dimensional arrays, 539
typeof operator, 597, 598

U

undefined keyword, 410
underline tag (<U>), 451
unloadMovie() method, 318
unloadMovieNum action, 225, 237
Up state, 111, 132, 134–135
updateAfterEvent action, 168, 332, 345
URLs
    absolute vs. relative, 200
    getURL action and, 200–206
    input text and, 440–441

V

values
    assigned to properties, 96–97
    returned by functions, 557–558
var identifier, 388
Variable field, 444
variables, 387, 388–389
    concatenating, 416–418
    counter, 434, 437
    data types of, 389, 597–598
    deleting, 391
    displaying a list of, 593–594
    dynamically referencing, 417–418
    global, 397
    initializing, 390, 397
    iterant, 437
    loading external, 398–405
    LoadVars class, 402–404
    local, 555
    modifying, 413–415, 418, 600
    scope of, 395–396
    storing/sharing, 406–412
    tracing, 596–598
    using, 393–394
    Watch list for, 601–602
$version property, 263, 594
vertical scrolling, 462–464
vertical text, 444
video, 41–72
    advanced options, 48–49
    bitmap sequences from, 67–69
    compression settings, 44, 45–47
    copying motion from, 64–66
    editing, 51–55
    embedding, 43–45
    exporting, 60–62
    external, 238–243
    Flash elements added to, 56–59
    importing, 42–50
    interactive controls for, 58–59

    linking to external, 50
    motion tweens applied to, 57–58
    quality tips for, 47
    rotoscoping, 64–66
    simulating, 67–72
    updating, 54
video clips, 52–53
    combining, 53
    creating, 52
    deleting, 53
    modifying, 53
    rearranging, 53
Video Import Wizard
    Advanced settings, 48–49
    Editing options, 51–53
    Embed video option, 43
    Encoding options, 43–47
    Link to external video option, 50
_visible property, 448
volume
    dynamic controls for, 368–373
    setting for sounds, 360

W

Watch list, 601–602
Web browsers, 200–220
    framesets and, 205–209
    GET and POST methods and, 215–216
    JavaScript and, 209–214
    local files and, 203–204
    navigating Flash content with, 218–220
    Web links and, 200–202
    windows and, 208–214
    XML objects and, 217
Web sites
    linking to, 200–201
    opening in frames, 207–208
    opening in new windows, 208–209
while statement, 434–435
windows
    JavaScript control of, 209–214
    opening Web sites in, 208–209
    properties of, 210
Windows systems
    device fonts on, 445
    export movie options for, 63
    viewing ID3s of MP3s on, 383
with actions, 187–189
    how to use, 188
    nested, 189
wrapping text, 483

X

Y